Cruising Guide to Coastal South Carolina and Georgia

OTHER BOOKS BY CLAIBORNE S. YOUNG

Cruising Guide to Coastal North Carolina
Cruising Guide to Eastern Florida
Cruising Guide to the Northern Gulf Coast
Cruising Guide to Western Florida

Claiborne Young also publishes a *free* quarterly newsletter called *The Salty Southeast*. This newsletter updates new marinas, bridge schedules, changes in aids to navigation, and other timely cruising information. If you are interested in receiving this free newsletter write:

Watermark Publishing
P.O. Box 67
Elon College, North Carolina 27244-0067

Cruising Guide to Coastal South Carolina and Georgia

by Claiborne S. Young

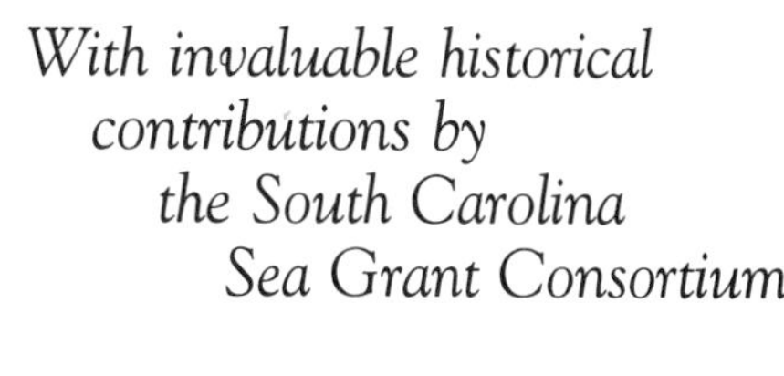

With invaluable historical contributions by the South Carolina Sea Grant Consortium

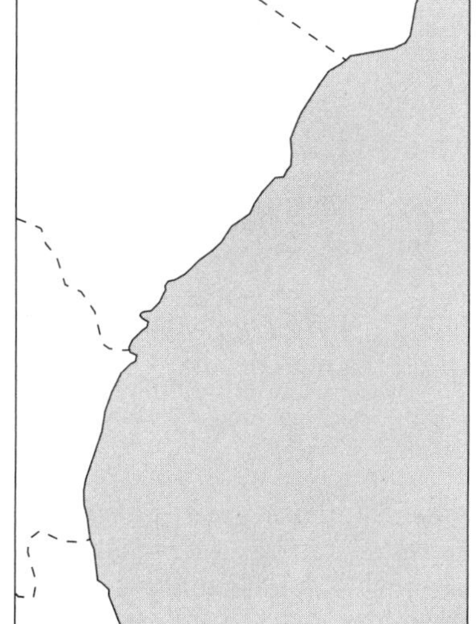

John F. Blair, Publisher
Winston-Salem, North Carolina

Designed by Debra Long Hampton
Cover photograph by Bernard Carpenter
Black and white photographs by the author and his first mate unless otherwise noted
Composition by The Roberts Group
Printed by R. R. Donnelley & Sons

Revised Third Edition © 1996

Library of Congress Cataloging-in-Publication Data

Young, Claiborne S. (Claiborne Sellars), 1951-
Cruising guide to coastal South Carolina and Georgia / by Claiborne S. Young ; with invaluable historical contributions by the South Carolina Sea Grant Consortium. —Rev. 3rd ed.
p. cm.
Includes index.
ISBN 0-89587-145-9 (alk. paper)
1. Yachting—South Carolina—Guidebooks. 2. Yachting—Georgia—Guidebooks. 3. Intracoastal waterways—South Carolina—Guidebooks. 4. Intracoastal waterways—Georgia—Guidebooks. 5. Inland navigation—South Carolina—Guidebooks. 6. South Carolina—Guidebooks. 7. Georgia—Guidebooks. I. South Carolina Sea Grant Consortium. II. Title.
GV815.Y68 1996
797.1'09757—dc20 96–12970

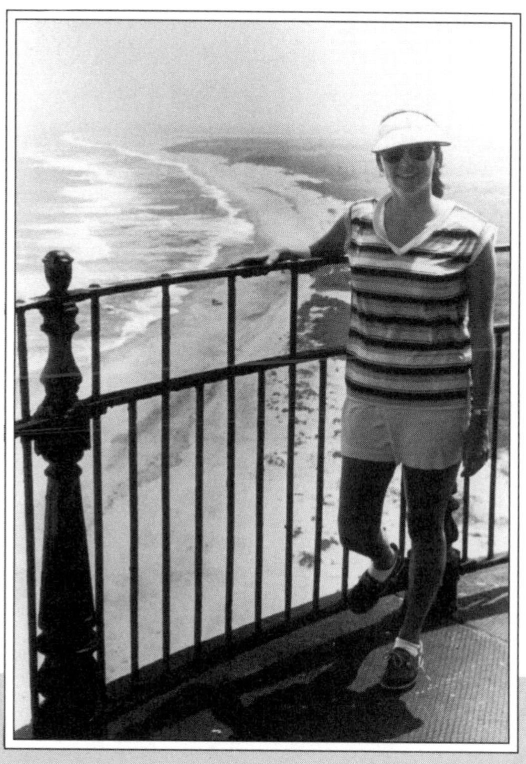

This book is dedicated to
my partner in life, Karen Ann,
without whose loving help as
research assistant, navigator, and
proofreader this guide would not
have been possible.

Contents

Acknowledgments

First and foremost, I want to thank my first-rate first mate, Karen, without whose help as an experienced navigator, research assistant, photographer, and partner this book would not have been possible. I would also like to extend a very warm thanks to my mother for all her encouragement.

Very special thanks also go to the South Carolina Sea Grant Consortium for its many invaluable historical contributions.

Rhett Wilson, Jack Keenar, and Margaret Davidson deserve particular recognition for their tireless efforts to make the most reliable historical data available to this writer. Without their aid, many of the historical sketches here presented could not have appeared in this guide.

To my research assistants, Earle "Bud" Williams, the late John Horne, Vic and Debbie Harllee, and Kerry Horne, goes my heartfelt gratitude for their efforts to help me complete the seemingly endless research necessary to put this guide together.

I gratefully acknowledge the aid of the May Memorial Library of Burlington, North Carolina, the South Carolina State Library, and the South Caroliniana Library for their aid in helping me to accumulate the vast body of historical information needed for this project. Special mention should also be made of the long-suffering efforts of research assistant Earle Williams to acquire all this data and forward it to me.

Many thanks go to Herbert Berle for all his aid and assistance. To the Georgetown and Beaufort Chambers of Commerce also goes a special note of thanks for their ready aid and for permission to reproduce their tour maps of the Georgetown and Beaufort historical districts.

To the following publishers, I extend my gratitude for permission to quote from the works listed: the Georgetown Rice Museum, *No Heir to Take Its Place*, by Dennis Lawson (1972); South Carolina Federal Bank, *A Brief History of Beaufort*, by John Duffy (1976); and the University of South Carolina Press, *Charleston in the Age of the Pinckneys*, by George C. Rogers, Jr. (1980). Thanks are also due to author Nell S. Graydon for permission to quote from her two books, *Tales of Edisto* (Sandlapper Publishing, 1955) and *Tales of Beaufort* (Beaufort Book Shop, 1963); to Mrs. J. Stevenson Bolick for the use of material from *Ghosts from the Coast*, by her late husband, J. Stevenson Bolick; to Edith Bannister Dowling for the use of her poem "For This Your Land," previously published in *One for Sorrow, Two for Joy* (1967) and *A Patchwork of Poems about South Carolina* (1970); to the University of Georgia Press, *Georgia's Land of the Golden Isles*, by Burnette Vanstory (1956, 1970, 1981); and to The Georgia Conservancy, *A Guide to the Georgia Coast* (1989).

Finally, I express my most heartfelt thanks to the staff of John F. Blair, Publisher, for their enthusiastic support and encouragement during this project.

Introduction

"To know the coast (of South Carolina) is to love it." Of the many coastal visitors and residents who have no doubt expressed this sentiment at one time or another, writer James Henry Rice, Jr., was perhaps the most inclined to eloquence. Describing the region in his 1925 *Glories of the Carolina Coast*, Rice spoke of "vast avenues of live oaks and magnolias flanked by towering pines, whose crowns are masses of wisteria dropping purple blooms and at whose feet azaleas bloom. . . . I think of winding rivers and pictured shores; of tillandsia, streaming from the trees, groves alive with birds, the haunting silence of deep woods where wild creatures revel . . . and I feel pity for people with toy houses and tiny yards."

Without a doubt, the coast of South Carolina is about as close to a cruising paradise as pleasure boaters are ever likely to find. The possibilities are endless. At times, your greatest problem will be to choose among the various intriguing alternatives.

In this second post–Hurricane Hugo edition, the Georgia coastline again receives complete coverage. With a natural, undeveloped coast very similar in nature to the South Carolina Low Country, Georgia's "coastline of the Golden Isles" should make a memorable addition to any cruiser's itinerary.

The beauty and the diversity of coastal South Carolina and Georgia waters are undeniable. Whether viewing the silent cypress swamps of Waccamaw River, the huge grass savannas of Santee Delta that seem to extend beyond the horizon, or the tall, mysterious oaks of the southern Sea Islands, the visitor to this enchanting land will come away enriched by his experience.

In addition to the breathtaking natural scenery so aptly described by Mr. Rice, there are also many historical sites readily visible from the water. These include lovely plantation homes that have never lost the flavor of the Old South, sleepy villages such as McClellanville, and the vast harbors of Charleston, Beaufort, and Savannah. The cruising boater who is not captivated by the very special qualities of coastal South Carolina and Georgia must possess truly numbed sensibilities.

In September 1989, a memorable event took place that has seriously affected coastal South Carolina ever since. Powerful Hurricane Hugo came roaring ashore just north of Charleston. This storm, the strongest to hit the South Carolina coast in decades, cut a swath of death and destruction as far north as Georgetown. Many buildings were heavily damaged in the "Holy City" of Charleston, and storm-surge tides rose to 4 feet or better as far inland as the restaurants around the Old Market. Sullivan's Island and the Isle of Palms to the north were practically laid waste. The boats and docks of Wild Dunes Yacht Harbor were bodily lifted out of their protected cove and deposited on the opposite side of the Waterway. At McClellanville, a huge tidal surge rolled inexorably up Five Fathom Creek inlet and smashed into the small village. Many of the local shrimp trawlers were deposited in the local residents' front yards. Georgetown was also hard-hit, and its marinas suffered extensive destruction. It is said that following the storm's assault, there was not a single commercial or private dock left standing between Charleston and Georgetown. Fortunately, the Sea Islands south of Charleston suffered much lighter damage, and the Georgia coast was hardly affected. One BBC commentator reported that after Hugo, Charleston was "gone with the wind."

This writer is happy to report that practically all the storm damage is now but a distant bad memory. Charleston and Georgetown are once again as charming as ever. If it weren't for the forest of uprooted trees along the Waterway between Minim Creek and Charleston Harbor, present-day visitors might not even realize that there had ever been such a natural catastrophe. Just ask the locals, though, and they'll quickly remind you of that awful night.

The sidewaters along the South Carolina and Georgia coastline offer a huge selection of overnight anchorages. Many of these are quite isolated, which can make for memorable evenings spent under the stars. Sometimes, it's possible to drop the hook within sight of a historic plantation home. It is a very special experience to watch the sun set over these grand old homeplaces. (Remember, however, that most of these plantations are privately owned. Please don't abuse your privilege by trespassing.) Anchoring on the waters of coastal South Carolina and Georgia need never be dull or repetitive.

Marina facilities in the Low Country are numerous and of good reputation. The vast majority of South Carolina's marinas cater to transient boaters and are eager to serve the cruiser. This writer and his mate were impressed time and time again by the friendly greetings and offers of assistance from the various facilities we visited. This friendly attitude seems to prevail in both large and small marinas. Cruising boaters can approach most of South Carolina's facilities with confidence.

Georgia marina facilities are also friendly and accommodating, but not nearly as plentiful. To be sure, good boating facilities exist around Savannah and Thunderbolt and St. Simons and Jekyll Islands. In between, however, are long, lonely stretches of the ICW where the marsh grass seems to go on forever. All captains should be sure their crafts are well fueled and in top condition before tackling the Georgia section of the Waterway.

From north to south, the geography of coastal South Carolina and Georgia presents many striking contrasts. The northern section, which runs from the North Carolina line to Winyah Bay, exhibits high banks and is pierced by only a few minor inlets. This section includes the Myrtle Beach area, usually seen by the boater from the none-too-attractive Pine Island Cut Canal, and the lovely Waccamaw River, which resembles a ghostly primeval cypress swamp.

Winyah Bay provides the first reliable access to the sea below Little River. The old port town of Georgetown sits at the strategic confluence of the bay and four major rivers.

South of Winyah Bay, the coast begins to change. The land quickly drops to the seemingly endless grass savannas of the Santee Delta. The marsh grass dominates much of the shoreline from Winyah Bay to Charleston Harbor. A few minor Sea Islands border the ocean in this section, but they are surrounded by relatively small, mostly shallow streams. Inlets are shoal and dangerous.

The "Holy City" of Charleston sits astride one of the finest natural harbors on the East Coast of the United States. The tidal Cooper, Wando, and Ashley Rivers extend far inland from the port city and provide many additional cruising opportunities.

South from Charleston, the nature of the coast quickly changes yet again. This is the land of the fabled South Carolina Sea Islands. These historic landmasses form an irregular, broken chain that shields the mainland from the Atlantic. They are surrounded by a bewildering maze of rivers, creeks, and inlets. There are also three large sounds. Along with Winyah Bay to the north, St. Helena, Port Royal, and Calibogue Sounds share the distinction of being the largest water bodies in all of South Carolina.

Savannah River introduces boaters to the natural character of the Georgia coastline. Sporting many wide rivers and seven mighty sounds, the "Golden Isles" waters are truly memorable. While the city of Savannah can boast one of the finest ports in the world, and some development is encountered near St. Simons Island and Brunswick to the south, the vast majority of Georgia waters are overlooked by marsh grass that has never known the hand of man. In fact, fully 60 percent of the Georgia coastline is either publicly owned or under the sway of lumbering and wood-pulp companies that have no interest in urban or residential development.

Our waterborne odyssey comes to an end at St. Marys River. This beautiful stream serves as the natural boundary between Georgia and Florida. One last port of call, the historic village of St. Marys, sends out her siren's call and tempts visiting cruisers to linger awhile before entering the Sunshine State.

The coast of South Carolina and Georgia presents a wide array of attractions waiting to greet the cruising boater. Perhaps the greatest single attraction is the coastal native. Born in a tradition of hospitality that is known and respected worldwide, he will greet you with a word of cheer in his inimitable accent. Like most people who have lived to, and depended upon, themselves for many years, the coastal resident does not take kindly to strangers telling him how something can be done better. He is likely to inform you that it has worked this way just fine for many generations. On the other hand, if you approach the coastal resident with respect and a genuine interest in his past, you will be welcomed into the heart of that special land that is coastal South Carolina and Georgia.

Another attraction well worth your notice is the many fine restaurants dotting the South Carolina and Georgia coastline. This is deep-fried seafood country, and this special cuisine has been perfected in the Low Country. The preparation of fowl is another specialty of the area. Duck, quail, turkey, and chicken are often prepared in sauces whose recipes have been handed down from generation to generation.

This tradition of fine food has its roots deep in the past. In his memorable book, *Charleston in the Age of the Pinckneys*, George C. Rogers, Jr., explained that these recipes might have come "from a French grandmother or a Santo Domingan grandmother or a German passing through Charleston. . . . It was some combination of Old World culinary arts with the New World staples." This writer is pleased to report that the tradition of eclectic cuisine and fine dining is alive and well today on the coast of South Carolina and Georgia.

It is not this guide's purpose to discuss the many angling opportunities of coastal South Carolina and Georgia, but it is certainly worth noting that both saltwater and freshwater fish are readily taken all along the coast. The upper reaches of Cooper River have long been known for bass and bream fishing. If you are interested in trying your luck, I suggest you find a friendly local native and engage him in a conversation about what's been biting lately. Judging from my observations during research, your efforts are more than likely to meet with success.

Certainly, South Carolina's three important coastal cities, Georgetown, Charleston, and Beaufort, rank as major attractions for passing boaters. All three towns offer a wide variety of historical attractions and numerous facilities for the cruising boater. Each has its own special charms, beckoning the passing cruiser to stop for a few days or even a week to explore and gain a sense of the past. This writer highly recommends that you heed this call.

The major Sea Islands south of Charleston are another significant cruising attraction. Here and there, beautifully restored plantation homes gaze serenely out upon rivers and creeks they have watched over for more than 100 years. Cruising amid the old oaks and moss-draped cypresses of the islands, it is not difficult to imagine that time has somehow lost its course and you have strayed into a far-removed era. Few will remain unmoved by the faded grandeur of the South Carolina Sea Islands.

Within the last several decades, developers have transformed several of the Sea Islands into plush seaside resorts. Many consider these to be one of the coast's principal attractions. Happily, some of this development has been carefully managed to coexist with the fragile coastal ecosystem. Others, unfortunately, have not followed this wise course of action. Many of these luxurious retreats do not offer facilities for transient boaters. Hilton Head Island, to the south, is a major exception. Boasting seven marinas, the island eagerly waits to greet visiting cruisers.

Many boaters cruising South Carolina and Georgia waters will be fortunate enough to experience some entertaining moments courtesy of a group of remarkable creatures. Large schools of bottlenose dolphins, or porpoises, can often be seen at play along the coast's rivers and creeks. These beautiful creatures add their unique and amusing charm to the waters of the South Carolina and Georgia coast.

The city of Savannah, guarding the border between the two sister states, vies with Charleston as one of the most beautiful communities in America. The original town plan put forward by James Oglethorpe, the colony's founder, called for the city to be built around a series of squares. Many of these were set aside as green areas with bountiful trees. This has lent the city a grace and dignity so very lacking in most of our modern urban communities. Savannah's beautiful homes and distinguished buildings are also very reminiscent of Charleston and are highly regarded in their own right.

South of Savannah, three resort islands—St. Simons, Jekyll, and Sea Islands—can lay as much claim to fame as their northerly sisters, Hilton Head and Kiawah. They feature a host of luxurious accommodations set amidst numerous historic sites, and passing cruisers are urged to fully experience these magical isles and sample their rarefied charms.

Even farther to the south, Cumberland Island has an enchanting history that is almost dream-like in its romantic quality. Today, visitors can go ashore to an all but deserted island under the care of the National Park Service. The reminders of richer, broader days are still very much in evidence.

Within the body of this guide, this writer has endeavored to relate all the information cruising boaters may need to take full advantage of coastal South Carolina and Georgia's splendid cruising potential. I have paid particular attention to anchorages, marina facilities, and danger areas. All the navigational information necessary for a successful cruise has been included. In the guide, these data have been screened in gray for ready identification. Readers will *also* find chapter introductions and marina services screened with a gray background. Longtime followers of my guides should keep this new design in mind to avoid confusion.

Each and every water body, large and small, has been personally visited and sounded for the latest depth information. However, remember that bottom configurations do change. The cruising boater should always be equipped with the latest charts and "Notices to Mariners" before leaving the dock.

The maps presented in this guide are meant to locate marinas and anchorages as well as impart a general knowledge of the coastline. They should *not* be used for navigation under any circumstances!

This guide is not a navigational primer. It is assumed that you have a working knowledge of piloting and coastal navigation. If you don't, you should acquire these skills before tackling these waters.

The inland waters of coastal South Carolina and Georgia are mostly deep and well marked. Many smaller sidewaters hold good depths from shore to shore and do not require aids to navigation. Thus, successful navigation of the states' waters is relatively simple.

You must not be lulled to sleep, however, by the generally forgiving nature of South Carolina and Georgia waters. The unwary boater can still pile up on a hidden sandbar if he does not pay attention to his sounder. Always have the latest chart on hand to resolve quickly any questions that might arise. Observe all markers carefully, and keep alert. You are also advised to study the navigational information contained within the body of this guide before your cruise. This basic planning will help to ensure an enjoyable cruising experience.

Many South Carolina water bodies are well sheltered and seldom give rise to rough conditions. Others, such as Winyah Bay and Charleston Harbor, can produce a healthy chop when winds and tides are contrary. For the most part, however, your cruise of the Low Country's waters will be quite pleasant as long as the fickle wind stays below 15 knots.

While Georgia also boasts many sheltered sections of the ICW, this coastline harbors seven wide sounds and more than a few broad rivers that can produce more than their share of choppy waters during inclement weather. Boaters should consult the latest weather forecast before beginning their sojourn across these wide waters. By all accounts, you should approach St. Catherines Sound with the greatest respect.

Boaters from the Middle Atlantic states will be struck by the tidal nature of South Carolina and Georgia waters. Currents run swiftly indeed, and 7- to 8-foot tidal ranges are often the norm. You will find that many marinas have floating docks to compensate for this phenomenon. If you do berth at fixed piers, leave plenty of slack in your lines.

Because the tidal ranges are so wide, this writer and his mate made every attempt to perform our soundings at low tide. Where that proved impossible, we compensated for higher tides, always leaning toward the conservative in our estimate. Nevertheless, if you enter waters just deep enough for your draft, feel your way in and watch the sounder closely.

Sailcraft and single-screw trawlers must be alert for the side-setting effect of the swift tidal currents. Be sure to look to your stern as well as the course ahead to quickly note any slippage.

All boaters should have a well-functioning depth sounder on board before leaving the dock. This is one of the most basic safety instruments in any navigator's arsenal of aids. The cruiser who does not take this elementary precaution is asking for trouble. An accurate knotmeter/log is another instrument that will prove to be quite useful. While not as critical as a sounder, it is often just as important to know how far you have gone as to know what course you are following. On the other hand, GPS or Loran is not a serious consideration for inland passage of South Carolina or Georgia waters. Of course, if you plan to cruise offshore extensively, a well-functioning GPS (or Loran) would be highly beneficial.

In this guide, lighted daybeacons are always called "flashing daybeacons." I feel this is a more descriptive term than the officially correct "light" or the more colloquial "flasher." Also, to avoid confusion, daybeacons without lights are always referred to as "unlighted daybeacons." Similarly, lighted buoys are called "flashing buoys."

Autumn is the ideal cruising season for the South Carolina and Georgia coastline unless a hurricane is threatening the area. From the middle of September all the way through November, coastal weather is usually at its best. Bright, shining days are frequent, usually with just enough wind for a good sail. Fall storms occasionally break this pattern of good weather, but the nontropical variety are usually of short duration. It always surprises this writer how many boaters never even visit the coast after Labor Day. Those who make this mistake will miss the most beautiful season the coast has to offer.

Summer is also a good time for cruising the twin states' coastline. However, heat and humidity during July and August can leave the air sticky and breathless. Fortunately, the frequent sea breezes do offer some relief. South Carolina and Georgia are also noted for their afternoon thunderstorms, which can reach severe proportions from time to time. To avoid any last-minute surprises, it is a good idea to check the latest weather forecast before beginning your summer cruise.

Spring comes early to the South Carolina and Georgia seashore. Warm-weather boating can often resume as early as the first of March. The trouble is that the spring weather is more than a little capricious. As seems to be true all along the eastern seaboard, weather from the first of March to the middle of May can range from beautiful, sun-draped days of light breezes to overcast days full of rain-driven gales. Be sure to include the latest weather update in your springtime cruising plans as well.

Many boaters continue their cruising through the cold winter months of December, January, and February. While freezes are possible, the visitor from northerly climes will be amazed by the mild character of coastal South Carolina and Georgia winters. If you choose to join the ranks of these adventurous "frostbite" cruisers, be sure to dress warmly and check the forecast in case a hard freeze is due. Small craft should not leave the dock in weather that threatens a danger of capsizing. The cold waters could quickly bring on hypothermia. Otherwise, consider giving South Carolina and Georgia winter cruising a try. It may not be for you, but on the other hand, it may prove to be a most enjoyable adventure.

In addition to the raw navigational data presented in this guide, this writer has included numerous historical sketches and coastal folk tales to enrich your cruising experience. South Carolina and Georgia enjoy one of the richest historical heritages of all the American states, and cruising boaters must acquire some sense of the area's colorful past if they are to fully enjoy their visit.

Founded as one of the original 13 colonies, South Carolina was prominent in American affairs until the close of the Civil War. Because the colony was blessed from its beginnings with rich soil, natural harbors, and navigable rivers, South Carolina became an agricultural giant in the New World. The cultivation first of indigo, then of rice, and finally of Sea Island cotton brought almost unimaginable wealth to some planters and gave rise to a system of large plantations that characterized the South Carolina lifestyle and economic base until the Civil War.

It is not too much to say that South Carolina led the whole South in that time of crisis and conflict. Little did the state's enthusiastic politicians realize that their policies would lead to the destruction of a society that had been built by many proud and struggling generations.

The Civil War decimated South Carolina, as it did much of the South. Coastal South Carolina became an underutilized land of small farms and poor villages. Wilderness reclaimed many a field that had once waved with cotton or rice. The coast of South Carolina was a land whose greatness seemed locked in the past.

During this difficult period, some were wise enough to see the coast's potential. In *Glories of the Carolina Coast*, written during the troubled twenties, James Henry Rice, Jr., stated, "We must . . . remember also that the sixty years which have elapsed since the Confederate War are less by a third than the period of the coast's glory. Time is the test of enduring worth and when the rest of the State shows a record equal in producing men eminent for character, intellect and achievement, and, finally, equal in promoting human happiness, it will be time enough to institute a comparison."

Mr. Rice's faith has at last been justified in the twentieth century. The coming of large-scale tourism to coastal South Carolina has clearly breathed new life into the region. Many of the surviving plantations have been restored as vacation homes, and some of the Sea Islands have been carefully developed as multimillion-dollar resorts. Yet for all this welcome activity, nostalgia for the "old" way of life persists and is at times almost a tangible entity. This vague feeling of regret and sorrow seems to be the key to understanding the very special aura of romance and mystery that bathes coastal South Carolina in its warm glow.

There are very few states indeed that can lay claim to such a colorful heritage. Today's South Carolinian is justly proud of his storied past. Thanks to the efforts of a number of excellent writers, many books on the history and folklore of the state are available today for anyone who wishes to partake of this rich tradition. The coastal visitor would do well to make the acquaintance of at least a part of this large body of literature before his trip. There is perhaps no surer way to get in touch with the spirit of the land and its people.

Georgia can also boast of a rich and colorful history, though its story began very differently from that of its northerly sister. In 1723, an extraordinarily enterprising Englishman, James Oglethorpe, was appointed to head a committee investigating British prisons. The results were horrifying. It was discovered that many of the prisoners were simple debtors. Working with Dr. Thomas Bray, founder of the Society for the Propagation of the Gospel in Foreign Parts, Oglethorpe secured a charter to found a colony south of the Carolinas. To this new land, Oglethorpe planned to take former prisoners, the underprivileged, and those simply down on their luck.

South Carolinians were enthusiastic about the establishment of the Georgia colony. While some of this good feeling was most certainly due to genuine charity and helpfulness, there is no denying that the South Carolina government correctly foresaw that Georgia would act as a ready barrier between itself and the hostile Spanish and Indians in Florida.

Oglethorpe founded Savannah in February 1733. He developed a town plan that called for many "green squares," what we would today call parks. Surprisingly enough, this sensible pattern has been maintained down through the years by Savannah's wise city leaders, even as the community expanded.

Under Oglethorpe's leadership, the colony's board of directors decreed that no colonist was to receive more than 500 acres of land, and that slavery was forbidden. These prohibitions were in keeping with Oglethorpe's idea of making Georgia a colony for the common man. As an additional inducement to settle in Georgia, full religious freedom was granted to all but Roman Catholics. This policy soon began to attract religiously persecuted settlers from all of Europe. Their diverse ethnic backgrounds were to add immeasurably to Georgia's character.

In 1742, a strong Spanish expeditionary force sailing north from St. Augustine attacked the English outpost on St. Simons Island established by Oglethorpe. Even though the English defenders were vastly outnumbered, the Spanish were soundly repulsed at the Battle of Bloody Marsh. This ended the Spanish threat from Florida, and all of South Carolina must have breathed a sigh of relief.

In spite of these early successes, Georgia was rapidly losing population by the 1750s. The restrictive land policies and lack of slavery made the large-scale agriculture of the day, practiced so successfully in South Carolina, impractical.

In 1752, the English Crown took over the Georgia colony and removed these rules once and for all.

From that time forward, the history of coastal Georgia has been a reasonably close approximation of that of its sister to the north. Rice was grown profitably both before and after the American Revolution.

While portions of Georgia (notably St. Johns Parish) were decidedly patriot during the Revolutionary War years, the colony was very dependent on England for many of the products that allowed everyday life to continue. For this reason, the soon-to-be state took a rather conservative approach during those troubled years.

Following the successful close of the Revolution, plantation life took even firmer root in the fertile Georgia soil. Rice was still grown profitably, and by the late 1700s Sea Island cotton had been successfully introduced to coastal Georgia, as it had on South Carolina's Sea Islands to the north. As in its sister state, vast quantities of wealth became concentrated in the hands of a relatively few planters.

Savannah became a great cotton- and rice-shipping port during this era and rivaled Charleston as one of the greatest shipping depots in America. The city expanded, and many of the beautiful homes and buildings that amaze us today were built with immaculate craftsmanship during these years.

While secession fever was far less fervent in Georgia than in its northerly neighbor, the state followed South Carolina's lead and joined the ill-starred Confederacy. The Georgia coastline fell to Union forces early in the war, and there was little military activity for several years until Sherman's infamous "march to the sea." Much of the coast was then laid in ruins, though Savannah survived Northern occupation without major damage.

During Reconstruction, Georgia recovered more quickly than many other Southern states. A timber boom was well under way by the 1870s, and tourism was becoming important to Georgia by the end of the nineteenth century.

The coming of the automobile and good roads secured the future of the Georgia coastline. Sumptuous resorts were established at St. Simons, Jekyll, and Sea Islands. Savannah also began to attract large numbers of visitors.

The twentieth century has seen the development of successful commerce along the Georgia coastline based on tourism, port facilities, lumber, and wood pulp. One cannot visit this fortunate land without gaining a swift and sure impression that this is an area on the move that still has a healthy respect for the fragility of the coastal ecosystem. The future seems bright, which is only to be expected for the coastline of the "Golden Isles."

If by now you have detected a certain rampant enthusiasm for coastal South Carolina and Georgia on the part of this writer, then you are on the right track. In my cruising experience, I have never found any other waters that combine breathtaking natural scenery, historic character, and ease of navigation in such perfect measure. The coast of South Carolina and Georgia sits shimmering in the summer sun, waiting to greet you. Boaters everywhere should rejoice in its promise.

And just in case your boating appetite has not been sufficiently whetted, consider this unforgettable description of cruising down a South Carolina river by James Henry Rice, Jr.: "A summer trip along one of the coastal rivers will show the giant yuccas in flower and the magnolia, the royal woman of the Southern wood, with its creamy white blossoms laid on shining green leaves, the cypresses clad in vivid green and lilies floating on still waters while the wampee shows forth its blossoms—everywhere blooms run riot. On the uplands tall brooding pines sway in the wind and murmur things unutterable. Huge wood ibises stalk along the shore; redwings chatter and quarrel; rails cry in the reeds; coots and gallinules patter over the lily pads; the bald eagle soars, often a speck in the empyrean, while coppices are snow white with egrets; and nonpareils cling to grass stalks, eating seeds. All is life, life omnipresent—bird and beast, insect and flower, reptile and fish."

Good luck and good boating!

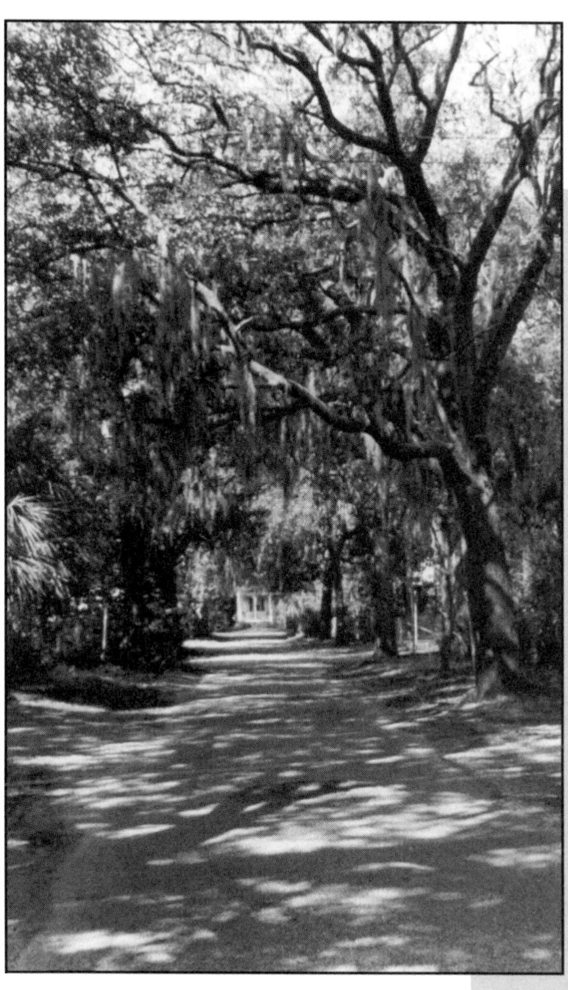

For This Your Land

*For this your land you have shown me I
feel a familiar love:
Its water vistas, quiet marshes, dear
sunshine, and hymnsong of trees,
These manly, majestic trees, with Gothic
moss hanging and swaying Like fairytale
mermaid hair, in the soft shore breeze;
And the rustling, stiff-barked palmettoes;
the brown marsh grasses,
Brown by the blue of wide rivers and
flame of great skies
Of the sunsets we saw, together, before
the red moon
And all the stars, and the darkness, took
over with wonderful arms,
Here there is grandeur, and joy, and
continuing peace.
Always the tides of the ocean, the wave-
break and the return, Promising,
giving, always. Ah, the sounds of these
waters
And all the choirs of the birds . . .
For these things, not contained, given
thanks for, in words,
I feel a familiar love.*

Edith Bannister Dowling

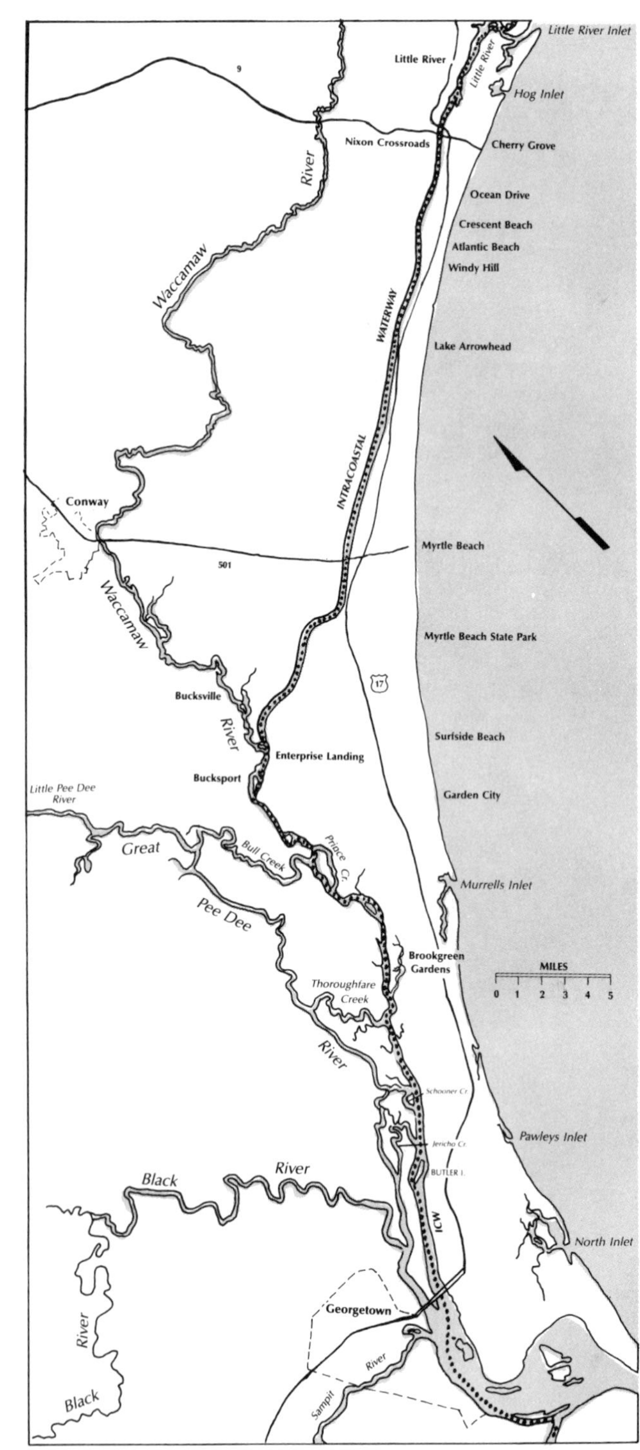

Little River Inlet
Little River
Little River
9
Hog Inlet
Nixon Crossroads
Cherry Grove
Ocean Drive
Crescent Beach
Atlantic Beach
Windy Hill
Waccamaw
River
INTRACOASTAL
WATERWAY
Lake Arrowhead
Conway
Myrtle Beach
501
Waccamaw
River
Myrtle Beach State Park
17
Bucksville
Enterprise Landing
Bucksport
Surfside Beach
Little Pee Dee
River
Garden City
Great
Pee Dee
Bull Creek
Prince Cr.
Murrells Inlet
Brookgreen
Gardens
MILES
0 1 2 3 4 5
Thoroughfare
Creek
River
Schooner Cr.
Jericho Cr.
BUTLER I.
Pawleys Inlet
Black
River
ICW
North Inlet
Georgetown
River
Black
Sampit
River

Little River to Winyah Bay

The waters of northeastern South Carolina present a study in contrasts for the cruising boater. Little River, a part of the ICW for approximately 5 nautical miles, is a typical but undramatic section of the Waterway. From the river, the Waterway enters a man-made canal known as Pine Island Cut. This is one of the least-attractive sections of the entire ICW. Additionally, the presence of numerous underwater rock ledges gives good cause for concern. Fortunately, the canal eventually leads into Waccamaw River, considered by many to be one of the most beautiful sections of the ICW. Its reputation is richly deserved. The river winds its way lazily to the south for some 22 nautical miles until it finally intersects the headwaters of Winyah Bay near Mile 400 of the Waterway.

Coastal South Carolina's northerly waters present excellent opportunities for the cruising boater in a variety of settings. From gunkholing to historic cruising, the region has something for everyone. While a few sections may not warrant much of the boater's time, others beg to be explored and cruised. Take the time necessary for a full appreciation of the region.

Charts

You will only need one chart to navigate this section of the South Carolina ICW:

11534 covers all South Carolina waters from the state line to Winyah Bay

ICW TO WACCAMAW RIVER

South Carolina's northernmost waters consist almost solely of the ICW's channel through Little River, followed by the man-made Pine Island Cut. Most of the route has treeless shores, often marred by visible evidence of dredging. This cut is, in this writer's opinion, one of the least-enjoyable portions of the entire South Carolina ICW. Anchorages are very few and far between. Marina facilities are available at the villages of Calabash and Little River, while the Myrtle Beach region to the south boasts several excellent marinas. Those who like a bustling, resort atmosphere will find Myrtle Beach, located to the east of the Waterway, and the nearby Grand Strand communities worth their while. Otherwise, except for the excellent area marinas, most boaters will be glad to put this stretch behind them.

Little River Inlet

From north to south, Little River Inlet is the first South Carolina seaward cut available to cruising boaters. The inlet provides reasonably reliable access to the open sea. Most of the cut's aids to navigation are not charted, as they are frequently shifted to follow the ever-changing sands. A check in late 1995 showed that the channel was well marked and reasonably easy to follow during daylight hours. Minimum depths were 10 feet, though this reading could be dramatically altered by the time of your visit. If you are lucky enough to spot a local craft putting out to sea, you might consider following in its wake. It is also a wise practice to check the current inlet conditions at Marsh Harbour Marina in Calabash or The Pier at Little River Marina.

Calabash Creek

Calabash Creek, just to the northeast of the Waterway's intersection with Little River Inlet, provides the first and one of the only opportunities for overnight anchorage on this section of the ICW. Some shoaling has occurred at the creek's southwesterly mouth (northeast of the ICW's unlighted daybeacon #2) but is not noted on the latest edition of chart 11534. Boaters can now expect typical low-water depths of 5½ to 6 feet over the entrance bar. Similarly, the channel farther upstream, between flashing daybeacon #4 and unlighted daybeacon #6, has shoaled along its eastern flank. Local reports indicate that this area is slated for dredging in 1996. Depths should improve markedly after that time.

Good anchorage is found along lower Calabash Creek's eastern and northeastern shores between the creek's unlighted daybeacon #2 (not to be confused with unlighted daybeacon #2 on the ICW) and flashing daybeacon #4. Low-water depths of 5½ to 9 feet run within 20 yards or so of shore between #2 and unlighted daybeacon #3. Similar depths are found between #3 and the creek's sharp swing to the north near flashing daybeacon #4. Swinging room should be sufficient for boats as large as 40 feet. Shelter is excellent from all but particularly strong southern winds that blow straight in from the creek's mouth. The eastern and northeastern banks are overlooked by a few attractive homes, while the marsh island to the west is undeveloped.

Calabash Creek leads north and northeast to the village of Calabash, barely within the borders of North Carolina. A marked channel holding minimum 6- to 8-foot depths is, for the most part, easily followed to the village waterfront. There are no formal marinas on the Calabash waterfront, but the diplomatic boater may be able to negotiate dockage for the night at one of the many commercial docks.

Fortunately, the longtime problem of finding a slip in or near Calabash has now been solved with the addition of a fine facility, Marsh Harbour Marina. A well-sheltered dockage basin sporting 120 slips has been dredged northwest of the creek's unlighted daybeacon #8. Entrance depths in the marina channel run 7 to 9 feet, while boaters will find 8 to 17 feet of water dockside. Marsh Harbour also holds the distinction of being the closest marina to Little River Inlet.

Transients are cheerfully accepted for overnight or temporary dockage at concrete-decked floating docks with water and power connections up to 50 amps. Gasoline, diesel fuel, and waste pump-out services are readily available, and shoreside showers are at hand. Some mechanical repairs can be arranged through local independent contractors. It's only a quick walk into downtown Calabash, where you will find a host of restaurants. Some of the local dining establishments also feature free dockside pickup and delivery for visiting cruisers. Ask the dockmaster for advice.

Recently, Marsh Harbour has completed three condo units and a large clubhouse overlooking the northwest corner of the dockage basin. More condos are planned in the near future. For a small additional fee, boaters may use the heated pool and exercise room in the clubhouse. Those who would like to take a break from the liveaboard routine will discover that "luxury condos" are usually available for rent, with an attractive discount for those who arrive by water.

Marsh Harbour Marina (910) 579-3500

Approach depth: 6–9 feet
Dockside depth: 8–17 feet
Accepts transients: yes
Concrete floating docks: yes
Dockside power connections: up to 50 amps
Dockside water connections: yes
Showers: yes
Waste pump-out: yes
Gasoline: yes
Diesel fuel: yes
Mechanical repairs: independent contractors
Restaurants: many nearby

The village of Calabash has long been famous for its fried seafood. You may want to step ashore and test its reputation for yourself. Better hurry, though. Locals declare that if one more restaurant is built, the entire town will sink into the ocean.

Historic Boundary House

As you pass flashing daybeacon #4 on Calabash Creek, look to the north and you will see a golf course and a clubhouse. These mark the approximate site of the old Boundary House. This establishment served as a resting place for colonial travelers on the King's Highway between North and South Carolina.

Little River

The village of Little River lines the Waterway's northern banks near flashing daybeacon #9. This waterside community offers a single facility catering to cruising boaters. Northside

Marina, once located just east of the principal village waterfront, is now long out of business. Similarly, an abandoned dock lining the northern banks west of flashing daybeacon #9 has been long unused. This structure has become dilapidated, and boaters should not attempt to tie off on the unstable pilings.

The Pier at Little River Marina lies along the northerly shores in the heart of the village. This facility welcomes the transient boater and provides fairly extensive overnight berths on a long fixed-face dock with water and power connections. Several 50-amp hookups are available, while 30-amp connections are more numerous. Low-tide dockside depths run around 6, and occasionally 5½, feet. Gasoline and diesel fuel are readily available, and mechanical repairs can sometimes be arranged. The marina maintains a small bait, tackle, and variety store on the docks.

Showers are usually available for visiting cruisers at the motel (open year-round) just behind the marina. A number of down-home, high-quality seafood restaurants are found adjacent to the marina docks. Captain Jewels and Fisherman's Hide-a-Way are worth the gastronomical attention of any who fancy Southern fried seafood. The Pier at Little River also maintains its own restaurant with a surprisingly sophisticated menu. Give the French lamb chops (sauteed with capers, mushrooms, and Chardonnay) or the Shrimp and Scallops Provencale (sauteed with tomatoes, mushrooms, shallots, and a touch of garlic) a try. Your palate will be ever so happy!

Several shops, including a convenience store, a video store, and another motel, can be accessed by way of a five-block walk. These businesses are all located on U.S. 17.

The Pier at Little River Marina
(803) 249-1220

Approach depth: 10–12 feet
Dockside depth: 5½–6 feet (low water)
Accepts transients: yes
Fixed wooden piers: yes
Dockside power connections: 30 and 50 amps
Dockside water connections: yes
Showers: yes
Gasoline: yes
Diesel fuel: yes
Mechanical repairs: local independent contractors
Variety store: small
Restaurants: on-site and nearby

Little River History The village of Little River is quite old. It was established before the Revolutionary War as a center of trade. Many of the original residents were from the Northern colonies, and the community was first known as "Yankee Town." For many years, logging was the mainstay of the local economy. Old piles still line the shore, marking the former sites of sawmills. As logging declined, commercial fishing assumed increasing importance. In recent times, sportfishing has become popular in Little River. Several fishing tournaments are held during the course of the year. Charter boats that put to sea from Little River Inlet are available for anglers.

Coquina Harbor

Study chart 11534 for a moment and notice the charted pool of water with a connector canal making in to the Waterway's northern banks west of Little River near unlighted daybeacon #13 (Standard Mile 346). This impressive port of call is known as Coquina Harbor. Located along the shoreline of this deep and sheltered harbor are no fewer than three firms, two of which readily cater to cruising boaters. Plenty of dockage and fuel are available, but no haul-outs are to be found.

Believe it or else, this large body of water once served as a stone quarry. When developers connected the quarry to the ICW, they encountered a rather unique problem. A certain regulation prohibits joining any body of water that is deeper than the Waterway channel to the ICW. Consequently, sand had to be pumped into the old quarry to raise its depth to that of the Waterway. Now, boaters can expect impressive minimum entrance depths of 10 feet on the connector canal and soundings of 14 feet or better on the harbor's interior reaches.

As you move into Coquina Harbor, Lightkeeper's Village (803-249-5720) will come up on the western shores. This large townhouse and condo development maintains extensive floating docks for its patrons but accepts relatively few waterborne transients.

Coquina Harbor, Inc., boasts a whole bevy of ultramodern floating docks on the harbor's eastern banks, overlooked by yet another extensive condo development. Coquina gladly accepts transients or those seeking temporary dockage at its slips, which feature full water and power connections. Shoreside showers and a first-rate laundromat are readily available. Mechanical repairs can usually be handled by an on-site independent repair firm. The harbor management owns and operates Umberto's at Coquina Harbor restaurant, perched on the cove's northeastern corner. While this writer did not have the opportunity to sample the fare, reports from local boaters paint a picture of gastronomic delight.

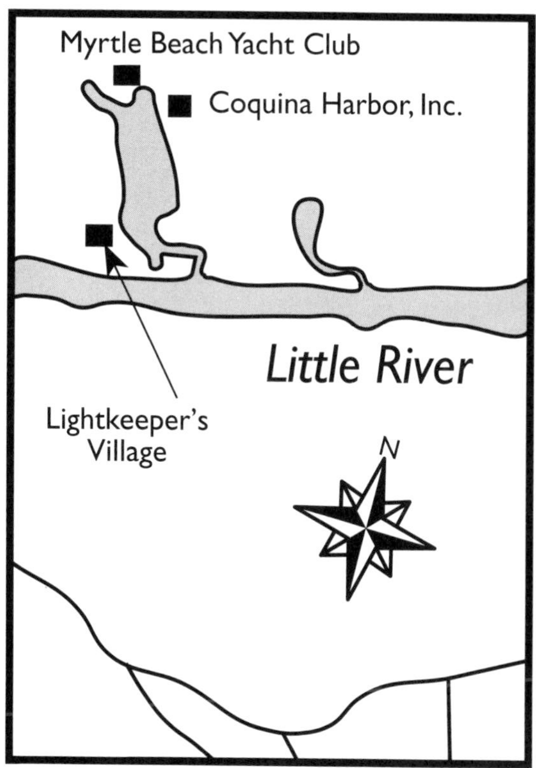

Entrance to Coquina Harbor

Coquina Harbor, Inc. (803) 249-9333

Approach depth: 10 feet
Dockside depth: 13+ feet
Accepts transients: yes

Floating wooden piers: yes
Dockside power connections: up to 50 amps
Dockside water connections: yes
Showers: yes
Laundromat: yes
Mechanical repairs: independent repair firm on-site
Ship's store: nearby
Restaurant: on-site

Myrtle Beach Yacht Club guards the harbor's northerly (innermost) shores. In spite of its name, this nautical establishment is a first-class marina that gladly accepts transient dockers. Berths with water, cable television, and power connections up to 50 amps are available at the floating wooden-decked piers. Clean showers, a full laundromat, waste pump-out service, and a well-stocked ship's store are at hand. Gasoline and diesel fuel can be purchased dockside. Mechanical repairs can usually be arranged through independent technicians, but no haul-outs are available.

Cruising visitors to Myrtle Beach Yacht Club are welcome to make use of the adjacent swimming pool and tennis courts. Umberto's restaurant is only a short step away. Little River Diner, just across U.S. 17 from the dockage basin, is open 24 hours a day and serves good, if simple, food.

Myrtle Beach Yacht Club
(803) 249-5376

Approach depth: 10 feet
Dockside depth: 13+ feet
Accepts transients: yes
Floating wooden piers: yes
Dockside power connections: 30 and 50 amps
Dockside water connections: yes
Showers: yes
Laundromat: yes
Waste pump-out: yes
Gasoline: yes
Diesel fuel: yes
Mechanical repairs: independent technicians
Ship's store: yes
Restaurant: on-site

Nixon Crossroads Facilities

Three facilities are found near the twin bridges spanning the Waterway at the small village of Nixon Crossroads. North Myrtle Beach Marina guards the northern banks 0.4 nautical mile east of flashing daybeacon #14. This establishment's large dry-stack storage building is readily visible from the ICW. Transients are infrequently accepted for overnight dockage, and wet-slip space is limited. Dry storage of small power craft is clearly this marina's primary occupation. If you do secure a berth, you will find concrete-decked floating docks sporting water connections and power connections up to 30 amps. The marina maintains a ship's and variety store on the premises. Gasoline can be purchased, and both mechanical repairs (gas and diesel) and below-waterline haul-out repairs are available. Haul-outs are accomplished by either a marine crane or a new 60-ton travelift. Next door, famished cruisers can slake their appetites at the Riverboat Restaurant. This on-the-water dining establishment is housed in a boatlike structure resembling (you guessed it) a riverboat. While the restaurant has a few slips of its own, these are only appropriate for small power craft.

North Myrtle Beach Marina
(803) 249-1000

Approach depth: 10–12 feet

Dockside depth: 6–9 feet
Accepts transients: limited
Concrete floating piers: yes
Dockside power connections: up to 30 amps
Dockside water connections: yes
Gasoline: yes
Mechanical repairs: yes
Below-waterline repairs: yes
Ship's and variety store: yes
Restaurant: on-site

West of flashing daybeacon #14, Anchor Marina (formerly Palmetto Shores Marina) overlooks the ICW's southerly banks just east of the Little River high-rise bridge. This newly minted, ultrafriendly facility is glad to welcome cruising visitors and offers not only dockage but full-service repairs as well.

Most of the marina's docks are located in a sheltered basin (6-foot depths) connected to the ICW via a small canal-like stream. There is one less-protected dock that fronts directly onto the Waterway. Transients are gratefully accepted at Anchor's floating wooden-decked piers, which feature full power and water connections. Showers are available shoreside, and extensive waste pump-out facilities are also offered. By the time you read this account, gasoline and diesel fuel should be ready to pump dockside. The marina also maintains a ship's store adjacent to the dockmaster's office. When it comes time to satisfy the old appetite, the on-site Blue Marlin restaurant and lounge is very convenient (lunch and dinner only).

Anchor Marina really shines in its repair capabilities. Full-service mechanical (gas and diesel), electrical, fiberglass, and below-waterline repairs are very much in the offing. Haul-outs are accomplished by way of a 35-ton travelift. This writer was very impressed with this facility's extensive service capabilities, coupled with a genuine "can do" attitude. I suggest that you give Anchor Marina a try when next your Waterway travels bring you to the Little River region.

Anchor Marina (803) 249-7899

Approach depth: 10-12 feet
Dockside depth: 6 feet (in dockage basin) 6½ + feet (dock on ICW)
Accepts transients: yes
Floating wooden docks: yes
Dockside power connections: 30 and 50 amps
Dockside water connections: yes
Showers: yes
Waste pump-out: yes
Gasoline: planned
Diesel fuel: planned
Mechanial repairs: extensive
Below-waterline repair: extensive
Ship's store: yes
Restaurant: on-site

Fabulous Harbour Gate Marina occupies the charted square cove abutting the ICW's southern banks between the two Nixon Crossroads bridges. The marina is designated as facility #18 on chart 11534. Harbour Gate's motto is "The best staff in the Southeast," and they truly mean it. Seldom in this writer's lengthy travels along the ICW have I received a warmer welcome. Visiting cruisers can be assured of the same enthusiastic reception.

Harbour Gate opened for business some seven years ago, but the docks and buildings look as if they have been newly minted. A huge building complex overlooks the westerly banks at the cove's mouth. This imposing structure contains offices and, most important, the Marker 350

Harbour Gate Marina at Nixon Crossroads

Harbour Gate Marina (803) 249-8888

Approach depth: 7 feet (minimum)
Dockside depth: 7–10 feet
Accepts transients: yes
Floating wooden piers: yes
Dockside power connections: up to 50 amps
Dockside water connections: yes
Showers: yes
Laundromat: yes
Gasoline: yes
Diesel fuel: yes
Mechanical repairs: independent contractors
Ship's store: yes
Restaurant: on-site

Restaurant. Believe you me, this dining firm is ready to handle the most ravenous appetite.

The dockage basin itself was dug out of the shoreline when the marina was constructed. Minimum entrance depths run around 7 feet, with 7 to 10 feet of water at the well-sheltered piers. Transients are eagerly accepted for overnight dockage at the marina's absolutely first-rate floating docks, which feature every conceivable power and water connection. Gasoline and diesel fuel are readily available, and mechanical problems can often be referred to independent contractors. Shoreside, boaters will discover spotless showers and an excellent laundromat. The on-site ship's store is one of the nicest you will find anywhere. Future plans call for the installation of a waste pump-out service and the construction of a motel just across the street. Without a doubt, this facility has acquired an excellent reputation among local boaters, particularly powerboat captains. Advance reservations would be a wise precaution.

The Marina at Dock Holidays

About 1 nautical mile southwest of the Little River swing bridge, the Marina at Dock Holidays (formerly Vereens Marina) will come abeam along the southeastern shore. This site bears facility designation #17A on chart 11534. Passing cruisers would have to have lost their eyesight entirely to miss the huge restaurant building overlooking the Waterway. Dock Holiday's well-sheltered dockage basin sits just southwest of the restaurant.

After having been closed following the failure of the former Shooter's Restaurant, this facility has reopened, and the new managment is obviously intent on doing things right. One visit to the on-site, full-line ship's, variety, and clothing store (doubling as the dockmaster's office) convinced this writer and his mate that this was the sort of place we wanted in our cruising itinerary.

Transients are eagerly accepted at floating wooden-decked piers. Depths in the sheltered basin run 7 to 10 feet. However, Dock Holidays' fuel dock fronts directly onto the ICW immediately northeast of the restaurant building. Approach depths to this pier have shoaled to only 6 feet or so. Captains whose craft draw better than 5½ feet should approach with caution.

All berths feature full power and water connections. Ultranice showers and a full laundromat are available within an easy step of the dockage basin. Gasoline and diesel fuel are both very much available, and mechanical repairs can sometimes be arranged through independent local technicians. Visitors will also discover a first-class ship's and variety store along the harbor's northeastern shores.

Of course, hungry cruisers will find the on-site Dock Holidays Island Grill most convenient. This writer found this to be what a research assistant once dubbed a "yuppie restaurant." The food was good, but the atmosphere was a trifle noisy.

Three other restaurants—Oak Harbor, the Marina Raw Bar, and Santa Fe Station—are also found within a quick step of the docks. An A&P supermarket is just across the street, and there is also a Food Lion three blocks away.

All in all, this writer recommends The Marina at Dock Holidays for its many services, sheltered dockage, and close access to resupply. Compared to a wonderfully isolated anchorage off the Waccamaw River—well, you will just have to make that decision for yourself.

The Marina at Dock Holidays
(803) 280-6354

Approach depth: 10-12 feet
Dockside depth: 7-10 feet (dockage basin)
6 feet (fuel dock on ICW)
Accepts transients: yes
Floating wooden piers: yes
Dockside power connections: yes
Dockside water connections: yes
Showers: yes
Laundromat: yes
Gasoline: yes
Diesel fuel: yes
Mechanical repairs: independent technicians
Ship's and variety store: yes
Restaurant: 4 on-site

Barefoot Landing

Barefoot Landing (803-272-8349), a huge shopping and dining complex, overlooks the southern shores of the ICW some 1 nautical mile east of Standard Mile 355. This sprawling facility maintains a long floating-face dock fronting directly on the Waterway; passing boaters are welcome to tie up while shopping or eating in the complex. Depths alongside run around 5 to 8 feet, with the better water found along the western end of the piers.

At the current time, visiting cruisers are welcome to dock overnight (three-day maximum stay), but no power or water connections or shoreside marine services are available. The docks are essentially unattended.

Hague Marina

Hague Marina is a well-managed full-service facility sheltered in a loop on the Waterway's southern shore some 2.4 nautical miles southwest of the Myrtle Beach high-rise and railroad bridge, near Standard Mile 369. The marina is designated as facility #21 on the current edition of chart 11534. Transient craft are gladly accepted at the facility's well-protected fixed wooden piers. Approach and dockside depths range from 6 to 8 feet. Full power and water connections are available, as are gasoline and diesel fuel. Hague Marina specializes in repairs both above and below the waterline. The yard's travelift is rated at 35 tons. If you are having mechanical or prop difficulty, it would be a good idea to put in here before proceeding on your way.

The marina maintains a fine ship's and parts store, along with good showers and an on-site laundromat.

The Maryland Crab Restaurant is within walking distance, but the fare here is rather plain. A better choice is Mancuso's Restaurant, which will dispatch complimentary transportation to pick up and return visiting cruisers to their slips. Ask any of the friendly marina staff for help.

Hague Marina is the closest facility to the town of Myrtle Beach, but it is still necessary to obtain motorized transportation to visit the resort. Hague Marina does have one courtesy vehicle which visiting cruisers are welcome to use for resupply runs or visits to the nearby Grand Strand.

Hague Marina (803) 293-2141

Approach depth: 6–8 feet
Dockside depth: 6–8 feet
Accepts transients: yes
Fixed wooden piers: yes
Dockside power connections: 30 and 50 amps
Dockside water connections: yes
Showers: yes
Laundromat: yes
Gasoline: yes
Diesel fuel: yes
Mechanical repairs: yes (gasoline and diesel)
Below-waterline repairs: yes
Ship's store: yes
Restaurants: within walking distance, or will send complimentary transportation

Socastee Bridge

Southwest of Standard Mile 370, one of the most troublesome spans on the South Carolina ICW crosses the Waterway. With a closed vertical clearance of only 11 feet and a restrictive opening schedule, the Socastee bridge has been plaguing boaters for years.

Now, a new, modern high-rise (fixed) bridge has been constructed just east of the old swing bridge. Unfortunately, there is still automobile traffic on the old span. Consequently, there is still a restrictive schedule for the swinging span. Consult the next section of this chapter for an opening schedule.

Myrtle Beach–Horry County History Myrtle Beach and the adjacent Grand Strand communities, all within the confines of Horry County, have grown into South Carolina's most popular resort area. Thousands of tourists make the annual trek to these famous beaches. Such popularity, however, was not always the case.

In colonial days, Horry County was one of the most sparsely populated areas of the state. Many of those who did settle here migrated from the north. They established a small-farms culture very unlike the plantation system to the south, which spread from Charleston. Development was further impeded by the presence of vast swamps in the district.

It was not until 1899 that the area received its first great boost. In that year, a railroad was completed from Conway to Myrtle Beach. Originally built to transport crops grown in the area, it was later to have much greater impact. In 1926, John Woodside of Greenville, South Carolina, and Colonel Holmes B. Springs began an intensive promotional effort. The railroad brought in crowds of vacationers. Myrtle Beach was incorporated in 1938 and has never looked back. Its popularity has grown at a miraculous rate since World War II.

Today, the visitor will find a bustling community crowded with motels, hotels, condos, restaurants, and amusements of all descriptions. There are also several very popular fishing piers along the beach.

Boaters who prefer the quiet of an isolated anchorage may find the Grand Strand a bit robust. However, there is certainly no denying the resort's longtime popularity. As the saying goes, "All those people can't be wrong," so if you are so inclined, take the time to rent a car and explore the beach's many possibilities.

Enterprise Landing

The modern boater will note the small village of Enterprise Landing mostly as the northerly entrance to Waccamaw River. There is little left of the hustle and bustle of the days when ferries plied the waters of the upper Waccamaw here. They provided the only reliable means of travel south from the Horry County area. Certainly, the construction of modern bridges has greatly facilitated transportation for all. As you pass, however, take a minute to reflect on the color of that era when travel was a real adventure, not just an everyday occurrence.

ICW TO WACCAMAW RIVER NAVIGATION

Navigation in this section of the South Carolina ICW is a fairly straightforward business of holding to the mid-width of the Waterway. Pine Island Cut requires additional attention, as detailed below.

Soon after crossing the state line, you will approach the intersection of Little River Inlet, Calabash Creek, and the ICW. Be on the watch for strong tidal currents. Slow-moving craft should be particularly alert for side-setting currents.

Little River Inlet Good minimum depths of 10 feet or so are currently maintained in the Little River Inlet channel from its intersection with the ICW to its exodus into the ocean at flashing buoy #LR. While several of the markers are charted, many are not. This indicates that the channel is changeable. The configuration of the inlet's aids to navigation, as well as its depths, could be very different by the time you visit.

To enter the seaward cut, turn southwest off the Waterway some 50 yards northwest of the ICW's flashing daybeacon #119. Cruise into the mid-width of the broad passage, which will open out before you. Point to come abeam and pass unlighted daybeacon #20 on its westerly quarter. South and southeast of #20, most of the channel markers are uncharted. As you are now headed out to sea, take red markers to your port side and green beacons to starboard. Ignore the charted "Markers" north of the inlet's passage out into the open sea. An on-the-water check revealed that these so-called aids to navigation are nothing but unadorned pilings set amidst shallow water.

Little River Inlet's passage into the ocean is

sheltered between twin stone breakwaters to the east and west. Currently, best depths can be maintained by slightly favoring the western side of the marked channel as you approach the passage between the breakwaters. As recommended earlier, if you are unfamiliar with the cut, you should try following a local craft or inquiring about current conditions at one of the nearby marinas. Aside from these precautions, just take it slow and keep a wary eye on the sounder and you should run the cut without any problem.

Calabash Creek To enter Calabash Creek, leave the Waterway just before reaching the ICW's unlighted daybeacon #2 by turning 90 degrees to the northeast. This maneuver is complicated by the presence of another unlighted daybeacon #2, which acts as the first marker on the Calabash Creek channel. Don't become confused by the numbering similarity of these two aids to navigation.

Favor the eastern shore a bit as you enter the creek. As you would expect, pass all red markers to your starboard side and green beacons to port as you head upstream to Calabash. The shallowest portion of the channel is encountered between the creek's entrance and Calabash Creek's unlighted daybeacon #2. Cruisers can currently expect some 5½-foot depths at low water.

After passing Calabash Creek's unlighted daybeacon #2, the channel begins a lazy turn to the northwest. Avoid the port-side banks between #2 and flashing daybeacon #4. Shallow water abuts the western and southwestern banks along this stretch of the stream.

As mentioned earlier, a popular anchorage can be found along the creek's eastern and northeastern banks between #2 and #4. Simply feel your way a short distance off the channel, drop the hook, and settle down for a night of peace and security.

Northwest of unlighted daybeacon #3, Calabash Creek forks. Avoid the branch leading to the west. Depths are more than suspect on this branch of the stream. Instead, follow the north fork past flashing daybeacon #4.

A new shoal known locally as "the parking lot" has built up along the channel's eastern flank between flashing daybeacon #4 and unlighted daybeacon #6. Favor the westerly side of the cut between #4 and #6 to avoid this hazard.

The entrance to Marsh Harbour will be spied along the northwestern banks hard by unlighted daybeacon #8. The channel is currently marked by two small, unlighted spar-type buoys.

A series of markers leads farther upstream on the main creek through good depths of 8 to 10 feet to Calabash village. Northeast of unlighted daybeacon #9, Calabash's waterfront opens out on the port shore. If you continue upstream, be sure to pass flashing daybeacon #10 to your starboard side. The first dock you will encounter is a long pier owned by Calabash Fishing Fleet.

Currently, there is little in the way of dockage for pleasure craft on the Calabash waterfront. Most cruising boats would do better to berth at Marsh Harbour Marina, just downstream, and then walk into the village.

Don't attempt to continue tracking your way upstream on Calabash Creek past the village waterfront. Depths soon rise to grounding levels.

On the ICW Avoid the offshoot of Calabash Creek intersecting the northern shores of the ICW west of unlighted daybeacon #6. Even though it looks good on chart 11534, this stream has now shoaled to depths of 3 feet or less.

West of unlighted daybeacon #8, the Waterway soon begins its approach to the Little River village waterfront, which abuts the northerly banks.

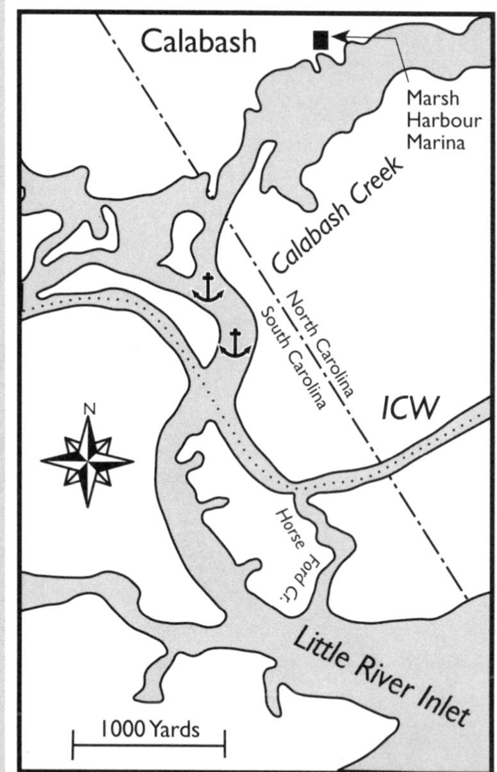

Flashing daybeacon #9 is almost abeam of The Pier at Little River Marina's docks. Large power craft should slow to idle speed when cruising past the various docks and piers.

Mariner's Pointe, a huge, new condo complex, guards the Waterway's northern shoreline east of flashing daybeacon #11. No services are available for transients.

The entrance to the protected basin serving Coquina Harbor, Lighthouse Village, and Myrtle Beach Yacht Club comes up along the ICW's northerly banks immediately east of unlighted daybeacon #13.

A quick jog to the west-southwest down the ICW will put you abeam of flashing daybeacon #14. From this aid, southbound boaters will soon exchange greetings with the Little River fixed high-rise bridge at charted Nixon Crossroads. This span has a vertical clearance of 65 feet. Slow down as you approach the bridge and continue at idle speed until you are well southwest of the second span.

The older Little River swing bridge crosses the Waterway a short distance southwest of the high-rise. Harbour Gate Marina occupies the southeasterly banks between the two spans. The swing bridge has a closed vertical clearance of only 7 feet, but fortunately it opens on demand.

Pine Island Cut West and southwest of Nixon Crossroads, the ICW enters the infamous Pine Island Cut. Running the canal presents more than its share of problems. Often referred to as "the Rock Pile," Pine Island Cut hides numerous partially submerged rock shelves on both sides of the channel. Because of these hazards, extreme caution must be exercised in the canal, particularly in passing situations. It is most important to hold strictly to the mid-width when at all possible. This is often made difficult for slow-moving craft by the strong tidal currents that may be encountered in the canal. Don't allow your attention to wander; be alert at all times when running the cut.

When you do meet another vessel, slow down to idle speed and hope it does the same. The slow speed will allow you to pass each other closely without undue wake and without having to encroach on the channel's edge.

Overtaking another vessel also calls for special attention. Often, this situation is the result of a powerboat overtaking a sailing vessel. It is an excellent practice for the sailcraft to squeeze just a bit to the side of the mid-width and slow down as much as possible. The powerboat should then

Sailcraft meets powerboat on Pine Island Cut

continue forward with just enough speed to pass the sailcraft. Failure to abide by this commonsense practice could result in some very frayed tempers and possible damage to both vessels.

As if the rock ledges were not problem enough, the canal is cursed with an abundant supply of flotsam. Floating logs and debris of all kinds abound, carried into the cut by the swift tidal currents. Keep a sharp watch for these hazards, or bent shafts and props could be your unlucky reward.

The Army Corps of Engineers has placed a whole series of lighted and unlighted daybeacons along the track of Pine Island Cut. Most of these aids to navigation are now shown on the current edition of chart 11534. While some of these markers serve only to help keep track of your progress, others warn of particularly nasty outcroppings of the rock shelf. Southbound boaters should be *sure* to pass all red markers to the boater's starboard side and green beacons to port. Ignore these markers only at your great peril.

On the ICW Southwest of unlighted daybeacons #18 and #19, the ICW runs hard by the Myrtle Beach airport, which overlooks the southeastern banks. The charted "Vortac" tower is readily visible from the Waterway. South of this point, the rock shelves described above seem a bit less of a problem. Nevertheless, visiting cruisers are still strictly advised to keep to the mid-width until entering Waccamaw River.

The long floating-face dock associated with the Barefoot Landing shopping and dining complex will be obvious on the southern banks just east of the small, charted dimple due north of Briarcliffe Acres (near Standard Mile 354). Slow down as you pass the docks. A large wake could damage any vessels moored to the piers.

Some 3.7 nautical miles southwest of the "Vortac" tower, you will pass under a cable car and a suspended power line. Minimum vertical clearance for these overhead obstructions is charted as 67 feet. The cable conveyance carries golfers across the Waterway to a course located on the northwestern shore. There is also a restaurant overlooking the canal at this point, but there is no dockage for boaters.

Passing cruisers will spy the sprawling Myrtlewood Golf Course lying along the southeasterly banks between unlighted daybeacons #19 and #20. The course makes for an impressive sight from the water.

Pine Island Cut meanders its way generally southwest through Myrtle Beach's railroad bridge and fixed highway bridge. The railway span is now apparently unused and remains open. The highway bridge has a vertical clearance of 65 feet. The Waterway turns again to the southwest near charted (but impassable) Socastee Creek.

The loop creek serving Hague Marina is located on the southern shoreline as the Waterway follows a long, slow track to the west. An official No Wake zone protects the docks of this facility. Slow down as you approach the marina and proceed at idle speed until you are well past the creek.

About 2.5 nautical miles southwest of the entrance to Hague Marina, passing cruisers will encounter the first South Carolina bridge with restricted operating hours. Despite the opening of a high-rise fixed bridge over this portion of the Waterway, the continued heavy automobile traffic on the older Socastee swing bridge (closed vertical clearance 11 feet) has necessitated a restrictive opening schedule. Currently, the Socastee swing bridge opens only 15 minutes after and 15 minutes before the hour from 6:00 A.M. to 10:00 A.M. and from 2:00 P.M. to 6:00 P.M., Monday through Friday. On weekends and holidays, the span opens 15 minutes after and 15 minutes before the hour between 10:00 A.M. and 2:00 P.M. At all other times, the bridge opens on demand.

Once through the troublesome swinging span, boaters will quickly pass under the new fixed high-rise. This bridge sports a vertical clearance of 65 feet.

South of the Socastee bridges, the land begins to change. Shores begin to rise and the banks become heavily wooded. You are now beginning your approach to Waccamaw River, and this scenery is just a taste of what is to come. At unlighted daybeacon #27, the Waterway intersects the beautiful Waccamaw.

WACCAMAW RIVER

Waccamaw River has long been known as one of the loveliest sections of the entire Intracoastal Waterway. As one slowly cruises along its cool length, pondering the ancient cypress forests that line the shores, it's easy to understand how this reputation was acquired. Stop your engine for a moment and listen. There are very few houses along this section, and the silence of the swamps can be eerie. Watch the shoreline carefully and you may well catch sight of an alligator lying in the sun or slithering into the water. It is easy to imagine that you have somehow slipped into a time far removed, long before the age of automobiles and factories. This primeval character can lend your cruise a feeling of adventure that is all too often absent in our modern, well-planned world.

Waccamaw River presents a multitude of possibilities for the cruising boater. Isolated, well-protected anchorages abound on the many deep creeks leading off the river. Some of these make fascinating side trips as well. Good marina facilities are found at Bucksport and Wachesaw. Tours of Brookgreen Gardens, one of the most lavish outdoor spectacles of flora in the Southeast, can sometimes be arranged from this latter facility.

The upper Waccamaw, abandoned by the ICW, offers a most interesting side trip. Stretching some 15 statute miles inland, the stream eventually leads boaters to the town of Conway, where two small marinas are located. It is seldom indeed that cruisers are presented with such a wide array of pleasurable choices in such a small span of distance.

From a navigational perspective, the Waccamaw is a delight. Good depths run almost from shore to shore. Sidewaters are almost invariably deep and invite serious gunkholing. About the only hazard you need to watch for is the presence of flotsam. While not as great a problem here as in Pine Island Cut, floating logs and snags are encountered from time to time.

By now, you have undoubtedly discerned that this writer has a great deal of enthusiasm for the Waccamaw. I believe that any serious cruising boater will have a similar reaction. Plan your cruise to allow ample time for full appreciation of this river's exceptional charms.

Waccamaw River History Waccamaw River was the site of many beautiful plantations before the Civil War. Sadly, only a few proud homes survive today. These vast farms were first based on the cultivation of indigo, but later came to depend on the growing of rice. In the next chapter, the rice culture that dominated the lands around Georgetown will be discussed. The plantations of the Waccamaw area were a part of this remarkably affluent era.

During the summer months, the planters usually fled their plantations and spent the season at coastal retreats, not to return until the first hard frost. Believing that the dreaded malaria, or "swamp fever," arose from the nearby swamps, they sought the more "healthful" breezes of the ocean. Little did these proud aristocrats suspect that their real enemy was the ignoble mosquito and that the sea breezes merely helped to disperse the foe.

Before the first hot spell, the entire household would be packed aboard a small fleet of pirogues. These were boats of various sizes made by hollowing out logs. As the slaves rowed the master and his family down the river, they would sing certain songs peculiar to their plantation. It is said that knowledgeable natives could recognize the origin of a particular party long before it passed simply by listening to the slow and sad singing that came before it. There are those who will tell you that on quiet spring nights, one may still hear ghostly singing along the river's banks. Perhaps it is only the wind remembering the grandeur and tragedy of long-lost days.

Upper Waccamaw River

Adventurous boaters can, if they so choose, abandon the ICW at Enterprise Landing and follow the upper reaches of Waccamaw River for some 15 statute miles to Conway. Two entrance routes are available. The wider of the two strikes to the northwest immediately southwest of flashing daybeacon #27A. The other, smaller feeder stream is found northwest of unlighted daybeacon #27.

Most of the upriver route is uncharted, but it is well marked, and the channel holds depths of 6 to 20 feet as far as Conway. During daylight hours, the navigational difficulties on the stream are limited to a few sharp bends and a fair number of snags. As the stream approaches Conway, it remains consistently deep but narrows somewhat. Consequently, this side trip is not recommended for craft over 40 feet. Visiting cruisers must also be able to clear one fixed

Old warehouse on upper Waccamaw River at Conway

bridge with approximately 35 feet of vertical clearance in order to reach the facilities and anchorage at Conway. Obviously, use of the city waterfront is confined to powerboats and small sailcraft. Be sure to read the upper Waccamaw River navigation section presented later in this chapter before trying the cut for the first time.

Boaters traversing the upper Waccamaw River will spot the beautifully restored plantation home of Henry Buck (see the Bucksville history section below) overlooking the port-side shore just upstream from unlighted daybeacon #8. Another short upriver jog brings you abeam of an easily spotted, large concrete chimney standing alone. This is all that is left of Buck's mighty sawmill, which once bustled and thrived along the Waccamaw.

The upper Waccamaw is well protected. The boater may choose to drop his hook almost anywhere along the stream. River traffic is light, so just select a likely spot and settle down for a peaceful evening. To be on the safe side, be sure to show an anchor light.

For those who make it all the way to Conway, one of the best spots to drop the hook is found just upstream from Kingston Point Marina. Here, the river divides in a wide fork and is soon blocked by low-level bridges. Boats up to 36 feet can easily anchor in the crook of this fork. Minimum depths are about 10 feet. The shores display an interesting mix of old buildings and natural areas. Protection from inclement weather is superb.

The city of Conway now boasts two small marinas. First up is Conway City Marina. The small canal leading to this facility will come abeam on the port-side shore (headed upstream) soon after you spot the twin smokestacks of the Waccamaw Power Plant broad off the port beam. Minimum entrance depths run around 5 feet on the canal, while boaters will find soundings of 6½ to 10 feet dockside. Conway City Marina provides limited overnight dockage at fixed, concrete-decked floating piers with water and 30-amp power connections. The piers are probably not adequate for boats larger than 40 feet. Gasoline is available, but diesel fuel is not offered. A small, concession-operated ship's, variety, and tackle store is located on the marina grounds, but a hike into the adjacent downtown business district will be necessary for any serious restocking. Frostbite cruisers may well find this marina in a semicomatose state during the winter months.

Approaching Conway on upper Waccamaw River

Conway City Marina (803) 248-6391

Approach depth: 5 feet (low water)
Dockside depth: 8–10 feet
Accepts transients: yes
Floating concrete-decked piers: yes
Dockside power connections: 30 amps
Dockside water connections: yes
Gasoline: yes
Ship's and variety store: small
Restaurants: several nearby

Kingston Point Marina guards the port banks just upstream from Conway City Marina. This

Conway City Marina

facility is associated with a large group of condos readily visible from the river's waters. No transient services are currently available at this marina.

For the most part, the shoreline of the upper Waccamaw is in its natural state. As you approach Conway, residential development along the river's banks picks up, but there are still many natural stretches as well. Few will count a cruise of the Waccamaw's upper reaches as anything but an eye-pleasing experience.

Conway History Conway was originally settled in 1734 as the town of Kingston. The name was changed in 1802 to honor Robert Conway, a hero of the Revolutionary War. Most of the village's early settlers were from North Carolina and Virginia; the dense swamps to the south made it difficult for settlers to migrate northward from Charleston. Since colonial days, Conway has been a leading center of government and politics for this section of South Carolina. Today, the visitor can still view a number of historic sites within walking distance of the marina. Ask at the office for directions.

Bucksville History In the mid-1800s, Henry Buck emigrated to the Waccamaw area from New England with the intention of founding a great lumber enterprise. Buck was a man of enormous energy and resource. He soon established three sawmills. The lower plant was at Bucksport on the Waccamaw; the second, or middle, mill was at Bucksville; and the third was at Bucksville Plantation, just upriver from unlighted daybeacon #8. The plantation house survives at this upper site. It is readily visible from the water. Look just to the right of the house and you will see an old chimney. This is all that remains of the once-busy sawmill.

By 1875, Buck was shipping large consignments of lumber to the North. His mills were busy, bustling places. Always looking for a new way to turn a profit, Buck decided to try his hand at shipbuilding. His intention was to compare the cost of building a ship on the Waccamaw with that incurred by the shipwrights of his native New England. The product of this experiment was a three-masted sailing ship, the *Henrietta*. Surprisingly, Buck's neighbors objected to his new enterprise. Bowing to their wishes, Buck built no more ships at the mills. The *Henrietta* survived for 19 years and was finally sunk in a violent hurricane near Japan in 1894. Her long service is evidence of Henry

Bucksville Plantation

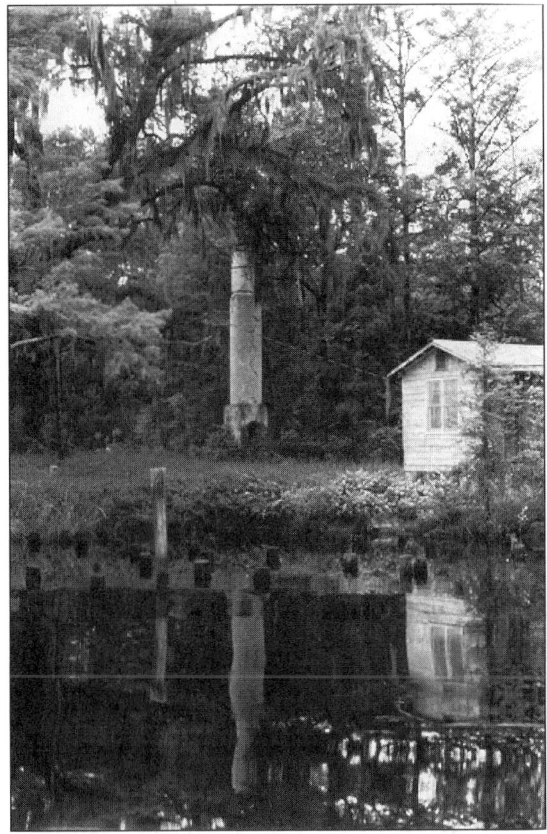

Old chimney marking the site of Bucksville Plantation sawmill

Buck's remarkable craftsmanship, so typical of all his work.

The ICW and Waccamaw River

From Enterprise Landing, the ICW follows the splendid Waccamaw for some 22 nautical miles south to the headwaters of Winyah Bay. Good facilities and a wide array of anchorages are available along the route.

Island Anchorage

Just northeast of flashing daybeacon #29, a branch of the river splits off to the northwest and loops behind a small island. Minimum depths are 9 feet. There is enough swinging room for boats as large as 36 feet on the loop's southwesterly entrance, while cruising craft as large as 40 feet should find enough elbow space near the stream's northeasterly mouth. The shoreline is in its natural state, and no facilities are available in the area. This is a good overnight anchorage, even though it lacks some of the adventurous feeling of the creeks to the south. If it has been a long day and you have seen enough of what's around the next bend for the moment, don't hesitate to drop the hook here.

Old River

Old River is a rather small stream that splits off from the Waccamaw's northwestern banks immediately southwest of flashing daybeacon #36. The stream's southwestern reaches are within sight of Bucksport Plantation Marina. Minimum depths are 12 feet, but there is really only one spot with sufficient swinging room for craft over 28 feet in length to anchor.

Old River's southwesterly mouth darts behind a small, undeveloped island found just north of #36. Boats up to 38 feet in length can anchor behind (west of) this small body of land with fairly good protection. Minimum depths run around 15 feet, with some soundings going all the way up to 25 feet. The banks are beautiful in their natural state. Local reports indicate the bottom is foul, so it would be best to set a trip line on your anchor.

Farther to the north, Old River narrows considerably. While depths remain good, boats larger than 30 feet will probably be a bit cramped. Leave exploration of the river's upper reaches to small power craft.

Bucksport Plantation Marina

Just south of flashing daybeacon #36, Bucksport Plantation Marina will come abeam on the western shore. This friendly facility welcomes transients and provides overnight dockage at fixed wooden-face piers with all power and water connections. Dockside depths are an impressive 7 feet or better. Gasoline and diesel fuel are readily available, and there is a well-stocked ship's and variety store on the grounds that can meet most of your grocery needs. Showers are also available.

Bucksport Plantation Marina features its own on-site restaurant. This well-known eatery offers a wide menu including seafood, steaks, and chicken. Through windows fronting onto the river, patrons can watch the passing Waterway traffic while they dine. The food is absolutely superb and is highly recommended by this writer.

Take a moment to investigate the old house behind the marina store. It is one of the homes Henry Buck built to serve his needs at the lower mill. Sadly, the once-proud structure is now in poor condition. Perhaps in the near future, some enterprising soul will undertake the task of restoring the old homeplace to its former glory.

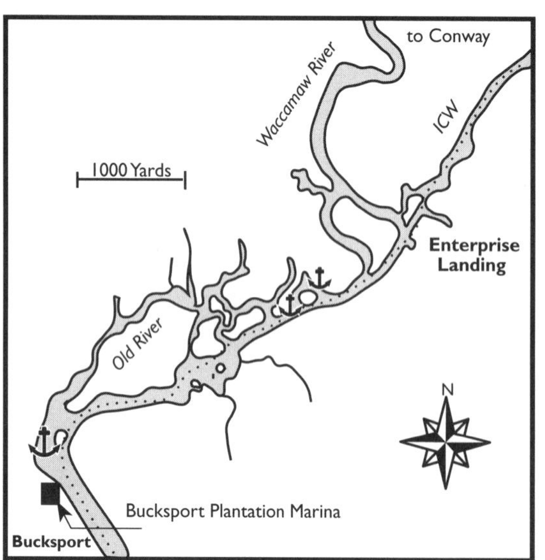

Bucksport Plantation Marina

All in all, Bucksport Plantation Marina is a good facility for the visiting boater. If it's near the end of your cruising day and you are nearby, don't hesitate to stop for a pleasant evening.

Bucksport Plantation Marina
(803) 397-5566

Approach depth: 10–12 feet
Dockside depth: 7–12 feet
Accepts transients: yes
Fixed wooden piers: yes
Dockside power connections: 30 and 50 amps
Dockside water connections: yes
Showers: yes
Gasoline: yes
Diesel fuel: yes
Ship's and variety store: yes
Restaurant: on-site (803-397-6300)

Prince Creek

The northern entrance to Prince Creek is found just east of flashing daybeacon #44. The creek loops inland to the southwest and rejoins the Waccamaw at flashing daybeacon #53. The beautiful shoreline is entirely in its natural state, covered for the most part with tall cypresses and hardwoods. No facilities are available in the area. Minimum depths are 12 feet for the creek's entire length, running to 30 feet in a few places.

Boaters with craft measuring between 30 and 38 feet in length will find the best swinging room near the northern and southern entrances. The creek narrows on its inner reaches, and while most any boat under 48 feet can safely use this portion of the stream as a super gunkhole, there is really not enough room to throw out the hook comfortably. This stream offers excellent protection from heavy weather.

Prince Creek gives the cruising boater his first opportunity to experience the charms of an overnight anchorage on the enchanting Waccamaw south of Bucksport. A few other spots may offer more swinging room, but for natural beauty, Prince Creek need not take a backseat to any sidewater on Waccamaw River.

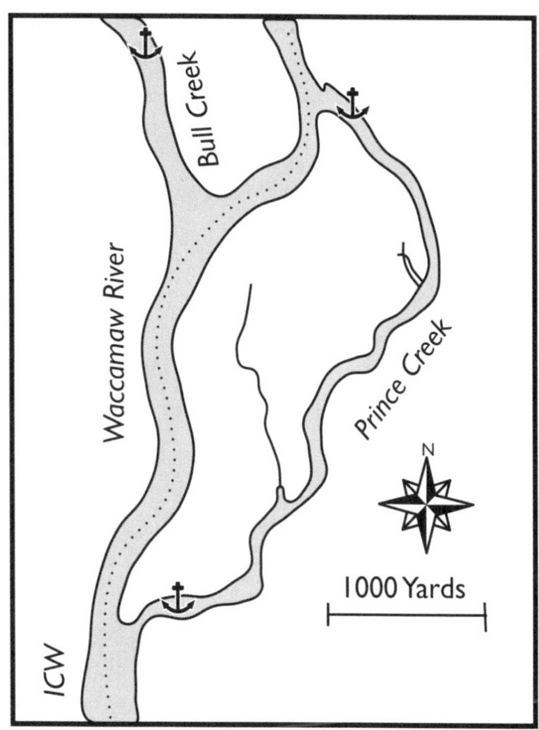

Bull Creek

Bull Creek, a major sidewater of the Waccamaw, makes in to its larger sister's northwesterly banks southwest of flashing daybeacon #48. It is one of the largest auxiliary streams on the river and provides what is unquestionably one of the finest anchorage opportunities north of Georgetown. The creek's considerable width gives plenty of swinging room for craft up to 45 feet. Minimum depths of 14 feet are held far upstream, though there is one (mostly) unmarked shoal at the entrance that must be avoided. The shoreline is entirely undeveloped, with lush cypresses and other hardwoods overlooking the banks.

Boaters can suit their fancy as to the best spot to anchor on Bull Creek east of the charted split (which is itself east of Bull Island). One of the best havens is found where high ground abuts the southerly and southeasterly banks as the creek follows a sharp turn to the west-northwest a short distance east of the split.

Seldom will cruising boaters find an overnight anchorage that combines so many fortunate qualities. Even if you usually frequent marinas, consider spending a night on the tranquil waters of Bull Creek. You may find that it is an evening to remember.

Wachesaw Landing

Boaters will discover what in this writer's opinion is the best marina facility on Waccamaw

River soon after passing unlighted daybeacon #56. Wacca Wache Marina, located in the heart of the village of Wachesaw Landing and hard by flashing daybeacon #57, is a far cry from its former incarnation a decade ago. Visitors will first spy a modern, recently expanded ship's store, snack bar, and fixed wooden fuel dock looking out proudly over the river's banks. The latest in floating wooden piers are found along the southern shores of the charted, well-sheltered, eastern-flowing stream just south of #57.

Transient boats up to 100 feet are cheerfully accepted for overnight or temporary dockage at berths with 30-, 50-, and 100-amp power and freshwater connections. Minimum dockside depths in the inner harbor run 5 to 7 feet, while boaters will find some 5 to 6 feet of low-tide depths at the fuel dock. Gasoline, diesel fuel, and free waste pump-out services are readily available, and some mechanical repairs can be arranged through independent contractors. Shoreside, cruisers will be delighted with the ultraclean showers as well as the fine laundromat. The ship's and variety store is well stocked and has been recently expanded. There is a nice snack bar inside the store that passing boaters might consider for a quick breakfast or lunch. When it comes time for the evening repast, several restaurants at nearby Murrells Inlet dispatch cars to pick up and return hungry diners. Ask any of the superfriendly marina staff for help.

Wacca Wache Marina at Wachesaw Landing

Tours of Brookgreen Gardens, not far to the south, can be arranged at Wacca Wache Marina. There is no longer any access by water to the gardens, so if you want to visit, you must make your reservations here.

Wacca Wache Marina (803) 651-7171

Approach depth: 5–10 feet
Dockside depth: 5–7 feet
Accepts transients: yes
Floating wooden docks: yes
Dockside power connections: 30, 50, and 100 amps
Dockside water connections: yes
Showers: yes
Laundromat: yes
Waste pump-out: yes
Gasoline: yes
Diesel fuel: yes
Mechanical repairs: independent contractors
Ship's and variety store: yes
Snack bar: yes
Restaurants: nearby

Wachesaw Legends

In his book *Ghosts from the Coast*, master storyteller J. Stevenson Bolick described the Wachesaw area thus: "Those who love the romantic and the beautiful fall in love with the spot on sight. The verdant subtropical vegetation, the bright flowers and berries, the great live oaks with their pennants of Spanish moss waving lazily with the breeze, the towering pine forests, and the green, green grasses and marshes that change color with the changing seasons all add to a charm and loveliness hard to surpass. Many who stop here for a short visit find the place so much to their liking that they end up buying plantations, farms, or resort homes in the vicinity."

It is in this idyllic setting that one of the many ghostly tales of the upper South Carolina Low Country is set. In the 1920s, work was begun on a new home atop Wachesaw Bluff. (Today, you can see a whole line of newly built townhouses and condos atop this promontory just south of Wacca Wache Marina.) The preliminary excavations unexpectedly revealed a number of human skulls and bones. Work was suspended, and the Charleston Museum was notified. Careful digging revealed many human skeletons, some of enormous size and others buried in huge urns. Also unearthed were many tools, weapons, and other artifacts, from which it was possible to identify the remains as those of early Native American tribes. It may well have been that the Wachesaw area was an ancient burial ground for many different Indian peoples.

While the archaeological work was going forward, an epidemic of diphtheria broke out in the area. Some said that the germs had been unearthed with the old remains. Others said that the scourge was the result of an Indian curse on those who disturbed the dead.

A related tale recounts the hair-raising experiences of a young man who worked at the dig. One night, so the story goes, he took home several arrowheads and spearheads that he had unearthed during the day. That night, his sleep was troubled by a strange dream. He seemed to hear loud wailing coming from the direction of the burial ground. When he awoke, the strange sounds ceased, but for a long time he was too afraid to sleep again. When he finally dropped off, the strange dream was repeated.

The next night, he dreamed that he saw an unusually large Indian warrior dressed in full battle regalia standing in the next room, sifting through the artifacts. As the restless nights passed, more and more warriors appeared to the unhappy man. Finally, on the sixth night, he was awakened by a violent thunderstorm. The lightning flashes revealed a blood-chilling scene with their phantom light. The warriors in the next room were fighting over the relics. Suddenly, to his horror, the wretched man realized that he was not dreaming this time. The strange spirits were actually present!

Too terrified to move, the young man huddled in his bed till dawn, when, as soon as he could persuade his frightened limbs to move, he rushed from the house and went in search of the museum officials. Finding them after a time, he immediately turned over his relics and said that he never wanted to see the accursed articles again. That was the last of his haunting. Perhaps the spirits of the ancient warriors were appeased at last.

If you think this tale a bit fanciful, you may be surprised to learn there are many in the South Carolina Low Country who believe it implicitly. The coastal ghost lore is quite old and is not to be dismissed out of hand. Many of these tales have given more than one visitor a goose pimple or two.

Murrells Inlet and Pawleys Island

Murrells Inlet and Pawleys Island, to the east of Wachesaw Landing, are two very popular resort communities whose roots are deep in the past. While neither village is accessible by water from the ICW, you may want to consider securing the use of a courtesy or rental car for a visit. Murrells Inlet is famous for its many fine seafood restaurants, and Pawleys Island is one of the most frequently visited resorts between Myrtle Beach and Georgetown.

Both communities were originally summer retreats for wealthy planters fleeing the Low Country's "fever season" of malaria. As you might well imagine, the long history of summer occupation by the romantic planter class gave rise to many legends. In *Ghosts from the Coast*, J. Stevenson Bolick does a masterful job of relating several of these fascinating yarns. Similarly, Nancy Rhyne presents a number of very moving legends concerning the Pawleys Island–Murrells Inlet area in two of her books, *Tales of the South Carolina Low Country* and *More Tales of the South Carolina Low Country*.

While little evidence remains today of the planters' occupation, these villages seem still to remember the grandeur of those lost days. If you have the chance to visit, take a few minutes to stroll along the beach and picture, if you can, the planters' wives and daughters dressed in their long white gowns, looking from their porches across the ever-moving sea. One cannot help wondering what their thoughts and dreams might have been.

Murrells Inlet Legends

The natives of Murrells Inlet will tell you that they and their fathers before them have long known the origin of hurricanes. A very old legend holds that whenever a mermaid is captured and held captive at the inlet, a great storm begins to build in the south. Its strength increases, and unless the child of the sea is released, the hurricane sweeps with devastating fury upon Murrells Inlet's shores. Just such a storm is the setting for the legend of the phantom lights.

Tradition tells us that in the period following the American Revolution, an ambitious young man lived on the shores of Murrells Inlet. His dream was to acquire a sailing craft to make coastal cruises and go on fishing expeditions. At last, after many years of being a ship's officer, he made his dream a reality. He purchased a beautiful schooner from a wealthy Georgetown rice planter and proudly sailed his new craft out of Winyah Bay with his whole family aboard. They took an extended ocean voyage and visited Wilmington, New Bern, Baltimore, and New York. Finally, the new master brought his shining vessel to his own dock at Murrells Inlet. The boat caused quite a stir, and people came from miles around to admire the young captain's purchase. Some commented on the running lights, which were covered with thick Venetian glass in rich shades of ruby and emerald.

For a time, all went well. The captain enjoyed a profitable cargo voyage and a successful fishing trip. Then came the September gale season. It was not long before a severe storm hit the coast. As the storm became more and more violent, the proud craft was driven relentlessly against its piling and began to suffer damage. The creek was too narrow for anchorage, so the master set sail with a few trusted hands with the intention of riding out the storm just offshore. Before leaving, the captain told his wife to keep a light burning in the window so he could maintain a bearing on the shore. Arriving offshore within sight of the beach, the crew set the anchor. As the wind rose, the anchor dragged repeatedly. Time and again, the anxious watchers ashore saw the distinctive running lights disappear, then reappear as the craft was masterfully piloted back toward the lighted window until the hook could again be set.

On the next day, the storm reached the height of its violence. Trees were uprooted, and the tide was frighteningly high. As the long afternoon drew to a close, the watchers lost sight of the ship in a blinding rainstorm. When night fell, all ashore strained for a glimpse of the ship's lights, but they were nowhere to be seen.

As the great storm finally abated, search parties were launched, but no trace of the proud ship was ever found. The captain's saddened wife continued to place a lamp in her window every night. It became a symbol to her of the promise she had made to her husband to keep the light burning. One year to the day after the tragic event, the captain's wife happened to look out of her upstairs window and was startled to see lights on the ocean bearing an amazing resemblance to those of the lost bark. Other family members were summoned, as were several neighbors. An anxious vigil was kept throughout the night. The lights were visible until just before dawn, but when it was daylight at last, not a ship was to be seen on the horizon.

Many will tell you that those desperate but beautiful lights may still be seen across the sea on September nights. Who can say? In the romance of Murrells Inlet, perhaps love is stronger than death.

Brookgreen Gardens

In the 1930s, the fabulously rich Archer M. Huntington acquired several of the old plantations along Waccamaw Neck. Many of these had originally belonged to the prominent Alston family. (One plantation, The Oaks, was the home of ill-fated Theodosia Burr Alston, whose story will be presented in the next chapter.) When the properties were joined, Huntington began to construct a huge garden to serve as a setting for the artistic creations of his wife, sculptor Anna Hyatt Huntington. No expense was spared, and as the years passed, the beautiful gardens were counted among the great splendors of the Southeast. Following Archer Huntington's death, the gardens were left to the people of South Carolina. Now, all who are inclined may enjoy this talented couple's amazing creation. The gardens remain a timeless monument to their determination and their love for the people of South Carolina.

Once upon a day, the charted creek southeast of flashing daybeacon #66 provided waterborne access to the fabulous gardens. Sadly, a wooden barrier now blocks this stream, and you must make landside arrangements to visit the estate.

Cow House Creek

The northern entrance of Cow House Creek makes off from the western shore of Waccamaw River just across from Wachesaw Landing and flashing daybeacon #57. The stream holds minimum depths of 7 feet and provides very sheltered overnight anchorage for any craft of 38 feet or less. Larger boats may find the creek a bit small for adequate swinging room. The shoreline is in its natural state, and no facilities are available on the stream. While not the most attractive of all the Waccamaw anchorages, Cow House Creek can certainly serve as a snug haven for the night.

Sandhole Creek

This small but inviting stream guards the Waccamaw's northwesterly shoreline near flashing daybeacon #66. The southeasterly reaches of Sandhole Creek (near its entrance from the Waccamaw) can serve as a good anchorage for boats up to 34 feet when winds are not blowing too harshly. Minimum depths of 7 feet may be held if you can avoid an unmarked shoal at the creek's entrance. The surrounding shores are wonderfully undeveloped. Strong winds from the southeast sometimes raise an unwelcome chop in this anchorage.

To be sure, there are roomier anchorages nearby, but if you are of a mind and your craft fits the size requirements, by all means give Sandhole Creek your most serious consideration.

Thoroughfare Creek

Thoroughfare Creek is a major sidewater of Waccamaw River and can lead adventurous skippers into the waters of the upper Pee Dee River. The stream breaks off from the ICW's northwestern banks opposite flashing daybeacon #73. Thoroughfare Creek itself is quite deep, holding 10-foot minimum depths until it joins the Pee Dee. The natural shoreline is particularly attractive and affords excellent protection. Once past the entrance to Guendalose Creek—a narrow but deep offshoot on the western shore of Thoroughfare Creek—the stream becomes wide enough to afford plenty of swinging room for large craft to anchor comfortably.

Thoroughfare Creek provides yet another excellent overnight anchorage opportunity for boaters traveling along Waccamaw River. While cruisers can really drop anchor almost anywhere they wish on this fortunate body of water, one of the best spots is found near the charted site of Belin. Here, high sandbanks overlook the eastern and northeastern banks just before the stream follows a long turn to the southwest. Depths run from 10 to 19 feet, and there is ample room for a 42-footer.

Hasty Point is located on the banks opposite the intersection of Thoroughfare Creek and Pee Dee River. Tradition claims that its name is derived from the "hasty" retreat of Francis Marion, "the Swamp Fox," during one of his many Revolutionary War campaigns.

For those boaters who can stand some 3- to 4-foot depths, it is possible to cruise south on the Pee Dee for a short distance until Exchange Plantation comes abeam on the western shore. One and a half stories tall, the house can be identified by its prominent central dormer window. The plantation, which dates back to 1825, supposedly acquired its name because it was given in exchange for another plantation.

Further passage south or north on this portion of the Pee Dee is not recommended, as depths become uncertain at best.

Exchange Plantation on Pee Dee River

Waverly Creek

Waverly Creek is a small stream that enters the eastern bank of the Waccamaw south of flashing daybeacon #77. The creek maintains minimum depths of 6 feet but is too narrow for anchorage by all but small craft. A few private docks are located along the stream's banks.

During the years prior to the Civil War, a number of rice mills carried on their bustling trade along the creek's shores, forming a small community known as Waverly Mills. The land was subdivided after the demise of the rice industry, and the old mills have disappeared entirely.

Butler Creek

Butler Creek is a small stream on the river's northwestern shore just southwest of flashing daybeacon #78. The creek holds minimum depths of 6 feet, deepening to 13 feet in a few places. Nevertheless, there is really not enough room on the inner reaches to safely accommodate any vessel larger than 28 feet.

This stream is actually joined to Schooner Creek (see below) by a narrow but surprisingly deep cut-through that intersects Butler Creek on its western shores near the "4 FT" indication on chart 11534. While the narrow cut boasts minimum depths of 8 feet, it is most certainly too slim for cruising-sized craft.

Schooner Creek

Schooner Creek, just below Butler Creek (nearly opposite flashing daybeacon #79), is an offshoot of the lower Pee Dee River. The stream holds minimum depths of 6 feet for a good distance upstream and sports an enchanting shoreline.

While the creek's lower reaches are a bit narrow for effective anchorage, the stream widens a bit as it swings to the north. The waters broaden further shortly before passing through the charted sharp swing to the east. Here, craft as large as 34 feet can safely anchor with superb protection from all winds. Be sure to read the navigational material on Butler and Schooner Creeks presented later in this chapter before cruising either stream or attempting the small cut joining the two.

Jericho Creek

Jericho Creek makes in to the Waccamaw's northwestern banks just northeast of flashing daybeacon #83. This stream is an offshoot of the lower Pee Dee River and will be covered in the next chapter. It is a lovely, enchanting body of water that is well protected and easily navigable all the way to the Pee Dee. It can serve as a good overnight anchorage for craft under 45 feet.

Fast boats on the larger side of this size range may want to follow the stream as it eventually turns to the southwest on its way to join Pee Dee River. The creek widens appreciably in this region. Just be *sure* to drop the hook *well away* from the charted "Cable Areas."

Butler Island

Southwest of flashing daybeacon #83, Butler Island bisects Waccamaw River. The ICW continues down the southeastern arm, but the northwestern branch also maintains a wide, deep channel. Even though this spot is recommended by another well-respected guide as an overnight anchorage, this writer considers it too open for effective shelter in any but the lightest of airs. Unless you are in immediate need of anchorage, it would be better to make use of the many havens to the north.

Arcadia Plantation

As you begin your approach to flashing daybeacon #90, watch the southeastern shore carefully. Soon, you will spot a long canal flanked by a large collection of old piles. If you peer carefully up the cut's length, you may catch a quick glimpse of the Arcadia Plantation house. Don't attempt to cruise up the canal for a closer look. It is quite shoal.

Arcadia is actually a collection of several old plantations that were consolidated by the Emerson Vanderbilt family in the early 1900s. One of Arcadia's former plantations, Clifton Plantation, had the distinction of entertaining George Washington on his tour of the Southern states following the American Revolution. Many of Arcadia's other plantations serve as settings for popular legends. Interested readers should consult J. Stevenson Bolick's tale "The Suicide Room," found in *Ghosts from the Coast.*

WACCAMAW NAVIGATION

Generally, navigation of Waccamaw River is a delightful process requiring only commonsense piloting. However, don't let the beautiful stream lull you into too great a sense of security. Snags and flotsam are encountered from time to time, and there are a few shoals along the way to avoid. Have chart 11534 handy at all times and keep a sharp watch. Nighttime passage is not particularly recommended because of possible encounters with unseen snags.

Upper Waccamaw River As stated earlier, depths remain consistently good (minimum 6 feet) on the upper Waccamaw as far as Conway. Most of the route is uncharted, but it is well marked and relatively easy to follow if you watch out for the various forks along the way. As the river approaches Conway, it begins to narrow a bit. For this reason, the upper Waccamaw is not recommended for boats over 40 feet. A fixed bridge with approximately 35 feet of vertical clearance found along the approach to Conway limits accessibility to power craft and small sailboats.

Give points a wide berth and be on the lookout for flotsam and snags. Otherwise, armed with the navigational information presented in this guide, don't hesitate to take advantage of this fascinating side trip off the beaten path.

Boaters have a choice of two routes to enter the upper Waccamaw from the ICW. A cut-through runs northwest from unlighted daybeacon #27 and intersects the river at unlighted daybeacon #2. This small channel maintains minimum depths of 8 feet but may be a bit narrow for large craft. The main entrance breaks off to the northeast from unlighted daybeacon #1 southwest of the ICW's flashing daybeacon #27A.

While cruising from the upper Waccamaw's entrance to Conway, pass all red markers to your starboard side and all green beacons to port. Following this rule, leave #1 to your port side as you enter the stream along its mid-width. Pass unlighted daybeacon #2 to your immediate starboard side and bear off to the north-northwest into the river's main branch.

Unlighted daybeacon #3 marks a channel that cuts off a loop of the river. This writer no longer recommends entering the side loop, as it is now choked with snags. Be sure to pass #3 to your port side and bear off to starboard.

Shortly before reaching unlighted daybeacon #4, boaters will encounter an unmarked fork in the river. Take the port-side fork and you will soon spot #4. Pass unlighted daybeacon #5 to port and bear off sharply to starboard. As you enter the branch marked by #5, you may see a small sign marked "Conway," with an arrow pointing up the cut; the sign is nailed on a shoreside tree. Pass unlighted daybeacon #6 to starboard and bend sharply to port. Don't be tempted to enter the starboard-side fork at #6. While it looks inviting as an anchorage, on-site research revealed that depths quickly rise to 4 feet or less on this errant arm.

Soon, you will encounter the small community of Bucksville along the port shore. Unlighted daybeacon #8 directs you into a port fork and should be passed to starboard.

After passing #8, watch the port shore and you will soon spy the Bucksville Plantation house. The old chimney marking one of Henry Buck's sawmills can be seen just to the right of the house.

Pass unlighted daybeacon #10 to starboard and bear to port. At unlighted daybeacon #12, hold a straight course and pass the aid to starboard. Look behind as you continue upriver and you will see that this daybeacon marks a fork for southbound boaters. Pass unlighted daybeacon #14 to starboard. This aid denotes a patch of shallow water on the river's starboard bank. At unlighted daybeacon #16, bear off to port and pass the aid to starboard. Soon, you will begin to pass shorelines that are more developed, followed by an unmarked fork of the river. Take the port branch. As you begin to enter the outskirts of Conway, the 35-foot U.S. 501 bridge will be spotted dead ahead. Continue through and begin watching to port. Soon, you will spy the twin red-and-white smokestacks of the Waccamaw Power Plant broad off your port beam, followed closely by a No Wake sign guarding the starboard shore. The entrance canal leading to Conway City Marina will come up on the port-side banks soon thereafter.

Upstream from Conway City Marina, passing

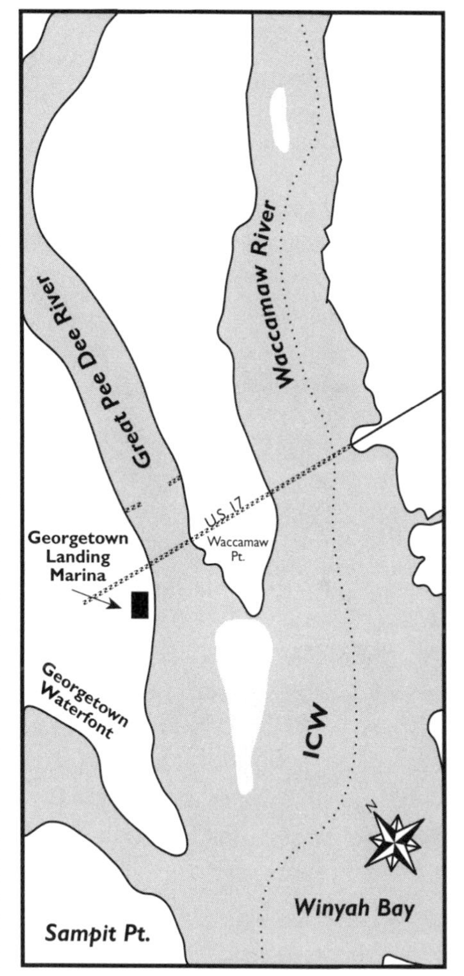

cruisers will soon come abeam of private Kingston Point Marina, also to port. As you sight another high-rise highway bridge ahead, the stream promptly forks. The port branch is blocked by a low-level fixed railroad bridge, and the starboard fork is cut off by an old swing railroad bridge that has obviously not operated for years. Boats up to 36 feet can easily anchor in the crook of the fork.

Loop Anchorage Back on the main path of the ICW traversing the lower Waccamaw River, cruise into either entrance of the loop anchorage north of flashing daybeacon #29 by following its mid-width. Drop the hook so as to swing well away from the shoreline.

On the ICW Southwest of flashing daybeacon #33, the Waterway begins its approach to Bucksport and enters a potentially confusing portion of the channel. A small, undeveloped island bisects the river southwest of unlighted daybeacon #35. The ICW continues down the southeasterly fork. Be sure to come abeam of and pass flashing daybeacon #36 to its southeasterly side.

Old River Chart 11534 correctly pictures a small, unmarked channel running from #35 past the northern tip of the island discussed above and into Old River. It would be better for visiting cruisers to enter this body of water from its primary mouth, west of #36. However, if you do attempt the passage north of the island, favor the southern side of the cut-through.

Old River should be entered on its mid-width by passing flashing daybeacon #36 to its southern and western sides. Drop anchor once behind (west of) the small island. Only small power craft should attempt to continue following the narrowing track of Old River to the north and northeast.

On the ICW Slow to idle speed as you pass flashing daybeacon #36. Bucksport Plantation Marina lines the westerly banks south of this aid. After following several more twists and turns in the Waterway, passing cruisers will observe the northerly mouth of Prince Creek making in to the easterly shores at flashing daybeacon #44.

Prince Creek Enter the northerly mouth of Prince Creek on its mid-width. Good depths open out almost from shore to shore. You will find the best swinging room on the initial portion of the creek before it begins a long, very slow turn to the southwest.

Continue following the centerline as you work your way down this long, enchanting body of water. Eventually, you will begin your approach to the creek's southerly intersection with the Waccamaw. Good swinging room again opens out as you move into this portion of the stream. Favor the southeasterly banks slightly as you cruise through Prince Creek's southerly mouth back into Waccamaw River and the ICW.

On the ICW Flashing daybeacon #47 marks a shoal and a large snag. Pass #47 well to its northwesterly side. Flashing daybeacon #48 warns against a similar patch of shallow water on the river's northwesterly shore. Be sure to pass #48 well to its southeasterly quarter.

Bull Creek Successful entry into Bull Creek is complicated by the correctly charted shoal building out from the northeasterly entrance point. These shallows have now surrounded flashing daybeacon #48. Stay well away from this aid. Enter Bull Creek by favoring the westerly banks. After cruising at least 200 yards upstream past the entrance, cut back to the mid-width. Good depths now open out along a broad path along the stream's centerline at least as far as the charted split in the creek southeast of Bull Island.

On the ICW Slow to idle speed as you approach flashing daybeacon #57. Excessive wake could damage boats docked at Wacca Wache Marina on the eastern banks.

West of #57, boaters interested in anchoring-off, rather than visiting the docks of Wacca Wache Marina, can enter Cow House Creek.

Cow House Creek Enter Cow House Creek from its northerly genesis by favoring the south-side shoreline. Soon, the stream turns to the south. Cruise back to the centerline and hold to the mid-width as you cruise along. Shoal water abuts certain portions of the shoreline along this portion of the stream. Cruise back into the Waccamaw opposite unlighted daybeacon #61 on this entrance's mid-width as well.

Sandhole Creek Boaters will spot the entrance to Sandhole Creek on the northwestern banks hard by flashing daybeacon #66. Enter on the centerline and drop the hook before cruising through the first sharp turn to the north. Depths become highly uncertain as the creek splinters into several branches farther upstream.

Thoroughfare Creek Successful navigation of Thoroughfare Creek is a simple matter until the stream intersects the upper Pee Dee River.

As is the norm all along Waccamaw River, hold to the middle as you enter Thoroughfare Creek. Soon, the stream cuts sharply to the north. Begin watching the easterly banks for the high ground near the charted location of Belin. This is a super spot to anchor. The canals shown on chart 11534 south of the Belin anchorage were apparently meant to serve some sort of development that has never come to fruition.

Most cruising-sized craft would probably do well to retreat to the Waterway before encountering the intersection of Thoroughfare Creek and Pee Dee River. Depths have lessened on the latter stream since the last time this writer visited the area. Currently, a bare 3 to 4 feet of minimum low-water depths can be held moving south on the river as far as the area abeam of Exchange Plantation.

Butler Creek If you choose to enter Butler Creek, cruise through the mid-width of its southeasterly mouth. Good depths continue upstream only so far as the charted cut-through to Schooner Creek.

Schooner Creek Navigation of Schooner Creek is straightforward until the creek flows through a sharp swing to starboard. As you round this bend, watch for a bad snag near the starboard shore. As shown on chart 11534, the creek eventually begins to widen as it joins the lower reaches of Pee Dee River. Do not approach these waters, as 4-foot depths are quickly encountered.

On the ICW The entrance to Jericho Creek makes in to the northwestern flank of the ICW just northeast of flashing daybeacon #83. This body of water will be addressed in the next chapter as part of Pee Dee River.

Southwest of flashing daybeacon #83, the Waterway slips southeast of Butler Island. Flashing daybeacons #84 and #85 and unlighted daybeacon #86 mark this section of "the Ditch." Unlighted daybeacon #86 marks a long shoal building out from the southwestern toe of Butler Island. Be *sure* to pass #86 to its southeastern quarter.

Keep a sharp watch for flashing daybeacon #90 after leaving unlighted daybeacon #89 behind. This latter aid marks a patch of very shoal water. Pass #90 well to its southeasterly side.

South and southwest of #90, the Waterway quickly begins its approach to Winyah Bay. Be sure to pass unlighted daybeacon #91 to its northwestern side. This beacon denotes a large shelf of shoal water abutting the eastern and southeastern banks.

Southwest of #91, the Waterway soon exchanges greetings with the U.S. 17 high-rise fixed bridge. This span has a vertical clearance of 65 feet.

Slow down after passing under this span. The next few miles along the southward-tracking ICW are far more navigationally challenging that any waters thus far along our sojourn through the Low Country. Continued navigation of the ICW and area rivers is presented in the next chapter.

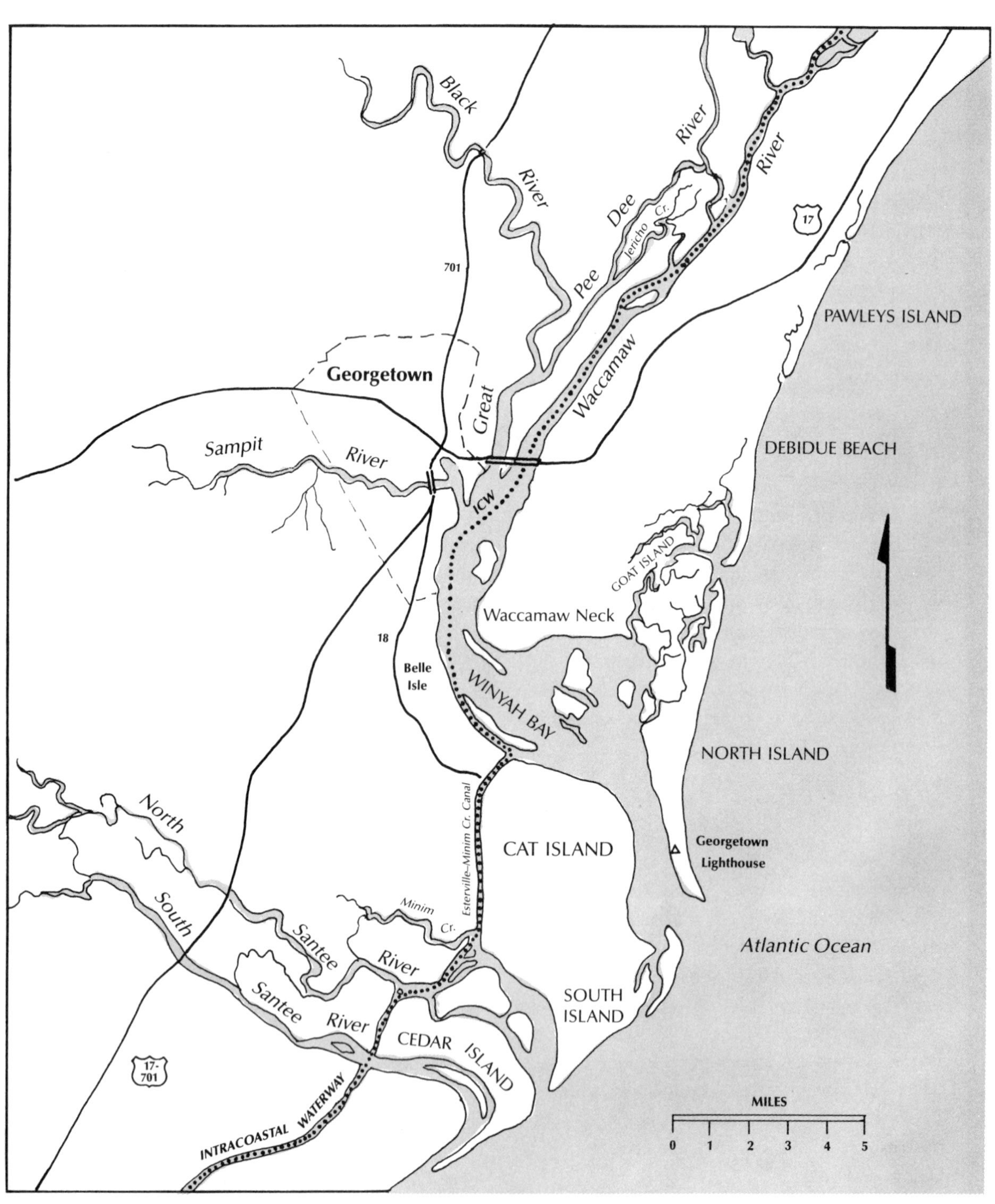
Black
River
Pee
Dee
River
Jericho
Cr.
River
Waccamaw
17
701
Georgetown
Great
Sampit
River
ICW
PAWLEYS ISLAND
DEBIDUE BEACH
GOAT ISLAND
Waccamaw Neck
18
Belle
Isle
WINYAH BAY
NORTH ISLAND
North
Esterville–Minim Cr. Canal
CAT ISLAND
Georgetown
Lighthouse
South
Santee
Minim
Cr.
River
Atlantic Ocean
Santee
River
SOUTH
ISLAND
CEDAR
ISLAND
17-
701
INTRACOASTAL WATERWAY
MILES
0
1
2
3
4
5

Georgetown

Sitting astride the confluence of Winyah Bay and Sampit River, present-day Georgetown constantly calls to mind its storied past. Long the most important South Carolina port north of Charleston, the town retains the character of bygone years alongside a new spirit of success. Fortunate cruising boaters who make Georgetown a port of call will find a quiet, beautiful, and historic town waiting to greet them.

Prior to the Civil War, Georgetown was the seat of a fabulously rich rice culture still remembered with pride and romance. Go quietly as you pass, and perhaps you may still hear the delicate tinkle of crystal glasses at an elegant garden party or the hoofbeats of the master's horse as he rides to check his fields in the early-morning mist. The heritage of the rice culture is an almost tangible entity here, and you cannot fully appreciate Georgetown and its surrounding streams without an understanding of this remarkable era.

Anyone who takes a few moments to study the charts will realize that Georgetown is ideally situated to take advantage of waterborne commerce. The waters of the Black, Pee Dee, Waccamaw, and Sampit Rivers all converge at the port to form Winyah Bay. Together, these waters present a multitude of cruising opportunities for the pleasure boater. The various streams—for the most part quite deep and easily navigable—offer many miles of isolated cruising and a host of overnight anchorage opportunities, as well as a fair share of delightful surprises. Just when it seems that you are truly in the middle of nowhere, the next bend of the river or creek reveals one of the fabulous plantation houses that have survived the trials of the years. It would take a very hard-bitten boater not to be smitten by the charms of Georgetown's rivers.

Charts

You will need two NOAA charts to cover the waters in the Georgetown area:

11534 covers the ICW through Winyah Bay and south on the Minim–Estherville Creek Canal, as well as the Pee Dee and Black Rivers

11532 details Winyah Bay, including its inlet channel and the upper reaches of Sampit River

Winyah Bay provides reliable access to the open sea and cruising opportunities of its own. Good facilities are found on the southern shore, and side trips to several historical sites are possible.

The waters surrounding Georgetown offer the state's widest array of cruising opportunities north of Charleston. It's enough to set any true cruiser to dreaming. The newly rebuilt town waterfront is simply bursting with shoreside attractions, including a potpourri of fine restaurants and interesting shops. The waterfront, coupled with the wonderful homes of Georgetown's historical district, should inspire every boater to put a red circle around this delightful port of call. Those who rush by without making the acquaintance of Georgetown and its rivers will miss one of the greatest cruising opportunities in all of South Carolina.

GEORGETOWN

What a delight it is to spend an evening, a week, or a month docked on the Georgetown waterfront! Snug in your slip, docked in the shadow of the Rice Museum's historic clock tower, you might be excused for forgetting that you are in the twentieth century. Fortunate indeed is the cruising boater who finds his way along Sampit River to Georgetown.

After those glowing words, it must be noted that Georgetown has one problem for visitors. A large paper mill is located on the southwestern portion of the Georgetown loop along the lower Sampit River. Fortunately, the prevailing winds tend to keep the worst of the smell away from the city, but it's only fair to note that the mill is there. When the fickle wind chooses not to cooperate, the smell of progress is not so sweet.

Most of Georgetown's facilities, including the new city docks, are located on the northeastern portion of Sampit River's northern loop (north of flashing daybeacon #42). This portion of the stream comprises the town's principal waterfront. While all the marinas are fairly small, they are quite friendly, and most cater to transient boaters.

Georgetown Marinas

Moving southeast to northwest, the first facility you will come upon is Hazzard's Marina. This facility has taken on a definite commercial flavor since this writer last visited Georgetown. While transients are occasionally accepted for overnight or temporary dockage, this practice is now clearly the exception rather than the rule. Boaters who do secure a berth will tie their lines to old, fixed wooden piers with water connections and 30- and 50-amp power connections. Depths alongside run 6½ to 8 feet. Gasoline can be purchased dockside; surprisingly, diesel fuel is not available. Hazzard's Marina offers mechanical repairs for both gasoline and diesel power plants, as well as haul-out service via a 30-ton marine railway. As is the case from all the waterfront marinas, the historical district and the newly revitalized downtown business section are just a quick step away.

Georgetown waterfront

Hazzard's Marina (803) 546-6604

Approach depth: 12+ feet
Dockside depth: 6½–9 feet
Accepts transients: limited basis
Fixed wooden piers: yes
Dockside power connections: 30 and 50 amps
Dockside water connections: yes
Gasoline: yes
Mechanical repairs: yes
Below-waterline repairs: yes
Restaurants: several nearby

Moving upstream, you will next find The Boat Shed Marina (formerly Georgetown Exxon Marina) guarding the northeastern banks. This ultrafriendly facility gladly accepts transients of all varieties. Low-water depths at the innermost slips run around 7 feet, while boaters will find 10- to 12-foot soundings at the outer docks. Berths at the fixed wooden piers feature all power and water connections. Small power craft can moor to a single floating dock. Gasoline and diesel fuel can be purchased, and visiting cruisers will be pleased to find showers on the premises. The marina maintains a medium-sized ship's store and a dry-stack storage building just behind the docks. Mechanical repairs for gasoline engines (mostly outboards and I/O's) are offered. Small boats can be hauled out via a forklift. This is another of Georgetown's small but likable marinas where visiting cruisers can expect a warm and knowledgeable welcome.

The Boat Shed Marina
(803) 546-4415

Approach depth: 12+ feet
Dockside depth: 7–12 feet
Accepts transients: yes
Fixed wooden piers: yes
Dockside power connections: 30 and 50 amps
Dockside water connections: yes
Showers: yes
Gasoline: yes
Diesel fuel: yes
Mechanical repairs: outboards and I/O's mostly
Ship's store: yes
Restaurants: many within walking distance

Cathou's Boat Yard (803-546-5441) is just beside The Boat Shed Marina. Some below-waterline repairs can be arranged here (haul-outs are on a marine railway), but the greatest attraction at Cathou's is the fresh seafood that is often for sale. This writer and his mate were amused one evening to see a local citizen pounding on the shop's door seemingly long after business hours. To our great surprise, the door swung open, an old yellow light was switched on, and flounder caught that same day was soon forthcoming.

The last commercial pleasure-craft center on the principal Georgetown waterfront is Harborwalk Marina (formerly Gulf Auto Marina). Harborwalk's management continues Georgetown's friendly tradition. Transients are welcomed with open arms.

Since the onslaught of Hurricane Hugo in 1989, fuel (gasoline and diesel) at Harborwalk has been dispensed via long hoses stretched from shoreside tanker trucks. This is not really a problem, however. We had no trouble topping off our tanks with the aid of the accommodating staff.

Transient and resident berths at Harborwalk Marina feature fixed wooden piers and good depths plus full power and water connections. Shoreside showers are available, and mechanical repairs are in the offing for both gasoline and diesel power plants. Some mechanical work is farmed out to local independent technicians. A laundromat is located 8 blocks away. Future plans call for the installation of a waste pump-out facility, but the opening date for this service could not be determined at the time of this writing. Harborwalk Marina is the closest of the commercial waterfront marinas to the downtown historical and business district. Cruisers who want to avoid walking more than necessary may want to take this advantage into account.

Harborwalk Marina (803) 546-4250

Approach depth: 12+ feet
Dockside depth: 8–11 feet
Accepts transients: yes
Fixed wooden piers: yes
Dockside power connections: 30 and 50 amps (new)
Dockside water connections: yes
Showers: yes
Gasoline: yes
Diesel fuel: yes
Mechanical repairs: yes
Ship's store: small
Restaurants: many nearby

Georgetown's largest and most modern marina is not located on the town waterfront. Georgetown Landing Marina is found on Pee Dee River's western shore just south of the U.S. 17 bridge, some 1.1 nautical miles northeast of the ICW's junction daybeacon #W. This fine facility was totally devastated by Hurricane Hugo but now features all-new modern slips at both floating and fixed piers. Boaters can count on minimum depths of 10 feet on the well-marked approach channel from the ICW, with 6 to 20 feet of water dockside. Transients are eagerly accepted at the marina's piers, which feature full power and water connections. Spotlessly clean shoreside showers and a complete on-site laundromat are at hand. Diesel fuel, gasoline, and waste pump-out service are all available. The marina can usually arrange mechanical repairs through local independent contractors. A well-stocked ship's and variety store overlooks the dockage basin.

Georgetown Landing Marina used to be enclosed by a partially submerged breakwater composed of old automobile tires. Most of this barrier was destroyed by the hurricane, and it has been replaced only on the south side of the harbor.

Land's End Restaurant sits perched just be-

Harborwalk docks on Georgetown waterfront

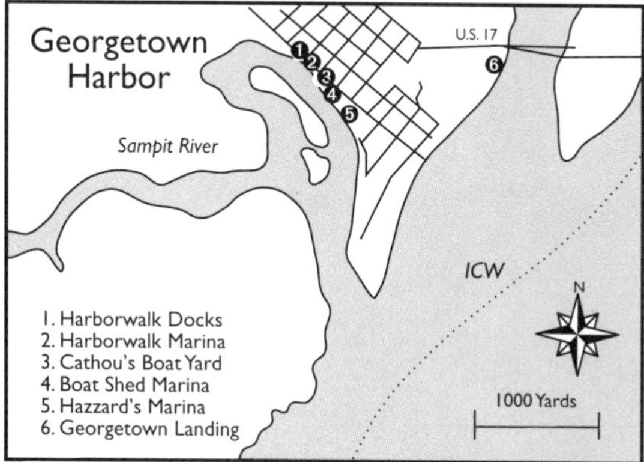

hind the piers at Georgetown Landing Marina. It is a very pleasant spot to rest after a long day of cruising. The restaurant's large plate-glass windows look out over the marina and Pee Dee River.

It's a 15- to 20-minute walk from Georgetown Landing Marina to the historical district and downtown section, but those used to long strolls will find it child's play. If you prefer, taxis are available. Call Stadium Taxi Service (803-546-5550), Friendly Cab Company (803-546-6315), or Moonlight Taxi Service (803-527-4441).

Georgetown Landing Marina
(803) 527-1376

Approach depth: 10 feet (minimum)
Dockside depth: 6–20 feet (low water)
Accepts transients: yes
Fixed and floating piers: yes
Dockside power connections: 30 and 50 amps
Dockside water connections: yes
Showers: yes
Laundromat: yes
Waste pump-out: yes
Gasoline: yes
Diesel fuel: yes
Mechanical repairs: independent contractors
Ship's and variety store: yes
Restaurant: on-site

Downtown Georgetown and Harborwalk

Upstream from Harborwalk Marina, the Georgetown waterfront has undergone a remarkable transformation. Where there was once only a small city pier that did not allow overnight dockage, most of the town waterfront has been magnificently renovated and incorporated into a lovely boardwalk complex which goes by the name of Harborwalk. The large green area in the center of the development is known as Francis Marion Park. Two additional parks are located at either end of the Harborwalk complex.

Three sets of floating piers associated with the Harborwalk project readily serve the needs of visiting cruisers. Mooring to the long fixed-face docks lining the entire Harborwalk project is not allowed. During many visits, this writer has usually found the first (southeasternmost) set of floating docks, just behind the Rice Museum, and the second pier in the middle of the Harborwalk complex (abeam of Francis Marion Park) to be more appropriate for cruising-sized vessels than the moorings farther upstream. While dockage for cruising-sized craft is allowed at these piers during inclement weather or when some difficulty is in the offing, it is usually best to anchor-off and then dinghy ashore. Depths alongside are a very impressive 9 to 13 feet at low water, but no power or water connections or other marine services are available at the city piers themselves. Of course, it is only a short jog back downstream to one of the commercial marinas if you need fuel or repair services. Showers are not currently available at the city docks.

The local Piggly Wiggly supermarket will be glad to dispatch a car to pick up and return cruisers who need to stock up their larders. Give them a call at (803) 546-5445 or take a taxi (see the numbers under Georgetown Landing Marina above). A laundromat located at the corner of Church and Cleland Streets can be reached via a five-block walk. The Georgetown Public Library is located directly across the street from the laundromat. With all these wonderful amenities, boaters can anchor or dock at Harborwalk confidently, with the added advantage of being moored in the heart of the revitalized downtown district.

As mentioned above, anchoring off the Harborwalk docks is encouraged. Happily, there are not yet any restrictions on this practice, as is all too often true in present-day Florida. Be sure to leave plenty of room in the channel by favoring the southwestern banks when you drop the hook. Show an anchor light! Depths run at least 10 feet. You may even want to consider a Bahamian-style mooring to minimize your swinging room, not because the anchorage is cramped, but to avoid swinging into the channel's midwidth should the wind and/or tide change.

Once the hook is down, it's a simple matter to dinghy ashore and tie up to one of the floating piers before exploring the downtown area. Protection from inclement weather is quite good.

Keeping pace with the Harborwalk complex is a wonderful revitalization of Georgetown's downtown business district. Thanks to this district and the community's enchanting historic residential section (see below), Georgetown can boast of attractions second to none in northeastern South Carolina.

Front Street runs parallel to the downtown Georgetown waterfront. This byway has been completely rebuilt over the last several years, with wider sidewalks and numerous planters. Front Street is also home to many fine shops and restaurants.

Harbor Specialties (732 Front Street, 803-527-3229), owned and managed by this writer's good friends Len Anderson and Susan Sanders, is a must stop for every cruising visitor. Specializing in personalized nautical clothing, this well-managed and fully outfitted shop offers something of interest to anyone journeying on the water.

This writer should also note in passing that Len and Susan have taken it upon themselves to formulate and deliver a welcome packet to every boater anchoring off Harborwalk. This delightful package is filled with information about local businesses and services. Be sure to get yours upon arriving in Georgetown.

Cruisers interested in learning more about local history or just finding the latest Tom Clancy novel should check out Mark Twain Bookstore (723 Front Street, 803-546-8212). This writer has always found a stroll through this delightfully ramshackle old building to be a genuine delight.

As you are wending your way down Front Street, don't be surprised to sniff the heavenly aroma of baking bread. Follow your nose to the Kudzu Bakery (714 Front Street, 803-527-7844). Here, you will find not only fresh bread but some of the most scrumptious chocolate chip cookies imaginable.

Just next door to Kudzu, Miss Emma Jane's (716 Front Street, 803-546-7844) offers gourmet coffees, teas, and other gifts. There is even a tearoom in the back.

Two gift shops of note are The Osprey's Nest (711 Front Street, 803-546-5877) and Pinckney's

Exchange (709 Front Street, 803-527-6664). Both firms offer a wide variety of tasteful gifts which should delight even the most discriminating customer.

Georgetown Restaurants

Famished cruisers will most certainly want to make the acquaintance of Thomas's Cafe (703 Front Street, 803-546-7776), hard by the historic Rice Museum, for breakfast or lunch. This longtime favorite serves some of the finest down-home Low Country cuisine you will ever enjoy. This writer particularly recommends the hot cakes for breakfast.

The venerable River Room Restaurant (802 Front Street, 803-527-4110) once overlooked what is now the northwestern tip of Harborwalk. Several years ago, this excellent dining spot moved into larger quarters astride the midsection of the town waterfront, just beside Francis Marion Park. It is conveniently located behind Harborwalk's middle set of floating docks. The seafood is absolutely extraordinary, whether you choose char-grilled catch of the day or a more elaborate crab casserole. Don't miss the South Carolina shrimp-and-grits appetizer, and (if you have room left)the peanut butter pie for dessert. You simply can't go wrong, no matter what your choice may be. To say the least, this writer gives the River Room Restaurant his highest recommendation.

A second outstanding restaurant in Georgetown is the Rice Paddy (408 Duke Street, 803-546-2021). Cruisers will need to trek four or five blocks from the waterfront to reach this dining spot, but the extra effort will be more than justified. Again, the food here is all that any patron could ask for. If you are into lamb, the Rack of Lamb Moutarde is to die for, and (if it is available during your visit) the Scallops au Gratin are memorable. There are many other succulent choices, so bring a good appetite along.

Another interesting dinner choice is Daniels (713 Front Street, 803-546-4377), on the west side of the street between the River Room Restaurant and the Rice Museum. This is a more informal dining choice, with waterfront tables available during fair weather. Entree choices range from burgers to grilled salmon.

Anyone for a tearoom repast? Well, if so, stop by The Pink Magnolia (719 Front Street, 803-527-6506). The decor is as ritzy as it gets, and the food is nothing to sneeze at either. Don't miss the shrimp salad.

For something really different, make a call on the Orange Blossom Cafe (107 Orange Street, 803-527-5060). This little cafe specializes in Greek dishes, and residents swear by its food.

For more information, check at the helpful Georgetown Chamber of Commerce and Visitor's Center (800-777-7705), now located on the corner of Front and Broad Streets. The people there will be glad to furnish you with useful information.

To summarize, the downtown Georgetown business district has undergone a rebirth during the last decade. What is so encouraging is that all the renewal and renovation have enhanced, rather than destroyed, the town's unique historical character. Boaters who pass Georgetown without a thought are quite simply missing one of the true gems of the South Carolina Low Country.

Georgetown Lodging

If it's time to take a night or two off from the

live-aboard routine, historic Georgetown is ready to accommodate with a host of fine motels and bed-and-breakfast inns. Three of these inns are located in the heart of the historic district and are well worth your attention.

The Dozier House (220 Queen Street, 803-527-1350 or 800-640-1350) is a delightfully rambling 1770-vintage house which offers three guest rooms. This writer and his mate found the Dozier House to be wonderfully informal, with a husband-wife innkeeper team (Tom and Chris Roach) who are just about as friendly as any hosts you will ever find. We were particularly taken with the superb breakfast consisting of fresh strawberries, coffee cake, and an egg, cheese, and sausage casserole.

The Kings Inn (230 Broad Street, 803-527-6937 or 800-251-8805) is Georgetown's largest and arguably most eloquent inn. The house was built around 1825 and displays something of the magnificence so characteristic of the Georgetown rice culture. The inn's furnishings look as if they have been laid out for a photo shoot by *Southern Living* or *Colonial Homes* magazines.

The 1790 House (630 Highmarket Street, 803-546-4821) is another excellent choice when considering shoreside lodging in Georgetown. This writer was particularly taken with two of The 1790 House's six guest rooms. The first is known as the "Slave Quarters." Located in the basement, this thoroughly renovated room did actually serve as the living quarters for several black slaves prior to the Civil War. Visitors to The 1790 House will also want to consider the "Dependency Cottage." With its own private entrance, its large Jacuzzi, and an expansive view of the enchanting backyard gardens, this room is a favorite with newlyweds.

Georgetown Historical District

The Georgetown historical district sits on some 220 acres of land and includes approximately 46 historical buildings. It is bounded to the south by Sampit River, to the east by Meeting Street, to the north by U.S. 17, and to the west by Wood Street. Begin your visit with a stop at the local chamber of commerce, on the corner of Front and Broad Streets. Here, you can obtain complete information on the historical area from the helpful staff. This writer particularly recommends the pamphlets *A Guide to Historic Sites in Georgetown County, South Carolina* and *A Guide to Historic Tours in Georgetown County, South Carolina.* The latter pamphlet lists dozens of tours. These excursions are perhaps the very best method for first-time visitors to get in touch with Georgetown. This writer highly recommends Miss Nell's Tours, which leave from the chamber building Tuesday through Thursday, Saturday, and Sunday. Call the chamber ahead of time for more information.

The Georgetown Chamber of Commerce has graciously consented to the reproduction of its historical-district map in this guide. A quick study of this excellent cartographical guide reveals many interesting homes and buildings worthy of exploration. Only a few of this writer's favorites can be mentioned here. It would be well worth your time, however, to take full advantage of the splendid historical sightseeing that the district affords.

Visitors interested in antiques and Revolutionary structures should check out the Kaminski House Museum (1003 Front Street, 803-546-7706). Filled with many period treasures, it features a fifteenth-century Spanish wedding chest and a Chippendale dining-room table, handcrafted in Charleston. The old home's interior features original floorings and moldings.

Prince George Episcopal Church, Winyah, is located on the corner of Broad and Highmarket Streets. The congregation dates from 1721, but the building was finished in 1750. With its cracked bricks and mortar, the old church seems to exude an almost tangible atmosphere of age. Stroll through the graveyard to the left of the church. It affords an excellent view of the tower, added in 1824. Among the graveyard's interesting headstones are many dating from the 1700s. Finally, take a moment to go inside. The doors are usually open, and respectful visitors are welcome. Standing amid the old-style box pews, one can almost picture the planters and their wives dressed in their best Sunday broadcloth and taffeta, listening soberly to a long sermon.

Prince George Episcopal Church

The Henning-Miller House, circa 1800, is located at the corner of Duke and Screven Streets. Like many Georgetown homes, this fine old building has its ghost story. The spirit, however, is most helpful. Tradition claims that during the British occupation of Georgetown, an officer staying at the house fell to his death on the main stairway. He is said to have lost his footing during a nighttime alarm. It is whispered that to this day, his ghost firmly grasps the shoulder of anyone who might trip on the stairs, saving that person from a fall.

The charming Waterman-Kaminski House is located at 620 Highmarket Street. This old home, circa 1770, was the scene of two tragedies. There is the sad story of a young boy who pined away at an early age. His thin little spirit is well known. The upstairs room opening onto the central dormer was the scene of another kind of tragedy. An old tale speaks of a young girl who was in love with a sea captain but who discovered her lover to be untrue. Heartbroken,

Interior of Prince George Episcopal Church

she took her own life in the upstairs room. On summer nights, her ghost is said to appear in the dormer window, patiently watching for the return of her faithless lover's ship.

The Winyah Indigo Society Hall is located on the corner of Prince and Cannon Streets. Organized in 1740 as a social club for wealthy planters, the Winyah Indigo Society eventually established a free school, founded a library, and served as both a business and social organization. The society survives to this day and still meets on a regular basis.

Just across the street from the Winyah Indigo Society Hall is the Morgan-Ginsler House. This building was used during the Civil War as a hospital for Union soldiers. It is said that strange noises have been heard from time to time in the dining room. There are those who claim that

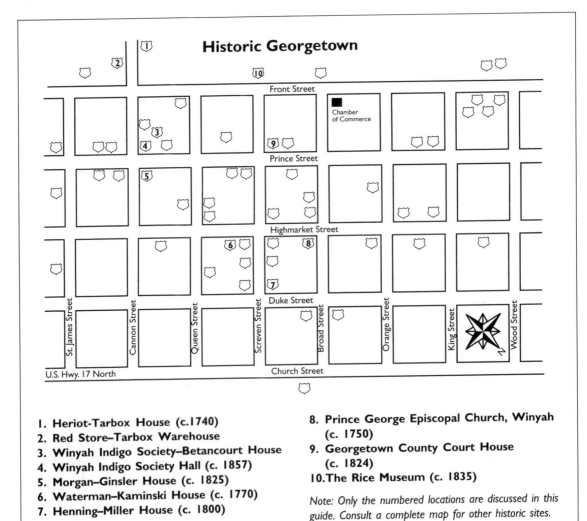

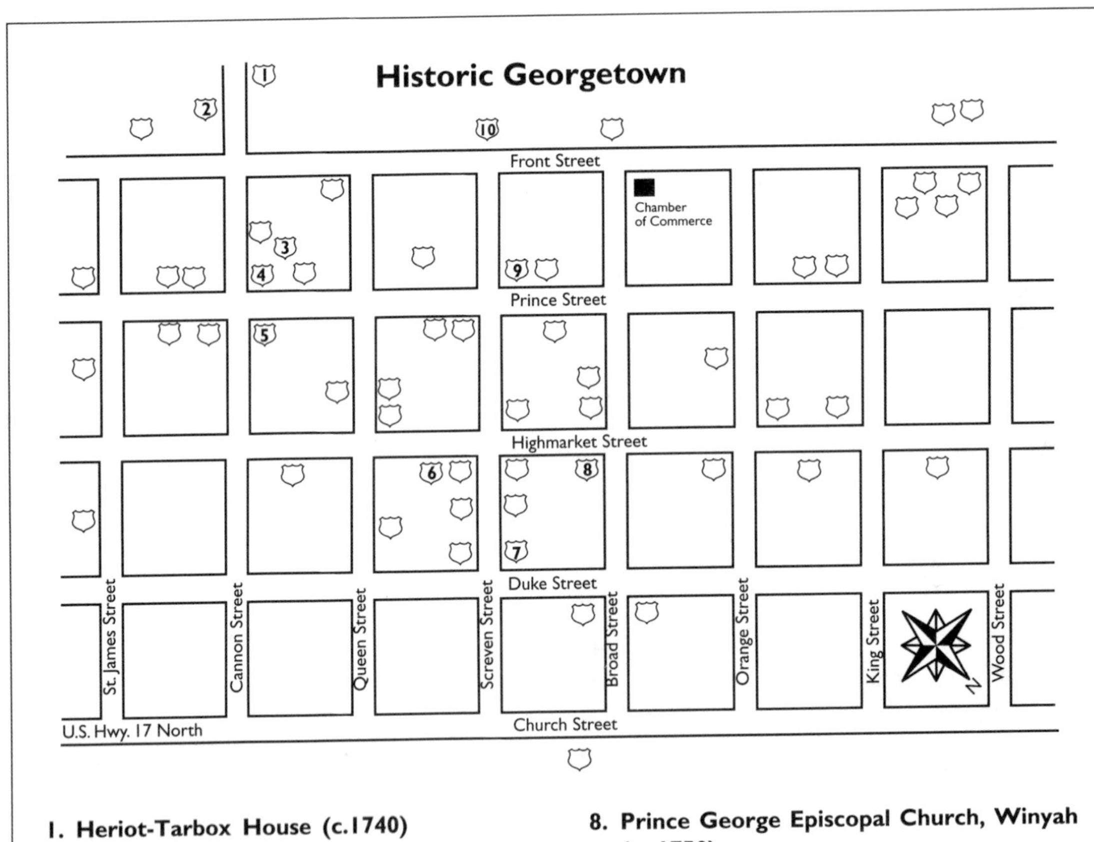

10. The Rice Museum (c. 1835)
Note: Only the numbered locations are discussed in this guide. Consult a complete map for other historic sites.

Winyah Indigo Society Hall

the ghostly noises are the sounds of Satan driving back the souls of the unfortunate soldiers who died there, making them relive their last few moments of misery on earth. This writer has a deep suspicion that a Southern sympathizer was the originator of this tale.

Two of Georgetown's historical points of interest are at the foot of Cannon Street fronting onto Sampit River. To the left is the Red Store–Tarbox Warehouse. In 1812, Theodosia Burr Alston, daughter of politician Aaron Burr, sailed from the warehouse docks on an ill-fated voyage to New York. The ship on which she sailed ran into a fierce gale off North Carolina and was apparently lost at sea or wrecked somewhere on the coast. Although there has been much speculation about her fate (one compelling version of her story is found in Charles Harry Whedbee's *Legends of the Outer Banks and Tar Heel Tidewater*), nobody really knows what happened to Theodosia.

Across the street from the warehouse is the Heriot-Tarbox House, one of the loveliest homes in Georgetown and the setting for what may well be the area's most touching legend.

Legend of the Heriot-Tarbox House

Some years before the Civil War, a wealthy family lived in this beautiful homeplace by the river. They had only one child, a daughter, on whom they showered all their love and attention. The girl was closely guarded by her parents to ensure a proper upbringing. She grew into a great beauty and was known by all the town's citizens for her gracious manners and shy nature.

The young enchantress was very fond of pets and always kept several dogs of rare pedigree. One day as she was throwing balls into the yard to see which dog was the swiftest retriever, a young officer from a ship docked at her father's warehouse happened to walk by and was captivated by the girl's loveliness. He retrieved one of

Heriot-Tarbox House, Georgetown

the balls that had fallen nearby and carried it up the broad steps to the shy maiden. Perhaps it was love at first sight. Before long, the two began to see each other on a regular basis, and their relationship blossomed with the passing of the days.

The young woman's tutor became worried about the seriousness of the affair and spoke to the girl's father, who was outraged. What made a common ship's officer think he could pay court to *his* daughter? He marched straight on board the ship and demanded that the captain forbid any further contact between the two lovers. Returning home, the father informed his daughter that she was never to see the young man again.

The captain did not take kindly to the father's demands, especially since the officer in question was his favorite nephew. Perhaps he aided the young couple. At any rate, the two lovers found a way to meet. When all those within the house were asleep, the girl would put a light in her upstairs window, and the young officer would know that all was safe. The two would then meet in the garden for a few brief but tender stolen moments.

The young woman would wed no other man and continued to live in her parents' house. Whenever the officer's ship was in port, the couple held their romantic trysts. Then, without explanation, the officer's visits suddenly ceased.

The heartbroken girl continued to place a lamp in her window every night. After a time, the light came to be a symbol of the love that she could never forget, yet that was doomed never to be. Eventually, she became a recluse and was rarely seen outside of the house. Following her parents' death, the servants and the dogs were her only companions.

As the Civil War drew its dark wings about Georgetown, stealthy blockade runners used the light in the window of the Cannon Street house for navigation. The saddened but loyal woman still faithfully placed the lamp in the window every night. Most thought she was doing what she could to aid the Southern cause. Only a few knew the real reason for this strange practice.

It was not long after the war that neighbors, alerted by barking dogs, discovered the poor woman's body in the house. She had apparently died of a heart attack. Some might say that it was a broken heart.

In the years that followed, many families lived in the old house. Strange noises were heard from time to time, and a light was often seen shining from the upstairs window. One resident even saw the form of a beautiful girl walking down the front steps into the garden. Others told of seeing a ghostly visage surrounded by barking dogs. The house was finally abandoned for many years, during which it acquired a sinister reputation.

In the 1930s, the house was restored to its former glory. It became one of the great showplaces of the Georgetown historical district. Its whitewashed walls and bright windows now look proudly over the harbor, recalling the grandeur of lost days. But there are many who will tell you that the sad ghost still maintains her lonely vigil each night from the upstairs window.

Lest you think this story too fanciful, several years ago the late owner herself told this writer that there was indeed "a ghost in the attic." While the spirit never appeared to her, she had

A street in Georgetown

seen the lights on the second floor many times. Even on a warm summer morning, this tale seemed to bring a bit of a chill to the air.

Georgetown History In 1526, the Spanish visionary Lucas Vasquez de Ayllon attempted to found a settlement in the Georgetown area. Little is known of this early attempt at colonization save the fact that it was a total failure. Some historians claim that only 150 of the original 500 colonists survived. Nevertheless, this effort, however futile, was one of the first European colonies in the New World.

Georgetown was laid out in 1729 by William Swinton at the request of newly appointed Royal Governor Robert Johnson. Johnson, one of South Carolina's most able and popular colonial governors, sought to ease the hardships of the settlers living north of Santee River, whose legal business had to be prefaced by a long and exhausting trip to Charleston and whose exports had to be shipped over tortuous land routes to the capital city. Finally, in 1732, the new town was declared a port of entry, and the first Royal customs officer took up residence.

Under British rule, Georgetown quickly became a prosperous port. England placed bounties on naval stores and indigo, both readily produced in the lands about the port. Many ships sailed from the Georgetown waterfront for the mother country with valuable cargoes of lumber and dye.

Shipbuilding began in Georgetown by 1738. As the wealth of the Georgetown merchants increased with expanding trade, it became profitable for them to acquire their own ships rather than share profits with a shipping agent.

In 1735, the citizens of the Winyah area petitioned the colonial assembly to "set forth the necessity of laying buoys and erecting beacons or landmarks, and maintaining pilot boats to attend the bar of the harbor of Georgetown." Clearly, the town was well on its way to becoming a bustling port.

As the clouds of war spread across the colonies, voices in Georgetown cried for American rights. Georgetown planters made substantial contributions to aid Boston when its harbor was closed after the Tea Party. In December 1774, Georgetown had its own tea party. When local patriots discovered that a ship in the harbor had a cargo of taxed tea in her hole, they demanded that the ship's master dump his cargo overboard. He soon complied with the less-than-gentle demands of the patriots. While it did not have the far-reaching implications of the more famous Boston incident, the Georgetown Tea Party certainly demonstrated the resolve of the local citizenry.

For the first four years of the Revolution, Georgetown was little touched by the war, although it was visited by one of the war's great heroes, the Marquis de Lafayette. In 1777, the marquis made landfall at nearby North Island and traveled through Georgetown on his way to Charleston.

Georgetown was occupied by the British in July 1780. It was not long before Francis Marion, the famed "Swamp Fox" of history and legend, began to strike at the English forces from the dark recesses of the Pee Dee swamps. Marion is credited with being the father of guerrilla warfare. He and his band of irregulars repeatedly struck the vastly superior British forces gathered around Georgetown and then melted away into the seemingly impenetrable wilderness.

In January of the same year, Marion had joined forces with Lighthorse Harry Lee to briefly overrun the town. Lacking sufficient artillery, Marion was forced to withdraw, but in 1781 he drove the British from Georgetown once and for all. The liberation of the port was followed by a disastrous fire set by an English raiding party. The fire consumed more than 42 houses.

In the latter stages of the Revolution, Georgetown was most important to the American cause. With Charleston still in British hands, the port served as an invaluable supply depot.

Following the war, the area's rice culture began its rapid rise. Free from the constraints of the British trading system and the requirements of war, the Georgetown rice planters began to carve a great empire from the muddy recesses of the tidal swamps. By 1840, the Georgetown area was said to produce 45 percent of all the rice grown in America. Fabulous fortunes were won, and the opulence of the rice culture became a standard for others to envy.

Surprisingly, Georgetown did not benefit as much from the rise of the rice culture as might be expected. Many rice planters sent their goods directly to Charleston for transshipment to other markets. The prestige of the capital port, with its long transcontinental shipping tradition, persuaded many planters to bypass Georgetown's shipping facilities. Georgetown was never able to compete effectively with its rival to the south.

Additional problems were caused by the shallow Winyah Bay inlet bar. It carried only some 10 to 12 feet of water, a bit shallow for oceangoing ships of that era. This problem led to various schemes to build an artificial inlet across North Island and a canal connecting the bay with Santee River. All of these projects ended in failure. Georgetown had to wait until the 1880s, when the Mosquito Creek Canal successfully joined the bay to Santee River.

Georgetown was spared the worst pains of battle during the Civil War. The town was not occupied until February 1865, and little damage was done to the historical buildings.

The end of the war saw the beginning of the end of the rice culture. Georgetown suffered through the years of Reconstruction, as did most other Southern cities. Times were hard until the twentieth century, but the town's economy began to improve when the ICW was opened in the 1930s. There followed the stabilization of the Winyah Bay inlet channel and the location of modern port facilities on Sampit River.

Today, Georgetown is a small but busy port that retains, for the most part, its charm and historical character. An active chamber of commerce and local historical society work diligently to maintain the mementos of the port's days of glory. Every visitor is indebted to their efforts. Those desiring to learn more of Georgetown's history should acquire Ronald E. Birdwell's excellent booklet, '. . . *That We Should Have a Port*. . . .' It gives a very readable account of Georgetown's maritime history from 1732 to 1865. The book is available at the Georgetown Rice Museum.

Rice-culture History Rice was grown in South Carolina as early as the 1690s, but it was not until McKewn Johnstone perfected the tidal-flow method of rice cultivation in 1758 that "Carolina Gold" became king of Georgetown County. In his fascinating booklet, *No Heir to Take Its Place*, Dennis T. Lawson comments, "From the earliest settlement at the beginning of the eighteenth century until the first decade of the 1900s rice was synonymous with Georgetown County. . . . The history of Georgetown until the modern era is the history of its rice culture. . . . It is likely that no other area of the United States has ever been as dependent for as long a period of time on this one crop."

Following the invention of the tidal-flow irrigation system, rice planting settled down to a regular pattern in the Georgetown area. First, swampy areas were cleared, then diked by building banks along the rivers. Then the fields were subdivided by smaller earthen banks so their flooding could be individually controlled. Floodgates, or trunks, were installed in the large banks. These most important devices controlled the time and level of the fields' flooding. Highly skilled slaves known as "trunkminders" were solely responsible for the maintenance of the floodgates. Bank mending was another unending chore.

Since the fields were flooded on a regular basis, the fertility of the soil was continually renewed. This practice was in sharp contrast to that of the cotton plantations, which habitually exhausted their fields. The rice plantations retained their fertility until the end of the rice culture.

The clearing of the fields, the construction and maintenance of the banks, and the cultivation of the crop were very labor-intensive tasks calling for hundreds of workers, almost exclusively black slaves. As this writer stood on the banks of an old rice field one summer afternoon with the sun hot on the back of my neck and flies buzzing around my head, I could not help reflecting on the backbreaking toil of the many slaves who once worked there. Without their labor, there would have been no affluent lifestyle for the rice master. When considering the romance of the rice culture, one should remember just what terrible sacrifices were required to maintain such a way of life.

Because the cultivation of rice was so labor-intensive, large landowners with heavy capital reserves were better suited for success than small farmers. By the mid-1800s, the great wealth of the rice culture was concentrated in the hands of a few large planters, such as "King" Joshua John Ward, the greatest planter on the Waccamaw. In 1850, he produced almost 4,000,000 pounds of rice on six plantations with more than 1,000 slaves. The Black and Pee Dee Rivers also had extensive rice fields.

The Civil War spelled the doom of the rice culture. Without slave labor, profits declined every year. Rice planting began in the Gulf States following the war. The firmer soil of the Gulf region was suitable for mechanized cultivation, while South Carolina's swampy earth would not support the use of farm machinery. Several great hurricanes struck the South Carolina coast from 1894 to 1906, severely damaging the rice crops. Finally, in the early 1900s, rice cultivation was abandoned almost entirely, marking the end of an age for the Georgetown area.

Only the barest outline of the rice culture is presented in these pages. To learn more, plan a visit to the Georgetown Rice Museum, located along the city's waterfront. It is easily recognized by its tall clock tower. Here, you can learn the full story of the fabulous rice culture. Dennis T. Lawson's booklet, *No Heir to Take Its Place*, is also highly recommended. As you come to understand the flavor of that era, you may agree with Lawson that the bygone rice culture truly left no heir to take its place.

Georgetown Rice Museum

GEORGETOWN NAVIGATION

There is nothing particularly complicated about navigation of the channels serving Georgetown or the approach to Georgetown Landing Marina at the southwestern foot of Pee Dee River. The various passages are well marked and resonably easy to follow.

After passing through the U.S. 17 high-rise bridge on Waccamaw River, set a careful compass course to come abeam of and pass flashing daybeacon #94 to its southeasterly side. As you will notice after a quick study of chart 11534, there is very shallow water on both sides of the Waterway channel along this stretch. Stay on course and watch for excessive leeway.

From #94, continue on the same track, carefully pointing to come abeam of flashing junction daybeacon #W by at least 30 yards to its southeastern quarter. Flashing daybeacon #94 and flashing junction daybeacon #W mark a long, long tongue of shoal water stretching southwest from Waccamaw Point. Be *sure* to stay to the southeast of #94 and #W. Notice, though, that there is shallow water abutting the southeastern side of the Waterway channel as well.

From flashing junction daybeacon #W, point to come abeam of flashing daybeacon #40 to its northwesterly side. You will quickly note that marker colors have now reversed. This is only as it should be. From Georgetown, the ICW converges with the Winyah Bay entrance channel as far as Belle Isle. The inlet channel takes precedence, and, as you are now headed toward the open sea, you must pass all red markers to your port side and take green beacons to starboard.

Flashing daybeacon #40 marks a strategic intersection. The entrance to Sampit River and the principal Georgetown waterfront lies to the north-northwest, while a jog to the northeast will take you into Pee Dee River and the approach to Georgetown Landing Marina. The ICW and the Winyah Bay channel continue on their combined way to the southwest.

Passage to Georgetown Landing Marina From flashing daybeacon #40, set course to the northeast and follow the well-outlined channel. Take red markers to your starboard side and green beacons to port.

While the channel is quite broad, chart 11534 correctly forecasts shoal depths on both sides of the cut. Be sure to identify the various aids to navigation and follow their track carefully.

Georgetown Landing Marina lies along the western banks between unlighted daybeacon #6 and the fixed U.S. 17 bridge. Be sure to enter the marina by way of the marked cut in the breakwater on the eastern side of the complex. Two lighted aids outline this passage.

Georgetown Waterfront Channel Fortunate boaters bound for the Georgetown waterfront should cut north-northwest from flashing daybeacon #40 and set course to traverse the mid-width of the broad passage between flashing daybeacons #41 and #42. This route will bring you into the southeastern mouth of Sampit River. Continue dead ahead, keeping a sharp watch for flashing daybeacon #S marking the well-charted split in the river. As you approach to within some 100 yards of this aid, bear off to the northeast and enter the eastern portion of the Georgetown loop. Soon, the town's facilities will begin to come abeam on the eastern and northeastern banks. First up is Hazzard's Marina, followed by The Boat Shed Marina and Cathou's Boat Yard. As you cruise the lengthy gap between The Boat Shed Marina and Harborwalk Marina, watch the eastern banks for a good view of the magnificent Heriot-Tarbox House.

North and northwest of Harborwalk Marina, the large clock tower of the Georgetown Rice Museum overlooks the water. This landmark hails the southeasterly limits of the Harborwalk complex. Watch carefully for the floating docks, anchor-off at a likely spot, and dinghy ashore.

Many boaters will wisely choose to discontinue their exploration of the Georgetown loop at the northwesterly end of Harborwalk. A large scrap-metal plant flanks the loop's northwesterly banks opposite flashing daybeacon #48. The commercial traffic in this area can be considerable from time to time.

Should you decide to explore anyway, simply pass all red markers to your port side and the one charted green daybeacon to starboard. After rounding the loop, you will soon come abeam of the entrance to upper Sampit River west of your course.

UPPER SAMPIT RIVER

The main body of upper Sampit River breaks off to the west from the Georgetown loop. The initial portion of the river's upper reaches is very commercial, with large ships often docked along the northern shores. Also located in this area is the paper mill mentioned earlier.

The river channel is quite deep and holds minimum 15-foot depths for several nautical miles upstream of the 65-foot fixed bridge. Boaters who persevere (and who can clear the correctly charted 61-foot fixed power line) will eventually leave the commercial waterfront behind and pass into an undeveloped portion of the river. This spot makes a good anchorage, with excellent protection from all winds. While it's quite a trek off the beaten path, boaters who enjoy cruising and anchoring where few of their number have been before may well be taken with the upper Sampit.

UPPER SAMPIT RIVER NAVIGATION

You may enter upper Sampit River by one of two routes. Cruisers docked or anchored in downtown Georgetown can follow the western portion of the loop and enter the river south of flashing daybeacon #47. Those bound directly from the ICW and Winyah Bay for the upper Sampit can bear northwest at flashing daybeacon #S marking the initial split in the river (instead of turning to the northeast to visit Georgetown) and cruise directly to the entrance.

Enter upper Sampit River on its mid-width and keep a close watch for commercial traffic. Soon, the river is spanned by a 65-foot fixed highway bridge. Upstream of this point, sailors must be on guard for the charted 61-foot power line.

Continue tracking your way upstream until the paper mill and commercial docks have been left behind. Consider dropping anchor here. Farther upstream, depths become less certain.

PEE DEE RIVER

Pee Dee River, sometimes known as the Great Pee Dee, is a disappointing body of water for cruising purposes. To enter the river from Winyah Bay, you must be able to clear a fixed bridge with only 20 feet of vertical clearance. There are no marina facilities available anywhere on Pee Dee River or Jericho Creek.

Some 4.5 nautical miles northeast of the stream's juncture with Black River, the Pee Dee enters a delta region where depths become too inconsistent for most cruising craft. As noted in chapter 1, the upper Pee Dee is accessible from Waccamaw River via Thoroughfare Creek, but this area, too, has its navigational problems. All but the largest pleasure craft can enter the deeper portion of the lower Pee Dee from Waccamaw River via Jericho Creek. However, it's a long cruise, particularly for sailors, from the Waccamaw to the Pee Dee by way of this route.

The lower Pee Dee River maintains minimum 7-foot depths from Winyah Bay to Jericho Creek and the delta region. While the stream is unmarked and there are a few shoal areas to avoid, navigation on this part of the river is fairly simple and does not present any real problem.

Despite its limited reaches, the lower Pee Dee does offer good cruising ground in a backwater atmosphere. This part of the river has lovely, undeveloped banks and offers anchorage possibilities. Much of the shoreline is composed of abandoned rice fields. Watch carefully as you cruise along; you can still see several old floodgates along the eastern shore.

One of the best spots to anchor on the Pee Dee is located southwest of the stream's intersection with Black River. Here, there is enough swinging room for anything smaller than the *Queen Mary*, and the surrounding shores are delightfully in their natural state. While this portion of the river is a bit wide for good protection in really nasty weather, visiting cruisers should be secure in light to moderate breezes.

Nightingale Hall Plantation on Pee Dee River

Jericho Creek

Jericho Creek is a large stream that splits off from the Pee Dee and winds generally northeast into Waccamaw River. The creek maintains minimum depths of 8 feet and affords good overnight anchorage on its southwesterly reaches, near Pee Dee River. Protection is excellent, even in heavy weather. The southwesterly portion of the stream has enough swinging room for craft as large as 45 feet. Beware of the charted "Cable" area northeast of the intersection.

The entire shoreline is undeveloped and composed mostly of abandoned rice fields. There are no facilities available on the creek. Jericho Creek has a true feeling of isolation. Consider dropping the hook here for an evening of peace and security.

Good depths continue upstream all the way to Waccamaw River. The stream does narrow a bit, however, and cruising-sized craft may find it a bit cramped for comfortable anchorage on the upper section of the stream.

Nightingale Hall Plantation

Some 1.2 nautical miles to the north of the Pee Dee River–Jericho Creek intersection, the Nightingale Hall Plantation house is readily visible on the western shore. This plantation was one of the many holdings of the illustrious Alston family. Following the Civil War, the Alston properties were broken up, and Nightingale Hall was sold.

PEE DEE RIVER NAVIGATION

Immediately after leaving Georgetown Landing Marina, the Pee Dee channel passes under the U.S. 17 fixed bridge, with a vertical clearance of 20 feet. Boats needing more vertical clearance must enter Pee Dee River via Jericho Creek from Waccamaw River.

After passing under the fixed bridge, watch carefully to the east and west for the remnants of an old low-level span. The outer tips of this derelict are now marked by aids to navigation. Unlighted daybeacon #10, marking the east-side portion of the old bridge, is mounted atop its own tripod of pilings, but unlighted daybeacon #9 is actually set on the west-side portion of the old bridge. Pass between the two aids carefully. Once through, stick to the mid-width. Keep a sharp watch for crab pots on this section of the stream.

Black River splits off from the Pee Dee's northern shore some 2.2 nautical miles north and northeast of the U.S. 17 bridge. This stream will be covered in the next section. Avoid the point of land separating the two rivers. Shoal water extends well southwest from this point.

Continue to cruise on the mid-width. Northeast of the intersection with Black River, the Pee Dee provides enough shelter for overnight anchorage.

Another upstream cruise of 2.6 miles brings you to the southwestern entrance of Jericho Creek. Good anchorage is available on the initial stretch of this stream, though you must be careful to avoid the charted "Cable" area. Good depths of 8 feet or more are held all the way to the Waccamaw.

The northwestern branch of the Pee Dee begins to enter its shallow delta region upstream of the intersection with Jericho Creek. The Pee Dee does remain navigable for another 1.2 nautical miles above Jericho Creek. North of this point, depths become inconsistent, to say the least. Just south of the shallow-water area, Nightingale Hall Plantation is visible on the northwestern shore.

BLACK RIVER

Black River is, quite simply, one of the most beautiful streams in northeastern South Carolina. The Black's shores are a study in pleasing contrasts. Abandoned rice fields alternate with heavily wooded banks and even a few sandy shores. Most of the shoreline is undeveloped, though here and there a few houses overlook the water. Even in a region where beautiful shorelines are the rule, Black River's banks can bring a sigh of contentment from the most indifferent cruiser.

Although the stream is unmarked, good depths open out from shore to shore. Unfortunately, the river holds problems for sailors. Obviously, sailcraft of any size will not be able to clear the 20-foot fixed bridge at the Pee Dee's southwesterly entrance. Even if you enter Black River by way of the Jericho Creek–Pee Dee River route (thereby avoiding the fixed bridge), there are still several navigational worries, at least if you try to explore the river all the way to the fixed U.S. 701 bridge. For one thing, you must negotiate an uncharted passage around a marsh island, but more important, there is a set of uncharted power lines to worry with. This writer has not been able to find any published vertical clearance for this shocking obstruction, but I estimate the lines' height at no more than 40 feet. Of course, you can always explore Black River south of the power lines, as such a plan allows sailors to experience the better part of the stream's delightful track. Power-craft skippers

Old ferry house on Black River

can glide speedily by without worrying with the overhead problems.

Take a moment to look at your wake and you will quickly discover how the river derived its name. Colored by vast cypress swamps to the north, the waters of Black River are a dark, brownish hue. This natural phenomenon somehow adds to the feeling of adventure one experiences while exploring this beautiful body of water.

The entire river is well sheltered and presents a wealth of anchorages. There is plenty of swinging room for large craft. The stream's upper reaches are fit for heavy weather, while the lower sections are fine for light to moderate airs. Simply select a spot that strikes your fancy and set the hook for a memorable night.

Rotting docks and old pilings dot the banks, evidence of the brisk rice and indigo trade that once flowed along this lovely stream. Before the rise of the rice culture, the finest indigo in South Carolina was said to be grown along Black River. The river winds through the lands of several historical rice plantations, though only one house is visible.

Over and above all these attributes, there is an indefinable quality of isolation and adventure that seems to permeate Black River's cruising grounds. Boaters who enjoy the feeling that every turn of the wheel or puff of wind takes them farther away from the ordinary will find Black River to be just what they are looking for.

Windsor Plantation

Windsor Plantation guards the west bank of Black River approximately 1 nautical mile from the Pee Dee intersection. Although the present house was built in 1937 to replace the original structure, the plantation itself dates from 1762. During the latter stages of the Civil War, Federal troops tried to burn the homeplace but were stopped by the daring resolve of 80-year-old Miss Hannah Trapier, the owner of the property. This story should lay to rest some of the traditional notions concerning the shy and retiring character of Southern belles.

Windsor Plantation on Black River

BLACK RIVER NAVIGATION

Simply follow the river's mid-width as you travel upstream. After cruising for several miles, you will spy a small island that bisects the river. For best depths, pass the small landmass to your starboard side.

As you leave the charted confines of Black River, begin keeping a close watch for the above-mentioned power lines. Sailboats should come about well short of this potentially deadly obstacle.

Some 7.8 nautical miles upstream from the Pee

Dee intersection, a fixed bridge blocks further upstream passage on Black River. As you approach the bridge, look to the northern shore. There, you will see a large clapboard ferry house, which was used until the local ferry was replaced by a bridge in the 1930s. The building is now part of a private estate.

This guide's coverage of Black River ends at the fixed bridge. Only small power craft should attempt to explore farther upstream, where depths are far from certain.

WINYAH BAY AND THE ICW

Winyah Bay is the largest body of water on the South Carolina coast north of Charleston. It stretches for some 16 nautical miles from the Atlantic to the confluence of the Waccamaw and Pee Dee Rivers. The inlet is less than 1 mile in width, but the main body widens to some 4.5 miles at Mud Bay. Winyah Bay covers 25 square miles.

Much of the bay is shallow, but two well-marked channels traverse its length. One offers reliable access to the open sea, while the ICW route leads the Waterway traveler to the Minim Creek Canal.

Navigation of Winyah Bay must not be taken lightly. Unlike the waters to the north, this bay demands that cruising boaters stick to the channel in most cases or risk prop and keel damage.

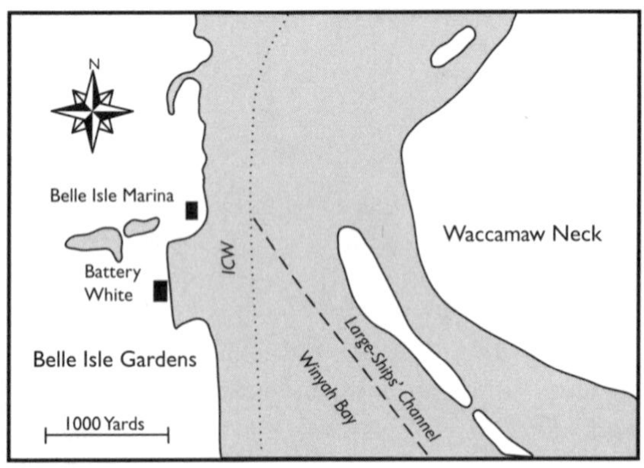

Study charts 11534 and 11532 carefully before entering these waters to familiarize yourself with the many aids to navigation. Five or six years ago, the various markers on Winyah Bay were completely reconfigured. Be sure to have the latest editions of charts 11534 and 11532 on board before beginning your passage.

Winyah Bay Inlet is the first truly reliable seaward passage south of North Carolina's Cape Fear River. The channel is used on a regular basis by large cargo ships entering the Georgetown port facilities. It is well marked and reasonably easy to navigate. However, like all inlets, it can be rough when winds and tides oppose each other. If at all possible, pick a fair-weather day before running the cut.

The bay has one good facility but lacks protected anchorages. It is not the sort of place one would want to spend the night swinging on the hook.

Several historical sites are located along Winyah Bay's shoreline. A number are readily visible from the water, while one calls for an adventurous side trip.

Winyah Bay is an attractive body of water that provides pleasant cruising in fair weather. However, in stormy conditions the bay can daunt the hardiest pleasure boater. Treat Winyah

Bay with respect and you will enjoy your cruise. Take the bay too lightly and you may find yourself in need of assistance.

Belle Isle Marina

Belle Isle Marina occupies the charted sheltered cove indenting Winyah Bay's western banks southwest of flashing buoy #30. Belle Isle is a modern facility under friendly, responsive management that gladly accepts transient boaters. This otherwise fine marina had a problem after Hurricane Hugo. The entrance channel shoaled, and it proved difficult to get the necessary permits to dredge. Fortunately, full dredging was at last completed in late 1994, and visiting cruisers can now expect to find some 7 feet of water in the entrance channel, with 7½ to 10-foot soundings dockside. Belle Isle is once again heartily recommended by this writer.

Belle Isle Marina offers overnight berths at both floating and fixed wooden-decked piers with all power and water connections. Showers are at hand to wash away the day's salt, and there is an on-site laundromat to help catch up on the wash. Gasoline, diesel fuel, and waste pump-out services are available, as are mechanical repairs. A small ship's and variety store guards the westerly end of the piers. While there is no longer a restaurant on the Belle Isle grounds, the management will usually loan transients a car to travel into town and slake their appetites.

Belle Isle Marina (803) 546-8491

Approach depth: 7 feet
Dockside depth: 7½–10 feet
Accepts transients: yes
Fixed and floating piers: yes
Dockside power connections: 30 and 50 amps
Dockside water connections: yes
Showers: yes
Laundromat: yes
Waste pump-out: yes
Gasoline: yes
Diesel fuel: yes
Mechanical repairs: yes
Ship's and variety store: yes
Restaurants: management will usually lend car

Belle Isle Marina is located on the lands of Belle Isle Plantation. The brother of Francis Marion, "the Swamp Fox," lived here during Revolutionary War times. General Marion's plantation, Pond Bluff, was flooded by the construction of Lake Marion back in the 1930s. The war hero's grave can be seen on Belle Isle.

Belle Isle Plantation also harbors acres of beautiful gardens, which are open to the public. A visit to these serene grounds is definitely recommended for those who have seen too many waves.

Battery White

Another historical site within walking distance of Belle Isle Marina is Battery White. This Civil War fortification is difficult to see from the water. It is located several hundred yards south of the marina. It was constructed during the Civil War to protect Winyah Bay, but it proved ineffective.

Hobcaw Barony and Anchorage

One of the largest landholdings in South Carolina was once located along the eastern

Hobcaw Barony, resort home of Bernard Baruch

shores of Winyah Bay east-southeast of flashing buoy #36. Hobcaw Barony was a huge estate. Over the years, the property was broken up into a number of large plantations.

From 1905 to 1907, Bernard Baruch acquired most of the original holdings of the barony and rejoined the various tracts. Baruch was a great duck hunter who entertained sporting guests on a lavish scale. Franklin D. Roosevelt and Winston Churchill were two of his most famous guests.

Today, the property is held under the auspices of the Belle W. Baruch Foundation. Extensive research in marine biology is carried on at the foundation by the University of South Carolina. Clemson University also uses the facilities for forestry experiments.

The main house is difficult to spot from the main channel, but there just may be a way to have a closer look. In spite of what chart 11534 would lead you to believe, it is quite possible for especially adventurous boaters to find their way to the waters abutting the charted position of the old Hobcaw Barony mansion, and even to anchor snugly for the night. This trip is not recommended for boats that draw more than 4 feet and should only be undertaken by skippers who are willing to risk finding the bottom. The route currently holds 5 to 5½-foot depths, but it is unmarked and tricky. Please read the navigational information presented below carefully before making the attempt.

If you successfully traverse the tricky approach route, the waters adjacent to Hobcaw Barony offer a good spot to drop the hook. This anchorage is well sheltered from eastern or western blows, and there is some protection from southern breezes as well. Strong winds from the north and northeast clearly call for another strategy. The shores of Rabbit and Hare Islands to the northwest are comprised of undeveloped salt marsh, while the mainland to the east is occupied almost exclusively by the Hobcaw Barony mansion.

Dover Plantation

Dover Plantation can be seen just to the southwest of flashing daybeacon #98. It features one of the most beautiful plantation houses visible from the water between Little River and Charleston. Although the house dates to 1810, it was moved to its present site in the 1940s from land now flooded by the Santee-Cooper watershed project. Anyone viewing this magnificent edifice will certainly agree that it was well worth saving from destruction.

Estherville Plantation

Estherville Plantation is just visible to the southwest of flashing daybeacon #100. Seasonal vegetation can interfere with the view from the water, but it is well worth a look. In 1758, Estherville Plantation was the site of the first

Dover Plantation, Winyah Bay

successful experiments with tidal cultivation of rice. The house and grounds have been carefully restored by the present owners.

Georgetown Lighthouse

Rising to a height of 85 feet, the Georgetown Lighthouse watches benignly over the entrance to Winyah Bay from the western shore of North Island. Lighted in 1812 after numerous delays, the present lighthouse is actually the second to occupy this location. The first, built in 1801, was a wooden tower and was toppled by a strong gale in 1806. The light is not readily visible from the ICW channel. A voyage down the inlet channel is necessary to view this old lighthouse, which speaks so eloquently of an age of the sea now long departed.

WINYAH BAY NAVIGATION

If you have an old edition of either chart 11532 or 11534, throw it away. As alluded to earlier, the aids to navigation along the Winyah Bay channel are entirely different from what they were five or six years ago. The channel markers were renumbered and added to at the request of the commercial pilots who regularly ply the waters of Winyah Bay.

Be sure to use chart 11532 for navigation of the Winyah Bay inlet channel. Chart 11534 is sufficient for the ICW route only! Pay attention to business while piloting in the bay. Watch your depth sounder! You cannot afford to be as casual with navigation here as on the deeper waters to the north.

Note that marker colors reverse at the intersection of the ICW and the Georgetown Harbor channel (at flashing daybeacon #40). The large-ships' channel takes precedence over the Waterway route, and the markers are configured as if you were putting out to sea, red to your port side and green to starboard. The standard Waterway markings resume where the ICW channel splits off from the seaward passage below Belle Isle at flashing daybeacon #96.

On Winyah Bay and the ICW Channel From flashing daybeacon #40, set your course south-southwest, pointing to come abeam of flashing buoy #38 to its western side. Continue to flashing buoy #36, passing it to the same quarter. Along the way between #38 and #36, you will come abeam of and pass flashing daybeacon #37 west of your course line. Shallow water lies west of #37, so be sure to pick up this beacon. South of #36, northbound boaters can make use of a charted range that helps them keep to the channel.

It's a fairly long but straightforward jog down the channel to flashing buoy #34. As you would expect, come abeam of this aid to its westerly quarter. Do not slip too far to the west on this run. The clearly charted shallows are waiting to trap the unwary.

Hobcaw Barony Channel In spite of the depths shown on charts 11534 and 11532, it is possible for shallow-draft vessels to cruise east from a position midway between flashing buoys #36 and #34 to view the main house at Hobcaw Barony, or even to anchor abeam of the old mansion. This side trip should be attempted only by wild-eyed skippers piloting craft less than 36 feet in length and drawing no more than 4 feet (and preferably less). It is best to time your cruise to coincide with a rising tide.

If you choose to make the attempt, cruise south from #36 for some 0.4 nautical mile, following the main channel. Then cut 90 degrees to the east and set a course parallel to the southern shore of Rabbit and Hare Islands, keeping the banks about 100 yards off your port side. As you approach the mainland shore, you will sight the house just to the east. Deep water opens out in a broad band to the northeast.

You may either drop the hook abeam of the Hobcaw Barony mansion or cruise several hundred yards farther to the northeast in depths of 8 feet or more. Retrace your course to the west in order to rejoin the main channel.

On Winyah Bay and the ICW Channel The channel remains fairly simple to follow as far as flashing buoy #30. Some of the aids are rather widely spaced, and the careful cruiser should be ready to run compass courses over the various legs of the channel.

Come abeam of flashing buoy #30 to its westerly side, just as you would expect. At this point, the Winyah Bay channel and the ICW break off from each other. To continue south on the Waterway, set course from #30 to come abeam of flashing daybeacon #96 to its easterly quarter. Between #30 and #96, you will pass the marked entrance to Belle Isle Marina northwest of your course.

At flashing daybeacon #96, the standard ICW marker colors resume. Southbound cruisers will pass red aids to the boaters' starboard side and take green beacons to port.

Boaters wishing to run the Winyah Bay channel to its inlet should swing to the southeast and follow the plentiful markers out to sea. Have chart 11532 at hand to quickly resolve any questions that might arise.

ICW Channel South of flashing daybeacon #96, the ICW channel is wide and deep but scantily marked. It is an excellent idea to run compass courses between aids to avoid confusion. Beware of the shoal water along the eastern and northeastern sides of the Waterway. Have chart 11534 handy and pay attention to what you are doing.

From #96, point to eventually come abeam of flashing daybeacon #98 to its eastern side. Watch the southwestern shoreline as you pass #98 for a good view of Dover Plantation.

Continue following the Waterway by passing flashing daybeacon #100 to its northeastern side. The Estherville Plantation house is visible on the southwestern banks just southeast of #100.

At flashing daybeacon #2, the Waterway takes an almost 90-degree turn to the southwest and enters the Minim Creek Canal. Continued navigation of the ICW route is presented in the next chapter.

Old Homeplace in Georgetown Historic District

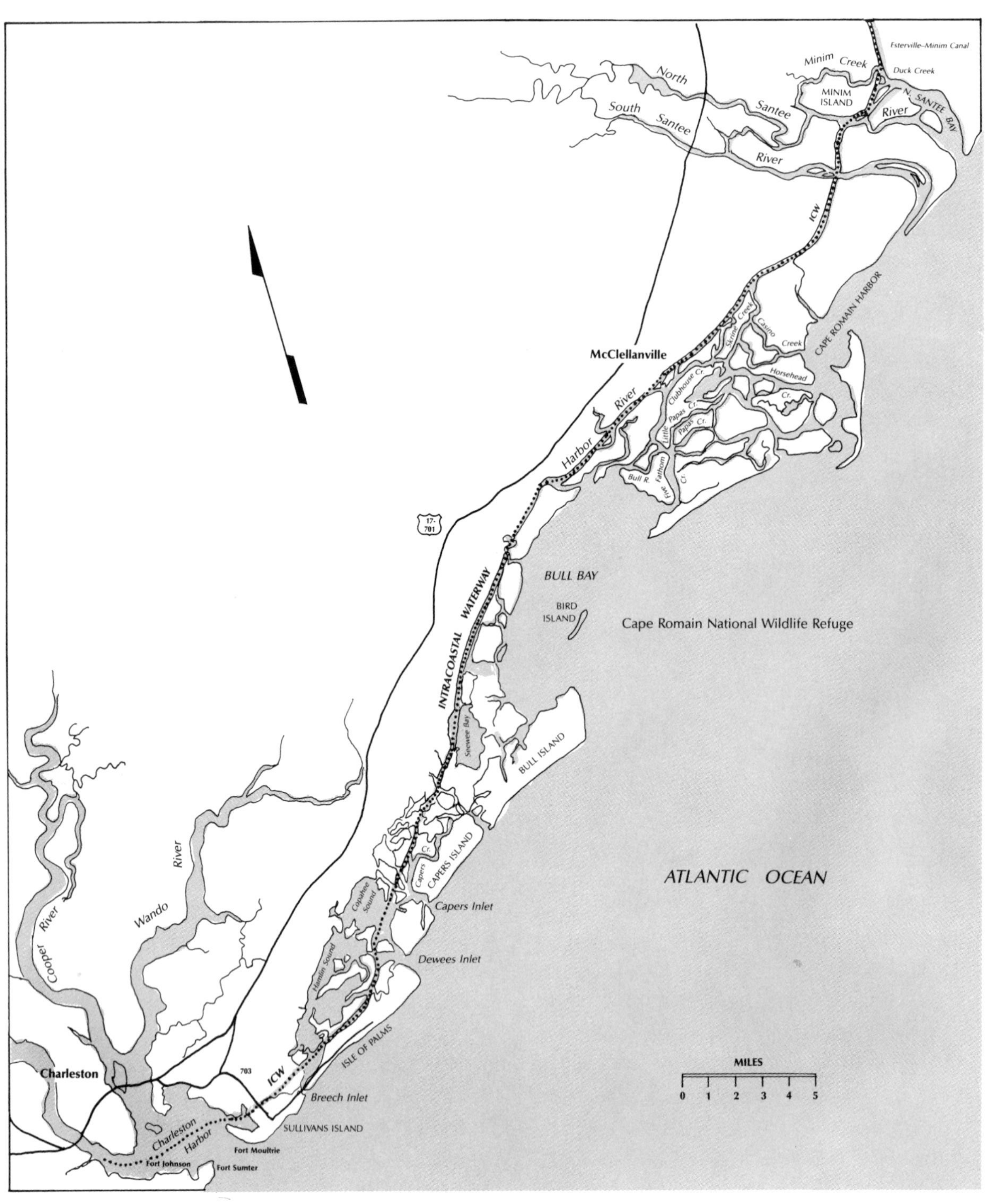

Esterville–Minim Canal
Minim Creek
Duck Creek
MINIM ISLAND
North
Santee
South
Santee
River
N. SANTEE BAY
River
ICW
CAPE ROMAIN HARBOR
Casino
Creek
Skrine Creek
McClellanville
Clubhouse Cr.
Horsehead
Cr.
Little Papas Cr.
Papas Cr.
River
Harbor
Bull R.
Five Fathom Cr.
17-701
BULL BAY
BIRD ISLAND
Cape Romain National Wildlife Refuge
INTRACOASTAL WATERWAY
Seewee Bay
BULL ISLAND
River
Wando
Cooper
River
Cr.
Capers
CAPERS ISLAND
Copahee Sound
Capers Inlet
ATLANTIC OCEAN
Dewees Inlet
Hamlin Sound
ISLE OF PALMS
MILES
0 1 2 3 4 5
703
Charleston
ICW
Breech Inlet
Charleston
Harbor
SULLIVANS ISLAND
Fort Moultrie
Fort Johnson
Fort Sumter

Winyah Bay to Charleston

Most boaters leaving Winyah Bay on the South Carolina ICW lean on the throttles or set the spinnaker and make a beeline for the waters of Charleston Harbor, never suspecting they are bypassing some unique cruising opportunities. The Santee Delta, Cape Romain Wildlife Refuge, and the small village of McClellanville offer excellent anchorages and numerous side trips on waters seldom visited by pleasure boaters.

Most of the rivers and creeks along the way are deep and reliable. However, there are some notable exceptions, particularly in the Santee and Cape Romain area.

The scenery here is very different from that along the northern rivers. Forested shorelines quickly give way to low-lying saltwater marshes. At times, it seems as though the seas of grass go on forever.

Facilities are very few and far between on the northerly portion of this stretch. One marina accepts transients at the charming village of McClellanville, but otherwise the boater is on his own until reaching the Isle of Palms, many miles to the south. Several facilities are located along the approach to Charleston.

In contrast to the relative scarcity of marinas, good overnight anchorages abound along the entire run. Many are seldom used, making for peaceful evenings. On the other hand, the grassy shores do not provide the protection afforded by the higher banks to the north. In heavy weather, one must be very cautious in picking a spot to drop the hook.

For adventurous skippers who are not in a hurry, the ICW between Winyah Bay and Charleston can provide many hours of contented gunkholing. However, be warned that shallow water is found here. Take your time and watch the sounder and some very unusual cruising experiences will be your reward.

Charts

You will need several NOAA charts for successful navigation of all the waters discussed in this chapter:

11534 covers the ICW from Winyah Bay to Casino Creek

11518 details the Waterway from Casino Creek to Charleston Harbor

11532 gives a good overview of the Santee River area

11531 is a small-scale, large-coverage chart covering the coastline from Winyah Bay to the Isle of Palms; this chart is required for navigation of many sidewaters off the ICW

MINIM CREEK CANAL TO MCCLELLANVILLE

The Minim Creek–Estherville Canal leads Waterway cruisers south from Winyah Bay to the waters lying about the two Santee Rivers. Along the way, the Cat Island ferry traverses the canal on a regular basis. Another series of canals and dredged cuts allows passage through the Cape Romain region and its adjoining wildlife refuge. Finally, the old fishing village of McClellanville comes into view on the northwestern shore. Along the way, many deep creeks offer anchorage and interesting side trips, but no facilities are available anywhere until reaching McClellanville.

Minim Creek

Minim Creek breaks off to the west of the ICW near the southern foot of the Minim Creek Canal, just past flashing daybeacon #4. The stream holds minimum depths of 8 feet until the charted 5-foot shoal just upstream of the creek's first sharp swing to the west. The eastern section of the creek between its entrance and the 5-foot shoal affords good overnight anchorage. Boaters will find the most swinging room southeast and south of a private dock along the northwestern banks. There should be adequate elbow room for a 50-footer. The low, undeveloped grass shores do not give adequate protection for winds over 20 knots.

Cat Island ferry

West of the 5-foot shoal, gunkholers may well find several shallow-water patches with only 4- to 5-foot depths. Passage along this portion of Minim Creek is not recommended for large cruising craft. However, small powerboats drawing 3 feet or less can navigate the creek all the way through to North Santee River.

If you should find yourself cruising the upper reaches of Minim Creek west of the Cork Creek intersection, look to the north and you may be able to spy what appears to be a huge barn with a cupola on the roof. This structure is one of the few threshing-type rice mills left standing. The small cupola apparently housed some of the pulleys used in the mill's machinery.

Santee Rivers

Southwest of flashing daybeacon #12, the Waterway quickly moves toward its intersection with the Santee Rivers and their delta. The Santee makes up the largest water complex in South Carolina. The great stream is formed by the junction of the Congaree and Wateree Rivers just below the state's capital city of Columbia. The river has a watershed of 15,414 square miles and drains most of the lands of northern South Carolina and western North Carolina. As it approaches the coast, the stream splits into two branches, the North and South Santee Rivers. Extensive shoals guard the seaward and inland passages of the two streams. For this reason, successful navigation of these waters can be tricky.

Santee Delta

The Santee's huge drainage has created the vast grass savanna known as the Santee Delta, shown on chart 11532 as the Santee Swamp. The delta spans the South Carolina coast from the southern foot of Cat Island to Cape Romain. At times, the area's immensity is almost overwhelming. This writer was reminded of his travels in the Florida Everglades. Here, as there, the grass seems to go on and on, sometimes to the edge of the horizon. Boaters without charts and adequate navigational knowledge can become confused on the delta's sidewaters. However, if you pay attention to what you are doing, the Santee Delta's wild, untamed marshes can be the setting for a great cruising adventure.

North Santee Bay and Duck Creek

The entrance to North Santee Bay makes in to the ICW's southeastern flank northeast of unlighted daybeacon #5. An alternate deepwater entrance can be made via Duck Creek to the east of flashing daybeacon #7. The vast majority of North Santee Bay is quite shallow, with 2 to 4 feet of water being the norm. However, both entrances hold minimum depths of 8 feet. It is quite possible to successfully circumnavigate the small island separating the principal entrance from Duck Creek, thereby reentering the Waterway to either the northeast or southwest. Even though chart 11532 indicates a fairly broad tongue of deeper water stretching east and southeast on North Santee Bay for some 1.1 nautical miles, this channel is unmarked and more than slightly tricky. The bay is a bit wide open for anchorage anyway, so it would probably be best to avoid these waters. Big Duck Creek to the southwest is also relatively shallow and best left alone.

The unnamed northeasterly entranceway can serve as an overnight anchorage in light to moderate breezes. There is plenty of swinging room for vessels as large as 48 feet. Strong winds can create a very healthy chop, though, and it would be better to look elsewhere during heavy weather. Fresh northerly or southerly breezes blowing directly up or down the stream can be a particular problem.

In spite of the soundings shown on chart 11534, Duck Creek holds minimum low-water depths of 7 feet and can also make for a good overnight stop. Swinging room here is comparable to that of its northeasterly sister stream, and the same beautifully undeveloped marsh-grass shoreline is present. Again, protection is not adequate for a real storm, but there is fair protection from northerly and southerly winds.

North Santee River

The broad seaward passage of North Santee River enters the Waterway southwest of flashing daybeacon #15. Minimum depths of 6 feet can

Old rice-threshing mill on Minim Creek

be carried until the creek swings back to the east-northeast some 0.8 nautical mile from its intersection with the Waterway. Just as chart 11532 predicts, depths rise to 5 feet, or sometimes considerably less, east of this point. The westerly portion of the river holds 6-foot minimum entrance depths, with depths of up to 20 feet. This deepwater stretch can serve as a light-air anchorage, but protection is not adequate for heavy or even moderate winds. The surrounding shores are composed of the usual marsh grass. Frankly, there are better anchorages not far away, but if this lonely spot strikes your fancy, don't hesitate to drop the hook here in fair weather.

The entrance to the mainland branch of North Santee River is found northwest of flashing daybeacon #18. This arm of the North Santee exhibits reliable depths of 7½ to 20 feet for a considerable distance upstream to the U.S. 17 fixed bridge.

The stream's lower reaches, hard by the ICW, are adequate for anchorage in light to moderate breezes. The seldom-visited upper portion of the river is bounded by higher ground and affords enough shelter for all but the strongest storms. Swinging room is ample all along the stream short of the fixed bridge.

Upstream from the ICW, the undeveloped shoreline is at first comprised of saltwater marsh but rises to wooded banks as one travels to the west. The U.S. 17 twin fixed bridges, with a vertical clearance of 29 feet, span the river some 7 nautical miles upstream from the Waterway. Passage farther upstream is not possible for tall sailcraft.

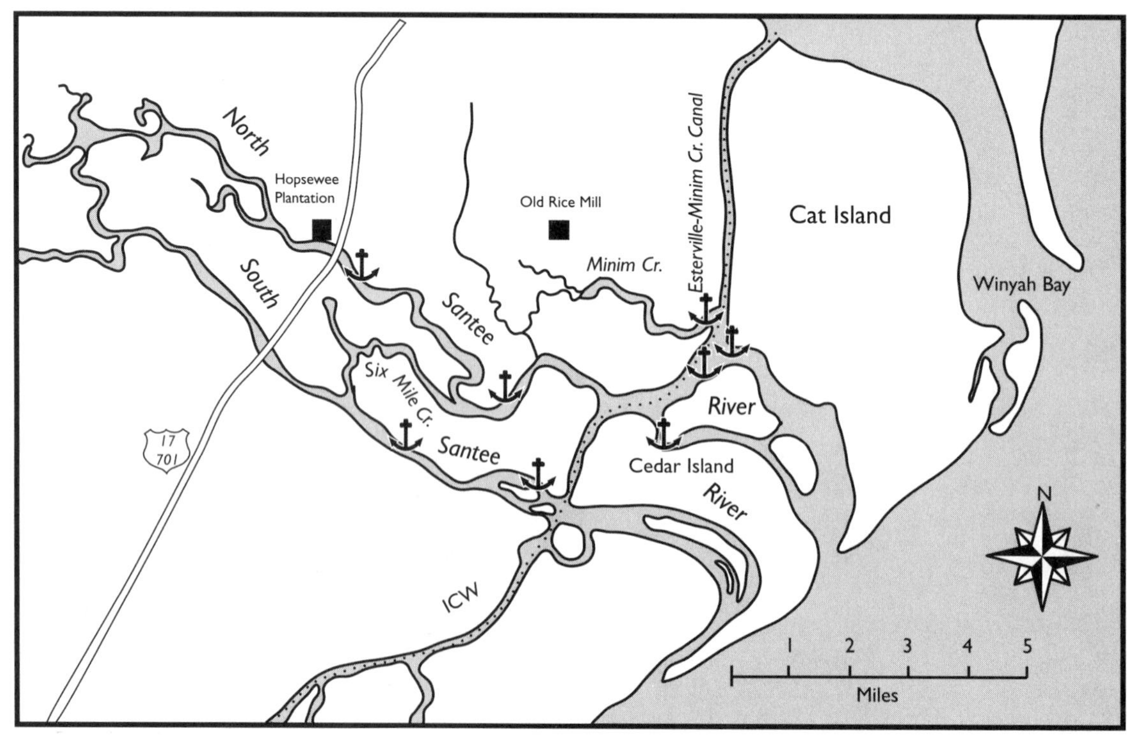

Hopsewee Plantation

Just west of the U.S. 17 span, Hopsewee Plantation is clearly visible on the northern shore. Hopsewee was the one-time home of Thomas Lynch, a fierce patriot of the Winyah district. His radical stand against England during the Revolutionary War period immortalized his name among South Carolina's great patriots. Now, his plantation is open to the public and is well worth your time. Tours are currently conducted daily March through October from 10:00 A.M. to 5:00 P.M. Seldom will visitors find such a beautifully preserved house of this age open for all to enjoy.

Hopsewee's old docks along the river are shoal and rotten and cannot be used. Just east of the bridge, there is a small-craft launching ramp with a small dock that might be adequate for craft under 28 feet. Otherwise, drop the hook and break out the dinghy. Once ashore, walk north along U.S. 17 until you see the plantation entrance on the left-hand side of the road.

South Santee River

South Santee River crosses the ICW southwest of flashing daybeacon #22. Depths on the mainland stretch (the northwestern branch) of the South Santee have improved significantly since the mid-1980s. While there are still several unmarked shoals to avoid, the careful gunkholer can now cruise through 7-foot depths to several good anchorages northwest of the Waterway.

The South Santee is a typical stream of the region. Its banks have barely been touched by development. Indeed, most of the shoreline is composed of the all-too-usual marsh grass, but one patch of higher ground does flank the southwestern banks west of charted Brown Island.

Visiting cruisers will discover the most accessible anchorage on the charted 13- and 15-foot waters off Brown Island's northeasterly reaches. Most cruisers with an understanding of coastal navigation should be able to safely reach this haven. There is good protection from northerly winds and fair shelter from southerly and westerly breezes. Strong blows from the southeast are another story.

While depths of 8 feet can be held west of Brown Island, as mentioned above, the channel is unmarked, and cruisers who miss the channel can wander into 5-foot depths. For this reason, the anchorage farther upstream reviewed below is not recommended for vessels drawing more than 5 feet.

After successfully avoiding the shoals near Brown Island, boaters that can stand the 5-foot depths can follow the unmarked channel west to the charted high ground abutting the southwestern banks. You will eventually sight a private dock along this shore. Anchor more or less abeam of this structure for good shelter in all but particularly strong northwestern winds.

Hopsewee Plantation on North Santee River

The river's seaward lane lies to the southeast of flashing daybeacon #22. It is possible to hold 7-foot minimum depths for 1 nautical mile to the east, but only by following an unmarked channel. Boaters might consider anchoring well west of charted Grace Island. However, this is to say the least a wide-open refuge appropriate only in fair weather.

Cape Romain

Cape Romain is an absolutely fascinating region that is rarely visited by pleasure boaters. In *Glories of the Carolina Coast*, James Henry Rice, Jr., writes of the "solitude where Cape Romain Light warns mariners of the treacherous reefs, off the mouth of Santee, a region so wild that you can readily believe yourself in Asia or Africa." Rice's description is entirely accurate. Cruising the backwaters of Cape Romain, it is as if you have entered another world very far from modern hustle and bustle. The grass savannas seem to stretch forever. Your only companions are likely to be the many different birds that populate the marshes. Stop your engine for a moment. The silence is eerie; then, suddenly, it is broken by the call of a lonely gull or hawk. If you crave the adventure that is so sadly lacking is our modern, well-planned world, Cape Romain is just what you seek.

The entire Cape Romain area is part of a huge wildlife refuge stretching from Alligator Creek, just south of unlighted daybeacon #26, to Five Fathom Creek. The refuge encompasses some 60,000 acres and at least 20 miles of shoreline. More than 250 species of birds live within the confines of the refuge. The cape is truly a bonanza for nature lovers.

While the lighthouse that Rice referred to in

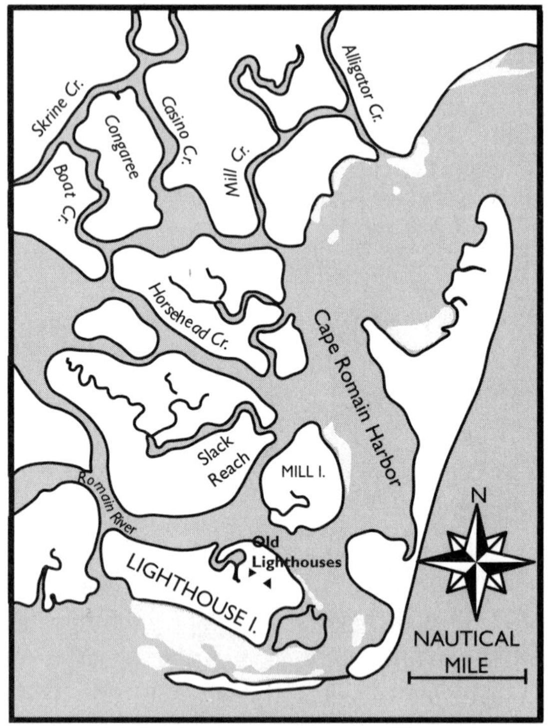

his book is now dark and empty, it remains as a mute monument to a far-removed age of the sea. For many a year, the old lighthouse warned mariners of the vast Cape Romain shoals. Today, it is a rarely used daymark. Adventurous boaters can, in fact, see two lighthouses on the cape. The shorter structure, lacking any crown, dates from 1827, while the other light was first used in 1866. The newer tower continued to operate until 1947. With some effort, you might catch a glimpse of the taller lighthouse from the Waterway, but a closer inspection calls for a long trip through the twisting and sometimes shallow streams of the cape.

Cape Romain encompasses the largest collection of shallow water on the South Carolina coast. Depths seem to have deteriorated even more since Hurricane Hugo. Several of the creeks with 6-foot minimum depths this writer used to recommend can now only be relied upon for 5-foot soundings, or even slightly less, at low tide. Boats drawing 4 to 5 feet must now carefully time their entrance and exit to coincide with a rising tide, while skippers whose craft need 6 feet of water to stay off the bottom should bypass these fascinating waters entirely. This writer would be very hesitant to commit any craft larger than 36 feet to a cruise of the Cape Romain streams, no matter what her draft. In any case, successful navigation of the cape's streams calls for extreme caution. Be sure to read the Cape Romain navigation section presented later in this chapter before attempting entry.

Cape Romain National Wildlife Refuge

Casino Creek and Other Cape Romain Streams

Casino Creek serves as the principal entrance to the waters of the Cape Romain region. Boaters should enter by way of the stream's easterly mouth, east of flashing daybeacon #29. Depths at the mouth of this creek have definitely shoaled over the past several years. There is now an unmarked patch of shallows to avoid at the stream's mouth. Even after you bypass this hazard, some low-tide depths of 4½ to 5 feet can be expected. Yet another shallow spot is encountered before the waters deepen near the intersection of Casino and Skrine Creeks.

South of this juncture, the charted depths on Casino, Skrine, Congaree Boat, and Horsehead Creeks are more or less accurate. Careful boaters intent on exploration of this fascinating sea of grass and marsh can cruise all these streams for at least some of their length and enjoy respectable depths, particularly on a rising tide.

Congaree Boat Creek once provided access to the charted Cape Romain watchtower. This structure was apparently destroyed by Hurricane Hugo.

Cruising-sized craft will find themselves a bit cramped for swinging room on most any of the Cape Romain creeks and streams. Boats up to 28 feet may be able to anchor normally, if their skippers pick their spots carefully. Larger vessels will most certainly want to consider a Bahamian-style mooring or even a stern anchor.

McClellanville

The old fishing village of McClellanville sits

perched on the eastern shores of Jeremy Creek to the north of flashing daybeacon #35. The town is the site of the first facilities available to the cruising boater south of Winyah Bay. Jeremy Creek holds minimum low-water depths of 7 feet and provides reliable access to the village waterfront.

McClellanville is a very pleasant stop for anyone who enjoys getting away from it all. Among a host of sleepy, charming coastal villages, McClellanville strikes this writer as one of the most easygoing of the lot. Progress has made only a few small inroads here. To be sure, the village has modern conveniences, but a leisurely walk along the quiet, tree-shrouded lanes reveals that little has changed in a very long time. Beautiful, old white homes line the streets, which are overhung by huge oaks trailing long beards of gray moss. Here and there, an old-style drainage ditch still fronts the neighborhood yards. This writer and his mate spent an enjoyable hour sitting on the waterfront watching two fishermen mend their nets. Besides the quiet banter of the men at work, the only sound was the sighing of the wind.

Once a year, the village's atmosphere of peace and quiet is traded for the friendly crowds that attend the "Blessing of the Fleet." This traditional ceremony, held on the second Saturday in May, has evolved into a seafood extravaganza. Seafood of all types, both familiar and exotic, is prepared by a host of local cooks for all to enjoy. For one day, the resident population of some 300 souls is swollen by 10,000 visitors, many of whom return year after year for the happy event.

Old home at McClellanville

There was perhaps no community harder hit by Hurricane Hugo than McClellanville. A tidal surge of 9 feet or better swept up Five Fathom Creek and through the surrounding marshes straight into the mouth of Jeremy Creek. Boats were picked up bodily from their seemingly secure moorings and deposited in people's front yards. To say the very least, damage to shoreside buildings and property was extensive. The docks at Leland Marine Service were laid waste.

We had occasion to visit McClellanville a few weeks after the tragedy, and the scene that met our eyes was absolutely awesome. With all the debris from the storm, beached boats, and dilapidated buildings, this writer and his mate could only wonder if this fair town would ever be the same again. Most of the beautiful old oaks lining the town's lanes had survived, at least.

So it was with some trepidation that we sailed into Jeremy Creek on a warm spring day in 1992. Both this writer and his mate were thrilled to see that many of the scars of the storm had been removed and that the marina had been rebuilt and was open for business. If you looked for it, there was still evidence of storm damage, but clearly the memory of that horrible night was mercifully fading into the background. Today, the storm is even more of a distant memory, with very few signs left of the former devastation. The village's residents can be excused for hoping that such a storm never comes their way again.

The rebuilt piers of Leland Marine Service sit proudly on the northern shores of Jeremy Creek near the stream's charted turn to the west. Leland Marine Service still offers dockage to the transient boater, but it is only fair to note that the post-Hugo incarnation of this marina is definitely more commercially oriented that its predecessor. The overnight berths feature fixed wooden-face piers with all power and water connections. Low-water depths alongside run around 6 feet. Gasoline and diesel fuel are available, and some mechanical repairs can be arranged. A laundromat is located within walking distance.

Leland Marine Service (803) 887-3641

Approach depth: 7 feet (minimum)
Dockside depth: 6 feet (low water)
Accepts transients: yes
Fixed wooden piers: yes
Dockside power connections: 30 and 50 amps
Dockside water connections: yes
Showers: yes
Laundromat: nearby
Gasoline: yes
Diesel fuel: yes
Mechanical repairs: independent contractors
Restaurants: nearby

There's more to see and do ashore in McClellanville than just stroll the quiet lanes and admire the old oaks. T.W. Graham's Grocery Store and Cafe (803-887-3331) is accessible by way of a four- or five-block walk from the waterfront. Breakfast and lunch are served regularly, and dinner is available Friday and Saturday evenings. The simple but tasty fare here is the best in town.

Just across the street, Village Creations Cafe (803-887-3469) is another choice, but this writer and his mate have found its hours of operation to be so erratic that we are hesitant to recommend this dining spot.

The nearby Crab Pot Restaurant (803-887-3156) will dispatch a car to pick up famished cruisers. The seafood at this long-lived establishment is quite good.

For those who need some time off the water, McClellanville now offers its own bed-and-breakfast inn. Laurel Hill Plantation (803-887-3708) features ultrafriendly management, four antique-furnished guests rooms and a panoramic view of the surrounding marshlands. The innkeepers will be glad to pick up and return guests to their berths at Leland Marine. The inn is actually located some 4 miles north of downtown McClellanville.

If you should find yourself cruising along the waters adjacent to Cape Romain at the end of a long day, this writer highly recommends that you stay for the night at McClellanville and give the village's magic a chance to soothe your cares. Don't be in such a hurry to reach the "Holy City" of Charleston that you pass McClellanville without a thought.

McClellanville History The present-day visitor to McClellanville would probably be surprised to learn that the town has an illustrious past. It began in 1822, when a devastating hurricane destroyed several summer houses on nearby Cedar Island. These homes belonged to wealthy planters, a list of whose names reads like a who's who of post–Revolutionary War South Carolina, including the Palmer, Pinckney, Lucas, and Doar families. Understandably, the planters immediately sought a safer haven for the hot summer months. They purchased land on the northern shores of Jeremy Creek from the McClellan family, and the town was born.

Following the Civil War, summer visits by the affluent planters ended. The community turned to commercial fishing for its livelihood. During Prohibition, rumrunning was a popular occupation. As the years passed, McClellanville remained a small fishing village, and it survives pretty much in that state to this day.

Five Fathom Creek and Associated Streams

Five Fathom Creek is entered from the ICW via a well-marked channel through Town Creek just southwest of flashing daybeacon #35. Five Fathom Creek provides fairly reliable access to the open sea and is the only marked inlet available to cruisers between Winyah Bay and Charleston. Entrance depths from the Waterway run around 8 feet, deepening to some 15 feet of water on the creek's interior reaches. The outlet to the sea, while well marked, is changeable, as you would expect. As of early 1995, minimum depths in the seaward passage were 8 feet, with many soundings far deeper. It might be a good idea to ask at Leland Marine Service in nearby McClellanville about current inlet conditions before attempting the cut.

Five Fathom Creek offers quite a few potential anchorages along its own length and on several deepwater streams that make in to their larger sister between the ICW and the inlet. The first of these havens is found on the upper portion of Five Fathom Creek's main branch, bypassed by the entrance channel coming through from Town Creek. Boaters entering this haven should take a lazy turn to the northeast around flashing daybeacon #28 (near the southwestern mouth of Town Creek). Currently, depths are not quite as deep as the soundings shown on chart 11518, but visiting cruisers can still count on at least 7 feet of water. Boats up to 45 feet with find ample elbow room. The surrounding undeveloped marsh-grass shores afford none too good a shelter in rough weather. Strong winds from the southwest blowing directly up this arm of the creek clearly call for another strategy.

Bull River makes in to the southwestern banks of Five Fathom Creek between unlighted daybeacons #24 and #22. It is surprising that this relatively small body of water has been designated a river. To be sure, there are far larger streams in the South Carolina Low Country that bear the lesser moniker of "creek." Bull River holds minimum depths of 8 feet, but there is only enough swinging room for boats as large as 32 feet. This is perhaps the least likely of the anchorages associated with Five Fathom Creek, and most boaters should probably choose an alternate haven.

The combined mouths of Papas and Little Papas Creeks cut the northeastern banks near unlighted daybeacon #22. An uncharted bar has raised depths at the entrance to low-water soundings of 6 feet, but any boat with a draft of less than 6 feet should not have a problem. Depths northeast of the bar as you approach the split in the streams deepen to 10- and 20-foot levels. Skippers piloting craft as large as 38 feet can anchor short of the fork. Strong southwestern winds can stir up an unwelcome chop in this anchorage.

Little Papas Creek splits off to the north and boasts at least 10 feet of water, with enough swinging room for a 34-footer. Its larger sister, Papas Creek, plunges off to the east. This stream holds 10 feet or better and can provide a 36-foot vessel with enough room for a snug overnight stay. These streams are surrounded by undeveloped marsh grass that gives scant protection when things turn nasty.

During on-site research of Five Fathom Creek, this writer and his mate observed a beautiful sailcraft anchored behind Sandy Point Beach west of unlighted daybeacon #18. While these waters are a bit too open for anchorage in all but light to moderate winds (particularly if they are blowing from the west), this is a great spot to wait for the morning light before running the inlet, or for resting up from a late-afternoon entry. Depths are an impressive 20 feet or more. The surrounding shoreline is in its natural state and quite impressive. If the weather cooperates, this is our choice for an unforgettable anchorage on Five Fathom Creek.

ICW TO MCCLELLANVILLE NAVIGATION

Navigation along this section of the Waterway is rather simple and fairly straightforward. Hold to the Waterway's mid-width and be on guard against any side-setting currents, particularly near the North and South Santee Rivers. Several of the sidewaters along the way call for greater caution and careful piloting. Boaters must be particularly alert for shoals on Cape Romain's waters. Otherwise, keep an eye on the sounder and your cruise should be a delight.

Cat Island Ferry Some 0.7 nautical mile south of the Minim Creek–Estherville Canal entrance, the Cat Island ferry crosses the Waterway on a regular basis. Signs displaying flashing red lights warn boaters approaching from the north and south to slow down. "No Wake" is strictly enforced for several hundred yards on both sides of the ferry route. Slow down and proceed at idle speed until you are well past the sign at the opposite end from your approach.

Minim Creek To enter Minim Creek (abandoned by the ICW), cruise west into the main body of the stream southwest of flashing daybeacon #4. Watch for a private dock on the starboard-side banks near the "Piles PA" notation on chart 11534. You would probably do well to anchor here, as there are unmarked shoals farther upstream.

Soon, Minim Creek turns sharply back to the west. This writer noted a tree growing in the charted 5-foot shoal along this stretch; you must heavily favor the northern shore to bypass this hazard. Good depths continue on Minim Creek through a turn to the north and another jog to the west. Soon after this second turn is left behind, shoal water is much more in evidence. It is best to leave exploration of the creek's upper reaches to small, shallow-draft powerboats. Should you continue upstream, the old rice-threshing mill described earlier can be seen to the north as you approach the intersection of Minim and Cork Creeks.

On the ICW Swift tidal currents are often encountered in the Santee section of the ICW. Sailcraft and trawlers should be particularly alert for side-setting currents as the Waterway cuts across North Santee River south and west of flashing daybeacon #15. Another area of concern is the passage across the South Santee at flashing daybeacon #22. Keep a careful watch over your stern to quickly note any leeway slippage.

North Santee Bay Boaters have a choice of two routes to enter the navigable section of North Santee Bay. Both the principal entrance, northeast of unlighted daybeacon #5, and Duck Creek, at flashing daybeacon #7, hold minimum 7-foot depths as far as the southeastern tip of the small island separating the two channels. Don't attempt to cruise farther to the east on the bay, as the channel is unmarked and more than slightly tricky.

On the ICW Southwest of the Duck Creek–ICW intersection, the Waterway channel borders on shoal water to the northwest. Be sure to come abeam of flashing daybeacon #12 to its southeasterly side.

At #12, the channel takes a jog to the southwest. You can pick up the charted range to help you along the way. The seaside branch of North Santee River will come abeam to the southeast immediately after you pass flashing daybeacon #15.

At #15, the ICW begins skirting the southerly shoreline to avoid the charted shallows to the north. Point to eventually come abeam of flashing daybeacon #18 to its fairly immediate southerly side. Boaters choosing to visit the inland portion of North Santee River can break off from the Waterway east of #18 and cruise into this impressive stream's southeasterly mouth.

North Santee River To enter the seaward branch of North Santee River, favor the eastern shore a bit until reaching the stream's first sharp turn to the east. Swing back to the mid-width here. Minimum depths of 6 feet continue for some 0.8 nautical mile east of the entrance.

Successful navigation of the North Santee's mainland entrance is a simple matter. Just follow the mid-width of the stream as it cuts to the northwest. Use chart 11532 for navigation of the river's upper reaches. On-site research in early 1996 did not reveal the charted 6-foot patch, but be ready for it anyway.

Soon after leaving the ICW channel, you may sight several uncharted U-shaped dump buoys on the river's southwestern shore. Keep clear of these waters.

Continue on the stream's mid-width. Good depths are held at least as far as the fixed, twin-span U.S. 17 bridge, which crosses the North Santee some 7 nautical miles west of the river's intersection with the Waterway. The higher, wooded banks on the stream's westerly section afford better protection for overnight anchorage than the lower, grassy shores to the east. In light airs, feel free to drop the hook almost anywhere, but in a heavy blow, it is better to cruise upstream for several miles before selecting a spot.

The U.S. 17 twin fixed bridges have a vertical clearance of 29 feet. This guide's coverage of the North Santee ends at these spans, but remember that you can anchor short of the bridges and dinghy ashore to the public launch area on the northern banks. It's then only a short walk to Hopsewee Plantation.

On the ICW The ICW enters a long, sheltered landcut known as Fourmile Creek Canal southwest of flashing daybeacon #18. The passage remains quite straightforward until reaching South Santee River at flashing daybeacon #22.

South Santee River Those boaters who choose to cruise the mostly shallow seaward branch of South Santee River should enter on the stream's mid-width. As shown on chart 11534, best depths can be held by favoring the southern shore after proceeding downstream for 200 yards or so. Shallow water is encountered 300 yards short of Grace Island's western tip, which bisects the river.

Enter the mainland branch of South Santee River on the mid-width of the broad band of deep water north and northeast of the two charted islands. Be on guard against the shallower water directly northwest of flashing daybeacon #22. Begin favoring the northeastern banks after cruising upstream for 200 yards. You should continue following this shoreline as you pass Brown Island south and southwest of your course.

As you approach the westerly tip of Brown Island, slow down and begin to feel your way cautiously with the sounder. This is the most difficult portion of the river channel. As can be seen from a study of chart 11534, what you must do is begin a slow cruise toward the southerly banks while entering the river channel west of Brown Island. This is a lot easier on paper than it appears on the water, so take your time and proceed with the greatest caution. Be on guard against the charted shoal abutting the southeasterly mouth of Pleasant Creek. You must also avoid the shallow water off the westerly tip of Brown Island.

Leland Marine Service, McClellanville

After bypassing all these shoals, favor the southern shoreline to bypass yet another charted patch of shallows, this time on the northern banks. Soon, the river begins a lazy turn to the northwest. Cruise back to the mid-width as you enter this turn. Watch the southwestern banks for a private dock. This writer suggests that you anchor as this structure comes abeam. Farther upstream, unmarked shoals are even more plentiful.

On the ICW The Waterway enters another long, protected canal-like stretch southwest of South Santee River. The entrance to this passage is heralded by unlighted daybeacon #24. It's an easy cruise down the delightful channel until you encounter the northeasterly entrance to Casino Creek just east of flashing daybeacon #29.

Cape Romain As stated earlier, the Cape Romain region is one of the shallowest stretches on the South Carolina coast north of Charleston. Do not attempt to enter unless your craft is less than 36 feet in length and draws 4 feet or less (unless you enter *and* leave on a rising tide). Chart 11518 covers the entrance, but you must use chart 11531 for the interior portion of the cape.

For best depths, enter Casino Creek via the mid-width of the small creek to the east of flashing daybeacon #29. Even though depths in this cut have now shoaled to some 4½- and 5-foot low-tide soundings, the cut is still deeper than the principal mouth of Casino Creek, southwest of #29.

Favor the western banks heavily as you enter the creek. A new bar has built out over much of the entrance's eastern reaches. Expect some low-tide readings of as little as 4½ feet as you pass through the mouth.

Depths improve temporarily as you cruise to

the south but shoal again as the stream follows a sharp turn to the west on its way to join Casino Creek.

Enter Casino Creek on its mid-width and turn to the south to follow its principal track into Cape Romain. From this point, the best advice is to hold scrupulously to the mid-width and keep chart 11531 immediately at hand. While this writer would not pretend to enumerate all the possible cruising permutations on the Cape Romain streams, you might consider following Skrine Creek to Congaree Boat Creek, or you might carefully cruise through the small stream connecting Congaree Boat Creek to Horsehead Creek.

To obtain a good view of the lighthouses described earlier, carefully cruise downstream on Casino Creek until the stream intersects Cape Romain Harbor. Do not proceed any farther! Depths quickly fall off past the intersection of the creek and the harbor. Look to the south and you will have a good view of the lights on Lighthouse Island. You can catch an even better view of the old sentinels while cruising on Congaree Boat and Horsehead Creeks. Additionally, the adventurous captain who takes this fascinating side trip will likely encounter many interesting birds. Do *not* attempt to enter Muddy Bay to the west. Its waters are shoal and dangerous.

McClellanville Boaters visiting Jeremy Creek and the charming village of McClellanville should turn 90 degrees to the north at flashing daybeacon #35 and cruise into the stream's mid-width. Depths are adequate for large craft well upstream. Several seafood docks will soon come abeam to starboard. At these small firms, it is sometimes possible to purchase seafood caught the same day. Farther along, the docks of Leland Marine Service will come into view along the northern banks as Jeremy Creek meanders through a slow turn to the west.

Five Fathom Creek The entrance to Five Fathom Creek (via Town Creek) makes in to the ICW southwest of flashing daybeacon #35. The creek's upper reaches are quite deep and well marked. Cruising craft of almost any size can confidently navigate the stream short of its inlet. As stated earlier, the seaward passage is changeable, and knowledge of local conditions is desirable, though not absolutely necessary, for using the inlet. Chart

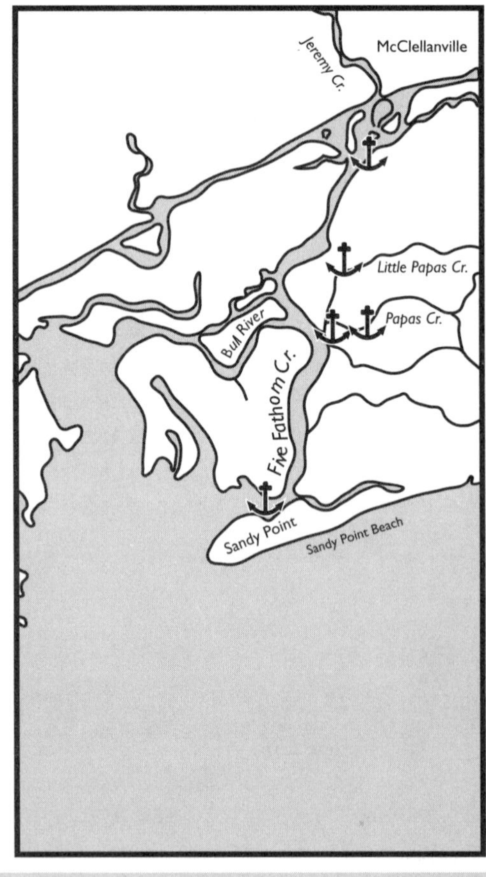

11518 covers the stream's upper section, but you will need chart 11531 to cover navigation of the inlet.

Most boaters will probably want to enter the creek by way of the marked Town Creek channel at flashing daybeacon #35. This small cut soon leads to the main body of the creek. As you are now headed toward the sea, take red markers to your port side and green beacons to starboard.

Northbound cruisers on the ICW may choose to enter the area by using Mathews Creek northeast of flashing daybeacon #38. Be warned, though, that you will now find some 5½-foot low-tide depths at the intersection of Mathews and Five Fathom Creeks.

Boaters choosing to anchor in the unmarked extreme upper northeastern reaches of Five Fathom Creek east of flashing daybeacon #28 should give the point of land southeast of #28 a wide berth. Cruise into the upper stream's mid-width, but be sure to discontinue your exploration well before reaching the charted shallows to the northeast.

A large patch of shoal water bisects Five Fathom Creek northeast of unlighted daybeacon #25. Come abeam of and pass #25 to its southeasterly side. Don't allow leeway to ease you to the north or northwest.

Between unlighted daybeacons #24 and #22, Bull River breaks off from Five Fathom Creek to the southwest. Enter on the centerline. Good depths continue downstream as far as ultrashallow Bulls Bay.

Northeast of unlighted daybeacon #22, Papas and Little Papas Creeks enter Five Fathom Creek. Stay away from #22. It marks a shoal building in from the northwestern point. Otherwise, simply follow the usual rule of holding to the mid-width for best depths. Don't attempt to follow Little Papas Creek past its first sharp jog to the east, where the charted soundings on 11518 end. Similarly, depths fall off on Papas Creek as the channel rushes through a lazy turn to the east.

At unlighted daybeacon #18, the Five Fathom Creek channel begins to enter its seaward passage by cutting west around Sandy Point. At flashing daybeacon #9, the cut turns sharply to the south and heads out into the open sea. Watch for additional uncharted markers along this stretch of the channel.

Continue following the marked channel out to sea at least as far as flashing buoy #2. For best depths, set a compass course from #2 for unlighted can buoy #1. The wide, blue ocean will now be before you.

MCCLELLANVILLE TO CHARLESTON HARBOR

South of McClellanville, the ICW follows the upper reaches of Harbor River for several miles. The Waterway then enters a long, dredged cut that carries the boater through the shallow waters of Bulls and Sewee Bays. As the ICW begins its approach to the Isle of Palms, the route continues to track through extensive saltwater marsh that is sometimes dignified with the designation of "sound." Finally, the Waterway passes both the Isle of Palms and Sullivan's Island to the south and enters Charleston Harbor.

Formerly, this stretch of the Waterway was without any fixed bridges. Sailcraft with masts

McClellanville's harbor

taller than 65 feet had the option of tracking their way down the ICW from Winyah Bay to Charleston Harbor. That situation has now changed with the erection of a 65-foot fixed span north of Breach Inlet. Tall-masted sailors take note.

The wide but shallow reaches of Bulls and Sewee Bays, as well as Copahee and Hamlin Sounds to the south, can allow enough fetch for a sharp chop when winds exceed 15 knots. Small craft should be alert for these conditions before venturing out on this section of the Waterway.

While the vast majority of the so-called bays and sounds between McClellanville and Charleston Harbor are quite shallow, the Waterway is pierced at regular intervals by deepwater creeks that can serve as overnight anchorages. Without exception, however, these streams have low, grassy shores that give inadequate protection in high winds.

Several streams just north of the Isle of Palms lead seaward to shallow inlets. All are unmarked and unreliable.

From McClellanville, cruising boaters must follow the ICW south for some 22 nautical miles before coming upon any facilities. This is a fairly lonely stretch, so make sure your tanks are topped off before leaving McClellanville behind. On the Isle of Palms, one of the finest marinas in the state welcomes transient boaters, and additional facilities are available near Breach Inlet.

Sullivan's Island guards the southern flank of the ICW's entrance into Charleston Harbor. Here, old Fort Moultrie is a constant reminder of the great battle that helped give South Carolina her state flag.

While certainly not as attractive as some stretches of the South Carolina Waterway, the run from McClellanville to Charleston Harbor does have its moments. Some anchorages are available, and good facilities are to be found on the southern portion of the run. All in all, the cruising boater will enjoy this passage while anticipating the glories of Charleston.

Awendaw Creek

Awendaw Creek makes off to the south from flashing daybeacon #48. The stream holds minimum depths of 8 feet, with soundings ranging up to 30 feet or better, until it intersects the shallow waters of Bulls Bay. The stream can serve as a light-air anchorage, but protection is not sufficient for winds over 15 knots. Maximum swinging room is found after the creek takes a sharp turn to the east. Here, depths run 8 to 13 feet. Boaters will not have to use as much anchor rode for a proper 6-to-1 scope here as is necessary on the deeper portion of the stream near its intersection with the Waterway.

Graham Creek

Graham Creek cuts the southeastern shores

of the ICW northeast of unlighted daybeacon #64. This stream is one of the best overnight anchorages in the area for craft under 45 feet. The western bank of the creek is much higher than the norm for this region and gives good protection in southwestern breezes. Minimum depths of 8 feet are held well into the stream's interior reaches. The shoreline is comprised of beautifully undeveloped banks.

Price Creek

Boaters traveling south on the ICW will intersect the Price Creek portion of the Waterway southwest of flashing daybeacon #80. Two channels make in to the southeasterly arm of Price Creek (abandoned by the ICW) between unlighted daybeacon #84 and flashing daybeacon #86. This southeasterly portion of Price Creek is a deep stream that eventually leads to a small, unmarked inlet. While there used to be a barely manageable passage out to sea via this errant cut, the seaward channel, which was none too good to begin with, seems to have shoaled in almost entirely. This writer guesses that Hurricane Hugo may have had more than a little to do with the alteration.

Boaters should enter and exit Price Creek only by way of the southwesterly approach. Please be sure to read the navigational information presented below before attempting first-time entry.

The northwesterly portion of the creek (northwest of the inlet) maintains minimum depths of 8 feet and can serve as an anchorage in light to moderate winds. On-site research seemed to indicate that the best spot to anchor is in the area of the charted 25-foot sounding just as the creek begins to follow a jog to the south. Boats up to 38 feet should find this anchorage roomy enough. The surrounding shores display common marsh grass. Protection should nevertheless be adequate for winds blowing from the northeast and southwest. Fresh breezes wafting in from the northwest or southeast blow almost directly up or down the creek and can make for a bumpy night.

Bull Narrows Creek, which cuts off to the northeast from the main body of southeasterly Price Creek, gives relatively good protection, but its swinging room is only sufficient for craft under 32 feet.

Capers Creek

Capers Creek is a large stream that leads south and then southeast from the ICW's unlighted daybeacon #94 to an impassable inlet. This body of water has four branches opening onto the ICW. The central-southwestern branch is known as Toomer Creek. All four branches maintain minimum 5-foot depths on their mid-width, with most soundings ranging from 7 to as much as 20 feet. The banks are shoal, however, and depths on the central-northeastern stream's channel are now too tricky for large, deep-draft vessels.

The three principal entrance streams and the main body of the combined inlet heading to the southeast are a bit too broad for anchorage consideration in all but the lightest of airs. The southwesternmost stream is far too narrow for anchorage by cruising craft.

If you are taking a leisurely cruise and the weather is fair, consider following Capers Creek to a point just short of its inlet. The Capers Island shoreline to the northeast is quite attractive. These waters are seldom visited by pleasure boaters and offer a good opportunity for serious gunkholing. Be sure to read the navigational information presented later in this chapter before entering any of these streams.

Whiteside Creek

Whiteside Creek is yet another deep stream that can serve as a light- to moderate-air anchorage for craft under 40 feet. It is found on the Waterway's northwestern shore northeast of flashing daybeacon #96. Minimum depths are around 10 feet, but there is one shoal to avoid on the creek's interior. The shores are undeveloped.

The majority of cruising-sized vessels will probably be most comfortable dropping the hook between the stream's mouth and its first sharp turn to the northeast. Swinging room is at its maximum here, and the 10- to 11-foot depths don't call for a mile of anchor line.

Toomer Creek: Mainland Branch

The mainland branch of Toomer Creek, northeast of flashing daybeacon #99, holds minimum depths of 6 feet until the stream splits as it moves inland. Protection is adequate for anchorage in winds of less than 20 knots blowing from any direction except the southeast. There may not be enough swinging room for vessels over 36 feet. The shoreline is undeveloped saltwater marsh.

Dewees Creek

The eastern (seaside) branch of Dewees Creek, lying to the south of unlighted daybeacon #109, leads to another impassable seaward cut. While the main body of the stream holds minimum depths of 10 feet, deepening to 45 feet of water in a few spots, the inlet is surrounded by shoals as it passes into the ocean.

The deeper westerly and northwesterly reaches of the seaside creek are bounded by saltwater marsh, but the interior section borders Dewees Island to the northeast and the Isle of Palms to the southwest. Dewees Island has high, well-wooded, attractive shores with some light residential development.

The main body of Dewees Creek is too open for effective overnight anchorage. However, the stream has an unnamed northeastern branch skirting the northeastern edge of Big Hill Marsh that affords good protection in all but heavy weather. Depths run between 10 and 25 feet until the waters abeam of the northern tip of Big Hill Marsh. There is plenty of swinging room for large craft. This stream is one of the best anchorages available to the cruising boater on this run. Do not attempt to reenter the Waterway

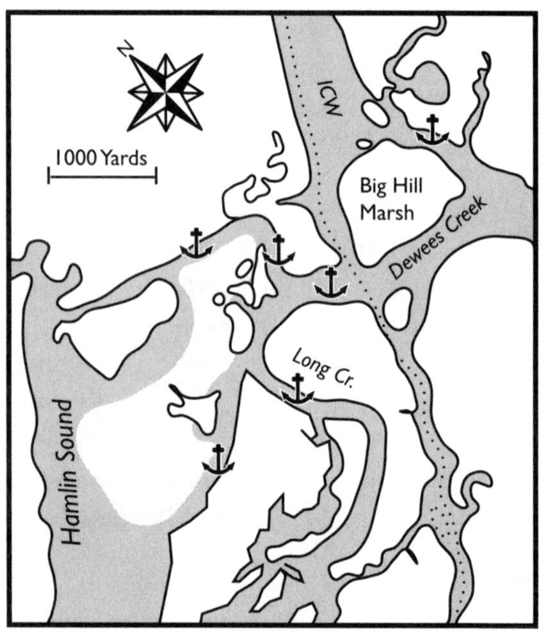

from this branch, however, as depths decline upstream.

As shown on chart 11518, the landward stretch of Dewees Creek (northwest of the ICW) looks like a three-fingered hand. The northeasterly finger is unnamed on chart 11518, but the southeasterly branch is called Long Creek. This area is much larger than a casual inspection of 11518 would lead one to believe. Protection afforded by the undeveloped marsh-grass shores is less than ideal for winds over 20 knots. All three streams eventually lead inland to shallow Hamlin Sound and Gray Bay. Do not attempt to cruise into the waters of these small sounds. Shallows are quickly encountered, as this writer's bent prop can readily attest.

The easterly reaches of all three fingers hold 8-foot minimum depths, with most soundings showing much deeper water. The main (central) branch of Dewees Creek boasts minimum 10-foot readings. Anchorage is a practical possibility on all these waters, but the unexpected breadth of the central stream short of its intersection with Long Creek relegates its use to fair-weather periods. The unnamed northeasterly fork makes for a great anchor-down spot, particularly on its initial stretch just north of its mouth. Here, boaters can drop the hook in some 18 to 20 feet of water. As the stream rounds a sharp bend to the west-northwest, depths temporarily go up to 30 feet or better, calling for a longer anchor line. Soundings again rise to 20-foot levels just short of the point where the creek splinters into several shallower branches. Boaters willing to trek a bit longer can find good anchorage short of the forks as well.

Long Creek affords yet another good anchorage opportunity, though again the stream's breadth, coupled with the marsh-grass shores, do not make for sufficient shelter from fresh winds. Depths run 15 feet or better in a broad band stretching out from the centerline.

The main branch of Dewees Creek continues southwest past its intersection with Long Creek toward shallow Hamlin Sound. Boaters can anchor along this portion of the creek short of the sound, but protection is clearly inferior to the havens discussed above.

Wild Dunes Yacht Harbor

Southwest of flashing daybeacon #116, one of the most modern facilities available to the cruising boater north of Charleston guards the Waterway's southeastern shore. Wild Dunes Yacht Harbor was one of the marinas hardest hit by Hurricane Hugo. Happily, the marina has been completely rebuilt since that tragic time, and there is scarcely a clue left of the stormy destruction.

Wild Dunes Yacht Harbor gladly welcomes transient boaters and provides overnight berths at well-sheltered, wooden-decked floating docks featuring water and 50-amp power connections. Thirty-amp splitters are provided for boats needing that sort of connection. Minimum dockside soundings are an impressive 8 feet. Gasoline, diesel fuel, and waste pump-out services are readily at hand. Future plans call for the construction of a dry-stack storage building. Wild Dunes Yacht Harbor features a fully stocked ship's and grocery store, with the emphasis on food and variety-store items. Ultraclean showers and a fine laundromat are located on the marina grounds. The on-site repair firm, Carolina Marine Service, provides complete mechanical service for both diesel and gasoline power plants. The nearby Tradewinds Restaurant serves the freshest of seafood and seems popular with the local crowd.

Wild Dunes Yacht Harbor
(803) 886-5100

Approach depth: 10–12 feet
Dockside depth: 8 feet (minimum)
Accepts transients: yes
Floating docks: yes
Dockside power connections: 50 amps (splitters available)
Dockside water connections: yes
Showers: yes
Laundromat: yes
Waste pump-out: yes
Gasoline: yes
Diesel fuel: yes
Mechanical repairs: yes
Ship's and variety store: yes
Restaurant: yes

It is not a good idea to attempt entry of Charleston Harbor at night without local knowledge, so if you are in the Isle of Palms–Sullivan's Island region at the end of the cruising day, it would be a good plan to dock at this unusually well-appointed facility and wait for the light of morning before approaching the "Holy City."

Isle of Palms History The Isle of Palms was known as Long Island until modern times. The island was rarely visited until a sort of carnival resort was developed on the strand in 1898. Visitors rode the trolley from Charleston to enjoy the seashore, the hotel, and the amusement rides at the carnival. It was not until the 1940s that a private developer purchased the land and residential development began. A bridge was built connecting the Isle of Palms with Sullivan's Island in 1945, and the resort's development has continued unabated ever since.

Wild Dunes Yacht Harbor

Hamlin Creek

West-southwest of unlighted daybeacon #117, Hamlin Creek cuts south and then west between Little Goat Island and the Isle of Palms waterfront on its way to an intersection with Breach Inlet. Hamlin Creek was formerly one of the best anchorages between McClellanville and Charleston Harbor, but things have changed a bit for sailcraft. As referred to above, a new 65-foot fixed bridge has been built across the ICW west-southwest of unlighted daybeacon #117. Unfortunately, this same bridge spans the northeasterly entrance to Hamlin Creek, and this portion of its passage does *not* provide 65 feet of clearance. This writer and his mate have been unable to find any officially listed clearance for the Hamlin Creek portion of the fixed bridge, but it appeared no taller than 40 feet to us. Sailors take note!

Many private docks border the southern shore of Hamlin Creek, but there are no facilities for transients along the way. The stream is well protected and is still one of the best anchorage possibilities, particularly in heavy weather, for craft under 48 feet on this section of the ICW assuming they can clear the bridge. Minimum depths of 6 feet hold to a point just short of Little

Goat Island's southwestern tip. Here, an unfortunate shoal bars further passage by all but shallow draft vessels.

About the only other problem associated with anchoring on Hamlin Creek is the considerable small-craft traffic the stream sometimes supports. Pick a spot far enough away from the island docks to avoid passing craft, and drop the hook for a night of security.

Swinton Creek

West of flashing daybeacon #118, Swinton Creek strikes into the northern shores of the ICW. The stream holds 5 to 15 feet of water well upstream. It exhibits typical grassy, undeveloped shores that give only enough protection for anchorage in light to moderate winds. There is probably not enough swinging room for craft over 35 feet.

Inlet Creek

The mainland branch of Inlet Creek cuts the Waterway's northern banks immediately west of unlighted daybeacon #119. Some shoaling flanks the eastern portion of this stream's entrance and calls for careful navigation. Otherwise, minimum depths of 8 to 10 feet carry for quite some distance upstream. The shoreline consists of undeveloped, grassy marsh.

Boats as large as 36 to 40 feet might seriously consider setting the hook on Inlet Creek south of its first sharp turn to the northeast. Depths along this portion of the stream run 11 to 18 feet, and protection is fairly good from northern, eastern, and western blows. Strong winds from the south blow directly up the creek and may make you imitate a Mexican jumping bean.

Breach Inlet

Breach Inlet is a small seaward cut that separates the Isle of Palms from Sullivan's Island. The channel is spanned by a low-level fixed bridge between the two islands that renders the cut useless to large pleasure craft. This cut is also quite shoal.

Isle of Palms Marina is located east of the bridge on the westerly tip of the Isle of Palms. This small facility offers limited dockage space for transients. Berths (if you can get them) include water, power, telephone, and cable-television connections. At low tide, visiting cruisers will find at least 5 to 6 feet of water alongside the floating piers. A variety store and a restaurant are located just behind the docks on top of the hill.

Isle of Palms Marina (803) 886-6599

Approach depth: 10+ feet
Dockside depth: 5–6 feet (minimum)
Accepts transients: yes
Floating piers: yes

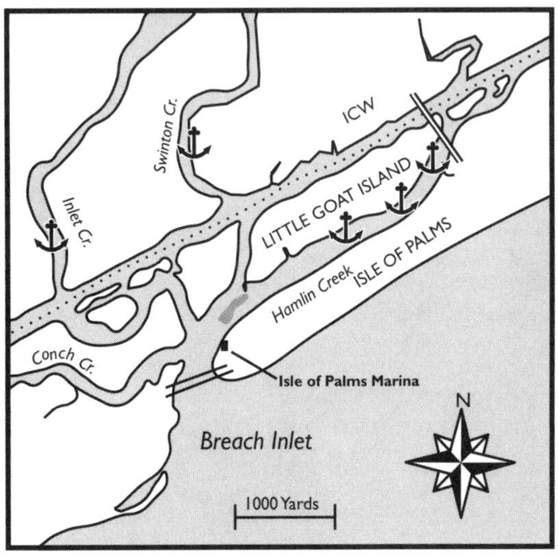

Dockside power connections: 30 and 50 amps
Dockside water connections: yes
Variety store: yes

Breach Inlet and Isle of Palms Marina can be approached by five separate channels leading from the Waterway. At least two of these cuts are deep and reliable. Make sure to read the Breach Inlet navigation section later in this chapter before attempting entry.

Conch Creek

The mainland branch of Conch Creek, just north of unlighted daybeacon #121, can serve as a light- to moderate-air anchorage for craft under 32 feet. Minimum depths run around 6 feet. The grassy shores are undeveloped. Frankly, there are better havens nearby, but if you are one of those captains who simply must see it all, navigational directions are presented below.

Toler's Cove Marina

Toler's Cove Marina guards the Waterway's northwestern shore southwest of the Sullivan's Island swing bridge. This fine facility is a truly memorable stop on the South Carolina ICW.

In the past, Toler's Cove had a bit of a shallow-water problem, but dredging in 1995 has relieved this situation. Visiting cruisers can now expect at least 8 feet of water in the approach channel, with soundings of 8 feet or more dockside.

Toler's Cove is an ultramodern, extrafriendly marina surrounded by a condo development. Extensive transient dockage is readily available at concrete floating docks featuring every conceivable power and water connection. Gasoline and diesel fuel are at hand, as are spotless shoreside showers and a full laundromat. The adjacent ship's store is particularly convenient. The helpful marina staff can easily arrange transportation to a host of nearby restaurants and a shopping center with a grocery store.

Toler's Cove Marina (803) 881-0325

Approach depth: 8 feet (low water)
Dockside depth: 8+ feet (low water)
Accepts transients: yes
Concrete floating docks: yes
Dockside power connections: 30 and 50 amps
Dockside water connections: yes
Showers: yes
Laundromat: yes
Gasoline: yes
Diesel fuel: yes
Mechanical repairs: independent technicians
Ship's store: yes
Restaurants: several available via marina-arranged transportation

Sullivan's Island

A small cut leads southeast from flashing daybeacon #125 to a National Park Service dock on the northeastern shore of Sullivan's Island. This once-deep creek has now shoaled to low-tide depths of as little as 4 feet. You must carefully follow an unmarked channel to maintain even these meager soundings. Passing boaters who can stand the depths, and who are of the devil-may-care variety, are welcome to moor to the park-service docks if they can find room amongst the official boats. The historic monument at Fort Moultrie is only a short walk away. The old fort makes for a fascinating visit.

This small stream also affords a good view of the Sullivan's Island Lighthouse. The black-and-white rectangular tower, 163 feet tall, is readily visible to the southeast. Designed to withstand even the gales of a hurricane, it exhibits, according to the South Carolina Sea Grant Consortium, "the brightest light . . . in the Western Hemisphere." Apparently, the designers did their job well, because the tower survived Hugo.

Sullivan's Island History Sullivan's Island was named for Captain Florentia O'Sullivan, a member of the original Charles Towne colonization party. As early as 1706, the military value of the island was recognized, and a makeshift fort was built on the island's eastern tip. During the Revolutionary War, Colonel William Moultrie supervised the construction of Fort Moultrie on the same point. The heroic story of Colonel Moultrie and his men will be related later in this chapter.

Following the Revolution, Sullivan's Island was used as a quarantine station for imported slaves. During the early 1800s, Charlestonians began building summer homes on the island to escape the oppressive heat of the city. By 1817, more than 1,000 seasonal residents flocked to the island's four hotels and 200 resort homes. In 1854, a severe hurricane nearly leveled all development, but loyal vacationers began rebuilding immediately thereafter, and Sullivan's Island has remained a popular resort to the present day.

In a situation reminiscent of the 1854 storm, many, if not most, of the resort homes on Sullivan's Island were flattened by Hurricane Hugo. New building has gone forward at breakneck pace since the modern-day storm, and the island has again become one of the most popular Charleston retreats.

Fort Moultrie History It was June 1776, and news had been received in Charles Towne that a massive fleet commanded by Sir Peter Parker was voyaging south from New York with the express intention of making the city a base for British operations in the South. On board were Sir Henry Clinton and an army of several thousand seasoned veterans. The English were confident that their powerful force could easily defeat any defensive measures the patriots threw in their way.

Meanwhile, Charleston patriots were feverishly preparing the city's defenses. Warehouses bordering the waterfront were torn down to clear a path for cannon fire. Continental companies drilled daily. Citizens with military experience predicted that the battle would very likely hinge upon the fight for the outer harbor. If the Americans could stop the British there, the British naval and infantry superiority could not be brought into play.

On the southern tip of Sullivan's Island, Colonel William Moultrie was supervising the construction of a new fort. Palmetto logs were cut on Capers Island to the north and quickly brought south by horse-drawn cart. The fort's double walls were built of thick palmetto planks reinforced by a layer of sand in between. Moultrie's men worked night and day, expecting to sight the enemy on the horizon at any minute.

There were those who did not believe in Moultrie's plan. Some said that the cannons of the British fleet would obliterate the small fort in the first broadside. It was only a waste of lives and resources to continue with such folly. Why not draw back and muster the defenses at the lower tip of the peninsula? Well, if Moultrie was stubborn enough to try the fool scheme, he could go ahead, but he wouldn't be allowed to squander the city's whole powder supply.

Moultrie turned a deaf ear to his critics and urged his men to even greater speed. By the time Sir Peter Parker sighted the Charles Towne bar, the patriots had accomplished the miraculous. Stout walls faced the enemy on three sides, and a host of cannons were mounted on their platforms. The rear quarter of the fort, however, still lay open to attack.

The British generals laid their plans carefully. While the great fleet pounded the fort in a bold frontal assault, Sir Henry Clinton would land his army on undefended Long Island to the north. From there, he would cross shallow Breach Inlet, thrusting aside the small force of patriots stationed there, and sweep against the fort from the rear. Parker and Clinton probably thought Charles Towne would be in their hands within a week.

On the morning of June 16, a strong contingent from the British fleet rolled out its massive cannons and stood in toward the impudent patriots blocking its way. No challenge was yet heard from the fort's cannons. Unknown to the British, the defenders were saving their scant powder supply until the fleet was at point-blank range.

Suddenly, the waters of Charles Towne Harbor exploded with British fire and smoke. Over 300 guns smote the walls of Fort Moultrie in a single cannonade. Confident shipmasters waited for the smoke to clear and reveal the shattered walls. What astonishment must have shown on the face of every sailor, from the lowliest tar to the fleet admiral, when they saw that the fort's spongy palmetto logs had simply soaked up the British cannonballs with no apparent damage!

Then it was Moultrie's turn. The patriots' cannons spoke. When the smoke cleared this time, the fort's defenders cheered as they surveyed the broken spars and shattered decks of the once-great force in front of them.

The battle continued throughout the day. At one point, Moultrie's powder ran so low that only a few cannons were in action. A new supply was rushed out from the city, and the battle was again joined in earnest. The English tried to maneuver several ships around to the fort's unprotected rear, but the vessels ran aground and were riddled with shot. The fort's proud crescent-moon flag was shot away, only to be retrieved by a Sergeant Jasper. This soldier's brave effort is immortalized by a statue on the South Battery in Charleston.

Meanwhile, Clinton's 2,200 troops had successfully landed on Long Island, only to discover that Breach Inlet was far too deep for the men to ford. The determined band of patriots guarding the inlet's southern banks kept the enemy at bay with grapeshot and rifle fire. Eventually, it was necessary to reembark the British troops to the fleet offshore.

By the time the sun set on that amazing day, the British naval force that had attacked the fort was in tatters. Sir Peter Parker even had the ignoble fate of being wounded in the buttocks by flying splinters. Within the fort's walls, Moultrie's men stared out to sea with powder-blackened faces. They could hardly believe it. The British forces were limping away, glad to leave the fury of Fort Moultrie behind. The defenders had faced the might, the very cream, of the British navy and bested that confident force in a pitched battle. Their victory was to remain one of the soundest English defeats of the entire war.

Following the Revolution, the South Carolina legislature adopted the palmetto tree as a part of the state flag, along with the crescent moon, which symbolizes liberty. The flag has since waved proudly over the Palmetto State, forever a memorial to those brave men who fought against such overwhelming odds on that hot June day in 1776.

MCCLELLANVILLE TO CHARLESTON HARBOR NAVIGATION

Running this stretch of the ICW means sticking to the marked channel. While tidal currents can run swiftly, particularly in the vicinity of inlets, they are not usually as severe as those found in the Santee region. Sailcraft and trawlers should nevertheless be on the lookout for excessive leeway. Also, be on guard for some official No Wake signs posted near several private docks on this run.

Most sidewaters can be entered simply by sticking to their mid-width. Streams that call for more caution are noted below. Be careful not to cruise too far upstream on any of these sidewaters. Almost without exception, they eventually lead to shallow water, which could result in a most unpleasant grounding far from the Waterway channel.

On the ICW South of McClellanville, the South Carolina ICW flows through the so-called Mathews Cut into the deep reaches of Harbor River. Southwest of flashing daybeacon #48, a dredged landcut knifes through portions of several shallow bays and sounds. The surrounding marsh is often covered at mid- or high tide, and the waters can be much wider than you might expect from a study of chart 11518. Fresh winds can also bring on more than a spot of chop. Visiting cruisers should be prepared for these less-than-ideal conditions.

The mouth of Tibwin Creek is located northwest of unlighted daybeacon #42. While this stream may look good on the chart, it is too narrow for comfortable anchorage by large pleasure craft.

Awendaw Creek Be sure to use Awendaw Creek's primary entrance, to the south of flashing daybeacon #48. For best depths, cruise directly from #48 into the entrance's centerline and continue along the mid-width as you cruise downstream. The two small streams that make off from the Waterway near unlighted daybeacon #49 and eventually lead into the main branch of Awendaw Creek are both shoal and should not be used by cruising craft. Don't attempt to cruise far past the sharp, charted turn to the east on Awendaw Creek. Depths rise sharply in Bulls Bay to the southeast.

On the ICW Boaters southbound on the ICW will come upon a No Wake zone near flashing daybeacon #50. The Waterway borders Francis Marion National Forest's recreation area along this stretch, and the minimum-speed zone is in place to protect a launching ramp associated with the complex. The regulations are in effect as far as unlighted daybeacon #51.

Graham Creek Favor the western banks slightly as you enter Graham Creek. Depths begin to drop off as the stream takes a sharp turn to the east. Discontinue your exploration of the creek before reaching this bend.

On the ICW At flashing daybeacon #80, the Waterway enters a dredged portion of Price Creek. Between unlighted daybeacon #84 and flashing daybeacon #86, the ICW abandons Price Creek. The southeasterly branch of this stream (northwest of its inlet) can serve as an overnight anchorage.

Price Creek Entry into Price Creek is complicated by the charted marsh island bisecting the entrance's mid-width. This small body of grass is covered completely at high tide or even mid-tide, but believe you me, it's there. On-site research in 1995 revealed that the best approach is from the southwestern flank of the entrance. Favor the southern and southwestern shores heavily as you make your way into Price Creek. Soon, you will swing back to the southeast, and good depths will open out in a broad band to within 200 yards of the charted power lines that cross the inlet. Depths become inconsistent east and southeast of the power lines. All cruisers should most certainly discontinue their exploration of the creek at that point.

Bull Narrows Creek can be easily accessed via its mid-width. Good depths continue upstream to the charted split. Remember, though, this body of water is a bit too narrow for anchorage by cruising boats.

Capers Creek All four entrances to Capers Creek have some shoaling problems. Slow down and watch the sounder until you are on the stream's main body. The northeasternmost branch is probably the best anchorage possibility, but notice the correctly charted 5-foot depths blocking direct entrance from the ICW. Captains piloting vessels that need more water must enter and exit this arm of Capers Creek from the stream's main body to the southwest.

Most of the central channel opposite flashing daybeacon #96 holds plenty of water, yet again there is a charted but unmarked shoal to worry with. Notice the patch of 4-foot depths abutting the westerly side of the channel, clearly pictured on 11518. You must favor the easterly shores slightly to avoid this hazard. Of course, you can't approach the easterly banks too closely, either, or shoal water will again be encountered. This is perhaps the most difficult of Capers Creek's principal entrances, and it is not particularly recommended.

Make sure to avoid the point of land separating the central-northeastern and northeasternmost entrance cuts. This point has built well south into the main body of the combined creeks. Those entering the northeasternmost fork from the main, seaward-flowing portion of the creek will probably do well to continue cruising south and southeast until just before meeting up with the correctly charted patch of 5-foot soundings. Boaters can then curl back around to the north-northeast and safely enter the northeasternmost stream.

The southwest-central channel, known as Toomer Creek (northeast of flashing daybeacon #99), is the smallest of the three principal entrances but carries good minimum 6- to 7-foot depths on its mid-width. Be sure to carefully avoid the northeastern point as Toomer Creek flows into the main passage of the combined streams. As correctly predicted on chart 11518, yet another shoal is building out from this point.

The southwesternmost entrance stream is a small body of water that is best left to our outboard- and I/O-powered brethren. Larger craft are advised to keep clear.

Cruising southeast beyond the northeastern and southwestern points of land that guard Capers Inlet's flanks is strictly not recommended. Depths rise quickly, and massive breakers are soon encountered.

Whiteside Creek Enter Whiteside Creek on its centerline. Good depths hold through the stream's first sharp bend to the northeast and even continue a short distance upstream as the creek turns back to the northwest. Cruising vessels can anchor on the initial portion of the stream near the charted 11-foot soundings. Do not attempt to follow Whiteside Creek too far past its turn to the northwest. The stream quickly splinters into several branches, and depths become more than suspect.

Toomer Creek: Mainland Branch The northwestern portion of Toomer Creek, directly opposite its seaside sister, can be entered safely by favoring the southwestern banks slightly. After cruising upstream for some 150 yards, swing back to the mid-width. Stop your forward progress well before reaching the small, charted creeks making in to the northeastern banks.

On the ICW Southwest of flashing daybeacon #99, cruisers traveling the ICW will come upon the unexpectedly broad waters of Copahee Sound. As mentioned earlier, the charted mud flats are covered completely at high or even mid-tide. This can be a quite a shock for first-time visitors. As you would expect, all the sound's waters outside of the Waterway are exceedingly shallow, so stick strictly to the marked ICW channel.

Dewees Creek The main body of Dewees Creek flowing southeast from the Waterway does not present any navigational problems. However, do not attempt to enter the stream by way of its northeastern cut at unlighted daybeacon #105 or the southern arm near flashing daybeacon #111. Both channels are too shallow and unreliable for cruising boaters.

If you choose to enter the northeastern arm from the creek's interior to anchor, avoid the point that separates the two branches.

Again, as with the two inlets to the north, depths begin to drop off rapidly as the stream approaches the ocean. Do not cruise farther downstream than the power lines charted on 11531.

Enter the landward branch of Dewees Creek on its mid-width. While good depths are held well upstream on all three branches of the creek, they eventually lead to very shallow water. Obviously, you should stop well short of these correctly charted shallows.

Do not attempt to explore the charted dump area located on the upper reaches of Long Creek. The waters are much too shoal for boats of any size, as the author's bent prop can attest.

On the ICW All boaters should slow to No Wake speed southwest of flashing daybeacon #116. The docks of Wild Dunes Yacht Harbor will soon be sighted on the southeastern banks. Continue at idle speed until well southwest of the piers.

New Bridge West-southwest of unlighted daybeacon #117, a new, fixed high-rise bridge has been built over the ICW and the northeasterly mouth of Hamlin Creek. The current edition of chart 11518 shows only a "Bridge under construction" notation, but the new span is now finished and open to automobile traffic.

The new span's vertical clearance is 65 feet over the ICW passage but considerably less as its passes across Hamlin Creek.

A thick strip of new homes, private docks, and small condos has recently been built along both banks of the ICW a short hop east-northeast of the new high-rise. Power craft should slow to idle speed while cruising through this stretch.

Hamlin Creek The deepwater entrance to Hamlin Creek is easily accessible west-southwest of unlighted daybeacon #117. Remember that the new bridge described above is considerably lower as it spans the northeasterly mouth of Hamlin Creek. This writer estimates its heighth at 40 feet or so.

Otherwise, you need only stay within shouting distance of the centerline for good depths short of the correctly charted 4-foot waters off the southwestern tip of Little Goat Island.

Don't attempt to approach Breach Inlet from Hamlin Creek. The extreme southwesterly tier of the stream is shoal, with some 4-foot depths in evidence.

Breach Inlet There are five possible entrances to the waters lying about Breach Inlet. One, Hamlin Creek, was discussed above. Of the other four, all but one are basically reliable.

To successfully navigate the east-central branch (opposite Swinton Creek), you must favor the eastern shore as you enter. Begin favoring the northwestern banks as the channel curves southwest to Breach Inlet.

The central-western channel, just west of unlighted daybeacon #119, is the most navigable of the entrances. Simply follow the mid-width until you begin to approach the Breach Inlet bridge. You will spy Isle of Palms Marina on the western tip of the land abutting Breach Inlet's eastern flank. Don't cut in toward the facilities too quickly. There is shoal water to the east and northeast, as noted on chart 11518. Continue on the main channel until you are about 25 yards from the bridge. Then cut 90 degrees to port and enter the marina.

The westernmost cut, known as Conch Creek, can also be used to reach the main channel. The stream has two mouths opening onto the ICW. However, the lower of the two, just east-northeast of the Sullivan's Island bridge, has only 4 feet of water near its entrance and is quite narrow. The branch near unlighted daybeacon #121 is far more reliable.

Swinton Creek As usual, boaters making in to Swinton Creek should enter via the stream's centerline. Expect some low-water soundings of 5 feet as you track your way from the ICW channel into the creek.

Don't attempt to follow Swinton Creek past its charted bend to the north, where an unnamed creek splits off to the east-southeast and chart 11518 indicates a 19-foot sounding.

Inlet Creek Some shoaling, possibly courtesy of Hurricane Hugo, has impinged upon the eastern side of Inlet Creek's southern entrance. Favor the western banks while cruising into the creek to avoid this potential trouble spot.

Good minimum depths of at least 8 feet run well upstream until the creek splinters into several shallow branches. Most large vessels will do well to drop anchor between the ICW and the creek's first turn to the northeast.

On the ICW West-southwest of unlighted daybeacon #121, the Waterway soon exchanges greetings with the Sullivan's Island (Ben Sawyer) swing bridge. This span was left dangling precariously by Hurricane Hugo and was for a time a real impediment to Waterway traffic. Fortunately, all has now long been set right, but the bridge still has a restricted opening schedule. Captains whose craft cannot clear the 31 feet of closed vertical clearance should know that the bridge does not open at all Monday through Friday from 7:00 A.M. to 9:00 A.M. and from 4:00 P.M. to 6:00 P.M. On Saturdays, Sundays, and legal holidays, the span opens only on the hour from 9:00 A.M. to 7:00 P.M. At all other times, it opens on demand.

Immediately after passing under the bridge, you will spy the entrance to Toler's Cove Marina on the northwestern shore.

Sullivan's Island Channel The small channel leading to the Fort Moultrie National Park dock is just to the southeast of flashing daybeacon #125. Remember that depths on this small cut have now shoaled to low-water soundings of only 4 feet in places. If you decide to enter anyway, hold to the mid-width and watch to starboard. The dock will soon come abeam.

Entrance to Charleston Harbor At flashing daybeacon #125, the Waterway cuts sharply northwest and begins its approach to Charleston Harbor. This is a potential trouble spot for newcomers, as there are a host of navigational aids to sort out and some strong tidal currents to boot.

Be sure to pass unlighted nun buoy #126 to its southwesterly side. This aid marks the ruins of an old bridge that once connected Mount Pleasant and Sullivan's Island. Be on guard for this hazard at night.

Come abeam of flashing daybeacon #127 to its northeasterly quarter. Past #127, the channel turns west-southwest and the wide expanse of Charleston Harbor opens out dead ahead. Continued navigation of the ICW and the Charleston area is presented in the next chapter.

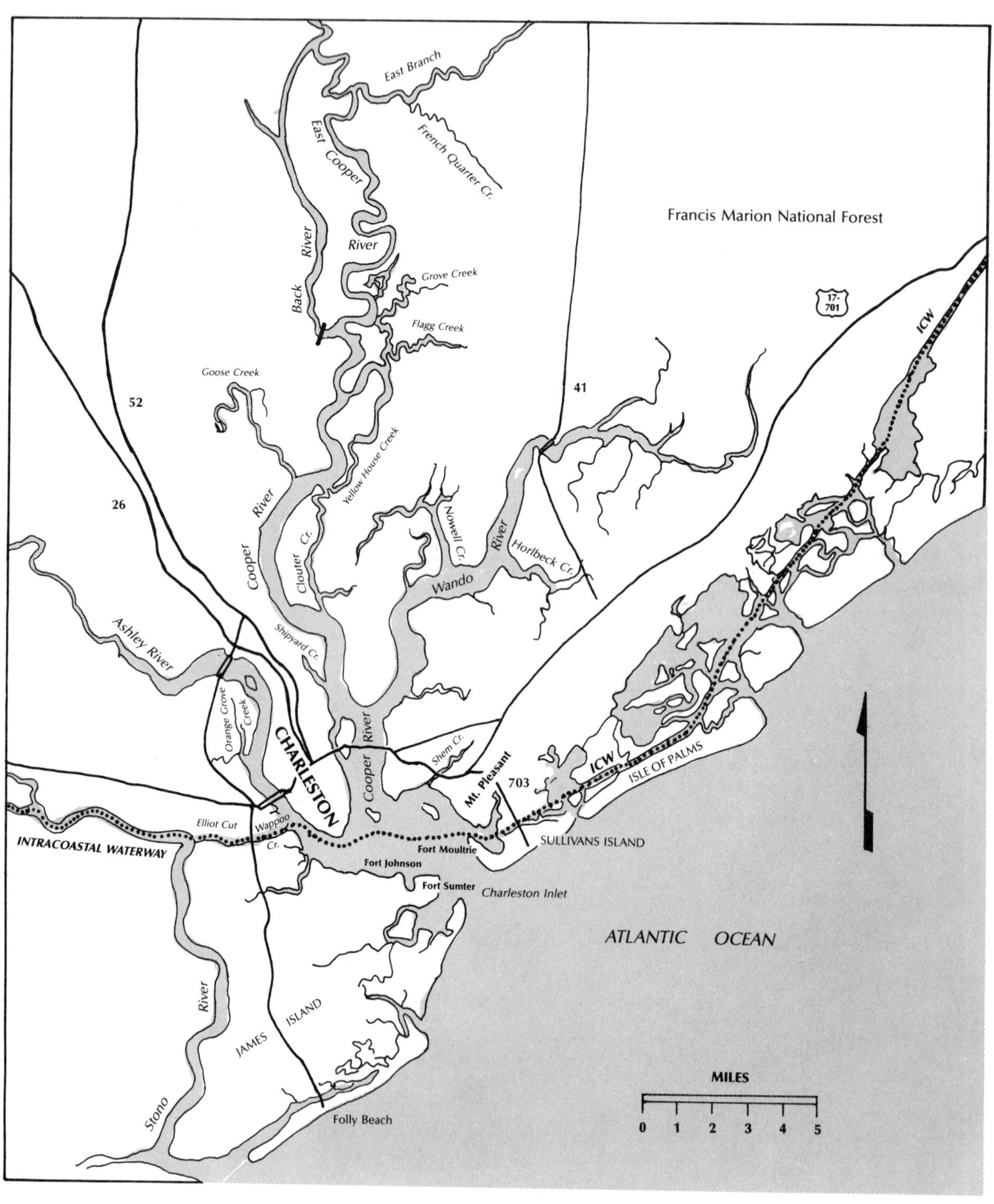

East Branch
French Quarter Cr.
East Cooper River
Back River
Grove Creek
Flagg Creek
Francis Marion National Forest
17-701
Goose Creek
52
41
ICW
Yellow House Creek
26
Cooper River
Clouter Cr.
Nowell Cr.
Wando River
Horlbeck Cr.
Ashley River
Shipyard Cr.
Orange Grove Creek
CHARLESTON
Cooper River
Shem Cr.
Mt. Pleasant
703
ICW
ISLE OF PALMS
Elliot Cut
Wappoo Cr.
INTRACOASTAL WATERWAY
Fort Moultrie
SULLIVANS ISLAND
Fort Johnson
Fort Sumter
Charleston Inlet
ATLANTIC OCEAN
Stono River
JAMES ISLAND
MILES
0 1 2 3 4 5
Folly Beach

Charleston

As you round the point from Sullivan's Island, the spires of Charleston will begin peeping over the horizon to the north. Shimmering in the summer haze, the city often looks as if it has been plucked from the pages of an old novel. You can almost feel the romantic promise of exciting Old World opportunities. The cruising visitor need not fear disappointment. The reality of Charleston is even more fascinating than its promise.

Charleston is clearly *the* stop on the South Carolina ICW. Boaters who fail to make the acquaintance of Charleston will miss what is, quite simply, one of the most beautiful and exciting cities in the world. The city stands ready to greet you with a mind-boggling array of attractions. Beautiful old mansions that look as if they have stepped out of another era, countless fine restaurants, and a multitude of interesting shops and businesses are only a part of the town's attractions. There are movies to see that reveal much of the Charlestonian character, and native craftsmen and artists to watch as they go about their traditional tasks. It would take months to fully appreciate all of the city's attractions, but fortunately, many can be enjoyed in the space of a few days.

With the possible exception of McClellanville, Charleston was impacted harder by Hurricane Hugo than any other community in coastal South Carolina. One BBC commentator reported after the great storm's passage that Charleston was "gone with the wind."

That report proved to be exaggerated. While many buildings in the city suffered extensive damage, the historic structures survived surprisingly well, often far better than more modern construction.

Charts

You will need several charts for complete coverage of the Charleston area:

11518 follows the Waterway across Charleston Harbor and into Wappoo Creek

11523 covers Charleston Inlet and the outer harbor

11524 is the principal Charleston Harbor chart, covering the lower sections of the Cooper, Wando, and Ashley Rivers; this is the single most important chart in the Charleston area

11527 provides navigational information for the upper Cooper River, including the "Tee"

11526 details the upper Wando River; unless you gain access through the usually closed highway bridge, this chart will not be needed

Restoration has gone forward at a steady clip since 1989, and today's visitor to this timeless city will find very few reminders of the great tempest. We can all celebrate the fact that even such a storm as Hugo was not able to vanquish the unique Charleston way of life.

In the following pages, this guide will explore the often vague, sometimes fleeting, but always exciting qualities that make Charleston a city apart from all the rest. You may confidently use this information as a base of reference for your visit. However, various publications recommended in the following sections can arm you with additional knowledge of the city. The fortunate cruising visitor who makes Charleston a port of call will do well to acquire all the information that he or she can before embarking on his or her journey through this timeless city.

CHARLESTON

Native Charlestonians will tell you that the Ashley, Cooper, and Wando Rivers flow down their respective channels to form first Charleston Harbor and then the Atlantic Ocean. While this may be at variance with accepted geographic theory, it clearly shows what a high regard this city has for its waters. Indeed, until very recent times, Charleston's waterways were its highways of commerce.

Currently, four full-service marinas serve the Charleston area. Three are located on Ashley River, while a fourth is now found on Cooper River. All gladly accept transients. However, sailcraft must be able to clear a 55-foot fixed bridge to reach two of the Ashley River facilities.

The Charleston historical district is within walking distance of all the Ashley River marinas, but it is a fairly long hike of 30 minutes or so. In order to see as much of the city as possible within a fairly short period of time, it may be necessary to arrange for an auto rental. Call Budget Car Rentals (803-760-9025) or Enterprise Rent-A-Car (803-723-6215), both of which have offices in downtown Charleston. Taxis are another possibility for transportation. This writer was impressed by the unusually prompt and courteous service of Charleston cabbies. Call Yellow Cab (803-577-6565) or Airport Limo (803-552-5639).

For many years prior to Hurricane Hugo, the most popular transient stop in Charleston was the George M. Lockwood Municipal Marina (otherwise known as the Charleston Municipal Marina). This facility's harbor, partially enclosed by a concrete breakwater, lies northeast of unlighted can buoy #5. It is not being too dramatic to say that this marina was laid waste by Hugo. The docks were either completely destroyed or heavily damaged, and many of the moored boats were cast upon the shore. In addition to the destruction of the docks, a huge quantity of mud was washed into the harbor, raising depths to less than a foot in spots during low tide.

Until recently, in marked contrast to all the other facilities discussed thus far in this guide, the Charleston Municipal Marina had not reopened. Now, things have taken a turn for the better, though all is not as it once was. Aggressive private management has now taken over this facility and renamed it The City Marina. Due to permit problems, the harbor has still not been dredged, but transients are once again being accepted at several of the outer docks. Depths run from 5 to 7 feet, with the deeper soundings obviously found on the outer slips. Future plans call for these outer slips to be expanded to the southeast. When completed, it seems likely that the new berths will not be afforded breakwater protection.

In any case, the existing berths consist of floating wooden-decked piers with water and 30- and 50- amp power connections. Upgraded showers and laundromat facilities should be in place by the time you read this account. Gasoline, diesel fuel, and waste pump-out services should be on line for dockside purchase by June 1996.

The popular Marina Restaurant and the variety store are still in their longtime location just behind the dockage basin. The breakfasts here remain the best early-day dining bargain in Charleston.

Additionally, a second building located just a short hop southeast of the restaurant houses the Armchair Sailor Bookstore and a wonderful wine shop. These two firms are worth the time of every boater who finds his way to this fortunate city. Be sure to stop by the Armchair Sailor (803-577-0254). If you need advice about local navigational conditions or anything at all in the way of nautical publications, this is the place to be. The adjacent wine shop (803-577-3881) carries a wide selection of fine wines. This writer was very impressed with the many vintners, both domestic and overseas, represented in the inventory.

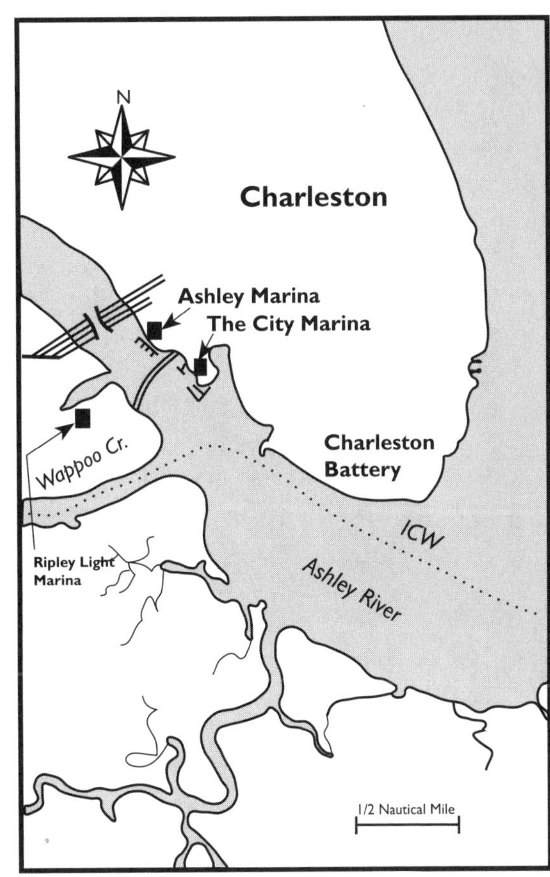

The City Marina (803) 723-5098

Approach depth: 7-10 feet
Dockside depth: 5-7 feet
Floating wooden piers: yes
Dockside power connections: 30 and 50 amps
Dockside water connections: yes
Showers: yes
Laundromat: yes
Waste pump-out: yes (available June 1996)
Gasoline: yes (available June 1996)
Diesel fuel: yes (available June 1996)
Ship's and variety store: yes
Restaurant: on-site

The Charleston Yacht Club (803-722-4968) resides just behind and a bit northwest of the municipal-marina basin. This fine club is happy to welcome members of other yacht clubs with reciprocal privileges to its clubhouse and dining room, but there are currently no dockage facilities available. However, you can easily berth at nearby City Marina or Ashley Marina and walk down to exchange a few cruising yarns.

In spite of loud protests, sailors will still have to contend with a 55-foot fixed high-rise bridge spanning the Ashley from northeast to southwest between The City Marina and the active marina facilities a bit farther upstream. Sailcraft that cannot clear the 55-foot height are out of luck when it comes to exploring the upper Ashley River.

For many years, visiting cruisers have made use of an anchorage southeast of what is now The City Marina. This haven has silted in a bit, but it is still possible for pleasure craft of most any size to feel their way carefully northeast off the channel (northwest of unlighted nun buoy #4) and drop the hook safely for the night in depths of 6 feet or better. Care must be taken to guard against the shallows that have built out from the northeasterly banks. Protection is good from all but strong southeasterly and northwesterly breezes, which blow directly up and down Ashley River. It's a quick dinghy trip ashore at the old city basin, but at low tide even dinghies may touch bottom.

If indeed the new pier construction at nearby City Marina proceeds as planned, the docks may well encroach on this anchorage and reduce swinging room considerably. Check on the latest conditions upon your arrival in Charleston.

Northwest of the 55-foot high-rise bridge, popular Ashley Marina maintains an extensive collection of wooden-decked floating piers along the northeastern banks between the new fixed span and the charted18-foot bascule bridge. With the Ashley's tidal range, the marina's floating piers are a distinct advantage over fixed structures. Transients are eagerly accepted at a considerable number of slips set aside for visitors. Each berth offers complete power, water, and telephone hookups. Dockside depths remain an impressive 15 feet or better. Additionally, an office building just behind the docks houses a first-rate ship's store, ultraclean bathrooms, and a complete laundromat. Gas, diesel fuel, and waste pump-out are offered. Ashley Marina can also boast its own mechanic, who is ready to service both diesel and gasoline power plants. Of course, a host of Charleston's finest restaurants are a quick taxi ride or a fairly long hike away.

To facilitate your visit to historic Charleston, Ashley now offers a courtesy van to its patrons. This motorized transportation is also very handy if it's time to restock the galley.

For breakfast or a quick meal any time of day, you can always walk down to Marina Restaurant at The City Marina.

Ashley Marina's popularity is richly deserved, and this writer highly recommends this unusually well-appointed facility. The only problem you might encounter when visiting the marina is the swift tidal currents that regularly scour Ashley River. All vessels, but particularly sailcraft and single-screw trawlers, should be on maximum alert when maneuvering into a slip. Fortunately, the attentive dockmasters greatly minimize any problems of this nature.

Ashley Marina (803) 722-1996

Approach depth: 15+ feet
Dockside depth: 15+ feet
Accepts transients: yes
Wooden floating docks: yes
Dockside power connections: 30 and 50 amps
Dockside water connections: yes
Showers: yes
Laundromat: yes
Waste pump-out: yes
Gasoline: yes
Diesel fuel: yes
Mechanical repairs: yes
Ship's store: yes
Restaurants: nearby

Lying almost opposite Ashley Marina on the river's southwesterly banks, Ripley Light Marina offers a warm welcome for visiting cruisers. Its concrete floating piers line the southeasterly shoreline of the dredged tongue of water almost due west of unlighted can buoy #5.

Ripley Light has an ongoing problem with shoaling along its approach channel. This cut was last dredged in 1994, and currently 5½-foot low-water depths can be maintained if and only if you hold strictly to the entrance's mid-width.

Conversely, the inner harbor slips had just been dredged at the time of this writing and new piers have been installed at the rear of the dockage basin. Depths at these docks now run 6 to 8 feet. The same cannot be said for the outer slips near California Dreaming Restaurant (see below). At low tide, these slips are all but bare of water.

The staff at Ripley Light Marina is eager to accept transients for overnight or temporary dockage. In fact, this marina makes it clear that transients are a very important part of its business. All berths feature full power and water connections. The shoreside bathroom, shower, and laundry facilities are first-rate. Full mechanical repairs, fueling services, and waste pump-out are offered, and small boats can be hauled out with a forklift. A shopping center with a grocery store is within walking distance, and Ripley Light even has a courtesy van. When entering the harbor, you will sight a large brick-and-glass building to port. This structure houses California Dreaming restaurant. It's not exactly in sync with the Low Country, but this dining spot is undeniably popular. Many boaters may alternately choose to take a taxi (see phone numbers above) or the courtesy van into the historical section of Charleston to visit the many superb restaurants located there.

Ripley Light Marina (803) 766-2100

Approach depth: 6–7 feet (low tide)
Dockside depth: 4–6 feet (low tide)
Accepts transients: yes
Concrete floating piers: yes
Dockside power connections: 30 and 50 amps
Dockside water connections: yes
Showers: yes
Laundromat: yes
Waste pump-out: yes
Gasoline: yes
Diesel fuel: yes
Mechanical repairs: yes
Below-waterline repairs: very limited
Ship's and variety store: yes
Restaurants: on-site, with several nearby

There is a third choice for visiting cruisers who make their way between the fixed bridge and the 18-foot bascule span. The waters just off the southwestern side of the main channel have become a popular city-sanctioned anchorage. Depths run 15-plus feet, and there is good shelter from eastern, northeastern, western, and southwestern winds. As with the anchorage farther downstream, fresh southeastern or northwestern breezes tend to blow directly up or down the river and can foster a healthy chop. Boaters must also be aware of the strong tidal currents that are a regular feature on this portion of Ashley River. Be sure the anchor is well set and holding steady before heading below for a well-earned toddy.

Two smaller marinas offer additional services for boaters who venture farther upstream on Ashley River through the 18-foot bascule bridge. Dolphin Cove Marina guards the Ashley's eastern shores north of unlighted daybeacon #16 (near the charted "R TR"). This medium-sized facility accepts transients at its wooden floating piers, which feature water hookups and power connections up to 50 amps. Currently, 6-foot depths are found at the innermost slips and the fuel pier. The outer docks feature better than 15 feet of water.

Dolphin Cove Marina features full mechanical services, and small vessels' bottoms can see the light of day via a forklift. The marina also offers gasoline, diesel fuel, and shoreside showers. When it's time to eat, your best bet is probably to take a taxi into the historical downtown section.

Dolphin Cove Marina (803) 744-2562

Approach depth: 8–10 feet
Dockside depth: 6–15+ feet
Accepts transients: yes
Floating wooden piers: yes
Dockside power connections: 30 and 50 amps
Dockside water connections: yes
Showers: yes
Gasoline: yes
Diesel fuel: yes
Mechanical repairs: yes
Below-waterline repairs: very limited
Ship's store: small

Finally, Duncan's Boat Harbor flanks Ashley River's northeastern banks a short distance upstream of unlighted daybeacon #28 (downstream of the 35-foot fixed bridge). This facility caters almost exclusively to small power craft. Some limited transient dockage is available for that type of vessel at the marina's floating wooden docks. Full power and water connections are at every slip. Gasoline can be purchased, and there is an on-site ship's and variety store. Showers are also available.

Duncan's Boat Harbor (803) 744-2628

Approach depth: 7 feet (minimum at low water)
Dockside depth: 5–9 feet (low water)
Accepts transients: yes
Wooden floating piers: yes
Dockside power connections: 30 and 50 amps
Dockside water connections: yes
Showers: yes
Gasoline: yes
Mechanical repairs: yes (gasoline)
Ship's and variety store: yes

Charleston's newest pleasure-craft facility is located along the western banks of Cooper River northwest of flashing buoy #48. Newly minted Cooper River Marina maintains an extensive set of floating concrete decked piers off the northern point of charted Shipyard Creek's eastern entrance.

This facility is located in the heart of the

now-defunct Charleston Naval Base. In fact, it was originally set aside for the use of military personnel, and service people still receive a special price when docking here. After the shutdown of the naval facility, Charleston County took over the marina, and seems intent on developing it into an attractive alternative for pleasure-craft skippers.

Currently, it is only fair to note that Cooper River Marina is out in the middle of nowhere, though the accommodating dockmasters can sometimes provide a courtesy vehicle for grocery runs or a quick visit to the historic section. No restaurants or other shoreside support facilities are within walking distance.

Transients are eagerly accepted at berths with fresh water and 30-amp power connections. Depths in the partially breakwater-enclosed dockage basin run 10 feet or better. The harbor is enclosed on three sides and is well protected from all but fresh northern and northeastern blows. New showers and maybe even a laundromat should be in place by the time this account finds its way into your hands.

The dockmaster's office is actually located better than a mile to the north of the harbor. This writer suggests calling the dockmaster on VHF (channel 16) as you pass under the Cooper River high-rise bridge. During daylight hours, someone will meet you at the docks upon arrival.

While it lacks the ready access to historic Charleston afforded by the Ashley River marinas, this facility does offer the first real pleasure-craft services on Cooper River. Cruisers who enjoy docking a bit off the beaten track should give it a try.

Cooper River Marina (803) 554-0790

Approach depth: 15-20 feet
Dockside depth: 10+ feet
Accepts transients: yes
Floating concrete piers: yes
Dockside power connections: 30 amps
Dockside water connections: yes
Showers: by early 1996
Laundromat: planned

For those who have seen one wave too many and want to escape for a while, Charleston offers a wide assortment of inns and hotels. Some of the finest are located in historic homes. Two of this writer's personal favorites are the Lodge Alley Inn (803-722-1611) and Two Meeting Street Inn (803-723-7322). The fortunate visitor who stays at one of these romantic establishments for a night or two cannot help but move closer to an understanding of the city.

The Heart of Charleston

"Charleston isn't a city. Charleston is a way of life." This writer and his mate reflected on the truth of that singular statement by tour guide Timmy Mallard as we enjoyed the Charleston Battery by horse-drawn carriage one cool spring afternoon. Long rows of lovely mansions slipped dreamily by, followed by a breathtaking view of the harbor. As the cool sea breeze hit my face, I reflected that the more one knows Charleston, the more one comes to understand what a unique city it really is. Indeed, without an understanding of Charleston's very special character, you cannot fully enjoy your visit as you should.

Charleston has had many titles since it first

began as a struggling colony on the banks of Town Creek in 1670. Those designations are at least a partial key to understanding the city's character. Charleston has often been called a living museum. While America's past has been recreated in such places as Williamsburg, Virginia, and Sturbridge Village, Massachusetts, those centers are monuments to our heritage. In Charleston, local citizens live and work every day in the city's historic homes and buildings. You might say they are actually living in the framework of the past, not just remembering times that are now far removed. This unique condition seems to impart a very special quality to Charleston. It is almost as though the past were somehow a closer and more tangible entity.

Charleston is also called the "Holy City." This title refers to the many steeples that dot the skyline. Certainly, Charleston has always been a very religious community, usually in the very best sense. The roots of religious tolerance stretch far back into the colonial era.

It takes far more than titles, however, to understand the very special community that is Charleston. In his book *Charleston in the Age of the Pinckneys*, George C. Rogers, Jr., lays bare the soul of the city in a clear, concise, and very readable manner. While there are many other works that detail Charleston's history, there is perhaps no other that offers such penetrating insight into the background of the city's unique character.

Rogers divides the social history of Charleston into two eras. The first he terms the "Open City." This period lasted from colonial days until the 1800s. During that time, Charleston acted as a giant sponge, soaking up education, culture, and science from all over the world. The

Charleston Battery

port's vast waterborne commerce made contact with other American and European cultures an everyday occurrence. Charlestonians picked from the very best of these influences and founded a social order that was admired throughout the Western world. Education flourished, and intellectual societies were established. There was no rigid social order. Men of ability were often admitted to the highest echelons of society even if they were not of noble birth. It was an exciting time to live and work in Charleston. Who among us does not have at least a little envy for those fortunate enough to have lived in those golden days?

The second era, which Rogers terms the "Closed City," began in the early 1800s. It was during this period that large sums of money began to be concentrated in the hands of wealthy, slave-owning planters. A rigid planter aristocracy developed, and the Charlestonian way of life began to change. No longer was it open to the influences of the outside world. The planters believed they had found the perfect existence. The lower classes were there to toil, and the aristocracy was there to reap the benefits. This way of life was to be jealously guarded, and the traditions of the past were to be preserved at all cost. Those who argued for change were the enemy. It was this attitude, coupled with economic friction, that helped lead to the Civil War.

Yet for all its closed-mindedness and social injustice, this period produced much that was glamorous and romantic. Many of the tales and beautiful homes that so enthrall us today had their roots in the planter society. Indeed, you cannot understand Charleston if you do not appreciate the vague but ever-present sorrow that permeates the city, a sorrow for that gracious way of life that is lost forever.

In the final pages of his book, Rogers records a young woman's description of her travels back to her native Charleston following the War Between the States. This touching passage can perhaps do more than any other to put the reader in touch with that very special bittersweet quality that will forever be the heart of Charleston: " 'Scarcely a farm house, not an elegant and hospitable plantation residence on the way, all ruin, ruin . . . I journeyed with a coffin where was laid my love and earthly hope, and came home.' " What she saw was a city devastated, her home plundered of all books, private papers, pictures, her church's cemetery filled with the debris and overgrowth of four years of war and neglect. Yet many flowers bloomed amid the ruins. And so she sighed: 'I could not help thinking yesterday, as I saw the flowers look up and smile, when the superincumbent weight and decay and ruin were removed, that they set us a good example politically. But then, flowers have no memory.' "

Charleston History In 1663, all of what was to become North and South Carolina was granted by King Charles II to eight "Lords Proprietors." These eight men were friends of the king who had helped him regain power following the death of Oliver Cromwell. Though in later times the colony was to come under Royal authority, the early years, for good or ill, were presided over by the Lords Proprietors.

In 1669, three ships set sail from England to found a colony in the new land of Carolina. The expedition made landfall at Port Royal Sound, but on the advice of the cacique of Kiawah, the expedition removed to the banks of Ashley

Interior of French Huguenot Church

River to the north. Here, on the shores of Town Creek, they founded Charles Towne, named by the colonists in honor of their king.

Around 1680, the small settlement was removed to Oyster Point, located on the neck of land separating the Ashley and Cooper Rivers. The site was deemed to be (and still is) ideally situated for waterborne commerce. Plans were carefully laid out for streets and lots before the move took place, making Charles Towne the first planned community in America.

In 1680, the young colony got a boost from the arrival of a number of French Huguenots. Fleeing religious persecution in their homeland, these first immigrants presaged many others who would brave the wave-tossed Atlantic to take advantage of South Carolina's religious tolerance. Eventually, the colony was influenced by Dutch and German immigrants as well, though the French influence was certainly the strongest of the lot. This melting-pot atmosphere is often credited for Charleston's resiliency and worldliness.

A strong Spanish-French fleet threatened the small colony in 1698, but the intruders were soundly defeated both by land and by sea. This event was typical of the courage and bravado that Charlestonians have always exemplified in times of military threat.

By 1730, Charles Towne had become an important, bustling port. Tragically, in 1740, the town was the victim of a great fire that burned many houses. Over the course of its history, Charleston has suffered many major fires, several violent hurricanes, and even a strong earthquake. As George C. Rogers, Jr., so aptly commented, "It is a wonder that Charleston still looks like an eighteenth-century city."

As the Revolution approached, Charles Towne took a decidedly patriot point of view. The news of the Battles of Lexington and Concord was greeted by a parade of South Carolina militia as well as a resolve by the assembly to raise three regiments and prepare the colony for war. Charlestonians did not have long to wait. In the battle described in the previous chapter, the British were soundly repulsed at Fort Moultrie. The English returned, however, in 1780, and after a brief siege captured the city. The fall of Charleston and the loss of New York were to rank as the worst American defeats of the war. The main English army was defeated by Washington at Yorktown in 1781, but it was not until December 1782 that Charleston was evacuated by the British, thus effectively bringing the war to an end.

Following the close of the war, the Charles Towne council changed the name of the city to Charleston. It seems that the local citizens no longer relished the idea of their fair town bearing the name of an English sovereign.

The years between the Revolution and the Civil War were mostly prosperous. Both the developing rice culture to the north and the rise of Sea Island cotton to the south aided Charleston's economy. Vast quantities of goods left the city's wharves bound for European and Northern ports. Rich planters built many residences in the city. It was quite fashionable to have a "city house" in addition to one's plantation. During this period, many of the small creeks and ponds on the Charleston peninsula were filled in to make room for further development. Several modern-day streets are located atop the one-time passage of these small streams.

The South Carolina economy continued to be highly agricultural, as did that of most of the Southern states. When the economic interests of the agrarian South conflicted with those of the industrialized North, confrontation became inevitable. In a fight with the federal government over tariff laws, South Carolina's great statesman, John C. Calhoun, argued for the doctrine of Nullification, an affirmation of a state's right to reject federal laws with which it could not agree.

Finally, of course, this war of words turned into a military conflict that began within sight of Charleston. The story of Fort Sumter will be told later in this chapter; for now, it is sufficient to note that the Civil War's first major conflict occurred between South Carolina forces at Fort Johnson on James Island and Federal troops occupying Fort Sumter.

Though Beaufort, to the south, fell to Northern forces early in the war, it was not until February 1865 that Union troops occupied Charleston, and then only after the Confederate army evacuated the city. South Carolina Confederates fought valiantly throughout the war, time and again denying the passages to Charleston to vastly superior Union forces.

Though Charleston suffered some damage from bombardment, it was not grievously decimated by the war, as were many other South Carolina cities. There has been much speculation about why Sherman, the usually cold-blooded Union commander, did not put the torch to Charleston as he did to other proud cities. He had visited Charleston before the war and admired the community, and some claim that he spared the city simply because he liked it. Others argue that he had promised friends in the North that he would preserve the town. Another theory claims that he did not act because the war was nearly over when Charleston's turn came. Whatever the reason,

Sidewalk art show, Charleston

Charleston survived the war better than any other major city in South Carolina.

The years following the Civil War were hard ones for Charleston. It was not until World War II that Charleston began to prosper again. This long depression proved to be a hidden boon for the city. While other communities were busy tearing down their historic buildings and widening their streets, Charleston was forced by lack of capital to make do with what it had. In the 1950s and 1960s, Charlestonians awoke to the unique opportunity afforded by a city that still retained its historic character. Renovation projects began on a wide scale, and they continue to this day. While some areas are still not fully renovated, vast sections of the historical district have been restored to their former glory. How fortunate we are that times were too hard in Charleston for "modern improvements" following the War Between the States!

Many visitors to Charleston will want to read more detailed accounts of the city's fascinating history. Inspiring tales and colorful figures enliven the story of Charleston. Several very readable accounts of the city's heritage are readily available. This writer's personal favorite is *A Short History of Charleston*, by Robert Rosen.

As you tour Charleston, pause often to reflect on the history of this great city. There are few places in America that can lay claim to such a treasure trove of tradition and heritage. Listen carefully and perhaps you can still hear faint music from the old Dock Street Theatre, or the powerful voice of John C. Calhoun arguing forcibly for states' rights. For those who seek knowledge, Charleston never fails in her reward.

Charleston Attractions

Charleston boasts a wide array of attractions waiting to fascinate cruising visitors. Some of this writer's favorites will be reviewed in the following pages. For a more complete listing of the city's many sights, however, you will need to purchase one of the Charleston guidebooks. My favorite is actually a monthly magazine known as *Gateway to Charleston*. This excellent publication helps the visitor sort out the city's bewildering selection of tourist attractions.

First-time visitors should begin their tour at the Charleston Visitor Center (803-724-7474), located at 375 Meeting Street. There, you will see a remarkable multiscreen slide show. The presentation not only helps put you in touch with the spirit of Charleston but also serves as an excellent introduction to the city's sights and attractions. The center is too far away from the city marinas for walking. You will need a rental car or a taxi for a visit.

The Old Market is definitely one of Charleston's premier attractions. It is enclosed by North and South Market Streets and, to the west and east, Meeting and East Bay Streets. You will often hear the area referred to as the "old slave market," which is a misnomer, as slaves were never sold here. The land was given to the city by the Pinckney family with the stipulation that it must always be used as a marketplace. In earlier days, the market served as a giant farmers' fair. Over the years, it has evolved into a huge craft show, though fresh vegetables can still be bought in season. The visitor who strolls through the Old Market on any day, but particularly on a Saturday, will find a wide array of handicrafts ranging from traditional dolls to baskets. The

A Portion of Historic Charleston

1. Visitor Information Center
2. The Old Market
3. St. Philip's Episcopal Church
4. St. Michael's Church
5. The Nathaniel Russell House
6. Calhoun Mansion
7. Heyward–Washington House (1730)
8. Edmonston–Alston House
9. White Point Gardens
10. The Battery Carriage House
11. Two Meeting Street Inn

black women of the city weave the baskets from native sweet grass. Their art has been passed down through the generations, reaching far back into the slave era.

A large collection of gift shops and restaurants is found around the Old Market. Here, you can dine at some of the city's finest eateries or select from many gifts and handicrafts. The market is certainly one of the best spots for shopping and dining in the city.

Several horse-drawn carriage lines depart regularly from the Old Market for tours of the city's historical district. This writer highly recommends these interesting excursions. The witty and knowledgeable tour guides provide thorough, often humorous insight into Charleston's past. Be sure to ask why ladies shouldn't wear red shoes during the evening when strolling south of Broad Street.

St. Philip's Episcopal Church lays claim to the oldest congregation in the city. The present church stands near the intersection of Church and Queen Streets. The first building on the site was occupied sometime between 1710 and 1724. This structure burned and was replaced by the present building in 1835. The tall, gray stone steeple is a striking sight at night, when it is lit with soft lights. The old sentinel seems to be a warm friend overlooking the city.

St. Philip's Cemetery is bisected by Church Street. According to tradition, only native-born Charlestonians can be buried in the section adjacent to the church. Those born elsewhere, no matter how famous, are interred across the street. John C. Calhoun, perhaps South Carolina's greatest statesman, was laid to rest at St. Philip's in 1850. Though he was universally beloved in Charleston, Calhoun was born in Columbia. Thus, he was buried in the western portion of the cemetery. As the Civil War entered its last dark days, patriotic citizens feared the desecration of Calhoun's grave by Union troops. One night, they stealthily moved his coffin to an unmarked grave next to the church. Some years later, Calhoun's remains were returned to their original resting place, where his gravestone may still be seen today. This writer and his mate heard one tour guide comment that not only was John C. Calhoun the state's greatest political figure in life, he was one of the most traveled in death.

St. Michael's Episcopal Church is located at the corner of Broad and Meeting Streets. It was built on the original site of St. Philip's in 1751,

St. Philip's Episcopal Church

when for reasons now lost in the mists of the past the congregation split into two church bodies. St. Michael's is a beautiful white building with a tall, stately spire and mellow bells that toll the time of day.

Before the Civil War, Charleston was plagued by fires. The inefficient means used to fight the frequent blazes greatly contributed to the problem. Until well after the war, there were a dozen or more private firefighting companies in the city. If you wished to be protected, it was necessary to purchase a badge from one of the companies and affix it to your building or home. During the night, a constant fire watch was kept from the steeple of St. Michael's. If flames were sighted, the alarm was given, and all the companies turned out. They were guided to the blaze by lanterns swinging from the steeple. When they at last arrived, the company whose badge was in evidence fought the fire while everyone else went home.

Located at 21 East Battery Street, the Edmondston-Alston House is one of the few homes in the city open to the public. This proud structure is perhaps the best example of an affluent planter's Charleston home. Dating from 1835, it was acquired soon after it was built by one of the illustrious Alstons, a family of wealthy Waccamaw rice planters. Guided tours of this striking house are conducted throughout the day by the Historic Charleston Foundation. Be sure to visit the second-floor balcony and take in the magnificent view of the harbor. Those lucky enough to catch a sea breeze will begin to appreciate what a wonderful experience it was (and still is) to live on the Charleston Battery.

The extreme southern tip of the Charleston peninsula is known as the High Battery. In Charleston's early years, a little-frequented saltwater marsh was located at the point. Beginning in 1737, the first in a series of forts and batteries was constructed there. These military fortifications were built and rebuilt throughout the city's conflicts until the end of the Civil War. The

Carriage tour passing in front of Edmondston-Alston House

View from balcony of Edmondston-Alston House

area's name is derived from the one-time presence of the batteries.

In 1820, a stone seawall was completed along the point's shoreline. The new wall replaced several earlier brick structures, which had been decimated by a series of strong hurricanes. Extensive repairs were necessary following a severe storm in 1893, but otherwise the wall has lasted to the present day.

In 1837, a park now known as White Point Gardens was established between South Battery Street and the point. It was to this vantage point that many Charlestonians flocked in 1861 to watch the fateful battle for Fort Sumter. Since that time, the park has never again been put to military use. It is now the site of numerous war memorials.

After the Battery was walled, some of the state's most affluent citizens began building large mansions just north of the park. This location was highly prized for the cooling sea breezes that blew across the harbor. Over the years, some of the most beautiful homes in the city were built here. Most have been in the same family for many generations and are in excellent condition. Stroll along South Battery Street at your leisure and admire these graceful, luxurious old homes.

The park itself contains an old bandstand where open-air concerts are still held from time to time. There is an excellent view of the harbor from the shade of the grounds. Truly, the visitor who has not seen the High Battery and White Point Gardens has not really seen Charleston.

Charleston Walking Tour

One of the best ways to see the Charleston historical district is by foot. This writer advises first taking one of the carriage tours described earlier to get your bearings. Once you are oriented, however, feel free to strike out on your own. There are many, many possible walking tours. This writer's favorite route is detailed below.

Begin your tour at the Old Market. Walk south on Church Street. You will soon encounter St. Philip's Episcopal Church and its interesting cemetery. Continue along Church as far as Broad Street. In Charleston's early years, many lawyers, doctors, and other professionals kept their offices on Broad.

Turn right on Broad and walk to Meeting Street. Here, you can stop to admire the cool, white serenity of St. Michael's Episcopal Church. Then turn left on Meeting and continue for several blocks. The Nathaniel Russell House and the Calhoun Mansion, both open to the public, are found along this section of Meeting Street.

Retrace your steps toward St. Michael's and turn right on Tradd Street. This street was named for the first male child born in the Charles Towne colony and is lined by some of the oldest surviving homes in the city.

Turn left where Tradd intersects Church Street. Here, you can visit the Heyward-Washington House. Built in 1730, the old edifice was the home of Thomas Heyward, a signer of the Declaration of Independence. George Washington was entertained here during his tour of the Southern states following the Revolution. Note the twin circular entrance staircases at the Heyward-Washington House. They are known as "welcoming-arms stairs." Tradition claims that the genteel ladies of the Old South would ascend one side while their gentleman companions climbed the other. That way, the ladies' ankles would not be on public display.

Go back to Tradd Street and continue east to East Bay Street. Turn right and you will soon approach the Battery. The Edmondston-Alston House is to the right. Pause in your tour for a few moments to stroll along the parapet of the Battery seawall. There is usually an excellent view of the harbor and Castle Pinckney. On a clear day, you can also see Fort Sumter.

Continue your tour by turning right up South Battery Street. Here, you can see many of the magnificent mansions mentioned earlier. There are also two inns along this street. Both the Battery Carriage House (803-727-3100) and Two Meeting Street Inn (803-723-7322) are located in historic homes and afford an unforgettable experience for those fortunate enough to lodge there a night or two.

Turn right on Meeting Street and retrace your steps to the Old Market. You have now seen some of Charleston's history and are just in time for a cold drink at one of the Old Market's many restaurants.

Charleston Restaurants

Charleston boasts a multitude of fine restaurants with a wide array of cuisine. In fact, with the possible exception of New Orleans, this writer has never discovered a city that can boast so many fine and varied dining attractions. Everything from the most sophisticated continental offerings to fried and broiled seafood is readily available. It would take weeks to sample all of Charleston's gastronomical delights. The wonderful guidebook *Dining Out in Charleston* lists dozens of restaurants well worthy of visitors' attention. This publication is highly recommended for first-time visitors. As only a few of this writer's favorite establishments can be mentioned here, you are encouraged to experiment. Charleston is one of those magical places where every corner can lead the visitor to an obscure little eatery just waiting for someone to discover its charms.

Eighty-two Queen (803-723-7591) is a restaurant named for its address. If one were to attempt to compile a list of Charleston's best restaurants (a foolhardy venture), this unique dining spot would certainly be somewhere near the top of the list. Consistently voted the favorite and most romantic restaurant by Charlestonians, 82 Queen should be on every visitor's list of must-experience places. Veal, chicken, beef, and the freshest of seafood are all prepared in inimitable fashion by the master chefs of 82 Queen.

One secret of the establishment's popularity is its lovely decor. The restaurant is laid out in a series of glass-enclosed buildings overlooking a central garden. In nice weather, the outdoor tables are at a premium. Eighty-two Queen is a very popular spot among both locals and tourists. Reservations are almost mandatory. For weekend meals, it is often necessary to call several days in advance to secure your desired seating time.

For one of the best dining experiences in this city of unforgettable culinary delights, consider a visit to Carolina's (10 Exchange Street, 803-724-3800). The food here could be accurately described as upscale continental cuisine. The atmosphere is relaxed, and this writer has always found the food to be in keeping with Charleston's tradition of fine dining.

After a while, cruising travelers may just want

a break from the seafood regimen. No matter how fresh or tasty the fish, the palate can begin to crave a change of pace. If this description fits, Garibaldi's (49 South Market Street, 803-723-7153), flanking the southern side of the Old Market, is for you. This writer and his mate have been privileged to partake of some of the finest Italian cuisine available in America and never have we found any better than the succulent offerings at Garibaldi's. The various veal dishes are particularly noteworthy, but the fresh seafood and beef preparations are equally striking. Make your reservations well ahead of time and groom your palate for a real treat.

During this writer's second carriage tour of Charleston, the tour guide made the unusual observation that Charleston chefs are surely bound for heaven. When queried about this bold claim, the tour guide responded that once the Almighty got a taste of Charleston cooking, nothing else would do. After enjoying the city's restaurants, you may not find this statement very difficult to believe.

CHARLESTON HARBOR

Charleston Harbor often reminds this writer of author Mike Greenwald's description of the Mediterranean. It is like "the girl with green eyes. There is often a surprise behind her smile." Indeed, on a day of moderate breezes, if the current is contrary, the harbor can still bear a wicked chop. On the other hand, the sightseeing opportunities are many and varied. Charleston Harbor boasts several historic sites of great interest. It is a true thrill to see Fort Sumter and the aircraft carrier *Yorktown* from the water. The cruising boater has the opportunity to view these monuments from a perspective that is denied the landlubber.

Be sure to study the latest edition of chart 11524 carefully before attempting entry of the harbor, and have this cartographical aid close at hand while cruising. The harbor is crisscrossed by a bewildering maze of buoys and other aids marking a variety of channels. These varied markers and channels can be very confusing to boaters not familiar with the harbor. Nighttime passage is particularly wrought with peril.

To make matters worse, Charleston Harbor has extensive shoals. While all of these are well marked, you must be readily able to interpret the buoys if you are to stay off the bottom. To say the least, cruising boaters must take navigation seriously on these waters, or a very unpleasant grounding could be the result.

There are practically no facilities for the pleasure boater on the harbor itself. Shem Creek, in the extreme northeasterly corner of the water body, offers a few restaurant docks. Otherwise, you are on your own while cruising Charleston Harbor.

Similarly, there are no opportunities for protected anchorage in Charleston Harbor. If you choose not to proceed on to the city marinas, select an anchorage to the north along the ICW and enter the harbor the next morning.

Unlike the off-the-beaten-path spots discussed earlier, Charleston Harbor hosts many pleasure boaters. You are likely to find yourself among numerous fellow pleasure craft on your cruise. Join them in an unforgettable cruising experience.

Charleston Inlet

Charleston Inlet is the most reliable seaward cut on the entire South Carolina coast. It is deep and very well marked. In fact, it's lit at night like the proverbial Christmas tree. The channel has served the port of Charleston reliably since its earliest years. Today, many large freighters and tankers use the inlet on a regular basis. If you plan to put to sea anywhere along this section of the coastline, Charleston Inlet is your best bet.

Shem Creek

Shem Creek is located in the extreme northeasterly corner of Charleston Harbor north of charted Crab Bank and the town of Mount Pleasant. It is a lovely stream with many interesting sights and several dining opportunities.

The Mount Pleasant Channel leads generally northwest from the ICW's flashing daybeacon #130 to the mouth of Shem Creek. This cut was dredged in 1993 and currently holds minimum 6-foot depths. Typical soundings range from 7 to 10 feet in the channel. This track is subject to shoaling, and skippers whose craft draw more than 5 feet might want to enter and leave on a rising tide.

Careful navigation must be practiced when running the Shem Creek approach channel. On the creek itself, depths are a more respectable 8 to 12 feet. Upstream passage is eventually blocked by a low-level fixed bridge.

Once on the stream's interior reaches, you will be delighted with the many picturesque shrimp trawlers docked along the banks. A large number of Charleston's commercial fishermen make their homes on Shem Creek. Have your camera ready for some shots with true Low Country flavor.

Shem Creek is the home of several waterside seafood restaurants, some with their own docks. Reagan's Cafe and Bar (803-881-8671) and Ronnie's Seafood Restaurant (803-884-4074) are both located on the stream's northwestern banks. This writer highly suggests that all cruisers set their sights on the docks of RB's Restaurant (803-881-0466), which guard the creek's southeastern shoreline . While RB's piers are not extensive, there should be room for two 30-footers to squeeze in together. Low-water depths alongside run 5 to 6 feet. RB's has a widespread reputation for serving the finest in fresh seafood. It is a warm, informal, and convivial establishment with a nautical bar where you can wait for your table on crowded evenings. Consider the crab spread for an appetizer. This writer also recommends the jumbo shrimp stuffed with crabmeat as an entree. All in all, a visit to RB's is sure to be remembered as a gastronomical delight.

A bit farther upstream, The Trawler restaurant (803-884-2560) also overlooks the south-

Dining dockside at RB's Restaurant, Shem Creek

eastern banks. This dining establishment has been serving fine seafood for many a year. Its longevity speaks well of its quality cuisine.

While many tourists have come to know and love the Shem Creek restaurants, the stream seems to be consistently overlooked by visiting cruisers. This writer highly recommends that the reader take advantage of this tasty body of water.

Mount Pleasant

Cruisers following the channel to Shem Creek will spy many beautiful homes on the northeastern shore. These lovely showplaces are part of the old community of Mount Pleasant. Originally, the village consisted of five separate communities that were established in the 1700s. Two were built around ferries that provided passage across Shem Creek, while another sprang up around a water-powered rice mill/lumbermill. Following the Revolution, all these separate settlements were combined into the single community of Mount Pleasant.

Fort Moultrie

The previous chapter told the story of the courageous battle at Fort Moultrie during the opening months of the Revolution. There used to be an excellent view of that old fort from Charleston Harbor northwest of unlighted nun buoy #2. Unfortunately, some concrete riprap, obviously placed to slow beach erosion, has impeded the view for those looking from the low vantage point of a sailcraft cockpit. Power cruisers piloting from a fly bridge will not have this problem.

Home at Mount Pleasant

You will catch sight of the walls just northeast of nun buoy #2 on the western banks of Sullivan's Island. It is possible to cruise within some 75 yards of shore and still hold 7-foot depths. Feel your way in carefully and be on guard against the correctly charted shoal to the east of #2.

Fort Moultrie was much altered during the Civil War, and today's visitors gaze on masonry walls rather than the palmetto logs that stood so bravely against British fire.

Fort Sumter

To the west-southwest of flashing buoy #25, Fort Sumter, one of Charleston Harbor's great historical sites, is readily visible.

In 1829, the federal government began to stabilize the shoal west of Fort Moultrie. Here, it constructed Fort Sumter, which was named after Revolutionary War general Thomas Sumter. In 1860, although the work on Fort Sumter was not yet complete, a small Union garrison of less than 100 men at Fort Moultrie was transferred to Sumter by command of Major Robert Anderson. Feeling that conflict with Southern forces was inevitable, Anderson believed the newer fort was more defensible.

As the garrison left Fort Moultrie, it spiked the cannons. South Carolina governor Andrew

Fort Sumter, Charleston Harbor

Pickens considered this a hostile act. State troops were mobilized, and shoreside batteries were quickly constructed bearing upon Sumter. Following a failed conference in Washington, D.C., General Pierre G. T. Beauregard, commanding the South Carolina forces, called upon Anderson to surrender. He refused, and a 30-hour assault on Sumter began on April 12, 1861. Eventually, Anderson was forced to surrender, and the first battle of the Civil War was over.

Fort Sumter was quickly manned by the Confederates. From 1863 to 1865, the fort was under almost constant Union bombardment. In 1863, a Union amphibious assault was beaten off, with heavy Northern losses. The South Carolina Sea Grant Consortium notes that the fierce resistance of Fort Sumter became a "symbol of courage for the South." The fort was finally abandoned in 1865, when Federal troops occupied the area from the rear.

Today, cruising visitors can easily view this monument, which has been lovingly preserved as a memorial to the brave men who fought so long against such overwhelming odds. While the inner fortifications have been carefully restored, the outer walls are mostly original. Cruise to flashing buoy #25 and work your way slowly to the southwest. Be on guard against the shallow water to the west and southeast. There is a small floating dock on the northeastern corner of the fort where pleasure craft are welcome to tie. Depths run 8 to 10 feet at low tide. Tour boats also leave The City Marina on a regular basis. These are well worth your time.

Fort Johnson

Prior to the construction of Fort Sumter, Fort Johnson, located on the northern shore of James Island, was a strategically important site in the defense of Charleston Harbor. Today, a group of modern buildings some 1 nautical mile west (and south) of flashing buoy #26 marks the spot where the fort once stood.

Fortifications were first constructed here during Queen Anne's War. A brick powder magazine was built in 1766; it still survives. In 1775, South Carolina patriot forces seized the fort and feverishly began to prepare its defenses for the assault that eventually fell on Fort Moultrie.

The fort was refurbished during the War of 1812 but was decimated by a severe hurricane in 1813. In 1861, batteries at Fort Johnson fired on Fort Sumter. Fort Johnson was finally abandoned in 1865, when Federal troops occupied Charleston and the harbor.

It is a strange twist of fate that an area that has seen so much hostility is today being put to such

Fort Johnson, Charleston Harbor

important peaceful use. Housed in the buildings that now occupy the site are many agencies engaged in maritime and marine research studies. Located at Fort Johnson are offices and laboratories of the College of Charleston, the National Marine Fisheries Service, the United States Fish and Wildlife Service, the South Carolina Wildlife and Marine Resources Department, the Medical University of South Carolina, and this writer's good friends at the South Carolina Sea Grant Consortium. There is no provision for pleasure-craft dockage at the center. However, if you can obtain the use of a rental car, a visit is well worth your while.

Morris Island Lighthouse

Look to the southeast from Fort Johnson and you will spy the Morris Island Lighthouse. The island has been used to light the harbor entrance since 1673. In 1767, a 102-foot brick tower, one of the first in the country, was built near the present lighthouse site. This light was severely damaged by the fierce fighting that took place on Morris Island around Fort Wagner during the Civil War. It was replaced in 1876 by the present tower. With the construction of the Sullivan's Island Lighthouse in 1962, the Morris Island Lighthouse fell into disuse. Since that time, it has been used as an unlighted daymark.

Marshlands Plantation

Marshlands Plantation can be seen through the trees just west of the Fort Johnson complex. Built in 1810 by John Ball, the elegant house was originally located on the shores of Cooper River. When that land was acquired by the United States Navy, the old home was moved by barge to its present location in 1961.

Castle Pinckney, Charleston Harbor

Castle Pinckney

Castle Pinckney is located on the southern tip of Shutes Folly Island well north of flashing buoy #32. This small fort served as an inner defense for Charleston Harbor, but as far as this writer has been able to determine, it never fired a shot in anger. Built in 1798, it was renovated in 1800 and again in 1808. The small fortification was named in honor of Charles Cotesworth Pinckney, one of South Carolina's greatest statesmen.

After the seizure of Fort Sumter, the Union troops taken prisoner were transferred to Castle Pinckney, where they were imprisoned until the end of the war. High tides forced the miserable prisoners to stand in water up to their waists.

Surprisingly, Shutes Folly Island was planted

Marshlands Plantation, Charleston Harbor

in orange trees during the early 1700s. Over the years, erosion has taken a heavy toll on the small island, and there is no evidence left of the once-luscious orchards.

Patriots Point

East of flashing buoy #10 at the southern foot of Cooper River, Patriots Point boasts the "Largest Maritime Museum in the World." The huge exhibit includes the aircraft carrier *Yorktown* and the *Savannah*, the world's first nuclear-powered merchant ship. Several other naval vessels are also exhibited, including the *Clamagore*, one of the last oil-powered submarines in the United States Navy. Surprisingly, an 18-hole golf course is also part of the complex.

Currently, it is best to view the exhibit from the main channel of Hog Island Reach. While charts 11524 and 11518 show an unmarked channel leading in to the ships, it is too treacherous for visiting cruisers.

The *Yorktown* is the most visible of the ships. It sits broadside to the channel. The large white ship docked perpendicular to the river is the *Savannah*. You will need a rental car or a taxi for a tour of the facility by land. If you have the time, this is an attraction that should not be missed.

CHARLESTON HARBOR NAVIGATION

Successful navigation of Charleston Harbor for nonresident boaters is a far more exacting process than one might expect. To be sure, there are many deep, well-marked channels that are used on a regular basis by large commercial and naval craft. However, the multiplicity of channels and markers can readily lead to confusion. Charleston Harbor is also cursed with many shoals that can bring the unwary boater to grief. This writer has talked with a professional captain who entered Charleston Harbor at night from Sullivan's Island and became immediately confused by the many lights. Even though he slowed to idle speed, a hard grounding was the eventual result of his consternation.

Nighttime entry into Charleston Harbor is strictly not recommended for nonresident boaters. Even in daylight, have charts 11524 and/or 11518 at hand and keep a wary eye on the sounder. If you take your time and actively practice good navigation, a cruise of Charleston Harbor can be one of the most pleasurable experiences offered by South Carolina waters. Failure to take the proper precautions, however, can result in an afternoon spent contemplating the value of good navigation while hard aground on one of the harbor's shoals.

Entry from Sullivan's Island All boaters entering Charleston Harbor via the ICW passage at Sullivan's Island should come abeam of flashing daybeacon #127 to its northeasterly side. Continue on the same course for a short distance until reaching a point just before coming abeam of the charted forward range marker to the east-northeast. At this point, the channel swings sharply to the west-southwest and sweeps out into Charleston Harbor. Once abeam of the forward range marker, immediately cut to the west-southwest and set course to come abeam of flashing daybeacon #130 to its southerly quarter. The great body of the harbor now lies directly before your bow. At #130, the Mount Pleasant Channel splits off to the north and leads to Shem Creek.

Mount Pleasant–Shem Creek Channel The Mount Pleasant–Shem Creek Channel is wide and well marked, but it is flanked by shoal water on both sides. To enter the cut, continue past flashing daybeacon #130 for some 100 yards, then swing 90 degrees to the north and point to pass between unlighted daybeacons #1 and #2. You will most likely find the shallowest stretch of the channel as your pass between #1 and #2. Low-water soundings can drop to 6 feet.

Continue to the north by passing between unlighted daybeacons #3 and #4. You should next point to come abeam of and pass unlighted daybeacon #6 and flashing daybeacon #8 by some 25 yards or so to their westerly sides.

At #8, the channel begins to bend to the west. Pass unlighted daybeacons #10, #12, and #14 to their southerly sides. Set a course to come abeam of flashing daybeacon #16 to its southerly side as well. Continue on course for some 10 to 15 yards and then turn 90 degrees to starboard to enter the main body of the creek. Watch for the docks of RB's Restaurant along the southeasterly banks.

Into the Harbor From flashing daybeacon #130, boaters wishing to follow the ICW or enter Cooper River should set a compass course to the mid-width of the Rebellion Reach Channel, well southeast of flashing buoys #1 and #2. Be mindful of the shallows to the north around Crab Bank.

At Rebellion Reach Channel, cruisers have several choices. A swing to the northwest leads to the wide Cooper and Wando Rivers. A turn to the southwest carries the boater to Ashley River, the Charleston marinas, and the ICW route. Charleston Inlet beckons to the southeast.

Entrance to Cooper River To cruise northwest into Cooper River, follow the well-marked Rebellion Reach, Folly Reach, Shutes Reach, and Horse Reach Channels. Be careful to avoid the considerable patch of shoal water that surrounds Shutes Folly Island to the southwest of the Shutes Reach Channel.

Charleston Inlet To enter the reliable Charleston Inlet, turn southeast on Rebellion Reach Channel and follow the well-marked Mount Pleasant and Fort Sumter ranges to the open sea. Be on guard against the twin jetties flanking the inlet to the northeast and southwest past the tips of Sullivan's and Morris Islands.

There is a shortcut channel that breaks off to the south at flashing buoy #19. The cut runs through a break in the southern jetty marked by unlighted can buoy #1 and unlighted nun buoy #2. The channel skirts several unmarked shallows and borders some breakers. This passage is not recommended for boaters without local knowledge.

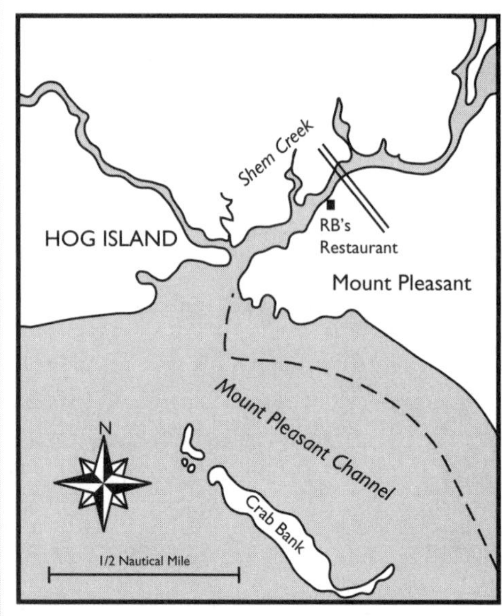

Ashley River and the ICW To enter Ashley River and follow the ICW route, set course from Rebellion Reach Channel to come abeam of flashing buoy #26 to its southeasterly side. At #26, the Waterway channel turns almost due west and begins to make its way past the tip of the Charleston peninsula. Point to eventually come abeam of flashing buoy #32 by some 300 yards on its southerly quarter. It is a rather lengthy run of some 1.6 nautical miles between #26 and #32. The charted South Channel range may help you keep to the channel along this stretch. Watch to the south when cruising between #26 and #32 for a view of the Fort Johnson complex.

At #32, boaters can choose to follow the confusing channel west of Shutes Folly Island into Cooper River. If you do make the attempt, avoid the large charted shoal making southeast off the Charleston Battery, and stay away from Shutes Folly Island.

Most boaters continue by way of the ICW route to Ashley River by pointing to come abeam of flashing junction buoy #BP to its southerly side. From #BP, the channel sweeps northwest and enters the mouth of Ashley River.

Boaters following the Waterway should set course to eventually come abeam of unlighted nun buoy #2 to its southwesterly side. Be on guard against the considerable body of shallow water building southeast from the Charleston Battery while cruising this portion of the Waterway channel. You will have a good view of the magnificent houses along the Battery while cruising between #BP and #2.

Shrimp trawlers on Shem Creek

Unlighted nun buoy #2 heralds your entrance into Ashley River. Upstream from this aid to navigation, good water runs in a broad band along the northern and northeastern banks to the Wappoo Creek cutoff.

For best depths, pass flashing daybeacon #3 by some 50 yards or more to its northeasterly side. Adjust course slightly to the northwest and point to come abeam of unlighted nun buoy #4 by some 20 yards to its southwesterly side.

Abeam of #4, the main body of Ashley River will be obvious to the northwest, while The City Marina lies along the northeasterly banks. You will have to be just about blind to miss the 55-foot fixed high-rise bridge barring further upstream passage on the Ashley. Those who can clear this span will find Ashley Marina flanking the northeasterly shoreline, with Ripley Light Marina lying to the southwest.

At unlighted nun buoy #4, the ICW cuts sharply west-southwest and soon enters the mouth of Wappoo Creek. Cruisers continuing directly south on the Waterway should point to come abeam of and pass the unnumbered, quick-flashing, red, 20-foot forward range marker denoting Wappoo Creek's entrance well to its southeasterly quarter. Continue on the same course, passing unlighted daybeacons #1 and #3 to their northwesterly quarters. Continued navigation of the ICW is presented in the next chapter.

COOPER RIVER

Cooper River offers Charleston's greatest variety of cruising opportunities. Everything from modern naval shipyards to historical buildings and industrial complexes is waiting to greet the Cooper River cruiser. The river also borders acres of abandoned rice fields along its upper reaches and affords another glimpse at the remnants of that old culture. If you have only enough time to cruise one of Charleston's rivers, the Cooper should be your choice.

For the most part, the Cooper is a navigational delight. The river is well marked as far inland as Bushy Park. Upstream, there are a few shoals to avoid, but careful attention to chart 11527 should see you through. The stream divides into two branches about a mile above the Dean Hall industrial site. This area, known as "the Tee," can lead the adventurous boater to some obscure, unspoiled cruising finds. Many abandoned rice fields border the channel in this section, but it is far easier to pick out the correct passage than a cursory examination of chart 11527 would lead you to believe.

The Cooper's shoreline offers widely varied sightseeing. Completely undeveloped areas alternate with the wharves of the now-defunct naval shipyard. Cruising the Cooper is never a dull experience.

Good anchorage can be found on the upper Cooper, but there is almost no opportunity for an overnight stay until you are well upstream from the old U.S. 17 twin bridges.

With the addition of Cooper River Marina, described earlier in this chapter, visiting cruisers will now have the opportunity to spend a night or two on the waters of this impressive stream. Just remember to bring your own supplies.

All in all, Cooper River is an enchanting, readily navigable stream that is consistently overlooked by cruising boaters. This writer suggests that you make it a point to explore this fascinating body of water before pushing on to the south.

Cooper River History Settled early in the history of colonial South Carolina, Cooper River became the second-richest rice-growing region in the state before the Civil War. Only in Georgetown to the north was the growing of "Carolina Gold" a greater enterprise. Sadly, there is little evidence left today of this fabled way of life. Only a few plantations survived the turmoil of the war years, and none of these is visible from the water. Nevertheless, a cruise on the river, particularly on "the Tee," is like journeying back to another era. It does not require too much imagination to see the old tidal flats heavy with rice heads and hear them echoing with the sad singing of the slaves at their sweaty work. Cooper River is part and parcel of the South Carolina Low Country tradition, and its place should not be forgotten.

Twin Entrances

Visiting cruisers have two routes that they might choose when entering the upper reaches of Cooper River. The more straightforward passage is known as Town Creek Reach. The channel skirts the westerly shores of Drum Island and borders extensive commercial wharves.

Alternately, you might choose to follow Hog Island Reach under the huge Cooper River

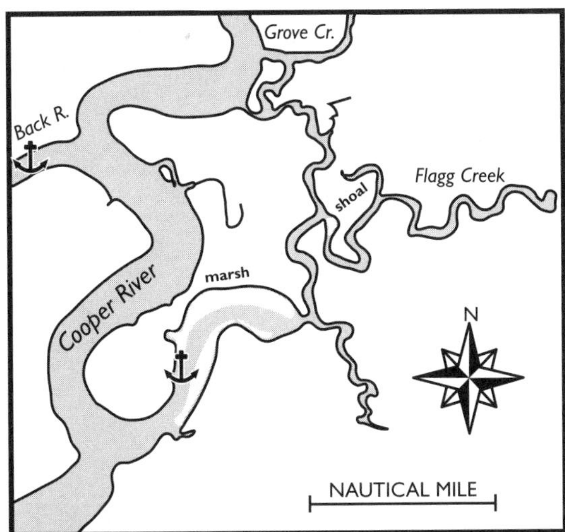

high-rise bridge and then cut northwest on Drum Island Reach to rejoin the main track of Cooper River. The Hog Island Reach portion of this route is used mostly by boaters making for Wando River, but if you are of a mind to avoid the lower Charleston port facilities, this passage is the ticket.

Charleston Shipyard

While cruising up the western entrance to Cooper River on Town Creek Reach, you will pass one of Charleston's major port facilities on the western shore. Here, large freighters can usually be observed loading or unloading their cargo. Watch your wake and you are welcome to make a close inspection.

Shipyard Creek

Shipyard Creek is a deep stream on the Cooper's western shore north of flashing buoy #48. As mentioned repeatedly above, this stream's north-side entrance point plays host to Cooper River Marina, the only pleasure-craft facility on the river. Check out the account of this facility presented earlier in this chapter.

Shipyard Creek is also home to several large wharves and commercial repair facilities. There is no room for anchorage by pleasure craft, but a slow cruise of the stream is highly recommended. The many large commercial ships usually docked there make for a most interesting visit.

Clouter Creek

Clouter Creek is a long, unremarkable stream that makes in to the river's northern shores northeast of flashing buoy #50. It snakes its way north for some 3 nautical miles and then rejoins the Cooper at flashing buoy #66. While this writer used to recommend a cautious cruise of Clouter Creek, new, extensive, unmarked shoaling at the stream's northern and southern entrances has rendered this body of water off-limits to all but small, shallow-draft outboard craft. Low-water entrance depths have now risen to 4 feet or less.

Should you be able to stand these shallow entrance soundings, Clouter Creek does lead to one small-craft facility along its eastern banks north of the charted "dam." Daniel Island Marina (803-884-1000) is primarily concerned with dry-stack storage of small power craft. Some wet-slip dockage is also available for shallow-draft vessels, and gasoline can be purchased.

Freighter passing under Cooper River Bridge

Charleston Naval Base

Big changes have taken place along the Cooper's western and southwestern shores just above Clouter Creek. Where once you would have spied a whole collection of United States Navy vessels, possibly including a nuclear submarine, you will now gaze sadly at empty wharves and docks. As has been so well documented in the news media, the Charleston Naval Base was deactivated some two years ago. Fortunately, some private industries have begun to occupy a portion of the grounds, but there is still a big hole on the river and in the local economy.

The land on which the now-defunct naval base sits was once a part of Belmont Plantation, owned by the illustrious Charles Cotesworth Pinckney, chief justice of South Carolina. Justice Pinckney's wife, the former Eliza Lucas, carried on extensive experimentation with the culture of silk. While her efforts never produced enough of the prized material to be commercially successful, she did manage to weave cloth for two silk dresses, which are now on display in the Charleston Museum.

North Charleston Port Terminal

The North Charleston Port Terminal flanks the Cooper's northwestern shore near flashing daybeacon #58. The wharves are overshadowed by a massive concrete building that is apparently used for grain or phosphate storage. It makes a very impressive sight for the boater cruising up the river.

Patriots Point, Cooper River

Goose Creek

Goose Creek is a surprising stream that breaks off from the northwestern banks of Cooper River northwest of flashing buoy #62. For the first 100 yards or so, the creek is lined with a less-than-eye-pleasing collection of old army barges and tugs. However, farther upstream, past extensive saltwater marsh, the creek runs past some beautiful homes and a golf course. There is swinging room for craft under 30 feet only, as well as fair protection from inclement weather. The entrance and main body maintain 7-foot depths well upstream, though there is one shoal area to avoid.

Yellow House Creek

Yellow House Creek, also known as Slack Reach, enters Cooper River along its southeastern shoreline at flashing buoy #66. The creek holds minimum 8- to 10-foot entrance depths, but there are some unmarked shoals to avoid. Once into the main body, waters deepen to 10- and 20-foot readings and continue well upstream. Large dolphins line the creek for a considerable distance. While no commercial craft were moored here during this writer's research, somebody certainly put the piles there for a purpose.

The stream's southwestern section is wide enough for anchorage by craft less than 36 feet in length. However, the creek's considerable depth calls for a great deal of anchor scope. The shores are mostly undeveloped saltwater marsh, though the starboard banks are a bit higher and do provide some protection in a southern blow.

While not suitable for heavy weather, Yellow House Creek offers one of the best anchorage opportunities on the lower Cooper River. If you draw less than 5 feet, don't hesitate to enter, but be sure to read the Yellow House Creek navigation section presented later in this chapter.

Flagg Creek

Flagg Creek makes off from the Cooper's eastern shore opposite unlighted can buoy #75. Minimum entrance depths run around 8 feet, but there is one shoal area to worry with. The banks are undeveloped marsh and provide only minimal shelter.

Flagg Creek's lower reaches near the river are wide enough to serve as anchorage for craft under 40 feet in length. However, as noted, protection is not adequate for heavy weather.

If you choose to enter, be sure to read the Flagg Creek navigation section presented later in this chapter. Extensive shoals, shown on the latest edition of chart 11527 but still unmarked by any aids to navigation, are waiting to trap the unwary.

Back River

Back River once opened onto the Cooper's western shore near unlighted daybeacon #86. In the 1930s, the stream was dammed in order to provide a ready source of fresh water for the industrial complexes at Cote Bas and Dean Hall. Today, a wide, deep cove cuts in toward the dam. The small bay's shoreline is mostly undeveloped, though it is a bit higher than the norm in this region. Back River holds minimum depths of 9 feet and provides adequate shelter for light- to moderate-air anchorage. It is one of the most readily accessible havens on all of Cooper River.

If you need supplies, a small grocery and tackle shop overlooks the cove's southwestern corner. Ice and snacks can also be purchased here. To visit, anchor within about 50 yards of shore and break out the dinghy.

Grove Creek

Grove Creek is a small stream that cuts into Cooper River's eastern banks north of unlighted daybeacon #87. It eventually leads to Grove Plantation, but no historic buildings are visible from the water. Most of the shores are undeveloped marsh. Minimum depths are 8 feet, and craft under 30 feet in length can anchor on the creek's western reaches, near the river. Protection is not adequate for heavy weather.

Moreland Plantation

Moreland Plantation was once located along the eastern banks of Cooper River in the sharp loop that cuts to the west below Cote Bas. Its former location is noted on chart 11527. Today, the only traces of the plantation are the many bricks and pilings lining the shore.

Cote Bas

The charted Cote Bas industrial complex is readily visible to the west as the Cooper flows through a hairpin turn to the west and then back to the east. The exceptionally large building that can be seen for many miles is a manufacturing facility formerly run by General Dynamics.

Dean Hall Plantation

Old Dean Hall Plantation gazes out over

Cooper River's western shore near privately maintained flashing daybeacon #C. From the water, the plantation is hidden from view by several industrial buildings. It is nevertheless one of the Cooper's greatest attractions. In the early 1900s, Dean Hall's owner, Benjamin R. Kittredge, donated a large portion of his property to the city of Charleston. Here, Kittredge improved upon the magnificent cypress trees growing naturally in the impounded fresh water by planting many flowering shrubs. He named his creation Cypress Gardens, and it soon became one of the great showplaces in coastal South Carolina. Unfortunately, there is no access to the gardens by water. You will need to rent a car in the city to visit Kittredge's magnificent achievement.

East Cooper River

As noted earlier, Cooper River splits into eastern and western arms at "the Tee." The eastern branch provides wonderful cruising ground, anchorage opportunities, and at least one historic site. These waters are seldom frequented by large pleasure craft, and those hardy cruisers who venture this far will be rewarded by the special excitement that comes from exploring where few have gone before. The twin branches are frequented by fishing skiffs, however. This writer observed dozens of hopeful anglers during his research. One might infer from the number and the devotion of its fans that the area produces a plentiful catch of bass and bream.

Minimum depths on the river's mid-width are around 8 feet. However, you must be careful not to mistake the large, abandoned rice fields bordering the stream for the main channel. Because the river is relatively narrow and there is a possibility of becoming entangled in the old flats, neither of the upper Cooper's branches is recommended for craft over 38 feet or those drawing more than 5 feet.

Abandoned rice fields, East Cooper River

While there are no facilities on this arm of the river, the entire region provides enough shelter for all but heavy-weather anchorage. Simply select a likely spot, drop the hook, and settle down for a restful evening.

Most of the river's shoreline is undeveloped, though you will sight a house from time to time. The banks consist mostly of tidal flats, but in other spots the shores rise to heavily timbered woods. Select the wooded areas for best protection when anchoring.

At one point, a Girl Scout camp borders the northern bank. It is built on land once owned by Edward Rutledge, a signer of the Declaration of Independence.

French Quarter Creek

East Cooper River boasts only one sidewater of significant proportions. French Quarter Creek cuts into the river southwest of charted Bonneau Ferry. The creek is named for several French Huguenot families who once lived alongside its length.

While the stream is too small for anchorage by all but small craft, adventurous skippers with craft of 28 feet or less can follow the stream for a considerable distance holding 6-foot minimum depths. The trip offers a chance to observe several old rice fields at close quarters. Again, you must be careful to differentiate the flats from the channel.

Pompion Hill Chapel

Perhaps the East Cooper's greatest attraction is historic Pompion Hill Chapel, which sits on the southern banks near the river's eastern cruising limits for pleasure craft. Its location is clearly charted on 11527.

The small church was built as a "chapel of ease" in 1765, according to the South Carolina Sea Grant Consortium. Locally, the chapel is known as "Punkin Hill." There is a magnificent view of the stately but humble old chapel from the East Cooper. Don't try to land, as the shore is littered with old pilings placed there to slow erosion. If you make it this far, you will be treading waters that have known almost nothing but small fishing skiffs for the last 100 years.

Pompion Hill Chapel, East Cooper River

West Cooper River

The western branch of Cooper River runs far inland to Lake Moultrie. This great lake was created in 1942 by the huge Santee-Cooper Project, which has since generated many a kilowatt. Much of the water that used to flow into Santee River was diverted through this arm of the Cooper by the several dams constructed during the project.

Unfortunately for large pleasure craft, passage on the western branch is soon barred by a railroad bridge. While this span supposedly opens on demand, its hours of operation are erratic. It is a good idea to discontinue your cruise at the bridge anyway. Minimum soundings of 8 feet are held as far as the span, but depths become uncertain thereafter. Small power craft may choose to continue upstream all the way to Lake Moultrie through a series of locks. This is a lengthy cruise that passes beyond the confines of this guide.

Near the beginning of the West Cooper's second sharp turn to the west, you will spy a ruined building on the eastern shore. This old derelict is all that is now visible of Rice Hope Plantation, once the abode of Royal Governor Nathaniel Johnson. The structure was apparently used as a warehouse for goods bound for Charleston.

The upper reaches of Back River enter the West Cooper's southwestern banks at the second sharp turn to the east. While the entrance and the canal that follows hold 6-foot minimum depths, passage is soon blocked by two low-level fixed bridges with only 6 feet of vertical clearance.

Just short of the West Cooper railroad span, the old town of Childsbury watches over the river's northeastern banks. This community was founded by James Childs in 1707 and was once the site of horse races held between gentleman planters.

Quite frankly, the West Cooper is not as appealing as the eastern branch, but it does share that same isolated, unexplored quality. So if you are one of those skippers who has to see it all, don't hesitate to cruise as far as the bridge.

COOPER RIVER NAVIGATION

There are two routes by which the pleasure boater may enter Cooper River. Both are wide, well-marked channels used regularly by large commercial and naval craft.

The more direct passage follows Town Creek Reach between the eastern banks of the Charleston peninsula and the western shores of Drum Island. After paralleling the Charleston shore for about 1 nautical mile, the channel passes the lower Charleston port-facility wharves to the west. The channel then flows quickly under the twin high-rise spans of the U.S. 17 bridge. With the bridge's vertical clearance of 135 feet, even the tallest sailcraft have no cause for concern.

As you cruise upstream from the highway bridge, watch to port for flashing buoy #7. This aid marks a long pier that once served as a coal-exporting facility. Today, the old piles are abandoned and dilapidated.

The second entrance follows Hog Island Reach north from Charleston Harbor. The channel passes between Hog and Drum Islands. Along the way, Patriots Point and the USS *Yorktown* aircraft carrier are passed to the east. Soon, the channel passes under the twin Cooper River fixed spans. Again, minimum vertical clearance is set at an impressive 135 feet. The route then cuts sharply to the northwest and follows Drum Island Reach past the northern tip of Drum Island, rejoining the main Cooper River channel near flashing daybeacon #46A.

From this point, the Cooper remains well marked and easy to follow for many miles upstream. Simply stick to the channel and have charts 11524 and 11527 ready at hand to resolve any questions that might arise.

Shipyard Creek and Cooper River Marina Cruisers bound for Cooper River Marina will spot the breakwater-enclosed harbor just north of Shipyard Creek's easterly mouth. Continue cruising upstream on the Cooper until the harbor's entrance is directly abeam to port. You can then turn into the breakwater's entrance without difficulty.

To enter the interior section of Shipyard Creek, continue cruising on the main Cooper River channel until the stream's mid-width comes abeam to the west. Only then should you turn into the creek. While Shipyard Creek has a broad entrance channel, there is some shallow water to the north and south that is easily avoided by the maneuver outlined above.

Clouter Creek The entrance to Clouter Creek is no longer recommended by this writer for cruising-sized vessels. A quick study of the charted but unmarked shallows shown on 11524 should convince you of the wisdom of this omission.

On Cooper River North of unlighted nun buoy #56A, a large, fixed high-rise bridge spans the

Cooper River. This structure has an impressive vertical clearance of 138 feet.

Yellow House Creek Shoals guard the northeastern and southwestern flanks of the entrance to Yellow House Creek. If you decide to enter, proceed at idle speed. Strike a course to enter the stream's mid-width, and keep a wary eye on the sounder until well into the creek's interior.

Inside the main body, depths improve for several miles upstream to Venning Lodge. You will soon spy the dolphins described earlier lining the port side of the stream's mid-width. For best swinging room, do not proceed too far upstream before dropping the hook.

Goose Creek Favor the port side of the creek when entering from the Cooper to avoid the charted shoal on the northeasterly banks. Cruise back to the centerline after leaving the stream's mouth behind. For the first several hundred yards, Goose Creek is lined by old barges, ships, and tugs. The creek then takes a sharp turn to the northeast (starboard). Favor the port shore slightly as you round this turn. There is some shoal water on the opposite banks.

Continue cruising down the creek on the mid-width and watch to port. Soon, you will catch sight

Nuclear submarine and tender, Cooper River

of several large white homes overlooking the stream from high ground. If there is sufficient swinging room for your craft, you can anchor in this area with enough protection for all but heavy weather.

Flagg Creek Chart 11527 accurately portrays one patch of shoal water on the mid-width of the otherwise deep entrance to Flagg Creek. To avoid this hazard, favor the southern shore when entering. Farther upstream, depths improve markedly. Discontinue your cruise on the creek well before reaching the charted shoal abutting the southeastern banks in the body of a sharp turn to the east. Farther upstream, there are far too many unmarked shoals for large cruising craft.

Back River The arm (cove) of Back River that is accessible from this section of Cooper River (opposite unlighted daybeacon #86) is wide, deep, and easily navigable. Simply enter anywhere near the mid-width and drop your hook at a likely spot. Good depths continue almost to the banks.

On Cooper River As you begin your approach to the Back River intersection at unlighted daybeacon #86, it's time to start concerning yourself with shoals. Initially, most of these hazards are marked, but farther upstream, boaters must depend on chart 11527 and good coastal navigation to avoid that unhappy sound of keel meeting mud.

Be sure to pass well west of unlighted daybeacon #86. Shallow water lies east and north of this aid.

Similarly, unlighted daybeacon #87 marks an extensive region of shoal water along the Cooper's northern banks. Pass well to the south of #87 and favor the eastern and southeastern shores as the river turns to the north.

Grove Creek Grove Creek's entrance is

relatively small but quite deep. Strike a course to enter on the stream's mid-width and you should not have any difficulty. Avoid the arm of the creek that turns off to the south just east of the entrance. Depths are too uncertain in this branch for large cruising craft.

On the Cooper The Cooper's last official aid to navigation is unlighted daybeacon #87. While there are several unmarked shoals to avoid farther upstream, they can be easily bypassed. Take your time, have chart 11527 ready at hand, watch the sounder, and you should not have any undue difficulty. Some of the river's best scenery is found in this area, so don't hesitate to continue if your craft draws 5 feet or less.

Cooper River's first significant shoals lie along the river's northern shore as the stream cuts sharply to the west above charted Lynan Creek. Favor the southern shore to avoid this trap.

Another area of very shallow water is found on the Cooper's mid-width in a sharp loop to the northwest located northeast of the industrial facilities at Cote Bas. Heavily favor the southwestern shoreline as you pass.

Just before entering the bend described above, boaters will pass under a charted power line with 75 feet of vertical clearance. With that height, there is nothing to worry about.

From here to "the Tee," no further shallows (less than 8 feet deep) are encountered. Stick to the mid-width and enjoy the sights.

East Cooper River It is much easier to follow the deep channel on the two branches of the upper Cooper River than a casual inspection of chart 11527 would lead you to believe. The small islands that separate the channel from the tidal flats are more readily identifiable than you might expect. Again, as is true with all unfamiliar, isolated waters, you should proceed slowly while maintaining a careful watch on the sounder. If you do become confused, slow to idle speed, study the chart, and select the correct passage.

To enter the Cooper's eastern branch, cut sharply to the east upon entering "the Tee." Follow the southern shore around the sharp turn, which leads first to the east and then almost due south, by favoring the starboard banks. From here to Pompion Chapel, stick to the channel's mid-width and you should meet with no difficulty. Depths begin to drop off past the old church. Discontinue your cruising at this point.

If you choose to anchor, just select any likely spot and drop the hook. Have the fishing rod ready at hand. Rumor has it that the fishing on the upper Cooper's two branches can be spectacular.

French Quarter Creek East Cooper River's only significant sidewater is French Quarter Creek. While the stream holds minimum 6-foot depths on its mid-width, it is too narrow for any craft over 28 feet in length. If you choose to enter, be careful to avoid the tidal flats lining much of the stream's banks.

Lower Charleston Port Terminal, with Cooper River Bridge in foreground

West Cooper River To enter West Cooper River, turn 90 degrees to the west-southwest (port) just after entering "the Tee." Stick to the mid-width and don't be fooled by the many tidal flats flanking both sides of the river. The channel is free of shoals as far as the railroad bridge which will often open on demand. The stream soon leaves the confines of chart 11527, and depths become uncertain. If you choose to continue, feel your way along.

Back River reenters the Cooper on its southwestern banks just before the stream cuts sharply to the east and heads toward Rice Hope Plantation. While this entrance holds minimum depths of 6 feet, the stream is blocked a short distance downstream by two low-level fixed bridges.

WANDO RIVER

Wando River splits off from the Cooper at Remley Point and strikes to the northeast for some 10 nautical miles before it encounters a low-level highway bridge. This span opens only with 24 hours' notice. While the Wando is quite attractive, it offers relatively few anchorage opportunities. For those who have the time to cruise its blue length, some beautiful scenery and one first-rate repair yard with transient dockage are the reward.

Large tracts of the Wando's shoreline are higher and more heavily wooded than is typical of most streams in this section of coastal South Carolina. Here and there, pockets of residential and commercial development break the natural landscape just enough for a pleasing variety.

Wando River is well marked by a renovated system of aids to navigation. These revitalized beacons are a considerable improvement over the older nun and can buoys. The channel is wide and relatively easy to follow, though some aids are so widely spaced that it might be a good idea to run compass courses between markers. Outside of the marked channel, good depths often hold well into shore, but there are several patches of shallower water as well. Wise cruisers will stick mostly to the marked cut.

Just short of the low-level highway bridge, a commercial fish house is located on the southwestern shore. It is often possible to tie to the docks here long enough to purchase seafood caught the same day.

With the addition of reliable transient dockage on the Wando, many more boaters will be setting their course for the river's delightful waters than in times past. It is indeed fortunate that marina facilities are now available on this fortunate river. This writer highly suggests that you heed its siren's call.

Dry-dock facility, Wando River

Wando River Port Facilities

A large containerized-cargo port facility will be spotted on the Wando's southeastern banks northeast of flashing buoy #4. Here, passing cruisers can often watch as huge oceangoing cargo ships are loaded with containers by several large cranes. Watch your wake and you can cruise quite close to the facility for a good view.

Nowell Creek

Nowell Creek is a fairly large stream that makes in to the Wando's northern shore hard by unlighted daybeacon #17. The stream offers the best opportunity for safe overnight anchorage on Wando River. Minimum depths of 6 feet are carried well upstream, though as usual there are one or two unmarked shoals to avoid. The marshy shores are entirely in their natural state. No facilities are available on the creek.

In fair weather, it is certainly possible to drop the hook along Nowell Creek's lower reaches not far from the Wando. For a more secure spot, boaters might consider continuing upstream until the stream begins to pass through a slow turn to the west. Here, you will find plenty of swinging room for boats as large as 42 feet and good protection from all winds. Depths range from 9 to as much as 20 feet. This spot would be my choice every time.

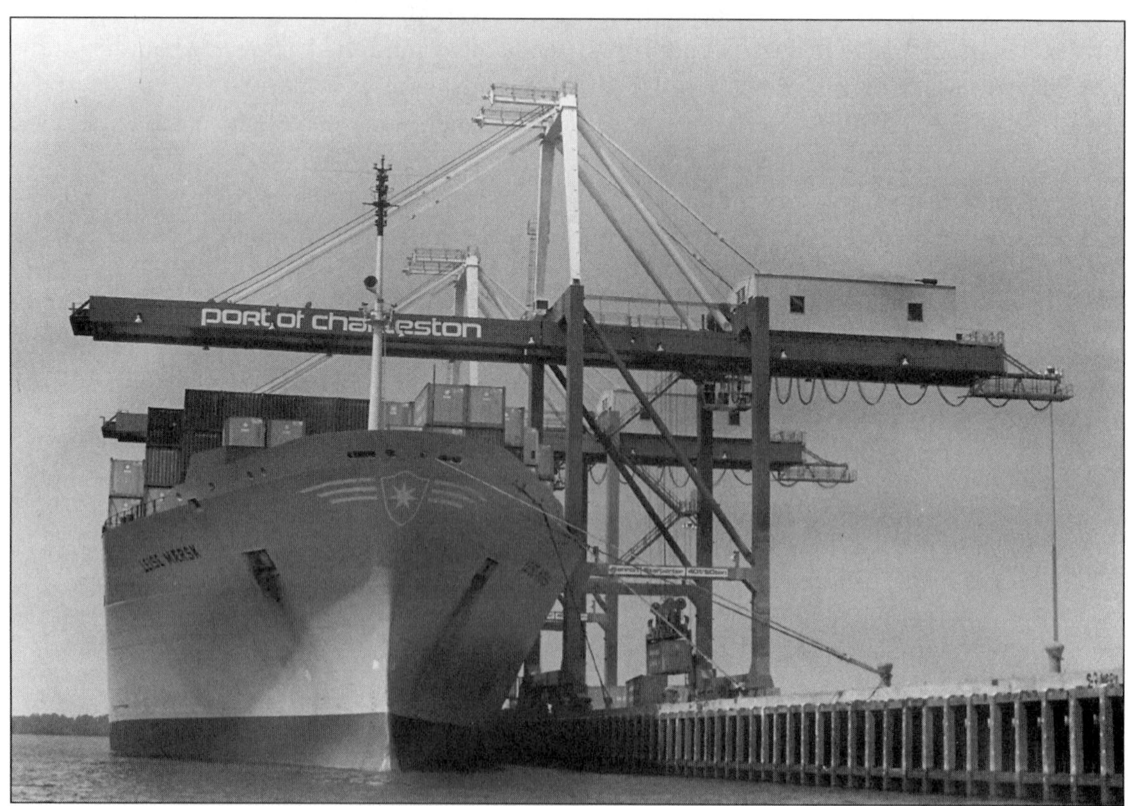

Port facility, Wando River

Horlbeck Creek

Horlbeck Creek is located on the river's eastern banks near unlighted daybeacon #24. This stream leads inland to fabulous Boone Hall Plantation and its famous mile-long avenue of live oaks. The plantation is one of the great showplaces of the South Carolina Low Country. Unfortunately, numerous unmarked shoals make entry into the creek too hazardous for large cruising craft. Furthermore, it is only possible to catch a fleeting view of the house from the water. This writer recommends that you visit by rental car from Charleston.

Halsey Boat Yard

Wando River boasts a full-service boatyard and marina guarding its northwestern banks opposite unlighted daybeacon #40 (hard by the charted position of Cainhoy). This friendly facility offers not only complete haul-out (via a travelift or a marine railway) and mechanical repairs, but transient dockage as well. Overnight or temporary berths are cheerfully provided at floating piers with water and 30-amp power connections. Entrance and dockside depths are a very respectable 9 to 10 feet. Shoreside, boaters will find showers and a large parts department. Hungry cruisers can walk into nearby Cainhoy for a bite to eat. Halsey Boat Yard also features outside winter storage. It is indeed fortunate that boaters now have such a fine facility to go hand in hand with Wando River's wonderful scenery.

Halsey Boat Yard (803) 884-3000

Approach depth: 9–10 feet
Dockside depth: 9–10 feet
Accepts transients: yes
Floating piers: yes
Dockside power connections: 30 amps
Dockside water connections: yes
Showers: yes
Mechanical repairs: yes
Below-waterline repairs: yes
Ship's store: yes
Restaurants: nearby

Avenue of oaks, Boone Hall Plantation near Charleston

Basket lady at Boone Hall Plantation

WANDO RIVER NAVIGATION

Successful navigation of Wando River from its intersection with the Cooper to the low-level highway bridge is a simple matter of following the deep, well-marked channel. Gaps of almost 1 nautical mile separate some of the Wando's aids to navigation. Prudent captains will run compass courses between the various buoys.

Entrance from Cooper River Split off from Cooper River abeam of flashing buoy #43 just before entering Drum Island Reach. Set your course northeast and point to come abeam of and pass flashing buoy #2 to its northwesterly side. Continue on the same course, pointing to eventually pass between flashing buoys #3 and #4. From this point, the Wando remains mostly deep and well marked all the way upriver to the low-level highway span.

Northeast of unlighted nun buoy #12 and unlighted can buoy #11, Charleston's new interstate bypass spans the Wando. Vertical clearance is set at a prodigious 138 feet.

Nowell Creek Enter Nowell Creek by striking a compass course from unlighted daybeacon #17 to avoid the shoal water to the east and west of the stream's mouth. Once on the interior, stick scrupulously to the mid-width.

After proceeding a short distance upstream, you will sight the rotten remains of a large, partially sunken derelict along the eastern shore. The wreck appears as a green square on chart 11524 and is marked as "PA" (position approximate). Several barges, lashed together and anchored in the creek, apparently burned here some years ago.

The channel is squeezed between two 5-foot shoals abeam of the sunken barges. If your craft draws more than 4½ feet, you must take more care than usual to hold strictly to the centerline. Soon, good depths again open out in a broad band abutting both sides of the stream's middle.

Eventually, Nowell Creek winds its way lazily through a turn to the west. Favor the northeastern and northern banks slightly as you begin to enter this bend. Many boaters will want to anchor in the initial portion of this turn. Don't attempt to cruise farther upstream.

On the Wando **Cruisers** continuing upriver on the Wando past Nowell Creek will find that the channel remains clearly outlined to unlighted daybeacon #40. At #40, the river turns sharply to

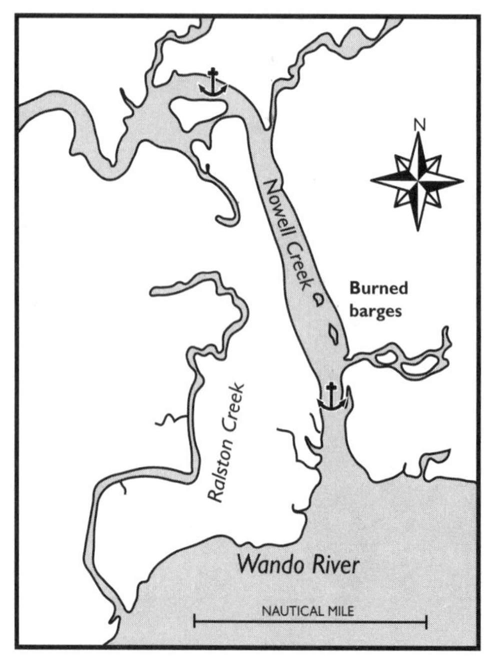

the east and hurries on toward a seldom-opened low-level highway bridge. Boaters traveling this portion of the river will need to use the Wando River inset on chart 11524.

Northwest of #40, boaters are encouraged to visit Halsey Boat Yard. This facility offers the only transient dockage on Wando River.

The charted swinging span crossing the Wando southeast of Cainhoy has a bare vertical clearance of 6 feet. The bridge opens only with advance notice, and even then I wouldn't hold my breath.

ASHLEY RIVER

Ashley River is Charleston's most improved body of water for cruising purposes. The addition of several new marinas plus an enhanced system of navigational aids allows boaters to track their way safely much farther upriver than was possible in years past.

Pleasure craft of most any size and draft that can clear the bridges can readily navigate Ashley River as far as the stream's fourth major highway bridge, northwest of unlighted daybeacon #28. Minimum depths are 7 to 9 feet, with most soundings considerably deeper.

At one time, many large and lovely plantations lined the Ashley's shores. Unfortunately, most of these were destroyed during the Civil War, and the ones that survived are not accessible to large cruising craft from the water.

The eastern shoreline of the lower Ashley River is dotted here and there with commercial docks, while the western banks exhibit light residential development. This section of the Ashley is not particularly attractive. Very few of Charleston's historical sites are visible, and no plantations grace the western banks.

As mentioned earlier, Charleston's principal collection of marinas is located along the Ashley. The City Marina will be spied northeast of unlighted can buoy #5. Ashley Marina is also on the northeastern shoreline just upstream, past the 55-foot fixed bridge. Ripley Light Marina sits just opposite Ashley Marina. Dolphin Cove Marina and Duncan's Boat Harbor are located farther upstream, past the 14-foot bascule bridge.

Protected overnight anchorage is practically nonexistent on Ashley River above the 14-foot bridge. There are no sidewaters worthy of the name, and the river itself is far too broad for consideration.

With Ashley River's reliable markers and marinas, boaters may consider a cruise along the Ashley as a prime boating prospect. The scenery doesn't hold a proverbial candle to the Cooper's, but the stream is still worth your time.

Pesky Bridge

It's worth noting one more time that a 55-foot fixed bridge now crosses Ashley River a short distance northwest of unlighted can buoy #5.

As previously mentioned, all but one of the Ashley's marina facilities must be accessed by first passing under this span. Tall sailcraft that need more than 55 feet of vertical clearance must forgo passage on the upper Ashley River.

Old Town and Orange Grove Creeks

Old Town and Orange Grove Creeks cut into the Ashley's western shore. These streams were the site of the original Charles Towne settlement before the town was moved to its present location around 1680. During the bicentennial celebration of 1976, the state of South Carolina constructed a very impressive commemorative park near the twin streams. Unfortunately, shoaling not noted on chart 11524 has raised the low-tide depths of both creeks to 4 feet or less. Cruising boaters can visit the park by obtaining ground transportation from Charleston.

The Citadel

Just east of unlighted nun buoy #6A, passing boaters will observe the campus of The Citadel. This military school was founded in 1842 as a response to fears of slave uprisings.

Cadets from The Citadel touched off the Civil War's first shots. Manning a cannon at Fort Johnson, they fired on the Union ship *Star of the West*, which was attempting to resupply the Federal garrison at Fort Sumter. Little did they suspect that their shot was the death knell of the Old South. Those same cadets and their fellows served valiantly for the next five years in the defense of Charleston. Their contribution is part and parcel of the great Charleston tradition.

The campus was originally located farther

New Ashley River bridge under construction

inland and was moved to its present site in 1922. The Citadel continues as an active four-year military college and enjoys an excellent academic reputation. There are still many reminders of the school's storied past preserved in its archives. Few will ever attend a school with a prouder tradition.

ASHLEY RIVER NAVIGATION

Ashley River can be successfully navigated by sticking to the well-marked channel as far as unlighted daybeacon #28. Past this aid, the channel, or what there is of it, is unmarked and precarious. The river is plagued by shoal areas outside of the marked cut, so follow the various aids and chart 11524 carefully.

Northwest of unlighted can buoy #5, visiting cruisers will quickly encounter the 55-foot fixed span discussed above. Be *sure* to slow to idle speed as you cruise between this span and the bascule bridge just upriver. The anchored boats, as well as the craft moored at the adjacent marinas, will be ever so grateful.

The old U.S. 17 twin bascule bridge northwest of Ashley Marina has a closed vertical clearance of 14 feet. The span is closed from 7:00 A.M. until 9:00 A.M. on weekdays and from 4:00 P.M. until 7:00 P.M. seven days a week. Otherwise, the bridge opens on the hour and half-hour for pleasure craft.

North of the bascule bridge, the Ashley's channel opens out in a broad band before you. Those bound upriver should take red aids to the boaters' starboard side and green markers to port.

Note the correctly charted 3-foot obstruction south of unlighted nun buoy #6A. Be *sure* to pass well west of #6A.

North of unlighted daybeacon #12, shallow water abuts the river's western banks for several miles upstream. Favor the eastern side of the river, just as the markers indicate.

At unlighted daybeacon #16, Ashley River begins a slow, lazy turn to the west. The third bridge crossing the river is located west of unlighted daybeacon #20. This fixed span has a vertical clearance of 50 feet.

Moving upstream from this 50-foot span, boaters must execute a series of sharp maneuvers. After passing under the bridge, point to pass unlighted daybeacon #21 by some 20 yards to its northerly side. Turn sharply to the southwest, pointing to come abeam of and pass unlighted daybeacon #22 to its southeasterly side. Set a new course to come abeam of unlighted daybeacon #23 by some 20 yards or so to its northerly side. Be mindful of the correctly charted shallows to the north when cruising between #22 and #23.

Pass to the south of unlighted daybeacon #24 and switch to the "Continuation of Ashley River" inset on chart 11524. At unlighted daybeacon #28, the charted channel poops out just short of the 35-foot fixed bridge. Cruising craft should halt their upstream explorations at #28.

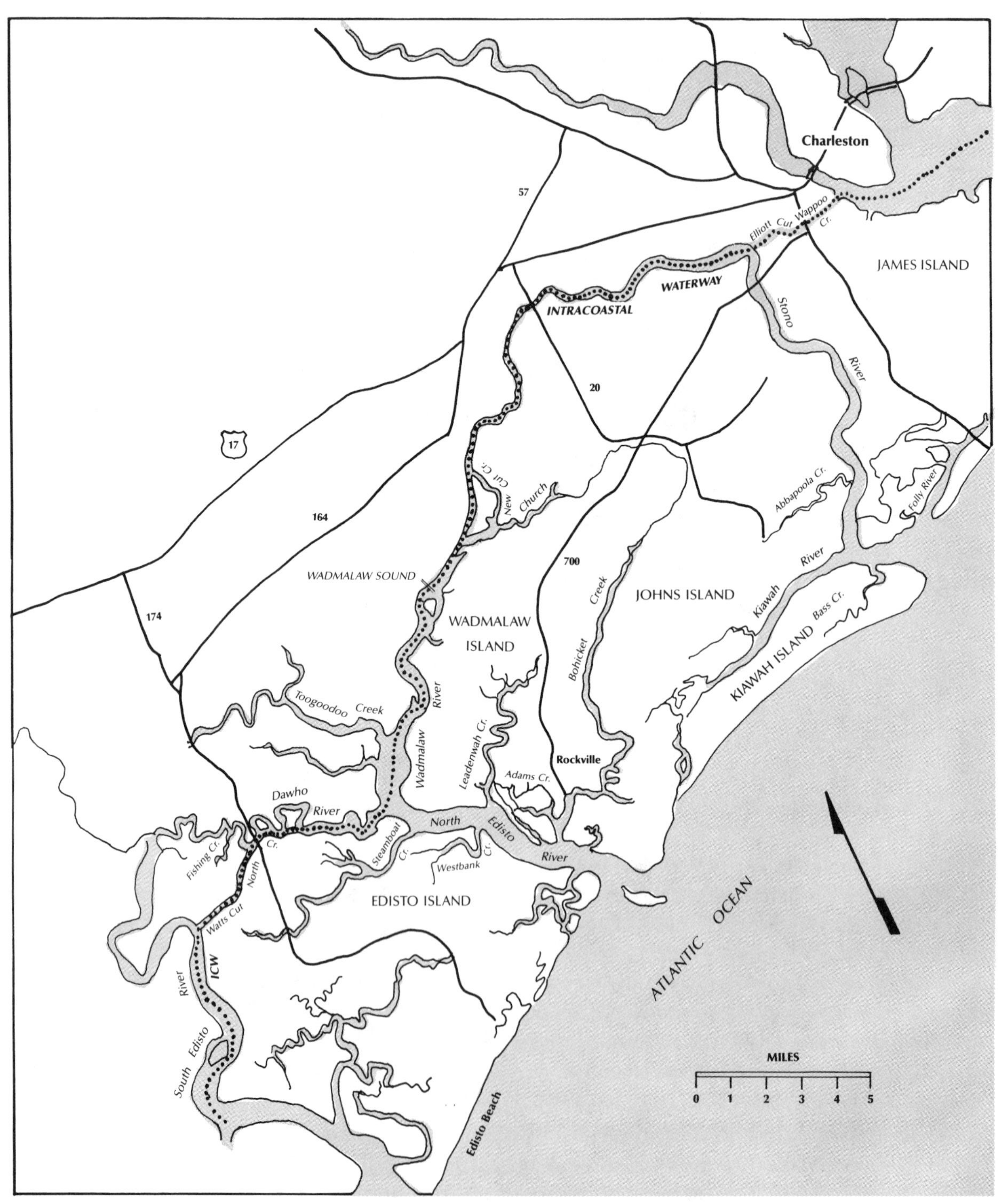

Charleston
57
Elliott Cut
Wappoo Cr.
JAMES ISLAND
WATERWAY
INTRACOASTAL
Stono River
20
17
164
New Cut Cr.
Church
Abbapoola Cr.
Folly River
700
WADMALAW SOUND
JOHNS ISLAND
Bohicket Creek
Kiawah River
Bass Cr.
174
WADMALAW
ISLAND
KIAWAH ISLAND
Toogoodoo Creek
Wadmalaw River
Leadenwah Cr.
Rockville
Adams Cr.
Dawho River
North Edisto River
Steamboat Cr.
Westbank Cr.
Fishing Cr.
North Cr.
Watts Cut
EDISTO ISLAND
ATLANTIC OCEAN
ICW
South Edisto River
MILES
0 1 2 3 4 5
Edisto Beach

Wappoo Creek to South Edisto River

South of Charleston, the state's coastline begins a radical transformation. Gone are the simple patterns of rivers and streams found to the north. The boater now faces an increasingly complicated and often bewildering maze of creeks, rivers, and inlets, all of which flow around the plentiful Sea Islands. These small, often marshy islands are the most striking feature of the southern South Carolina coast. Separated from the mainland by multiple streams, they provide some of the most historic and romantic cruising grounds in the state.

The main water bodies in the northern section of "Sea Island country" are Stono and North Edisto Rivers. The smaller Wadmalaw and Dawho Rivers join these two principal streams and are followed by the ICW as the Waterway snakes its way south.

Both the Stono and the North Edisto boast excellent facilities, though long stretches of isolated waters separate the various marinas. Good overnight anchorages abound. Many of these are quite isolated and can make for adventurous evenings far from the most remote vestiges of civilization. Some are even within sight of historic plantation homes that watch benignly over the waters as they have for more than 150 years.

Charts

You will need two charts for navigation among the Sea Islands covered in this chapter:

11518 covers the ICW through the entire area from Wappoo Creek to South Edisto River

11522 details the lower sections of both Stono and North Edisto Rivers, as well as the upper reaches of Toogoodoo Creek

Shorelines vary greatly along the two rivers and connecting streams. While the saltwater marsh so much in evidence to the north is still quite plentiful, there are also higher, heavily wooded banks. Large undeveloped stretches alternate with commercial and residential sections. Here and there, a historic plantation is visible from the water. These old homeplaces are elegant reminders of the Sea Island culture's past majesty, and many are the settings for fascinating legends. Several of these tall tales will be explored in this chapter.

Cruising the waters of the South Carolina Sea Islands is a refreshingly different experience. While performing research, this writer was reminded of the rivers of Albemarle Sound in North Carolina, which are also largely bypassed by cruising boaters. In the Sea Islands, too, it is relatively rare to spot other cruising craft far from the ICW channel. Yet it is clear that those who pass up the chance to cruise the rivers south of Charleston are missing one of the most historic and colorful experiences offered by coastal South Carolina.

ICW TO STONO RIVER

Wappoo Creek and Elliott Cut provide access from Charleston's Ashley River to Stono River via the ICW. While the two interconnecting streams are well marked and mostly free of shoals, incredibly strong tidal currents regularly scour the channel. This problem seems to be particularly acute at the Stono River intersection. Sailcraft and trawlers must be especially cautious in these swift waters. Some sailors may even want to consult the tide tables and time their entry for a tide setting in the direction they are voyaging.

There are no formal facilities on the two creeks, and there is only one anchorage opportunity. East of unlighted daybeacon #9, a deep loop of the river cuts in toward the southern shore. Here, boats up to 55 feet can anchor in minimum 9-foot depths. This is a good spot to wait for morning light or a favorable tide before entering the Ashley or the Stono. Just be sure the anchor is well set before heading below. In light of the cut's swiftly moving waters, dragging anchor is a genuine concern.

Immediately west of the charted 33-foot bascule bridge, the Charleston Crab House restaurant (803-795-1963) guards the southerly banks. This notable dining establishment maintains a small floating dock fronting directly on the Waterway for the use of its patrons. There should be room enough for one 30-footer, but no more. Depths alongside run around 5 feet at mean low water.

Wappoo Creek and Elliott Cut are spanned by two bridges. The easternmost structure is a fixed high-rise with better than 65 feet of vertical clearance. The older, western bascule bridge has a closed vertical clearance of 33 feet and a very restricted opening schedule.

If possible, tidal currents may pick up even more west of the bascule bridge. All hands should be ready for instant action if the current thwarts your forward progress.

The cut's shoreline exhibits fairly heavy residential development. Here and there, some truly elegant homes overlook the water, and at least one historical site is visible to the careful observer.

McLeod Plantation

Just before passing under the Wappoo Creek bascule bridge, look toward the southern banks and you will catch a quick glimpse of McLeod Plantation's white columns through a long avenue of oaks. The house is set back a good distance from the water, so you will have to look carefully.

This beautiful home was built in 1858 and extensively remodeled in the early 1900s. Though not visible from the water, a few slave cabins still stand near the plantation's remaining fields.

During the Civil War, the plantation was used as a hospital and headquarters for Confederate forces. Later, it housed a local office of the Freedmen's Bureau, an agency set up after the war to aid the emancipated blacks.

Wappoo Creek History North of unlighted daybeacon #9, the shallow upper reaches of Wappoo Creek (abandoned by the ICW) make off to the northwest. This seemingly insignificant body of water was the scene of one of the most important agricultural developments in the early years of South Carolina.

In the 1740s, a remarkable young woman, Eliza Lucas, lived on the shores of Wappoo Creek. Her father, the governor of Antigua, moved Eliza to South Carolina with her mother, who was in failing health. Mr. Lucas was hurriedly summoned back to Antigua to deal with Spanish hostilities, leaving his young daughter in charge of the family plantation.

A woman of extraordinary drive, Eliza was not content merely to oversee the day-to-day operation of the plantation. She began to experiment with the preparation of indigo dye. She was familiar with the plant from her days in the West Indies and believed that it could prosper in South Carolina.

There followed many trials for the determined lady. Her first planting was killed by frost, and her second was eaten by worms. A successful third crop was processed incorrectly by an assistant dispatched by her father from the West Indies. Eliza persevered, and finally her father was able to send her an old slave from Antigua who revealed the secrets of the complicated preparation process.

As a direct result of Eliza's eventual success, South Carolina's first great agricultural dynasty was born. With a generous bounty offered by the British government, indigo was grown and exported in great quantity until the Revolution. Vast fortunes were accumulated by indigo planters throughout coastal South Carolina. After the Revolution, the bounty was no more, and indigo was cultivated less and less. The final blow came as the Western world began to learn the process of preparing dyes from coal tar.

The growing of indigo is but a distant memory in South Carolina today. It is most fitting, however, to remember the courage and diligence of Eliza Lucas and to reflect on just how much can really be accomplished by a single individual who possesses the necessary drive.

Sea Islands History The Sea Islands continued to shape South Carolina's economic and agricultural history during the early and middle 1800s, when they were host to the state's last great agricultural dynasty. Planters discovered that the warm, humid climate was well suited for the growth of long-staple cotton. Much as Egyptian cotton is prized to this day for its long fiber, Sea Island cotton was very much in demand during the 1800s. The successful cultivation of this valuable commodity concentrated fantastic wealth in the hands of a few planters. There evolved among the Sea Island planters an affluent way of life that the modern mind can scarcely imagine.

Such wealth led to the construction of beautiful plantations. Many of these old estates have a tradition of colorful folklore that the romantics among us find hard to resist. It is apparent from reading the tales of the Sea Islands that the planters were a fiercely independent breed of men and women with fascinating characters. Their tradition lives on in the plentiful Sea Island legends.

Surprisingly, it was not the Civil War but a small insect that spelled the doom of Sea Island cotton. Following the war, cotton was again grown profitably despite the absence of cheap labor. However, the coming of the boll weevil in the late 1800s was the final act in the Sea Island tragedy. The cotton fields were decimated, and many who once hoarded great fortunes were suddenly bankrupt. Only within the last several years have scientists learned to break the life cycle of the boll weevil. Perhaps this discovery will eventually bring the snowy fields of cotton back to coastal South Carolina.

Over the years, the face of the Sea Islands has changed. Here and there, descendants of former slaves have established rural communities on the sites of former plantations. Many plantation homes fell victim to the ravages of war or the passing of the years. Several of the old homes still survive, however, particularly on Edisto Island. Some of the structures stand empty, while others have been restored to their former glory. Either way, they speak eloquently of an age that will never come again.

ICW TO STONO RIVER NAVIGATION

As already mentioned, boaters must be on guard against the strong currents that regularly plague Wappoo Creek and Elliott Cut. Sailcraft should proceed under auxiliary power and be ready for quick course corrections. All vessels should be alert for the side-setting effect of the currents. Remember to watch your stern as well as your forward progress so that you may quickly note any excessive leeway.

West of unlighted daybeacon #3, boaters will pass under a 65-foot fixed bridge. West of unlighted daybeacon #4, cruisers will meet up with the Wappoo Creek bascule bridge. This span has a closed vertical clearance of 33 feet. Sailors must deal with one of the most complicated set of opening times in all of coastal South Carolina. The span is closed year-round Monday through Friday between 6:30 A.M. and 9:00 A.M. and between 4:00

P.M. and 6:30 P.M. From 9:00 A.M. to 4:00 P.M. the span opens weekdays only on the hour and half-hour . On Saturdays, Sundays, and holidays, the bridge opens on the hour and half-hour between 6:00 A.M. and 6:00 P.M. Be sure to plan your cruise around these opening times; otherwise, you may experience long delays. This writer knows it's a complicated schedule! Write your congressman.

"No Wake" regulations are strictly enforced on the Waterway west of the bascule bridge to the Stono River intersection. The Charleston Harbor Police are known for their vigilance in this area. Slow to idle speed and spend your time observing the pleasant residential development on the shores.

Wappoo Cut Anchorage The entrance to the cut's single anchorage is found on the southern banks a short distance west of the 33-foot bascule bridge (east of unlighted daybeacon #9). Enter on the mid-width of the stream's eastern mouth. Drop the hook once you are between the marsh-grass island and the mainland.

Minimum 8-foot depths are now maintained through the western mouth, where you can rejoin the ICW near unlighted daybeacon #9. For best depths, give #9 a wide berth. Some shoal water seems to be building west around this aid to navigation.

On the ICW The Waterway enters Stono River as it leaves the western mouth of Elliott Cut at flashing daybeacon #B. The ICW follows the upper reaches of the Stono into Wadmalaw River. This account now turns to the cruising opportunities of the lower Stono River. Continued description and navigation of the ICW route will be presented later in this chapter.

STONO RIVER

Stono River is the first major body of water that cruising skippers will encounter south of Charleston. When this writer first reviewed the Stono back in the mid-1980s, navigation of the river was an exacting process, courtesy of numerous unmarked shoals. Now, I am happy to report that a comprehensive system of aids to navigation has vastly simplified a cruise along this notable body of water.

Folly and Kiawah Rivers are two major sidewaters of the Stono. Both streams join their larger sister near the Stono's inlet and offer excellent cruising opportunities. The Folly sports an improved channel and one good marina.

The Stono's shoreline is generally attractive. The river is bordered along most of its length by James Island to the east and Johns Island to the west. Both landmasses have figured prominently in the history of the South Carolina Low Country. A few historical sites are visible along the Stono's banks among tracts of light residential development.

The Stono's inlet is flanked by Folly Island to the east and Kiawah Island to the west. Both bodies of land have been extensively developed as resorts. The inlet is subject to continual change and probably should not be attempted without local knowledge. Check at one of the Stono marinas before making the attempt.

Facilities along the lower Stono River are excellent. Two full-service marinas are close by the ICW on the western shore, near the

U.S. 701 bridge, and a third facility is located on Folly River.

Stono River presents far fewer anchorage opportunities than its sister streams to the south. Only a few creeks offer adequate shelter with enough swinging room for large craft.

The Stono is an attractive body of water with uncrowded cruising grounds, good facilities, and several historic sites. Boaters who like to get away from the crowd should enjoy a leisurely cruise on this storied stream.

River Anchorages

In recent years, some boats traveling the ICW have started anchoring on Stono River's charted deep waters north and south of Wappoo Creek–Elliott Cut's westerly mouth. Good depths of 15 feet or more hold to within 50 yards of the residentially developed easterly shoreline for 200 yards or so north and south of the cut's westerly entrance. There is good protection from easterly winds and some shelter from moderate northerly breezes, but there is minimal protection from fresh southwesterly blows. By all accounts, this is not a heavy-weather anchorage, but in fair weather, it is a convenient spot for northbound craft to wait for the morning light or a fair tide before running Wappoo Creek and entering Charleston Harbor.

Buzzards Roost and Stono Marinas

Two marinas catering to cruising transients flank the western banks of Stono River near the U.S. 701 swing bridge. Buzzards Roost Marina is located on the northern side of the span. It is without a doubt one of the finer pleasure-craft facilities in all of coastal South Carolina. This marina suffered a complete loss of its dockage during Hugo, but new wooden-decked floating piers have now been in place for several years.

Transients are gladly accepted at overnight berths featuring all power, water, and cable-television connections. Low-water depths alongside range from 7 to 10 feet or better. Gasoline, diesel fuel, and waste pump-out services are readily available. The adjacent showers and laundromat are as fine as any cruiser could ask for. There is also a full-line grocery and ship's store on the premises, as well as a refreshing swimming pool open during the summer, late spring, and early fall.

Cappy's Seafood Restaurant, located just behind the marina, is widely renowned for its succulent seafood. No less a celebrity than Tom Selleck has been attracted on occasion by Cappy's charms. Fried, broiled, or steamed, the seafood has the flavor that comes only from the freshest ingredients prepared with care and pride. This

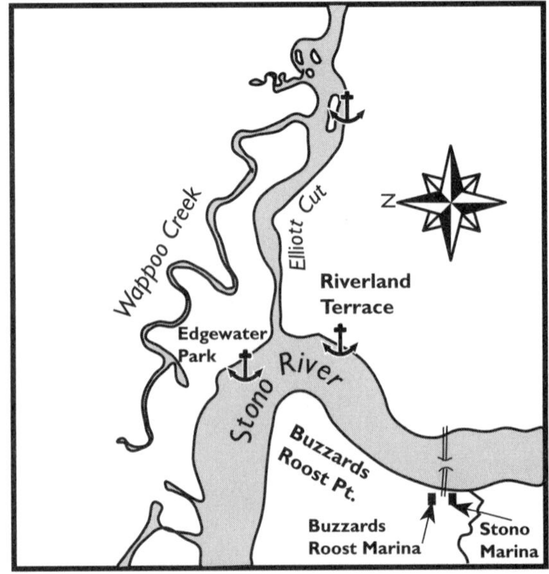

writer particularly recommends the combination fried shrimp and oyster platter. The chocolate mousse is a notable entry in the dessert line.

Over and above these impressive features, Buzzards Roost Marina is managed by one of the friendliest families in this land of fine hospitality. It is a genuine pleasure to find such a caring establishment. Certainly, Buzzards Roost can be recommended without the slightest hesitation.

Buzzards Roost Marina (803) 559-5516

Approach depth: 12+ feet
Dockside depth: 7–10 feet (low water)
Accepts transients: yes
Wooden floating piers: yes
Dockside power connections: 30 and 50 amps
Dockside water connections: yes
Showers: yes
Laundromat: yes
Waste pump-out: yes
Gasoline: yes
Diesel fuel: yes
Ship's and variety store: yes
Restaurant: on-site

Stono Marina is a medium-sized facility located on the southern side of the Stono bridge. This establishment does not offer either gasoline or diesel fuel, but transients are gladly accepted for overnight dockage at well-maintained wooden floating piers. As you would expect, water and power connections up to 50 amps are available. Minimum dockside depths run 9 to 10 feet or more. Showers are located in an enclosed building constructed directly on the docks. Waste pump-out facilities are available for paid transients and regular month-to-month customers only. Stono Marina boasts a resident mechanic, but the management has informed this writer that it's just about all he can do to satisfy the demands of the resident boaters. A ship's store sits perched just behind the piers.

Come dinnertime, it's a quick step across the street to Cappy's Seafood Restaurant, reviewed above. While not as large as some, Stono Marina is a friendly facility that transient boaters can use with confidence.

Stono Marina (803) 571-5159

Approach depth: 12+ feet
Dockside depth: 9–10 feet (minimum)
Accepts transients: yes
Floating wooden piers: yes
Dockside power connections: 30 and 50 amps
Dockside water connections: yes
Showers: yes
Waste pump-out: yes (paid customers only)
Mechanical repairs: limited
Ship's store: yes
Restaurant: nearby

James Island History James Island comprises the eastern banks of Stono River from Elliott Cut to Folly River. The island was settled as early as the 1670s. Since that time, the landmass has figured prominently in the history of the region.

Perhaps James Island's first claim to fame was its noted shipbuilding trade during the 1700s. In 1763, the *Heart of Oak* was launched from one of the island's shipyards. The proud ship weighed 180 tons and could carry more than 1,000 barrels of rice in her hold.

In 1780, Sir Henry Clinton used James Island as the final staging ground for his encirclement of Charleston. He was not to be the last enemy who would attempt to use the island as a back door to the "Holy City."

In June 1862, a vastly superior Union force was defeated on James Island at the Battle of Secessionville. The high command of the Northern forces was so impressed with the Confederate defenses that it chose to redirect the efforts against Charleston to nearby Morris Island. Many fierce and bloody battles followed, and it was not until 1865 that Union forces finally occupied James Island.

Accounts of the courage and hardships of the defenders on James and Morris Islands are awe-inspiring. One Confederate was heard to say following the evacuation of Fort Legarre on Morris Island that he would never fear hell again because it couldn't be worse than Fort Legarre. If you would like to read more about the valiant but vain struggle for James Island, this writer highly recommends the book *James and Related Sea Islands*, by James P. Hayes.

Johns Island History In 1739, an event took place on Johns Island that had a profound effect on the South Carolina view of slavery. Known as the Stono Slave Rebellion, the incident began at the urging of an educated slave named Cato. With the backing of Spanish authorities in Florida, he encouraged other slaves to revolt. His plan was to head for Florida, freeing fellow slaves along the way. The mob first stormed an arms warehouse, killing two white guards stationed there. Then the ragged army began to travel south.

It was not long before they were observed by a small group of white planters, including the governor of South Carolina. The planters rushed to nearby Willtown Presbyterian Church, where a service was in progress. In those days, it was the law that everyone must go to church armed. This law was apparently a vestige of the days of Indian attacks.

The armed white congregation immediately set out in pursuit and found the rebellious slaves in a nearby field. They fired upon the mob, killing the ringleader, Cato, in the first volley. Several of the other leaders were hanged, and many of the remaining slaves were severely punished by their masters.

Following the Stono Slave Rebellion, fear of black uprisings ran rife through the white population. Heavily outnumbered by the slaves, the whites believed that the blacks had to be carefully controlled or other, more dangerous revolts would be the result.

As a direct consequence, a new, strict, uniform Slave Code was adopted by the state of South Carolina. Among other harsh measures, the new law made it a crime to teach any slave to read or write. A series of nightly patrols throughout the countryside was instituted by the planters to hunt for fugitives and to monitor any slave gatherings. In short, the fear of uprisings engendered by the Stono Slave Rebellion affected South Carolina history until the Civil War.

Battery Pringle

Though obscured by seasonal growth, Battery Pringle is visible to the careful observer on the eastern shore of the Stono a short distance south of unlighted daybeacon #12. This Confederate battery was built early in the Civil War to protect Stono River from attack. Look east just as you swing back to the south after passing #12 (heading downriver) and you will see the earthen walls near the shoreline.

Abbapoola Creek

Abbapoola Creek is a wide stream that cuts into the Stono's western banks south of unlighted daybeacon #6. The stream holds minimum 6-foot depths on its centerline for some distance upstream, but there are several unmarked shoals abutting the shoreline. Boats as large as 34 feet will find sufficient swinging room for overnight anchorage on the eastern portion of the creek. One good choice would be to drop the hook just before the stream turns sharply south-southeast and chart 11522 indicates a sounding of 28 feet. The creek's shores are comprised of saltwater marsh and give only minimal protection in heavy weather. Consequently, the creek is recommended only for light- to moderate-air anchorage.

Abbapoola Creek was once host to Legareville, a summer retreat for wealthy planters. As you enter the creek, watch ahead for a tin roof in the distance. Of all the original dwellings at Legareville, this structure is the sole survivor. Unfortunately, you must enter the shallow section of the creek in order to have a good view of the house. Don't make the attempt unless your craft draws less than 3 feet.

Green Creek

Green Creek makes in to the eastern shore of Stono River south of unlighted daybeacon #3. Cautious navigators can find their way past the stream's mouth with minimum depths of 5½ to 6 feet, but one false move can land you in 3 feet of water lying atop an unmarked shoal. This writer does not recommend Green Creek to any captain piloting a vessel that draws more than 4½ (preferably 4) feet.

If you do negotiate the difficult entrance, anchorage is a practical possibility for boats up to 32 feet. The best swinging room is discovered as the creek swings back to the east-southeast just where chart 11522 shows a sounding of 14 feet.

The surrounding shores are composed of the usual salt marsh, which gives only minimal protection during inclement weather. Nevertheless, Green Creek has a feeling of true isolation, so if your size and draft requirements fit the bill, give every consideration to spending a night tucked in the confines of this beautiful stream. Just don't forget that tricky entrance.

Kiawah River

Kiawah River is a large body of water intersecting the Stono on the western banks near its inlet. Unlighted daybeacon #A marks the Kiawah's eastern mouth. The river divides Johns, Seabrook, and Kiawah Islands. While deep and easily navigable for much of its length, the Kiawah presents surprisingly few genuine cruising opportunities. It is too wide for effective anchorage in all but light airs, and there are no marinas in the immediate vicinity. Little can be seen of the sumptuous Kiawah Island resort to the south. Your most immediate companion for a cruise of the river is likely to be the familiar saltwater marsh grass. Some higher ground is visible on Kiawah Island.

There is one exception to this rather plain character. Large schools of bottlenose dolphins often frequent the river. Sometimes, if you anchor quietly, these beautiful creatures will swim right up to your craft. Have the camera ready and you might be rewarded with the picture of a lifetime.

Kiawah Island

Kiawah Island is one of the premier resorts in all of coastal South Carolina. Representing a splendid example of an effective compromise between developers and environmentalists, large portions of Kiawah Island have been left in their natural state, while other tracts have been developed in the most lavish style. Condominiums, hotels, sports complexes, and restaurants dot the island's central district. Many residents of coastal South Carolina have told this writer that they would rather vacation on Kiawah than anywhere else in the world.

Kiawah Island's careful planning bore unexpected fruit during Hurricane Hugo. While beachside developments to the north at Sullivan's Island and the Isle of Palms were laid waste, Kiawah escaped with only minimal damage. Of course, winds and tidal surges were worse north of Charleston, but there is still much to be said for the development practiced on Kiawah Island.

Unfortunately, there is no water access to the resort at this time. Plans for a marina on Kiawah River have apparently been shelved for the present. To visit Kiawah, make your reservations from Charleston.

Bass Creek

Bass Creek is a small stream found along the Stono's southwestern banks south of unlighted daybeacon #2. While the interior portion of the creek holds 8-foot minimum depths, the entrance is flanked by several unmarked shoals. Adventurous skippers can enter Bass Creek, but they must be sure to hold strictly to the midwidth and feel their way in cautiously to avoid the shoals. By all accounts, you should consider entering only if you pilot a craft under 32 feet that draws 3½ feet or less.

The Bass Creek shoreline is mostly saltwater marsh, but the banks are a bit higher here than is the norm. They give good protection in all but the heaviest of weather. If you make it through the entrance, there is just enough swinging room for boats under 32 feet to anchor. You might want to set a Bahamian-style mooring to minimize your swinging to and fro on the hook.

Folly River

Folly River joins the Stono on its northeastern banks just short of the inlet. While the channel may look none too good on the current edition of chart 11522, boaters can rejoice in the knowledge that the United States Coast Guard dredged and re-marked the channel in 1991. Currently, minimum 6-foot depths can be held in the marked cut all the way upriver to Mariner's Cay Marina. Most soundings range from 8 to as much as 20 feet.

We boaters often complain about the Coast Guard or Army Corps of Engineers being stingy with their aids to navigation. Visiting cruisers will encounter just the opposite problem on the Folly River channel. The markers are in places so plentiful as to be confusing. This problem is further fueled by the omission of most of the river's beacons from chart 11522. The careful captain should still be able to make his way safely upstream by remembering the old, faithful red-right-returning rule, but this is definitely not the place to go charging along at full speed, navigating casually by eye.

Two marinas are located on Folly River. Boaters may be able to buy gasoline and diesel fuel from a very small establishment on the southeastern shore just upstream from unlighted daybeacon #17. However, the river's principal facility lies along the northern banks just short of the charted fixed bridge.

Mariner's Cay is a large marina-condo complex that now welcomes visiting boaters. While the dockmaster has informed this writer that only a few transients have thus far made the trek down Stono River to the marina's docks, the staff is ready to greet any who arrive.

Mariner's Cay Marina features both wooden and concrete floating docks with water hookups and power connections up to 50 amps. Minimum depths alongside run about 6 feet. Gasoline, diesel fuel, and waste pump-out services are readily available. There is an unusually nice variety and ship's store on the premises where cruisers can restock their larders. Clean showers and a nice laundromat are close at hand. The well-respected Bushy's Restaurant, serving excellent fried seafood, is within an easy walk of the docks. Without putting too fine a

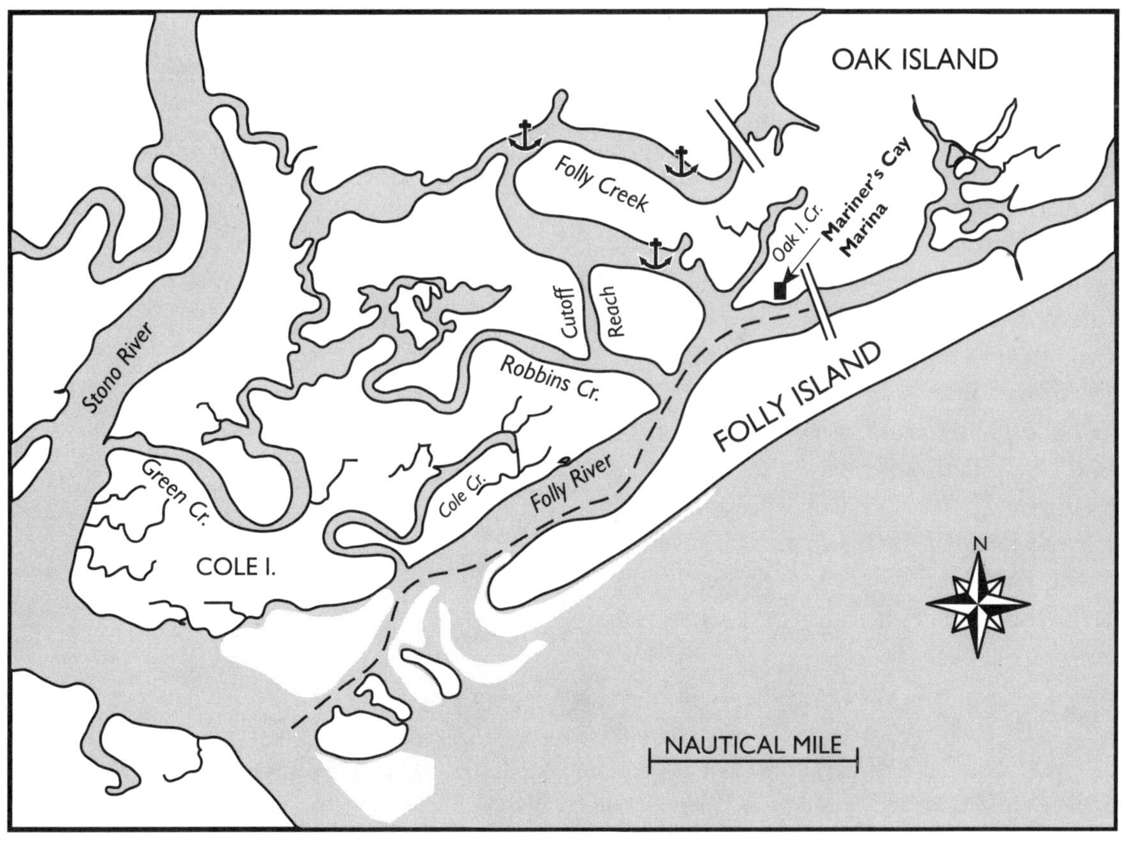

point on it, this writer urges his fellow cruisers to take advantage of this well-appointed facility, which has hitherto been mostly bypassed.

Mariner's Cay Marina (803) 588-2091

Approach depth: 6–20 feet
Dockside depth: 6–12 feet
Accepts transients: yes
Floating wooden piers: yes
Dockside power connections: 30 and 50 amps
Dockside water connections: yes
Showers: yes
Laundromat: yes
Waste pump-out: yes
Gasoline: yes
Diesel fuel: yes
Ship's and variety store: yes
Restaurant: nearby

Folly Creek

Folly Creek, Robbins Creek, and Cutoff Reach are mostly deep sidewaters of Folly River that make in to the larger stream's northwestern banks west of the 10-foot fixed bridge. There are some unmarked shoals on all these waters. Because of the shallow obstructions, these streams are not recommended for craft over 38 feet. If you choose to enter, make sure to read the Folly Creek navigation section presented later in this chapter.

Anchorage on Folly Creek is possible for craft up to 38 feet, but the marshy shores give inadequate protection in heavy weather. Robbins Creek and Cutoff Reach are a bit too narrow for comfortable anchorage by large cruising craft. However, all are interesting and mostly deep gunkholes.

Two potential havens on Folly Creek deserve particular attention. The creek's waters southeast of the charted marsh island (itself north of the Cutoff Reach intersection) boast minimum 12-foot depths and enough swinging room for boats up to 38 feet. You might also consider anchoring along the body of the long hairpin loop northwest of the marsh island. Protection is a bit better here than at the downstream anchorage described above. Depths range from 18 to as much as 27 feet.

Eventually, Folly Creek is blocked by a fixed bridge with 10 feet of vertical clearance. Just south of the bridge, a fish house and dock are located on the creek's southeastern shore. Here, you can sometimes buy seafood caught the same day. Skippers could anchor just short of the bridge, but this writer prefers the two havens farther downstream reviewed above.

Folly Island

Folly Island separates Folly River from the ocean. Since 1930, the island's beaches have been one of the most popular weekend getaways in coastal South Carolina. Over the years, Folly Island has steadily eroded toward the mainland, but this natural regression does not seem to have injured the beach's popularity.

STONO RIVER NAVIGATION

As already noted, successful navigation of Stono River is now facilitated by a complex system of aids to navigation. If it were not for a few shallows that are a special concern, navigation of the Stono could be summarized with the old saw about passing all red beacons to your port side and green markers to starboard (since you are now heading toward the open sea). But just to be on the safe side, have chart 11522 at hand and keep a wary eye on the sounder. Do not attempt to run the river at night! If you follow these simple rules and study the navigational data presented in this section, your can look forward to a most enjoyable cruise.

Entrance from Wappoo Creek-Elliott Cut Flashing daybeacon #B marks the western terminus of Elliott Cut. Past #B, the ICW spills out into Stono River. Cruisers following the Waterway will want to swing west-northwest and enter the Stono's upper reaches, but those planning to visit the marinas by the U.S. 701 bridge or explore Stono River's lower length should swing south and point to pass unlighted daybeacon #19 by at least 30 yards to its eastern side. This maneuver will cause you to favor the eastern banks, thereby avoiding the charted shoal west and south of #19. Continue favoring the eastern shore heavily as you work your way to unlighted daybeacon #18.

South of #18, good depths open out almost from shore to shore as far as the swing bridge. Boaters continuing downriver should point for the U.S. 701 bridge's central pass-through.

The U.S. 701 Stono River bridge has a closed vertical clearance of only 8 feet, but fortunately it opens on demand. Just before you reach the span, Buzzards Roost Marina will come abeam on the western shore. Once through, you will see Stono Marina, also on the western banks.

South of the bridge, point to pass unlighted daybeacon #16 to its immediate westerly side. Be mindful of the correctly charted shoal abutting the easterly banks. Similarly, pass unlighted daybeacon #15 to its easterly quarter. This aid marks a smaller patch of shoal water to the west.

South of #15, the Stono follows a long bend to the southeast. Be sure to pass well southwest of unlighted daybeacons #14 and #12A. An extensive shoal flanking the northeasterly shoreline is marked by these beacons.

Unlighted daybeacon #12 denotes a southerly turn in Stono River. Soon after leaving #12 behind, keep a close watch on the easterly banks for a quick view of Battery Pringle.

Anyone making even a cursory study of chart 11522 will note that unlighted daybeacon #11 must be passed to its easterly side to avoid a small shoal. South of #11, the river follows yet another turn, this time to the southwest. Unlighted daybeacon #9 warns of shallows along the northwestern bank.

At unlighted daybeacon #7, the Stono continues its serpentine path by cutting to the south. Be sure to pass unlighted daybeacon #6 well to its westerly side to avoid the charted shoal.

Abbapoola Creek Enter Abbapoola Creek on its mid-width. West of its entrance, the stream follows a series of turns and bends. The creek first turns to the south-southeast, then to the southwest, then to the north, back to the south, and finally to the west-northwest. Discontinue your cruise before reaching this last turn. Depths drop off to 4 feet or less at this point.

On the Stono South of the intersection with Abbapoola Creek, boaters cruising downstream on Stono River must exercise unusual caution. The shoal west of unlighted daybeacon #4 has built much farther out into the river than is shown on chart 11522. While always staying a bit to the west of #4, you must favor the eastern and southeastern banks heavily to avoid this considerable hazard. Of course, don't approach the eastern and southeastern shoreline too closely, as there is a much narrower ribbon of shoals shelving out from this shore as well.

Green Creek Chart 11522 reveals a tongue of 3-foot water that runs well southwest from Green Creek's northwesterly entrance point. This obstruction complicates successful entry into the creek.

Continue cruising south on Stono River until you are at least 0.2 nautical mile past the creek's entrance. Only then should you cut back around to the north-northeast and point for the entrance. Heavily favor the easterly shoreline to avoid the long shoal. Once into the creek, cruise back to the centerline. Good depths continue at least through the long, slow turn to the north some distance upstream.

Kiawah River When entering Kiawah River, slightly favor the southern shore and be sure to pass unlighted daybeacon #A by at least 20 yards to its southern side. The shoal marked by #A is building south and has already encroached upon this aid to navigation. Otherwise, simply stick to the mid-width. Good depths are held for several miles upstream.

As you cruise the river, watch to the south for an occasional glimpse of the homes on Kiawah Island. A small dock fronts onto the river's southern shore some 3 nautical miles from the entrance. This pier is for the use of residents and guests of the Kiawah resort. Here, you may see a few small craft moored, but there is no room for large cruising craft.

Signs along the shoreline denote an uncharted cable area east of Bryans Creek. Obviously, you should not anchor anywhere near this hazard.

Depths begin to fall off on Kiawah River as the stream passes through an extensive marshy patch west of Bryans Creek. Discontinue your cruise before proceeding too far.

Folly River The Folly River entrance channel is prolifically marked and holds 7-foot minimum depths. Those cruising upriver should, just as you would expect, pass red markers to the boaters' starboard side and take green beacons to port. Watch for excessive leeway, which can quickly ease you out of the channel into shoal water unless you keep a wary eye to your stern.

The Folly River channel is subject to change and re-marking. The configuration of aids to navigation could be very different from that described below by the time of your visit. Check in advance with Mariner's Cay Marina for the latest information.

Enter Folly River by passing between flashing daybeacon #9 and unlighted daybeacon #10. Point to pass unlighted daybeacon #11 to its fairly immediate southeasterly side.

The current edition of chart 11522 shows a broad shoal lacking any aids to navigation east and northeast of #11. Fortunately, the chart does not represent the situation as it now exists on the water. This is the most changeable portion of the river channel, and the current markers are so plentiful as to be almost confusing.

From #11, point to pass between flashing daybeacon #12 and unlighted daybeacon #13. You should take unlighted daybeacon #12A to your starboard side and pass unlighted daybeacon #13A to your port side. After leaving #13A behind, you will next spy flashing daybeacon #14. Pass it to its northwesterly side and continue upriver to flashing daybeacon #15. Come abeam of #15 to its southeasterly quarter.

At #15, the Folly River channel takes a jog to the east-northeast, and good water broadens out in a wide ribbon before you. There are still some shoals abutting the northern and northwestern banks, however, so be sure to pass unlighted daybeacons #16 and #16A to their immediate northwestern side and come abeam of unlighted daybeacon #17 by at least 25 yards to its southeastern quarter. Shoal water building out from the northwestern banks has encroached on #17. Stay away from this aid.

At unlighted daybeacon #17, the channel shifts again, this time back to the northeast. There are currently no additional aids to navigation upriver from #17, but there is really only one other shoal to worry with, and it is located immediately past #17.

Continue favoring the southeasterly shores to avoid the correctly charted shoals jutting out from the northwesterly shoreline. As the mouth of Robbins Creek comes abeam to the northwest, good depths at last open out almost from shore to shore. You need only stay within shouting distance of the centerline to hold good depths as far as the 10-foot fixed bridge. Just before reaching this span, Mariner's Cay Marina will come abeam on the northerly banks.

Robbins Creek Enter Robbins Creek on its mid-width. Good depths of 8 feet or more are maintained as far as Cutoff Reach. Past this point, shoaling not noted on chart 11522 has apparently occurred. Low-tide depths of 4 to 5 feet are soon encountered. Anchorage may be possible on the lower, wider sections of Robbins Creek for craft under 33 feet in length. However, a better spot is just to the north on Folly Creek.

Cutoff Reach Cutoff Reach is a small stream that provides reliable access from Robbins Creek to Folly Creek. Minimum depths of 8 feet are held between the two creeks. The reach is too narrow for anchorage by all but small craft. However, don't hesitate to use this advantageous shortcut if you wish to reach Folly Creek from the interior of Robbins Creek.

Folly Creek Folly Creek, as already noted, can be entered via Robbins Creek and Cutoff Reach. Its principal entrance is located on Folly River just northwest of Oak Island Creek. When cruising through this passage, favor the port (western) shores slightly until coming abeam of Oak Island Creek's mouth to the east. Once past this small stream, cruise back to the mid-width for the next 0.4 nautical mile. As you make your approach to the intersection with Cutoff Reach to the south, begin to favor the southern shore heavily. As clearly shown on chart 11522, there is shoal water along the northern banks lying about the charted marsh island.

Past this point, Folly Creek begins a loop that eventually curves back to the southeast, then sharply to the north-northeast. Stick to the mid-width in this section. You will soon encounter a fixed bridge with only 10 feet of vertical clearance. The fish house described earlier will come abeam on the eastern shore just before you reach the span.

ICW TO NORTH EDISTO RIVER

From the mouth of Elliott Cut, the ICW follows the upper reaches of Stono River as the stream makes a long loop to the west. The route then traverses a short man-made landcut into the headwaters of Wadmalaw River. The Wadmalaw, in turn, leads Waterway cruisers to the intersection of Toogoodoo Creek and North Edisto River.

The upper Stono is fairly well sheltered and usually boasts smooth cruising. However, for much of its length, Wadmalaw River is flanked by large areas of saltwater marsh that are covered completely at high tide. Stiff breezes have more than enough fetch to make for a bumpy ride.

Several small creeks along the way offer good overnight anchorage for craft under 42 feet. Larger vessels will have to find anchorages farther along, on the North Edisto. One facility on the initial (easterly) portion of this run offers transient dockage, gasoline, and diesel fuel, but otherwise you are on your own along this stretch of the Waterway.

The shoreline along this passage varies from undeveloped saltwater marsh and mud flats to higher, wooded shores with light residential development. This is an attractive section of the Waterway and should provide an interesting cruise.

Ross Marine

A full-service boatyard and marina flanks the southeastern banks of the ICW's path through the upper Stono River northeast of flashing daybeacon #25. Ross Marine specializes in full-service mechanical repairs (gas and diesel power plants) and below-waterline haul-out repairs. The firm maintains two travelifts (30-ton and 70-ton) and a marine railway (300-ton capacity).

Within the last two years, Ross Marine has shifted its focus from commercial vessels to pleasure craft. The yard still engages in some commercial work, but visitors will now find far more cruising boats on the ways than ever before. Ross Marine has its own machine shop and features electrical and fiberglass repairs as well. In fact, this yard is known far and wide as a "fiberglass painting specialist." In short, if you can't get it fixed here, better find out how the new-boat market has been doing lately!

Ross Marine can now boast a modern set of floating wooden piers, set directly along the shores of the ICW. Depths alongside run around 7 to 8 feet at low water. While there is sufficient shelter for most weather conditions, this would not be the spot to ride out a heavy blow.

Transients are welcome at these new piers. All berths feature water and 30- and 50- amp power hookups. Gasoline and diesel fuel are available as well. Unfortunately, no showers or laundromat are currently in the offing. Also, there are no restaurants within walking distance, but you could take a taxi ride into Charleston or to nearby Cappy's Seafood Restaurant.

Ross Marine (803) 559-3172

Approach depth: 10 feet
Dockside depth: 9 feet
Accepts transients: yes
Floating wooden piers: yes
Dockside power connections: 30 and 50 amps
Dockside water connections: yes
Showers: yes
Laundromat: yes
Gasoline: yes
Diesel fuel: yes
Mechanical repairs: extensive
Below-waterline repairs: extensive

Stono River Anchorage

Chart 11518 pictures a loop-shaped creek with 10- to 20-foot depths northwest of flashing

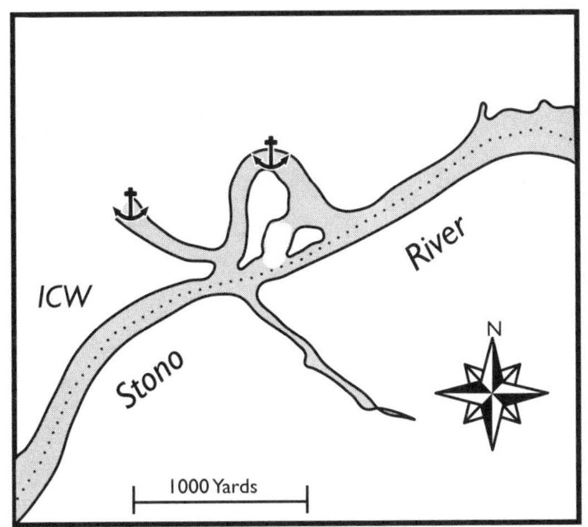

daybeacon #39. The northeasterly portion of this loop makes a good anchorage for boats up to 36 feet. There are several unmarked shoals to avoid, but if you can stay in the channel, minimum depths are 7 to 8 feet. The undeveloped marsh-grass shores do not provide the best of shelter. The charted marsh island fronting the loop is covered almost completely at high tide. Anchoring abeam of this errant body of mud and grass offers scant protection. Instead, track your way carefully upstream to a point just short of the hairpin loop, where chart 11518 notes a sounding of 20 feet. This spot should make a good haven for the night. Be sure to read the navigational information presented later in this chapter before attempting first-time entry.

Another branch of this creek leads northwest off the Waterway immediately northeast of unlighted daybeacon #41. This section of the stream maintains minimum depths of 10 feet, though care must be taken when entering to avoid an unmarked shoal at the stream's mouth. Swinging room is sufficient for anchorage by craft under 36 feet. Shelter is adequate for light to moderate airs. The creek is eventually blocked upstream by a low-level railroad bridge. Select any likely spot to drop the hook short of this span.

Farther upstream on Stono River near unlighted daybeacon #52, cruisers will pass the general area where the Stono Slave Rebellion took place. This infamous uprising was discussed earlier in the chapter.

New Cut Creek

The mouth of New Cut Creek is found southeast of unlighted daybeacon #64. As chart 11518 notes, shoals guard the entrance. Don't attempt to access the stream via this passage. New Cut Creek can be entered from Church Creek, as discussed below.

Church Creek

Church Creek, east of flashing daybeacon #77, offers the best overnight anchorage on Wadmalaw River. Its entrance channel is broad and deep. The western portion of the creek's interior is wide enough to accommodate vessels up to 45 feet. Minimum depths of 10 feet or more hold upstream at least as far as New Cut Landing. For maximum shelter, consider dropping the hook abeam of New Cut Landing's charted

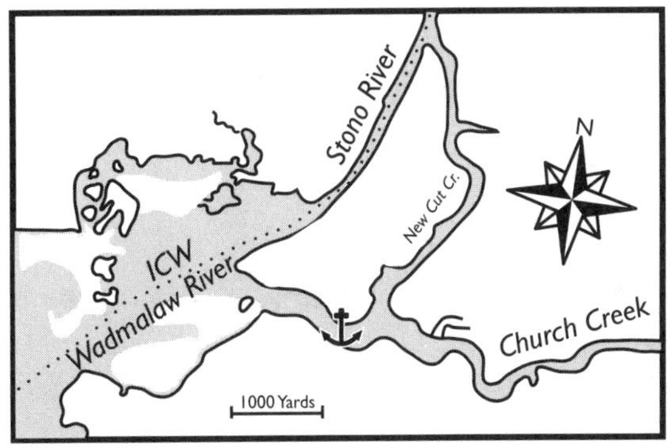

position. The high ground abutting the southwestern banks renders good protection when winds are blowing from this quarter.

A beautiful old home overlooks Church Creek at New Cut Landing. This venerable structure was actually built in nearby Rockville in 1842. It was moved to its present location in 1900.

Upstream, Church Creek splits. New Cut Creek leads off to the north. Continued passage southeast on Church Creek is not recommended, and only adventurous skippers should consider cruising New Cut Creek. If you choose to enter, make sure to read the Church Creek navigation information below.

Wadmalaw River

Southwest of flashing daybeacon #77 and Church Creek, the ICW begins to follow the indefinite reaches of the upper Wadmalaw River. Extensive marsh flats surround this stream, and these shallows are completely covered at high tide. Boaters are presented with a far broader stretch of water than they might expect from studying chart 11518. There are no facilities for pleasure craft on this body of water, and there are few anchorages as well.

Oyster House Creek

Oyster House Creek strikes in to the northwestern shores of the Wadmalaw near flashing daybeacon #86. This stream affords a good overnight haven for small craft that can stand some 5-foot readings. The creek's entrance is guarded by shallows, but vessels under 34 feet in length that draw 3½ feet or less should not hesitate to make use of the creek, providing proper caution is exercised. Actually, it's possible to maintain minimum 8-foot depths if you know where to find the tricky channel, but as this cut is unmarked and often hard to find, the creek is only recommended for vessels of this size and draft.

Old house on Oyster Creek

Most of Oyster Creek's shoreline is undeveloped marsh, but there is one beautiful home on the entrance's southwestern point. This writer has not been able to learn the history of the stately structure, but it's a safe bet that it has guarded the creek's mouth for many a year. Wise boaters will drop anchor just upstream from the stream's mouth soon after passing the old house. Don't try to cruise upstream more than 100 yards or so past this point. Unmarked and uncharted shoals are all too quickly encountered.

ICW TO NORTH EDISTO RIVER NAVIGATION

The South Carolina ICW between the Wappoo Creek-Elliott Cut and North Edisto River presents some real navigational challenges. While the upper Stono River section is not too difficult, the wide mud flats and shoals of Wadmalaw River are another matter entirely. Some years ago, one of this writer's good friends wrote a very popular, albeit sad, cruising story about a young couple who lost their boat on a hidden shoal on these waters. So take a word to the wise: Proceed with caution and keep the sounder in continuous operation.

Entrance from Elliott Cut When leaving the westerly mouth of the Wappoo Creek-Elliott Cut, continue cruising due west for some 25 yards past flashing daybeacon #B. Then cut west-northwest and set course to come abeam of unlighted daybeacon #19A to its fairly immediate northerly side.

Continue on course, pointing to come abeam of and pass unlighted daybeacon #20 on its southerly quarter and to come abeam of flashing daybeacon #21 on its immediate northerly side. Be on guard against the large, charted shoal shelving out from the Stono's northerly banks between #19A and #21.

On the ICW Study chart 11518 for a moment and notice the oblong 4-foot shoal west of #21. Be sure to favor the northern side of the channel when passing this obstruction to avoid an unpleasant meeting of keel and sand. You might also consider using the charted range northwest of flashing daybeacon #21A to help keep to the channel along this run.

At flashing daybeacon #21A, the ICW and Stono River begin a slow curve to the southwest. Watch out for the correctly charted shoal abutting the northwesterly shore between flashing daybeacons #23 and #25. Northbound boaters can make use of another range between #25 and #23.

Flashing daybeacon #25 marks a sharp bend to the northwest in the Waterway channel. Be sure to stay north of #25 and northeast of unlighted daybeacon #27.

After leaving #27 behind, boaters must negotiate yet another bend in the ICW passage. Cruise from #27 to a position some 20 yards southwest of the forward, charted range marker #C. At this point, you should cut sharply to the west and point to pass unlighted daybeacon #28 to its southerly side.

The ICW winds its way hither and yon for another few miles to the John F. Limehouse swing bridge, southwest of unlighted daybeacon #37. Several charted ranges along the way should help you keep to the good water. This seemingly ancient swinging span has a closed vertical clearance of 12 feet and offers a restrictive opening schedule. From Monday through Friday (except legal holidays), the bridge opens only on the hour, 20 minutes past, and 40 minutes past from 7:00 A.M. to 9:00 A.M. and from 4:00 P.M. to 6:00 P.M. At all other times, it supposedly opens on demand.

Stono River Anchorage Favor the northeastern shore as you enter the northeastern side of the loop creek northwest of flashing daybeacon #39. Remember that the charted marsh island bisecting the entrance is all but covered at high tide.

As you cruise into the main branch of the loop, begin heavily favoring the starboard (northeasterly) banks to avoid the charted 1-foot shoal flanking the opposite shore. Consider dropping the hook as soon as this hazard is left behind, before entering the hairpin turn a bit farther to the northwest.

To enter the other branch of the stream north-northeast of unlighted daybeacon #41, favor the port-side shore. After proceeding some 25 yards upstream of the creek's mouth, cruise back to the middle and continue holding to the centerline as you work your way along. You will find the best swinging room about 50 yards upstream from the mouth. Passage on the creek is eventually blocked by a low-level fixed railway bridge.

On the ICW The shoaly northeasterly entrance to New Cut Creek makes in to the ICW opposite unlighted daybeacon #64. Do not try to enter the creek from this position unless you relish the idea of finding the bottom.

Southwest of flashing daybeacon #69, boaters will come upon the mud and marsh flats lying about Wadmalaw River. If you happen to arrive during high tide, the logic behind all this writer's previous warnings about this area will be quite apparent.

Church Creek If you choose to make use of Church Creek's excellent anchorage, continue on the Waterway channel until you are some 50 yards southwest of flashing daybeacon #77. Then swing around to the east and point toward the mid-width of the creek's entrance, passing #77 by some 30 yards to your port side.

Once on the stream's interior, continue cruising on the mid-width. Good depths are maintained as far as the intersection with New Cut Creek.

Eventually, Church Creek intersects the southern mouth of New Cut Creek. Continued passage east or southeast on Church Creek is not recommended, as depths soon become uncertain. New Cut Creek can be cruised for some distance upstream by adventurous captains with craft under 35 feet in length. However, the creek does not offer as much swinging room or protection as the lower section of Church Creek. If you choose to cruise New Cut Creek anyway, stick to the mid-width and discontinue your passage long before reaching the shoals that block the northern entrance.

On the ICW The Waterway skirts a whole series of shoals between flashing daybeacons #77 and #82. Study chart 11518 very carefully and be sure to observe all markers with the greatest care. This is an unusually tricky section of the ICW, and it demands your strictest attention.

Oyster House Creek Remember, do not enter Oyster House Creek unless your boat draws 3½ feet or less. For best depths, favor the port banks heavily when entering. Continue upstream until the house described earlier comes abeam to port. Consider dropping the hook here, as depths become even more uncertain farther upstream.

On the ICW Southwest of Oyster House Creek, the ICW rounds a long turn and parallels a large commercial barge facility flanking the western banks at the charted location of Yonges Island. Large power craft should probably slow to minimum wake speed. You will also want to watch carefully for several seemingly derelict barges anchored along the Waterway's eastern edge.

Be sure to pass well north of flashing daybeacon #83 and unlighted daybeacon #85. These aids sit hard by the charted shallows to the south. Similarly, pass unlighted daybeacons #87 and #89 to their westerly quarters. These aids mark another side of the same shoal.

Successful navigation of the Waterway remains fairly straightforward from the Yonges Island commercial facility to the intersection with Toogoodoo Creek and North Edisto River. Still, there are several more shoals to avoid. While all are well marked, the cautious mariner should keep chart 11518 close at hand to quickly resolve any questions.

Southwest of flashing daybeacon #102, the Wadmalaw rushes to meet Toogoodoo Creek. These two streams join to form the fabled North Edisto River. Let's now turn our attention to the cruising possibilities of Toogoodoo Creek, followed by those of the lower North Edisto River. A continuing account of the ICW will resume later in this chapter.

TOOGOODOO CREEK

Indian-named Toogoodoo Creek is such a large stream that one wonders why it is not called Toogoodoo River. Certainly, smaller streams in coastal South Carolina bear the more important designation.

Another well-respected cruising guide warns against entrance of Toogoodoo Creek by any craft. That guide claims shoaling has raised the bottom to dangerous levels. However, this writer's extensive and detailed on-site research revealed that cruisers who navigate the stream's tricky entrance with care can hold minimum depths of 7 feet. Since no shoals were found between the creek's mouth and the area where it splits into upper and lower branches some 3 nautical miles upstream, this writer recommends Toogoodoo Creek, but again, you must take care when traversing the stream's entrance.

Below the split, large sections of the creek's shoreline exhibit the usual marsh grass, but other portions border higher ground. These waters are quite attractive and seem to be excellent cruising ground. With winds less than 20 knots, boaters may choose to drop the hook anywhere to their liking short of the split. Of course, the havens fronted by the higher banks offer the best protection.

Of the two branches formed at the split, the western fork affords the better cruising opportunity. The eastern branch, known as Lower Toogoodoo Creek, is peppered with unmarked shoals that render navigation a bit too tricky for large cruising craft. The western arm, on the other hand, offers good depths well upstream, excellent protection, and several sights worth your attention.

The usual marshy shores give way to higher, well-wooded banks several hundred yards up the western branch of Toogoodoo Creek. Several fine homes overlook the water, and a project is under way to stabilize the lower shoreline with concrete riprap. This portion of the creek makes an ideal spot to drop the hook for almost any craft under 40 feet. Protection should be sufficient for heavy weather. One of the best anchor-down spots is found just beyond the first sharp turn to the west. Here, the northern shore is lined with tall pines and hardwoods, which afford good protection.

Farther upstream, good depths continue for some distance. Eventually, you will spy the rotting remains of an old car ferry. When this writer first saw this derelict some 10 years ago, it was in pretty good shape. It now resembles nothing so much as a haphazard pile of lumber.

Lem's Bluff Plantation

The house at Lem's Bluff Plantation is readily visible to the northwest at the fork of Toogoodoo

Ruins of ferry on Toogoodoo Creek

Creek. Built in 1842, the home was enlarged extensively in the 1960s. Watch the starboard shore carefully as you cruise up the western branch and you can catch a glimpse of the older section of the house atop a high earthen bank.

TOOGOODOO CREEK NAVIGATION

Successful navigation of Toogoodoo Creek can almost be summed up by saying, "Find your way past the entrance and you've got it made." The creek's mouth is flanked by an extensive collection of obscure but charted shoals to the west and northwest and a smaller course of shallows stretching southwest from the point separating Toogoodoo Creek from Wadmalaw River.

To enter Toogoodoo Creek, continue following the Waterway passage as it cuts southwest on North Edisto River. Maintain this track until you are at least 500 yards past the point of marsh separating Toogoodoo Creek and the Wadmalaw (southwest of flashing daybeacon #102). Only then should you turn back to the north and point for the creek's entrance.

Favor the eastern and southeastern side of the channel as you make your approach! The black, slimy, muddy shoal that flanks the western and northwestern side of the creek's entrance is extensive and is not accurately represented on chart 11518. Of course, you can't afford to approach the east-side banks too closely either. Perhaps this maneuver can be summed up by saying that all boaters should favor the eastern and southeastern third of the creek's mouth.

Past the entrance, good depths open out almost from shore to shore and continue to a point just short of the split. Hold to the center and you should not encounter any obstacles.

After a run of some 1.5 nautical miles, the port shore will begin to rise. If storms or strong winds are not in the offing, simply select a spot that strikes your fancy and drop the hook.

Begin favoring the southwestern banks heavily as you approach the split. A large body of very shoal water extends out from the eastern shoreline. Curve around to port and enter western Toogoodoo Creek on its mid-width.

As you are performing this maneuver, look to the northwest and you will see the newer section of the house at Lem's Bluff Plantation. The western stream first bends to the north but soon cuts back sharply to the west and leaves the chart. Watch the starboard shore before reaching the western turn to catch sight of the older section of the house at Lem's Bluff. Even though western Toogoodoo Creek soon leaves chart 11522, good depths continue far upstream. Remember to stop after coming abeam of the old ferry.

Tidal currents on upper Toogoodoo Creek are absolutely fierce. This is another one of those South Carolina Low Country anchorages where you must be sure the anchor is secure and not dragging before heading for the galley to begin preparations for the evening meal.

NORTH EDISTO RIVER

North Edisto River is, quite simply, one of the finest bodies of water for cruising in all of coastal South Carolina. It is a beautiful stream, free from shoals and readily navigable. The shores

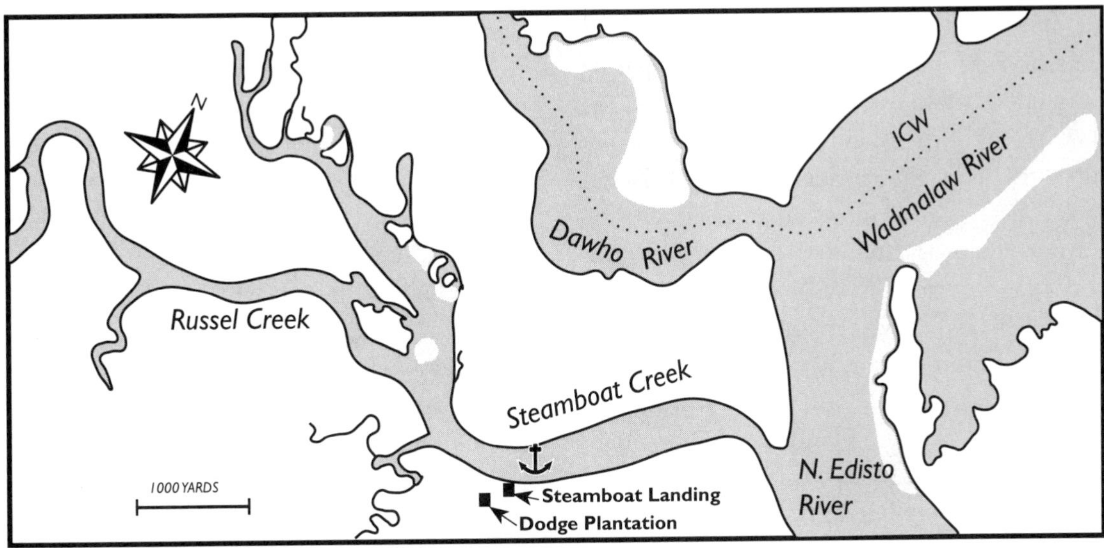

present a sometimes dramatic contrast between marsh grass and higher, forested banks. The river boasts a number of sidewaters, several of which are well suited for overnight anchorage. The North Edisto also has good facilities. Two marinas are located on Bohicket Creek not far from the river's inlet. One is a full-service facility with an on-site restaurant and all the amenities, while the other is a revitalized boatyard offering incredibly conscientious service.

Additionally, many historical sites are readily visible from the waters of the North Edisto and its creeks. You can pause to contemplate fine old plantation homes that once overlooked vast fields of Sea Island cotton. Many of these estates have fascinating legends attached to their history. Several of these tales will be reviewed in this chapter.

About the only drawback to the North Edisto is the sharp chop sometimes spawned by strong breezes on the river's ample width. Pick a day of light to moderate airs and you should not have any difficulty.

To summarize, North Edisto River has just about every quality the cruising boater could ever desire. Easily navigable, attractive, and historical, this storied stream waits eagerly to greet you.

Edisto Island

Edisto Island borders the western reaches of North Edisto River for most of its length. Like most other Sea Islands, Edisto hosted a thriving cotton culture before the Civil War. Unlike many others, however, most of Edisto Island's plantations survived the war. Edisto was abandoned by most of the white population before Union occupation. The beautiful homes left behind were used to house Yankee troops and freed slaves. Edisto's families later returned and reclaimed their homeplaces. While some plantations have fallen victim to the years, many are still intact, and some have been restored to their former glory.

Not only the plantation homes have survived on Edisto Island. So has the colorful history of the place. Among a host of historical and folk accounts that this writer reviewed in preparing this guide, the late Nell S. Graydon's fascinating descriptions of the island planters clearly stand out as the most unforgettable of the lot. In her book *Tales of Edisto*, Graydon gives a haunting portrait of Edisto Island as it is today and as it was in days long gone. Listen as she describes her beloved island. "Forty miles southwest of Charleston . . . within the arms of two tidal rivers, lies a fabulous Island. An aura of mystic and alluring charm hovers over the Island and its old homes. Weird gray moss shrouds with ghostly grandeur the queenly magnolias and gnarled live oaks around the plantation houses. . . .

"In the stillness of the early evening, the faint haunting melody of a slave lullaby drifting through the twilight, the galloping of a horse passing by, the echo of a footstep, or the swish of a silken skirt can bring forth half-forgotten memories of long ago. Then, if you have been welcomed into the homes and hearts of the Island, you may hear stories of the people and the land. . . .

"Edisto changes, but somehow remains the same. Today, there is the hum of automobile tires on the highway and the bustle of holiday crowds on the beach. But the phantoms of the past persist. Amid the roar of the ocean surf . . . a wave slaps the beach with the sound of a pistol shot. The gray moss streams from live oaks like plumes from the helmets of young men dressed in the armor of the tournament. An old Island resident bows in passing with the courtesy and the calm assurance of a bygone era. Just as surely as the flood tide leaves its imprint on the shore, life marks a land."

Tom Point Creek

Tom Point Creek is a lovely, deep stream that makes in to the western shores of North Edisto River north of White Point. Some of the stream's upper reaches border high, well-wooded banks and make for secure anchorage in all but gale-force winds. Swinging room is a little skimpy, and captains with craft larger than 36 feet may be a bit crowded. You may want to employ a Bahamian-style mooring to minimize swinging room. Minimum depths on the centerline run about 7 feet.

For maximum elbow room, try the water west-northwest of the creek's first short but sharp jog to the southwest. Depths run 8 to 12 feet, and protection is good from all winds. This is a delightful, undeveloped portion of Tom Point Creek, and it is highly favored by this writer. The shoreline is mostly in its natural state, though here and there a private home breaks the green landscape.

There is an off-the-beaten-path feeling about Tom Point Creek that many cruisers will find unforgettable. While not as large as some, and lacking the historical sites so readily visible from several of the Edisto's other streams, Tom Point Creek nevertheless remains a place to savor.

Steamboat Creek

Steamboat Creek and its sister stream, Westbank Creek, are two of the most historical bodies of water along the storied course of North Edisto River. Besides offering good overnight refuge, Steamboat Creek provides views of several sites of interest on Edisto Island.

The eastern mouth of Steamboat Creek thrusts into the North Edisto's southwestern flank south of the ICW's exodus from the Edisto via Dawho River. Steamboat Creek's mouth is marked by unlighted daybeacon #2. The stream is free of shoals as far as its intersection with Russel Creek and boasts minimum depths of 8 feet.

While a bit wide for effective shelter during really nasty weather, the waters of Steamboat Creek are usually tranquil unless an unusually fresh breeze is blowing. If you do not anticipate a heavy blow, consider dropping the hook here for a night spent on some truly historic waters. For this writer's money, the waters abeam of the old octagonal steamship house (described below) are the first choice every time.

While most of the shoreline is composed of the usual marsh grass, a stretch of higher ground is located on the southern shore some 1.2 nautical miles upstream from the entrance. Here, not one but two historical sites well worth your attention can be observed.

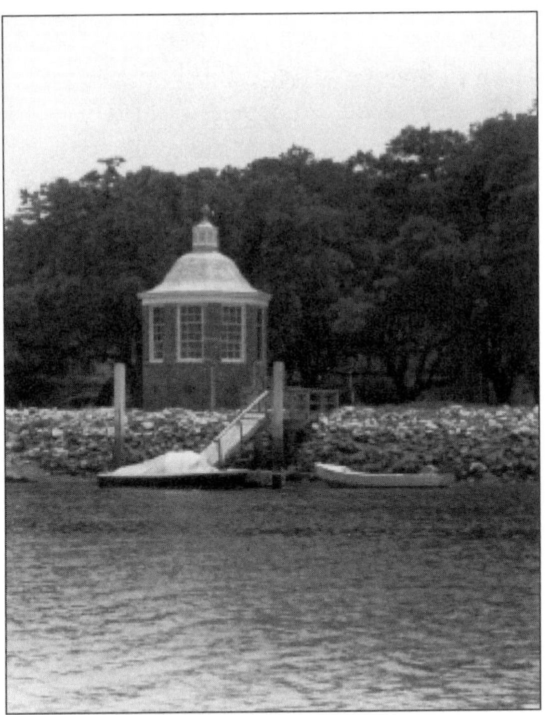

Octagonal house, Steamboat Creek

Exploring cruisers will first catch sight of a small, octagonal brick building with high windows. This interesting structure was used by island residents as they waited for the steamboats that regularly plied the waters between Edisto Island and Charleston before the Civil War. Apparently, this quaint mode of transportation also gave the creek its name.

William Seabrook Plantation

You must look carefully to the southeast behind the octagonal building to catch sight of the William Seabrook Plantation house, now known as Dodge Plantation. According to the South Carolina Sea Grant Consortium, it was built in 1810 and represents "the wealth brought to island planters by their fine long-staple cotton crops. This house set the style of houses built on the island by many other planters."

In *Tales of Edisto*, Nell S. Graydon describes the one-time grandeur of Seabrook House: "The house is close to the water's edge, with an iron railing bordering the portico and the double front steps. [William] Seabrook had his initials molded across the front of the ironwork. . . . Between Steamboat Creek and the house was a formal garden with a multitude of walkways bordered with boxwood. Here, on warm afternoons in the early spring and late fall, tea was served, and many a frosted glass of julep sipped."

In 1825, Seabrook House received one of the most honored guests it has ever known. The Marquis de Lafayette was on a tour of the new

United States and accepted an invitation to visit the island home. The entertainment and hospitality shown to the dashing hero of the Revolution were in the best sumptuous Sea Island tradition.

While Lafayette was in residence, he was asked to name the youngest daughter of William Seabrook, born just a few days before the marquis' visit. Without hesitation, Lafayette dubbed her Carolina Lafayette Seabrook. We shall meet this remarkable woman again in connection with another Edisto Island plantation.

Some years later, William Seabrook's son returned from a trip abroad and proceeded to hold forth at great length about the pomp and glitter of Paris. Eventually, according to Nell S. Graydon, the elder Seabrook had enough of his young son's colorful descriptions, and "lapsing into the Gullah of the Island said, 'Yuh like 'um son, I buy 'um fur yuh.' " To be sure, Seabrook wasn't serious, but this laughable episode shows how the Sea Island planters had become so accustomed to their wealth that the purchase of an entire European capital did not seem too extravagant.

Westbank Creek

The mouth of historic Westbank Creek fronts onto the southwestern banks of North Edisto River some 2.3 nautical miles southeast of Dawho River. Happy waterborne explorers of this stream have the opportunity to anchor abeam of not one but two memorable plantations, each with its own unique story.

Westbank Creek maintains 6-foot minimum depths on its mid-width and affords sufficient swinging room for craft up to 36 feet. There are a few unmarked shallows to avoid, but most cautious navigators can bypass these obstacles.

The shores of Westbank Creek are mostly saltwater marsh and mud flats, but a section of higher ground flanks the southern shores as the stream enters a long loop to the north. Here, two splendid plantation homes watch serenely over the creek. Both were built during the height of the Sea Island cotton culture. The presence of these two landmarks makes a cruise of Westbank Creek an unforgettable experience.

Many boaters will find it convenient to anchor in the body of the first hairpin turn on Westbank Creek, in the area where chart 11518 shows a sounding of 8 feet. Depths actually range from 8 to as much as 20 feet along this stretch of the creek. In addition to good protection courtesy of the high ground to the south and southwest, this haven is overlooked by historic Cassina Point Plantation, described below.

Another good anchorage is abeam of Oak Island Plantation, where 11518 predicts a sounding of 22 feet or so. This spot is very similar to the refuge described above, save that it offers slightly less swinging room.

Cassina Point Plantation

The beautifully restored Cassina Point Plantation house is the first of the two historic structures you will encounter on Westbank Creek. The lovely house sits back some distance from the water, but the marsh grass cannot hide the quiet grandeur of this old homeplace.

Cassina Point Plantation was the home of Carolina Lafayette Seabrook and her husband, James Hopkinson. They lived here peacefully until the end of their days, but their great house was not built without some difficulty.

Carolina was raised in an atmosphere of unbelievable wealth in her father's house. She grew into a beautiful woman by all accounts and eventually left South Carolina for a grand trip abroad to the courts of Europe.

Returning to the United States, Carolina made the rounds of the party circuit in the Northeast. There, she met James Hopkinson, dashing grandson of a New Jersey signer of the Declaration of Independence. He became so infatuated with Carolina that he followed her home to Edisto Island. Here, he quickly grew to love the island and adopted coastal South Carolina as his home.

Carolina, however, had other ideas. She delighted in the attention commanded by her beauty and reputation in Northern society and wished to make her home in the Northeast. When Hopkinson asked for her hand, she consented on the condition that he would agree to live in the North. The young man had already planned a grand plantation on Edisto Island, and so he refused Carolina's request. So strong was the young girl's will that the lumber for Cassina Point sat on the site for three years before Carolina finally relented and the grand house was built at last.

Cassina Point Plantation, Westbank Creek

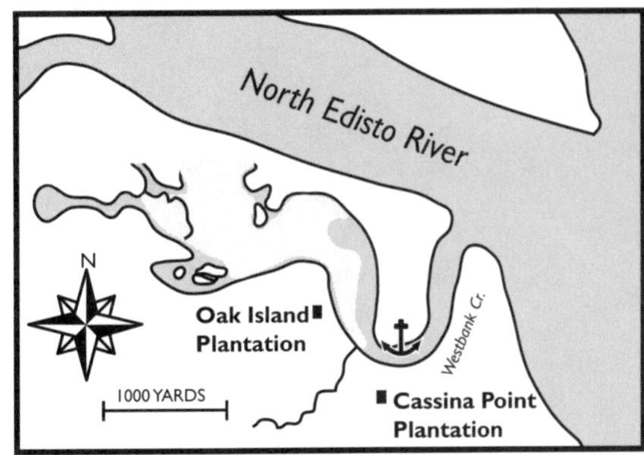

Within the last several years, Cassina Point Plantation (803-869-2535) has been opened as an exclusive inn. Unfortunately, there is no ready access to the inn by water, and even those who arrive by land will need directions from the innkeepers. Nevertheless, a night or two spent in this romantic homeplace with its memories of days long gone will be an experience to remember always.

Oak Island Plantation

Oak Island is the second of Westbank Creek's plantations. It sits closer to the water than Cassina Point Plantation, and visiting cruisers should have an excellent view of the noble structure. This plantation house, too, has been lovingly restored. It is a haunting sight from the placid waters of the creek.

Oak Island Plantation was built by the brother of Carolina Seabrook Hopkinson, William Seabrook, Jr. Here, he lived with his wife, Martha Edings, in the greatest luxury imaginable. Shortly after the Civil War, the couple's son wrote his reminiscences of Oak Island Plantation as it was in its days of glory. Recounted by

Oak Island Plantation, Westbank Creek

Nell S. Graydon in *Tales of Edisto*, this passage is almost dreamlike in its description not only of the house and its grounds, but of the lifestyle of the Sea Island planters: "I became so accustomed to its grandeur it ceased to impress me . . . lawns encircling the house occupied acres, outbuildings of every description, camellias of every known species, 1500 varieties of roses, an apiary and fish pond in the middle of which there was a latticed house covered with roses. A rustic bridge crossed to the Island. Walkways were covered with crushed shells. At the end of the avenue there was a park with many deer—including a white one. There was a quaint brick house where an iron chest of select wines were kept. Near the water was a dairy, a building made of crushed shells. Just beyond the dairy was a large longboat house. Sail and row boats were kept there and above were the bath houses. In the carriage house were seven or eight vehicles. The family used to ride to Virginia Springs and carriages were kept there during their stay and sent home the first of September when the family went to New York."

Leadenwah Creek

Leadenwah Creek cuts the northeastern banks of the North Edisto directly across the river from Westbank Creek. This stream has numerous unmarked shoals, making navigation quite tricky for cruising craft. If you can find it, there is a fairly deep channel with 6-foot minimum depths, and the creek does offer some anchorage possibilities. Because of its hazards, Leadenwah Creek is recommended only for craft under 35 feet drawing 4 feet or less, captained by adventurous skippers.

The creek's starboard shore supports fairly extensive residential development, but the port banks are the familiar saltwater marsh. One particularly beautiful home sits prominently on the fork of the creek near its mouth.

Those who successfully navigate Leadenwah Creek might consider dropping the hook between the first fork in the creek and the main stream's next turn to the east. Be sure to cruise upstream past the charted shallows flanking the northwestern banks before anchoring. Set your hook so your craft will swing well away from the thin, correctly charted band of shoals along the eastern side of the stream.

Another possible overnight stop lies along the southern banks of Leadenwah Creek upstream of its first sharp bend to the east. Here, chart 11522 correctly predicts minimum 15-foot depths, though you must be on guard against the considerable shoal and the marsh islands to the north and northwest.

All boaters should be *sure* to read the navigational account of Leadenwah Creek presented later in this chapter before attempting the stream. Even then, many captains will want to think long and hard before tackling this navigationally demanding body of water.

Bohicket Creek

Bohicket Creek is a large stream on the northeastern shores of the North Edisto near the river's inlet. This important water body is host to the region's best facilities and to numerous historical sites as well. Cruising boaters traveling on North Edisto River will certainly want to make the acquaintance of Bohicket Creek.

The channel serving Bohicket Creek is well marked but still tricky in places. Shoal water is very much in evidence on the stream, though all such hazards are marked. Visiting cruisers must follow the aids to navigation and chart 11522 carefully, or they might spend the afternoon perched on a sandbar or mud bank contemplating the value of good coastal navigation. Minimum depths in the marked channel are currently 8 feet, with most soundings ranging from 9 to as much as 30 feet.

Bohicket Marina Village, one of the finest facilities of its kind in all of coastal South Carolina, is located 3 nautical miles upstream on the creek's southeastern banks (upstream of unlighted daybeacon #8). This ultramodern marina-retail complex gladly accepts transient boaters and boasts just about any service that mariners might ever require. The marina's docks are set well out into the stream and are overlooked by a semicircular complex of shops and restaurants. The visual effect is rather dramatic from the water.

All berths at Bohicket Marina Village feature wooden-decked floating piers with freshwater connections and 30- and 50-amp power hookups. Depths alongside are an impressive 12 feet or better. Gasoline and diesel fuel are readily available, as is a full-line ship's and variety store. First-rate showers and a laundromat are conveniently located just behind the dockage basin. The facility also offers dry-stack storage for small power craft.

Rectory house, Rockville, Bohicket Creek

There are now four on-site restaurants at Bohicket Village, including a pizza parlor. Rosebank Farms Cafe serves both lunch and dinner. The Privateer restaurant is well known throughout this part of the Low Country for its wide-ranging evening meals. By the spring of 1996, Abaco's Steakhouse will also be a part of

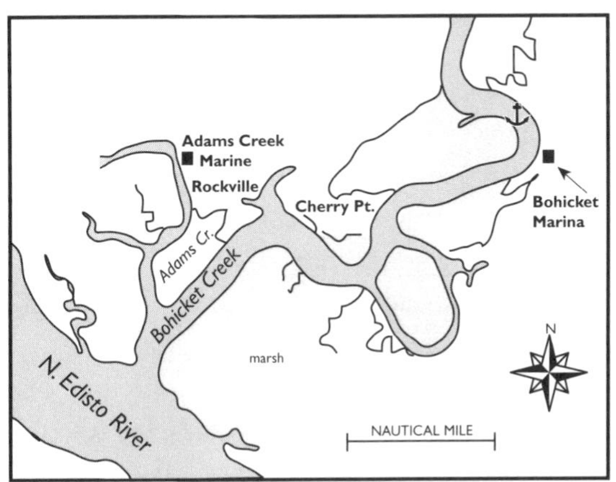

the village, serving three meals a day.

In addition to the marina and the ship's store, the Bohicket Village complex boasts a number of other gift shops and offices. It's an interesting spot to spend an hour or two strolling about while sampling its many offerings.

Bohicket Marina Village is about as good a spot as you will ever find to coil the lines and rest from your travels. With all the adjacent facilities and shops, plus the attraction of nearby Kiawah Island, it's not hard to understand why veteran South Carolina cruisers set their course for this fine facility year after year.

Bohicket Marina Village
(803) 768-1280

Approach depth: 8 feet (minimum)
Dockside depth: 12+ feet
Accepts transients: yes
Floating wooden piers: yes
Dockside power connections: 30 and 50 amps
Dockside water connections: yes
Showers: yes
Laundromat: yes
Gasoline: yes
Diesel fuel: yes
Ship's and variety store: yes
Restaurants: 4 on-site

While the resourceful skipper can certainly find a place to drop anchor on the marked section of lower Bohicket Creek, the surrounding shoals make for some cramped spaces. Additionally, the waters on this portion of the creek are a bit wide and do not afford the best shelter. There is also quite a bit of small-craft traffic, particularly on weekends.

Instead, consider anchoring in the loop just north of Bohicket Marina Village. High ground fronts both shores and offers good protection when winds are blowing from the east or west. The banks of the loop to the north and south also give good protection when winds are blowing from these quarters. Minimum depths are 9 to 10 feet, and there is enough swinging room for boats as large as 55 feet.

Past the marina, Bohicket Creek extends for some 12 nautical miles to the north and northeast until it finally peters out in a marshy area above Hoopstick Island. While most of this route holds minimum depths of 7 feet, there are numerous unmarked shoals to avoid. This portion of the creek (above the just-reviewed anchorage) is not recommended for craft that draw more than 4 feet or those over 35 feet in length. If you choose to cruise upper Bohicket Creek, take your time and watch the sounder.

The shoreline of Bohicket Creek offers a variety of scenery to the visiting boater. The familiar saltwater marsh is very much in evidence, as you would expect. Other sections present higher, wooded shores with moderate residential development. Many of the homes on the upper reaches of the creek have long piers extending across the marsh grass to docks fronting the deep water. Just upstream from Bohicket Marina Village, a Girl Scout camp borders the port shore. Unquestionably, though, the most impressive sight on the shores of Bohicket Creek is the village of Rockville.

Rockville

Established in the 1800s as a summer watering place for the Sea Island planters, Rockville is perhaps the best-preserved example of those warm-weather retreats. Today, Rockville sits serenely on the shores of Bohicket Creek and looks quietly over the creek's waters much as it has for over 150 years. The village's simple but beautiful homes are a lovely sight from the water. More than one passing boater has paused in his travels to admire their quiet elegance.

Every summer, the quiet community erupts in pageantry and enthusiasm when the annual Rockville Regatta is held on Bohicket Creek. Begun in the 1890s, the yearly race has continued its unbroken tradition to the present day. If you happen to be cruising these waters during the celebration, don't fail to stop by and join in the festivities.

Adams Creek

Adams Creek is an offshoot of its larger sister, Bohicket Creek. The smaller stream breaks off to the north from the larger creek about 0.5 nautical mile from the North Edisto. Locally, the stream is known as Breakfast Creek because large numbers of breakfast shrimp are often netted here.

Adams Creek boasts minimum 10-foot depths and an easily followed channel with several interesting homes along the way. Vessels as large as 30 feet might find enough room to anchor, but skippers must be careful to select a spot that avoids the considerable commercial fishing traffic that often plies the creek.

One of the best spots to drop the hook comes up just past the last commercial docks as the creek takes a bend to the west. Depths here range from 10 to 13 feet, and the high eastern and northern banks give fairly good protection when winds are blowing from either of these directions.

Adams Creek Marine gazes proudly out over the eastern shore of the like-named creek just before the stream passes through the western loop discussed above. The present owners have transformed this facility from the seedy establishment it once was into one of the finest boatyards that boaters will ever be lucky enough to find. This writer has never encountered a boatyard staff that was so obviously concerned with customers' needs and so determined to provide absolutely first-quality work. If you are in need of mechanical repairs for either a gasoline or diesel power plant, or if you need below-waterline haul-out service, you need look no further.

Give the caring people at Adams Creek Marine a call and set a date. You can then relax, knowing your needs will be met in as sure and honest a fashion as you are ever likely to find in the boating game.

While most of the wooden floating docks at Adams Creek Marine are understandably reserved for service customers, the management has informed this writer that transients can occasionally be accommodated. However, the forte here is clearly service work, and dockage is very much a sideline.

Adams Creek Marine (803) 559-5594

Approach depth: 10 feet
Dockside depth: 6–9 feet
Accepts transients: limited
Floating wooden piers: yes
Dockside power connections: 30 and 50 amps
Dockside water connections: yes
Mechanical repairs: extensive
Below-waterline repairs: extensive
Ship's store: yes

North Edisto Inlet

North Edisto Inlet is much wider and more

stable than most South Carolina seaward cuts. It is marked by several charted aids, which usually imply the presence of a fairly stable channel. However, as is true with all inlets, it is subject to continual change and can quickly give rise to heavy seas. It would be most wise to check on current channel conditions at Bohicket Marina Village before running the cut.

NORTH EDISTO RIVER NAVIGATION

As noted, North Edisto River is wide, deep, and generally free of shoals. The cruising boater needs simply to avoid the few shallow areas noted on chart 11522 for successful navigation of the river.

There are very few aids to navigation on the North Edisto. While this does not present any real difficulty as far as staying off the bottom, you must practice good navigation to maintain a fix on your position. It's quite easy to cruise pleasantly down the North Edisto enjoying the river and the landscape, then suddenly realize that you do not know where you are. To avoid this problem, note the passing of the various creeks as you work your way downstream.

All boaters will need to turn south-southwest at flashing daybeacon #102 and enter the broad waters of the North Edisto. About 0.8 nautical mile downstream, the mouth of Tom Point Creek comes abeam on the western shore.

Tom Point Creek Enter the creek on its mid-width and continue to hold the middle ground as you cruise upstream. The waters with the most swinging room will be found as the stream makes its first turn to the west. Discontinue your cruise before reaching charted Park Island.

On the North Edisto South of Tom Point Creek, the next sidewater encountered is Dawho River. This stream is part of the ICW and will be covered later in this chapter. Stick to the mid-width of the North Edisto and it is a straightforward run south and southeast to the mouth of Steamboat Creek. Again, hold to the mid-width of the river and don't allow leeway to ease you onto the small shoal near Wadmalaw Point.

Steamboat Creek The entrance to Steamboat Creek is marked by unlighted daybeacon #2. Pass #2 to its southerly side and enter the creek on its mid-width. Continue holding to the centerline and you can cruise through 10-foot minimum depths as far as the intersection of Russel and Long Creeks. Watch the southerly shore for a good view of the octagonal steamboat house about halfway between the entrance and the split.

Under no circumstances should you consider cruising farther upstream than the confluence of Russel and Long Creeks. Unmarked shoaling has raised depths to dangerous levels on both creeks. Discontinue your passage of Steamboat Creek before reaching the forks.

On the North Edisto It is another straightforward southeasterly run of about 1.5 nautical miles to a point abeam of Leadenwah Creek to the northeast and Westbank Creek to the southwest.

Westbank Creek For best depths, favor the port (southeastern) shore a bit when entering Westbank Creek. As the stream begins to bend to the west, good depths open out almost from shore to shore. Watch the port banks and you will spy the two historic plantations on the creek's southern shoreline. This is an excellent spot to drop the hook. While good depths continue for some distance, the creek's upper reaches border extensive mud flats, and protection is minimal. This portion of the stream is not recommended for cruising craft.

Leadenwah Creek Successful navigation of Leadenwah Creek calls for cautious cruising. As can be seen from a quick study of chart 11522, the stream's entrance is flanked by unmarked shallows. The interior sections are also plagued with shoals. If you choose to enter, feel your way along at slow speed and keep an eagle eye on the sounder.

Be careful to avoid the considerable shoal protruding from the northwestern point when entering. You must also take care to bypass the shallow water abutting the eastern shore. Study chart 11522 carefully to familiarize yourself with the necessary maneuvers.

For best depths, proceed south down the North Edisto far enough to turn back north and enter the creek's mid-width. Once inside, good depths open out from bank to bank as far as the creek's first split.

Do not attempt to enter the western branch of the first fork. It is shoal and narrow. Favor the southeastern shoreline when entering the northeastern arm. This maneuver will enable you to avoid the shoal on the northwestern shore, clearly pictured on chart 11522.

Farther upstream, the creek takes a hairpin turn back to the east-southeast. Begin heavily favoring the southern banks as you enter the bend. Even a cursory glance at 11522 reveals the large body of shoal water and marsh flanking the northern and northeastern banks in the body of this bend.

Continued passage upstream is not recommended except for devil-may-care skippers. Unmarked shoals abound, and it is all too easy to run aground just when you think all is well. If you do choose to proceed, study the shoals marked on chart 11522 carefully. According to this writer's on-site research, the chart is accurate in this section.

Bohicket Creek To enter Bohicket Creek, pass well to the southeast of the forward North Edisto Inlet lighted range marker. Enter the creek on its mid-width, but begin favoring the southeasterly shoreline as you approach the intersection with Adams Creek. Point to eventually pass unlighted daybeacon #2 to your starboard side, and set course to come abeam of unlighted daybeacon #4 well to its northwesterly side. These two markers denote a large shoal southeast of their position.

While passing #4, you will observe the town of Rockville to the north and northwest. Take a few moments to admire the beauty of the community's historic homes. Good depths hold to within 50 yards of the shoreline.

Bohicket Creek now follows a long loop to the southeast and then cuts back to the north-northeast. Unlighted daybeacons #5 and #7 mark another large shoal abutting the northeastern shoreline. Obviously, you should pass #5 and #7 to their southwestern sides and favor the southern banks heavily through the bend.

Just before the creek takes another jog to the east, unlighted daybeacon #8 warns of shallow water on the easterly shore. Pass #8 to its westerly side.

Favor the southerly shore just a bit as you swing out of the easterly loop. Continue cruising upstream and Bohicket Marina Village will soon come abeam to starboard.

Exploration of Bohicket Creek past the loop

above Bohicket Marina Village is not for the faint of heart. While 7-foot minimum depths are held on the stream's mid-width for the most part, there are numerous unmarked shoals waiting to trap those who are a bit too adventurous. These waters are strictly not recommended for craft drawing more than 4 feet. Otherwise, if you simply must go where none have gone before, feel your way along, scrupulously avoid points of land, and, as always in suspect waters, watch the sounder.

Those who do cruise upstream will soon encounter the previously mentioned Girl Scout camp on the western banks. About 4 nautical miles farther along, two beautiful white homes with a wide expanse of green grass are visible on the western shores.

ICW TO SOUTH EDISTO RIVER

The ICW leaves the southwestern mouth of Wadmalaw River and follows the North Edisto to the southwest for 1.5 nautical miles. The Waterway then enters the eastern reaches of Dawho River and follows this stream until it intersects Watts Cut. The cut leads in turn to South Edisto River.

This section of the ICW used to be remarkable for its navigational difficulty. Fortunately, extensive dredging by the Army Corps of Engineers seems to have removed most of the shoals that used to encroach directly upon the channel. Of course, these obstructions might always develop again at some future date, and boaters are still advised to proceed with caution.

A quick inspection of chart 11518 would probably lead most boaters to think that a variety of good anchorages are available on Dawho River. Unfortunately, shoaling not noted on the chart has raised the bottom on all but one of these sidewaters to bare low-tide mud flats. With the exception of Fishing Creek, cruisers are strictly warned against any exploration of waters outside of the Waterway channel in this region.

The Dawho's shoreline is composed of marsh grass for the most part, but here and there some higher banks exhibit light residential development. There are also a few commercial fishing docks along the way.

Visiting boaters will not find any facilities along this stretch of the Waterway. In fact, the ICW traveler is pretty much on his own until reaching Beaufort, still many miles to the south.

Fishing Creek

Fishing Creek cuts the shoreline north-northwest of unlighted daybeacon #132, just southwest of the Dawho River swing bridge. This small but deep stream provides the only opportunity for sheltered overnight anchorage on Dawho River and Watts Cut. Even so, swinging room is sufficient only for boats under 34 feet in length. Minimum depths run between 8 and 10 feet, and much of the stream is deeper. The shoreline is flanked by the all-too-usual marsh grass, which gives scant protection from really heavy weather. Even so, Fishing Creek is a good bet for overnight anchorage if there is sufficient swinging room for your craft.

The long, straight stretch of the creek after its first sharp turn to the northwest is one of the best spots to anchor. Another good choice is located just before the creek's split. For the explorers among us, good depths continue far upstream.

ICW TO SOUTH EDISTO RIVER NAVIGATION

From flashing daybeacon #102 at the southwesterly extreme of Wadmalaw River, set course to come abeam of flashing daybeacon #110 to its southerly side. This aid to navigation is found hard by the easterly entrance of Dawho River. It is a lengthy run of 1.7 nautical miles between #102 and #110. Once abeam of #110, swing to the west-southwest and set a new course to come abeam of unlighted can buoy #111 to its fairly immediate northwesterly side.

The short run from #111 to pass between the next two aids, unlighted daybeacon #112 and unlighted can buoy #113, is fairly straightforward, but be aware of the correctly charted shallows to the northwest.

After passing between #112 and #113, set a new course to come abeam of unlighted daybeacon #116 to its fairly immediate southern side. Ignore flashing daybeacon #115, located near the southern banks. A patch of shoal water has built up between these two aids. The shallows are shown on chart 11518 as an area of 5-foot soudings. To avoid this shoal, favor the northeastern side of the Waterway slightly for some 200 yards northwest of #116. However, you must not compensate too much or you will strike the shoal to the north of #116.

Point to come between flashing daybeacon #119 and unlighted daybeacon #118. Note the shallow water southeast of #118.

The most welcome channel improvement on Dawho River is found between #118 and the next upstream aid, unlighted daybeacon #120. Boats used to run aground all too often by attempting to run a straight course from a position between #119 and #118 to #120. While it's still not a bad idea to favor the southerly banks slightly during the easternmost third of the run between #118 and #120, extensive soundings in 1995 showed that minimum 7-foot depths are held even when running almost straight between the two markers.

Past #120, the Waterway becomes easier to follow and is generally free of shoals. Don't attempt to enter the loop north of unlighted daybeacon #126 by either of its entrances. Both passages have shoaled to bare mud at low tide. Also, the small loop south of #128 holds only some 1 to 2 feet of water at low tide.

The Dawho River swing bridge will come up southwest of flashing daybeacon #130. The old 8-foot swing bridge still pictured on chart 11518 has now been replaced by a 65-foot fixed span. The old bridge has been removed entirely.

Fishing Creek The entrance to Fishing Creek is found just southwest of the swing bridge. To enter, favor the port shore heavily. On the interior portion of the creek, good depths stretch out almost from shore to shore.

On the ICW From Fishing Creek, the ICW follows Watts Cut to South Edisto River. Flashing daybeacon #143 marks the Waterway's entry into this impressive body of water. A continuing account of the ICW route is presented in the next chapter.

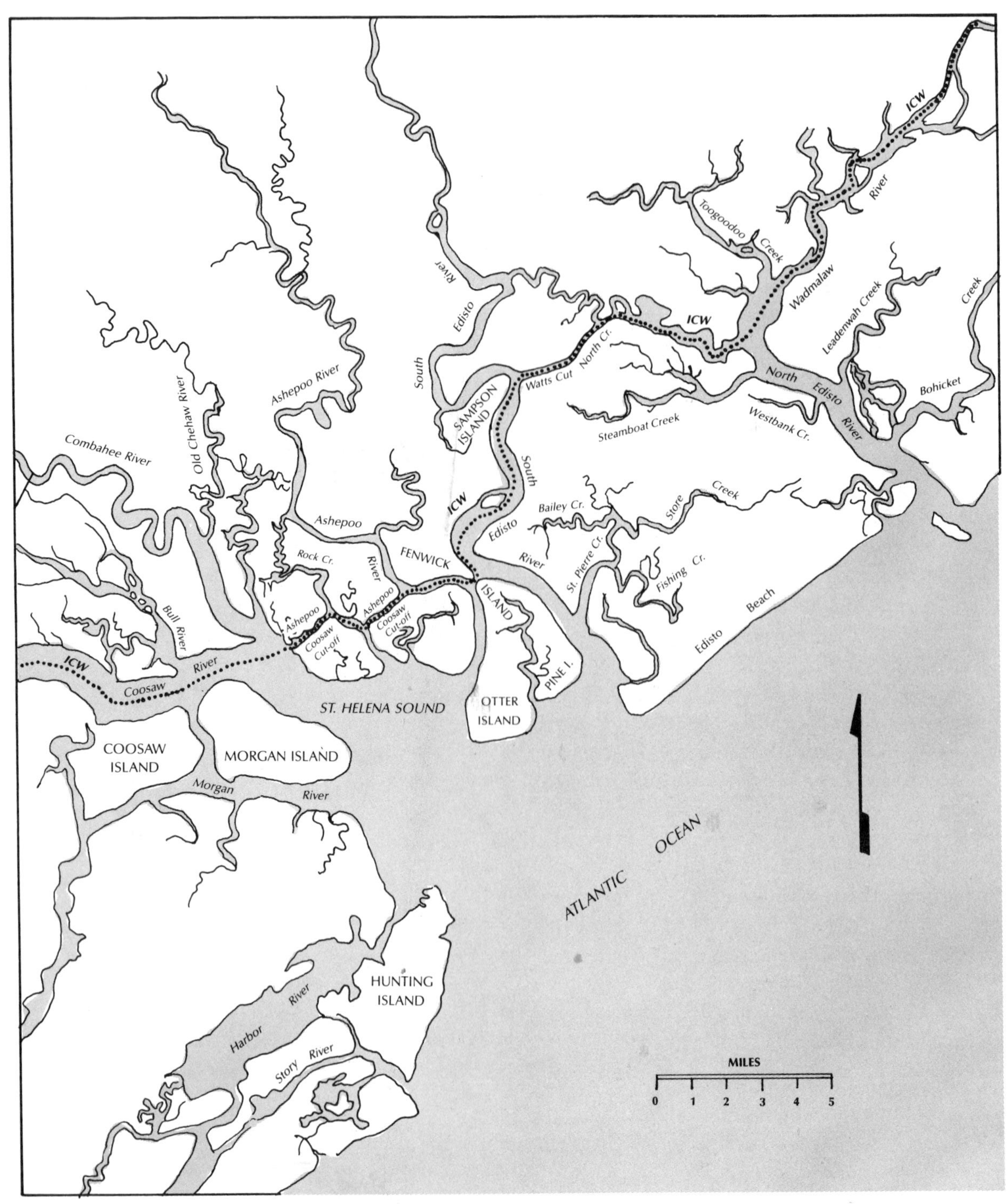

ICW
Toogoodoo Creek
River
Wadmalaw
Leadenwah Creek
Creek
River
South Edisto
Ashepoo River
Old Chehaw River
Combahee River
Watts Cut
North Cr.
North Edisto River
Bohicket
SAMPSON ISLAND
Steamboat Creek
Westbank Cr.
South Edisto River
Bailey Cr.
Store Creek
Ashepoo
Rock Cr.
River
FENWICK
St. Pierre Cr.
Fishing Cr.
ISLAND
Edisto Beach
Bull River
Ashepoo
Coosaw Cut-off
Ashepoo
Coosaw Cut-off
Coosaw River
PINE I.
ST. HELENA SOUND
OTTER ISLAND
COOSAW ISLAND
MORGAN ISLAND
Morgan River
ATLANTIC OCEAN
HUNTING ISLAND
Harbor River
Story River
MILES
0 1 2 3 4 5

South Edisto River to St. Helena Sound

A definite change in character becomes evident as one enters the waters of South Edisto River from the western mouth of the Dawho. Except for the ICW, friendly, well-traveled routes give way to some of the most forlorn waters in all of coastal South Carolina. This condition persists all the way south to the beautiful port city of Beaufort.

Between Dawho River and St. Helena Sound, three major bodies of water comprise the vast majority of the accessible cruising grounds: South Edisto River, Ashepoo River, and Rock Creek. All are traversed for a short distance by the ICW. Outside the Waterway's familiar confines, however, boaters will discover waters seldom visited by the passing cruiser. Captains who thrive on waters off the beaten path will find much to interest them here, while those who enjoy the lively atmosphere of coastal marinas may wish to put this stage of their journey quickly behind them.

Three marinas are available to the cruising boater between Dawho River and Beaufort River, but all require a fairly substantial cruise off the Waterway. Be sure to have plenty of fuel on board before beginning your sojourn.

On the other hand, anchorages abound. Several small streams and creeks stand ready to provide pleasant overnight stops miles from the most remote vestige of civilization. In a few cases, it is even possible to anchor within sight of a historic plantation for a truly memorable stay.

Charts

Two charts are required to cover the waters discussed in this chapter:

11518 details the ICW to St. Helena Sound and covers portions of the South Edisto and Ashepoo Rivers as well as Rock Creek

11517 covers the upper and lower sections of the South Edisto and Ashepoo Rivers

All these waters are relatively free from navigational hazards. The South Edisto, the Ashepoo, and Rock Creek are all mostly deep. There are exceptions, however, so be sure to consult the navigational sections in this chapter before venturing far off the ICW.

Much of the shoreline of the three streams consists of undeveloped saltwater marsh grass. A few small villages are found along the way, but the passing boater will not encounter a single major town on the water between Dawho River and Beaufort.

The ICW follows the course of South Edisto River for a short distance, then ducks across Ashepoo River and Rock Creek on its way to the wide Coosaw River. This section of the Waterway is relatively straightforward, with excellent shelter. Cruisers need not fear choppy waters unless the fickle winds exceed 20 knots.

The waters of the South Edisto, the Ashepoo, and Rock Creek provide excellent, often historical cruising ground for the interested boater. Take your time and have the charts ready at hand, and some fascinating sights may well be your reward.

SOUTH EDISTO RIVER

South Edisto River provides excellent cruising grounds for pleasure boaters, though there are several unmarked shoals to avoid. Don't be put off. Basic coastal navigation should see you through without any major difficulty.

Like its northern sister, the South Edisto boasts a wide inlet with several charted aids. While local knowledge is, as always, desirable, it is possible for cautious strangers to run the inlet successfully.

Numerous historical sites overlook the banks of the South Edisto and its auxiliary creeks. Most of the river's eastern shoreline is comprised of the western shores of storied Edisto Island. Several of the island's magnificent plantation homes can be seen from the waters of the South Edisto.

Two creeks offer overnight anchorage opportunities on the lower South Edisto below Fenwick Cut. North of Watts Cut on the upper South Edisto, only one small sidewater features a protected haven. A single marina on Big Bay Creek near Edisto Beach welcomes transients and visiting cruisers, but note that this facility sits hard by the river's seaward inlet three miles from the Waterway's track.

The ICW enters South Edisto River from Watts Cut and follows its course generally south for some 6 nautical miles before it darts to the southwest on Fenwick Cut. The river is navigable for a considerable distance both north and south of the Waterway channel. This account will first review the upper reaches of South Edisto River north of Watts Cut, then the ICW section, and finally the stream's lower (southern) reaches.

UPPER SOUTH EDISTO RIVER

The upper South Edisto River is plagued by several shoals, but they are well defined on chart 11517 for the first 5 nautical miles. Farther upstream, depths become too unreliable, and this section of the river should not be entered except by very small craft. While the undeveloped shores are lovely, particularly on calm, bright autumn days, this is a side trip recommended only for see-it-all boaters.

Anchorages are very few and far between. One small sidewater offers a spot for craft under 28 feet to anchor. Another possible anchorage can be found farther upstream west of Fishing Creek, between the northwestern shore and a small island that bisects the river near its practical cruising limits. Here, the boater, surrounded by a beautifully undeveloped natural setting, can drop the hook in 10 to 17 feet of water. Protection is adequate only for light winds.

Sampson Island Creek

Sampson Island Creek is a small stream that makes in to the southwestern shores of the South Edisto about 2 nautical miles above Watts Cut. The creek holds at least 6 feet of water until it splits into two branches. Good depths continue upstream for some distance on the southeastern fork, and there is enough swinging room for craft under 28 feet to anchor. The shores are the usual undeveloped marsh grass, which gives inadequate shelter for a heavy blow.

UPPER SOUTH EDISTO RIVER NAVIGATION

Those adventurous souls who choose to cruise the upper portion of South Edisto River should cut to the north once through the western mouth of Watts Cut. The river soon takes a sharp turn to the southwest. Begin favoring the southern and southeastern shoreline as you enter the turn. As charts 11518 and 11517 clearly indicate, there is shallow water abutting the northern and northwestern shore.

The river now takes another sharp jog to the north. You can cruise back to the stream's mid-width as you pass through this bend. The mouth of Sampson Island Creek will come abeam to the southwest in the body of this turn.

Sunken skipjack on South Edisto River

Sampson Island Creek Enter Sampson Island Creek on its mid-width and follow the left-hand branch. Consider dropping the hook before proceeding too far upstream, as the small creek becomes narrower.

On the South Edisto North of Sampson Island Creek, hold to the mid-width until the river takes a sharp turn to the east. Begin favoring the southern shore heavily as you come out of the turn. As depicted on chart 11517, there is a broad band of shoals along the northern shore. Next, the South Edisto takes a sharp bend back to the north. There is a wide patch of shallows abutting the eastern banks along this stretch. Favor the western shore heavily to avoid this hazard.

Continue favoring the western banks as the river takes a jog to the northeast. You will soon sight a small island bisecting the river. Look at chart 11517 and notice the long shoal running southwest from this small body of land. To avoid this trouble spot, boaters must continue to favor the western and northwestern shoreline heavily.

It is possible to cruise between the small island and the northwestern shore and hold minimum 7-foot depths, but you must halt your progress before coming abeam of the island's northeastern tip. Consider anchoring between the island and the mainland if winds do not exceed 15 knots. Past this anchorage, depths quickly fall off, and the twisting channels are much too treacherous for cruising craft.

ICW AND SOUTH EDISTO RIVER

The ICW section of South Edisto River runs through fairly open water until the channel darts to the southwest on Fenwick Cut and leaves the river. With winds above 15 knots, the chop can make for a dusty crossing. There are also several shoals along the way, but all are well marked. Be sure to observe all daybeacons carefully to avoid any unwelcome encounters with the bottom.

There is only one relatively open anchorage between Watts and Fenwick Cuts. The river's single marina facility is on Big Bay Creek, almost 3 nautical miles below Fenwick Cut.

In fair weather, cruising boaters should enjoy this small section of the Waterway. However, in heavy breezes, skippers may remember this stretch for an entirely different reason.

Prospect Hill Plantation

Northeast of unlighted daybeacon #152, Prospect Hill Plantation is easily visible from the water. This fascinating structure, which dates from 1790, is clearly defined with the designation "House" on chart 11518.

Ephraim Baynard was the plantation's first owner, and the stately design has been credited to James Hoban. Today, Prospect Hill Plantation makes a truly spectacular sight from the water. Few other coastal South Carolina plantations are so readily observed directly from the Waterway.

Prospect Hill Plantation Legends

Many ghostly tales have been told about the wandering spirits that inhabit Prospect

Hill. Ephraim Baynard was a great horse lover. Nell S. Graydon wrote that "when the wind is high . . . the sound of wheels, the crack of a whip, and the beat of horses' hooves" can be heard "sweeping up the driveway."

Another tale relates the story of a longtime black caretaker who complained to the new owners about being bothered by Baynard's ghost. According to the old servant, the ghost incessantly rapped on his bedroom door, calling loudly to him and disturbing his sleep.

The plantation's most famous tale relates how Ephraim Baynard lost one of his favorite mounts. One fine day, the story goes, Baynard rode alone to the nearby landing to collect several parcels he had ordered from Charleston for his wife and daughter. On the way home, he stopped by a friend's house for a few drinks, and it was quite dark before he again set out on the road home. Baynard was passing the Presbyterian churchyard when a sudden gust of wind caused him to look at the path behind him. Much to his astonishment, he saw a large white mass billowing directly behind his horse. In his fright, the planter set his spurs to the fiery horse and fled down the road like the wind. When he dared to look back, his hair stood on end. Not only had he failed to leave the phantom behind, but it seemed to be closer than ever. Baynard urged his prize horse on to even greater speed. As he entered his driveway, his horse collapsed, giving the master a nasty fall. The noble beast was dead, its heart burst by the great race. It was only then that the thoroughly bewildered planter realized that a long bolt of white linen had worked loose from one of the packages and had been trailing behind him. Ephraim Baynard must have been an embarrassed man when he realized that he had been frantically running from a few yards of cloth.

Alligator Creek

In fair breezes, boaters might consider anchoring off the southwesterly mouth of Alligator Creek north of unlighted daybeacon #157. Minimum depths of 7 feet or better hold to within 100 yards or so of the northwesterly banks. Depths on Alligator Creek itself are too suspect for large craft. This anchorage offers fair protection from northwesterly and northerly winds, but it is wide open to blows from all other directions. With good weather, this is a fair haven for the night, but if fresh breezes are in the offing, cruisers had better look elsewhere.

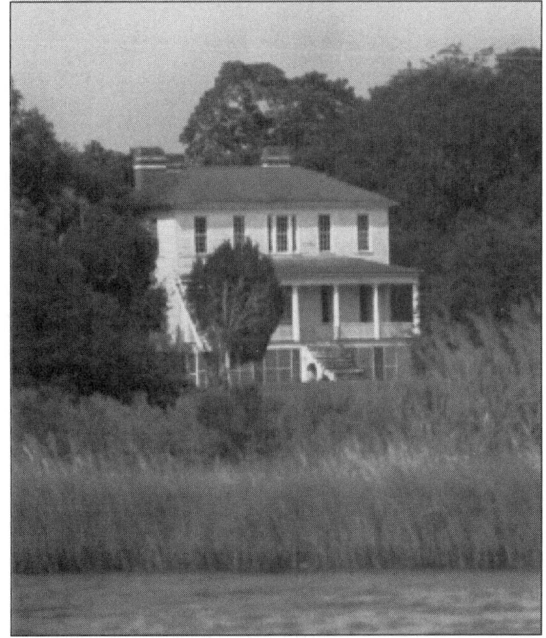

Prospect Hill Plantation, South Edisto River

ICW AND SOUTH EDISTO RIVER NAVIGATION

Pass flashing daybeacon #143 by some 20 yards to its northerly side and continue straight out into South Edisto River without cutting either corner of Watts Cut's westerly mouth. Some shoaling seems to be taking place to the north and south of the cut's westerly terminus. After finding your way well out into the river, swing sharply to the south and set course to pass unlighted daybeacons #145, #147, and #149 by 30 yards or so to their westerly sides. With this procedure, you will favor the easterly banks and avoid the shoals lining the westerly shore, which are clearly shown on chart 11518.

From #147, a set of range markers to the southwest helps you keep to the channel. Swing to the south-southeast some 50 yards before reaching the forward range marker and point to come abeam of flashing daybeacon #151 well to its westerly side. Don't allow leeway to ease you toward the large charted shoal flanking the easterly banks.

Continue on course and point to come abeam of unlighted daybeacon #152 to its easterly side. Look to the northeast and you will catch sight of Prospect Hill Plantation. If you avoid the shoal water to the north, it is possible to cruise to within 100 yards of the easterly banks for a better view.

Continue on the Waterway by setting course to come abeam of unlighted daybeacons #152 and #152A to their easterly sides. Swing to the southwest and set a new course to come abeam of and pass unlighted daybeacons #154 and #156 to their southeasterly sides. Be sure to avoid the charted shallow water northwest of the channel between #152A and #156.

From #156, another set of range markers leads you past unlighted daybeacon #157 to its northwesterly side. Swing to the south as you approach to within 75 yards of the forward range marker, then set a new course to come abeam of and pass unlighted daybeacons #159 and #161 to their westerly sides. The shoal shown on chart 11518 east of #159 and #161 is covered completely at high tide. You must be careful to avoid this area, or a most unpleasant grounding will be the result.

Alligator Creek Anchorage To visit this open, light-air anchorage, depart the Waterway abeam of unlighted daybeacon #157. Cruise to the north-northwest, pointing to keep at least 200 yards southwest of Alligator Creek's southeasterly entrance point. For best depths, begin feeling your way along at idle speed with the sounder as you approach to within 200 yards of the shoreline. Shallow water extends offshore for at least 100 yards.

On to Fenwick Cut It is a fairly straightforward run from unlighted daybeacon #161 to flashing daybeacon #162. Be on guard against the correctly charted shallows lining the channel's northeasterly flank. Flashing daybeacon #162 marks the northeasterly entrance to Fenwick Cut and the ICW's exodus from South Edisto River.

Come abeam of #162 well to its northeasterly side and continue cruising downriver until the mid-width of Fenwick Cut comes abeam to the southwest. You can then turn into this cut, passing #162 to its southeasterly quarter.

Our account will now turn to the cruising possibilities of the lower South Edisto River, abandoned by the Waterway. A continuing account of the ICW route will be presented later in this chapter.

LOWER SOUTH EDISTO RIVER

South Edisto River below Fenwick Cut is a delightful stream with only a few shoals, all of which are well marked. The attractive shores are mostly undeveloped and alternate between low marsh and higher, wooded shores. Several hospitable sidewaters offer safe haven for the night and interesting historical sites easily viewed from the water. Boaters will do well to include this inviting stream in their cruising plans.

St. Pierre Creek

St. Pierre Creek makes in to the northeastern banks of South Edisto River well southeast of unlighted daybeacon #3. This stream is the largest sidewater on the lower South Edisto and leads to several smaller creeks and numerous historical points of interest. Upstream, minimum depths of 10 feet are held to the intersection with Fishing Creek. As St. Pierre Creek begins its first slow swing to the east, the western and northwestern banks border the high land of Bailey Island. This stretch can readily serve as an overnight anchorage for craft of almost any size. The waters are a little too broad for a comfortable stay if the winds exceed 15 knots, but otherwise boaters can drop the hook here with confidence.

Another anchorage possibility is found north of Peters Point, just after the creek loops back to the north. Here, good depths open out from shore to shore, and high ground fronts the eastern banks. This is a more sheltered spot than the downstream anchorage and has sufficient swinging room for craft up to 40 feet in length.

Fishing Creek

Fishing Creek splits off from St. Pierre Creek at Peters Point and wanders off generally to the southeast. The stream holds minimum 7-foot depths at least as far as its first hairpin turn to the north. Swinging room is sufficient for craft up to 35 feet. One of the best overnight stops is found just downstream of the split, where the high ground of Peters Point borders the northeastern banks.

Until World War II, a large oyster cannery was located on the shores of Fishing Creek. Here, the famous Lady Edisto Oysters were canned. Longtime island residents will tell you they never tasted better canned oysters.

Bailey Creek

Bailey Creek branches off from St. Pierre Creek about 1 nautical mile north of Peters Point. The stream carries minimum depths of 7 feet for most of its length, but there are two small unmarked shoals to avoid. This is a good spot for craft up to 35 feet to drop the hook. Consider anchoring in the section that fronts the northern shore of Bailey Island, where chart 11517 indicates a sounding of 11 feet. The high ground gives good protection, particularly from southern, southeastern, and southwestern winds. The stream's shores alternate between the usual marsh grass and higher ground exhibiting light residential development. All in all, Bailey Creek can be recommended as an excellent anchorage or side trip.

In the 1880s, Bailey Creek enjoyed the distinction of being one of the few areas of coastal

South Carolina where subtidal oyster cultivation was practiced. At one time, as much as 20 watery acres of the creek were under cultivation. There is no evidence left today of this once-thriving industry. Like so many of the accomplishments of those days, it has faded into the fabric of the distant past.

Shingle Creek

Shingle Creek is a small offshoot of Bailey Creek. While the stream holds minimum depths of 5 to 6 feet for a short distance upstream, it is too narrow for anchorage by any but very small craft and should probably be bypassed by the cruising boater.

Store Creek

Store Creek, probably named for an old store once located along the stream, branches out to the east from its intersection with St. Pierre and Bailey Creeks. This body of water is a real cruising find. With only a few small, unmarked shoals to avoid, it offers good depths of 8 feet or more that continue well upstream. Anchorages abound, and at least two historical sites can be observed from the creek's waters.

While it is possible to drop the hook almost anywhere on Store Creek, there are three areas worthy of special consideration.

The first is found within the body of the hairpin loop encountered soon after entering the creek. Here, visiting cruisers will find enough swinging room for craft up to 45 feet, and the high southern and southwestern shores afford good protection.

Another good spot is found as the creek heads back toward the southeast upstream of the hairpin turn described above. Chart 11517 shows soundings of 17 feet on these waters. Here, Store Creek borders high ground to the north and northwest and is overlooked by historic Chisolm House. Protection is adequate even for heavy weather, and the view of the old homeplace is a considerable bonus.

Boaters can also anchor in the creek's third bend, found just before the stream heads northeast. Here, the high southern banks support moderate residential development and give good shelter.

Before entering Store Creek, be sure to read the navigational information presented later in this chapter. With this elementary precaution in mind, this writer highly recommends the extraordinary cruising opportunities of this remote stream.

Chisolm House Legend

Historic Chisolm House is located on Store Creek's northern banks as the stream enters its second major turn. This beautiful home was

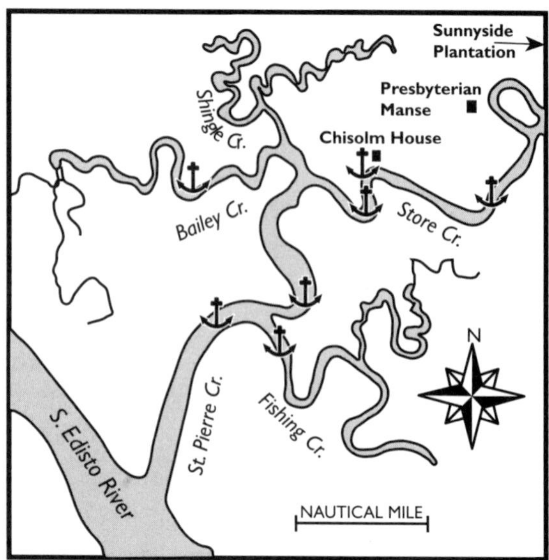

built by Dr. Robert Chisolm for his wife, the former Mary Eddings, in 1830. After many years of happiness and public service, the good doctor contracted an incurable disease. Racked with pain, Chisolm committed suicide. His body was interred in a nearby churchyard, but after a few weeks passed, an official informed Mary Chisolm that the church did not allow the burial of suicide victims within that hallowed ground.

Saying little, the grieving widow ordered the plantation's largest boat to be made ready for a trip to Charleston. On her trip to the "Holy City" the next day, she purchased bricks and mortar. Returning to the island in the dead of night, she instructed her slaves to build a thick masonry wall around her husband's grave. The following day, she defied anyone to disturb the late doctor's rest. No one ever did, and some years later the faithful widow was laid to rest beside her husband.

Presbyterian Manse

An old Presbyterian manse is visible to the northwest as you approach the practical cruising limits of Store Creek. Only very small shallow-draft boats can approach the house, but you can gain a good view of the old parsonage from the main body of the creek. Built in 1790, the home is a beautiful sight from the water.

Sunnyside Plantation

Depending on seasonal foliage, Sunnyside Plantation can sometimes be seen in the distance to the northeast just as depths begin to decline on Store Creek. While it can be viewed only from a distance by cruising craft, the house is yet another magnificent sight on this historic creek.

Sunnyside, constructed by Townsend Mikell in 1875, was one of the few plantation houses built on Edisto Island after the Civil War. There are tabby ruins of a much older structure in the front yard. Tabby was a popular building material in coastal South Carolina before the Revolution. It was made by burning limestone and seashells in an intricate process. The art of tabby making has been lost over the years and is now only a distant memory.

Big Bay Creek

Big Bay Creek is a large sidewater which cuts into the South Edisto on the river's eastern shore just northeast of flashing daybeacon #2. Minimum depths of 8 to 10 feet extend far upstream, and good anchorages abound. Most sections provide sufficient swinging room for craft up to 45 feet. Much of the creek is bounded by marsh grass, which gives minimal protection, but there are several exceptions.

As you enter Big Bay Creek from South Edisto River, the planned community of Edisto Beach lines the southern banks. Extensive residential development is encountered here. The large shrimping fleet that calls Big Bay Creek home can usually be seen along this section of the creek. The picturesque shrimpers make for interesting viewing.

For many years now, Edisto Marina has resided

Shrimpers on Big Bay Creek

on the southwestern banks of Big Bay Creek near the stream's northwestern mouth, between the charted 12- and 17-foot soundings. This facility features plentiful transient dockage at ultramodern wooden floating docks with every conceivable power and water hookup. Depths alongside are a very respectable 10 to 12 feet. Shoreside, boaters will find showers, a laundromat, and an expanded ship's and variety store. Bay Creek Restaurant is located upstairs above the marina store. Gasoline, diesel fuel, and waste pump-out service are at hand. Haul-outs can occasionally be arranged at the commercial shipyard next door. Mechanical repairs are also available through independent contractors.

Cruisers looking for a break from the live-aboard routine can rent one of the villas that are sprawled out just behind the docks. Advance reservations are a good precaution.

Located just 3 miles downriver from the ICW and Fenwick Cut, Edisto Marina is a fine addition to the South Carolina Low Country's pleasure-boating facilities. Boaters cruising the South Edisto will certainly want to make its acquaintance.

Edisto Marina (803) 869-3504

Approach depth: 10–20 feet
Dockside depth: 10–12 feet (low water)
Accepts transients: yes
Floating wooden piers: yes
Dockside power connections: 30- and 50-amps
Dockside water connections: yes
Showers: yes
Laundromat: yes
Waste pump-out: yes
Gasoline: yes
Diesel fuel: yes
Mechanical repairs: independent contractors
Below-waterline repairs: limited
Ship's and variety store: yes
Restaurant: on-site

Cruising craft can easily anchor on the lower section of Big Bay Creek east of Edisto Marina, though the waters here are a bit wider and less sheltered than those farther upstream. The extensive small-craft and commercial-fishing traffic on these waters can also be a nuisance. However, the high southern banks render good protection, and this spot is certainly worthy of consideration.

Upstream, the creek takes a long but sharp turn to the north. Soon after passing through the loop, you will spy a patch of high, wooded land on the eastern banks. This area is known as "the Mound" and is thought to have been the site of a sixteenth-century Spanish Jesuit mission. It is often forgotten that the Spanish were the first European residents of South Carolina and an influence in the state until the early 1700s. The section of Big Bay Creek adjacent to "the Mound" is another good anchorage, with minimum 7- to 8-foot depths and plenty of swinging room for boats up to 42 feet. Protection is good from all but strong southern winds.

Above "the Mound," the high ground that continues to border the eastern and northeastern shore is known as "the Neck." Tradition holds that a large plantation house once looked out on the creek from these banks but has long since washed away. Local residents claim that "the Neck" is one of the most haunted spots in all of coastal South Carolina. According to the South Carolina Sea Grant Consortium, such ghostly apparitions as "boodaddies, plateyes, and drolls that take shape and cry in the night" are supposed to make regular appearances. This writer was not privileged to meet any of these supernatural visitors during his research, but perhaps you will be more (or less) fortunate.

Unless you are concerned about ghostly visitations, this portion of the creek is also a good spot to drop the hook for the night, with swinging room and protection comparable to that of the anchorage described above. Depths finally drop off as the creek splits into several forks farther upstream.

South Edisto Inlet

Below Big Bay Creek, the generally reliable South Edisto Inlet runs seaward. If you plan to attempt this cut, read the navigational suggestions later in this chapter before proceeding.

LOWER SOUTH EDISTO RIVER NAVIGATION

South of Fenwick Cut, successful navigation of South Edisto River remains quite straightforward as far as unlighted daybeacon #3. Along the way, you should pass just south of unlighted junction daybeacon #SE. After leaving #SE behind, set course to come abeam of and pass #3 well to its northeasterly side. On-site research revealed that there has been some shoaling along the southwesterly shore in this area.

Hold to the mid-width as you continue downstream. Soon, the entrance to St. Pierre Creek will come abeam on the northeastern banks.

St. Pierre Creek Enter St. Pierre Creek on its mid-width. Be on guard against the small shoal extending into the river from the creek's northwestern point. Once inside, favor the western shore slightly.

Some 1.3 nautical miles upstream, the high ground of Bailey Island begins lining the northern and northwestern banks. You can drop the hook here and be assured of a restful night unless the wind exceeds 15 knots.

The creek soon takes a swing to the east and intersects Fishing Creek.

Fishing Creek Enter Fishing Creek on its mid-width. If you choose to anchor here, your best bet is to drop the hook where the high ground of Peters Point borders the northeastern shore. Depths begin to fall off as you approach Fishing Creek's intersection with the small stream that breaks off to the north, shown on chart 11518 as having 4-foot depths. Cease your exploration well before reaching this point.

On St. Pierre Creek East of the intersection with Fishing Creek, St. Pierre Creek takes a long turn to the north. This is another good spot to drop the hook. Hold to the mid-width through the bend, but begin heavily favoring the western shore as you enter the straight stretch leading north-northwest. With this maneuver, you will avoid the shoal on the eastern shore pictured on chart 11517.

As the creek enters another bend, this time to the northeast, begin favoring the southeastern shore. There is shoal water abutting the northwestern banks. St. Pierre Creek soon ends at the forks of Bailey and Store Creeks.

Bailey Creek Favor the eastern shore a bit as

you enter the mouth of Bailey Creek. Take the port branch at the fork with Shingle Creek. Hold to the mid-width until you approach the first bend to the west. Charts 11517 and 11518 mark a "Tree" on the northwestern shore in this turn. On-site research did not reveal any tree, but there is certainly very shoal water adjoining the northwestern and western banks. Favor the southeastern and southern banks as you pass through the turn.

Good depths continue well upstream until the creek splinters into several small branches. Simply select a likely spot before reaching this point and drop the hook .

Store Creek Enter Store Creek on its mid-width, but begin favoring the southwestern and southern shores slightly as you approach and pass through the creek's first hairpin turn to the north. After coming through this bend, begin immediately favoring the western banks. As shown on chart 11518, there is very shoal water on the eastern shore. The creek then takes a turn to the east-southeast. Watch the northern shore as you are passing through the turn and you will catch sight of Chisolm House. The waters abeam of and just past the house are an excellent spot to spend the night swinging on the hook.

As the creek takes a sharp jog to the northeast, begin to favor the northwestern shore heavily. A small shoal abuts the southeastern banks. Watch ahead and you will spy the old Presbyterian manse. Discontinue your cruise as you approach the small marsh island bisecting the creek. Past this point, depths become much too uncertain for large cruising vessels. Look to the northeast and you may be able to see Sunnyside Plantation house in the distance.

On the South Edisto South of St. Pierre Creek, set course to come abeam of and pass unlighted daybeacon #2A and flashing daybeacon #2 well to their westerly sides. These two aids mark a large shoal building out from the easterly shore. At #2, you may choose to enter Big Bay Creek to the east.

Big Bay Creek To enter Big Bay Creek, continue on course downriver past flashing daybeacon #2 for some 150 yards, as if you are putting out to sea. Only then should you turn back to the north and set a new course to pass #2 by some 100 yards to its eastern side. Follow the eastern shore and enter the creek on its centerline. From this point until the creek finally splinters far upstream, successful navigation is a simple matter of holding to the mid-width. Edisto Marina will come abeam on the southwestern shore between the charted 12- and 17-foot soundings.

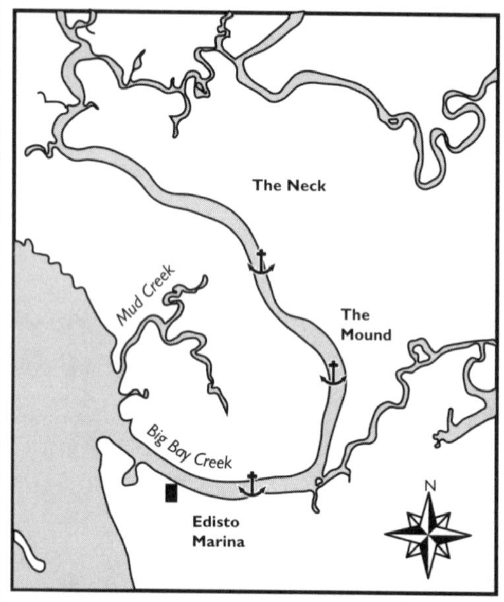

South Edisto Inlet If you choose to run the inlet, study chart 11517 carefully before making the attempt. If possible, follow in the wake of a local shrimper as he runs the cut. Otherwise, take your time and proceed with the greatest caution.

ASHEPOO RIVER

The ICW quickly darts through Fenwick Cut and enters the waters of Ashepoo River. The Ashepoo is quite frankly rather a "plain Jane" among coastal South Carolina rivers. There are no longer any reliable sidewaters along the stream's entire navigable length that offer enough protection for overnight anchorage, and only one historic site is visible from the water. Even this single point of interest calls for a very long cruise from the Waterway channel.

Of course, with a forecast of light winds (less than 10 knots), you can anchor on the Ashepoo itself above the Ashepoo-Coosaw Cutoff. If a summertime thunderstorm comes along unexpectedly, however, you might spend a few minutes imitating a Mexican jumping bean.

While most of the Ashepoo is deep and free of shoals, there are several unmarked patches of shallow water to avoid. Except for these hazards, the river can be easily navigated from St. Helena Sound to Airy Hall Plantation.

The Ashepoo's shoreline alternates between saltwater marsh and higher, wooded banks. There is very little development along the river, and sighting a house is a rare occurrence.

Many boaters choose to follow the Ashepoo only so far as the Waterway channel traverses its length. Captains with wanderlust in their souls, on the other hand, may want to consider the cruising possibilities both above and below the ICW channel.

Lower Ashepoo River

South of Fenwick Cut, Ashepoo River is abandoned by the ICW, but the stream remains deep and almost entirely free of shoals. The river leads to a marked deepwater entrance into St. Helena Sound. Boaters wishing to enter the sound can use this route with confidence.

There are no sidewaters offering anchorage on this section of the Ashepoo, nor are there any facilities. Most of the shore is undeveloped marsh grass. Fenwick Island and the Otter Islands, both located on the eastern banks, are exceptions.

Fenwick Island

Today, Fenwick Island is a rather isolated tract, with only a few buildings in the village of Seabrook. The island is split into two parts by Fenwick Cut. This passage through the narrow part of the island was opened many years ago to shorten the water passage from South Edisto River to the Ashepoo.

Before the boll weevil's unwelcome arrival, the Jenkins family, residents of nearby Edisto Island, planted Sea Island cotton on Fenwick Island. The Jenkins fortune was decimated when the entire crop was destroyed soon after the Civil War by a sudden plague of caterpillars. This writer has not been able to learn of any other such occurrence during the Sea Island cotton agricultural dynasty.

Otter Islands

The Otter Islands are several small patches of high ground to the east of Ashepoo River near its entrance into St. Helena Sound. A very grim story of human cruelty is attached to these sad little islands. During the Revolutionary War, British forces occupying South Carolina marooned captured slaves here and left them to die without food or drink. It is pitiful to read the accounts of the abandoned slaves swimming desperately after the English skiffs, only to be turned back or wounded by sword thrusts from the British soldiers.

The ICW and Ashepoo River

From Fenwick Cut, the ICW follows the course of Ashepoo River for just over 1.6 nautical miles as the river winds its way generally to the west. At flashing daybeacon #166, the Waterway cuts to the southwest on the Ashepoo-Coosaw Cutoff and leaves the river behind. This is a very straightforward, easily navigable section of the ICW. There are no accessible anchorages on this stretch.

Upper Ashepoo River

North of the Ashepoo-Coosaw Cutoff, Ashepoo River winds its way northward for almost 7 nautical miles before it is spanned by the Settlement Island swing bridge. Captains who cruise even farther upstream will find a pleasant anchorage near the one spectacular historical site the Ashepoo offers.

Mosquito Creek

Mosquito Creek enters the northeastern banks of Ashepoo River as the stream takes its first westward bend northwest of the ICW cutoff. This writer used to recommend the waters of this creek as a pleasant overnight stop. However, local fisherman have warned of new, uncharted sunken wrecks along the creek's course which could quickly bring cruising visitors to grief. With a healthy respect for these hidden hazards, this writer no longer recommends that any craft larger than a skiff consider entering the waters of Mosquito Creek.

Airy Hall Plantation

Airy Hall Plantation house overlooks the western shores of Ashepoo River from a high bluff about 2 nautical miles upstream from the Settlement Island bridge and 1 nautical mile downstream from the power line shown on chart 11517. The old home is a magnificent brick structure that dates from around 1825. It is surrounded by a collection of moss-draped oaks that lend an air of mystery and age to the grounds. The house has been lovingly restored and presents a magnificent sight from the water. Consider anchoring abeam of the plantation for the evening. You may find it a night to remember.

Airy Hall Plantation, Ashepoo River

ASHEPOO RIVER NAVIGATION

Flashing daybeacon #164 marks the southwestern entrance of Fenwick Cut, which is the ICW's entrance into Ashepoo River. Pass #164 to its southeastern side and continue straight out into the Ashepoo before turning either upstream or downstream. After leaving Fenwick Cut, the Waterway channel turns sharply to the west-northwest, while the river's lower reaches split off to the south.

Lower Ashepoo River Simply stick to the middle reaches on the lower Ashepoo as you move toward the stream's intersection with St. Helena Sound. As the Otter Islands come abeam to the east, set course to come abeam of unlighted daybeacon #2 by some 75 yards to its westerly side. Set a new course to come abeam of unlighted daybeacon #1 by some 100 yards to its easterly side. Stay away from #1. It marks a long shoal building south into St. Helena Sound. South of #1, a wide, easily followed channel leads south into the deep waters of the sound.

ICW-Ashepoo River Continue on course past flashing daybeacon #164 until you are on the river's mid-width. Swing 90 degrees to the west-northwest and follow the river's centerline past flashing daybeacon #165. Watch to the northwest for flashing daybeacon #166. Come abeam of #166 well to its southwestern side. At this point, the Ashepoo-Coosaw Cutoff is directly abeam to the southwest. Cut into its mid-width and continue through to Rock Creek. Unlighted daybeacon #172 marks the cutoff's southwestern entrance into Rock Creek. A continuing account of the ICW resumes later in this chapter.

Upper Ashepoo River If you choose to visit the upper Ashepoo River, continue cruising to the northwest past flashing daybeacon #166 and the Ashepoo-Coosaw Cutoff. Hold to the mid-width and all should be well. As the river enters its first westward bend north of #166, the entrance to Mosquito Creek will come abeam to the north.

Mosquito Creek With the danger of uncharted underwater wrecks and obstructions, entrance into Mosquito Creek is no longer recommended without very specific local knowledge. Most cruising skippers would do well to bypass this stream entirely.

On the Upper Ashepoo North of Mosquito Creek, simply hold to the Ashepoo's mid-width until you begin to approach the intersection with Rock Creek's northern entrance along the western shore. As shown on charts 11517 and 11518, a shoal abuts the northeastern shore along this stretch of the river. Favor the southwestern banks to avoid the hazard, but don't approach this shoreline too closely either. Do not attempt to enter Rock Creek from this access point. Its entrance is guarded by several unmarked shoals, and it is far too tricky for cruising craft.

Continue favoring the western shore as you move upriver. As shown on chart 11517, a large area of shallow water abuts the Ashepoo's eastern shore between Rock Creek and the river's next bend to the west.

You must begin favoring the eastern shore about 0.5 nautical mile before you reach the western bend. Again, as shown on chart 11517, there is a small patch of very shallow water on the western banks at the turn.

Beyond the turn, Ashepoo River opens out into a baylike body of water. Chart 11517 shows a marsh island in the middle of the stream, but this small mass is covered completely at high tide. To avoid this hazard, favor the southwestern and western shores heavily until the creek again narrows.

From this point to "Hole in the Wall," clearly shown on chart 11517, stick to the mid-width. At "Hole in the Wall"—which you should not attempt to enter—the main body of the Ashepoo takes a sharp bend to the north. Favor the port-side banks heavily as you round the sharp turn. Begin cruising back to the mid-width as you approach the Settlement Island bridge. This swinging span has a closed vertical clearance of only 9 feet, but it was opening on demand at the time of this writing. There is so little traffic on this portion of Ashepoo River that it is quite possible the span may lose its operator in the future. From here to Airy Hall Plantation, stick to the center for good depths.

Watch to the west after cruising some 3 nautical miles upstream from the bridge. You will spot Airy Hall Plantation atop a high bluff. Discontinue your explorations at this point. Depths fall off upriver, and the stream soon leaves the chart.

ROCK CREEK

The ICW enters Rock Creek from the southwestern terminus of the Ashepoo-Coosaw Cutoff, then follows the stream northwest for less than 1 nautical mile before it again cuts to the southwest on another man-made channel, also known as the Ashepoo-Coosaw Cutoff. Navigating this section of the Waterway calls for caution. While the route is well marked, there is one large shoal that can quickly bring careless boaters to grief.

Southeast of the Waterway channel, Rock Creek flows to join St. Helena Sound. This portion of the stream should probably be avoided by cruising boaters. There are several unmarked shoals to contend with, and the creek's entrance into the sound is flanked by numerous shallows. Also, this lower section of Rock Creek is too open for all but light-air anchorage.

On the other hand, northwest of flashing daybeacon #177 and the upper branch of the Ashepoo-Coosaw Cutoff, Rock Creek provides excellent anchorage for craft up to 45 feet in length. There are a couple of unmarked shoals, but they can be avoided by the cautious mariner. Otherwise, the creek holds minimum 6-foot depths, with most of the channel much deeper.

One of the best spots to drop the hook is found as the creek takes its first sharp bend to the west. Here, the eastern and northern shores border high ground, and protection is excellent, particularly from northern and northeastern breezes. Not only does this spot offer good shelter, but it has the most swinging room you will find on the creek.

Captains with vessels 36 feet and smaller can find many other anchorages as well. Just select a spot that seems to be sheltered and settle in for

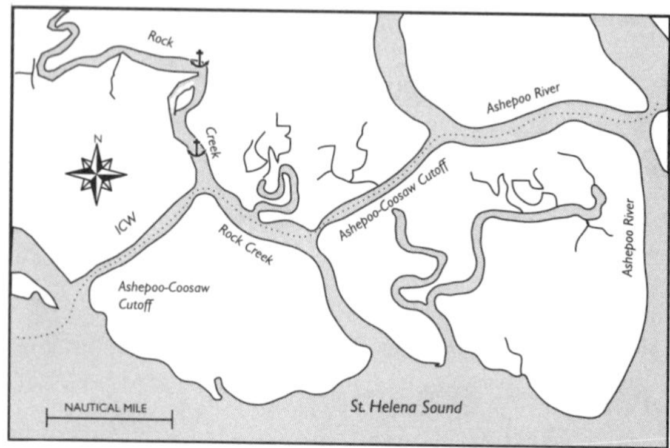

an undisturbed evening. Be sure to set the hook so as to swing well away from the correctly charted band of shallows abutting much of the creek's shoreline.

Adventurous boaters can follow Rock Creek for quite a distance upstream and hold good depths. Eventually, a small marsh island, located north-northwest of Beet Island and clearly shown on chart 11518, bisects the stream. Above this small landmass, Rock Creek begins to narrow and should probably be avoided by large cruising vessels.

ROCK CREEK NAVIGATION

ICW to Coosaw River Come abeam of unlighted daybeacon #172, located at the southwestern mouth of the Ashepoo-Coosaw Cutoff, to its southeastern side. Set course directly for flashing daybeacon #173 on the southwestern shore of Rock Creek. Don't let leeway ease you onto the shoals to the northwest.

Swing sharply to the west just before reaching #173, then carefully set course to pass the northwesternmost of the two range markers (set up for northbound craft) just to its northerly side. Come abeam of unlighted daybeacon #176 by some 30 yards to its southwesterly side. As you can see from a quick study of chart 11518, these maneuvers will help you avoid the considerable patch of shallow water abutting the northerly and northeasterly shores of Rock Creek.

Come abeam of flashing daybeacon #177 to its northeasterly side, then swing 90 degrees to the southwest and enter the mid-width of the lower Ashepoo-Coosaw Cutoff. Continue holding to the mid-width until coming abeam of flashing daybeacon #184. Southwest of this aid, the Waterway enters the wide waters of Coosaw River and St. Helena Sound. Continued description of the ICW route will be presented in the next chapter.

Upper Rock Creek Intrepid cruisers who choose to make use of the excellent anchorage opportunities on upper Rock Creek should abandon the Waterway abeam of flashing daybeacon #177. As you continue upstream, favor the eastern and northeastern banks to avoid the shoal bordering the southwestern shore, shown on chart 11518.

Soon, the creek follows a slow bend to the northwest. Begin favoring the western and southwestern banks as you pass through this stretch of the stream. Cruise back to the mid-width after traversing the next bend to the north-northeast. Farther upstream, hold to the centerline for good depths at least as far as the previously described small island north-northwest of Beet Island, where the creek begins to narrow.

Consider dropping the hook in the body of Rock Creek's first hairpin turn to the west. The high ground found here on the eastern and northeastern shoreline affords good protection.

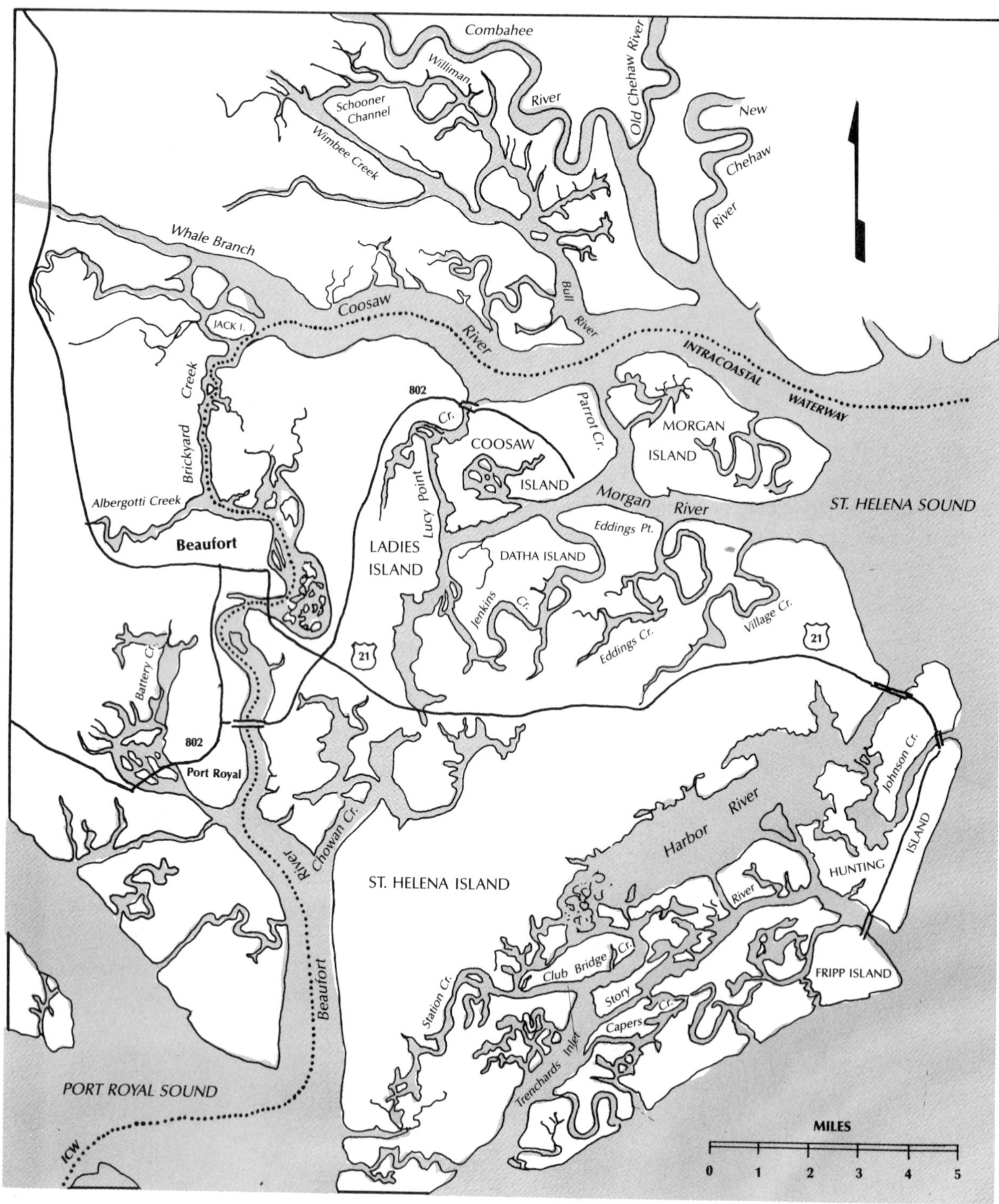

Combahee
Williman
River
Old Chehaw River
New
Chehaw
River
Schooner Channel
Wimbee Creek
Whale Branch
Coosaw
River
Bull
River
JACK I.
INTRACOASTAL
WATERWAY
Brickyard Creek
Albergotti Creek
802
Cr.
Parrot Cr.
MORGAN ISLAND
COOSAW ISLAND
Morgan River
ST. HELENA SOUND
Lucy Point
LADIES ISLAND
Beaufort
Eddings Pt.
DATHA ISLAND
Jenkins Cr.
Eddings Cr.
Village Cr.
21
21
Battery Cr.
802
Port Royal
Johnson Cr.
Harbor River
HUNTING ISLAND
Chowan Cr.
Beaufort River
ST. HELENA ISLAND
River
Club Bridge Cr.
FRIPP ISLAND
Station Cr.
Story
Capers Cr.
Trenchards Inlet
PORT ROYAL SOUND
ICW
MILES
0 1 2 3 4 5

St. Helena Sound to Beaufort

Charts

Several charts are required to cover the wide-ranging waters discussed in this chapter:

11518 details the ICW to Beaufort and covers portions of the Combahee and Bull Rivers; it also encompasses all navigable sections of the New Chehaw and Morgan Rivers

11517 covers all of St. Helena Sound and the Old Chehaw, Harbor, and Story Rivers

11519 provides coverage of the upstream portions of the Combahee and Bull Rivers

11516 details the Trenchards Inlet area

At flashing daybeacon #184, southbound Waterway travelers come upon the broad waters of Coosaw River and St. Helena Sound. Suddenly, the boater finds himself on mighty rivers and wide waters. Here, fresh winds can quickly set up a nasty chop, which often leads to rough crossings. This openness can be quite a shock after the mostly sheltered sounds and streams to the north. However, on days of fair breezes, the waters of St. Helena Sound and its many auxiliary streams offer some of the finest cruising in all of coastal South Carolina. Nevertheless, many are the boaters who have wisely taken a second glance at their charts—and the weather forecasts—before leaving the sheltered reaches of the Ashepoo-Coosaw Cutoff. You would do well to approach these waters with similar respect.

St. Helena Sound is host to many, many lesser streams and rivers. From the sound itself to little-known Trenchards Inlet, visiting explorers can contemplate a broad range of cruising opportunities. To the south, Morgan, Harbor, and Story Rivers beckon. These waters are seldom visited by cruising craft and can provide many fine hours of pleasant gunkholing. To the north, Combahee, New Chehaw, Old Chehaw, and Bull Rivers offer exciting off-the-beaten-path cruising possibilities of their own. Meanwhile, the ICW route works its way west on broad Coosaw River until it enters Brickyard Creek and begins its approach to the beautiful port city of Beaufort. This stretch is one of the most unprotected portions of the entire South Carolina ICW. Successful passage calls for caution.

Marina facilities have improved along this stretch of the South Carolina Waterway during the last several years. Boaters can traverse marked Parrot Creek and cut west on Morgan River to a full-service facility that welcomes visiting cruisers. Another marina sits hard by Fripp Inlet. These two marinas are still the only recourse for boaters on the wide waters between the Ashepoo-Coosaw Cutoff and Beaufort River. Neither is located directly on the Waterway. You should make sure your tanks are topped off and your craft is in top-notch working order before beginning a cruise south of North Edisto River.

Anchorages abound on all the area streams. While most of the shoreline is the usual saltwater marsh, some of the myriad Sea Islands along the way exhibit high ground and provide a pleasing contrast where their heavily wooded banks overlook the waters. It is often possible to anchor near one of these small oases miles and miles from the nearest sign of civilization. The adventurous souls among us may want to contemplate a quick trip ashore on one of these isolated islands, which may not have known the foot of man for many years.

Shoreside development along St. Helena Sound and its various streams is very sparse indeed. A few of the sound's streams exhibit a light smattering of private homes, but many look as if they have remained in the same pristine condition for several hundred years.

Coosaw and Morgan Rivers and St. Helena Sound are all relatively deep and free of hazards, while Combahee, Bull, Harbor, and Story Rivers are peppered with shoals and obstructions. Cruising captains should give careful consideration before leaving the safe confines of the ICW channel. To be sure, there are many interesting cruising opportunities, but almost all of them involve some hazard. Many boaters will find the risks to be more than justified. Others will wish to hurry on to the considerable charms of Beaufort. Whichever course you choose, take your time and practice good navigation.

This chapter will first review the waters of St. Helena Sound and the rivers south of the Waterway channel. Next, the rivers to the north—Combahee, New Chehaw, Old Chehaw, and Bull Rivers—will be explored. Finally, the ICW route will be followed until it begins its approach to Beaufort.

ST. HELENA SOUND

St. Helena Sound is a very impressive body of water. For those cruising on its central axis, the surrounding shores are barely visible. The sound also provides reliable access to the open sea. The inlet channel is wide, relatively deep, and well marked. Many of the inlet's aids are charted, a sure sign of a stable seaward cut.

The sound can quickly give rise to rough conditions with winds over 15 knots in the offing. Small cruising craft should consult the latest weather forecast before venturing onto St. Helena Sound's wide waters. The same holds true for its major sidewaters, particularly Morgan and Coosaw Rivers.

The St. Helena shrimping fleet can often be seen plying the waters of the sound for the abundant shellfish found here. Those cruising the sound or its large sidewaters may well be joined by several of these classic trawlers.

With one small exception, the sound itself offers few cruising opportunities to the visiting boater other than its reliable seaward passage. Fortunately, the same cannot be said of its sidewaters. Both Harbor and Morgan Rivers present multiple off-the-track cruising grounds.

Morgan Island

Morgan Island comprises the southern banks of upper St. Helena Sound and the northern banks of Morgan River. The island was named for Captain Joshua Morgan, a sea captain who settled on nearby St. Helena Island. According to the South Carolina Sea Grant Consortium, monkeys were raised here for experimental purposes during the early 1980s.

Morgan Back Creeks

A group of small streams known as the Morgan Back Creeks is found southwest of flashing daybeacon #13 (itself east of Marsh Island Spit) on the northern shore of Morgan Island. Navigation of these three small streams is quite tricky, but there is sufficient swinging room for craft from 30 to 35 feet to anchor in fairly good protection. If you can avoid the unmarked shallows, minimum depths in the channel run around 7 feet. These streams should be visited only by bold skippers who are willing to take a gamble in order to explore little-traveled waters. On-site research revealed that the charted marsh west of flashing daybeacon #13 no longer exists, or at least is covered completely at high tide. For this reason, the channel that chart 11518 shows running northwest from #13 should not be attempted.

The central branch of the creek affords the most swinging room. Here, craft up to 40 feet can anchor flanked by marsh grass on both shores.

The starboard fork has some 5-foot depths, but for those who can stand these readings, there is room for craft up to 35 feet to anchor.

The port fork is the deepest of the three but also the narrowest. There is only enough room for boats less than 28 feet to anchor.

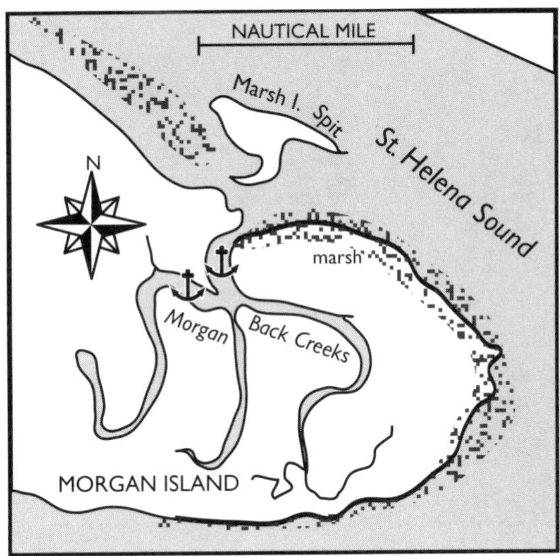

ST. HELENA SOUND NAVIGATION

Unless one's cruising plans call for a visit to Combahee River, all boaters entering Coosaw River from the Ashepoo-Coosaw Cutoff at flashing daybeacon #184 must turn south and set course to come abeam of flashing daybeacon #186 well to its southeasterly side. Don't cut the corner between #184 and #186. Shoal water is building to the southeast at a location just northwest of #186.

Morgan Back Creeks To visit the Morgan Back Creeks, set course from flashing daybeacon #186 to come abeam of flashing daybeacon #13, located east of Marsh Island Spit, by some 200 yards to its northeasterly side. Continue on course to the southeast for another 0.2 nautical mile. You can then swing back to the west and pass #13 by at least 100 yards to its southerly side. Point for the mid-width of the creeks' central branch, bearing in mind the large charted shoal to the northwest. As you approach the entrance, favor the starboard shore slightly in order to avoid a small patch of shallows guarding the southeasterly banks. Once on the stream's interior reaches, stick to the mid-width until the creek forks. The best swinging room is found in this central section short of the forks.

Only those craft that can stand 5-foot depths should consider entering the starboard fork, and only boats under 28 feet should enter the port branch. Don't cruise very far upstream on either creek, as depths soon begin to decline.

On St. Helena Sound From #186, the ICW continues westward, while a turn to the southeast leads to the lower reaches of St. Helena Sound. If you are making for the sound's seaward passage, set course from #186 for unlighted nun buoy #12, located to the southwest of Combahee Bank. This is a long run of 3.7 nautical miles, but it passes through deep water, and you should not have any difficulty. Pass #12 to its southwesterly side.

Moving seaward from #12, set course to come abeam of and pass unlighted can buoys #1 and #11 by at least 200 yards to their northeasterly side. These two aids mark shallow Pelican Bank and should be avoided like the plague.

Once abeam of #11, bend your course a bit farther to the southeast and point to come abeam of unlighted can buoy #9, also well to its northeasterly quarter. Notice the charted shallows south and southwest of #9.

Past #9, unlighted can buoys #7 and #5 mark a southward turn in the inlet channel. Set course from #5 for the red-and-white unlighted buoy to the south-southeast. Use unlighted nun buoys #4A, #4, and #2 and unlighted can buoy #1 to continue following the remainder of the inlet channel first south and then east to the open sea.

MORGAN RIVER

Morgan River is a wide, deep stream that enters St. Helena Sound west of Pelican Bank. This impressive river stretches westward between St. Helena and Datha Islands to the south and Morgan and Coosaw Islands to the north. Eventually, the stream takes a sharp turn to the south and becomes much too tricky for cruising-size craft. Along the way, numerous auxiliary creeks afford many anchorage opportunities and fascinating side trips.

Morgan River is a bit short of aids to navigation. One beacon warns of extensive shoals guarding the entrance's northern flank. Several markers west of Parrot Creek help boaters track their way to Dataw Island Marina. Otherwise, successful navigation of the Morgan is an elementary matter of sticking to the mid-width.

Morgan River is bounded by a pleasant mixture of mostly undeveloped marsh grass and higher ground. This writer has been struck time and time again by the great natural beauty of this stream. Few will count a cruise of Morgan River a waste of time.

Coffin Point Plantation

Coffin Point Plantation is visible to the south at Morgan River's eastern entrance. Built in 1801 for Thomas A. Coffin, this is one of the few St. Helena Island plantations that survived the turmoil of the Civil War. At the close of the war, the elegant house was used by Northern missionaries who came south as part of the "Port Royal Experiment," an effort to educate freed slaves. Sea Island cotton continued to be grown here by the missionaries until the coming of the boll weevil.

St. Helena Island

Before the Civil War, St. Helena was the richest Sea Island south of Edisto. Numerous cotton plantations dotted the landscape. Following the fall of Port Royal in 1861, the planter families fled, leaving their slaves behind. Most of the beautiful plantation homes were subsequently destroyed by Union troops. Northern missionaries established the Penn School soon thereafter with the intent of educating the emancipated blacks in academic, domestic, and craft skills.

Attempts were made to continue the cultivation of Sea Island cotton after the war to support the various educational efforts. The South Carolina Sea Grant Consortium commented that "although there were abuses and mistakes . . . valuable lessons were learned. . . . Today the Penn Center continues to be an important cultural and community center for the people of St. Helena."

Datha Island

Datha Island, which lines Morgan River to the south, was once the cotton empire of the wealthy Sams family. According to James Henry Rice, Jr., in *Glories of the Carolina Coast*, the family mansion "has long crumbled and no trace remains; but the live oak grove speaks with mute eloquence of taste and care in days gone by. Near it is another grove, where rest the dead of the family."

Coosaw Island

Coosaw Island flanks Morgan River to the north near its westerly cruising limits. Tradition holds that the island once supported large groves of orange and olive trees. The cultivation of these fruits was not commercially successful, but there are some reports of scattered trees surviving to this very day.

Village Creek

Village Creek is a small offshoot that makes in to the southern shore of Morgan River to the east of Pine Island. In spite of depths shown on chart 11518, the entrance has shoaled to 3 feet. Don't attempt to enter.

Edding Creek

Edding Creek enters the southern shore of Morgan River not far to the west of Village Creek. While some caution must be exercised in order to avoid several shallows, the stream carries minimum 7-foot depths well upstream. The western shore around Edding Point supports moderate residential development. The houses on the point itself are particularly pleasing to the eye. Otherwise, the shoreline consists mostly of saltwater marsh.

Edding Creek offers excellent anchorage for craft up to 45 feet. For best protection, consider dropping the hook where the creek fronts high ground along its eastern shores just south of the small, unnamed creek that makes in to the eastern banks. This is a very sheltered spot and is one of the best overnight stops on all of Morgan River.

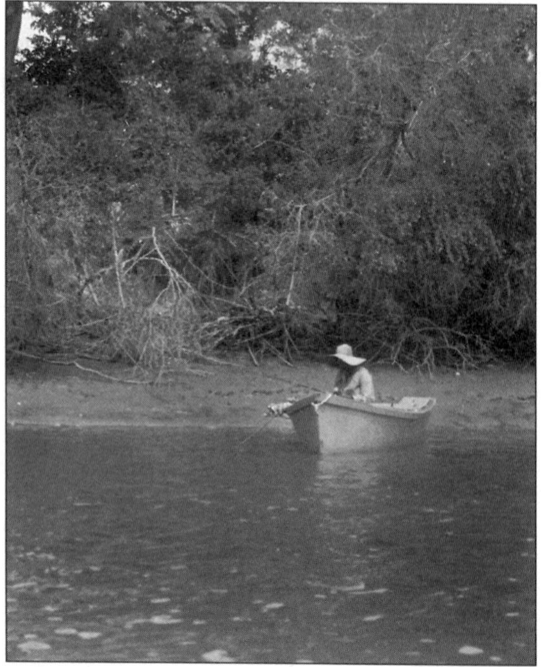

Fishing on Edding Creek

Small craft (32 feet and under) might also consider anchoring in the charted bubble of deep water just west of the creek's first sharp turn westward. Set your hook so as to swing well away from the charted shallows to the north and west.

Parrot Creek

Parrot Creek flows north from Morgan River between Coosaw and Morgan Islands. This well-marked stream provides reliable access from Coosaw River to Morgan River (and Dataw Island Marina) and features at least one anchorage opportunity on a small sidewater. The entire shoreline is composed of undeveloped marsh grass.

Charts 11518 and 11519 both note a shoal adjacent to unlighted daybeacon #2 near the creek's northern mouth. However, on-site research revealed that 8-foot minimum depths can now be held all the way into the deeper waters of Coosaw River. Apparently, dredging not shown on the charts has considerably improved depths in the channel. There is one other shoal to avoid, but good navigation should see you through.

Bass Creek

Bass Creek, a small sidewater of Parrot Creek, makes in to the larger stream's northeastern shore. Minimum depths of 7 feet are carried on the creek's mid-width as far as its first bend to the northeast. Swinging room is sufficient for craft up to 34 feet to anchor. The marsh-grass shores do not provide enough protection for heavy weather, but otherwise this is an excellent spot to drop the hook.

Dataw Island Marina

Dataw Island Marina occupies the charted high ground of Datha Island west of Jenkins Creek (along Morgan River's southern banks). This facility is part of the private Dataw Island development, but fortunately the marina is open to all boaters. Incidentally, don't let the difference in spelling between Dataw and (charted) Datha Islands fool you. They are one and the same. When the ALCOA aluminum company developed the island, it changed the spelling, which had already undergone several alterations in the past. However its name is spelled, Dataw Island Marina is a superfriendly, full-service, absolutely first-rate facility that all boaters can use with confidence.

At first glance, it might appear that the marina is on a rather exposed portion of Morgan River. Fortunately, the facility's designer saw fit to enclose the dockage basin with an outer pier that serves to shelter the harbor from all but the roughest weather. Transients are eagerly accepted at the ultramodern concrete floating docks, which feature all power, water, and telephone connections. Approach depths run 18 feet or better, and most slips boast at least 8 feet of water, with many of the outer docks having 15-plus feet of depth. Low-water depths at the fuel pier run 7 to 8 feet.

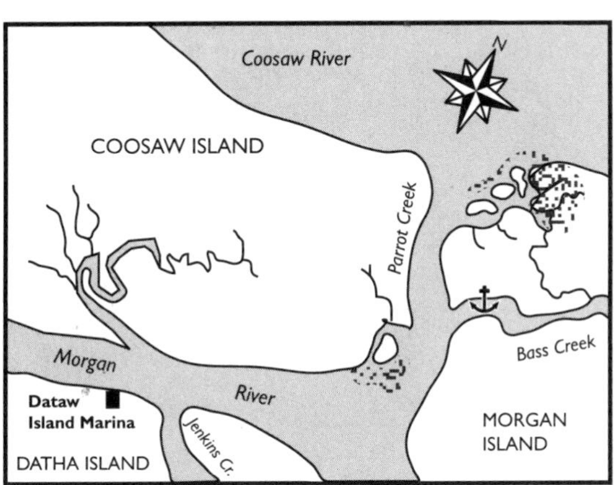

Transients can dine at the island's clubhouse and are free to use the nearby swimming pool, tennis courts, and golf course. There are even shoreside barbecue grills convenient to boaters. As you would expect, spotless showers and a full laundromat are at hand.

Full fueling facilities (gasoline and diesel) are available, as is a good ship's and variety store. A new addition to Dataw Island Marina is waste pump-out connections at each and every slip. There is even a full-service boatyard located just behind the docks. Both diesel and gasoline mechanical repairs are offered, and boats up to 48 feet in length can be hauled out via a unique transport system.

In addition to all these impressive services, nautical visitors can expect the kind of warm welcome that is something of an oddity in a large operation of this type. This writer and his mate were shown every courtesy during our visit, and the marina staff gave unstintingly of their time to help us with advice and suggestions about researching the nearby waters. In short, you will be doing yourself a big favor by setting your course to Dataw Island Marina during your next trip along the mighty Coosaw.

Dataw Island Marina (803) 838-8410

Approach depth: 15+ feet
Dockside depth: 8–17 feet
Fuel-dock depth: 7–8 feet (low water)
Accepts transients: yes
Floating concrete piers: yes
Dockside power connections: 30 and 50 amps
Dockside water connections: yes

Showers: yes
Laundromat: yes
Waste pump-out: yes
Gasoline: yes
Diesel fuel: yes
Mechanical repairs: yes
Below-waterline repairs: yes
Ship's and variety store: yes
Restaurant: on-site

Jenkins Creek

Jenkins Creek is located on Morgan River's southern shore east of Datha Island. The stream is home to a small fleet of shrimpers who dock on the eastern shore below the creek's first bend to the southeast. Anchorage abeam of the commercial piers is a definite possibility for boats under 36 feet in length. Most of the western shore is marsh, but the higher eastern banks give good protection in strong northeastern blows.

Several unmarked shoals render navigation of Jenkins Creek a bit tricky. If you stay in the channel, you can expect 8-foot minimum depths, but a navigational error could land you in 2 to 3 feet of water. Because of these difficulties, Jenkins Creek is not recommended for boats over 35 feet or those drawing more than 4½ feet. Be sure to read the Jenkins Creek navigation section presented later in this chapter before attempting entry.

Lucy Point Creek

Lucy Point Creek flows to the north as Morgan River takes a sharp turn to the south and heads for Warsaw Island. The creek is wide and mostly deep and offers reliable passage to Coosaw River for boats that can clear a fixed bridge with 14 feet of vertical clearance. The stream boasts many possible anchorages. There are a few unmarked shallows, but those who proceed carefully should come through unscathed.

Unlike many creeks in this region, most of this stream's western shore borders on high ground. Attractive modern houses watch over the creek from much of this shore. The eastern banks are mostly marsh, but even these are backed by higher land on Coosaw Island farther to the east.

Because of its high shores, Lucy Point Creek makes an excellent anchorage for almost any craft that can find sufficient swinging room. The creek's broad lower (southerly) reaches can accommodate boats up to 40 feet, while the

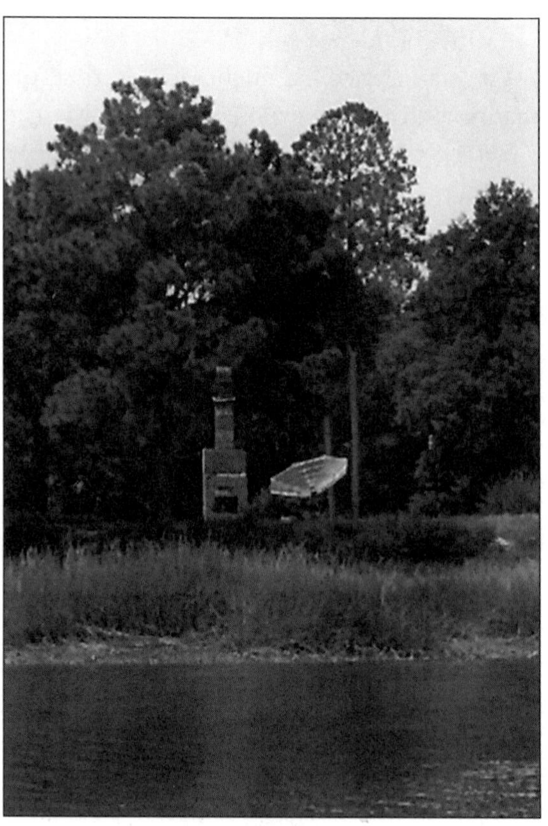

The old and the new on Lucy Point Creek

narrower upper sections can shelter craft as large as 32 feet.

Sams Point bridge spans Lucy Point Creek just south of the stream's intersection with Coosaw River. The fixed span has only 14 feet of vertical clearance, which effectively bars most sailcraft from using this route to reach the Coosaw. Just north of the bridge, there is a small dock on the eastern shore, but there are no facilities for transients.

Lucy Point Creek is a particularly attractive sidewater. The modern homes on the western shore are interspersed with woodlands, and together they make for very pleasant viewing from the water. Thanks to its many anchorage possibilities, this creek can be unreservedly recommended as a side trip for all craft and as a route to the Coosaw for boats that can clear the fixed bridge.

MORGAN RIVER NAVIGATION

To enter Morgan River from St. Helena Sound, continue seaward on the sound channel until you are about midway between unlighted can buoys #11 and #9. You can then cut back to the west-northwest and set a careful compass course to come abeam of unlighted can buoy #11 by at least 0.3 nautical mile to its southerly side. This aid, along with unlighted daybeacon #2 (lying to the west of #11), marks the 3- and 4-foot waters abutting charted Pelican Bank. Don't skimp and make your turn to the north-northwest too quickly. Shoals associated with Pelican Bank are clearly building well southeast past #11.

Bend your course farther to the west and point to pass unlighted daybeacon #2 by at least 0.2 nautical mile to its southern side as well. It's a long run of 3 nautical miles or so through open water from a position abeam of #2 to the eastern mouth of Morgan River. Fortunately, the channel is almost 0.5 nautical mile in width, but you should still use your compass and Loran or GPS (if you have them) to avoid the shallows to the north and south.

Enter the river on its mid-width between the eastern points of Morgan and St. Helena Islands. From here to the stream's eventual turn to the south, you can cruise on the Morgan's centerline with confidence.

As you begin your approach to Morgan River's eastern mouth, look to the south for a quick sighting of Coffin Point Plantation house on the northeastern point of St. Helena Island. Do not approach the old home, as the adjacent shores are shoal and dangerous.

Shortly after passing into the main body of Morgan River, both Coffin and Village Creeks will come abeam on the southern shore. Avoid both creeks, as entrance depths have shoaled to 3 feet.

Continue on the mid-width, but take care to avoid the shoals flanking the southwestern tip of Morgan Island. Watch to the south and Edding Creek will come abeam on the southern shore.

Edding Creek If you choose to enter Edding Creek, carefully set course to cruise into the stream's mouth while favoring the southeastern banks. A large tongue of shallow water guards the west-side entrance point, while a smaller band of shoals abuts the southeastern banks.

Once on the creek's interior reaches, favor the western shore slightly for best depths until the stream turns slightly to the south. Here, the deep water is found along the eastern shore, which fronts high ground. This may also be the best place on the creek to drop the hook.

To continue upstream, follow the centerline through the sharp westward bend. Once through this turn, begin favoring the northern shore heavily to avoid the correctly charted shoal on the southern banks.

As Edding Creek takes a sharp bend to the south, it leaves chart 11517, and depths become suspect. Discontinue your cruise at this point.

Parrot Creek Since many boaters will be entering Parrot Creek from the ICW (running through Coosaw River), the navigational account of this stream will run from north to south instead of the opposite direction.

From Coosaw River and the ICW channel, set course to come abeam of unlighted daybeacon #1 to its fairly immediate westerly side. The shallowest depths of the entire Parrot Creek channel are near #1, but you can still expect low-water readings of 8 feet or so.

From #1, point to pass into the central portion of Parrot Creek's northern mouth and to come abeam of unlighted daybeacon #2 by some 20 yards to its eastern quarter. Chart 11518 shows a shoal abeam of #2, but this obstruction has apparently been removed by dredging.

Continue to the south by passing unlighted daybeacon #3 to its fairly immediate westerly side. South of #3, boaters must watch out for the charted 4-foot shoal west of Bass Creek. This shallow spot did not show up during on-site research, but it's better to be safe than sorry. To avoid this potential obstruction, favor the southwesterly side of the channel as you approach a position abeam of Bass Creek. Once abeam of this sidewater, bend your course slightly to the south-southeast and point to eventually come abeam of unlighted daybeacon #4 by at least 30 yards to its easterly quarter.

Between #4 and unlighted daybeacon #6 (marking the intersection of Parrot Creek and Morgan River), favor the eastern side of the creek. This maneuver will help you avoid the long charted shoal south of #4. At high tide, it is surprisingly easy to mistake unlighted daybeacon #8, located well out into the main body of Morgan River, for #6. Such a mistake could land the navigationally impaired in the shallows off the southwestern corner of Parrot Creek's southern mouth.

Come abeam of #6 by some 0.1 nautical mile to its easterly side. A closer approach to this aid could encroach upon the shoal mentioned above. Continue out into the central portion of Morgan River before turning east or west.

Bass Creek To make use of the anchorage on Bass Creek, enter the stream by carefully avoiding the 4-foot shoal west of the north-side entrance point. The best way to accomplish this objective is to continue south on the main track of Parrot Creek past Bass Creek's entrance. You can then swing safely to the northeast and enter the stream on its centerline. Exercise caution and watch the sounder in case you accidentally approach the surrounding shallows. Once inside, drop the hook at any likely spot west of the stream's first swing to the northeast. Don't cruise past this turn, as depths begin to decline.

On Morgan River West of the Morgan River–Parrot Creek intersection, point to pass south of unlighted daybeacon #8. This is the last aid to navigation you will find as you move west on the Morgan, but the channel is quite broad, and the few shoals on these waters are rather close to the shoreline. Soon, you will come abeam of Jenkins Creek to the south.

Jenkins Creek Cruising Jenkins Creek calls for caution and careful navigation. Favor the eastern shore slightly when entering. As the creek takes a sharp southeasterly swing, the waters widen and extensive shoals line the southern and southwestern shores. Cruise to within 30 yards or so of the port banks and set your course parallel to the shoreline. Maintain this distance from the shore and follow the land until the creek narrows. Good depths open out from shore to shore where several private docks abut the northeastern banks. Don't attempt to cruise past the creek's next sharp bend to the west. Depths quickly fall off past this point.

On Morgan River After leaving the entrance to Jenkins Creek in their wake, westbound boaters on Morgan River will soon come abeam of Dataw Island Marina, perched on the charted high ground of Datha Island to the south. You can cruise straight into the marina basin with good depths.

Morgan River eventually takes a sharp turn to the south at its intersection with Lucy Point Creek. Good depths continue for a short distance upstream, but extensive unmarked shoals are soon encountered. Boaters who cruise this far on Morgan River are advised either to retrace their path or to use Lucy Point Creek to enter Coosaw River.

Lucy Point Creek Even though Lucy Point Creek is used on a daily basis by local craft of all sizes, navigation of the stream calls for some caution. One of the trickiest sections is the entrance from Morgan River.

To enter the creek, slightly favor the Morgan's southern banks until you are just to the east of the creek's southeastern entrance point. Turn northwest and enter Lucy Point Creek by heavily favoring the eastern banks. As you will quickly note from a study of chart 11519, this procedure will help you avoid both the shallows around Coosaw Island's southwestern point and the large shoal on the western shore of Lucy Point Creek's southern entrance.

Hold scrupulously to the centerline as you move upstream to the creek's first bend to the northwest. Be sure to avoid both shorelines before reaching this first turn. Some sections are quite shoal.

As you enter the bend, heavily favor the western shore. An oyster bank lines the eastern banks.

Lucy Point Creek now follows a long turn back to the east. From here to the Sams Point bridge, you need simply stick to the mid-width for good depths.

The Sams Point fixed bridge has a vertical clearance of only 14 feet. If you cannot clear this span, your only option is to retrace your route downstream to Morgan River. Boats able to cruise under the bridge should set course to come abeam of unlighted daybeacon #2 fairly close to its southeasterly side. From #2, the wide waters of Coosaw River open out before you.

HARBOR-STORY RIVER AREA

The Harbor-Story River area comprises the southernmost sidewaters of St. Helena Sound. Besides the two major rivers, a vast network of smaller streams and two inlets infiltrates this region around the various Sea Islands. The principal landmasses are Hunting and Fripp Islands. Both are the scene of extensive resort development.

There are perhaps no other waters in coastal South Carolina that present such a variety of navigational difficulties for visiting boaters. Many of the channels are unmarked and carry only 6 (and occasionally 5) feet of water. At high tide, most of the surrounding mud flats, bare at low water, are completely covered, and it becomes almost impossible to determine just where the deep water is located. A single error, even when trying to navigate carefully, can quickly result in a hard grounding on one of the many oyster banks lining the shores.

Due to these various navigational problems, this entire area should be entered only by truly adventurous skippers who pilot craft less than 38 feet in length that draw no more than 4 feet. Even then, boaters should attempt entry only at low tide, when it is possible to identify the channels.

Interestingly enough, one of the two marinas between South Edisto River and Beaufort is found among these difficult waters, on Old House Creek near Fripp Inlet. Associated with the resort development on Fripp Island, this facility offers limited services for visiting cruisers.

Both Fripp and Trenchards Inlets are surrounded by extensive shoals that render the two cuts impassable for cruising craft. Neither is marked, and boaters who stray onto their breaker-tossed waters do so at their own peril.

Several of the area creeks offer overnight anchorage, but almost all are lined by the usual undeveloped saltwater marsh, with minimal protection in strong winds. The marsh grass can become quite boring after a while, and one often wonders if it's ever going to end.

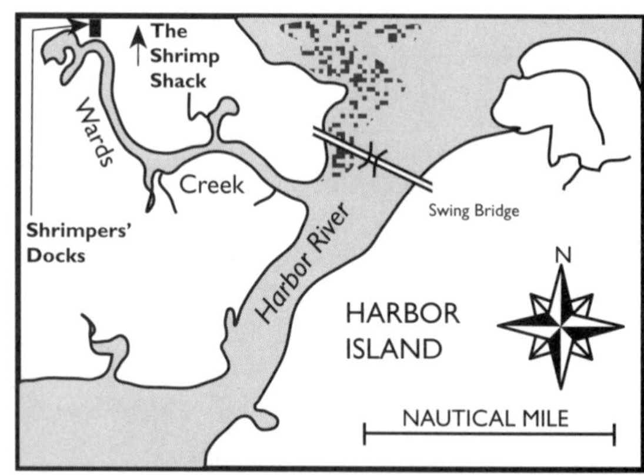

Unless they are interested in visiting the island resorts, most boaters will probably wish to bypass this entire region. However, if you are the wild-eyed type who is willing to risk touching bottom, there are many isolated streams miles away from the usual treks that can be visited. If you are numbered among these hardy souls, please proceed with the greatest caution.

Harbor River

Harbor River is the deepest body of water in the area. In spite of its depths, you must enter the river from St. Helena Sound by a narrow but well-marked channel holding 7-foot depths. This cut is used on a regular basis by local shrimpers and should not prove too taxing.

The river is spanned by a swing bridge near its northeastern mouth. The span has a closed vertical clearance of only 15 feet, but it does open on demand.

The upper Harbor River is too wide for effective anchorage and offers only one sidewater that may be entered by large pleasure craft. Eventually, depths begin to decline as the river peters out into extensive mud flats and salt marsh to the southwest. Here, a narrow, treacherous channel can lead the courageous captain south to Fripp Inlet. Chart 11517 shows a patch of 3- and 4-foot depths east and northeast of the cut leading to Fripp Inlet. These waters have apparently been deepened by tidal currents. On-site research revealed 5-foot minimum depths.

West of the cut-through to Fripp Inlet, good depths are maintained for a short distance on Harbor River as the stream snakes its way to the northwest. Here, boats up to 38 feet can anchor, but the marsh-grass shores provide only minimal protection with winds over 15 knots in the offing. Depths fall off markedly as the river cuts sharply to the southwest.

Wards Creek

Wards Creek enters the northwestern banks of Harbor River southwest of the swing bridge. While successful entrance into this stream can present more than a spot of difficulty, the creek is used on a daily basis by local shrimpers. It carries minimum 6-foot depths on its mid-width as far as the commercial docks on the northern banks of the creek's upper reaches. There is enough swinging room for craft up to 32 feet to anchor, but you may well be obliged to move aside early in the morning by the shrimp fleet that calls Wards Creek home.

A fairly large commercial dock used by the shrimpers is located on the upper reaches of Wards Creek astride the hairpin turn to the southwest. Here, it is possible to anchor abeam of the docks and take the dinghy ashore for an unexpected dining treat.

A fairly long walk from the shrimpers' piers will bring you to a small restaurant on the main highway with the unlikely name of The Shrimp Shack. The building lives up to its name. It is merely a screened porch where visitors eat on picnic tables and benches. The food is served drive-in style through small windows. But don't be put off! The shrimp served here are some of the finest this writer has ever enjoyed. I suspect that the restaurant's shrimp supply is garnered daily from the docks on Wards Creek. Don't be a late arrival. This unusual eatery closes at 7:30 P.M. and is not usually open during the winter and late fall.

Shrimper on Wards Creek

Hunting Island

For many years, Hunting Island, which lies southeast of Harbor River, was owned by several wealthy St. Helena Island planters. They used the land as a private hunting preserve and often spent weeks camping and hunting during the fall months. Until the Civil War, hunting was one of the chief leisure occupations of the Sea Island planters.

In recent years, Hunting Island has become the northernmost of the resort developments that stretch from St. Helena Sound south to Hilton Head Island. Five thousand acres of the island have been set aside as Hunting Island

State Park and are protected from commercial construction.

While cruising Harbor River, you may be able to catch a glimpse of the Hunting Island Lighthouse to the southeast. Built in 1875, the tower was cleverly constructed of movable parts so that it could be relocated if beach erosion threatened its base. Although located a quarter-mile from the surf line, the structure did indeed have to be moved in 1889. The old light remained in operation until 1933. It is now open to the public and commands an imposing view of the surrounding islands and streams.

Fripp Inlet and Associated Waters

Fripp Inlet is an impassable seaward cut. The only access for pleasure boats to the interior of the inlet is via a small, twisting cut from Harbor River. This channel is marked by two unlighted daybeacons, but it still isn't a walk in the proverbial park.

The inlet branches into several streams that might serve as overnight anchorages for visiting cruisers. Almost without exception, the various creeks have undeveloped marsh shores that do not afford much protection in winds over 15 knots. The fork leading from Harbor River maintains minimum depths of 7 feet once past the entrance shoals and has sufficient swinging room for craft up to 36 feet.

Northwest of the Harbor River cut, another branch of the inlet offers a wide, deep channel and swinging room for boats as large as 45 feet. This stream eventually forks. The southwesterly creek carries minimum soundings of 8 feet until it begins its first sharp jog to the north. Craft up to 35 feet will probably find enough swinging room short of this turn for safe anchorage.

The northerly fork has elbow room for craft up to 40 feet and minimum depths of 6 feet, but there is one unmarked shoal which must be bypassed.

An unnamed creek enters the eastern shore of Fripp Inlet northeast of unlighted daybeacon #12. This small stream holds minimum low-tide depths of 8 feet well upstream and can accommodate boats of up to 35 feet for overnight anchorage. Eventually, depths begin to rise as the creek takes its first sharp bend to the north-northwest.

Old House Creek

Old House Creek makes in to the southwestern shore of Fripp Inlet west of the inlet's fixed bridge. You must avoid several unmarked shoals, but prudent navigation should see you through. The channel carries minimum depths of 8 feet and is deeper for most of its length.

Fripp Island Marina is located on the shores of Old House Creek where the charted high ground of Fripp Island abuts the southeastern banks. This facility is glad to allow visitors to dock for a day or two at its wooden floating piers, which feature water and power connections, but boaters are discouraged from staying aboard overnight. Gasoline and diesel fuel are available, and some mechanical repairs can be arranged through independent contractors. A ship's store is located on the premises.

Fripp Island Marina (803) 838-5661

Approach depth: 8 feet (minimum)
Dockside depth: 8 feet
Accepts transients: dockage, but no stay-aboards
Floating wooden piers: yes

Dockside power connections: 30 and 50 amps
Dockside water connections: yes
Gasoline: yes
Diesel fuel: yes
Mechanical repairs: independent contractors
Ship's store: yes

Fripp Inlet Channel

Good depths continue on Fripp Inlet for some distance southeast of the fixed bridge that crosses the channel east of Old House Creek. This span has a vertical clearance of only 15 feet. The unmarked inlet channel eventually becomes much too treacherous without the aid of specific local knowledge. The wise cruiser will discontinue exploration a short distance southeast of the bridge.

Fripp Island

According to Nell S. Graydon, "It is possible that there are more legends connected with this lovely little island than any other on the South Carolina coast." Tradition has it that Fripp Island was one of the favorite hiding places of the notorious pirate Blackbeard. The many twisting creeks and small inlets that indent Fripp Island's shores would have been ideal for the brigand's purposes. Legend tells us that he buried many chests of his ill-gotten booty under the island's shifting sands. None has ever come to light, but if you are the prospecting type, you might try your luck at finding his treasure.

Another story tells how Blackbeard brought his new, unwilling wife, whom he had kidnapped in Charleston, to Fripp Island and left her there under heavy guard while he continued as a buccaneer on the high seas. Some say that she remained a prisoner until the end of her days, but others claim that eventually she became a loving wife and at last joined her pirate husband in the West Indies.

Story River

Story River leads wild-eyed boaters from Fripp Island to Trenchards Inlet and its several creeks, which split off to the northeast and west. At low tide, the river's channel is fairly easy to follow and holds minimum depths of 6 feet. However, at high tide, many of the surrounding mud flats become covered with a foot or two of water, and it is virtually impossible to pick your way along the unmarked channel. If you decide to attempt passage of the river, enter and exit at low tide only.

Story River is relatively sheltered and makes a good anchorage for craft up to 40 feet. One of the best spots is perched hard by the higher ground of Old Island, which borders the southeastern shore. Protection from southern and southeastern blows is quite good, though strong winds from the north can be a bit of a problem.

Northeast of Old Island, a branch of Story River splits off to the north-northwest. This wayward fork boasts at least 9 feet of water for quite a distance upstream and affords enough swinging room for overnight stops by craft up to 38 feet. As usual, the marshy shores give minimal protection in strong winds.

Trenchards Inlet

Trenchards Inlet is another of the impassable seaward cuts located along this stretch of the South Carolina Low Country. This writer was struck by the very real isolation of the inlet. From the main body, there was no sign of civilization, and it was easy to imagine that the shores had not changed at all in the last 300 years. If this sounds appealing, you might wish to exert every effort to reach this isolated water body, but bear in mind that successful passage is far from easy.

The interior portion of Trenchards Inlet holds good depths but is too open for effective anchorage. If the wind is not blowing, you might consider dropping the lunch hook anyway, just to savor the stream's wild character a bit longer.

To the north, Trenchards Inlet splits into two large creeks. Both offer cruising opportunities of their own, and one leads to a small community.

Club Bridge Creek

Club Bridge Creek comprises the northeastern fork of upper Trenchards Inlet. While the creek's lower reaches are probably too open for anchorage in any but light airs, the upper portion offers several opportunities to drop the hook far from the beaten path. Most of the shores are the usual salt marsh, and there is no development on the creek's banks.

The warning beacon shown on chart 11516 at the stream's intersection with its first sidewater consists of only a few pilings. North of the marker, the creek maintains good minimum depths of 9 feet for some distance upstream and has enough swinging room for craft up to 35 feet.

Farther upstream, Club Bridge Creek splits into three branches. In light to moderate winds, craft of almost any size can anchor on the creek's mid-width between the old warning beacon and the forks.

Each of the three upstream forks holds good depths for a short distance. These streams offer a bit more protection than the main creek, but all must be entered with caution. Pick a branch that appears appropriate for your size boat and carefully feel your way in.

Station Creek

Station Creek leads west from Trenchards Inlet to the small village of County Landing. Most of the stream is quite deep, with one spot holding a surprising depth of 60 feet. The upstream portion of the main creek and several sidewaters offer anchorage opportunities.

The easterly reaches of Station Creek near Trenchards Inlet are a bit too open for anchorage except in fair weather, but a wide sidewater leads off to the north less than 1 mile from the creek's mouth. This stream has minimum soundings of 9 feet and affords plenty of swinging room for almost any size craft to drop the hook in safety.

Farther upstream, Station Creek splits into three branches. The southernmost stream is shoal and should not be entered.

The middle cut holds low-tide depths of around 8 feet or more. There is enough room for boats of less than 36 feet to drop anchor. Do not try to reenter the main body of Station Creek at County Landing from this stream, as depths drop to 3 feet or less.

The northernmost fork is the main body. It has minimum depths of 7 feet, with most of the channel deeper. The stream eventually curves around to the south and borders the small village of County Landing on its western banks. Anchorage by boats up to 38 feet is a practical possibility on the creek as far as County Landing. Past the village, depths quickly decline.

HARBOR-STORY RIVER AREA NAVIGATION

Remember, navigation of this entire region calls for the most exacting use of chart, compass, log, sounder, and the information contained in this section. Enter the waters south of Harbor River at low tide only. Go slowly and exercise extreme caution at all times.

Harbor River Enter Harbor River by the marked channel west of Egg Bank. The direct route from St. Helena Sound calls for local knowledge and is too tricky for visiting cruisers.

Proceed from St. Helena Sound past unlighted daybeacon #2 as if you were entering Morgan River. Eventually, unlighted daybeacon #4 will come abeam well to the south. Continue upstream on Morgan River for another 100 yards, then turn back to the southeast and set course to come abeam of #4 fairly close to its easterly side. Study chart 11517 for a moment and notice the 5-foot shoal north-northeast of #4. If your boat draws more than 4½ feet, guard against this hazard as you approach #4.

Once abeam of unlighted daybeacon #4, immediately set a new course to come abeam of and pass unlighted daybeacon #6 to its fairly immediate easterly quarter.

Now comes the tricky part. You must track your way south to a position some 100 yards east of unlighted daybeacon #8 without encroaching on the very shoal water correctly charted east of #8. Study chart 11517 to illuminate this complicated procedure.

Continue cruising south from #8 for several hundred yards. You can then swing to the southwest and enter the broad Harbor River channel. Stick to the mid-width and stay well away from the shoal water to the northwest; excellent depths are carried well upstream to unlighted daybeacon #9.

Soon, your path will be blocked by the Harbor Island swing bridge. This span has a closed vertical clearance of 15 feet, but it does open on demand.

Wards Creek Favor the northern shore heavily at the entrance to Wards Creek. After passing into the stream's interior reaches, swing back to the mid-width. By holding scrupulously to the middle, you can expect good depths as far as the shrimpers' docks well upstream. If you choose to anchor, just select a likely spot and drop the hook. If possible, try to leave enough room for passing shrimpers.

On Harbor River Southwest of unlighted daybeacon #9, unmarked shoals guard the northwestern shores. Favor the eastern and southeastern banks as you approach the cut-through to Trenchards Inlet. If you choose to enter the upper reaches of Harbor River northwest of unlighted daybeacon #10, stick to the mid-line and be sure to cease your gunkholing before reaching the stream's first sharp bend to the south.

South to Fripp Inlet To enter the small cut leading south to Fripp Inlet, you must pass unlighted daybeacon #10 immediately to its eastern side, even though that maneuver looks wrong on the chart. Avoid the eastern banks, where an extensive shoal juts well out into the creek. If you happen to arrive during or near high tide, this passage can be all but impossible. Be sure to time your run on the channel for low water.

Once past #10, swing back to the mid-width. Good depths continue on the centerline as far as the creek's intersection with the main body of the inlet.

If you choose to explore the creek running northwest from the cut-through's junction with the upper reaches of Fripp Inlet, avoid the point of land separating the two streams. You should encounter no difficulties on the northwesterly creek until the stream splits into two branches. Even these small creeks are briefly navigable.

Enter the southwesterly fork on its centerline. Be sure to discontinue your explorations well before reaching the stream's first hairpin turn to the north.

To enter the northern branch, you should also hold to the mid-width initially. After proceeding upstream for some 75 yards, begin favoring the eastern banks, and continue to favor them until the stream cuts sharply to the west. Cruise back to the mid-width when you have rounded the turn. Discontinue your exploration before reaching the waters where the creek splits into several small branches.

Lower Fripp Inlet Hold to the center as you cruise to the south and southeast toward the bridge spanning the main body of Fripp Inlet. You will pass unlighted daybeacon #12 west of your course. This aid marks the entrance to Story River and will be covered in the next section. At #12, the inlet passage widens considerably and turns to the southeast. Watch to the southwest as you approach the bridge and you will soon spy the entrance to Old House Creek, home of Fripp Island Marina.

Old House Creek Be careful to avoid the large shoal flanking the northern point at the entrance to Old House Creek. Favor the southern banks when entering, but don't approach this shoreline too closely either. Watch to the north for the first point of land extending into the creek. As this point comes abeam, alter your course and begin to favor the northern shore as you approach the stream's first turn to the south.

Once around the turn, cruise back to the mid-width. From this point, successful navigation of the creek's practical cruising limits is a simple matter of holding to the center.

Begin watching the southeastern shores as the creek takes a sharp turn to the southwest. Fripp Island Marina will soon come abeam. Good depths continue until the stream swings sharply to the northeast and finally peters out. If you decide to anchor rather than make use of the marina, consider the long, straight section past the docks.

Story River Pass unlighted daybeacon #12 well to its southerly side and enter Story River on its mid-width. Some 1.3 nautical miles upstream, Story River divides. As described earlier, the northwesterly branch provides good anchorage. Enter on the mid-width and drop the hook at any likely spot. Depths fall off rapidly where the creek splits into three branches. Stop well southeast of this juncture.

The southerly branch of Story River runs generally southwest to Trenchards Inlet. Hold strictly to the mid-width and you should not encounter too many problems at low tide. At high tide, this section of the river is particularly susceptible to covered mud flats. During on-site research, this writer repeatedly failed to find the channel at high water. A word to the wise: Plan your cruise to correspond with low tide.

As Story River makes its entrance into Trenchards Inlet, the stream broadens appreciably. Hold to Story River's centerline as you cruise west-southwest into the main body of the inlet. Follow this course for at least 200 yards southwest

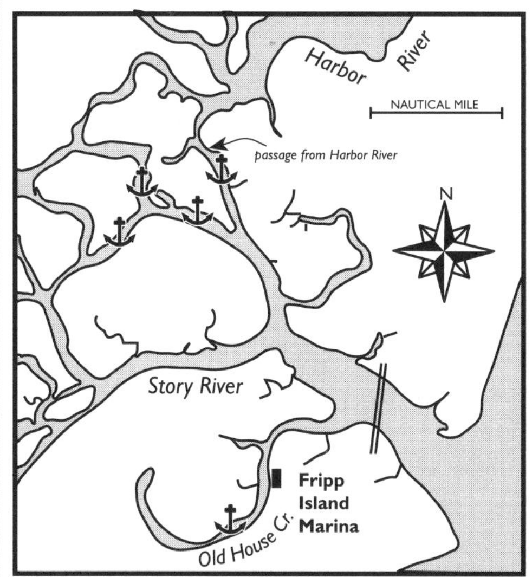

of the river's mouth before turning to the north or south. Very shallow water on both sides of the channel flanks the river's intersection with Trenchards Inlet. This section calls for extra caution. Feel your way along and keep an eye on the sounder.

Trenchards Inlet Trenchards Inlet holds excellent depths as far as Bull Point, on the southwestern tip of Capers Island. Further seaward passage is strictly not recommended without specific local knowledge.

To cruise north and enter either of Trenchards Inlet's two auxiliary streams, continue tracking west-southwest from the mouth of Story River until you come abeam of the inlet's mid-width. Turn to the north and point for the middle of the split.

Club Bridge Creek Favor the southeastern shores of Club Bridge Creek a bit when entering. Good depths soon spread out from shore to shore. Hold to the mid-width as the creek turns to the north-northwest. Watch for the three pilings near the eastern banks that serve as the charted warning beacon. Here, the creek's first sidewater will come abeam to the west.

If you choose to make use of this first creek, enter on the mid-width. Drop the hook anywhere you like, but be sure to halt your progress well before reaching the stream's hairpin turn to the north. Depths of 3 feet or less are encountered thereafter.

The main body of Club Bridge Creek between the warning beacon and the split is a good spot to drop the hook in all but the heaviest of weather. Don't attempt to enter the next large sidewater making in to the western banks. Depths are too uncertain for large cruising boats on this changeable stream.

Eventually, Club Bridge Creek splits into three branches. Adventurous skippers may enter any of these on the mid-width, but shallow depths are soon encountered on all three creeks.

Station Creek Station Creek features unusually deep readings along its central waters from the stream's intersection with Trenchards Inlet until it splits into three branches. If you choose to enter the first sidewater on the northern shore west of the split, do so on its mid-line, and don't cruise any farther upstream than the stretch where the stream splinters into several branches.

Soon, the main body of Station Creek splits into three branches. Do not enter the southernmost fork of Station Creek. It is shoal.

The center fork holds good depths until it encounters the waters of the northern branch looping south at County Landing. Depths of 2 feet or less wait to greet the unfortunate cruiser at this intersection. Drop your hook well before reaching the junction and retrace your path to the east-southeast when it is time to leave.

Enter the northern branch's center section and continue on the middle course until County Landing comes abeam on the western shore. Watch to starboard and you will spy a concrete launching ramp near the town's southern border. In spite of readings shown on chart 11516, depths drop to 4 feet or less past this point.

COMBAHEE RIVER

Combahee River is one of two major streams that cut into the northern shores of mighty Coosaw River's eastern reaches. The Combahee has two major auxiliary waters of its own, New and Old Chehaw Rivers. These two streams will be reviewed later in this chapter.

Despite its impressive size and rich history, Combahee River presents surprisingly few cruising opportunities other than those offered by the two Chehaw Rivers. No other sidewaters offer a safe haven for the night, and the river itself is too wide for protected anchorage. Most of the shores are salt marsh, except where the higher ground of Fields Point borders the northern and eastern shores east of Gunboat Island. This is probably the best spot to drop the hook if you must do so on the Combahee.

The Combahee has a number of unmarked shoals to avoid, and the stream leaves the charts north of Gunboat Island.

Quite frankly, the only reason visiting cruisers should consider entering Combahee River is for its fascinating sidewaters. However, a navigational sketch of the river as far as Gunboat Island is offered for those brave, hardy cruisers who simply must see it all.

Combahee River History Before the Civil War, the banks of Combahee River were one of the richest rice-growing regions in South Carolina. Sadly, there is very little left today of this once-thriving agricultural dynasty. An occasional sluice gate is sometimes spotted by adventurous explorers along the shore, and hunters still frequent the fields during the fall months, but the beauty and grandeur that once graced the river's banks are now only a distant, haunting memory.

COMBAHEE RIVER NAVIGATION

It is a simple matter to enter the main body of Combahee River from the southwestern mouth of the Ashepoo-Coosaw Cutoff. Cruise southwest past flashing daybeacon #184 on the ICW channel for some 300 yards, then turn sharply to the northwest. Soon, you will find yourself on the river's lower reaches.

Favor the northeastern shore to avoid the small, extremely shallow patch of water abutting the entrance's southwestern point, clearly shown on chart 11518. Once past these shallows, cruise back to the mid-width. If you intend to enter New Chehaw River, you should begin to make your way toward the northeastern banks as you cruise upriver.

To continue upstream on the Combahee, begin heavily favoring the southern and southwestern banks as you approach the first point of land on the southwestern shore. A large patch of shoal water bisects the river just to the north and northeast. Boaters will find it most convenient to maneuver around this shallow water by hugging the southwestern shoreline.

Watch to the east-northeast for a sharp point of land jutting into the river. As soon as this promontory comes abeam, ease back to the river's mid-width. Continue on the middle course to hold good depths for some distance upstream, until the river takes a hairpin turn to the south. Old Chehaw River's entrance will come abeam on the eastern banks some 0.8 nautical mile before you reach this turn.

After rounding the Combahee's sharp southern bend, immediately begin to favor the eastern banks slightly. As shown on chart 11519, a very shallow stretch of water lines the western shore. Notice also the much narrower band of 2-foot shallows abutting the eastern shoreline. Soon, the Combahee takes another 180-degree turn back to the north. Hold to the mid-width as you pass through this bend.

Favor the eastern shore slightly when approaching Fields Point. Boaters will find the best protection for anchorage on Combahee River where the high ground of Fields Point comes abeam to the north and northeast.

Cruisers continuing upriver to Gunboat Island should follow the river around its next turn to the west and begin favoring the southern banks after cruising upstream for 300 yards or so past the western bend. Gunboat Island will soon be sighted dead ahead. Continue favoring the southern shore and you can cruise to the south of the island in at least 20 feet of water.

Passage farther upstream is not recommended for cruising boats. Numerous unmarked shoals wait to trap the too-bold skipper, and the river soon leaves the chart. It may be possible to anchor in the southern lee of Gunboat Island, but it would be an uncomfortable night if the fickle wind gets up its dander. It would be much better to retrace your route down the Combahee and explore the fascinating cruising possibilities of Old and New Chehaw Rivers.

NEW CHEHAW RIVER

New Chehaw River is a lovely stream with at least two inviting anchorages. However, the river's entranceway is difficult and holds minimum depths of only 4½ feet. For this reason, the New Chehaw is recommended only for boats under 38 feet that draw less than 4 feet.

Past the troublesome entrance, good depths of 7 feet or more hold along the stream's mid-width. The lower reaches of the river are lined by marsh and are suitable only for light-air anchorage. Farther upstream, there are two more-sheltered spots that could make for a memorable overnight stay. The first is found where charted Boulder Island flanks the eastern banks in the body of a hairpin loop which curls first to the east, then back to the west. Tall pines overlook this haven, and the wind's sighing in the branches lulled this writer and his mate to sleep during our last visit.

This writer's personal selection for overnight anchorage on the New Chehaw is the stretch where the heavily wooded banks of charted Warren Island line the river's northwestern shore. Here, good depths run almost to the island's banks, and there is plenty of swinging room, coupled with excellent protection. The undeveloped woodlands of Warren Island beckon the intrepid visitor to come ashore and explore. We gave in to the temptation and found the remains of an old logging camp. Whether you stay on your boat and simply admire the woods' beauty or heed the pioneering instinct and go ashore, this is an anchorage you will not soon forget.

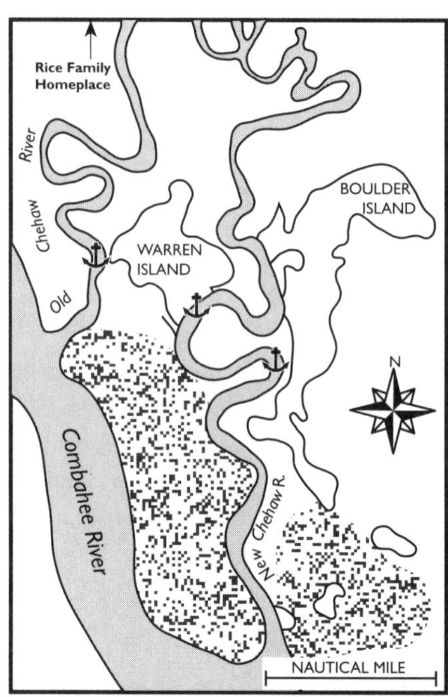

NEW CHEHAW RIVER NAVIGATION

New Chehaw River's southern entrance calls for very cautious cruising. Don't be in a hurry! Proceed at idle speed and feel your way through the river's mouth. Keep a weather eye on the sounder to quickly spot any encroachment on the surrounding shoals.

Begin heavily favoring the northeastern shores of Combahee River well southeast of the New Chehaw's entrance. Stay about 25 yards from the banks and follow the shore into the interior section of the river. Expect some 4½- to 5-foot readings in this area at low water. Take care not to drift to the west or southwest. As shown on chart 11518, a shoal flanks the mid-width of the river's mouth.

Continue favoring the eastern banks until the river narrows perceptibly. As the stream passes through its jog to the north-northeast, cruise back to the mid-width. From here to Warren Island, you need only stick to the middle for minimum low-tide depths of 7 feet, with most of the channel being deeper.

Upstream of Warren Island, good depths continue for some distance. However, depths finally decline as the river takes a sharp turn to the east-northeast. Wise cruisers will terminate their explorations soon after passing Warren Island's shores.

OLD CHEHAW RIVER

Old Chehaw River, another fascinating sidewater, makes in to the northeasterly banks of Combahee River well south of Fields Point. Like its southerly sister, New Chehaw River, the stream offers a multitude of anchorage opportunities, along with one historic site of great interest. Unlike its sister river, however, the Old Chehaw is easy to enter and maintains minimum depths of 8 feet on its mid-width to the stream's charted upstream limits. There are a few unmarked shoals to bypass, but competent navigators should come through safely.Boats of up to 40 feet that draw less than 6 feet can enter Old Chehaw River with confident caution.

Most of the shores lining the Old Chehaw's lower reaches are the usual marsh grass. These waters are suitable for anchorage only in light winds. Protection is much improved where the river briefly borders the western limit of Warren Island. Another excellent anchorage lies on the long, straight stretch of the river bounded by the high ground of Big Island to the east.

The Old Chehaw's most exciting anchorage is located just east of the small community of Wiggins (clearly marked on chart 11517), where high ground fronts the western banks and a tank symbol appears on the chart. Here, it is possible to anchor with excellent protection and solid holding ground within sight of a historical point of interest.

It is quite practical to cruise upstream on Old Chehaw River past the Wiggins area, but there are several unmarked shallows to worry with, and the river leaves chart 11517 near the abandoned course of the old South Carolina Railroad. The navigation is not difficult, however, so don't hesitate to continue your cruise as far as the old railroad if you are of a mind. Just be sure to read the navigational information presented in the next section before proceeding.

Rice Family Homeplace

Just east of Wiggins, the Rice family homeplace gazes boldly out on Old Chehaw River from a high bluff. This beautiful home was once the abode of James Henry Rice, Jr., whom this writer has had frequent occasion to quote in this guide. It is not difficult to picture Rice sitting on his porch with the magnificent river panorama before him, penning his immortal *Glories of the Carolina Coast*. With such inspiration, it is no wonder that Rice's phrases so vibrantly reflect the wondrous qualities of coastal South Carolina. The thoughtful visitor's imagination will surely be fired by the romantic word-portraits Rice painted of the land he loved so deeply.

During our research, this writer and his mate had occasion to anchor in the shadow of the Rice homeplace for a special evening. Nature

Rice family homeplace on Old Chehaw River

cooperated by providing a breathtaking sunset behind the old house, and we came a bit closer to a true understanding of why so many are lured back to this dreamlike land. That evening will always remain our fondest memory of traveling the South Carolina coast.

OLD CHEHAW RIVER NAVIGATION

Favor the northwestern shore slightly when entering Old Chehaw River from the Combahee. As shown on chart 11517, a patch of shoal water guards the entranceway's southeastern point. However, you must also be on guard for the long, correctly charted shoal stretching south from the entrance's northwestern point.

Once past the river's mouth, you need only hold to the mid-width as far as the Rice homeplace for successful navigation of the stream.

Hard by the Rice home, Old Chehaw River takes a 90-degree bend to the east. Begin favoring the southern shore and continue to do so until the stream again turns to the north. Using this procedure, you will avoid a patch of very shallow water lining the northern banks.

As the Old Chehaw turns to the north, cruise toward the western banks and favor this shoreline until the stream's next jog to the northeast. Past this turn, simply hold to the mid-width for good depths as far as the old railway.

BULL RIVER

Bull River flows into the northern banks of the Coosaw several miles west of Combahee River. An impressive stream for its size, the Bull affords a number of overnight anchorage possibilities. Surprisingly, not a single historic site is visible from the water. The many cotton plantations that once dotted the river's banks were entirely destroyed by Sherman's ruthless march during the latter stages of the Civil War.

As Bull River winds its way to the north and northwest, it soon splits into two large branches, Wimbee and Williman Creeks, which in turn offer numerous sidewaters of their own. Williman Creek eventually leads to Schooner Creek. Overnight anchorages abound on all these streams. Additional stops are afforded by several smaller streams that break off from the river's main body.

Bull River and its two main offshoots hold excellent depths for the most part. Several of Wimbee and Williman Creeks' sidewaters are shoal and much too treacherous for large cruising boats. If you choose to enter any of these auxiliary waters, proceed with caution and keep a steady watch on the sounder.

With only a few exceptions, Bull River and its various creeks are surrounded by marsh grass. High ground reaches the river's banks in only a few places. These shoreside conditions render minimal protection for overnight stops. None of Bull River's anchorages is particularly recommended for heavy weather.

Main-body Anchorages

Two small sidewaters on the Bull's eastern shore south of Williman Creek afford good anchorage for craft up to 34 feet in length. The southern creek is located south of Buzzard Island. This small stream carries 6-foot minimum depths, but there is a large unmarked shoal at the entrance. Past this hazard, the stream's interior waters provide visiting cruisers the opportunity to drop the hook in a primitive setting. Depths drop off in this creek sooner than chart 11519 would lead you to believe. Be sure to discontinue your exploration before proceeding too far upstream.

The northern creek is a bit larger and also holds 6-foot minimum depths in its unmarked channel. Here, too, there is a large shoal that must be worried with at the stream's entrance, but careful cruisers should be able to bypass this danger without too much difficulty. Select a likely spot on the mid-width of the inner creek and drop the hook for an evening spent far from the madding crowd.

Wimbee Creek

North of Summerhouse Point, Wimbee Creek, the western fork of Bull River, cuts to the northwest. The creek holds good depths as far as the small village of Chisolm on the southwestern banks. Here, almost any craft can anchor abeam of several private docks, but the creek is a bit wide for comfortable conditions if winds exceed 15 knots.

Don't attempt to enter the branch of Wimbee Creek that flows south from Williman Creek east of Chisolm. This stream can be entered from Williman Creek and offers good anchorage along its northern reaches, but shoals guard its intersection with Wimbee Creek. Its southern mouth is too treacherous for boaters who lack local knowledge. For the same reason, you should avoid the small offshoot northeast of Chisolm.

Northwest of Chisolm, frequent unmarked shoals pepper Wimbee Creek and render conditions too uncertain for cruising-sized vessels.

Williman Creek

Williman Creek is a deep stream that affords good anchorage in light to moderate airs. For more protection, boats of 34 feet or less can enter the northeasterly mouth of the small stream that flows south to Wimbee Creek. This sidewater holds 8-foot minimum depths on its mid-width before reaching the shoals that guard its southerly exit. If you choose to enter, be sure to use the lower (southeasternmost) of the two entrances from Williman Creek. The upper passage is quite shoal.

Eventually, Williman Creek splits. The deep northerly branch becomes Schooner Channel, while the southerly fork affords additional anchorage opportunities. The southerly stream eventually leads to a large patch of shoals that effectively bars reentry into Schooner Channel

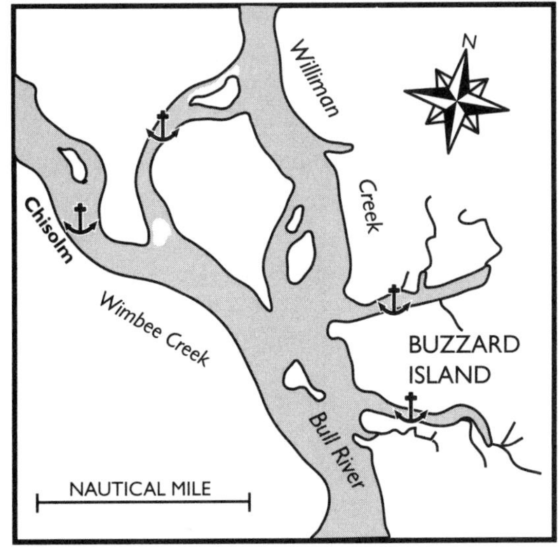

from this quarter. Before reaching the shoals, however, this stream offers excellent anchorage for boats up to 36 feet as it rounds its first sharp turn to the northwest. Here, the high ground of Williman Island to the southwest gives good protection.

Schooner Channel

Schooner Channel holds 8-foot minimum depths on its centerline until it rejoins the northwesterly reaches of Wimbee Creek. Boats up to 40 feet can easily anchor anywhere along the creek's length in light to moderate winds. Protection is not adequate for strong blows.

Though a channel continues upstream from this point, there are numerous unmarked shallows that can bring visiting boaters to grief. This writer highly recommends that you cease your exploration where Schooner Channel and Wimbee Creek meet.

BULL RIVER NAVIGATION

Exercise caution when cruising Bull River. While most of the river is deep, many sidewaters are blinds and traps waiting to surprise the careless boater. Be sure to read the information in this guide before attempting entry into any sidewater.

Enter Bull River on its mid-width from the Coosaw. Avoid the shallow water extending east-southeast from Bull Split, marked by an unnumbered and unlighted red-and-green daybeacon north of Parrot Creek.

Begin favoring the eastern banks just a bit as you cruise upriver. This procedure will help to avoid the large shoal, clearly shown on chart 11519, that lines the western banks south of Summerhouse Point.

You will soon observe an island bisecting the Bull. Don't approach this small landmass. It is surrounded by shallow water. You must now make a choice. If you want to visit Wimbee Creek, pass to the west and southwest of the island. If, on the other hand, you intend to explore Williman Creek or make use of the two small unnamed anchorages on the eastern banks, set your course to pass the island's eastern and northeastern sides.

Bull River Sidewater Anchorages The entrance to the unnamed creek south of charted Buzzard Island is flanked by very shallow water to the north. Favor the southern banks heavily when entering. Set the hook at a spot that strikes your fancy on the stream's interior waters. Don't attempt to cruise past the creek's first turn to the southeast. Despite the soundings recorded on chart 11519, 3- and 4-foot depths are immediately encountered.

The northerly stream's mid-width (north of Buzzard Island) is blocked by a shoal that is bared at low water but covered at high tide. Favor the southerly banks heavily as you traverse the entrance to avoid this hazard. Once past the stream's mouth, select a spot to anchor. Depths eventually begin to fall off as the stream splinters into several smaller creeks to the east-northeast.

Wimbee Creek Stick to the mid-width of broad Wimbee Creek as you cruise upstream to the charted position of Chisolm. Remember not to attempt entry of the branch connecting Wimbee and Williman Creeks or the loop separated from the creek's main body by a marsh island northeast of Chisolm.

Watch the southwestern shores and you will spy several private docks and a few homes. These are all that is visible today of Chisolm Island, once virtually covered by rich Sea Island plantations. Anchor a respectful distance from the piers.

Don't attempt to cruise farther up Wimbee Creek than the small island bisecting the stream east of Keans Neck. Numerous shoals lie beyond this point, and depths rise generally. You should also bypass South Wimbee Creek, northwest of Chisolm. It is too narrow for large boats, and depths quickly drop off.

Williman Creek Favor the eastern shore of Williman Creek slightly when entering the stream from Bull River, but don't approach the eastern banks too closely. Don't be fooled by the false entrance behind the two charted marsh islands on the western shore. These errant waters are choked with shoals and oyster banks.

From its southerly entrance until it splits, Williman Creek carries minimum 8-foot depths on its mid-width, with most of the channel significantly deeper. Boaters can anchor on this section of the creek in light to moderate airs, but winds over 15 knots can bring on an annoying "drub-drub."

Williman Creek Sidewater Anchorage If you choose to make use of the more protected anchorage on the small stream running south to Wimbee Creek, be sure to use its southeastern entrance. Hold to the mid-width and drop the hook at your convenience. Discontinue your cruise well before reaching the bend to the southeast where the creek begins to make its way into Wimbee Creek's northwestern banks.

Southerly Williman Creek Exercise caution when entering the southerly branch of Williman Creek from its split with Schooner Channel. Favor the southeasterly shores until the stream makes a sharp bend to the northwest. Cruise back to the center at this point.

Consider anchoring soon after passing around this bend. Farther upstream, numerous shoals guard the creek's intersection with Schooner Channel.

Schooner Channel Deep Schooner Channel does not present any navigational difficulties short of its intersection with the northwestern reaches of Wimbee Creek. Simply stick to the mid-width and drop the anchor anywhere you choose.

Be sure to cease your exploration before reaching the juncture with Wimbee Creek. Passage farther upstream calls for local knowledge and is strictly not recommended for cruising craft.

ICW TO BEAUFORT

From the southwestern reaches of the Ashepoo-Coosaw Cutoff, the ICW follows the mighty Coosaw River until it intersects the headwaters of Brickyard Creek, which in turn leads south to the historic community of Beaufort. The Coosaw section of the Waterway is broad and generally unsheltered. It is one of the most open stretches on the entire South Carolina ICW. Winds over 10 knots can quickly give rise to a sharp chop, and blows over 20 knots can make for a very rough crossing indeed. The Waterway traveler would be well advised to check on the latest weather conditions before tackling the Coosaw.

At unlighted daybeacon #209, the Waterway begins its turn to the south into Brickyard Creek. This stretch of the ICW boasts good protection and easy navigation. Several sidewaters offer convenient overnight anchorage.

Cruising boaters should approach the run from the Coosaw to Beaufort with a healthy amount of respect. With proper caution, however, you can enjoy your cruise to Beaufort and gain a broader perspective on the beautiful South Carolina Low Country.

Coosaw River

The broad Coosaw seems more like a sound than a river. More than one boater visiting South Carolina for the first time has sailed calmly out of the Ashepoo-Coosaw Cutoff only to stop short, amazed by the wide waters before him or her. Don't be put off. In fair weather, passage of the Coosaw can be a very pleasurable experience. Sailing skippers in particular may find that they have a good reach all the way to Brickyard Creek.

Airplane flying over Brickyard Creek

The only Coosaw sidewaters offering protected anchorage are Combahee and Bull Rivers, just described, and the two smaller creeks leading south to Morgan River that were reviewed earlier in this chapter. If you seek shelter, consider one of these auxiliary streams. Otherwise, with one possible exception, you must make your way to the protected waters of Brickyard Creek before finding safe haven.

While the vast majority of Coosaw River is quite deep, there are a few shoals along the way. Waterway-wise boaters will stick to the marked channel unless they decide to visit one of the sidewaters. It is often a long run between aids to navigation on the Coosaw. It is a wise procedure to run compass courses between the various markers to avoid errors.

This portion of the ICW presents a challenge to the cruising boater. The river's open waters can indeed provide a most humbling experience during foul weather. Still, this writer cannot help feeling a genuine fondness for this stretch of the Waterway. There is a very real sense of adventure that comes from the successful navigation of such broad waters with only undeveloped natural shorelines within your range of vision. This is an experience often absent along the well-marked ICW and one that passing cruisers should not dismiss too lightly.

Sams Point Anchorage

During times of light winds, or when moderate breezes are blowing from the southwest, Waterway cruisers occasionally anchor in the waters east-northeast of Sams Point and the northern entrance of Lucy Point Creek. Depths range from 10 to 15 feet if you avoid the charted shoals to the south and southwest. A few homes overlooking the banks from nearby Sams Point only add to this anchorage's unmistakable charm. It is hard to imagine a finer fair-weather spot to watch the evening's golden light fade from the surrounding waters.

Whale Branch

At flashing daybeacon #203, a broad fork of Coosaw River breaks off to the northwest and becomes Whale Branch. While it is possible to enter Whale Branch from Broad River to the west, the eastern entrance from Coosaw River is littered with unmarked shoals and is much too dangerous for any but shallow-draft skiffs. Visiting boaters are strictly advised to bypass this section of Whale Branch. The entrance from Broad River will be covered in chapter 9.

Brickyard Creek

The ICW's well-marked, easily followed channel leads south down Brickyard Creek to the charming community of Beaufort. Several small auxiliary waters along the way can provide good anchorage for boats under 40 feet. Stick to the channel in Brickyard Creek. Outside the marked cut, numerous shoals await your keel.

Jack Island Anchorage

West of unlighted daybeacon #209, an unnamed creek south of Jack Island offers very protected anchorage for craft up to 36 feet that draw less than 4 feet. A large, unmarked shoal guards the entrance, but careful navigation should see you through. Otherwise, the creek's channel carries 6-foot minimum depths until the stream takes a sharp bend to the north. In spite of soundings shown on chart 11519, shallow water is quickly encountered past this turn.

The creek's southern and southwestern banks support moderate residential development. The best anchorage is located abeam of the several private docks that serve these shoreside homes.

Loop Anchorage

A small, unnamed loop creek whose northerly entrance makes in to Brickyard Creek's easterly banks abeam of unlighted daybeacon #216 provides one of the best overnight stops on this portion of the Waterway. Minimum depths of 8 feet on the creek's southerly reaches combine with excellent protection from the surrounding shores to make a superior anchorage.

Entrance from the north, though possible, is a tricky passage not recommended for cruising boaters. The loop's southerly entrance is easily navigated and provides reliable access to the protected portion of the stream.

Watch to starboard at the rear (easternmost)

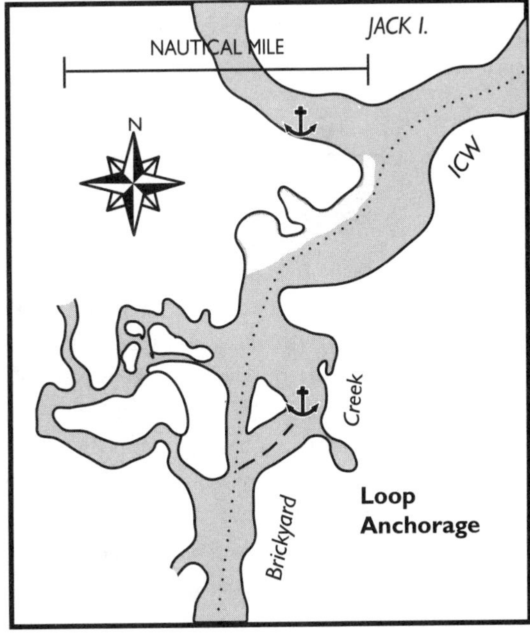

portion of the loop and you will spy a large private dock on the eastern shore. Consider anchoring abeam of or just slightly upstream of the pier. This is the most protected stretch of the creek. Farther to the north and northwest, depths become uncertain.

Albergottie Creek

West-southwest of unlighted daybeacon #226, two small buoys mark the entrance to Albergottie Creek. In spite of these markers, all boaters are advised to bypass this stream. It is associated with the local Marine Corps airfield and is off-limits to visitors.

Pleasants Point

Just across Brickyard Creek from unlighted daybeacon #226, boaters will note a beautiful home on Pleasants Point overlooking the Waterway. This property was originally owned by "Tuscarora Jack" Barnwell, one of the historical heroes of Beaufort. The present house was built in the 1920s, but it reflects the style of earlier times.

Brickyard Creek Anchorage

An offshoot of deep water abuts the northern banks of Brickyard Creek north of unlighted daybeacon #229A. While this area is rather exposed, it can be used as an overnight anchorage in light to moderate airs by craft up to 40 feet. However, anchored craft are exposed to the wake of all passing vessels, which can make for a rude awakening during the early morning.

On to Beaufort

East of unlighted daybeacon #229A, the Waterway flows around Pigeon Point, once a favored spot for duels. It then turns south on its way to the lovely city of Beaufort. Accounts of this marvelous port of call and the ICW route farther south will be presented in the following chapter.

ICW TO BEAUFORT NAVIGATION

Coosaw River presents some navigational circumstances seldom encountered on the South Carolina ICW. Markers are widely spaced, and the often-choppy waters can make it difficult to hold a steady compass course. These conditions make the practice of sound coastal navigation a real necessity rather than the nicety it sometimes is on other parts of the Waterway.

Brickyard Creek, on the other hand, is a typical section of the South Carolina ICW. The creek fairly bristles with markers; passing boaters would almost need to be asleep at the helm to encounter trouble. Stranger things have happened, though, so be sure to stay alert.

Coosaw River Begin bending your course slightly to the south-southwest as you exit the Ashepoo-Coosaw Cutoff at flashing daybeacon #184. After proceeding some 300 yards, swing almost due south for at least 0.2 nautical mile. Only then should you turn to the west and set a new course to come abeam of flashing daybeacon #186 to its southerly side. Do not try to short-cut your entrance into Coosaw River by passing between #186 and the southwesterly point of Combahee River. This point is building outward and could trick you into a most unpleasant grounding.

From #186, use your compass and chart to work your way west to flashing daybeacon #189, north of Coosaw Island. Along the way, you will pass flashing daybeacon #187 well south of your course and the unnumbered red-and-green warning daybeacon marking Bull River's southeasterly entrance to the north of your track. You may also spy unlighted daybeacon #1, the first of Parrot Creek's markers, south of your passage. If you are bound for Dataw Island Marina, cut south and follow Parrot Creek to Morgan River. This channel was thoroughly discussed earlier in this chapter as part of the Morgan River subsection.

Come abeam of #189 to its fairly immediate northerly side and then set a new course to pass between flashing daybeacon #191 and unlighted daybeacon #192. From here to flashing daybeacon #203, the Waterway channel is well marked and generally easy to follow. Come abeam of #203 by some 30 yards to its northerly side. Keep chart 11518 close at hand to quickly resolve any on-the-water questions that might arise.

Sams Point Anchorage If you choose to anchor near Sams Point when the winds are light or blowing moderately from the southwest, depart the ICW about halfway between #189 and #191. Work your way carefully to a point several hundred yards east-northeast of unlighted daybeacon #2, the northernmost of the markers leading to Lucy Point Creek. Remember that this stream is spanned by a fixed bridge with only 14 feet of vertical clearance. It was reviewed in the Morgan River subsection of this chapter.

Study chart 11518 for a moment and notice the correctly charted band of 1-foot shallows east-southeast of #2. Obviously, you should drop the hook far enough from this shoal so as not to swing onto the shallows if the wind or tide changes.

On the ICW Between #203 and the next westerly aid, unlighted daybeacon #206, a spoil bank flanks the southerly tier of the Waterway channel. Set course to come abeam of #206 to its immediate southerly side. West of #206, a pair of range markers helps you to avoid the spoil bank. Line the two markers up and stay on course until your track begins to bend a bit to the west-southwest as you approach the entrance into Brickyard Creek at unlighted daybeacon #209.

Jack Island Anchorage Use chart 11519 when navigating the unnamed creek south of Jack Island. To hold best depths, come abeam of unlighted daybeacon #209 and immediately turn 90 degrees to the west. Continue on course, favoring the northern banks heavily as you pass through the stream's mouth. Take extra care to avoid the large 2-foot shoal, clearly marked on chart 11519, that flanks the southwestern portion of the creek's entrance.

After leaving the creek's eastern mouth behind, watch the southern and southwestern shore and you will soon spy a series of private docks. As you begin your approach to these piers, slowly cruise toward the southwestern banks. Drop the hook as you come abeam of the docks.

Don't attempt to follow the creek past its first sharp bend to the north. In spite of depths shown on chart 11519, 3- and 4-foot readings are quickly encountered past the turn.

Loop Anchorage Skippers choosing to enter the loop stream lying along the Waterway's eastern flank between unlighted daybeacons #216 and #219 must remember to use its southern entrance, located just north of #219. Cruise into the creek on its mid-width and continue on the middle ground. Set your hook at any likely spot before the stream begins to bend back to the west. Past this point, depths become too uncertain for cruising-sized vessels. To rejoin the Waterway, retrace your route to the south.

On the ICW On-site research revealed that dredging has apparently removed the large, charted shoal on the Waterway's western banks between flashing daybeacons #221A and #224. To be on the safe side, favor the eastern side of the channel between #221A and #224.

As you approach #224, a large commercial dock facility will be visible on the western shore. Slow down and proceed at idle speed if any barges are loading.

Brickyard Creek Anchorage Boaters making use of the open anchorage on Brickyard Creek north of unlighted daybeacon #229A should continue cruising east on the ICW channel until they are some 0.2 nautical mile east of #229A. At this point, turn sharply to the north and cruise toward the shore. This procedure should help to avoid the finger of shoal water north of #229A that extends well to the east.

Some 40 yards before reaching the banks, swing sharply to port and cruise back upstream, staying within some 25 to 40 yards of the northern shoreline. Good depths continue until unlighted

Cruising on Coosaw River

daybeacon #229 comes abeam to the south.

Do not attempt to rejoin the Waterway by cruising to the west. Retrace your steps east to the ICW channel.

On the ICW As you round Pigeon Point, be sure to come abeam of and pass unlighted daybeacon #232 to its easterly quarter. Shallow water is found to the west of this aid.

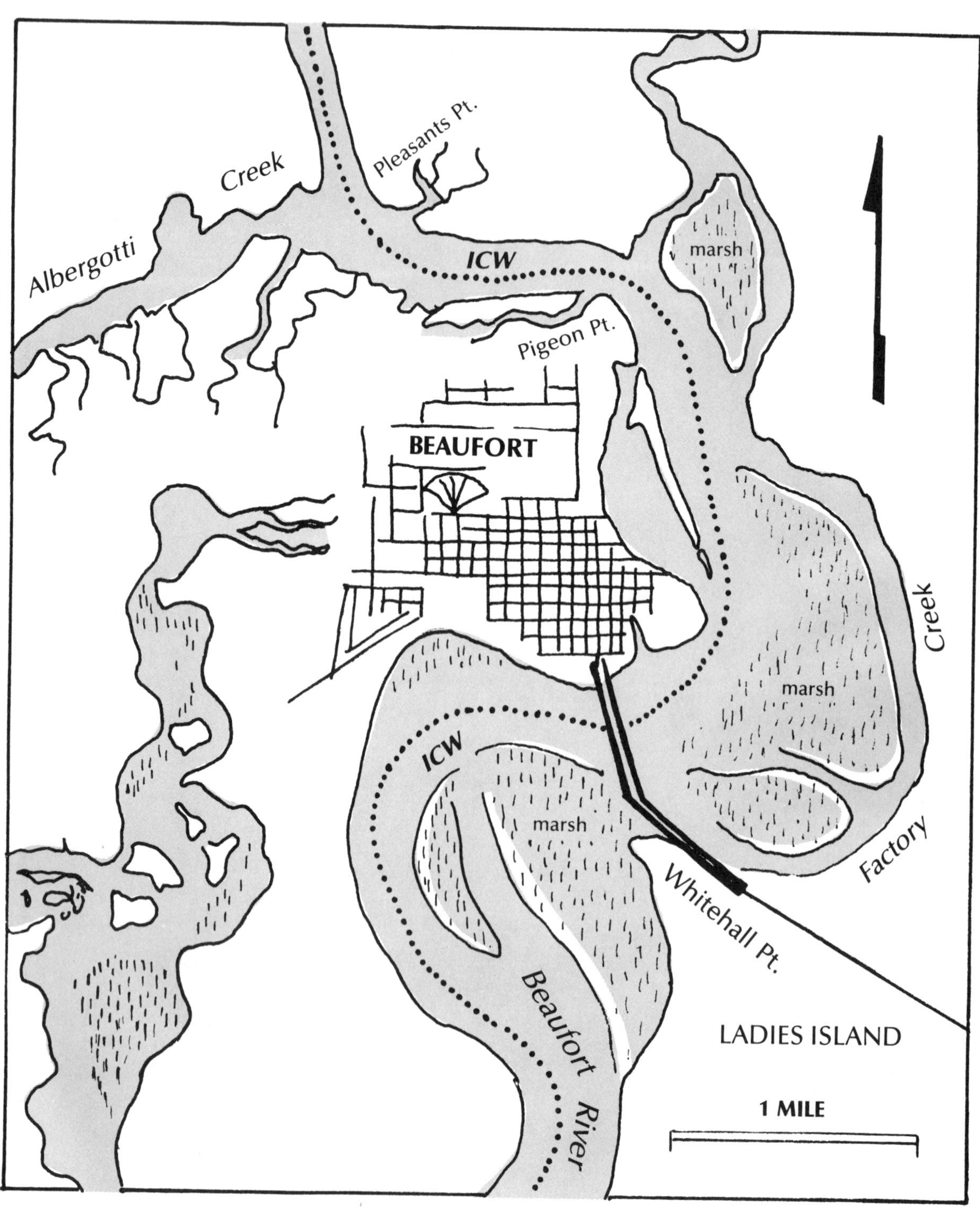

Albergotti
Creek
Pleasants Pt.
ICW
marsh
Pigeon Pt.
BEAUFORT
Creek
marsh
ICW
marsh
Factory
Whitehall Pt.
Beaufort
River
LADIES ISLAND
1 MILE

Beaufort

"Just after sunset . . . the writer, with several friends, viewed a beautiful phenomenon from the terrace of the Gold Eagle Tavern, Beaufort, S.C.

"With the heavens for a canvas, from zenith to the southwest horizon, the greatest of Artists, Nature, had painted another glorious masterpiece, the motif being continuous areas of variable size and contour, in a soft medium tone of ultramarine or lapis lazuli blue, each framed in clouds of brilliant silver, copper and gold, while the restless waters of Beaufort Bay were mirrored in exquisite pastel shades.

"On a pale pearl azure background, Luna, the Queen of Night, appears in luminous splendor, wearing, in honor of the Harvest Month, a royal robe of turquoise blue beneath a shimmering gossamer veil of silvery grey.

"The radiant picture now in its entirety presents an entrancing ensemble of color and beauty, suggesting in its enchantment an approach to the celestial Gates of Paradise—and adds another glory to the Carolina Coast."

Thus wrote Gilbert Augustus Selby in 1934 as a preface to a new printing of James Henry Rice Jr.'s *Glories of the Carolina Coast*. The Gold Eagle Tavern is gone now, but the breathtaking scene described above in such flowery terms can still be witnessed when nature chooses to cooperate. Just across the street from the old tavern site, Bay Street Inn still welcomes the weary traveler. From its second-story balcony, this writer and his mate were privileged to watch a sunset very much like the one described by Selby many years ago. The beauty of that evening will remain with us always.

Chart

You will only need one chart to cover all navigation in the Beaufort area:

11518 covers the ICW through Beaufort and all surrounding waters

Charleston may be the "Holy City" of coastal South Carolina, but this writer contends that Beaufort is certainly the coast's most romantic community. The many stately homes and the mysterious old oaks that surround them impart an air of romance and wonder that must be experienced to be understood. The atmosphere of age, coupled with a yearning for the simpler, more gracious life of bygone years, is a pervasive presence. The sensitive visitor sometimes feels that he or she can almost reach out and touch those far-removed days.

Beaufort is a "must" stop for those cruising the waters of coastal South Carolina. Those who pass by without stopping to make the acquaintance of this unique city will be less for the omission. And just in case you are not yet enticed, take a moment to listen to the haunting words of Robert W. Barnwell, one of Beaufort's many famous citizens of another era:

Called Back

I think if I could see once more
The tide at Beaufort sweep,
Just as the crimson fades to gray,
Just as the shadows creep.
Just as the star of evening glows
And the skimming swallows seek repose
There where the oleanders grow
Before my boyhood's home,
Stumbler and groper that I've been,
Panting on the mountain path,
Lost in the forest green,
Wrecked by the Ocean's wrath,
Stifled in throngs of men;
Come for the wanderer's rest
Come to the home loved best.

BEAUFORT

Beaufort sits poised on the banks of Beaufort River, waiting to greet visitors of the nautical persuasion. The town boasts three marinas and a first-rate boatyard. A number of noteworthy restaurants are within walking distance of the various shoreside facilities, and several inns wait to shelter those who have seen one wave too many. One particularly well-placed marina is located in the heart of the city's historical district. It is indeed fortunate that this fascinating town has such excellent accommodations for passing boaters.

For taxi service in Beaufort call Yellow Cab (803-522-1121), Griffin Cab Company (803-524-4410), or Beaufort Cab Company (803-524-4940).

Moving north to south, Beaufort's first facility, Marsh Harbor Boatyard, is located on an unnamed creek that makes in to the eastern shores of Beaufort River north of unlighted daybeacon #233. This establishment is primarily a service facility. The superfriendly management is very much in touch with the needs of cruising vessels, and the yard is highly recommended by this writer. Full below-waterline haul-out repairs are readily available via a 50-

ton travelift. Additionally, Marsh Harbor Boatyard can handle most mechanical repairs short of a complete overhaul for both gasoline and diesel power plants. There is a complete parts department on the premises. It should also be noted that this yard is one of the only service facilities this writer has ever reviewed that specializes in trawler repairs. If you are the captain of such an excellent cruising craft and need repairs, Marsh Harbor is the place to stop.

Minimum low-tide approach depths on the well-marked entrance channel run around 6 feet, with 5 to 6 feet of water dockside. If there is room, Marsh Harbor Boatyard accepts transients, but the management has informed this writer that only a few boats stop just for the night. Most of the slip space is usually taken up by service customers. Should you berth here, you will find full power and water connections at the wooden floating docks. The marina does not offer gasoline or diesel fuel.

All in all, this writer has seldom found a boatyard with such an upbeat, what-can-we-do-to-help attitude. If you are cruising the southeasterly portion of the South Carolina ICW and are in need of service, your search is ended.

Marsh Harbor Boatyard
(803) 521-1500

Approach depth: 6 feet (low tide)
Dockside depth: 5–6 feet (low tide)
Accepts transients: limited
Floating wooden piers: yes
Dockside power connections: 30 and 50 amps
Dockside water connections: yes
Mechanical repairs: yes
Below-waterline repairs: yes
Ship's store: parts department

Boaters approaching the Lady's Island swing bridge west of unlighted daybeacon #237 will note a marked channel on the Waterway's southern flank that comes abeam just before the span. This cut leads to Factory Creek. Lady's Island Marina sits perched on the southwestern shores of Factory Creek. Low-water entrance depths in the marked channel run around 6 to 7 feet, while cruisers will encounter at least 5 to 6 feet of water dockside at the marina.

This amiable facility gladly accepts transients for overnight dockage and offers berths at floating docks with all power and water connections. At the time of this writing, many of the available slips were taken up by resident boaters. It would be wise to give the marina a call well ahead of time and check on dockage availability before committing to a stay at this facility. Showers, a laundromat, and a small paperback exchange library are located on the premises. Gasoline and diesel fuel are readily available, and both mechanical and haul-out repairs can be arranged through the adjacent Boat Builders boatyard. Haul-outs are accomplished via a 22-ton marine railway. An on-site dining spot, Lady's Island Seafood Restaurant (803-525-1101),

View of Beaufort River from Bay Street

is quite good. Its fried seafood struck the fancy of this writer. A supermarket and a host of other shoreside businesses are located within walking distance, making for a great opportunity to stock up the on-board galley.

Famished cruisers might also choose a quick walk to Wilkop's White Hall Inn (803-524-0382), long one of the most famous restaurants on Lady's Island. To reach this notable dining attraction, walk from the marina toward the Lady's Island swing bridge. You will spot the restaurant to the left of the road just before reaching the span.

Yet another outstanding dining alternative is available to boaters berthing at Lady's Island Marina. Steamers Restaurant (803-522-0210) is located southeast of this facility along the main highway that passes behind the marina. Ask any of the marina staff for directions. Local boaters and non-mariners alike agree that this establishment offers some of the best seafood in the Low Country.

Lady's Island Marina (803) 522-0430

- Approach depth: 6–7 feet (low water)
- Dockside depth: 5–6 feet (low water)
- Accepts transients: yes (space may be limited)
- Floating wooden piers: yes
- Dockside power connections: 30 and 50 amps
- Dockside water connections: yes
- Showers: yes
- Laundromat: yes
- Gasoline: yes
- Diesel fuel: yes
- Mechanical repairs: yes
- Below-waterline repairs: yes
- Restaurants: on-site, with several nearby

Factory Creek may also be used for anchorage northeast of Lady's Island Marina. The best spot is found after the creek passes through a sharp bend to the north. Here, the starboard shores border high ground and give good protection. Boats up to 45 feet should find plenty of swinging room. Do not try to rejoin the Waterway through the creek's northwesterly entrance. Depths are much too uncertain on these waters for cruising craft.

The Downtown Marina of Beaufort is located in the heart of the city's historical district north of unlighted daybeacon #239 (a short distance west of the Lady's Island swing bridge). A host of shops and restaurants, not to mention dozens of dreamlike historical homes, are within an easy walk of the docks. The marina gladly accepts cruising boaters and offers ultramodern wooden and concrete floating docks with full power and water connections. Minimum entrance and dockside depths are better than 12 feet, allowing even the most long-legged vessels to make use of the slips comfortably. Gasoline, diesel fuel, and waste pump-out services are readily available, and there is a wide-ranging ship's and variety store on the premises. Clean showers and a laundromat are also found on the marina grounds. Mechanical repairs can usually be arranged through independent technicians. Obviously, the Downtown Marina is a very

Lady's Island Marina, Factory Creek

well-appointed facility that sees a hefty transient business, particularly when the "snowbirds" are winding their way north or south. Advance slip reservations are a smart precaution.

Tidal currents flow swiftly around the docks of this marina, so take care when maneuvering into your slip. Have all hands stand by with fenders just in case.

Downtown Marina of Beaufort
(803) 524-4422

Approach depth: 12+ feet
Dockside depth: 12+ feet
Accepts transients: yes
Fixed wooden piers: yes
Dockside power connections: 15, 30, and 50 amps
Dockside water connections: yes
Showers: yes
Laundromat: yes
Waste pump-out: yes
Gasoline: yes
Diesel fuel: yes
Mechanical repairs: yes
Below-waterline repairs: yes
Ship's store: yes
Restaurants: many within walking distance

The Downtown Marina of Beaufort is adjacent to a lovely riverside park that features fixed-face docks of its own set against a concrete seawall. These berths are managed by the Downtown Marina. Passing cruisers are welcome to berth at the park's docks, but most cruisers choose to stay at the marina. You would do well to imitate this practice. During the early-evening hours, many local residents gather on the banks of the park to watch the spectacular river sunsets that nature thoughtfully provides from time to time.

There is a local anchorage west of the Downtown Marina where boaters are welcome to drop the hook. Many of the craft in this basin are tied to mooring buoys, but anchoring by visiting cruisers is still allowed. Depths run 12 to 20 feet. Protection is far from the best, and this writer would not want to be caught out here if a heavy thunderstorm should happen by. Tidal currents are also rather swift, which can contribute to a dragging anchor. If you do decide to stay for the night, be sure to leave plenty of swinging room for nearby boats and drop the hook well away from the ICW channel to avoid any passing traffic.

Beaufort's fourth marine facility, Port Royal Landing Marina, is located farther downstream on Beaufort River, near the charted high-rise bridge. This marina will reviewed in the next chapter.

Boaters docking at the Downtown Marina of Beaufort and in need of culinary supplies are in for a real treat. Blackstone's Grocery and Deli (803-524-4330) is located just two blocks east of the marina at 915 Bay Street. This firm offers fine cheeses, meats, and gourmet food items of all descriptions. Blackstone's now serves breakfast. For lunch, the take-out deli sandwiches are nothing to sneeze at either. A trip to Blackstone's

Downtown Marina of Beaufort

is a real treat. Afterwards, you can sail away sipping on the best Chardonnay and munching the freshest Brie.

A number of truly notable dining establishments are located within a short walk of the Downtown Marina. For lunch and dinner, every single visitor to Beaufort should find his way to Plums Restaurant (904½ Bay Street, 803-525-1946). The main entrance is located down a small alley from the street, with an alternate approach from the waterfront park just behind the restaurant. Try to get a table overlooking the park and Beaufort River.

For a delectable evening meal, this writer suggests a trip to the Gatsby Restaurant and Tavern (822 Bay Street, 803-525-1800). Here, you can assuage your appetite on the finest in seafood, steaks, and prime rib. This writer and his mate have always been very impressed with the ultrafriendly, prompt service at Gatsby's. During our last visit, the Spanish-mackerel special was absolutely first-rate. May you, too, be so fortunate.

The Anchorage House Restaurant (1103 Bay Street, 803-524-9392) sits just across the street from the Downtown Marina. It is this writer's personal pick as the most elegant dining spot in town. Lunch and dinner are served Monday through Saturday.

Patrons of the Anchorage House have the opportunity to dine amidst truly historic surroundings. Built by William Elliott during the pre-Revolutionary period, the old house has passed through many different phases. At one time, it was used as an exclusive club, complete with gambling casino. Some years later, the commander of the nearby Parris Island Marine Base, Admiral Beardslee, came to admire the house greatly and purchased it upon retirement. Having spent several years in Japan, the admiral imported many pieces of heavily carved Oriental furniture. Though some of these rare articles were sold at auction many years later, others can still be seen today. Following the admiral's death, the house was operated as a tourist home for many years, until it was finally converted into an elegant restaurant.

The newest dining attraction in town is the Beaufort Inn (809 Port Republic Street, 803-521-9000). Housed in a 1907 homeplace, the inn rents out a collection of exquisite rooms furnished with antiques. Each room has been named for one of the local plantations.

In spite of its memorable lodging, the real star at the Beaufort Inn is the dining room, open to the public for both breakfast and dinner seven days a week. The food here can only be described as sumptuous. Give the Rosemary Honey Salmon Steak a try—you won't be sorry. It is only fair to note that dining at the Beaufort Inn is a bit on the formal side, and that the prices will never be accurately described as inexpensive. This is a place where you will want to dig out your last clean shirt—you know, the one buried under

Anchorage House, Beaufort

the forward V-berth. Nevertheless, considering that the Beaufort Inn's chef consistently wins the most presitgious awards offered anywhere, this is one dining spot where the extra effort is more than justified.

If you are looking for something totally yummy to take back to your own galley, give Sweet Temptations (205 West Street, 803-524-6171) a check. The breads, cakes, and pies (not to mention the sandwiches) are all palate-pleasers.

View of Lady's Island bridge from balcony of Bay Street Inn

Beaufort Lodging

Beaufort is a wonderful choice for weary cruisers who are ready for a break from their waterborne life. The town boasts a number of fine lodging establishments. Three of these are particularly convenient to the passing boater.

The Best Western Sea Island Inn (803-522-2090) is located just across Bay Street from the Downtown Marina of Beaufort. This modern hostelry occupies the same site once claimed by a much older inn of the same name. The renowned reputation of the old Sea Island Motel lives on in its well-managed modern counterpart. The motel is in the heart of the historical district and is convenient to all the city's major attractions. This writer found it a bit more pricey than was true just a few years ago.

The Rhett House Inn (803-524-9030) sits just behind the Best Western Sea Island Inn at 1009 Craven Street. As someone who has spent the last 20 years staying in bed-and-breakfast inns all over the nation, this writer can say without qualification that the Rhett House Inn is one of the most beautiful and charming of the lot. The recipient of a legion of awards, it was voted the most romantic lodging in the South by one prominent magazine several years ago. Built in 1820, the inn is housed in a historic Beaufort home. Robert E. Lee once visited here. The inn's present owners are designers, and their exquisite taste is brilliantly reflected in the lush but warm interior furnishings and decoration.

The Bay Street Inn (601 Bay Street, 803-522-0050) is four blocks east of the Downtown Marina docks. This notable inn is housed in yet another of Beaufort's historic homes. The house is readily visible from the water, and many a passing boater has no doubt admired its cool white porches and columns, never guessing that they were welcome to spend the night. The management is glad to provide transportation from the area marinas for cruise-weary guests.

The two-story inn was built by Lewis Sams in 1852. Apparently, Sams was very fond of sitting on the porch in the evenings, as he built his house with not one but two porches, one above the other. Both offer a magnificent view of the river. The breathtaking panorama provided by the upper balcony was alluded to in the opening section of this chapter. This writer cannot imagine a more peaceful evening than taking one's ease in the balcony's rocking chairs and watching the light slowly fade from the surrounding waters.

Beaufort History The long and colorful history of Beaufort stretches back to early exploration and colonization by the Spanish empire. The first European to visit the area was apparently Francisco Cordillo, who landed at Port Royal Island in 1520. It was he who named the nearby cape St. Elena, which with the passage of the years became St. Helena. In 1557, the Spanish attempted to establish a base in the area, but the colony failed.

In 1562, an adventurous Frenchman named Jean Ribaut led a group of French Protestants to the New World. The colonists built a settlement on nearby Parris Island and named their small town Charlesfort. For a time, all went well, but the colony was doomed to end in tragic and grisly failure.

Promising to return as soon as possible, Ribaut sailed back to France to obtain needed supplies. When the dynamic leader arrived in his mother country, he found the French nation torn asunder with religious conflict. Despairing of aid from his native land, Ribaut traveled to England, where for a time it appeared that he might obtain the help he needed. Finally, though, he was thrown into prison and vanished from the canvas of Beaufort's early history.

Meanwhile, the Parris Island colonists were quickly running through their inadequate supply of stores. Despite generous aid from nearby Indian tribes, starvation began to loom as a very real fear in the colonists' minds. It is curious that they could have feared hunger surrounded by forests teeming with game and waters jumping with fish, but for whatever reason, the settlers determined to build a small ship and sail for France. Once the vessel was finished, the desperate group quickly abandoned Charlesfort. But when the little boat was becalmed in the doldrums, food supplies were soon exhausted. It is whispered that the crew even resorted to cannibalism to fend off their hunger. At last, a passing English ship rescued the survivors, and France's colonization attempts along the South Carolina coast were brought to an abrupt end.

Spanish soldiers returned to Parris Island in 1566 and built Fort San Felipe. This small outpost was temporarily abandoned some years later and was then reoccupied for a single year. With the burning of St. Augustine, Florida, by Sir Francis Drake in 1566, Spanish efforts to maintain a foothold in the Beaufort area were brought to an end.

In 1660, following the restoration of the English monarchy, Britain sent an expedition under William Hilton to explore the Carolina coast. Hilton wrote glowingly of the Beaufort coastline: "The Ayr is clear and sweet, the countrey very pleasant and delightful; and we would wish, that all they that want a happy settlement of our English Nation, were well transported thither."

The English colonization party that eventually founded Charleston first put ashore at Port Royal in 1679. The local Indians were able to persuade the expedition's leader, Robert Sayle, that better lands were to the north. This advice led to the removal of the party to the banks of Ashley River. Some historians have labeled this series of events as a crafty move on the part of the cacique of Kiawah. However, it seems plain from later history that the Indians' advice was quite sound. For all their many qualities, neither Beaufort nor Port Royal could ever have become as great a port as Charleston.

In 1648, a group of adventurous Scotsmen established Stuarttowne near the present site of Port Royal. This ambitious settlement was completely wiped out by a Spanish raid in 1688, though the invaders were later soundly beaten at Charleston. By 1712, successful expeditions against the Spanish and the Indians of Florida had lessened the threat of attack. That same year, the South Carolina colonial legislature laid out plans for a new settlement in the area, to be known as the town of Beaufort.

Beaufort had been officially established for only a few years when the great Yemassee uprising broke out. Allied with the Creeks and other Indian tribes, the Yemassees slaughtered every white settler they could find in the Beaufort region. Peace finally returned in 1717 after the Cherokees allied with the English settlers, but continued fear of Indian and Spanish attacks retarded the development of Beaufort into the 1720s.

Indigo provided the first basis for agricultural wealth in the Beaufort–Port Royal area. Beginning about 1740, this cash crop brought continuing progress and prosperity. Nevertheless, this was a time of small farms and simple dwellings. The great plantations and townhouses that we admire today came much later.

As reported earlier in this guide, the British government paid a sizable bounty for indigo. For this reason more than any other, the citizens of Beaufort showed a marked dislike for the patriot cause at the outbreak of the Revolution.

Beaufort and Port Royal were occupied by British forces in 1779. The entire region became a staging ground for raids by rival parties of patriots and Tories.

Prosperity returned around 1790 with the rise of Sea Island cotton. Until 1860, the long-staple plant brought fabulous wealth to Beaufort, as it did to the surrounding Sea Islands. Great plantations sprang into being on nearby St. Helena Island, and the wealthy planters built sumptuous summer residences in Beaufort, where the cool river breezes helped to alleviate the sweltering heat.

Beaufort took a decidedly secessionist stance during the tragic train of events that led to the Civil War. One of the town's citizens, Robert Barnwell Rhett, gained the title of "Father of Secession." Other Confederate leaders actually considered Rhett too fiery and unrestrained, and he was denied a place in the new Southern government.

In November 1861, a strong Union fleet under the command of Commodore S. F. DuPont smashed the Confederate forts defending the entrances to Port Royal Sound. Under the orders of Robert E. Lee, the area was quickly abandoned by the few Southern forces left, and

Riverside docks on Beaufort waterfront

Beaufort remained under Union occupation for the rest of the war.

The nearby planters were caught by surprise. They had been told that the forts guarding the water approaches to the sound were impregnable. Most of the white population fled in panic, leaving their homes and possessions behind. Many of these estates were confiscated as abandoned lands and redistributed to freed blacks. Few residences were actually destroyed, and as a consequence Beaufort still boasts many beautiful homes built in the lavish antebellum style.

The Reconstruction period was a difficult time in Beaufort, as in all of South Carolina. Sea Island cotton was again grown, but the coming of the boll weevil erased this final mark of prosperity.

In 1893, a hurricane of astonishing violence struck Beaufort. The town and nearby islands were covered with 12 feet of water, and winds of more than 100 miles per hour wreaked havoc. According to one report, the receding waters left a large ship aground in the middle of present-day Bay Street.

Prosperity finally began a long-awaited return to Beaufort during World War I with the establishment of the Parris Island Marine Base nearby. This event was followed by the establishment of the Port Royal Port Authority in 1955 and the opening of a major shipping terminal at Port Royal in 1958. Improved roads and bridges further added to the development of Beaufort. In the 1960s and 1970s, the town began to enjoy the fruits of a thriving tourist trade. With recent historic restorations and a beautifully landscaped waterfront, Beaufort's future as a tourist attraction appears bright.

Every visitor to this beautiful port city should be thankful that the good sense and foresight of Beaufort's leaders have led to controlled development that has carefully preserved the town's historic character. In *A Brief History of Beaufort*, John Duffy comments, "It is heartening to note that much of Beaufort's wealth in the third quarter of the twentieth century has been used to restore the grandeur of old homes and buildings dating from its 'Periclean Age.' As a result Beaufort is one of the most attractive towns on the Atlantic coast."

Beaufort Attractions

The many period homes of Beaufort's historical district are clearly the city's star attraction. Thanks to the lack of extensive damage during the Civil War and to the diligent efforts of the local historical society and many private citizens, Beaufort still teems with lovely nineteenth-century homes. It is a very special treat to view these old homeplaces from the town's shady lanes. A walking tour of the historical district is not to be missed.

The map of Beaufort included in this guide points out some of the more prominent homes. For more information, you should acquire *A Guidebook to Historic Beaufort*, published by the local historical society. This fine publication gives a detailed history of most of Beaufort's historic homes and other points of interest. For those interested in the area's rich folklore, always a worthwhile concern, Nell S. Graydon's *Tales of Beaufort* relates many a touching story.

Begin your tour at the local chamber of commerce (803-524-3163), located just behind the Downtown Marina's ship's store. Here, you will find all sorts of information that will help to make your tour a more meaningful experience.

The books listed above can also be purchased at the office.

You will find it a good idea to choose which homes you wish to view before setting out. It is a rather long walk—though undeniably a pleasant one—from one end of the district to the other. By planning your tour, you can avoid unnecessary steps. It is impossible to list all of Beaufort's many historic homes or relate any reasonable portion of their history within the confines of this guide. For complete information, this writer suggests consulting one of the publications recommended above. However, some of the more prominent homes and their

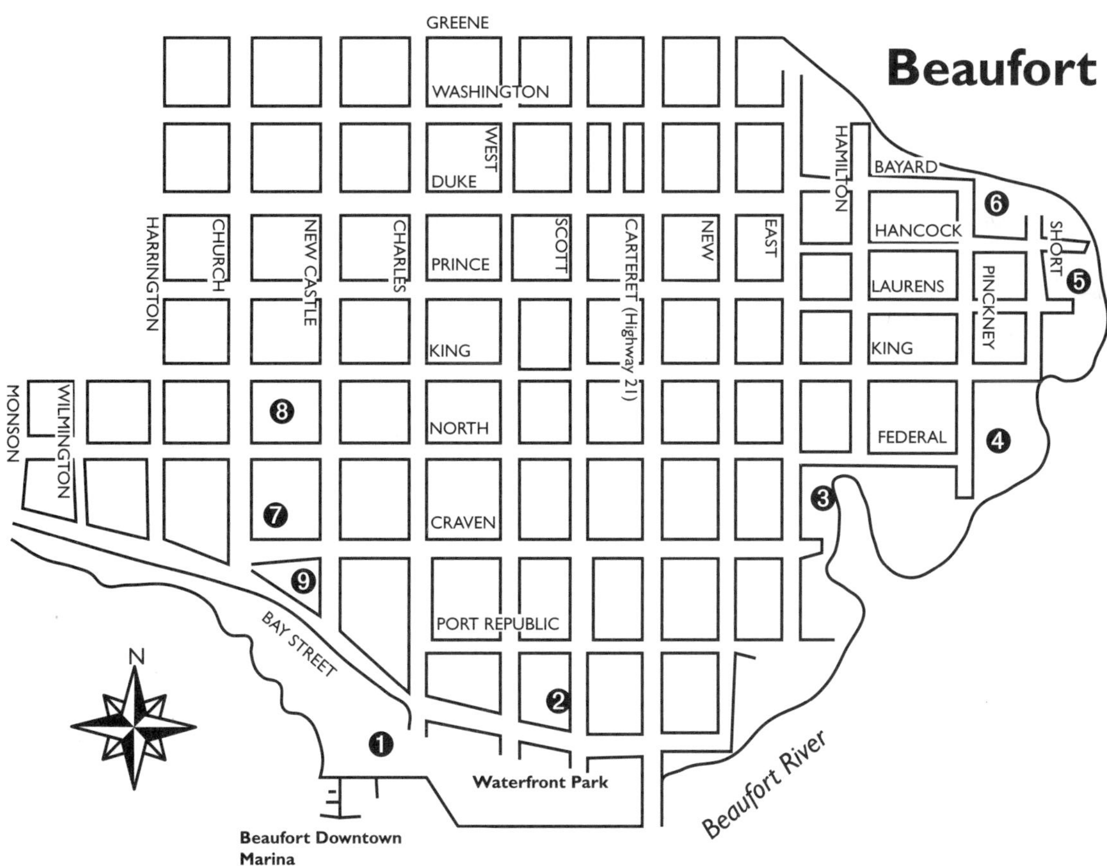

1. Chamber of Commerce
2. John Mark Verdier House Museum ("Lafayette House," 1790)
3. Joseph Johnson House ("The Castle," 1850)
4. James Robert Verdier House ("Marshlands," 1814)
5. James Fripp House ("Tidalholm")
6. Elizabeth Hext House ("Riverview," c. 1720)
7. Milton Maxey House ("Secession House")
8. St. Helena Episcopal Church (1724)
9. William Elliott House ("The Anchorage")

fascinating stories are reviewed in the following pages.

Lafayette House

The "Lafayette House," otherwise known as the John Mark Verdier House (801 Bay Street), was built in 1790. The structure was raised on a tabby foundation and styled in the Federal manner. John Verdier was a very successful merchant and factor. He did not hesitate to spend whatever sum was necessary to ensure that his home would stand the test of time. Verdier would be quite pleased to know that his proud homeplace has so well withstood the rigors of the passing years.

The Marquis de Lafayette paid a brief visit to Beaufort during his tour of the United States in 1825. For many days before his scheduled arrival, preparations went forward at a feverish pace for a grand reception. As the time for Lafayette's arrival drew near, huge crowds gathered at the city's wharves.

The crowds were destined to be disappointed. Lafayette was unavoidably delayed on Edisto Island for several hours. Tradition claims that his steamboat was stranded on the bottom by the ebbing tide. When he finally arrived in Beaufort, it was the dead of night. A messenger, sent on ahead, breathlessly informed anyone he could find that the Marquis was just a short distance away. The crowds were hastily reassembled, and they cheered the steamboat as it appeared around a bend of the river.

Lafayette was well behind schedule and did not really have the time for a stop in Beaufort. Being a true gentleman, however, he refused to disappoint the gathered multitude. He descended the gangplank and delivered a speech from the balcony of Verdier's home. The venerable residence has been known ever since as the Lafayette House.

Secession House

The foundation of Secession House (1113 Craven Street) dates to the 1740s. During the early 1800s, the present structure was built atop the old tabby base. In the 1850s, Edmund Rhett rebuilt the two upper floors in a modified Greek Revival style. He installed marble steps at the entrance and Italian marble mantelpieces above the fireplaces. Today, the proud home stands in all its grandeur facing Beaufort River.

Edmund Rhett, a United States senator from South Carolina, was one of the leading advocates of secession from the Union. He held many impassioned meetings at his magnificent house on Craven Street and continually advocated the cause of states' rights. Tradition claims that the last meeting of Beaufort's delegates to the Secession Convention was held at Rhett's house, and that they went directly from the house to their waiting boat amid the lusty cheers of many onlookers. To a man, the delegates voted for secession. Little did they realize that

Secession House, Beaufort

their vote was the death knell of the life they treasured so deeply.

The Castle

The Joseph Johnson House (411 Craven Street) has been known as "the Castle" for time out of mind. The title is well bestowed. Built by Dr. Joseph Johnson in 1850, the house has few rivals for pure magnificence. Fashioned in the Italian Renaissance style, the grand structure occupies a full city block. Curiously, the house's exterior color changes with the light. Sometimes it appears gray, sometimes tan, and on rare occasions it even seems pink. The large porches are supported by six massive columns. The house contains 79 windows and boasts four triple chimneys. Yet this massive structure is actually built on a crib of palmetto logs. The Castle had the distinction of serving as the centerpiece for a 1961 United States Department of Commerce poster. Many people feel that if you have not seen the Castle, you have not seen Beaufort.

As you might well expect of a homeplace like the Castle, the house has its ghost story. While Dr. Johnson was supervising the construction of his house, he saw a strange, dwarfish figure wandering the grounds. When he went to investigate, the apparition vanished. When the good doctor questioned a gardener working nearby, the worker nonchalantly informed him that the dwarf lived in the basement.

The Castle, Beaufort

Many have claimed to have seen the ghostly figure since those early days, and residents of the house have reportedly learned to live with furniture that is moved about and doors that are opened and closed by invisible forces.

Marshlands

The James Robert Verdier House (501 Pinckney Street) is one of the loveliest homes in all of Beaufort. Nicknamed "Marshlands," this beautiful house faces south on Beaufort River at Pigeon Point. Many boaters have undoubtedly admired its striking facade as they passed by.

Built in 1814 by Dr. James Robert Verdier, Marshlands is set high off the ground on a foundation pierced by multiple arches. The double entrance stairway runs parallel to the second-story porch and lends a very impressive look to the front of the home.

Dr. Verdier had a most illustrious medical career. He is credited with early successful treatment of yellow fever. This dread disease often ran rampant during the summer months and was greatly feared by whites and slaves alike. Verdier's crude but apparently effective vaccines helped to mitigate the horrors of epidemics in the Beaufort area.

Marshlands has the distinction of being the mythical home of Emily, the heroine in Francis Griswold's novel of the Civil War, *Sea Island Lady*. This fictional work remains popular in the South Carolina Low Country to this day.

Tidalholm

The house known as Tidalholm (1 Laurens Street) presents a strikingly beautiful view to the passing visitor. Surrounded by mighty oaks and enclosed by an impressive wrought-iron fence, this historic home has more than one claim to fame.

Legend tells us that following the Civil War, the old homeplace was put up for auction to pay back taxes. The owner, James Fripp, stood by with tears running down his cheeks because he didn't have enough money to make a bid. An unknown Frenchman visiting Beaufort and attending the auction was made aware of Fripp's plight. He bought the house and immediately presented the deed to the astonished owner. The two embraced and the Frenchman left, never to be heard from again.

In 1982, the house was the setting for the critically acclaimed motion picture *The Big Chill*. This touching story of the reunion of six college friends of the 1960s and how they deal with the realities of the 1980s seems altogether fitting for Tidalholm's romantic past. I'm sure James Fripp and the unknown Frenchmen would have approved.

Tidalholm ("The Big Chill House"), Beaufort

Riverview

The Elizabeth Hext House, also known as "Riverview," is one of Beaufort's oldest homes. Though simple in comparison to many of the town's antebellum mansions, Riverview maintains a feeling of intimacy that is often absent from grander structures.

Built about 1720, the house has been added to over the years. Many of the windows still contain the original glass. The floors in most of the house are the same 10-inch pine planks that were laid so long ago. The heavy old doors still swing on their H-hinges. The house is surrounded by huge shade trees and is set well back from the street. Even without its many ghost stories, the old home would be a point of interest.

According to persistent local legend, the original owner of Riverview was strolling the grounds when she noticed her faithful gardener digging holes in apparently random spots in the yard. When questioned about this strange practice, the old servant replied that he was searching for gold, as instructed by several visitors who had called on him the night before. The gardener described the strange callers' clothing, and the mistress was astonished to hear an accurate description of ancient pirate garb.

One morning, the excited servant informed his mistress that the strange visitors had come again and had promised to reveal their secret that very night. When the gardener did not appear the next morning, the mistress went to his house to see what was the matter. She found him speechless; he had suffered a stroke the night before. The old servant died soon thereafter without ever revealing whether he had learned the fateful secret.

Some may call this tale fanciful, but stories of

pirates and their buried treasure have been associated with Riverview for many a year. Strange apparitions are said to haunt the night, offering riches to any who will follow their instructions. For all these ghostly visitations, however, no treasure has ever been unearthed.

St. Helena Episcopal Church

Not all of Beaufort's attractions are to be found among the community's historic homes. St. Helena Episcopal Church is one of the most popular points of interest in the city. Built in 1724 for a congregation organized in 1712, the handsome edifice has twice been enlarged, and the steeple has been replaced in this century. The adjacent cemetery contains some notable graves, in particular that of "Tuscarora Jack" Barnwell. Old records note the burial of a man named Perry who, in great fear of being buried alive, instructed his friends to place a jug of water, a loaf of bread, and a hatchet in his coffin. If he regained consciousness, he could then stave off hunger and thirst while chopping his way out.

This writer had a rare experience associated with the church's graveyard while researching this new edition. One warm early-spring night, I found myself alone in Beaufort after putting my ace research assistant, Bud Williams, on a plane that same afternoon in Savannah. Never being one who enjoys motel rooms, I took a long walk and was soon accompanied by a friendly black Labrador. It was late, and few were stirring on the historic district's dimly lit streets. I happened to pass by St. Helena's cemetery and was attracted by the warm glow of several spotlights reflecting off the church's walls and casting long, silent shadows over the tombstones. I surprised myself by walking through the open gates and staring long at the utterly still scene around me. You might suspect that this was an eerie experience, but it was just the opposite. Somehow, the scene before me seemed to welcome the respectful visitor and encourage him to come look at what had gone before him.

During the Civil War, St. Helena Episcopal Church was used as a hospital by Union troops. Pews were removed, and gravestones were uprooted and used as operating tables. The old organ was destroyed and the walls much damaged.

The churchyard is graced by a number of unusually large oak trees, which lend a quiet,

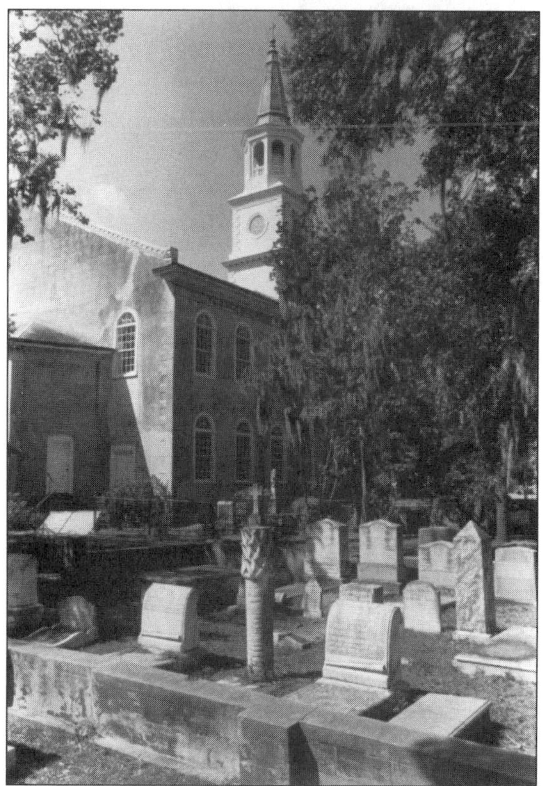

St. Helena Episcopal Church

shaded atmosphere to the old house of worship. The grounds are surrounded by a wall built of brick once used as ships' ballast. It is a very peaceful place indeed, and one you won't want to miss.

Bay Street Inn

BEAUFORT AREA NAVIGATION

South of unlighted daybeacon #232, set course to come abeam of unlighted daybeacon #233 to its westerly side. Don't let leeway ease you too far to the west. As shown on chart 11518, a large shoal flanks the Waterway's westerly edge. Between #232 and #233, the entrance to Marsh Harbor Boatyard will come abeam to the east.

Marsh Harbor Boatyard The entrance to Marsh Harbor Boatyard is well marked by unlighted daybeacons. As you would expect, pass red beacons to your starboard side and green markers to port. Continue cruising upstream on the creek's mid-width and the docks will soon come abeam to starboard.

On the ICW The northwestern reaches of Factory Creek make in to the eastern banks of

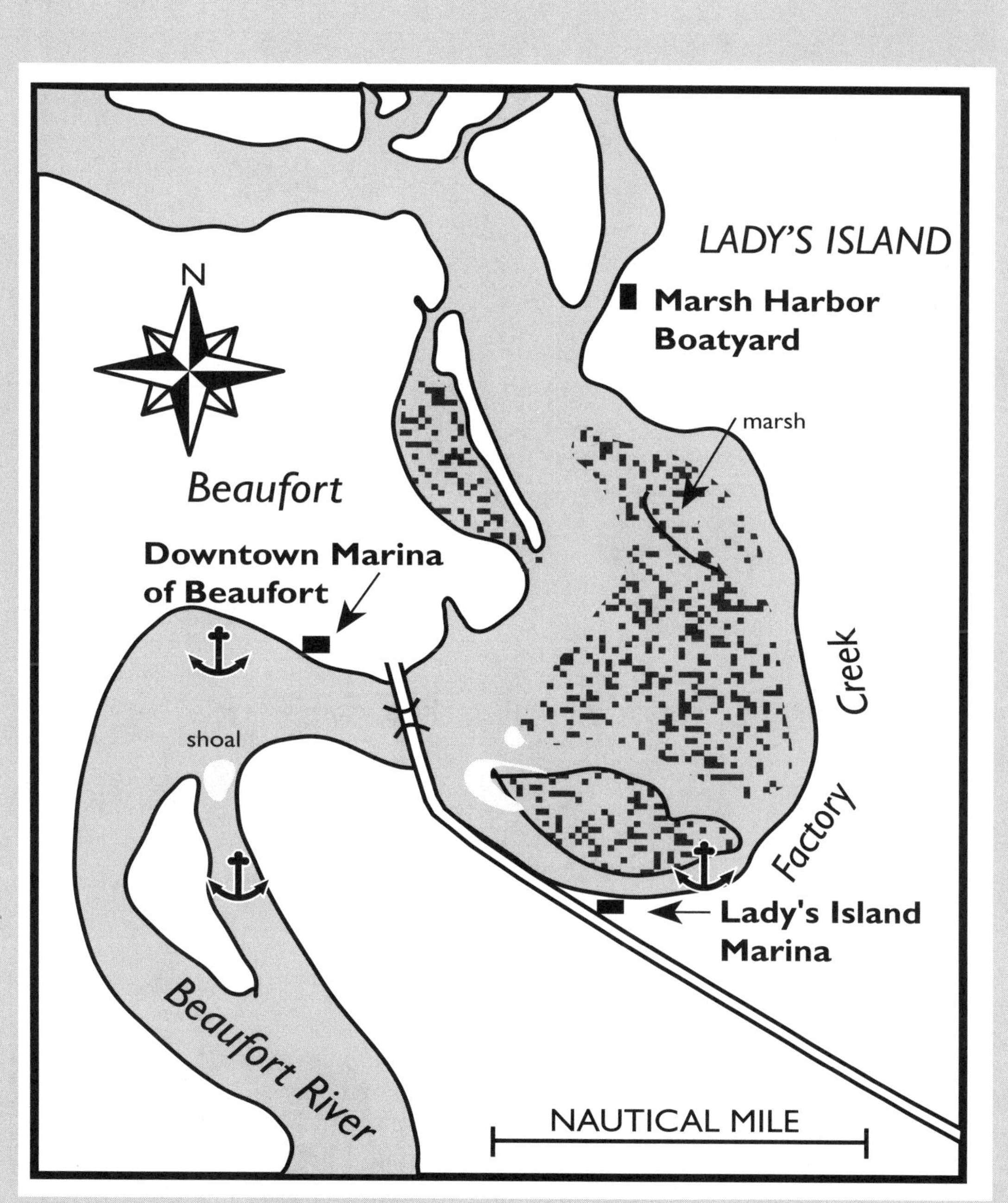
LADY'S ISLAND
N
Marsh Harbor
Boatyard
marsh
Beaufort
Downtown Marina
of Beaufort
Creek
shoal
Factory
Lady's Island
Marina
Beaufort River
NAUTICAL MILE

Beaufort River at unlighted daybeacon #233. Do not attempt to enter the creek from this quarter. The stream's mouth is flanked by mud flats and oyster banks which are covered at high water. The channel is much too treacherous for visiting cruisers who lack specific local knowledge.

From #233, point to come abeam of and pass flashing daybeacon #235 well to its westerly side. At #233, a sign on the easterly banks warns that all waters around Beaufort are a Minimum Wake Zone. Large power craft should proceed at slow speed from this point to flashing daybeacon #242.

From #235, set course to pass unlighted daybeacon #237 to its northwesterly side. The ICW turns west at #237 and hurries on toward the Lady's Island swing bridge. Just before you reach the bridge, the entrance to Factory Creek and Lady's Island Marina will come abeam to the south.

Factory Creek and Lady's Island Marina To enter Factory Creek, continue on the ICW channel until you are just short (east) of the bridge, then swing 90 degrees to the south and point to come abeam of unlighted daybeacon #1 by some 10 yards to its westerly side. Carefully set a new course to come abeam of unlighted daybeacon #3 by about the same distance to its southwesterly side. Be sure to favor the southwesterly side of the channel a bit as you cruise between the two markers. By doing so, you will avoid the very shallow water flanking Factory Creek's easterly and northeasterly banks. Be on guard against leeway. Watch your stern to be sure that you are not drifting to the east.

Past #3, good depths open out almost from shore to shore. You will soon spy the marina docks to starboard. Remember to proceed at idle speed as you approach the docks.

If you choose to anchor in Factory Creek rather than to make use of the facilities at Lady's Island Marina, continue upstream past the piers, holding to the mid-width. Once clear of the marina docks, simply drop your hook at any likely spot and settle in for the night.

Do not attempt to enter the small arm of Factory Creek that breaks off to the west just as the stream finishes its first long curve to the north. Also, be sure to discontinue your exploration of Factory Creek before it begins to bend to the northwest and rejoin the Waterway.

On the ICW The Lady's Island bridge at Beaufort has 30 feet of closed vertical clearance. Boats that cannot clear this height must contend with restrictive opening hours. Between 7:00 A.M. and 9:00 A.M. and from 4:00 P.M. to 6:00 P.M. Monday through Friday (year-round, except for legal holidays), the span opens only at 8:00 A.M. and 5:00 P.M. Also, from April 1 through November 30, the span opens only on the hour, 20 minutes past the hour, and 40 minutes past the hour from 9:00 A.M. to 4:00 P.M. At all other times, the bridge supposedly opens on demand, but the operator has sometimes been known to be rather slow on the draw. It might be best to call ahead on your VHF to avoid any unnecessary delays.

Beaufort anchorage, with Bay Street in background

Once you are through the bridge, the Downtown Marina docks will come abeam to the north. Entrance into this facility should present no problem, but watch out for swift tidal currents. The designated anchorage is just west of the marina.

West and south of unlighted daybeacon #239, the Waterway follows Beaufort River south toward Port Royal and Parris Island. A continuing account of the ICW to the Georgia line is presented in the next chapter.

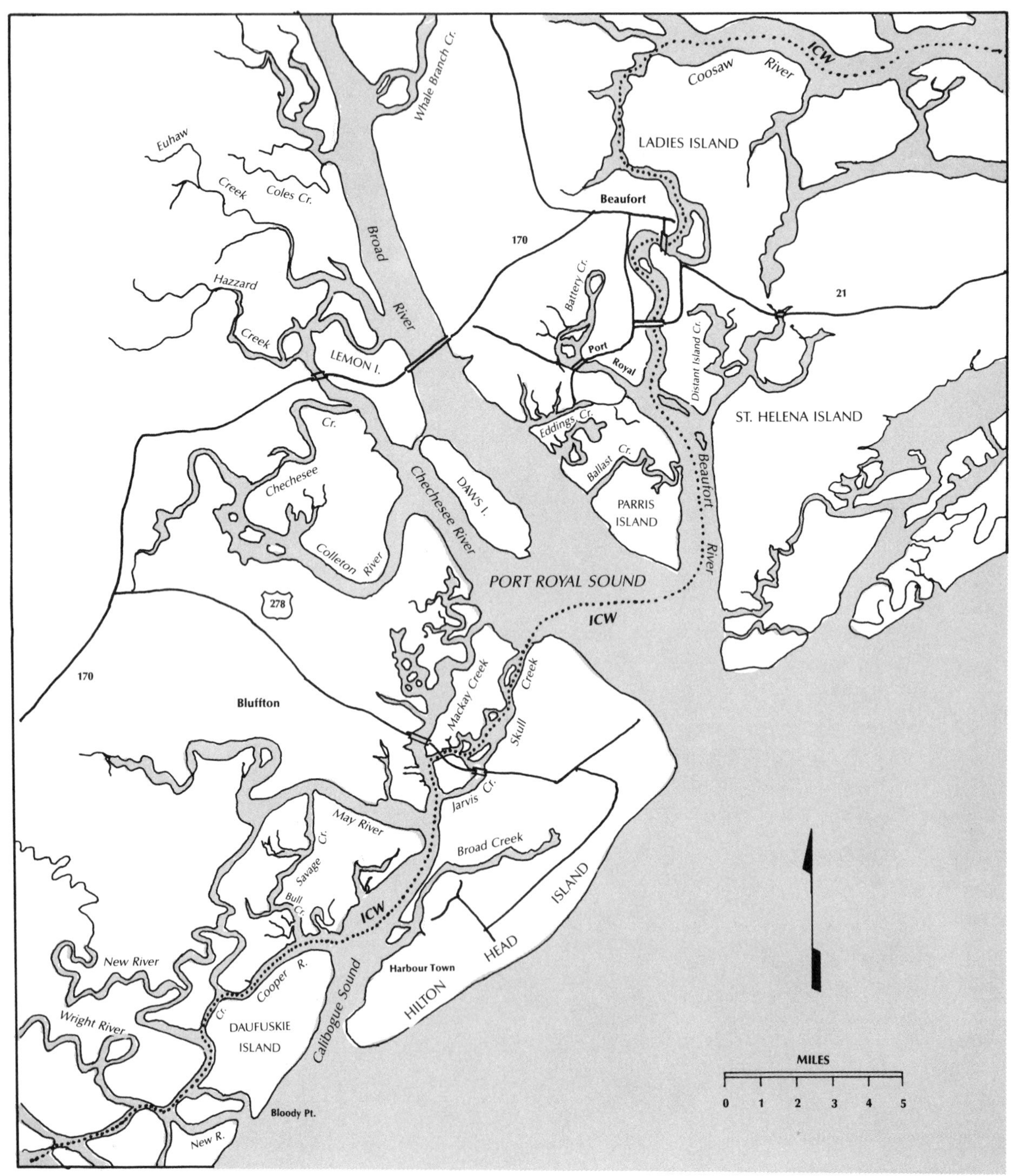

ICW
Coosaw River
Whale Branch Cr.
Euhaw Creek
Coles Cr.
LADIES ISLAND
Beaufort
Broad River
170
Battery Cr.
21
Hazzard Creek
LEMON I.
Port Royal
Distant Island Cr.
Cr.
Eddings Cr.
ST. HELENA ISLAND
Ballast Cr.
Chechesee
DAWS I.
Chechesee River
Beaufort River
PARRIS ISLAND
Colleton River
PORT ROYAL SOUND
278
ICW
170
Mackay Creek
Skull Creek
Bluffton
Jarvis Cr.
May River
Broad Creek
Savage Cr.
Bull Cr.
ICW
HILTON HEAD ISLAND
New River
Harbour Town
Cooper R.
Calibogue Sound
Wright River
Cr.
DAUFUSKIE ISLAND
MILES
0 1 2 3 4 5
Bloody Pt.
New R.

Beaufort River to Georgia

The waters of coastal South Carolina between Beaufort and Savannah River offer a very mixed bag of cruising opportunities to the visiting boater. To the north, Beaufort River, Port Royal Sound, and the sound's tributary streams provide cruising grounds off the beaten path. Anchorages are numerous, but facilities are sparse. Farther to the south, Calibogue Sound and Hilton Head Island boast no fewer than seven marinas waiting to greet transient boaters. Hilton Head is the largest resort in South Carolina, and its popularity seems unbounded. Several water bodies in the Hilton Head region are noted for their beauty and will appeal to those who like a bit more isolation.

After leaving Calibogue Sound behind, the Waterway abruptly plunges into another undeveloped tract. The ICW follows the Cooper, New, and Wright Rivers, joined by several man-made cuts, south to Savannah River and the Georgia state line. Along the way, the Waterway passes through lonely countryside with only a single marina and a few homes to break the landscape.

The waters between Beaufort River and Savannah River are some of the most interesting in the state. In few other places of such limited size does one find cruising conditions that range from islands bristling with marinas to small, secret, winding creeks.

Charts

Five NOAA charts are required for complete coverage of the waters from Beaufort to the Georgia state line:

11518 follows the ICW down Beaufort River as far as Port Royal

11507 details the ICW from Beaufort River to Georgia and includes many sidewaters off the Waterway

11516 covers Cowen Creek on Beaufort River, Port Royal Sound, the lower section of Broad River, and all of Colleton and Chechessee Rivers, as well as May River and Calibogue Sound (including Broad Creek)

11519 includes the upper section of Broad River and all the navigable sections of Whale Branch

11512 details the upper and lower portions of New and Wright Rivers

BEAUFORT RIVER

South of Beaufort, the river bearing the port's name becomes a wide stream that often spawns a healthy chop. Winds over 15 knots can make for a bumpy ride, but waves seldom reach a dangerous height. Approaching Port Royal Sound, the waters widen further and are even more likely to be rough in high winds. Should bad weather threaten, it would be a good idea to retreat to the marina near Port Royal or one of Beaufort River's anchorages and wait for fair conditions before attempting the run across Port Royal Sound to Skull Creek.

South of Beaufort, there is one marina just north of the 65-foot high-rise bridge, but otherwise no facilities are available on the southern portion of Beaufort River. In fact, except for one very small marina on a remote section of Chechessee River, cruising boaters are on their own until reaching Skull Creek and Hilton Head.

Three large creeks provide good overnight anchorage on Beaufort River. Two are suitable only for light to moderate winds, while the other can be used in all but the heaviest of weather.

Being part of the ICW, Beaufort River is easily traversed. South of Port Royal, a large-ships' channel is well defined by numerous flashing buoys. The Waterway follows this passage until cutting west across Port Royal Sound at flashing daybeacon #246. With a few exceptions, the river is deep and free of shoals. Most boaters need have no concern about successful passage of Beaufort River.

The northerly section of the river, near Beaufort, is bordered by high banks on its westerly shore. In fact, most of the Beaufort shoreline is composed of higher ground than is usually seen along this section of the coast. One exception is the extensive marshland of Parris Island that comprises the lower Beaufort River's westerly shore. Some buildings associated with the island's Marine Corps base are visible near flashing buoy #37. As you view the marsh, it does not take much imagination to understand why Parris Island is considered by many to be the toughest basic-training camp in the country.

Northerly Anchorage

East of flashing daybeacon #241, a wide, deep stream runs between the river's banks and a small marsh island. When entered from its southerly mouth, this stream carries minimum 10-foot depths for most of its length. Protection is adequate for anchorage in light to moderate winds. Depths finally drop off as the stream begins its reentry into Beaufort River to the north-northwest.

Spanish Point

West of flashing daybeacon #242, Spanish Point juts boldly into the waters of Beaufort River. In 1686, a group of daring Scotsmen founded Stuarttowne near the point. The settlement was later destroyed by a Spanish and Indian raid from Florida. The survivors fled to Charleston, where the attackers were soundly repulsed.

Port Royal Landing Marina

Several years ago, a new marina sprang up on the western banks of Beaufort River immediately north of the 65-foot fixed bridge. Port

Royal Landing Marina is more than glad to welcome transient boaters to its concrete floating docks, with water connections and power connections up to 50 amps. Approach and dockside depths are a very impressive 15 feet or more. The river's swift tidal currents can make docking at the marina's piers a bit tricky, but the attentive seven-day-a-week dockmaster and the facility's wide passages between the piers help to minimize this difficulty. Good showers and a full-service laundromat are available shoreside, as is a ship's and variety store. Gasoline and diesel fuel can be purchased, and minor mechanical repairs can be arranged through independent technicians. Waste pump-out service is also offered.

The on-site Stewbies Bar and Restaurant is convenient, but Port Royal Marina also maintains a courtesy car which visiting cruisers can use for a visit to historical Beaufort, including its many restaurants and food stores. This writer suggests that you take advantage of this useful service.

It should be pointed out that Port Royal Landing Marina sits in a fairly exposed position on Beaufort River. This relative lack of shelter can pose a problem in heavy blows.

Port Royal Landing Marina
(803) 525-6664

Approach depth: 15+ feet
Dockside depth: 15+ feet
Accepts transients: yes
Floating concrete piers: yes
Dockside power connections: 30 and 50 amps
Dockside water connections: yes
Showers: yes
Laundromat: yes
Waste pump-out: yes
Gasoline: yes
Diesel fuel: yes
Mechanical repairs: yes
Ship's and variety store: yes
Restaurant: on-site

Port Royal Landing Marina

Fort Frederick

The tabby walls of Fort Frederick are clearly visible near the grounds of the large hospital south of the Beaufort River high-rise bridge. Chart 11518 notes a "Surfaced Ramp" near the fort's position.

Fort Frederick was built between 1732 and 1734 to protect the Beaufort area from Spanish attack. It was abandoned after only a few years. The walls have survived the long years in remarkably good condition, a monument to the tabby makers of the day.

Battery Creek

The deep waters of Battery Creek make in to the western shores of Beaufort River near unlighted daybeacon #42 (well west of charted Cane Island). This stream leads to the modern shipping facility at Port Royal. Jean Ribaut once described Port Royal as "one of the greatest and fairest havens . . . where without danger all the ships in the world might be harbored." The port has never lived up to Ribaut's billing, but today the town's fortunes certainly seem to be on the upswing.

The terminals here are not as large as those of Georgetown or Charleston, but several seagoing freighters can usually be seen loading or unloading cargo at the docks. The waters northwest and west of the wharves offer anchorage for pleasure boats of almost any size. Your best bet is to drop the hook in the charted 18- and 22-foot waters northwest of unlighted daybeacon #47. Battery Creek is rather broad at this point and is bordered by marsh grass to the south. This is not a good spot to ride out heavy weather.

Farther upstream, a bridge with only 12 feet of closed vertical clearance bars the creek. This span is normally closed. Requests that the bridge be opened must be made to the South Carolina Department of Transportation 24 hours in advance, and even then the request will likely be denied unless the applicant has a very good reason.

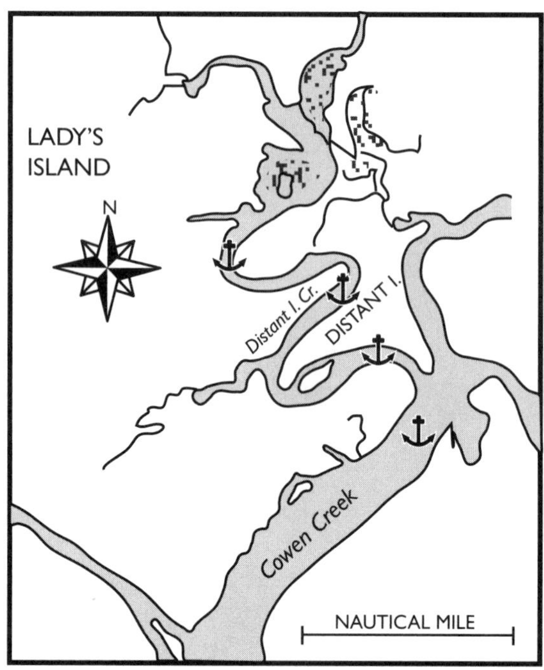

Cowen Creek

Cowen Creek cuts the eastern banks of Beaufort River north-northeast of unlighted can buoy #33. This wide stream eventually splinters into several branches. One of these forks, Distant Island Creek, is the best anchorage on the river.

Cowen Creek itself is a bit wide for effective anchorage in all but light airs. However, in light to moderate winds, boats requiring a great deal of swinging room can drop the hook just southwest of the split. Otherwise, craft under 42 feet should proceed to Distant Island Creek.

Cowen Creek's mouth from Beaufort River is bordered by extensive shoals to the west, but there is a wide entrance channel north-northeast of unlighted can buoy #33. Several unmarked shallows flanking the cut must be avoided, but good navigation should see you through. Because of these difficulties, Cowen Creek is not particularly recommended for boats over 45 feet or those that draw more than 5 feet.

Distant Island Creek

Boats as large as 42 feet can find sufficient swinging room on Distant Island Creek for comfortable anchorage. Certain portions of the creek are very well sheltered and can be used in heavy weather. Minimum depths are 7 feet, with most of the stream deeper.

There is one navigational problem on Distant Island Creek. At high tide, some of the mud flats bordering the creek's first hairpin curve to the northeast are submerged. While the careful boater should be able to pick out the correct passage,

Banks of Distant Island Creek

entry into this creek at high water does call for caution.

The shoreline of Distant Island Creek is most attractive, especially where the stream borders Distant Island. Currently, the banks are beautifully undeveloped, with many large oaks and other hardwoods overhanging the water. Distant Island was beginning to undergo development at the time of this writing, and some buildings may be in evidence before much longer.

Some sections of Distant Island Creek are better sheltered than others. The first well-protected spot lies just upstream of the intersection with Cowen Creek. The high banks of Distant Island border the creek along this stretch and provide a good windbreak. You need not pass around the mud banks mentioned above to reach this haven.

The second superior overnight refuge is located in the middle of the creek's second hairpin curve. Again, the high, wooded shores of Distant Island border the creek to the east, offering excellent protection.

The third and final sheltered spot is encountered short of the creek's second sharp bend to the northeast. A small section of high ground on Lady's Island flanks the creek to the south and southwest. This landmass provides particularly good protection in hard southwesterly blows. The creek narrows a bit here and provides only enough swinging room for craft up to 36 feet.

Ballast Creek

Ballast Creek enters Beaufort River from Parris Island west of unlighted nun buoy #36. Though the stream is marked by two aids, boaters should not enter. This is United States Marine Corps property and is off-limits to pleasure craft.

Station Creek

The southerly reaches of Station Creek enter the mouth of Beaufort River at its intersection with Port Royal Sound south and east of unlighted nun buoy #26. The creek has two aids to navigation along its track, but the extensive unmarked shoals flanking the stream's entrance are not easily avoided. Cruising boaters are advised to bypass this section of Station Creek unless they are armed with local knowledge.

BEAUFORT RIVER NAVIGATION

West of unlighted daybeacon #239, the ICW follows a broad turn in Beaufort River as the great stream bends slowly to the south. Simply stick to the river's centerline as far as flashing daybeacon

#242 and all should be well. Be sure to pass well west of flashing daybeacon #241 and unlighted daybeacon #241A. Very shoal water and marsh lie east of these aids to navigation.

Look to starboard as you cruise past #241. The high bluffs to the west are dotted with tasteful modern homes and a few larger structures. This is an attractive section of the Waterway.

North of #242, boaters may choose to enter Beaufort River's first anchorage.

Northerly Anchorage To enter the broad sweep of water between the mainland and the marsh island east of flashing daybeacon #241, continue cruising southeast on the Waterway channel until you are almost abeam of flashing daybeacon #242, then swing slowly around to the north and enter the stream on its mid-width. Good depths stretch almost from shore to shore. Select any likely spot and drop the hook. Do not attempt to reenter Beaufort River to the north, as this passage is all but blocked by extensive shallows. Discontinue your forward progress well before reaching these obstructions.

On the ICW South of unlighted daybeacon #244, the Waterway begins its approach to the high-rise Beaufort River bridge. The span has a vertical clearance of 65 feet. Port Royal Landing Marina is located along the western banks immediately north of the bridge.

South of the fixed span, there are no further markers until flashing buoy #41, which marks the intersection of the ICW and the Port Royal Shipping Channel. Fortunately, there are no shoals in the area. Stick to the river's mid-width and you should stay well away from a meeting with the bottom.

South and southeast of #41, the ICW follows the well-marked Port Royal Shipping Channel to Port Royal Sound. Colors are reversed here. Southbound cruisers should take red markers to the boaters' port side and green beacons to starboard. To the northwest, Battery Creek offers anchorage opportunities.

Battery Creek From flashing buoy #41, set course to pass between flashing daybeacon #43 and unlighted daybeacon #42. These two aids mark the southeasterly mouth of Battery Creek. Continue tracking your way upstream on the creek's centerline and you will soon spy the Port Royal wharves to the northeast. Just past the docks, unlighted daybeacon #47 marks the southwesterly shore. Pass #47 well to its northeasterly side.

The best anchorage is found just past #47 before the creek turns to the west. Good depths stretch from shore to shore. Set the hook near the lee shoreline and head below.

Passage farther upstream to the seldom-opened bridge is not particularly recommended. A large shoal flanks the northern shore, and the creek widens, making for even less protection.

On the ICW Watch to the west between unlighted can buoy #39 and flashing buoy #37 and you will observe some of the buildings of Parris Island Marine Base. Remember not to attempt entry into Ballast Creek west of unlighted nun buoy #36. North-northeast of can buoy #33, boaters may choose to enter Cowen and Distant Island Creeks.

Cowen and Distant Island Creeks To enter Cowen Creek from Beaufort River, set course from #33 toward the unnumbered, quick-flashing 16-foot forward range marker to the east (charted as "QK," for quick-flashing, on 11516 and "Q" on 11507). Some 100 yards before reaching the forward range marker, swing sharply to the north and set a new course to pass the marsh island well east of flashing buoy #37 by some 35 yards to the marsh's easterly side. Proceed with caution in this area. As you will note after a quick study of chart 11516 or 11507, extensive shallows border the channel to the east.

Continue past the island and follow the waters as they bend slowly to the northeast. Enter the creek on its mid-width. Cruise upstream, avoiding all charted shoals, until you reach the point where the stream splits into four branches. Be sure to avoid the large, charted marsh island southeast of Cat Island by passing well to its southeasterly side. Also, note the shallow waters abutting the southeasterly banks short of the split. If winds are light, you might consider anchoring before reaching the forks. If you choose to spend the night here, be sure to set the hook so as to swing well away from the shallows to the southeast. Otherwise, cut to the northwest and enter the extreme left-hand branch, Distant Island Creek.

Cruise into Distant Island Creek on its mid-width. Large craft may want to drop the hook within the entrance rather than continuing upstream. Those who choose to continue should approach the creek's first hairpin turn to the northeast with caution. Remember, at high tide some of the surrounding mud flats are covered completely. If you enter at high tide, choose what appears to be the central passage and feel your way slowly around the turn with the sounder.

Past the northeasterly bend, continued navigation upstream to both of the other anchorages is a simple matter of holding to the mid-width. Remember to cease your gunkholing soon after the creek takes its third sharp turn. Depths finally begin to decline past this bend.

On the ICW The ICW continues to follow the Port Royal Shipping Channel south to the sound. While the cut is very well marked, boaters might find it advisable to run compass courses between markers. Some are set fairly well apart.

At flashing buoy #27 and unlighted nun buoy #26, the Waterway abandons the large-ships' channel and cuts sharply to the west. Set course to come abeam of and pass flashing daybeacon #246 by at least 200 yards to its southerly side. A long shoal building south from Parris Island Spit has all but surrounded #246. Stay well away from this aid to navigation.

Once flashing buoy #27 is left behind, marker colors revert to the usual ICW system. Southbound cruisers will again want to pass red, even-numbered markers to the boaters' starboard side and take green beacons to port.

From #246, Port Royal Sound and its tributary streams offer many cruising possibilities to the north and northwest, while the ICW flows to the west and enters Skull Creek. This chapter will next review the waters to the north, after which a continuing account of the Waterway south to Hilton Head Island will be presented.

PORT ROYAL SOUND AND AUXILIARY STREAMS

Port Royal Sound is formed by the juncture of several large streams, all of which lead into the South Carolina mainland. Broad, Chechessee, and Colleton Rivers are all major bodies of water. Each offers many cruising possibilities and anchorage opportunities.

The vast waters of the Port Royal area are seldom visited by cruising boaters. Except for one tiny facility, there is not a single marina on any of the three rivers or their creeks. With only a few exceptions, the region's shoreline is undeveloped. Isolated residential settlements dot the banks here and there, but in between are vast stretches of untouched marsh grass and highlands. Most of the anchorages found north of the ICW provide only minimal shelter and are not suitable for winds over 20 knots.

Successful navigation of the three rivers is no simple matter. Numerous unmarked shoals call for careful cruising. There are only a few aids to navigation on the sound's streams. Consequently, you must practice your best coastal navigation in order to know your position at all times and keep off the bottom.

Still, the waters of the three rivers are not lacking in positive attributes. Seldom will cruising boaters find such wide-open waters, often fronting onto lovely, undeveloped shorelines, with so few other boats in evidence. The natural beauty and splendor of these rivers will delight all cruisers with wanderlust in their hearts. On the other hand, those who prefer a well-marked channel with several marinas close by will probably want to forgo these streams. Whether you choose to enter the Broad, the Chechessee, or the Colleton will depend on what type of cruising you enjoy.

Port Royal Sound

Port Royal Sound provides reliable access to the open sea via the Port Royal Shipping Channel. Boaters can use this well-marked seaward cut with confidence. Large ships enter and exit the channel on a regular basis, and the passage's aids to navigation are exhaustively charted. Otherwise, the cruising possibilities of the sound are limited to its northern tributary streams.

Broad River

Broad River is aptly named. The waters of the Broad are so wide that they often seem more like a sound than a river. In fact, Broad River is the northwestern extension of Port Royal Sound. The river remains a substantial body of water for its entire length until it intersects its feeder streams—the Pocotaligo, Tulifiny, and Coosawhatchie Rivers to the north.

Broad River is an exceptionally beautiful body of water. Both shorelines are readily visible. The southern section of the river is lined mostly by marsh grass, but much of the stream's northern reaches are bordered by high, wooded banks. On a calm, clear day, passage of Broad River can be a wonderful visual treat.

Despite its natural beauty, Broad River is surprisingly devoid of cruising possibilities. Only two sidewaters make interesting gunkholes and offer safe haven for the night. Even these creeks call for a long cruise from the safe confines of the ICW. None of the several streams that enter the river's western shore and lead to Chechessee River should be attempted by cruising captains. All are bounded by numerous unmarked shoals, and depths shown on chart 11516 cannot be trusted. To the northeast, several streams flow into the river from Parris Island. Chief among these is Archer Creek. Do not attempt to enter these sidewaters either. They are part of the Parris Island Marine Base and are off-limits to pleasure boaters.

The three northern feeder rivers are uncharted and consequently too risky for large cruising craft. This lack of charting is most unfortunate, as on-site research led this writer to believe that all three rivers would make excellent cruising grounds. Perhaps some enterprising Power Squadron will undertake the charting of these waters in the future.

Successful navigation of Broad River is an exacting process. There are several large unmarked patches of shoal water on the river's central section and along the banks. You will need to make careful use of chart, compass, log, and the information contained in this guide to stay off the bottom.

Broad River is crossed by a long fixed bridge some 7 nautical miles northwest of the intersection with Port Royal Sound. The current edition of chart 11516 shows a swing bridge at this location with only 12 feet of closed vertical clearance. However, on-site research revealed that the charted structure has been replaced by a fixed medium-rise span. This writer and his mate have been unable to find any published account of the bridge's height, but we estimate it to be at least 25 feet. Many sailcraft will have trouble clearing the span, but most powerboats should be able to pass without difficulty. Obviously, the upper reaches of Broad River and Whale Branch are off-limits to most sailors.

Broad River is not for the casual boater. The river's hazards call for a wary cruise. On the other hand, the wide-eyed explorers among us who can overcome these difficulties will reap rewards that few other boaters have known.

Boyd Creek

Boyd Creek enters the western shore of Broad River north of charted Hogs Neck. The stream has two unmarked shoals that could prove hazardous for cruising craft. Consequently, this creek should be entered only by daring skippers piloting boats of less than 34 feet that draw no more than 4 feet.

If and when these hazards are bypassed, Boyd Creek and its several auxiliary streams offer a number of spots suitable for overnight anchorage. With one exception, the various shorelines are undeveloped marsh and do not give enough protection for heavy weather.

Cole Creek breaks off to the south from Boyd Creek near the latter stream's intersection with Broad River. Cole Creek holds 8-foot minimum depths for a short distance. There is enough swinging room for craft up to 34 feet to drop the hook. Don't attempt to cruise past the stream's first turn to the southeast. Depths quickly become too uncertain for large pleasure craft.

Farther upstream, the main body of Boyd Creek splits into eastern and western branches. The western fork holds 7-foot minimum depths as far as Deloss Point, though there is one unmarked shoal to avoid. The best anchorage in the area is located on this stream. West of the creek's split but short of the stream's first turn to the north-northeast, the southern banks of the western branch border the high land on Boyd Neck. Here, boats up to 35 feet can anchor with good protection. Be on guard against the charted shallows abutting both shorelines immediately east of this haven.

The easterly fork of Boyd Creek holds 7-foot minimum depths until the stream peters out as its approaches Pilot Island. Some of the undeveloped marsh shores are shoal, and boaters must exercise care to hold to the mid-width. Do not anchor here if winds exceed 20 knots. Otherwise, you can drop the hook at any likely spot.

Whale Branch

Whale Branch is the second (and last) readily navigable auxiliary water of Broad River that offers overnight anchorage. The large stream makes in to the river's eastern banks north of the Boyd Creek intersection. Tradition claims that the creek was named for a whale that was stranded on its banks. If so, the whale picked a good spot to meet its end.

As if to make up for the Broad's lack of navigable creeks, Whale Branch's natural scenery is enough to make any cruiser sigh with contentment. There are only one or two unmarked shallows to worry with. Most of the stream holds minimum depths of 7 feet between its banks. All the stream's waters are quite sheltered, and beautiful anchorages abound. All you need do is select a spot to your liking sheltered from the prevailing breezes. There, you may drop the hook in an idyllic setting most boaters only dream about. Of course, remember that you must be able to clear the fixed bridge spanning Broad River to make your way to this delightful body of water.

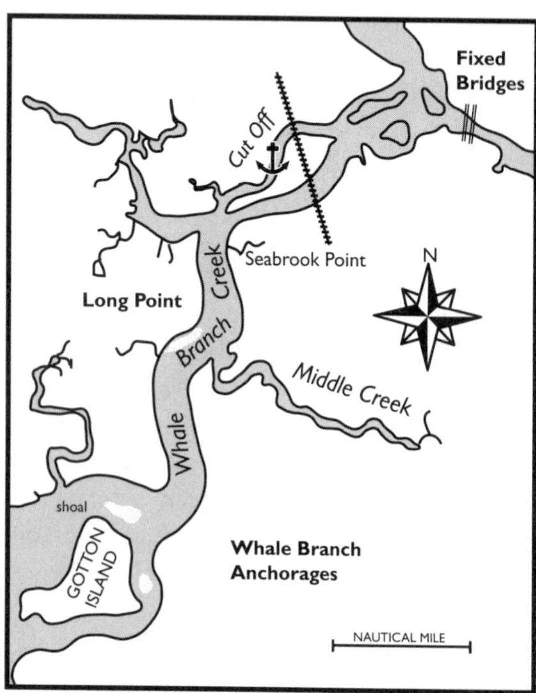

Whale Branch's shoreline is bordered for much of its length by high, heavily wooded banks. There is just enough marsh grass to make a pleasing contrast. Private homes overlook the creek here and there. One historical site graces the shores. It almost appears as if some landscape architect spent many months in the sky selecting the sites for the various homes to give the creek a perfect balance.

In heavy weather, Whale Branch offers at least one very sheltered anchorage with sufficient swinging room for craft up to 40 feet. Just west of the charted railroad bridge that crosses Whale Branch east of Seabrook Point, a fork of the creek charted as "Cut Off" splits off to the east-northeast. While care must be taken when entering this fork, minimum interior depths run about 8 feet, with most of the creek considerably deeper. The best place to anchor is just west of the railroad bridge. Here, high ground abuts the northern shore and gives excellent protection.

Whale Branch and "Cut Off" are both eventually blocked by a railroad bridge with only 5 feet of closed vertical clearance. The railway bridge is usually closed. Just to the east, Whale Branch is spanned by a twin highway bridge with 20 feet of vertical clearance. Both sides of this structure are now fixed spans. The current edition of chart 11519 still shows the easterly side as a 5-foot swing bridge, but this structure was removed and the fixed span added during the past several years.

Clarendon Plantation

The house at Clarendon Plantation is readily visible on the eastern shore of Whale Branch near the area marked "Corning Landing" on chart 11519. The present house was built in 1930. Even though it is relatively modern, the homeplace is an imposing brick structure and makes an impressive sight from the water.

The history of Clarendon Plantation stretches far back into the past. The property was once owned by Paul Hamilton, secretary of war under President James Madison. Hamilton is buried on the plantation.

Whale Branch Tale

In *Tales of Beaufort*, Nell S. Graydon relates an amusing tale about the Whale Branch bridge. The story took place before the Civil War, when the span was little more than a narrow wooden track. It seems that a certain gentleman from Beaufort was visiting friends to the north of Whale Branch one wintry evening. The party was warm and lively. As the gentleman prepared to return home, his host presented him with a fine bottle of Irish whiskey to be opened on a special occasion. The traveler departed and soon approached the Whale Branch bridge. Because it was a cold night, he decided to stop for a swallow from his host's gift. Finding the whiskey much to his liking, he concluded that now was as good an occasion as any and proceeded to drink freely.

Suddenly, there was a clatter on the bridge, and the ghostly specter of a camel appeared before the astonished traveler's eyes. This strange apparition was followed by the form of a huge elephant, and the gentleman even heard the unmistakable roar of a lion. Throwing the bottle

Clarendon Plantation, Whale Branch

away, he forswore strong drink then and there, and he never broke his promise.

Of course, it so happened that a small traveling circus was visiting Beaufort at the time and had incurred more bills than its owner could pay. He decided to make his escape by night and just happened to pass over the bridge as the Beaufort man was approaching from the opposite direction. The circus owner probably never knew that he had rescued a soul from the hands of John Barleycorn.

Chechessee River

Chechessee River is a large but erratic stream that enters Port Royal Sound northwest of unlighted nun buoy #2 (itself east of Dolphin Head). The river is littered with unmarked shoals, and great care must be taken to avoid an unpleasant juncture of keel and mud. It should be entered only by devil-may-care cruisers with boats of less than 40 feet that draw no more (and preferably less) than 4½ feet.

The Chechessee does offer several opportunities for overnight anchorage. There is even one tiny facility, Lemon Island Marina. This firm is located on the river's western banks north of the fixed highway bridge that spans the stream at

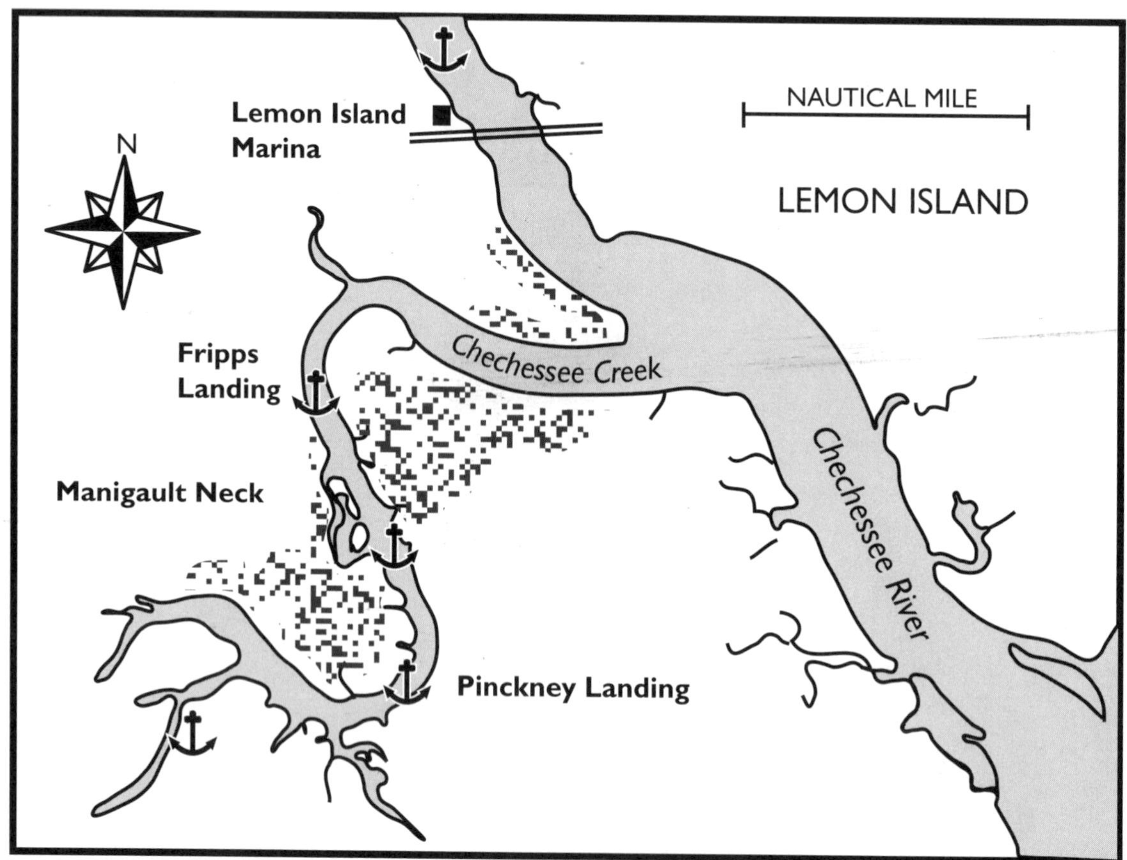

Chechessee Bluff. This span has a vertical clearance of 20 feet. Lemon Island Marina caters almost exclusively to small power craft. There are no facilities for transients and no diesel fuel, but gasoline can be purchased. Low-tide depths alongside are a scant 4 feet at best.

The shores of Chechessee River are not as attractive as others in this region. Most banks are composed of the usual saltwater marsh. Higher ground is rare on the stream. All in all, the best that can be said for the Chechessee is that it leads to several protected anchorages and to Colleton River, a beautiful stream covered later in this chapter.

Chechessee Creek

Chechessee Creek divides the western banks of its like-named river north of Spring Island. The stream carries minimum depths of 7 feet, though there are several unmarked shallows to contend with. These shoals are not too difficult, however, and boats up to 40 feet can drop anchor here with confidence.

One of the best anchorages is found after the creek takes a long, slow turn to the south-southeast. The high ground of Manigault Neck borders the stream on its western banks in the body of the bend and offers excellent shelter. Fripps Landing, a small community of resort homes, is located along this shoreline. Many private docks stretch out from the banks. Select any likely spot, but be sure to leave plenty of clearance between your craft and the nearby piers.

Another possible anchorage lies along the straight stretch of the creek where chart 11516 notes soundings of 10 to 12 feet. There is not nearly as much protection here, but there is plenty of swinging room. In light to moderate airs, this is a good spot for those who prefer an isolated anchorage.

A third overnight stop is found where the high ground of Spring Island borders the creek's southeastern shores at the charted site of Pinckney Landing. There is only light residential development at the landing, and the island shelters the stream from southern and southeastern blows. The creek does narrow a bit, providing only enough swinging room for boats up to 32 feet.

Chechessee River Anchorage

For those who can clear the 20-foot height of the fixed Chechessee River bridge, the waters just northwest of the span narrow sufficiently for anchorage consideration by pleasure craft of almost any size. If the winds are under 15 knots, there should be enough protection for a comfortable evening. The shores are marsh grass, so you might be obliged to seek better shelter if the wind rises.

Hazzard Creek

Chechessee River splits into two branches, both known as Hazzard Creek, about 0.7 nautical mile northwest of the fixed bridge. Both forks offer anchorage opportunities. The western branch holds 10-foot minimum depths in its channel, but care must be exercised to avoid several unmarked shallows. The stream briefly borders some high ground on its southern and southeastern banks at Bellinger Neck. A large pier juts into the creek at this point. The waters just upstream from this dock are a good place to set the hook.

The northerly branch of Hazzard Creek pierces a large marsh and eventually splinters into several smaller streams. As you approach this parting of the waters from the south, depths become shoal and dangerous. However, the stream's lower reaches south of the multiple split hold minimum 9-foot depths and can serve as an overnight anchorage in all but heavy weather.

Colleton River

Colleton River splits off from the western shores of the Chechessee at Foot Point. The Colleton's character is in sharp contrast to that of its sister stream. Colleton River is an absolutely beautiful body of water. Wooded shores with light residential development overlook the river from atop Victoria Bluff, and the high land of Spring Island borders a portion of the northern and northeastern shoreline. The small community of Copp Landing is noted on chart 11516 near the southwestern tip of Spring Island. Only one lone house is visible from the water. You may spy several shrimp boats plying their nets in the river. These classic craft add to the charm of this lovely stream.

The Colleton is free from shoals and other navigational hazards. Depths of 20 feet or more stretch almost from bank to bank. Any skipper would have to be soundly snoring at the helm to run aground on Colleton River.

On the other hand, the river is almost devoid of sidewaters and safe anchorages. One small stream, Sawmill Creek, penetrates the southerly banks opposite Spring Island, but minimum depths of 15 feet hold for only a short distance upstream, and there is only enough swinging room for boats under 30 feet. In fair weather or moderate northerly breezes, visiting cruisers might anchor in the lee of Spring Island abeam of charted Copp Landing, but southerly winds over 10 knots will bring on a bumpy evening.

West of Copp Landing, the river is bisected by a number of marsh islands, and the waters are littered with unmarked shoals. Halt your explorations east of charted Callawassie Creek.

Colleton River is one of those water bodies cruising boaters encounter from time to time that presents a clear case of good news-bad news. You will have to decide whether the river's great natural beauty justifies a long trip from the ICW with only a moderate chance of finding a secure place to drop the hook.

PORT ROYAL SOUND AND AUXILIARY STREAMS NAVIGATION

As already noted, navigation of Port Royal Sound and its tributary streams is not a laughing matter for casual boaters. If you choose to enter these waters, have your compass courses worked out beforehand. Run your intended tracks carefully while measuring your progress with a log. Go slowly, keep an eagle eye on the sounder, and with a bit of luck you may come through with nothing but good memories.

Port Royal Sound If you plan to make use of the Port Royal Inlet channel, simply continue following the marked cut south of flashing buoy #27. The channel is well marked by lighted buoys and is reasonably easy to follow. All other boaters should turn southwest at unlighted nun buoy #26 and set course to bring flashing daybeacon #246 abeam by some 300 yards to its southerly side. From #246, you have many choices. A cut to the northwest leads to Broad River and Whale Branch, while a westerly course brings boaters to the southeasterly mouth of Chechessee River.

Broad River To enter Broad River, you must set a northwesterly course from a position well south of flashing daybeacon #246, which will help to avoid the large shoal extending generally southeast for several nautical miles from Ribbon Creek on the Broad's northeasterly banks. Pass well to the west and southwest of this huge obstruction.

As you continue cruising northwest on Broad River, point to avoid the large patch of shallows guarding the river's mid-width northeast of Daws Island. After passing this shallow stretch, point northwest for the central pass-through of the Broad River bridge. There are no further shoals bearing directly upon the river's centerline between the Daws Island shallows and the span.

While making your run to the bridge, you will pass an unnamed creek southwest of your course that leads to Chechessee River south of Rose Island. Do not attempt this stream. It is surrounded by shallow water, with only 1 foot of depth in some places.

Bend your course almost due north after passing

the Broad River bridge. This maneuver will steer you clear of the charted shallow spot just northwest of the pass-through. From this point, you need only keep to the mid-width to maintain good depths as far as Whale Branch.

Euhaw Creek pierces the western shores of Broad River through several mouths north of the bridge. This stream, too, should be bypassed. Depths are much too uncertain for visiting boaters.

After leaving Euhaw Creek behind and cruising upstream for another 2 nautical miles or so on Broad River, it will be time to break out chart 11519. This cartographical aid describes the northern portion of Broad River and Whale Branch.

Boyd Creek Favor the southern banks when entering Boyd Creek, but don't approach this shoreline too closely either. Chart 11519 correctly predicts a huge patch of shallow water abutting the entrance's northern flank. Soon after leaving the creek's mouth behind, Cole Creek splits off to the south. If you choose to explore this small sidewater, favor the western banks slightly as you enter, then cruise back to the mid-width. Be sure to stop before the stream takes its first jog to the southeast.

To continue upstream on the main body of Boyd Creek, begin favoring the western banks heavily as the creek curves to the north-northeast. Follow the shore until the stream again cuts back to the west. Just short of this turn, be sure to keep at least 25 yards from the shoreline. Chart 11519 clearly identifies a shoal that can be bypassed by following this procedure. Cruise back to the mid-width after passing through the westerly turn and stick to the middle until the creek splits.

Favor the southern shore when entering West Branch Boyd Creek, but do not approach the bank too closely. Cruise back to the centerline as the creek takes a sharp turn to the north. From here to Deloss Point, you can expect good depths if you stick scrupulously to the middle of the stream. Don't approach either shoreline. Both banks are shoal and dangerous. Past Deloss Point, depths drop off to 4 feet or less.

To cruise East Branch Boyd Creek, simply stick to the mid-width. Discontinue your exploration before the creek enters a hairpin turn to the east abeam of Pilot Island.

Whale Branch The westerly reaches of Whale Branch join Broad River south of Barnwell Island. Cotton Island divides the entrance into two branches. Both are readily navigable, but both require caution.

If you choose to make use of the southern branch, enter the creek on its mid-width. Take care to avoid the finger of 4-foot water extending north from Port Royal Island on the entranceway's southern quarter. Stick to the middle until the creek takes a sharp turn to the north. Begin favoring the western banks and continue to do so until you enter the main body of Whale Branch at the eastern tip of Cotton Island.

Follow the mid-width of the northern entrance until the stream begins to bend to the east-southeast around Cotton Island. As shown on chart 11519, a shoal guards the center of the stream in this area. To avoid this hazard, favor the southern and southwestern shores until reaching the island's eastern tip.

Once on the main body of Whale Branch, you need simply hold to the mid-width as far as the railroad bridge. Chart 11519 shows a small shoal near the northwestern banks opposite Middle Creek. This shallow patch did not show up in on-site research, but to be on the safe side, favor the southeastern banks as you pass.

To enter the sheltered anchorage on "Cut Off,"

avoid the point that separates this creek from the main body of Whale Branch. A long shoal extends west-southwest from this marshy promontory. Otherwise, simply hold to the centerline and drop the hook anywhere before reaching the railroad bridge.

Begin slightly favoring the southern shore of Whale Branch as you approach the railroad bridge. There is a small shoal on the northern shore. Soon, your passage will be blocked by the usually closed railway span. Discontinue your cruise at this point.

Chechessee River To enter shoal-prone Chechessee River, set course from flashing daybeacon #246 to come abeam of unlighted nun buoy #2 (east of Dolphin Head) to the buoy's southerly side. Set a careful compass course to the northwest and enter the deepwater section of Chechessee River. Along the way, you will pass flashing daybeacon #1 well southwest of your course. This aid marks the northeasterly mouth of Mackay Creek, which will be reviewed later in this chapter.

Begin favoring the Daws Island (northeasterly) shores after cruising upriver for some 1.5 nautical miles past flashing daybeacon #1. As shown on chart 11516, a large shoal abuts the southwesterly banks southeast of Foot Point.

At Foot Point, the entrance to Colleton River will come abeam to the west. Navigation of this stream will be covered later in this chapter.

To continue upstream on the Chechessee, set a new course to pass between the marshes of Spring Island to the southwest and the small marsh island that bisects the river to the northeast. Begin working your way slowly back toward the northeastern banks as you approach Rose Island. After passing the three charted marsh islands to the southwest, set a new course to pass Chechessee Creek's south-side entrance point by some 150 yards to your port side. Study chart 11516 carefully before undertaking this complicated procedure. This is an extremely tricky section that calls for maximum alert.

Chechessee Creek If you choose to enter Chechessee Creek, favor the southern banks a bit. Shoal water extends into the creek from Chechessee Point, to the north. Once on the main body of the stream, hold to the mid-width. The creek eventually follows a long bend to the south-southeast and begins to border Fripps Landing. Continue cruising upstream on the mid-width until you approach Pinckney Landing. Here, the stream bends to the southwest; you should begin favoring the eastern and southeastern shores just before entering this turn. Discontinue your progress before passing through the creek's next turn to the west.

On Chechessee River Cruisers plodding northwest on Chechessee River to the fixed bridge should hold to the main stream's mid-width as they pass the entrance of Chechessee Creek to the southwest. Favor the northeastern banks slightly as you approach the point opposite the southern tip of Chechessee Bluff. Set a new course toward the central pass-through of the Chechessee bridge. This span has a vertical clearance of 20 feet. Craft that need more clearance must retrace their steps south and southeast to Broad River and Port Royal Sound.

Once through the span, look to port and you will spy Lemon Island Marina on the western banks. Continue upstream on the centerline, but begin to favor the eastern banks heavily about 0.4 nautical mile south of the Hazzard Creek split.

Notice the large shoal building out from the southern entrance point of the western branch of Hazzard Creek, correctly pictured on chart 11516.

Hazzard Creek To enter the western branch of Hazzard Creek, continue favoring the eastern shore of the main body until the centerline of the western creek is directly abeam to your port side. Then turn 90 degrees to port and enter the creek. As the sharp entrance point comes abeam to the south, begin favoring the southern and southeastern shores heavily. As shown on chart 11516, a large shoal guards the northwestern banks. Remember to discontinue your cruise before entering the wide stretch of the creek north of Bellinger Neck.

Cruise into the northern fork of Hazzard Creek on its mid-width. Good depths continue on the middle until the stream splinters south of Hazzard Neck. Stop well short of these waters.

Colleton River Avoid Foot Point on the southern quarter of Colleton River's entrance. Otherwise, simply stay at least 150 yards from either shore and you will be in deep water all the way to Copp Landing. Remember to stop before reaching Callawassie Creek.

If you pilot a boat under 30 feet and choose to anchor in Sawmill Creek, enter the stream on its mid-width. Don't attempt to cruise past the creek's first bend to the southeast. Depths quickly drop off to 3 or 4 feet.

ICW TO COOPER RIVER

Southwest of Port Royal Sound, the ICW enters the headwaters of Skull Creek and comes into contact with Hilton Head Island. Hilton Head comprises the southeastern banks of the Waterway until the route turns west off Calibogue Sound into Cooper River. Seven marinas are located on the island, and all eagerly accept transients. Nowhere else in coastal South Carolina are so many facilities for the cruising boater concentrated in so small an area.

Skull Creek leads the Waterway cruiser southwest to Calibogue Sound. Like most open bodies of water, Calibogue can foster choppy conditions when winds exceed 15 knots. The sound's inlet channel provides fairly reliable access to the open sea. Some markers are not charted, probably because they are frequently shifted. The inlet channel is used by fishing boats from Hilton Head Island on a daily basis. While not absolutely necessary, local knowledge is certainly desirable before attempting the inlet. Check on current conditions at one of the area marinas.

May River breaks off to the west near the northeastern headwaters of Calibogue Sound and provides beautiful cruising grounds as far inland as the historic community of Bluffton. A well-outlined channel and numerous anchorage possibilities add to this lovely stream's charms.

Unlike Port Royal Sound, the waters around Hilton Head Island are some of the most heavily used in the state. Their popularity is richly deserved. There are very few shoals or other navigational difficulties. Calibogue Sound in particular is blessed with great natural beauty. The numerous marinas are a real boon to visiting and resident boaters alike. Yet amid all this popularity, there is still the opportunity to cruise isolated waters. Seldom will cruising boaters find a water body so consistently overlooked, yet possessing such a lovely character, as May River. There are even a few creeks off Calibogue Sound that provide sheltered anchorage far from civilization. To summarize, the waters of and around the ICW from Port Royal Sound to Cooper River have just about everything the cruising boater could ever desire.

To arrange taxi or rental-car transportation on Hilton Head, call Taxi World (803-686-6666), Low Country Adventures (803-681-8212), Enterprise Rent-A-Car (803-689-9910), or Budget Car Rentals (803-689-4040).

ICW THROUGH CALIBOGUE SOUND

Skull Creek

The ICW enters the northeastern headwaters of Skull Creek at flashing daybeacon #6. The creek splinters into several branches at this point. The Waterway follows the northwesternmost fork. The marked route is more reliable, but it is worth noting that the southeasternmost branch holds minimum 9-foot depths and is readily navigable southwest to Skull Creek Marina. Boats up to 36 feet will find sufficient swinging room to drop the hook on the southwestern two-thirds of this creek. Be sure to anchor well away from the marina docks.

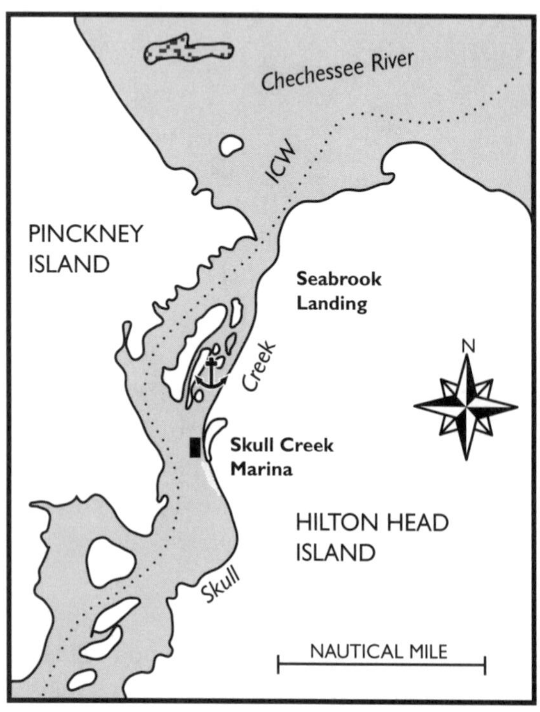

Skull Creek Marina

The huge dockage complex associated with Skull Creek Marina is readily visible east of unlighted daybeacon #9A. This unusually well-appointed, modern facility gladly accepts transients and features concrete floating docks with every conceivable power, water, telephone, and cable-television connection. As you would imagine, the showers and full-service laundromat are first-rate. Gasoline, diesel fuel, and waste pump-out services are available, as well as full below-waterline haul-out repairs (via a 30-ton travelift). Mechanical service can be easily arranged through local independent contractors. The on-site restaurant was closed at the time of this writing but should be reopened under new management by the spring of 1996.

Visiting cruisers are welcome to make use of the development's golf course. Reservations may be made at the marina office. A courtesy van is even available to ferry boaters to the nearby supermarket.

Skull Creek Marina struck this writer as an unusually friendly establishment where the visiting cruiser can be assured of a warm welcome. Advance dockage reservations are heartily recommended during the spring or fall transient seasons. It's really that popular.

Skull Creek Marina (803) 681-4234 or (800) 237-4096

Approach depth: 12+ feet
Dockside depth: 9-12 feet
Accepts transients: yes
Floating concrete piers: yes
Dockside power connections: 30 and 50 amps
Dockside water connections: yes
Showers: yes
Laundromat: yes
Waste pump-out: yes
Gasoline: yes
Diesel fuel: yes
Mechanical repairs: independent contractors
Below-waterline repairs: yes
Restaurant: on-site

Outdoor Resorts Yacht Club Marina

Outdoor Resorts Yacht Club Marina overlooks the ICW's southwestern shoreline opposite unlighted daybeacon #20. This facility maintains a floating, wooden-decked transient dock fronting directly onto the ICW. Shelter might not be adequate for really heavy weather. Some additional dockage is located in a sheltered cove just west of the transient pier, but these slips are occupied exclusively by resident boaters. Depths on the outer slips run 10 feet or better, with at least 8 feet of water on the inner berths. Full power and water connections are very much in the offing.

Gasoline and diesel fuel can be purchased at the marina, and some mechanical repairs can be arranged through independent technicians. Waste pump-out service is available by way of a portable system. Shoreside, boaters will find showers, a laundromat, tennis courts, a sauna, a swimming pool, and an on-site restaurant. Again, advance reservations during transient season are a wise precaution.

Outdoor Resorts Yacht Club Marina (803) 681-3256 or (800) 845-9560

Approach depth: 10+ feet
Dockside depth: 15+ feet at transient dock (projected)
Accepts transients: yes
Floating wooden piers: yes
Dockside power connections: 30 and 50 amps
Dockside water connections: yes
Showers: yes
Laundromat: yes
Waste pump-out: yes
Gasoline: yes
Diesel fuel: yes
Mechanical repairs: independent technicians
Ship's and variety store: yes
Restaurant: on-site

Windmill Harbor Marina

Hilton Head's newest and arguably most unique facility sits hard by the southwesterly mouth of Skull Creek north of unlighted daybeacon #27 (on the easterly banks). To this writer's knowledge, Windmill Harbor Marina is the Southeast's only facility accessible to visiting cruisers that features a "locked harbor." Boats docking at the fixed concrete piers need not contend with the rise and fall of the tide thanks to the harbor's lock gate. Of course, the basin is also thoroughly protected from any weather short of a hurricane by this same scheme.

The locked dockage basin's shores are beautifully landscaped and surrounded by tasteful condos and several larger buildings. One of these latter structures houses the South Carolina Yacht Club (803-681-4844). Visiting cruisers may request guest membership in this fine organization, and believe me, it's worth your time to take advantage of this extra service. The club is decorated in the most sumptuous nautical style that this writer has *ever* observed. Additionally, the bar and restaurant are absolutely first-rate. You will not find better food anywhere in the South Carolina Low Country.

Cruising boaters can rejoice in Windmill Harbor's decision to accept transients for overnight or temporary dockage. Most slips are fixed concrete structures featuring full water and power connections. The sheltered entrance channel leading to the lock has low-tide depths of 6 feet, with 8 to 10 feet of water in the tide-protected harbor.

Gasoline, diesel fuel, and waste pump-out services are at hand, as are shoreside showers.

Entrance to lock at Windmill Harbor Marina

Mechanical repairs can be arranged, and the marina features a small but nevertheless full-line ship's store.

Boaters seeking a unique, upper-crust cruising experience should do themselves a huge favor and give Windmill Harbor Marina a try. Need this writer even say that advance reservations would be one of the smartest precautions you could take on your cruise?

Windmill Harbor Marina
(803) 681-9235

Approach depth: 6 feet (low water)
Dockside depth: 8-10 feet
Accepts transients: yes
Fixed concrete piers: yes
Dockside power connections: 30 and 50 amps
Dockside water connections: yes
Showers: yes
Waste pump-out: yes
Gasoline: yes
Diesel fuel: yes
Mechanical repairs: independent contractors
Ship's store: yes
Restaurant: on-site

Calibogue Sound and Broad Creek Facilities and Anchorages

At flashing daybeacon #24, Skull Creek leads ICW cruisers into the northern headwaters of Calibogue Sound. Mackay Creek cuts back to the north and offers prime cruising ground and several excellent anchorages. Similarly, May River breaks off from Calibogue Sound west of flashing daybeacon #29. Both of these water bodies will be covered later in this chapter. The various facilities and anchorages of Hilton Head Island on Broad Creek and Calibogue Sound are reviewed immediately below.

Jarvis Creek

Jarvis Creek leads east into the main body of Hilton Head Island at flashing daybeacon #1, south of Ferry Point. The creek holds minimum 9-foot depths until it takes a sharp jog to the north well upstream, but the channel is surrounded by mud flats that are covered at high water. Consequently, it is sometimes difficult to pick out the deepwater passage at high tide. The mud flats also give virtually no protection from hard blows. Boaters will find enough swinging room for craft up to 34 feet to anchor, but their stay will be uncomfortable if winds exceed 10 knots.

Bryan Creek

Bryan Creek cuts into Calibogue Sound's northwestern banks well southwest of unlighted daybeacon #30. This stream makes an excellent anchorage for those who prefer an isolated haven for the night. Minimum depths run around 7 feet, with most of the stream deeper. There is sufficient swinging room for boats up to 38 feet.

The creek's entrance is surrounded by shoals and calls for careful cruising. However, there is a broad entrance channel, and cautious navigators should be able to keep to the deep water.

The creek's lower reaches are surrounded by marsh grass, but the higher ground of Bull Island flanks the western banks as the stream takes a turn to the north-northeast. Protection is excellent here.

Bryan Creek eventually splits into two branches. Both forks narrow considerably, and depths become uncertain.

Broad Creek Facilities

Broad Creek enters Calibogue Sound at unlighted daybeacon #1 north of the charted position of Harbour Town. This wide stream leads first northeast and then east into the heart of Hilton Head Island. No fewer than three marinas are located along the stream. All can accommodate visiting cruisers, with two of the three extending a particularly warm welcome.

Broad Creek has 7-foot minimum depths, but much of the stream's channel holds more than 10 feet of water. The passage is well marked by privately maintained daybeacons. Broad Creek is used on a daily basis by many local craft, and you should not have undue navigational difficulty.

Palmetto Bay Marina

Palmetto Bay Marina is the first facility you will encounter on Broad Creek. The marina is located on the creek's southern shore just east of the stream's first sharp bend to the east. It is designated as facility #2 on chart 11507.

Palmetto Bay is a large, modern marina that features a full-service boatyard. Transients are gladly accepted at the wooden-decked floating docks, which boast 8-plus feet of low-tide depths. Full power and water connections are available at every slip. Gasoline, diesel fuel, and waste pump-out are readily available. Showers and a laundromat are also on the grounds.

A complex of offices and retail businesses just behind the docks features two restaurants. Captain Woodies is a fine, informal dining spot open for lunch and dinner. The Chart House is a bit more "uptown" and serves evening meals only.

Palmetto Bay Marina's boatyard boasts two travelifts (one 16-ton, one 50-ton) and full mechanical repairs for both gasoline and diesel

Palmetto Bay Marina, Broad Creek

engines. Judging from this writer's observations, the yard is very popular with Hilton Head boaters. A marine canvas shop is also located at the marina.

Palmetto Bay Marina (803) 785-3910 or (800) 448-3875

Approach depth: 12+ feet
Dockside depth: 8+ feet (low water)
Accepts transients: yes
Floating wooden piers: yes
Dockside power connections: 30 and 50 amps
Dockside water connections: yes
Showers: yes
Laundromat: yes
Waste pump-out: yes
Gasoline: yes
Diesel fuel: yes
Mechanical repairs: yes
Below-waterline repairs: yes
Restaurants: 2 on-site

Broad Creek Marina

Broad Creek Marina is the second facility you will encounter on the creek of the same name. Located on the stream's northern banks just upstream from Palmetto Bay Marina, Broad Creek is the smallest facility on Hilton Head Island. The firm's principal business is the dry-stack storage of small power craft. The marina does offer some transient dockage on floating piers with power and water connections. Gasoline (but not diesel fuel) can be purchased dockside. Mechanical repairs are offered, and there is an on-site ship's store where snacks can be purchased.

Broad Creek Marina (803) 681-7335

Approach depth: 7 feet (minimum)
Dockside depth: 10+ feet
Accepts transients: yes
Floating wooden piers: yes
Dockside power connections: up to 30 amps
Dockside water connections: yes
Gasoline: yes
Mechanical repairs: yes
Ship's store: yes

Shelter Cove Marina

A prolific series of unlighted daybeacons leads boaters up Broad Creek to one of the finest facilities on all of Hilton Head Island (or anywhere else, for that matter). Shelter Cove Marina is perched in a man-made cove on the southeastern shores of Broad Creek near flashing daybeacons #22 and #23. The marina encourages transient business and offers a wide array of services. The only disadvantage to this facility is the fairly lengthy trek from the ICW and Calibogue Sound that is required to reach its basin. Many boaters will find the trip more than justified.

Minimum dockside depths in Shelter Cove's well-protected basin are a very impressive 8 to 12 feet. The docks are ultramodern concrete-decked floating piers that boast every sort of water, power, telephone, and cable-television connection. Gasoline, diesel fuel, and waste pump-out are readily available, and the marina maintains an excellent, full-line ship's and variety store. Some mechanical repairs can be arranged through independent contractors. Showers and a full laundromat are also available.

The adjacent Harbormaster Restaurant (803-785-3030) is very convenient and features fine seafood. Several additional dining choices (including a "Fuddruckers" restaurant) are only a short step away in an adjacent shopping complex. Here, you will also find a supermarket.In our cruising experience, this writer and his mate have seldom come across a better-equipped marina than Shelter Cove. We encourage our fellow boaters to take advantage of this unusually well-appointed facility.

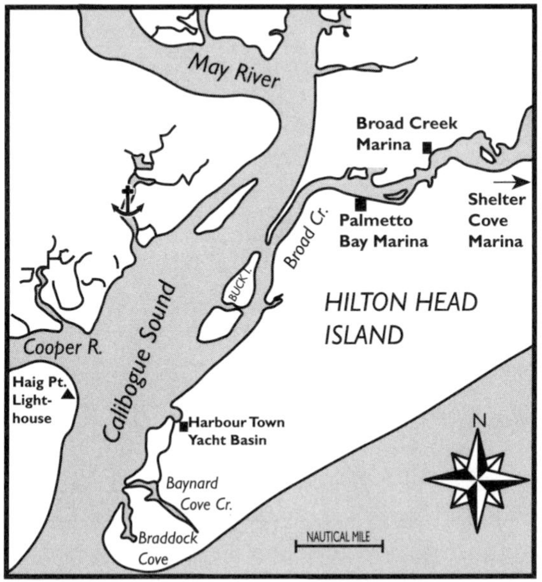

Shelter Cove Marina, Broad Creek

Shelter Cove Marina (803) 842-7001

Approach depth: 7-8 feet (low water)
Dockside depth: 8 feet (low water)
Accepts transients: yes
Concrete floating piers: yes
Dockside power connections: 30 and 50 amps
Dockside water connections: yes
Showers: yes
Laundromat: yes
Waste pump-out: yes
Gasoline: yes
Diesel fuel: yes
Mechanical repairs: independent contractors
Ship's and variety store: yes
Restaurants: on-site, with several nearby

Harbour Town Yacht Basin

Harbour Town Yacht Basin is certainly the best known of Hilton Head Island's many boating facilities. Its candy-striped red-and-white lighthouse has been admired for many years by cruisers traveling along the ICW. This special facility is located well southeast of flashing daybeacon #32.

Harbour Town Yacht Basin used to suffer from some fairly severe low-water depth problems and a bit of tidal surge at the docks. Both of these difficulties have been lessened by the construction of twin breakwaters flanking the dockage basin's entrance. These structures are marked by flashing daybeacons #3 and #4. At the time of this writing, approach depths had risen to some 5 feet at mean low water. Fortunately, maintenance dredging is scheduled for February 1996, with a projected depth of 9 feet. If past experience is a teacher, the entrance channel could shoal again in the future. Skippers whose craft draw more than 5½ feet may want to check with the marina staff ahead of time or enter and leave on a rising tide.

Harbour Town welcomes visiting boaters with ultramodern concrete floating docks. All slips feature every conceivable power and water connection. Gasoline, diesel fuel, and waste pump-out service are available, of course, and full mechanical service is now offered as well. Spotless showers and a full laundromat are only a step away. Visiting cruisers are welcome at the complex's swimming pool and tennis courts. The world-famous Harbour Town golf course is located nearby and is readily visible to starboard as you enter the harbor. Hold onto your wallet—the greens fees are something to behold.

Harbour Town's docks are grouped in a circular bay around a series of exclusive shops and restaurants. It's a bit like Palm Beach's Worth Avenue in the South Carolina Low Country. There are clothing and gift stores, book shops, and nautical retailers. Three restaurants stand ready to satisfy famished cruisers. One, the Cafe Europa (803-671-3399), overlooks the sound through glass walls. This writer particularly recommends the shrimp salad, with the cherry torte for dessert. With a view of the sun setting across the sound, a leisurely meal in such surroundings at the end of a long cruising day can be a memorable repast indeed. The Quarterdeck (803-671-2222) is located atop the Cafe Europa and features casual dining in a lovely setting. And if you're in the market for some tasty seafood, consider the Crazy Crab Restaurant (803-363-2722) for lunch or dinner. You simply can't do better.

While it's not on the harbor, nearby CQ's Restaurant (803-671-2779) may just serve the best food in Harbor Town. The fresh seafood, steaks, and poultry dishes are all consistently excellent.

Visitors are free to climb the Harbour Town Lighthouse. The view from the light's crown commands a wide panorama of the sound and Daufuskie Island to the west. Eastward, you can see much of Hilton Head. You must ascend many flights of steps to reach the top, but the view is well worth the climb.

Harbour Town Yacht Basin remains one of the most prestigious stops on the entire ICW. Visiting cruisers should know that all these sumptuous qualities do not come cheaply, but many will still find the experience worth the price. If you choose to set your course for Harbour Town, it would be a good idea to call ahead for reservations to avoid disappointment.

Harbour Town Yacht Basin, Hilton Head Island

Harbour Town Yacht Basin
(803) 671-2704

Approach depth: 9 feet (projected following February 1996 dredging)
Dockside depth: 9 feet (projected)
Accepts transients: yes
Floating concrete piers: yes
Dockside power connections: 30 and 50 amps
Dockside water connections: yes
Showers: yes
Laundromat: yes
Waste pump-out: yes
Gasoline: yes
Diesel fuel: yes
Mechanical repairs: yes
Below-waterline repairs: yes
Ship's store: yes
Restaurants: several on-site

Baynard Cove Creek and Braddock Cove

A series of private markers south of the Harbour Town Yacht Basin entrance denotes two channels leading into the western shores of Hilton Head Island. These channels serve two private dockage harbors that are associated with several condominium projects. At low tide, the two cuts carry only some 5 to 6 feet of water. Visiting boaters are advised to bypass both streams.

Hilton Head Island History Hilton Head Island was known as the "Island of the Bears" in early colonial times. The sands of Hilton Head have changed much since the noble bear was the island's principal resident.

William Hilton explored the region in 1663, and the island was subsequently named in his honor. He described the area in glowing terms: "The lands are laden with large tall trees—oaks, walnuts and bayes, except facing the sea it is mostly pines. . . . The country abounds with grapes, large figs and peaches; the woods with deer, conies, turkeys, quail, curlues, plovers, teile, herons, ducks and innumerable other water fowls. Oysters [are] in abundance. . . . The Rivers [are] stored plentifully with fish which we saw play and leap."

Once the danger of Indian attack lessened following the Yemassee Indian wars, families began to settle and build plantations on Hilton Head. Most of these have vanished with the passing years, but several are remembered in the names of modern resort developments.

During the Revolution, the settlers on Hilton Head took a decidedly patriot stand. This contrasted sharply with the Loyalist leanings of the Daufuskie Island citizenry across the sound. There were frequent skirmishes on Hilton Head between the two groups.

Hilton Head Island fell to Union forces in the early stages of the Civil War. Fort Walker had been hastily constructed by the Confederates to guard the island's southeastern point. The fort was attacked by a huge Union fleet, which landed more than 13,000 troops. After Fort Walker's fall, the Northern fleet used the island as a base of supply for its regional operations.

Following the war, Hilton Head was virtually abandoned until the Sea Pines Company pioneered a resort development in the 1950s. Today, the island hosts the largest collection of condominiums, hotels, restaurants, and marinas in all of coastal South Carolina. The automobile traffic problems have grown so severe that a new bypass bridge over Broad Creek is being discussed. Several golf courses, many tennis clubs, and a late-fall sailing race known as the Calibogue Cup are among the island's attractions. The island draws larger and larger crowds every year.

Hilton Head Island Stories

Hilton Head Island has its share of buried-treasure stories. One tale claims that the Frenchmen of the abortive Charlesfort colony on Parris Island salvaged over $1.5 million in gold recovered from Spanish wrecks by friendly Indians. Tradition holds that the French settlers buried their booty on Hilton Head.

Another old story begins with the successful raiding of Spanish treasure ships by the French navy off the South Carolina coast. The booty was subsequently buried on Hilton Head. When the Spanish conqueror Menendez captured a French colony in Florida, he was offered this treasure as ransom. The offer was refused, and the gold was lost. Who knows? Perhaps buried treasure still awaits some young lad with pail and shovel building sandcastles on the beach at Hilton Head.

ICW THROUGH CALIBOGUE SOUND NAVIGATION

Most of the waters between the northern entrance of Skull Creek and Cooper River are well marked and easily traversed. There are some exceptions, but generally cruisers can take a welcome break from their constant vigil over the sounder. Proceed warily nevertheless, and don't let the amiable nature of the waters lull you into too great a sense of security.

ICW to Skull Creek Set course from flashing daybeacon #246, south of Parris Island Spit, to come abeam of unlighted nun buoy #2 by some 25 to 50 yards to its southerly side. As you approach #2, you may spy flashing daybeacon #1 well south of your course. Do not approach #1. It is surrounded by shallows.

Set a new course from #2 to come abeam of flashing daybeacon #3, north of Dolphin Head, by some 50 to 75 yards to its northerly side. From #3, the Waterway bends to the southwest and begins its approach to Skull Creek's northeasterly mouth. Point to pass unlighted daybeacon #4 by some 50 yards to its southeasterly side and unlighted daybeacon #5 to its fairly immediate northwesterly quarter. Continue into Skull Creek by coming abeam of and passing flashing daybeacon #6 to its southeasterly side. From #6, the Waterway continues down the northwesternmost branch of Skull Creek and is easy to follow. Be sure to slow to idle speed when passing Skull Creek Marina.

Skull Creek Anchorage Adventurous boaters can cruise the creek's southeastern fork and either anchor there or follow the stream southwest to Skull Creek Marina. Unless you plan to drop the hook, it would be better to use the Waterway channel to access the marina. Also, boats over 35 feet may want to use the southeastern fork's southwestern entrance at Skull Creek Marina. This entrance is wider than the northeastern passage.

If you choose to enter the southeastern branch by way of its northeastern mouth, avoid the point of marsh separating this stream from the Waterway channel. Cruise along on the centerline until you spy a thin marsh island that divides the stream. Pass the island on its southeastern side. The creek now broadens, and there is plenty of swinging room. If you continue southwest, hold to the middle until reaching Skull Creek Marina.

On the ICW South of Skull Creek Marina, the Waterway flows southwest along a well-marked track. Favor the southern shores a bit between flashing daybeacon #19 and unlighted daybeacon #20. A long shoal abuts the northern banks between these two aids. Abeam of #20, slow to "No Wake" speed when passing Outdoor Resorts Yacht Club Marina.

Southwest of flashing daybeacon #22, cruisers will pass under Hilton Head's 65-foot fixed highway bridge. Watch the southeastern shores after passing under the fixed span. Soon, the entrance to Windmill Harbor Marina will come abeam.

At flashing daybeacon #24, the ICW enters the headwaters of Calibogue Sound. Cruise carefully between #24 and unlighted daybeacon #27. Don't allow leeway to ease you toward either side of the channel. There is shoal water abutting both flanks of the Waterway along this stretch. Some 0.3 nautical mile south past #27, good depths again open out almost from shore to shore.

South of flashing daybeacon #24, the ICW follows the waters of Calibogue Sound as they hurry seaward. The route is outlined by aids to navigation between unlighted daybeacon #27 and the ICW's entrance into Cooper River. However, it is a long run between some markers. You may want to run a compass course down Calibogue Sound to be on the safe side.

Don't approach Middle Marsh Island. It is surrounded by shallow water. Otherwise, the sound is pretty much free of shoals all the way to Cooper River.

Jarvis Creek If you choose to enter Jarvis Creek at flashing daybeacon #1, favor the northern shore slightly when entering. Once inside, keep to the middle and good depths will be held until the stream takes a jog to the north. Discontinue your cruise before reaching this point.

Bryan Creek Before approaching Bryan Creek, be sure to clear the tongue of shoal water extending southwest from Middle Marsh Island. Enter the creek on its mid-width, but begin favoring the western banks slightly once on the stream's interior. You can expect good depths as far as the creek's split if you continue to favor this shore. Past the forks, depths become too inconsistent for cruising craft.

Broad Creek Leave the Waterway and continue cruising southwest on Calibogue Sound until the private markers leading to Harbour Town Yacht Basin are almost abeam to the southeast; then curl slowly around to the northeast, passing unlighted daybeacon #1 by some 50 yards to its southeasterly side and coming abeam of unlighted daybeacon #2 by about 10 yards to its northwesterly quarter. These aids mark the entrance to Broad Creek. Stay away from #1—shoal water is building southwest around this beacon.

Cruise upstream on Broad Creek's mid-line. Pass unlighted daybeacon #4 to its western side

South Carolina Yacht Club at Windmill Harbor

along the way. At Opossum Point, the creek enters a long swing to the east. Many private docks dot the northern banks along this stretch. Watch to starboard as you round the bend and you will catch sight of Palmetto Bay Marina on the southern banks.

East of Palmetto Bay, cruisers heading upstream should take red beacons to the boaters' starboard side and green markers to port.

Eventually, the channel cuts southeast at flashing daybeacon #18 and unlighted daybeacon #19. You will soon enter Shelter Cove Marina's protected dockage basin. The harbor entrance is marked by flashing daybeacons #22 and #23.

Harbour Town Yacht Basin Pass between flashing daybeacons #1 and #2 and continue dead ahead between the two arms of the enclosing breakwaters. These structures are marked by flashing daybeacons #3 and #4. Once inside the breakwaters, continue cruising straight ahead into the harbor. Soon, you will spy the fuel dock to your port side. Stop here for dockage instructions unless you have called ahead on the VHF for advance arrangements.

Seaward on Calibogue Sound Remember, some of Calibogue Inlet's aids are apparently not charted. It would be best to check at Harbour Town Yacht Basin or one of the other nearby marinas before running the cut. Even better, follow one of the many fishing craft that frequently put out to sea from Hilton Head Island.

MACKAY CREEK

Mackay Creek leads north and northeast, back toward Port Royal Sound, from flashing daybeacon #24. A fixed bridge with 25 feet of vertical clearance spans the stream. It is followed by a power line with 43 feet of clearance. Boaters bound southwest on Mackay Creek from Chechessee River to Calibogue Sound should take careful measurements before cruising under this shocking obstruction.

Mackay Creek is an unusually pretty body of water. The high, heavily wooded banks of Pinckney Island to the east contrast pleasantly with the marshy shores to the west. Mackay Creek is bypassed by most cruising boaters, and its isolation, coupled with the stream's natural beauty, can make for a very pleasant cruise.

While there are a few shoals to avoid, most of the stream is readily navigable. A series of unlighted daybeacons helps the visiting cruiser avoid the shallows. Generally, boats up to 40 feet that draw less than 5½ feet can cruise the creek with confidence.

Several sidewaters offer good anchorage along Mackay Creek. South of Buzzard Island, a wide bubble of deep water shoots off to the northeast. Minimum depths of 9 feet are held for a short distance from the main channel. Boats of almost any size can anchor here, but protection is not sufficient for heavy weather. Feel your way along and drop the hook before cruising very far from the main body of the creek.

West of Buzzard Island, a small creek branches off to the west. This stream is marked by a series of unlighted daybeacons leading to a private dock and country club. There are no facilities for visitors, but anchorage in the stream short of the docks is a very good possibility. The waters between unlighted daybeacons #4 and #6 offer enough swinging room for boats up to 34 feet, but this spot is not very sheltered. Farther upstream, craft up to 36 feet can anchor past #6 upstream of the creek's first sharp turn to starboard.

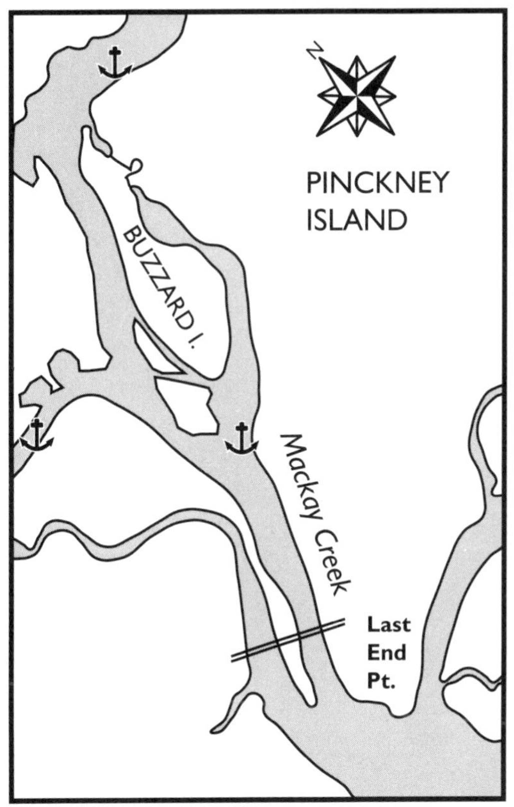

Back on the main body of Mackay Creek, cruising captains can confidently continue upstream, with several charted markers showing the way. South and southwest of unlighted daybeacon #8, the creek borders high ground on Pinckney Island. This spot is a good anchorage for almost any size of craft if the winds stay under 20 knots.

Mackay Creek eventually enters the southeastern reaches of Chechessee River. This entrance is currently marked by one flashing daybeacon and features minimum depths of 6 feet. Take care if you choose to use this passage. Proceed slowly and keep a sharp watch on the sounder.

MACKAY CREEK NAVIGATION

To enter the southern reaches of Mackay Creek, continue cruising on the ICW until you are at least 400 yards south of unlighted daybeacon #27, then turn toward the western banks and cruise until the centerline of Mackay Creek's southern entrance comes abeam to the north. Only then should you turn to the north and enter the creek. Study chart 11507 for a moment and you will see how these maneuvers will help you avoid the long shoal building south from Last End Point.

Begin favoring the eastern banks as you approach the 25-foot fixed bridge. Chart 11507 clearly and correctly shows a long, thin finger of marsh and shoals bisecting the river to the west.

Boaters should also know that the channel shown on 11507 bordering the westerly shoreline has now largely disappeared and should be avoided completely.

Remember that the power line with 43 feet of clearance lies just northeast of the 25-foot fixed bridge. Boaters bound to the southwest should take this critical measurement into account.

Watch to the east as you begin to approach Buzzard Island. You will quickly spot the large offshoot of deep water that makes off to the northeast. If you choose to anchor here, enter the stream on its mid-width, but be sure to stop well before coming abeam of Buzzard Island's southern tip.

Farther upstream on Mackay Creek, you will spy the marked but unnamed creek leading to the private country-club dock to the west. To enter, cruise between unlighted daybeacons #1 and #2. Continue on the middle, passing unlighted daybeacons #4, #6, and #8 to starboard. Drop the hook anywhere you choose, but be sure to leave plenty of room for passing vessels.

Between the unnamed creek and Port Royal Sound, Mackay Creek is marked by a series of helpful aids to navigation. Pass unlighted daybeacon #9 to its fairly immediate northwestern side. Don't drift too far to the northwest here. As chart 11507 notes, there is a large patch of shallow water along the northwestern and northern banks. Follow the creek as it bends to the east and pass unlighted daybeacon #8 to its southern side.

Be on guard against the charted shoal west of unlighted daybeacon #6. Be sure to pass #6 to its easterly side.

Northeast of unlighted daybeacon #5, Mackay Creek begins its run into the southeastern reaches of Chechessee River and Port Royal Sound. Slow down as you approach the entranceway. Look northeast and you will spy flashing daybeacon #1. Set course from the creek's mouth to come abeam of #1 to its fairly immediate northwestern side. Go slowly and watch the sounder. Don't attempt this passage if your boat draws more than 5 feet.

MAY RIVER

"Picturesqueness and variety, which characterize the lower coast, reach perfection . . . on the River May, lauded by all travelers from Ribault [*sic*] down." James Henry Rice, Jr., wrote those words in the 1920s, but they are as true today as they were then. This writer was impressed by May River as a microcosm of the many good features of coastal South Carolina. The beautiful shores are undeveloped except for two picturesque communities. Both Brighton Beach and Bluffton look out over the river and provide a pleasant break in the grassy shores. Bluffton is perched atop high earthen banks and is particularly impressive. There are no facilities for boaters at either village.

Viewed in the warm light of a fall afternoon, May River resembles the kind of "artist's rendition" of a lovely stream often seen in boating magazines but seldom discovered in reality. Strangely, few cruising boaters take advantage of the May's charms. This writer urges you to join the ranks of those fortunate few who have made this extraordinary river's acquaintance.

May River is well marked and reasonably easy to navigate. Several unlighted but charted daybeacons lead visiting cruisers to the shores of Bluffton. Past this point, depths become too uncertain for large craft.

The river boasts excellent anchorage abeam of Bluffton's high banks, but otherwise the stream's side creeks are not appropriate for most cruising vessels. Bass Creek, northwest of unlighted daybeacon #4, is surrounded by unmarked shoals, as is Bull Creek, southwest of unlighted daybeacon #5. Neither is particularly recommended for those without local knowledge.

Bluffton

Bluffton was settled before 1800 as a summer retreat for the rich planters of the day. Many famous families built residences here, and the old names read like a who's who of coastal South Carolina history. James Henry Rice, Jr., once described Bluffton as "retaining enough flavor of the old days to let one know he is within the pale, surrounded by the purple-born, who through storm and stress, war and misfortune, have clung tenaciously to their birthright."

In *Tales of Beaufort*, Nell S. Graydon relates a description of life in Bluffton before the Civil War, as told by a member of the famous Hayward family: "In the days before the war when splendor was in its glory and hoop skirts and tall silk hats held sway, the village was a place of wealth. . . . Families on surrounding plantations lived in palatial homes. . . . Life and gaiety, oldtime formalities and customs ran high. 'Marsuh' and 'Missus' sat in dignity while young sideburn 'Masters' courted young 'Missuses' in bonnets and curls. Tightwaisted, hoopskirted figures danced and flirted in innocence and mirth."

House at Bluffton, May River

As the dark days of the Civil War approached, Bluffton strongly favored secession. Some historians claim that the first secession movement in the state was organized here. A fiery speech supporting states' rights was delivered in the village by Dr. Daniel Hamilton under an old oak tree that is even today known as "the Secession Oak." The movement was carried forward by Barnwell Rhett of Beaufort, who had a summer home in Bluffton. In 1844, Rhett launched the "Bluffton Movement for a State Convention." According to Graydon, his message was direct and left no room for wavering: "I proclaim to you, if you value your rights, you must resist and submit not."

Unfortunately, many of Bluffton's historic buildings are not visible from the water. An exception is the Church of the Cross. This structure dates to 1854 and can be seen through the trees atop the bluffs overlooking May River.

MAY RIVER NAVIGATION

Pass well to the south of unlighted daybeacon #2, which marks the easterly mouth of May River. Shoal water is building south near this aid. Do not approach #2 closely.

Set course to come abeam of and pass unlighted daybeacon #4 by some 100 yards to its southerly side. Watch to be sure that leeway does not ease you to the north after passing #4. As shown on charts 11516 and 11507, there is shallow water north of the marker.

Continue upstream by setting a new course to come abeam of unlighted daybeacon #5 to its northerly side. A huge patch of shallow water is located south of #5 on the river's mid-width. On the water, it's hard to believe that 3-foot depths can be found on the centerline of such a broad river.

Follow the river as it makes a slow turn to the southwest. Favor the northerly shores slightly as you pass Brighton Beach. Pass unlighted daybeacon #6 to its southerly side and come abeam of unlighted daybeacon #8 to its southeasterly quarter.

South of #8, the marked channel follows a branch of May River that cuts first to the west and then back to the north, eventually leading to Bluffton. After passing #8, watch the western banks for the cut-through. Pass unlighted daybeacon #10 to your starboard side. Stick to the mid-width and point to pass unlighted daybeacons #11 and #13 to your port side.

Past #11, May River follows a long loop to the west. The high cliffs of Bluffton line the eastern shores along this stretch of the stream. From here until the river forks, you can anchor abeam of the village with good protection. Do not attempt to cruise beyond the forks located just past Bluffton. Depths are highly uncertain.

ICW TO SAVANNAH RIVER

The waters south of Calibogue Sound to Savannah River and the Georgia line are quite different from those surrounding Hilton Head Island. Gone are the marinas and condo projects, with one exception. Pleasure-craft skippers suddenly finds themselves in a wild, mostly uninhabited region, though more development can be seen from the water than was the case only a few years ago. Much of the Waterway passes through vast saltwater marshes and is not particularly pleasing to the eye.

Portions of the Cooper, New, and Wright Rivers, joined by man-made cuts, make up this section of the ICW. Other parts of these streams are abandoned by the Waterway. These waters are mostly deep and offer many anchorage possibilities. Unfortunately, the prevailing marsh banks do not give enough protection for stormy weather.

Those boaters who thrive on cruising waters off the beaten path but who don't wish to stray far from the ICW or contend with too many navigational difficulties may enjoy this region. Others will find this stretch of the Waterway quite dull and will be glad to reach the wide waters of Savannah River.

Haig Point Lighthouse

The old lighthouse at Haig Point has been privately restored and is visible through the trees on the northeastern tip of Daufuskie Island southwest of flashing daybeacon #32. The light was built in 1875 to mark the passage from Calibogue Sound to Savannah River. It was used as a range marker until 1936.

Cooper River

Cooper River breaks off from Calibogue Sound at flashing daybeacon #32. The river is mostly free of shoals and is easily navigated. The single

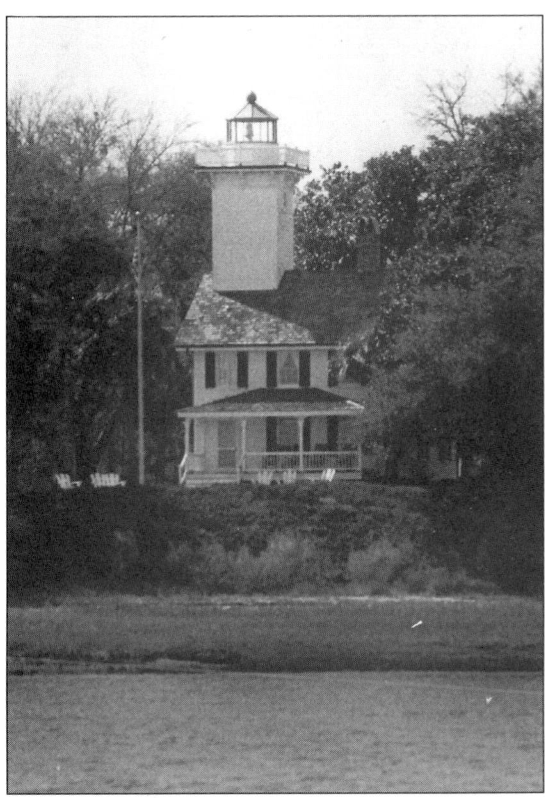

Haig Point Lighthouse, Daufuskie Island

shallow spot is marked by unlighted daybeacon #36. Not far into the river's interior, Bull Creek will come abeam to the north.

Bull Creek

Bull Creek knifes into the Cooper's northern banks immediately east of flashing daybeacon #34. This stream is one of the best anchorages between Calibogue Sound and Savannah River. The creek maintains minimum depths of 5 feet, with most soundings showing much more water. The lower reaches are bordered by marsh but provide enough swinging room for almost any size of pleasure craft. Farther upstream, the creek flows through a sharp turn to the west. The high banks of Bull Island line the stream's northern banks in the body of this turn. Boats up to 38 feet can anchor here with excellent protection. Just be sure to avoid the charted shallows along the northern portion of the bend. Set your hook so as to swing well away from this obstruction.

Farther upstream, there are unmarked shoals to contend with, and a power line with 46 feet of vertical clearance spans the stream. Only the wild-eyed explorers among us should attempt to cruise this portion of Bull Creek. Captains with boats drawing less than 5 feet might choose to make the attempt, but they should proceed cautiously and keep an eagle eye on the sounder.

Daufuskie Island

For much of its length, the ICW section of Cooper and New Rivers borders Daufuskie Island to the southeast. Until a few years ago, this body of land was one of the few remaining South Carolina Sea Islands that had not been developed as a resort. All that is changed now. A new complex of homes, condos, tennis courts, golf course, and other amenities has gone fitfully forward during the last seven years. Sadly, some of the old-time residents have been displaced. The quaint character of this long-undeveloped island is now fading all too rapidly into the past.

Daufuskie is an Indian word meaning "the place of blood." The island has lived up to this sinister title throughout its history. Before the Revolution, Daufuskie was a kind of no man's land between the English settlers to the north and hostile Indians to the south. There were frequent small battles between the Indians and the colonial militia on the island.

As the Indian threat lessened, English colonists began building plantations on Daufuskie

Island. For some unexplained reason, these settlers took a decidedly Loyalist point of view during the Revolution. This was in sharp contrast to the patriot stance of those living on neighboring Hilton Head. Daufuskie's ominous name was again confirmed by the many skirmishes that took place between these two groups during the war.

Following the Civil War, Daufuskie Island was virtually abandoned. Its only inhabitants were freed blacks. Until the coming of the Haig Point Plantation development, the island's population numbered only about 100 souls. The popular Southern writer Pat Conroy wrote a fascinating book, *The Water Is Wide*, about teaching black children on Daufuskie. The volume is highly recommended by this writer.

Melrose Landing Marina

One last facility is now available to cruising boaters between Cooper River and Georgia waters. Melrose Landing Marina sits hard by the southeastern shores of the ICW on Daufuskie Island opposite unlighted daybeacon #36.

This small- to medium-sized operation offers transient dockage at one long floating-face pier. Depths alongside are an impressive 15-plus feet. Transients are accepted at berths featuring water and 50-amp power connections. Y-adapters are available for those needing 30-amp hookups. A small ship's store is on the marina grounds, and there is a restaurant next door. Gasoline and diesel fuel are available.

Melrose Landing Marina
(803) 842-9998

Approach depth: 15+ feet
Dockside depth: 15+ feet
Accepts transients: yes
Floating wooden piers: yes
Dockside power connections: 50 amps (Y-adapters provided)
Dockside water connections: yes
Gasoline: yes
Diesel fuel: yes
Ship's store: yes
Restaurant: nearby

Upper Cooper River

The ICW abandons Cooper River and runs southwest on Ramshorn Creek at flashing daybeacon #37. The upriver section of the Cooper holds minimum 6-foot depths, with only one or two easily avoided shoals. Anchorage possibilities abound. You need only select a spot to your liking that is sheltered from the prevailing winds, then drop the hook for a peaceful evening. Swinging room is sufficient on most stretches of the river for boats up to 40 feet.

As the river takes a sharp turn to the north-

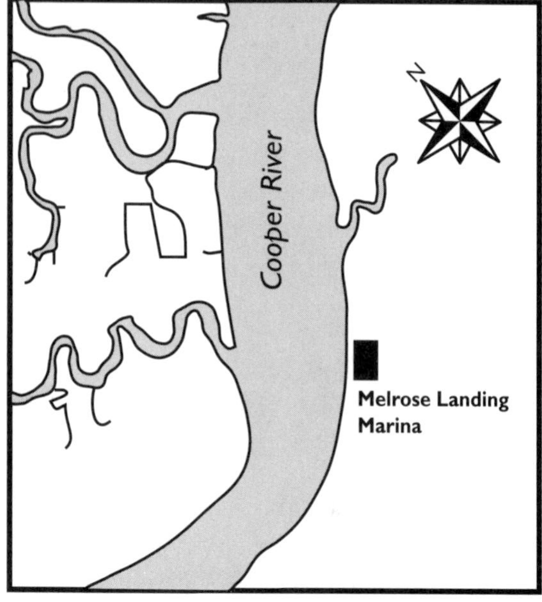

west, several power lines with 55 feet of vertical clearance cross the water. High ground abuts the river's northeastern shore immediately west of the lines. This is one of the most sheltered anchorages on the upper Cooper River for craft that can clear the power lines. Boats up to 45 feet can anchor here with confidence.

Past the power lines, two small creeks break off from the main body of Cooper River, as shown on chart 11507. Both streams are narrow and suffer from unmarked shallows. This writer suggests that you bypass both creeks.

Eventually, the Cooper leads into the deep waters of New River. It is a simple matter to follow the New back to the ICW.

New River

The Waterway enters the waters of New River from the southwestern reaches of Ramshorn Creek at flashing daybeacon #39. This is a tricky stretch of the ICW, particularly for northbound boaters. Be sure to read the navigational section on Ramshorn Creek below.

Northwest of the ICW's exodus from Ramshorn Creek, the upper section of New River offers overnight anchorage possibilities. Minimum depths are 6 feet, with most of the stream exhibiting much deeper soundings. Both shores are mostly marsh grass and provide only minimal protection. However, in winds under 15 knots, captains with boats up to 45 feet can drop anchor almost anywhere that strikes their fancy between the Ramshorn Creek intersection and the juncture with Cooper River. Farther upstream, unmarked shoals litter the river. Cruising boaters are advised to cease their explorations at the hairpin turn to the southwest just upstream of the Cooper River junction.

The ICW leaves New River at flashing daybeacon #42 and follows Walls Cut west to Wright River. The easterly reaches of New River remain deep as far as Bloody Point. This section of the river is open and provides very little shelter. While there is plenty of swinging room for boats of almost any size, this writer advises you to choose the more sheltered upriver section for an overnight stop.

Mungen Creek

For those who simply must cruise where no one has gone before, and who pilot craft under 35 feet that draw less than 4 feet, some consideration might be given to anchoring on the southern reaches of Mungen Creek north of

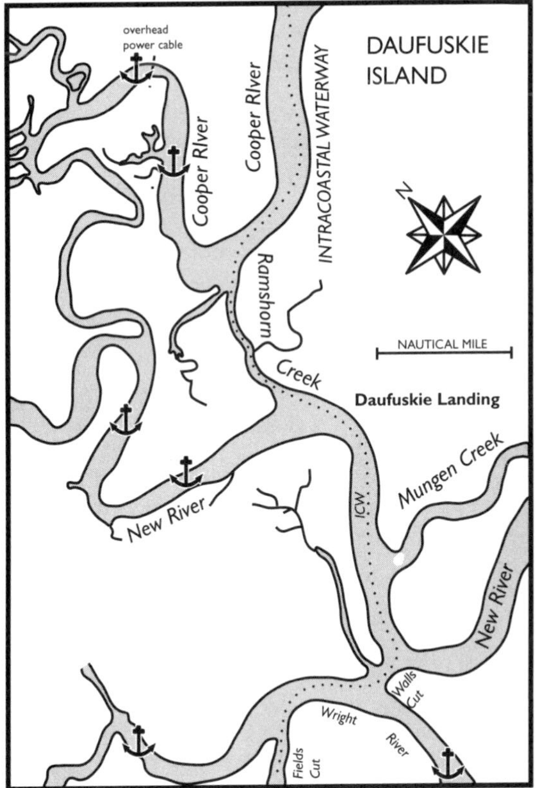

Bloody Point. This stream is entered from the lower reaches of New River, abandoned by the ICW, southeast of the ICW's flashing daybeacon #42.

The southerly portion of Mungen Creek is well sheltered by the high ground of Daufuskie Island to the north, but successful navigation of the creek is a very tricky business. If you choose to enter, be sure to read the navigational information presented later in this chapter before making your attempt. By all accounts, you should not cruise past the creek's first sharp turn to the west. In spite of soundings shown on chart 11512, depths drop off to 3 and 4 feet past this point.

Bloody Point

Bloody Point, located just below the intersection of New River and Mungen Creek, derives its name from a battle fought nearby during the early days of English colonization. In those uncertain times, Indians from Georgia and Florida often conducted raids on the settlers in Beaufort. They would carry off all they could, then hide on Daufuskie Island to enjoy the spoils.

On one occasion, an Indian raid so angered the white settlers that the colonial militia set out in hot pursuit of the attackers. The Indians had retreated to the southern point of Daufuskie. Supposing themselves to be safe, they lit cooking fires and fell to enjoying their plunder.

Meanwhile, the militia had learned of the raiders' position from friendly Indians. Landing on the northwestern portion of the island, the whites marched overland and surrounded the unsuspecting Indians. A hail of musket balls was the first evidence the Indians had of the militia's arrival. The raiders were cut off from escape and were slaughtered to a man. Ever since, the island's southern extreme has been known as Bloody Point.

Wright River

The ICW follows Wright River for only a brief distance before entering Fields Cut and hurrying southwest to Savannah River and the Georgia state line. Abandoned by the Waterway, the lower reaches of the Wright south of unlighted daybeacon #43 carry minimum depths of 7 feet for some distance downstream and boast enough swinging room for boats up to 45 feet. The stream is bordered entirely by salt marsh. Winds over 10 knots can give rise to a most unpleasant chop, and anchorage is recommended only in light airs. Eventually, depths drop off as the stream approaches a ruined bridge. Be sure to halt your cruise well before reaching this old wreck.

West of unlighted nun buoy #44B, the upper portion of the Wright holds minimum depths of 10 feet far upriver until it bends sharply westward to the east of charted Turnbridge Lodge. Though both shores are marsh and give questionable protection, there is enough swinging room for boats up to 45 feet. However, you must cruise through some 5- to 7-foot depths near #44B to gain access to the deeper portion of the river. In light of these restrictions, the river's upper reaches are recommended only for craft that draw less than 5 feet.

ICW TO SAVANNAH RIVER NAVIGATION

There are a few shoal-prone areas on the ICW between Cooper and Savannah Rivers, but most of the route is easily traveled. Similarly, most sidewaters throughout this area are deep and free of obstructions. Of course, there are always exceptions, and waters calling for special caution are discussed below.

Cooper River Pass well to the southwest of flashing daybeacon #32 and enter Cooper River on its mid-width. Look to the southwest as you pass #32 and you may be able to see the Haig Point Lighthouse on the northeastern tip of Daufuskie Island.

Begin favoring the northern and northwestern shores slightly as you approach flashing daybeacon #34. As shown on chart 11507, there is a small shoal on the southeastern shore, but the channel is quite broad here, and you need not have much concern. At #34, Bull Creek breaks off to the north.

Bull Creek Do not approach flashing daybeacon #34 when entering Bull Creek. Pass this aid well to its eastern side and enter the mid-width of the creek. As you cruise through the stream's first turn to the west, begin favoring the southern banks slightly.

A short distance beyond this turn, the creek follows another loop, this time to the northeast. You may be surprised to note a 60-foot reading on your sounder in one spot while traversing the turn.

Begin heavily favoring the southeastern shore as soon as you come out of the northeastern bend. As shown on chart 11507, there is a large shoal abutting the northwestern shore.

Melrose Landing Marina, Daufuskie Island

Beyond this obstruction, the creek soon takes a sharp jog to the east. Visiting cruisers are advised to discontinue their upstream journey at this point.

On the ICW From flashing daybeacon #34, continue on the mid-width of Cooper River until coming abeam of flashing daybeacon #35 to its northwestern side. Begin favoring the southeastern banks, passing unlighted daybeacon #36 to its southeastern side. As shown on chart 11507, there is shallow water west and north of #36. At flashing daybeacon #37, the Waterway leaves Cooper River and enters Ramshorn Creek.

Upper Cooper River With a few exceptions, the upper reaches of Cooper River, abandoned by the ICW, can be easily traversed all the way to the intersection with the upper New River by holding to the mid-width. The first exception comes just short of where the river, bending northwestward, is crossed by overhead power cables. Chart 11507 correctly notes a small shoal on the northwestern (port-side) shore just before this bend. Favor the southeastern banks until you round the turn and pass under the cables. Vertical clearance is set at 55 feet.

After leaving the cables behind, favor the

southern and southwestern banks until the first small sidewater comes abeam to the north. Cruise back to the mid-width and hold scrupulously to the middle through the river's various twists and turns until you eventually intersect the upper reaches of New River.

On the ICW The southwestern mouth of Ramshorn Creek is partially obstructed by a shoal and calls for great caution. Pass flashing daybeacon #39 to its immediate western quarter and hold course into the deepwater section of New River. Don't let leeway ease you to the west. The shoal on the creek's southwestern point is building outward. Watch your sounder! If depths start to rise, try giving way to the east.

The Waterway follows the lower portion of New River southwest to Walls Cut. The upper reaches of the river are also accessible to cruisers.

Upper New River Cruising the upper section of New River as far as its intersection with the upper Cooper River is an elementary matter of holding to the centerline. Be sure to stop immediately after rounding the next sharp turn to the southwest upstream from the junction. Unmarked shoals pepper New River past this point, and the stream soon leaves the chart.

On the ICW Favor the southeastern shore when rounding the turn at Daufuskie Lodge. A small shoal has built out from the opposite banks and encroached on flashing daybeacon #40. Don't approach this aid closely.

At flashing daybeacon #42, the Waterway follows Walls Cut for a short distance into Wright River. This passage is subject to continual shoaling, and depths often rise above ICW specifications between maintenance dredgings. Extensive soundings in 1995 found some low-tide depths of a mere 8 feet directly in the Waterway channel.

Boaters should also be on guard against swift tidal currents while cruising through Walls Cut. Take your time and keep a firm hand on the helm.

The southeastern section of New River, abandoned by the Waterway, offers cruising possibilities of its own for hardy explorers.

Southeastern New River The wide southeastern section of New River holds good depths on its mid-width as far as Bloody Point. Don't even think about proceeding farther. Depths soon fall off to less than 1 foot of water.

Those daring souls who attempt to enter the southern reaches of Mungen Creek must proceed with the greatest caution. To hold best depths, continue on the centerline of New River until the southeastern third of Mungen Creek's southern mouth comes abeam. Here, you may turn north into the creek, favoring the starboard banks. Don't approach this shoreline too closely either. Be sure to discontinue your exploration soon after the creek takes its first turn to the west. In spite of soundings shown on chart 11512, depths soon deteriorate.

Lower Wright River South of unlighted daybeacon #43, the lower reaches of Wright River can be cruised to within 1 nautical mile of the ruined bridge guarding the river's seaward mouth. Simply hold to the **mid-line** and don't go too far.

On the ICW The Waterway follows Wright River briefly before cutting southwest on Fields Cut. The entrance to this man-made canal has chronic shoaling problems and calls for caution. Come abeam of flashing daybeacon #45 to its fairly immediate northerly side and then curl slowly around to the southwest, pointing to pass unlighted nun buoy #44B to its immediate southeasterly side. The northeasterly entrance to Fields Cut will then be obvious dead ahead.

Upper Wright River To enter the western section of Wright River, abandoned by the Waterway, proceed on course as if you were entering Fields Cut until nun buoy #44B comes abeam. Cruise another 35 yards or so on the same course, then cut 90 degrees to the west and pass about halfway between #44B and the southern shoreline. Don't approach the southern banks too closely. A charted shoal seems to be building out from this shore. Beyond these shallows, favor the southern banks slightly until you approach the stream's first slow turn to the north. Cruise back to the middle as you enter the bend. Good depths can be held as far as the river's split east of Turnbridge Lodge by sticking to the mid-width. Be sure to give all points a wide berth.

On to Georgia Flashing daybeacon #48 marks the ICW's entrance into the wide Savannah River and the waters of Georgia. Watch for swift currents and shoaling problems at the cut's mouth. Now, the coastline of the "Golden Isles" and more superb cruising grounds lie before you.

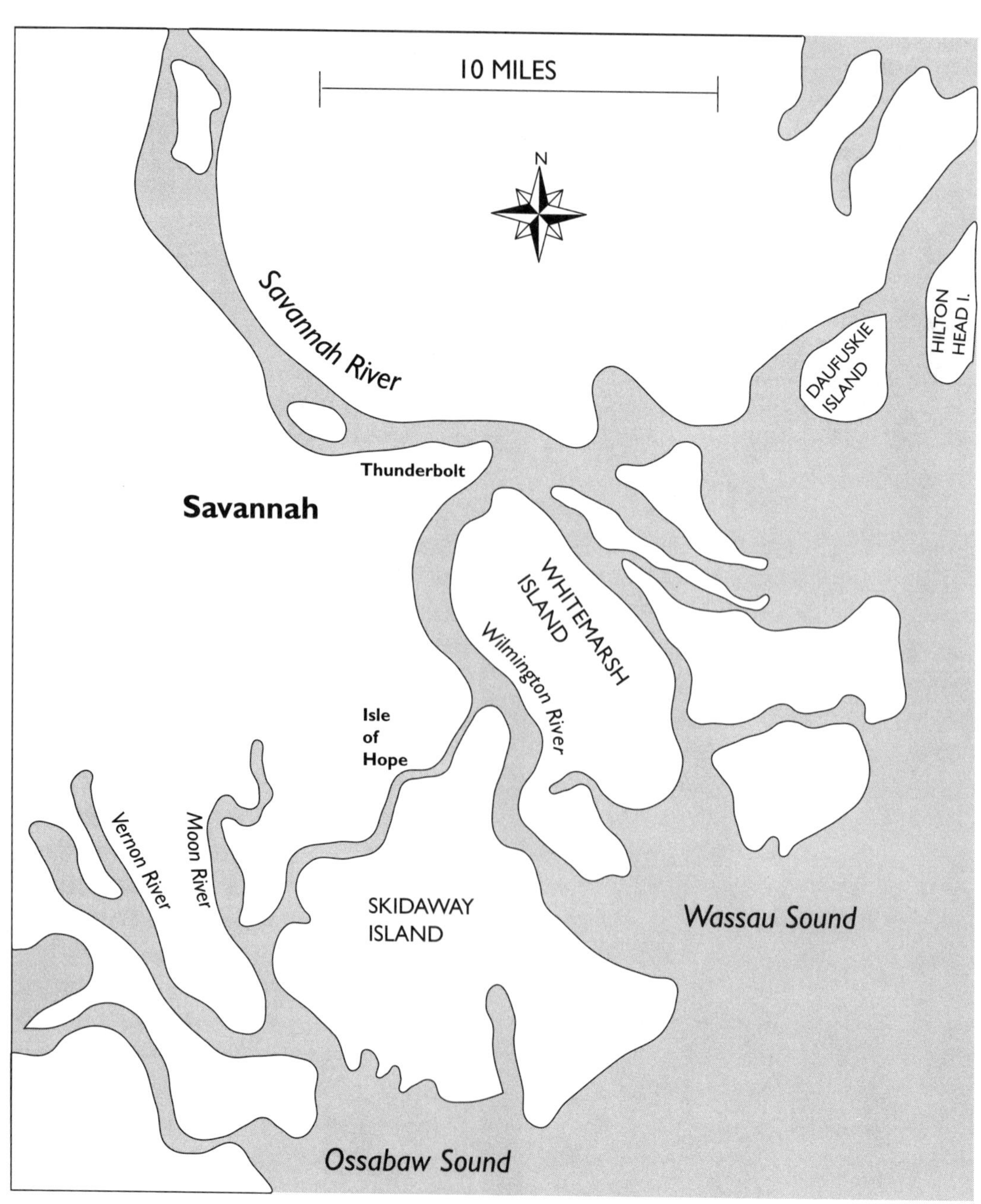

10 MILES
N
Savannah River
DAUFUSKIE ISLAND
HILTON HEAD I.
Thunderbolt
Savannah
WHITEMARSH ISLAND
Wilmington River
Isle of Hope
Vernon River
Moon River
SKIDAWAY ISLAND
Wassau Sound
Ossabaw Sound

Savannah River to Vernon River

A league and a league of marsh-grass, waist-high, broad
in the blade,
Green, and all of a height, and unflecked with a light or
a shade,
Stretch leisurely off, in a pleasant plain,
To the terminal blue of the main.
Oh, what is abroad in the marsh and the terminal sea?
Somehow my soul seems suddenly free
From the weighing fate and the sad discussion of sin,
By the length and the breadth and the sweep of the
marshes of Glynn.

The South Carolina Low Country most certainly had its James Henry Rice, Jr., and George C. Rogers, but the Georgia coastline can also boast many an inspired writer who attempted to portray some of the region's great natural beauty with the written word.

The famous poem "The Marshes of Glynn," by Sidney Lanier, quoted partially above, was inspired by the seemingly timeless and often interminable marsh grass set about the southeastern Georgia community of Brunswick. This account is arguably the most enthralling word-portrait of that very special beauty and nature that belongs uniquely to coastal Georgia.

Charts

Cruising skippers will need two or possibly three NOAA charts to cruise the waters of northeastern Georgia:

11507 is the principal ICW chart that carries boaters across Savannah River and south past Thunderbolt and Isle of Hope to Vernon River

11512 is an important large-format chart that details Savannah River's inlet, the passage upstream to the city of Savannah, and several sidewaters between Thunderbolt and Vernon River

11514 details Savannah River far inland past the confines of this guide; you may not require this chart unless you plan to cruise past Savannah upstream toward Augusta

If you are one of those cruisers who lives for the opportunity to travel far from the most remote vestige of civilization, then Georgia's coastline may well hold the key to your search. Seldom has this writer ever witnessed waters with such a multitude of anchorages set amidst miles and miles of undeveloped marsh and woodlands. In places, you may find yourself wondering just how far from a developed community you really are, as this writer and his mate did the day we ran out of fuel while researching a remote river. In fair weather, with the canopy of stars wheeling over your cockpit, it is all too easy to decide that dropping the hook in such a place is really what cruising is all about. Others may disagree, but there is simply no denying the charms of this seemingly far-off land and its waters.

On the other hand, if you are a boater who generally spends his nights docked securely at a marina with all the amenities, then the Georgia story may be different for you. To be sure, the state boasts excellent marina facilities, particularly around Savannah and St. Simons Island. In between, however, are vast all-natural tracts that have probably changed very little since Native Americans rowed their canoes past these same shores.

In many ways, the geography of the South Carolina and Georgia coastlines is very similar. Both coasts feature mostly deep waters with a multitude of streams set behind a chain of mostly undeveloped barrier islands. The waters of both coasts are very tidal, with swift currents and tidal ranges sometimes approaching 8 feet. This rapid water movement tends to keep the bottoms of even small creeks scoured out and deep, but there are certainly exceptions.

Conversely, you could roll Winyah Bay, Charleston Harbor, and St. Helena and Calibogue Sounds all into one and barely begin to equal Georgia's mammoth sounds and open rivers. The ICW traverses all these sounds to a greater or lesser extent. To say the least, these little-protected passages can make for some dusty crossings when the wind has its dander up. Small cruising craft in particular must plan their cruise among the Golden Isles with a ready and certain ear toward the latest NOAA weather forecast.

There is one good point about the large Georgia sounds that is sometimes overlooked. Several of these bodies of water lead to reliable inlets that can readily serve cruisers putting out to sea or sailors making a run for inland waters. The various seaward passages are mostly deep and well marked, though again boaters must be on guard for the occasional exception.

As alluded to above, most of the banks lining coastal Georgia's myriad streams consist of undeveloped marsh, just like the South Carolina Low Country. There is even more of the same here, and you can assume these shoreside conditions to be in place unless stated otherwise. Of course, acres upon acres of marsh have a charm of their own—witness their inspiration to Sidney Lanier in the lines that opened this chapter. It's just that after so long, one begins to yearn for tall trees and wooded banks. Keep the faith, as we will most certainly find some of that sort of shoreline in our travels.

Of course, marshy shores, as was discussed at length during this guide's review of the Low Country, do not give particularly good protection for overnight anchorage during heavy weather. Unfortunately, when it comes to the Georgia coastline, this condition is clearly a way of life.

There are exceptions to this marshy shoreline for boaters seeking sheltered anchorage. Any number of streams lead to pockets of higher, well-wooded ground that can serve as a ready windbreak. Of course, you must select these havens carefully, based on the current and predicted wind direction. Seldom will you find a stream on which all the shores are blessed with high-ground protection.

The coast of Georgia sits waiting to greet the cruising boater in a state little different from the far-removed times when James Oglethorpe first set foot on the future site of Savannah. Just as we launched our voyage of the Low Country with James Henry Rice Jr.'s ,inspirational description of cruising down a South Carolina river, let us pause to ponder William Barton's immortal sketch of boating down Georgia's Altamaha River:

"How gently flow thy peaceful floods. O Altamaha! How sublimely rise to view, on thy elevated shores, yon Magnolian groves from whose tops the surrounding expanse is perfumed. . . .

"The air was filled with the loud and shrill whopping of the wary sharp-sighted crane. Behold on yon decayed, defoliated Cypress tree, the solitary wood-pelican, dejectedly perched upon its utmost elevated spire. . . .

"Thus secure and tranquil, and meditating on the marvelous scenes of primitive natures, as yet unmodified by the hand of man, I gently descended the stream, on whose polished surface were depicted the mutable shadows from its pensile banks; whilst myriads of finny inhabitants sported in its pellucid floods."

SAVANNAH RIVER

Many boaters entering Savannah River from Fields Cut simply cruise upstream for a short distance and then exit to the southwest on Elba Island Cut. Little do they realize what an exciting opportunity awaits them after a short cruise up Savannah River to the like-named city. Charleston alone in the southeastern United States can lay claim to as rich and varied a past as the city founded by James Oglethorpe. From the richly green city squares to dreamlike homes and buildings to a multitude of fine restaurants and memorable inns, Savannah is a city that today greatly depends on tourism as a mainstay of its economy. Visitors are well cared for and shown a profusion of courtesy. This writer highly suggests that you heed the siren call of this unique city and experience its charms for yourself.

Of course, it should be noted that pleasure-craft dockage facilities on the heavily commercialized

Savannah waterfront are, to say the least, minimal. The city has constructed a river-walk park along a good portion of the river's passage, but these piers are really not appropriate for cruising boats. After seeing them, this writer is sure you will agree that the high seawall and naked concrete pilings are not the sort of place to rest from your travels.

Fortunately, the large downtown Hyatt Regency Hotel offers a single, long floating pier at which visiting cruisers are welcome. This facility is sometimes occupied by tour boats, so advance arrangements are almost a necessity.

Often, boaters dock at one of the many marinas in nearby Thunderbolt (reviewed in the next section of this chapter) and then drive into Savannah via a rental car or taxi. This is a viable alternative and one you may want to seriously consider. For taxi and car-rental service in Savannah, contact Airport Taxi (912-965-0213), Savannah Cab (912-236-9455), U-Save Rental Car (912-925-6444), or Savannah Car and Rentals (912-233-6554).

However you find your way to it, the city of Savannah is an absolute *must-see* stop on your cruise down the Georgia coastline. Clearly, those who pass by this timeless and historic community with scarcely a thought are forgoing the very best that these lands and waters have to offer.

It should also be noted that the shipping port supported by Savannah is one of the most active in America. Savannah River is the most commercially important stream in the state of Georgia. Hundreds of oceangoing cargo ships make their way up and down the river every year. You may very well spy one of these waterborne metal giants during your cruise. Feel free to have a good look, but remember that these large vessels have

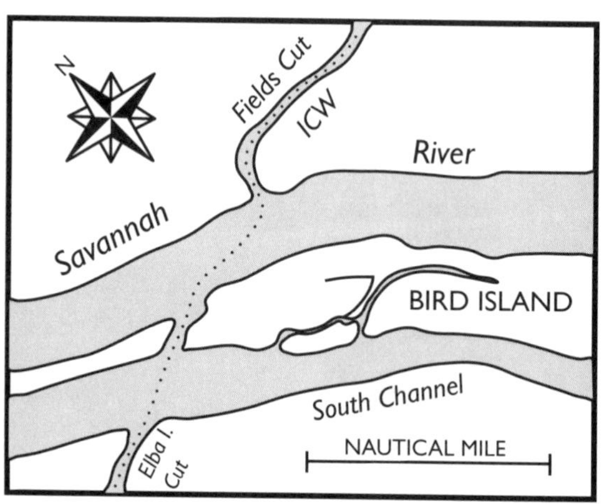

limited maneuverability and that it's up to pleasure-craft skippers to keep clear, regardless of the "rules of the road."

Savannah River to the Sea

Boaters leaving Fields Cut have three alternatives. While cruisers may turn northwest to Savannah or, more likely, follow the Waterway to the southwest, those seeking a ready passage to the open sea can cut southeast and follow an unusually well-outlined track to the briny blue. This passage is used daily by the large ships discussed above, and as you would imagine, it is well maintained and lit up with dozens of aids to navigation. The deep channel extends well out to sea.

Fort Pulaski

South of flashing buoy #25, boaters cruising seaward on Savannah River will sight the magnificent restored masonry walls of Fort Pulaski on the shores of Cockspur Island. This venerable military post was named for Polish general Casimir Pulaski, who fought in the Continental

Army under George Washington. The gallant general was fatally wounded in a combined American-French attack on the British forces entrenched in Savannah during the Revolutionary War.

The fort was built between 1829 and 1844 with a view to military control of the vital water route to the city of Savannah. It was constructed of massive brick walls with a wide drawbridge. The entire fort was surrounded by a deep moat. None other than the young Robert E. Lee, newly graduated from West Point, participated in the fort's design and engineering.

The fort's walls weigh many tons, and the most inventive engineering was required to support such a weight atop the mucky coastal soil. As Beth Lattimore Reiter and Van Jones Martin commented in their wonderful book, *Coastal Georgia*, the fort "literally floats on the mud on massive timber pilings."

Fort Pulaski was considered the state of the art in mid-nineteenth-century military fortifications. When the Civil War broke out with the assault on Fort Sumter in Charleston Harbor, Southern militia seized Fort Pulaski, thinking it to be an impregnable defensive position.

The date of April 11, 1862, marked a watershed event in military history. On that date, a Union battery on nearby Tybee Island opened fire on Fort Pulaski with new rifled-barrel cannon. This was the first time guns of such design were used in warfare. The deadly accuracy of the ordnance reduced a portion of the fort's walls to red dust after a 30-hour bombardment. The fortifications were quickly surrendered by the Confederate forces.

With the fall of Fort Pulaski, the days of coastal masonry forts were at an end, but as will be discussed later, Southern forces soon found an inventive approach to forestall the Northern invaders.

Now a national monument, Fort Pulaski is open to the public from 8:30 A.M. to 5:30 P.M. daily, with hours extended to 6:45 P.M. during the summer months. The fort is closed Christmas and New Year's Day. There is no access from the water. You will need a rental car to visit this attraction.

Cockspur Island Lighthouse

Look well south of the Savannah River channel as you are cruising between flashing buoys #25 and #21. You may be able to catch a glimpse of the old Cockspur Island Lighthouse at the eastern end of Cockspur Island. Originally lit in 1848, the light was extinguished by Southern forces during the War Between the States. Although it was in the direct path of fire between Fort Pulaski and Union batteries on Tybee Island, the lighthouse somehow survived. It was relit after the war and continued in operation until 1949.

Restored in 1978 by the National Park Service, the lighthouse is now open to the public. It operates on the same schedule as the nearby Fort Pulaski National Monument.

A strange and poignant story is told about Cockspur Island Lighthouse by old-time citizens of Savannah. In 1887, Florence Martus, the sister of the Cockspur light's keeper, chanced to meet a sailor from a ship docked in nearby Savannah. The budding romance continued whenever the sailor's ship was in port. The love affair eventually led to a proposal of marriage. Florence's sailor promised to give up the seafaring life and settle down after one last sail abroad.

As the sailor's ship cruised gaily out of Savannah River, so the legend tells us, Florence waved after it from the lighthouse with a white handkerchief. The sailor was lost at sea, never to return again. Nursing a broken heart, Florence soon developed the novel custom of waving at every passing ship with a white handkerchief in memory of her lost love. She continued this practice for more than 50 years. The sailors who regularly called on Savannah came to admire the woman, and it is said that many brought her presents from all over the world.

This is one of those coastal legends that is more fact than fiction. There are retired seamen living in Savannah to this very day who will tell you of seeing a strange apparition waving desperately with her white handkerchief from atop the old lighthouse.

Tybee Island

Tybee Island guards the southern flank of Savannah River's outlet to the open sea. This isle offers the only readily accessible beachfront property north of St. Simons Island.

The original township of Tybee was founded by 1733 by James Oglethorpe. The third lighthouse built in America rose over the island's shores to light the entrance to Savannah River.

It is whispered that honest mariners weren't the only ones to take advantage of this early aid to navigation. The infamous pirate Blackbeard, who is better known on this writer's native North Carolina coast, is rumored to have headquartered his forces on Tybee Island for a time. Persistent legends speak of a treasure hidden under the shifting sands, but no loot has ever been unearthed in modern times.

In 1779, a mammoth French fleet under Count d'Estaing dropped anchor off Tybee Island preparatory to the allied attack on the English forces entrenched in nearby Savannah. The assault failed, and the proud fleet limped dejectedly away.

Fort Screven guards the northern shores of Tybee Island and overlooks the southern flank of Savannah River's inlet. This military fortification dates back to 1808 and was in continuous use until 1945. The fort was then purchased by the city of Tybee. Today, visitors can tour the Tybee Museum and the lighthouse, both of which are contained within the walls of the one-time fort.

With its readily accessible beaches, Tybee Island has been a popular vacation resort since colonial times. Unfortunately, this popularity has led to heavy residential development during the twentieth century. Such questionable stabilizing structures as seawalls have been erected all along the shoreline. The natural sand dunes have been destroyed by modern construction. Tybee Island is already undergoing rampant beach erosion, and this process is liable to continue unabated into the next century.

Tybee Island Light

By 1736, a 90-foot wood-frame lighthouse sat poised at the mouth of Savannah River. Commissioned by none other than the colony's founder, James Oglethorpe, the tower lasted only a year before being knocked down by strong storm winds. A second structure arose in 1742. This light was adorned by a 30-foot flagpole perched atop its summit. Alas, this tower was toppled, too, as were two subsequent wooden structures. The federal government built yet another light in 1791, but this structure was destroyed by a fire kindled from its own candle-lit beacon.

Finally, in 1781, a masonry lighthouse was constructed on roughly the same spot as its earlier wooden counterparts. This tower was fitted with a new smokeless, hollow-wicked oil lamp that allowed air to flow around and through the wick, thereby creating a far brighter light than simple candles. In 1857, the lighthouse was raised to a height of 100 feet and outfitted with a modern, second-order Fresnel lens.

During the Civil War, retreating Confederate forces attempted to blow up the lighthouse by detonating a keg of gunpowder inside the tower. The light was extinguished, but the tough brick shell survived, and the light was relit in 1867. As part of its postwar restoration, the lighthouse was again raised, this time to a height of 144 feet. Outfitted with a first-order Fresnel lens that remains in place to this day, the light can be spotted 20 miles out to sea under ideal conditions.

Powerful storms in 1871 and 1878 generated cracks in the tower wall. This problem was worsened by an earthquake in 1886. Over the years, there have been many plans to rebuild the tower, but the project has never been undertaken. The modern-day visitor will find the light pretty much as it was following the disastrous conflict between North and South.

Savannah River to Savannah

The upriver passage to the Savannah waterfront is well marked and easy to run. The only tricky maneuvers you may be called upon to execute involve avoiding any large commercial vessels you might encounter cruising downriver. Fortunately, the passage is quite wide, and cruising boaters should be able to favor one side of the river or the other while watching their mammoth sisters pass in peace.

After sighting Fort Jackson on the southerly banks, boaters intent on a visit to Savannah should take the main, southwesterly branch of the river. This passage is charted on 11512 as "Wrecks Channel" along its easterly portion and "City Front Channel" on its track beside Savannah. The northwesterly fork is designated as "Back River" and is thoroughly commercialized. Pleasure craft should probably avoid "Back River."

The single floating pier of the Hyatt Regency Hotel will come abeam on the southern shore just short of the charted "Dome." During on-site research, this entire facility was occupied by two river tour boats and two ICW cruise ships. This writer has been assured that this was an unusual situation and that 200 feet of dockage space is usually available for transients.

Transients are accepted at the Hyatt's dock, and it is not necessary to lodge in the hotel to secure a berth. Full power and water connections are at hand. Dockside depths of 20 feet or better remove any grounding worries. There is a host of restaurants and shops adjacent to the pier. In fact, boaters who berth at the Hyatt will find themselves in the heart of Savannah's restored waterfront and historic district. The hotel can arrange for tours leaving directly from the pier. "Room service" is also available dockside.

Unless you decide to berth at one of the Thunderbolt marinas and motor into Savannah, the Hyatt's dock is the only game in town. Even though the pier is well off the Waterway, many boaters may want to consider stopping here. A night or two spent aboard your own vessel tied snugly to a dock in the heart of historic Savannah is not an experience to be dismissed lightly.

Hyatt Regency Hotel Docks
(912) 238-1234

Approach depth: 20+ feet
Dockside depth: 20+ feet
Accepts transients: yes
Floating concrete piers: yes
Dockside power connections: 30 and 50 amps
Dockside water connections: yes
Restaurants: many nearby

West of the Hyatt, Savannah's commercial wharves continue well upstream. While the various freighters and other vessels make for a fascinating view from the water, there are no other pleasure-craft facilities in the city. Savannah River is navigable far inland to the city of Augusta, but this route falls beyond the scope of this guide. The 136-foot fixed bridge northwest of the charted city-hall "Dome" marks the end of this guide's coverage of the great river.

Fort Jackson

Cruisers approaching Savannah will sight the prominent red-brick walls of Fort Jackson hard by flashing daybeacon #53. Fort Jackson is Georgia's oldest standing military fortification. Its history stretches back to the Revolutionary War. During the conflict between the mother country and the 13 American colonies, patriot forces erected a battery on the grounds of a former brickyard at the present site of Fort Jackson. An outbreak of malaria led to an evacuation of the battery before it ever fired a shot in anger.

In 1808, the government took over the property and began construction of what has been described as a "heavy artillery position." The War of 1812 brought a permanent garrison, and the fort was extensively renovated and strengthened in 1842.

During the Civil War, Fort Jackson served as a headquarters for the Confederate forces defending Savannah River. The fort held out to the end of the war and only fell after it was evacuated by the Confederates.

Today, visitors are welcomed to Fort Jackson by the Coastal Heritage Society on Tuesday through Sunday from 9:00 A.M. to 5:00 P.M. A self-guided tour is available, as well as a slide show. The fort's museum is housed in the actual rooms of the inner fort and features exhibits on construction, uniforms, and flags of the Civil War. Visitors also have the opportunity to view the "oldest known portable steam engine." A special 2½ hour program entitled "Trooping of the Colors" is presented on Saturday evenings during the summer months. This is a superb account of Savannah's military history. From Memorial Day to Labor Day, special live demonstrations are often held at Fort Jackson. Be sure to check with the staff (912-232-3945) well ahead of time about what may be in the offing during your visit to Savannah.

SAVANNAH

Upon the river-side in the centre of this plain I have laid out the town. . . . I marked out the town and common; half of the former is already cleared and the first house was begun yesterday in the afternoon.

James Oglethorpe to trustees,
February 10, 1733

I have the pleasure to address you My dear Eliza once more from this place, where I assure you I am very happy to find myself. . . . Every square in town is now enclosed with light cedar posts painted white and a chain along their tops, trees planted within, & two paved footpaths across, the remainder of the ground they are spreading Bermuda grass over, & upon the whole the Town looks quite another thing & very enchanting.

Robert MacKay to his wife, 1810

I write from the most comfortable quarter I have ever had in the United States. In a tranquil old city, wide-streeted, tree-planted, with a few cows and carriages . . . [there is] a red river with a tranquil little fleet of merchant men taking in cargo, and tranquil warehouses barricaded with packs of cotton—no row, no tearing northern bustle, no ceaseless hotel racket, no crowd drinking at the bar. . . . [I had] a famous good dinner, breakfast etc, and leisure all the morning to think and do and sleep and read as I like.

William Thackeray, 1855

Just what is the charm of this enchanting city that has inspired writers and called visitors back time and time again from the colony's first days to the present? This writer and his first-rate first mate, Karen, contemplated this question at length as we wandered the dreamlike streets of Savannah's historic district one cool March weekend. We walked the incredibly green city squares and admired their many statues and monuments. At times, the history was such a tangible entity that it seemed we could simply reach out and touch the likes of John Wesley, James Oglethorpe, and Nathanael Greene. We strolled down to the waterfront and admired the river walk while eating scrumptious pecan candies and enjoying the many colorful shops.

In the evening, the many lights playing across the squares made our walks even more special, if that is possible. Our visits to Savannah's wonderful restaurants increased our girth considerably and reminded us anew that there is really nothing to compare with traditional Southern cooking.

But what was this charm that held us in its sway? After much discussion, Karen observed with a note of finality, "Savannah is just the kind of place that makes you glad to be alive." There is really little else to add to that comment. We earnestly hope that you will have the chance to experience the same Savannah charm that held us in contented awe on that beautiful March afternoon.

Consider for a moment: Where else in our fair country can you find a coastline that features two such jewels as Charleston and

Savannah within a few days' cruising time? We don't know of any other shores so fortunate.

Certainly, any visitor to Savannah will find something to enjoy amidst the many attractions spread about the city's 3.3-square-mile historic district, the largest of its kind in the country. The district supports eight house museums, two living-history attractions, and three forts.

First-time visitors should begin their sojourn at the Savannah Visitors Center (912-944-0455), housed in the restored 1860 Central of Georgia Railway Station. The center is on Martin Luther King Boulevard (formerly Broad Street) directly across from West Liberty Street and between Louisville and Turner Streets. Here, you can obtain all the necessary information for an efficient and enjoyable tour of the city. Complete data on lodging and dining in Savannah is available as well. You may buy tickets for tours by bus or horse-drawn carriage at the center. There is also a fascinating slide show that features the people of Savannah. It should not be missed. The center is open from 8:30 A.M. to 5:00 P.M. on weekdays and from 9:00 A.M. to 5:00 P.M. on Saturdays and Sundays.

The Scarborough House is located a few blocks to the north of the visitors center. This striking edifice was designed by renowned English architect William Jay and built for wealthy merchant William Scarborough in 1819. Scarborough was one of the principal investors in the SS *Savannah*, the first steamship to successfully navigate across the Atlantic Ocean. President James Monroe visited Savannah in 1819 and was entertained at the Scarborough House. From 1878 to 1972, the structure served as a private school dedicated to the education of African-Americans. The house was recognized as a National Historic Landmark in 1974 and was restored by the Historic Savannah Foundation in 1976 as part of our nation's bicentennial celebration. It is now open to the public Monday through Friday from 10:00 A.M. to 4:00 P.M.

Savannah waterfront

Of course, no visit to Savannah is complete without a lengthy walk along the waterfront and a visit to Factor's Row. The red-brick buildings still preserved along River Street once housed Savannah's many wealthy cotton merchants and factors. Visitors will be interested to observe that these buildings are set upon a bluff and reach down to River Street. A few small streets extending from the waterfront allow the careful observer to see for himself how the various buildings were designed to follow the slope of the hill jutting up from the water's edge. Today, Factor's Row offers an eclectic selection of the city's finest gift shops and restaurants. A stroll along River Street is just about as much fun as anything this wonderful city has to offer. Of course, if it's mealtime, so much the better. Several of the fine restaurants along River Street will be covered in the discussion of Savannah's many dining choices later in this chapter.

As you walk along River Street, keep watch for the statue erected to the memory of Florence

Savannah Historic District

1. Savannah Visitors Center
2. Scarborough House
3. Factor's Row
4. Savannah Cotton Exchange
5. Emmet Park
6. Reynolds Square
7. Johnson Square
8. Wright Square
9. Juliette Low House
10. Chippewa Square
11. Madison Square
12. Lafayette Square
13. Andrew Low House
14. Cathedral of St. John the Baptist
15. Colonial Park Cemetery
16. Isaiah Davenport House
17. Warren Square
18. Telfair Square
19. Pulaski Square

Martus. It is located in a small park west of the cut-through to Emmet Park. You will remember Florence's tragic story from the discussion of the Cockspur Island Lighthouse earlier in this chapter.

The Savannah Cotton Exchange sits behind River Street on the upper side of the bluff overlooking the river; it is just east of the domed city hall. This handsome building was completed in 1887 and now houses private offices. It is fronted by one of the most impressive fountains this writer has ever witnessed. The Savannah Cotton Exchange is open to the public the first Saturday of every month from 10:00 A.M. to 3:00 P.M.

The striking Savannah City Hall sits proudly looking out over Johnson Square west of the cotton exchange. This structure features the golden "Dome" shown so prominently on chart 11512.

Legions of Girl Scouts make regular pilgrimages to Savannah to visit the birthplace of Juliette Gordon Low, founder of the Girl Scout movement in America. This exceptionally beautiful house at the corner of Oglethorpe Avenue and Bull Street was named Savannah's first National Historic Landmark in 1965 in recognition of its "architectural beauty, historical significance and exceptional furnishings." It is now owned and operated by the Girls Scouts and serves as the organization's national headquarters.

St. Johns Church graces the west side of Madison Square in the heart of the Savannah historic district. Visitors strolling along the square will be enchanted by the church's mellow chimes at the top of the hour. St. Johns Church was built between 1852 and 1853. The building has been altered very little since those days.

Nearby is the present-day parish house. Constructed in 1853 for wealthy cotton merchant Charles Green, this homeplace had the less-than-estimable distinction of serving as General William Sherman's headquarters when he "presented" Savannah to President Abraham Lincoln in December 1864. After the home passed through a series of owners—including a mayor of Savannah—following the war, St. Johns Church bought it and restored its striking Gothic facade. The parish house is open to the public Tuesdays, Thursdays, Fridays, and Saturdays from 10:00 A.M. to 4:00 P.M. unless a special church function is in progress.

The Andrew Low House is also special to the history of the Girl Scouts in America. This magnificent home was built in 1849 by Andrew Low, a wealthy English merchant. Low's son, William, lived in the house after his father's death. He married Juliette Magill Gordon in 1886. Following her husband's death, Juliette Gordon Low founded the Girl Scouts of America on March 12, 1912. In her will, she bequeathed the adjacent carriage house to the Girl Scouts.

The house itself is now owned and maintained by the Colonial Dames of America, who have restored its interior and furnished it with period antiques. It is open to the public daily except on holidays from 10:30 A.M. to 4:30 P.M. The balcony rising above the front is graced by some of the most impressive ironwork in the city.

Savannah's most striking house of worship, the Cathedral of St. John the Baptist, overlooks Abercorn Street near Lafayette Square in twin-steepled magnificence. Though the original building was partially destroyed by fire in 1898, the present structure was faithfully reconstructed on the original plan. Respectful visitors can step inside to see the high altar of Italian marble, the striking wall murals, and the lush Persian rugs.

Every visitor to Savannah should set aside a few moments to stroll through Colonial Park Cemetery, south of Oglethorpe Square. Many of the city's most famous citizens are buried here, including Button Gwinnett, signer of the Declaration of Independence. The Gwinnett family died out after the Revolution, and for several decades historians believed that the Button Gwinnett signature on the Declaration was a fake. Thankfully, that myth was long ago set right, and Gwinnett's grave is now marked with the appropriate honors.

During Sherman's occupation of Savannah, several corps of his troops camped in Colonial Park Cemetery. The soldiers despoiled and broke many of the headstones. Dozens of grave sites were lost, never to be found again. Modern-day visitors can still see many of the broken markers, now cemented against the cemetery's eastern wall.

A shady Savannah square

The Isaiah Davenport House, one of the most important historic sites in modern-day Savannah, sits proudly at the corner of State and Habersham Streets north of Columbia Square. This grand old family home was slated for demolition in 1955. A group of concerned citizens banded together and saved the house. This effort marked the beginning of the Historic Savannah Foundation, one of the most successful organizations of its type in the country. The foundation was further enlivened by the construction of a modern civic center. This building displaced one of the city's historic squares, and the citizenry was outraged. The upstart of all the agitation was the designation of downtown Savannah as a huge National Historic District. Since then, local leaders have found it far easier to control all the construction and destruction in the district. The Isaiah Davenport House and its gardens are open to visitors Monday through Saturday from 10:00 A.M. to 4:00 P.M. and Sunday from 1:30 P.M. to 4:00 P.M.

The reader will appreciate that it has only been possible to present a smattering of historic Savannah's many attractions in this account. This writer highly recommends that all visitors acquire the book *Sojourn in Savannah*, published by the city. It lays out the city's many points of interest in great detail. You can purchase the book at the visitors center or at any of the many Savannah bookstores.

The city of Savannah will also have the distinction of hosting the yachting and boating events of the 1996 Olympics. We will learn more about these exciting events in our review of Thunderbolt and its many marinas below.

Savannah Tour

There are many ways to tour Savannah—by car, bus, and horse-drawn carriage. This writer and his mate recommend that you take one or the other if you are new to Savannah. Armed with the knowledge gleaned from the always-witty tour guides, you can then strike out on foot to discover the city's many attractions for yourself. To our way of thinking, the choice among the three types of tours is obvious. The carriage tours are an infinitely more intimate experience, clopping along in the open air, with tourists able to chat one-on-one with their tour guides. Perhaps the abbreviated version of a Savannah tour presented here will whet your appetite for the real thing.

From the Savannah Visitors Center, head north on Martin Luther King Boulevard, then east on West Oglethorpe Street, then north on Barnard Street to Telfair Square. This square was named for a prominent Savannah family that bequeathed the magnificent building on the western side of the square to be used as a museum. Today, it houses the Telfair Academy of Arts and Sciences, the preeminent art museum in the city.

Alexander Telfair, the son of former governor Edward Telfair, made the bequest with one condition: No alcoholic beverages were ever to be served on the premises. This stricture was followed for many years, but finally the management relented, and champagne was served at an art reception. It so happened that a portion of the roof chose just that moment to cave in on the guests. Fortunately, no one was hurt, but the rumor soon spread that the Telfair ghosts were letting it be known that their wishes were to be honored in perpetuity.

Turn east down West York Street to Wright Square. Named for James Wright, the last of Georgia's Royal governors, the square is home to two monuments. A huge stone boulder in the southwestern corner commemorates the 1739 death of Tomo-Chi-Chi, chief of the Yamacraw Indians. This tribe and its chief were fast friends of the English colonists. The monument arching out of the square's middle is a tribute to William Washington, founder of the Central Georgia Railroad.

From Wright Square, follow Bull Street north to historic Johnson Square. This was the city's first square, laid out by founder James Oglethorpe and named for his friend Governor Robert Johnson of South Carolina. The early colonists used the square as the center of their community. A sundial was kept here, and the settlers came to find out the time of day. A reproduction of this quaint device can now be observed once again in the square. It was here that President James

Savannah carriage tour

Monroe was received by the citizenry during his 1819 visit and where the Marquis de Lafayette was honored with an enthusiastic reception in 1825.

Today, Johnson Square is dominated by a huge granite shaft at its center. During the latter stages of the American Revolution, the patriot cause was at a low ebb in the Southern colonies. George Washington dispatched Rhode Island general Nathanael Greene to take command of the Southern forces in the face of almost impossible odds. Greene's brilliant leadership has been credited with the eventual removal of British forces from the region.

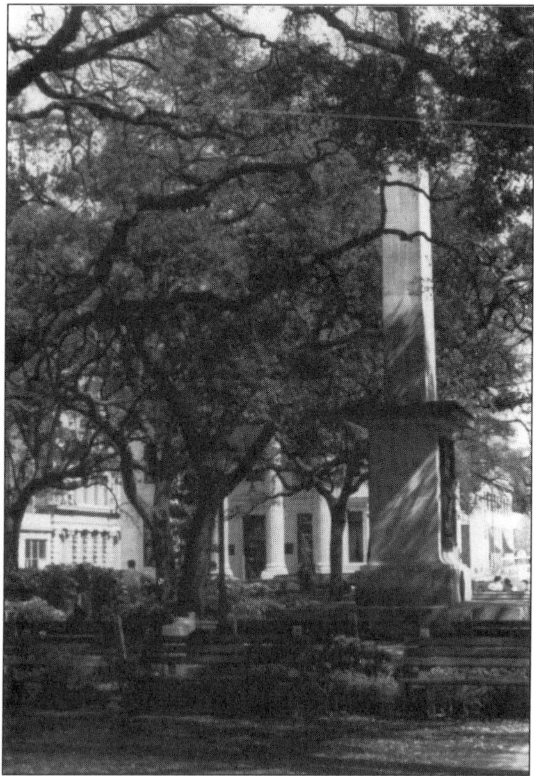

Monument honoring General Nathanael Greene, Johnson Square, Savannah

Following the war, Greene was understandably beloved by the citizens of the Southern colonies, who saw him, perhaps even more than Washington, as their savior. Many of the new states granted land to Greene. He took up residence for a short time on Georgia's Cumberland Island. Following his death, his remains were laid to rest in Savannah's Colonial Park Cemetery.

With the passage of the years, the exact location of Greene's grave became a matter of conjecture. Finally, his supposed grave was reverently opened, and the remains therein were determined to indeed be those of the general who had fought so brilliantly during our country's struggle for independence. Greene's body was reinterred with full military honors in Johnson Square, and the bold monument still there today was raised over his remains to forever honor this true American hero.

On a less serious note, Johnson Square is also known as the windiest square in the city. City hall is located just north of this square. Savannah tour guides may tell you, with a twinkle in their eye, that the locals believe the winds are a result of all the hot air flowing out of city hall.

From Johnson Square, head east on East Congress Street to charming Reynolds Square, which features a statue of John Wesley, founder of the Methodist Church. There is a little-known story that Wesley fell in love with a young girl while visiting Savannah. When his advances were spurned, the church leader supposedly left the colony in a huff.

The Olde Pink House Restaurant and Tavern overlooks the square's western flank. This wonderful dining spot is ensconced in an elegant 1789 homeplace built for James Habersham.

Entrance to Colonial Park Cemetery, Savannah

Broken headstones in Colonial Park Cemetery, Savannah

More about this gastronomical attraction will be presented in the discussion of Savannah's restaurants.

Continue east along East Congress Street to Warren Square. The attraction here is the beautiful houses set about the square. These structures survived the great fire of 1889 and are some of the oldest homes in the city.

Next, turn south on Habersham Street and proceed to Columbia Square to admire the Isaiah Davenport House, home of the Historic Savannah Foundation. The story of this historic house was presented above.

From Columbia Square, head west on East State Street, then turn south on Abercorn Street past Colonial Park Cemetery, the site of the desecration carried out by Sherman's Union troops.

Turn west on East McDonough Street to see Chippewa Square. A huge bronze statue of James Edward Oglethorpe dominates the center of this square. It was designed by Daniel Chester French, often considered to be the foremost American sculptor.

After you have seen Chippewa Square, return to Abercorn Street and cut south to Lafayette Square. This square was laid out and named for the Marquis de Lafayette soon after his visit to Savannah in 1825. The Andrew Low House is among the beautiful homes surrounding the park.

From Lafayette Square, it's only a quick westerly jaunt on West Harris Street to Madison Square, one of the most popular squares in the city. The central statue commemorates the heroism of William Jasper, a patriot soldier in the Revolution who was killed in the attack on Savannah. A quick glance at the square's restful benches may make you want to relax for a time in the shadow of Jasper's statue.

Finally, continue west on West Harris Street past Pulaski Square for a look at the special oak

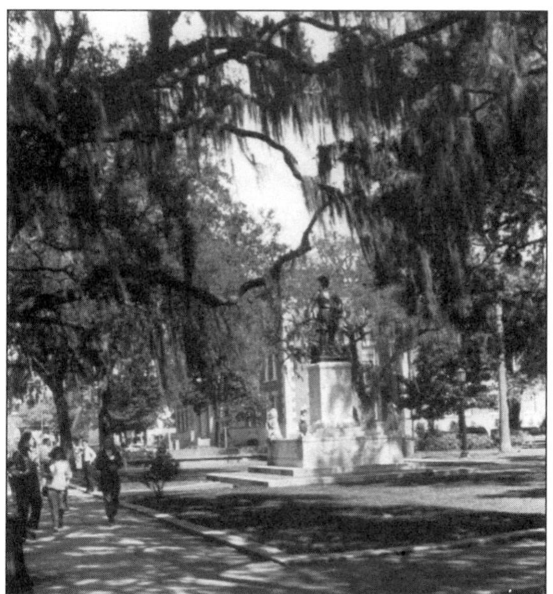

Statue of James Oglethorpe, Chippewa Square, Savannah

trees spread throughout the grounds. They never lose their leaves and are considered evergreens. The tillandsia, or Spanish moss, hanging from the oaks' limbs adds an air of mystery to the scene.

Now, it's only a quick jaunt west on West Harris and north on Martin Luther King back to the Savannah Visitors Center. This writer hopes you will feel encouraged to strike out on your own and experience the very special community that is Savannah.

Savannah Restaurants

The city of Savannah is replete with many fine places to dine. Only a very few of this writer's personal favorites can be mentioned within these pages. Visitors are encouraged to experiment. You never know when you might find a new culinary gem waiting just around the corner of the next square. Reservations at these restaurants are almost mandatory on weekends. It would be wise to call well ahead of time rather than risk disappointment.

Few would argue that Elizabeth on 37th (105 East 37th Street, 912-236-5547) is one of the most elegant dining experiences in Savannah. The food is described by the management as "gourmet Southern." Believe you me, that is an apt description. This writer highly recommends Elizabeth on 37th, but be aware that it is a trifle pricey.

A great place to take a break from the fresh-seafood regimen and rediscover the culinary value of fine beef is 45 South Restaurant (20 East Broad Street, 912-233-1881). The prime rib is outstanding.

The Pirates' House (also at 20 East Broad Street, 912-233-5757) specializes in regional fare. If you want to try any Georgia coastal specialties, this is the place.

This writer's personal dining favorite in Savannah is the historic Olde Pink House Restaurant and Tavern (912-232-4286) at 23 Abercorn Street, hard by Reynolds Square. You will have to experience the seafood for yourself, but suffice it to say it's akin to the taste of a fresh, fragrant loaf given to a starving man. There is also the added bonus of taking your meal in an elegant, historical home overlooking a lovely square. Who could ask for more?

On the Savannah River waterfront, Factor's Row is jammed with restaurants. For casual dining at a great price, give Dockside Seafood (201 West River Street, 912-236-9253) a try. The "Low Country Seafood Boil," a combination of incredibly fresh boiled shrimp, boiled potatoes, and corn on the cob, must be experienced to be understood. Quite simply, it's outstanding.

The River House Seafood Restaurant (125 West River Street, 912-234-1900) is also superb. My grilled salmon was all my taste buds could ask for, and my mate was equally thrilled with her red snapper. Don't miss the pecan pie for dessert. It's the house specialty.

We should not leave Savannah without one last word about a dining institution. If you yearn for good old Southern-fried chicken, fresh vegetables, mashed potatoes yellow with butter, and homemade pies, all served family-style, then do yourself a huge favor and visit Mrs. Wilkes' Boarding House (107 West Jones Street, 912-232-5997) for lunch. Reservations are *not* accepted. The crowd usually begins to gather by 11:15. Be early unless you can put up with a long wait. The smells wafting out of the door will make this ever so difficult.

Savannah Lodgings

Of course, many cruising visitors to Savannah will stay aboard their own vessels, whether they dock along the city waterfront or in nearby Thunderbolt. Thus, it is not this guide's purpose to present an exhaustive review of Savannah's many fine hostelries. However, for those who just want to get off the water for a night or two, there are three inns this writer feels merit special mention.

First in any discussion of Savannah lodgings must be the Ballastone Inn (14 East Oglethorpe Avenue, 912-236-1484). As old-time inn-hoppers, this writer and his mate can say with some authority that we have never stayed in more exquisitely decorated lodgings. Housed in a historic three-story Savannah home, the inn features a host of guest rooms each furnished in a unique style. From the wallpaper to the period antiques to the coffee and hot tea available in the sitting room and bar 24 hours a day, the Ballastone Inn has everything its patrons could ever desire.

Magnolia Place Inn (503 Whitaker Street, 912-236-7674) also has an elegant reputation for Old South hospitality. It features working fireplaces and period antiques. This writer has spoken with several satisfied cruising patrons who return year after year.

Finally, the 1790 Inn, Restaurant, and Lounge (307 East President Street, 912-236-7122) merits a mention. To our great misfortune, we have not had the opportunity to stay or dine at this establishment, but we are willing to accept the opinion of a knowledgeable tour guide who once told us and her other passengers that the food is superb and that the inn is (to use her word) "neat." We've always found the tips and advice of locals to be on the money.

Savannah History The English colony of Georgia, named in honor King George II, was founded by James Oglethorpe and a group of trustees with the avowed purpose of improving the plight of the common man, particularly individuals who were in prison for crimes no greater than being in debt. The first party of settlers arrived on the banks of Savannah River in February 1733.

Oglethorpe himself laid out the unique town grid, with its many green, parklike squares. His inspiration for the plan is a matter of historical debate, but wherever he got the idea, the city has benefited from his imagination ever since.

In 1736, a visitor described Savannah as "a mile and a quarter in circumference; it stands upon the flat of a hill. . . . The town . . . is built of wood. . . . The streets are very wide, and there are great squares left at proper distances, for markets and other convenience."

Savannah grew slowly, as did all of Georgia, largely due to the threat of Spanish attack from Florida. Following Oglethorpe's defeat of a Spanish expeditionary force on St. Simons Island at the Battle of Bloody Marsh in 1742, this threat was ended. By the opening of the Revolution, Savannah boasted a population of 2,500.

Savannah was invaded by the British early in the Revolution, and in spite of a determined attack by French and American forces, the English held the city until the close of the conflict. The war's depredations, along with serious fires in 1796 and 1820, destroyed much of colonial Savannah. Today, there are few homes that survive from that early era.

By the early 1800s, Savannah was fast on its way to becoming one of the most important ports in the southeastern United States. The town's limits now encompassed 12 squares. Vast quantities of rice and, a bit later, Sea Island cotton were stored in massive warehouses lining the river's edge and shipped from the city's wharves. Eli Whitney's invention of the cotton gin on a nearby plantation solidified the already growing cotton industry and added immeasurably to the port's burgeoning prosperity.

In 1819, President James Monroe visited Savannah and was entertained in lavish style. He took a ride on the steamship *Savannah*. This vessel would soon make the first successful transatlantic crossing using partial steam power.

Another great fire in 1820 laid waste the old section of the city between Broughton and Bay Streets. More than 463 buildings were burned. It was not long before the wealth that still poured into the port city was directed toward new construction. The Marquis de Lafayette visited Savannah in 1825, and by all accounts he found much to admire.

By 1850, antebellum Savannah was at its zenith. The city now numbered some 15,000 citizens. A rail line had been completed to Augusta, allowing for the ready shipment of cotton and other agricultural products to the Savannah wharves. A new city gasworks allowed street lamps to be powered with this novel source of energy. The river channel was dredged and the city wharves much improved. Many of the lovely homes and brick buildings so admired today were built during this heyday.

Georgia joined the conflict with the Northern states more reluctantly than did neighboring South Carolina. Though many of Georgia's barrier islands fell to Union forces early in the war, it was not until the latter stages of the conflict that William Sherman's infamous "March to the Sea" brought the horrors of war directly to the city by the banks of Savannah River. After the fall of nearby Fort McAllister to Sherman's forces, the Confederates evacuated Savannah, and Union troops marched into a virtually deserted city on December 21, 1864. Fortunately, for whatever reason, Sherman did not see fit to burn Savannah's proud homes and buildings, in contrast to what he had done in so many other Southern towns and cities. Nevertheless, the invasion was the harbinger of many tough years to come.

Savannah suffered through Reconstruction, as did the rest of the South. Some cotton was again exported, but the arrival of the boll weevil spelled the doom of that way of life. Fortunately, a new industry was at hand. By the late 1800s, the Georgia coastline was enjoying a timber boom, with Savannah as one of the principal beneficiaries. Thousands upon thousands of board feet of lumber were loaded aboard ocean-going ships at Savannah's wharves and sent off to Northern or European ports.

Savannah's port facilities continued their important role into the twentieth century. With the rise of tourism along the Georgia coastline, the long-term prosperity of the city was assured. It is every American's good fortune that the great foresight of Savannah's founders has been perpetuated by the vigilant members of the Historic Savannah Foundation. More tourists are drawn to the city's rarefied climes every year. The port along Savannah River is now one of the busiest in the world.

It would probably surprise James Oglethorpe to see what has become of the city he so carefully laid out along Savannah River. If he could see all the squares that his plan envisioned still carefully preserved, the many proud historical homes still in place, and most important, the harmony among Savannah's citizens, he would probably be very proud.

SAVANNAH RIVER NAVIGATION

If you run aground on Savannah River, let this writer suggest a complete review of *Chapman's*, or maybe a visit to your eye doctor. The channel is exceedingly well outlined by numerous flashing buoys and ranges, with the odd daybeacon thrown in for good measure. As with all of Georgia's waters, tidal currents run swiftly, so you must be on guard against excessive leeway. Sailcraft under auxiliary power and single-screw trawlers must proceed with the knowledge that their maneuverability may be impeded by the swiftly moving waters.

West of its inlet, Savannah River seldom becomes really choppy, though particularly strong winds blowing directly up or down the large stream can bring exceptions. Like any inlet, the river's seaward passage can spawn rough conditions when winds and tide oppose each other, but at least you will be shepherded along by one of the largest collections of aids to navigation that this writer has ever witnessed.

For the most part, though, you can relax while cruising Savannah River. Simply avoid any large vessels you might encounter and enjoy the domes and spires of Savannah as they appear over the horizon.

Entry from Fields Cut After exiting the southwestern mouth of Fields Cut, cruise straight out into the centerline of Savannah River. Soon, you will spot flashing buoy #35 dead ahead. Before reaching this aid, you should either cut southeast if you are planning to run the river's inlet or turn to the west if Savannah or the ICW's southern route is your destination.

Savannah River to the Sea From a position abeam of flashing buoy #35, turn southeast and point to pass flashing buoy #33 to its northeasterly quarter. You can then continue down the well-marked LI Crossing Range to flashing buoy #26, where the river takes a jog to the east. You are now heading downriver toward the sea, so take all red markers to your port side and green beacons to starboard, as you would expect.

As you approach flashing buoy #25, watch to the south for a view of old Fort Pulaski. It can usually be identified by the charted "Flagpole."

East of #25, the Savannah River channel begins to flow through a broad passage between extensive shoals into open water. Again, watch to the south for the charted Cockspur Island Lighthouse, located east of Fort Pulaski.

The channel begins a bend to the east-southeast after passing between flashing buoys #17 and #18. The still-active Tybee Island Light is visible to the south.

Flashing buoys #11 and #12 denote a further turn to the southeast on Bloody Point Range. The channel curves back a bit to the east after passing between flashing buoys #5 and #6. It's now a quick run through the remaining markers to the open sea.

Upriver to Savannah Cut almost due west once you are within 50 yards of flashing buoy #35 and set course to come abeam of and pass flashing buoy #36 to its southerly side. The river now cuts a bit to the northwest on the Upper Flats Range. Northwest of flashing buoy #40, three huge sky-blue tanks will come abeam on the westerly shoreline. They are a very impressive sight from the water, as is their filling and dispensary dock.

Flashing daybeacon #45 introduces upstream-bound boaters on Savannah River to a hairpin turn around Elba Island. West-southwest of flashing buoy #52, you will begin to approach the Back River split. Watch for Fort Jackson on the southerly banks. The forks will be obvious as you approach this historic fortification. Be sure to follow the main southwesterly branch (Wrecks Channel) as it quickly cuts west to the Savannah waterfront. Soon, the city's waterfront park and the old Factor's Row buildings will come into view along the southerly banks. Watch for the charted golden "Dome." The Hyatt Regency Hotel Docks will come abeam just short of this impressive structure.

Northwest of the city-hall dome, Savannah River flows under a fixed high-rise bridge with 136 feet of vertical clearance. This guide's coverage of the river ends at this point, but boaters should be aware that the stream remains navigable for many additional miles to the west.

ICW SOUTH FROM SAVANNAH RIVER TO VERNON RIVER

The northernmost waters of the Georgia ICW are home to the most prolific marina facilities on the state's entire coastline. Many of these boating havens are grouped around the village of Thunderbolt, while several others guard various creeks making off from the Waterway.

Cruisers who prefer to anchor for the evening are not forgotten either. While not quite as plentiful as those found a bit farther to the south, there are still any number of opportunities to pull off the beaten track. Few of these havens offer much in the way of heavy-weather protection.

This portion of the Georgia Waterway is more developed than most. To be sure, plenty of brown water and marsh grass are still there for you to contemplate, but passing boaters will also observe many private homes and even a few low-rise condos along the way. By the time you make your entrance into Vernon River, this sort of development begins to drop away, with only a brief reappearance in the Brunswick–St. Simons region, much farther to the south.

The ICW and Savannah River

Powerboaters cruising on Savannah River actually have a choice of two routes by which they can follow the Waterway south to Vernon River. Most skippers will want to use Elba Island Cut, which is just a hop, skip, and jump from Fields Cut's southwesterly mouth. This route, while straightforward, does call for some navigational caution. At unlighted daybeacon #18, Elba Island Cut leads cruisers into the upper Wilmington River. St. Augustine Creek cuts to the southeast abeam of #18 and tracks its way to a marina and several additional cruising opportunities.

Cruisers voyaging south from Savannah may alternately use the so-called South Channel to reach the ICW. This passage cuts off to the east-southeast abeam of Savannah River's flashing buoy #50. It is not nearly as reliable as Elba Island Cut. Some 7-foot low-water depths can be expected, and the channel is spanned by a fixed bridge with 35 feet of vertical clearance. Obviously, this route is not the correct choice for most sailcraft. The South Channel passage intersects the primary ICW northwest of flashing daybeacon #15. Navigation of the channel at this juncture calls for a steady hand on the helm.

St. Augustine Creek, Bull River, and Associated Streams

St. Augustine Creek departs the ICW south of unlighted daybeacon #18 and meanders its way to the southeast until it eventually joins Bull River. This latter stream features a reliable inlet passage to the open sea and several sidewaters of its own that boast anchorage possibilities for craft that can clear a 20-foot fixed bridge. Minimum depths of 9 to 11 feet are typical.

The initial section of St. Augustine Creek sports 18-foot minimum depths and enough swinging room for boats as large as 38 feet. For those who don't want to travel too far from the Waterway, good anchorage is found after the creek's first crook-like turn to the east. The creek is bordered by undeveloped salt marsh that renders unreliable protection if winds exceed 25 knots. Again, unless specified differently, you can expect this sort of shoreline.

At its intersection with the combined mouths of Richardson and Turner Creeks (making in to the southwestern banks), St. Augustine Creek flows directly into Bull River, and the combined waters soon approach a fixed bridge with 20 feet of vertical clearance.

Do not attempt to follow Turner Creek back to the ICW. While the lower portion of this stream, south of Thunderbolt, is readily navigable and plays host to several marina facilities, the passage from Bull River is narrow, with depths running to low-water soundings of as little as 3 feet.

Southeast of the 20-foot fixed bridge, Bull River Yacht Club Marina guards the southwestern shoreline. It is yet another of Georgia's friendly pleasure-boating facilities, and visiting cruisers can be assured of a warm welcome. Of course, unless you enter from the open sea via the Bull River–Wilmington River inlet, it is necessary to pass under the 20-foot bridge to reach the marina. This obviously renders Bull

River Yacht Club Marina off-limits to many sailing craft traveling the ICW.

Bull River Yacht Club gladly accepts transients for overnight or temporary dockage at wooden floating piers featuring every conceivable power and water connection. Depths alongside are an impressive 8 to 20 feet at low tide, with a few 6-foot soundings at the innermost slips. Gasoline and diesel fuel can be purchased, and full mechanical repairs are available through independent technicians. Clean showers are located on the premises, and the marina maintains a full-line ship's and variety store. The on-site Good Friend's Galley restaurant is a new addition to the dining scene.

Bull River Yacht Club Marina
(912) 897-7300

Approach depth: 9 feet (minimum)
Dockside depth: 6–20 feet
Accepts transients: yes
Floating wooden piers: yes
Dockside power connections: 30 and 50 amps
Dockside water connections: yes
Showers: yes
Gasoline: yes
Diesel fuel: yes
Mechanical repairs: independent technicians
Ship's and variety store: yes
Restaurant: on-site

Southeast of the marina, Bull River stretches generally south along a broad path and eventually meets up with the Atlantic Ocean. The river is so wide that anchorage should only be contemplated during light airs.

Deep and reliable Lazaretto Creek cuts into Bull River's eastern shores well south of charted Betz Creek. This fortunate stream leads to a host of anchorages, the resort community on Tybee Island, and even a tiny marina.

Bull River Yacht Club Marina, St. Augustine Creek

The westerly stretch of Lazaretto Creek maintains minimum 11-foot depths. While most of the shoreline is composed of the usual marsh, notice the charted higher ground fronting the southerly banks in the body of the stream's first hairpin turn. This is an excellent spot to spend the night, particularly if winds are blowing from the south or southwest. Swinging room is ample for a 38-footer.

Oyster Creek breaks off from Lazaretto Creek at the intersection with Morgan Cut. Oyster Creek also offers anchorage, with 12-foot minimum depths but no high ground.

Perhaps the region's most tempting cruising gem is Tybee Creek, which breaks off to the southeast and east from Morgan Cut. Minimum depths of as little as 6 feet are occasionally encountered, but typical soundings range from 8 to as much as 40 feet. This extensive body of water flows through acres of marsh toward the higher ground on Tybee Island. At one point, you will even have a pretty good, if distant, view of the old Tybee Island Light to the north. Anchorage is a practical consideration most anywhere on Tybee Creek short of the island development.

Tybee Creek turns sharply to the south near the charted intersection with Chimney Creek and rushes on toward a very shallow intersection with the ocean. Downstream of the creek's southward bend, the high eastern banks are overlooked by the dense residential development of the Tybee Island resort community. Small MarLin Marina is found in the midst of all the various structures. This facility was being upgraded at the time of this writing. A new on-site restaurant and bar (open for lunch and dinner) has been added. While most of the available wet-slip dockage is used for month-to-month rentals, transients are accepted. Depths alongside run 10 feet or better. All slips feature water and 30-amp power connections. Showers, fueling facilities, and waste pump-out service are planned for the future, but their completion date was indefinite as this guide went to press. A newly expanded ship's and variety store on the marina grounds is prepared to receive those who need nautical hardware or simple foodstuffs.

MarLin Marina (912) 786-7508

Approach depth: 7–40 feet
Dockside depth: 10+ feet
Accepts transients: yes
Floating wooden piers: yes
Dockside power connections: 30 amps
Dockside water connections: yes
Ship's and variety store: yes
Restaurant: on-site

Halfmoon River cuts off from its larger sister, Bull River, opposite unlighted daybeacon #4. In spite of soundings noted on the current edition of chart 11512, on-site research revealed water depths of 3 to 5 feet near the stream's easterly entrance. Cruising-size craft are advised to bypass Halfmoon River.

With careful navigation, it is possible to cruise from Bull River into the open sea by making use of Wilmington River's seaward channel. Be sure to read the navigational information presented in the next section of this chapter before making your first attempt at this passage.

Bonaventure Cemetery

Back on the ICW, boaters passing southwest of flashing daybeacon #25 should watch the western and northwestern banks. Soon, this shore rises to a high cliff, and you will spy a large cemetery perched atop the earthen banks. This tranquil spot is known as Bonaventure Cemetery, and it holds a unique place in the history of coastal Georgia.

Bonaventure was originally the site of Tattnall Plantation during the 1800s. The family began a cemetery that eventually developed into a public grave site after the plantation house burned.

In 1850, the graveyard was visited by one of the most extraordinary men in American environmental history. The young Scotsman John Muir had embarked upon a "Thousand Mile Walk to the Gulf," which originated in Louisville, Kentucky, and was to end at the tip of mainland Florida. Out of money and in great need of a place to rest and recuperate, Muir chanced upon Bonaventure and spent five days camping on the property, which he described in glowing terms: "It is one of the most impressive assemblages of animal and plant creatures I have ever met. . . . Never since I was allowed to walk the woods have I found so impressive a company of trees as the tillandsia-draped oaks of Bonaventure."

Upon the completion of his amazing journey, John Muir went on to become our country's most prominent early advocate of environmental protection. He was also one of the founders of the Sierra Club. The journal Muir kept during his journey is still avidly read by naturalists.

Thunderbolt

South of the 21-foot Causton Bluff bascule bridge, boaters will come upon a heavy concentration of marinas and related facilities grouped around the 65-foot Thunderbolt fixed bridge (south of flashing daybeacon #34). Taken as a group, the Thunderbolt marinas and boatyards comprise one of the most impressive collections of pleasure-craft facilities to be found anywhere.

As mentioned earlier, many cruisers berth at one of the Thunderbolt marinas and then take a taxi or rental car back into historic Savannah for dining or sightseeing. Consult the opening section of this chapter for information on local taxi service and car rentals.

First up is Savannah Bend Marina, which guards the eastern shores immediately north of the bridge. This friendly facility features a state-of-the-art dry-stack storage building for small powerboats, but cruising craft are also welcomed for overnight or temporary dockage. Berths at the concrete floating docks feature full power and water connections.

Depths alongside run 7 to 14 feet. Gasoline and diesel fuel can be purchased, and the marina offers light mechanical repairs for outboards and I/O's. There are shoreside showers and a full laundromat to help you recover from your salty days on the Waterway. A ship's and variety store just behind the piers features a bar and a small restaurant open for lunch and dinner. This dining spot features gourmet sandwiches and weekend seafood specials. Those who prefer dinner a bit more offbeat might consider Desposito's Seafood, a quick step from the marina grounds. Housed in what might be described as a "shack," this dining spot looks as if it has just stepped out of the 1950s.

Savannah Bend Marina (912) 897-3625

Approach depth: 12+ feet
Dockside depth: 7–14 feet
Accepts transients: yes
Floating concrete piers: yes
Dockside power connections: 30 and 50 amps
Dockside water connections: yes
Showers: yes
Laundromat: yes
Gasoline: yes
Diesel fuel: yes
Mechanical repairs: limited (outboard and I/O only)
Ship's and variety store: yes
Restaurants: on-site and nearby

You will spy the floating fiberglass piers of Tidewater Boatworks on the Waterway's western banks opposite Savannah Bend Marina. In this land of friendly yards and marinas,

Savannah Bend Marina, Thunderbolt

WHITEMARSH ISLAND
N
Grays Creek
Thunderbolt
Williamson Cr.
Sylvan Island
Herb River
DUTCH ISLAND
Skidaway R.
Wilmington River
Turner Creek

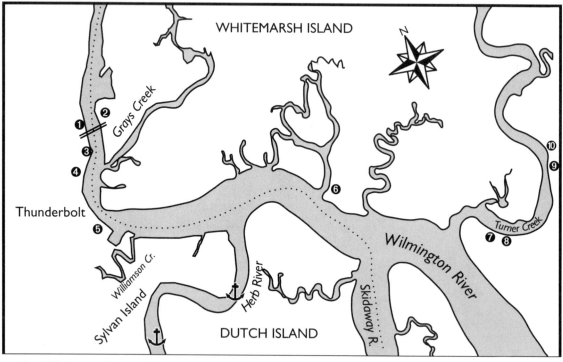

1. **Tidewater Boatworks**
2. **Savannah Bend Marina**
3. **Fountain Marina**
4. **Riverwatch Marina**
5. **Palmer Johnson of Savannah Marina and Boatyard (formerly Thunderbolt Marina)**
6. **Savannah Yacht Club**
7. **Sail Harbor Marina**
8. **The Yachtworks**
9. **Palmer's Seafood House Restaurant**
10. **Hogan's Marina**

Tidewater Boatworks stands out as one of the most helpful facilities of its type that this writer has discovered. To say that the staff and management are very much in tune with the needs of visiting cruisers is truly putting it mildly.

Tidewater offers complete below-waterline and mechanical repairs. Haul-outs are achieved by a 25-ton travelift or a 45-ton marine railway. Mechanical services ranging from minor tune-ups to complete rebuilds are available for both gasoline and diesel power plants, as well as for generators and marine air conditioners. Do-it-yourself work is also allowed in the yard. There is a full-line ship's and parts store on the marina grounds, which is particularly convenient for those performing their own work.

Thunderbolt waterfront

While transients are sometimes afforded space at the yard's wet slips, service work is clearly the forte here. The accommodating management has informed this writer that transients will not be turned away, but if slip space is available at one of the other nearby marinas, visiting boaters will usually be directed to those establishments. The fiberglass-decked floating docks at Tidewater Boatworks have full power and water connections, along with typical minimum soundings of 8 to 9 feet. Gasoline and diesel fuel are readily available. Several excellent restaurants are located within walking distance.

Tidewater Boatworks (912) 352-1335

Approach depth: 12+ feet
Dockside depth: 8–9 feet (minimum)
Accepts transients: yes
Floating piers: yes
Dockside power connections: 30 and 50 amps
Dockside water connections: yes
Gasoline: yes
Diesel fuel: yes
Mechanical repairs: extensive
Below-waterline repairs: extensive
Ship's and parts store: yes
Restaurants: several nearby

South of the 65-foot fixed bridge, three additional facilities line the western shoreline. The northernmost of these is Fountain Marina. This small firm sometimes has room for a few transients, but usually most of its wet slips are occupied by resident craft. Should you be able to secure overnight dockage, you will be berthed at a wooden-decked floating dock with water and 30-amp connections. Gasoline (but not diesel fuel) is available, as is dry-stack storage for small power craft. There are some showers on the premises, and light mechanical repairs are featured for outboards and I/O's. This facility may be purchased by Riverwatch Marina (see below) in the near future. If so, it will probably cease to function as a separate entity.

Tidewater Boatworks, Thunderbolt

Fountain Marina (912) 354-2283

Approach depth: 12+ feet
Dockside depth: 13 feet
Accepts transients: limited
Floating wooden pier: yes
Dockside power connections: 30 amps
Dockside water connections: yes
Showers: yes
Gasoline: yes
Mechanical repairs: outboards and I/O's
Restaurants: several nearby

Next up is Riverwatch Marina. This small but accommodating establishment has an expanded number of wet slips set aside for transients at its concrete-decked floating docks. All berths feature full power and water connections. Gasoline and diesel fuel are readily available, as are shoreside showers and a new waterside bar. Extensive dry-stack storage is available for small power craft. A full-line ship's store independent of the marina is located just across the street. Thunderbolt's full selection of restaurants is within walking distance.

As mentioned above, Riverwatch's management is currently negotiating the purchase of adjacent Fountain Marina. If this transaction is completed, the dockage at Riverwatch will expand markedly.

Riverwatch Marina (912) 355-8500

Approach depth: 12+ feet
Dockside depth: 12+ feet
Accepts transients: yes
Floating concrete piers: yes
Dockside power connections: 30 and 50 amps
Dockside water connections: yes
Showers: yes
Gasoline: yes
Diesel fuel: yes
Restaurants: several nearby

The southernmost of the three marinas south of the fixed bridge is fabulous Palmer Johnson of Savannah Marina and Boatyard (formerly Thunderbolt Marina). This extensive facility is located in and around the small, charted square cove south of unlighted daybeacon #35. When this writer and his mate first visited this combination marina and yard in 1992, it had just come under the ownership of Palmer Johnson. We were told at the time that the company had a commitment to transforming this facility into a repair yard and marina second to none. This writer will bear witness to the fact that the good folks at Palmer Johnson have now succeeded in that goal.

As far as the marina portion of the operation is concerned, additional docks have been constructed. Extensive transient berths are now provided at both floating wooden and concrete-decked piers. Depths alongside run 8 to 17 feet. Full power (up to 100 amps) and water connections are at hand, as are super clean showers and a full-service laundromat. Gasoline and diesel fuel are readily available dockside. The former gift shop just behind the docks has been taken over by Palmer Johnson and now features a fine selection of nautical gear, basic food, and snack items. Visitors will also find a small paperback exchange library in the dockmaster's office. Gasoline and diesel fuel are at hand, and waste pump-out service is planned for the near future. All the local Thunderbolt restaurants (see below) are within an easy step of the docks.

One look at the numbers and impressive sizes of the hauled craft undergoing repairs at Palmer Johnson will convince you of this yard's enviable reputation. Quite simply, it is one of the largest and most impressive repair operations along the eastern seaboard. Virtually any size pleasure craft can be hauled by either a 160-ton travelift or a 1,150-ton sinking lift. Mechanical repairs (gas and diesel) are complemented by full marine electrical, refrigeration, and fiberglass service work. If you can't get it fixed here, the old craft has real problems.

Cruisers plying the waters of northeastern Georgia are very fortunate to have a facility of Palmer Johnson's reputation and ability available to them. This writer unreservedly recommends this marina and yard to his fellow cruisers.

Palmer Johnson of Savannah Marina and Boatyard (912) 352-4956

Approach depth: 12+ feet
Dockside depth: 8–12 feet
Accepts transients: yes
Floating wooden and concrete piers: yes
Dockside power connections: 30, 50, and 100 amps

Dockside water connections: yes
Showers: yes
Laundromat: yes
Gasoline: yes
Diesel fuel: yes
Mechanical repairs: extensive
Below-waterline repairs: extensive
Ship's and variety store: yes
Restaurants: several nearby

The small village of Thunderbolt lies within a few steps of Palmer Johnson's docks. While there are a number of dining choices for famished cruisers, this writer strongly recommends either the River's End (912-354-2973) or Teeples Restaurant (912-354-1157). The latter is the more informal choice, but both offer some of the very best and freshest seafood to be found in coastal Georgia. Another good local dining choice is Fiddler's Restaurant (912-354-5903).

Herb River

Minimum depths of 9 feet, with typical soundings of 13 to 20 feet, escort boaters into Herb River south-southwest of flashing daybeacon #37. This stream features some residential development along its lower, southeasterly shoreline, but most of the various homes drop away as the river turns almost due south.

There are at least two good spots to drop the hook for the evening. The first is found abeam of the just-mentioned development. The high southeastern banks give good shelter when the fickle wind is blowing from that quarter or from the south. Boats as large as 40 feet should have plenty of elbow room.

Smaller vessels (up to 36 feet) might consider anchoring upstream of the river's first sharp turn to the south. High, well-wooded banks flank the westerly shores along a portion of this run. Unfortunately, correctly charted shoal waters abutting the easterly banks limit swinging room. If you choose to drop the hook here, be sure to set your anchor so as to swing well away from this hazard.

Savannah Yacht Club

Impressive Savannah Yacht Club (912-897-1314) overlooks the ICW's northeastern banks hard by the southeastern shores of the charted canal that lies southeast of unlighted daybeacon #38. This club does not extend reciprocity to members of other yacht clubs. Consequently, no guest dockage or other marine services are available to visiting cruisers.

Turner Creek and Associated Facilities

South and east of Herb River, the Georgia ICW follows the mighty Wilmington River. The Waterway soon departs this body of water by cutting south-southwest on Skidaway River at flashing daybeacon #40. Boaters can easily follow the broad path of deep water southeast into the lower portion of Wilmington River, abandoned by the Waterway. The mouth of Turner Creek will soon come abeam on the northeastern banks at the charted location of Turners Rock. This stream plays host to several marina facilities.

Turner Creek holds minimum depths of 6½ to 8 feet. There is one shoal to avoid, but navigators who pay attention to business should bypass this obstruction easily.

First up is Sail Harbor Marina, located on the southerly banks near the charted, privately maintained light. This marina has upgraded its facilities significantly since the last edition of this guide. Transient visitors are now welcomed at new, wider wooden-decked floating docks. Depths alongside run from 7 to 11 feet. The marina maintains showers and a laundromat on the premises, as well as a full-line ship's and variety store and a paperback exchange library. No fuel is available. The on-site Lightship Restaurant is popular with the local crowd.

Sail Harbor and the adjacent Sheraton Hotel complex will play host to the committee boats and much of the staff for the 1996 Olympic yachting races. Most of the racing vessels will be moored to temporary floating piers located out in the heart of Wilmington River. The races themselves will take place during July 1996. It goes without saying that more than a few boating people will be on hand for this event, and that transient dockage in Thunderbolt will be at a premium.

The Yachtworks boatyard is found adjacent to Sail Harbor Marina, and the two firms work closely together. The Yachtworks boasts haul-outs via a 30-ton travelift, as well as complete mechanical repairs for both gasoline and diesel engines. Do-it-yourself work is also allowed, and rental tools are available.

Sail Harbor Marina (912) 897-2896; The Yachtworks (912) 897-1914

Approach depth: 6½ feet
Dockside depth: 7–11 feet
Accepts transients: yes
Floating wooden piers: yes
Dockside power connections: 30 and 50 amps
Dockside water connections: yes
Showers: yes
Laundromat: yes
Mechanical repairs: extensive
Below-waterline repairs: extensive
Ship's and variety store: yes
Restaurant: on-site

Palmer's Seafood House Restaurant (912-897-2611) maintains several docks fronting onto Turner Creek's easterly banks near facility designation #10A on chart 11507. While a number of resident craft occupy much of the available dockage space at this dining attraction, there should still be room for a few boats up to 40 feet in length. Depths run 10 to 20 feet. The restaurant itself attracts many tourists. This writer found the seafood quite good, even if a bit pricey.

Hogan's Marina sits hard by the northern side of Palmer's Seafood House Restaurant. This friendly facility caters mostly to small power craft and features dry-stack storage. While transients are occasionally accepted, the management has informed this writer that cruising boaters are "not our market." The marina's one face-type pier is a floating wooden structure with water and 15-amp power connections. Dockside depths are 20 feet or better. Gasoline can be purchased, and some light mechanical repairs can be arranged through independent contractors. A small ship's store and snack bar are on the premises.

Hogan's Marina (912) 897-3474

Approach depth: 9 feet (minimum)
Dockside depth: 20+ feet
Accepts transients: very limited
Floating wooden pier: yes
Dockside power connections: 15 amps
Dockside water connections: yes
Gasoline: yes
Mechanical repairs: independent contractors
Ship's store: small
Restaurant: nearby

Wilmington River

South and east of flashing daybeacon #40, the lower track of Wilmington River, abandoned by the ICW, continues seaward down a broad, deep channel stretching in places almost from bank to bank. While the river itself is a bit wide open for protected overnight anchorage, there is one facility along the stream's route with limited services for visiting cruisers. The river's inlet is well marked and fairly reliable.

Many cruisers entering Wilmington River have wondered at the immense structure visible on the river's eastern banks just south of the Turner Creek entrance. This huge complex is the Sheraton Savannah Resort and Inn. While it is most certainly a premier vacation facility, it offers very little in the way of service for boaters, and the docks visible from the water are quite shoal, with depths of 4 feet or less.

Well south of flashing daybeacon #23, boaters cruising on Wilmington River will spot the protected, breakwater-enclosed harbor of The Landings on Skidaway Island at the charted location of Priest Landing. This friendly facility is part of a private development and is now under the ownership of The Landings Yacht Club. The marina is open to transients, though the number of visitors' berths is quite limited. Those lucky enough to secure a berth will discover fixed concrete piers with all power and water connections. Dockside depths of as little as 5 feet could be a problem only for long-legged sailcraft. Gasoline and diesel fuel can be purchased, and there is a combination gift shop and ship's store on the premises. There is one shoreside shower, but it's not going to win any awards.

Mechanical repairs are available for both diesel and gasoline engines, and the marina features extensive dry-stack storage of small power craft. No restaurants are within walking distance, so bring your own galley supplies.

In July 1996, The Landings on Skidaway Island will play host to the United States Olympic race team. The always-limited transient space will probably fall to nil during these events.

The Landings on Skidaway Island
(912) 598-0500

Approach depth: 15+ feet
Dockside depth: 5–8 feet (low water)
Accepts transients: limited
Fixed concrete piers: yes
Dockside power connections: 30 and 50 amps
Dockside water connections: yes
Showers: very limited
Gasoline: yes
Diesel fuel: yes
Mechanical repairs: yes
Ship's and gift store: yes

Wilmington River's inlet is bordered by huge shoals, but the passage is fairly well marked, and it should not prove too challenging for the careful navigator in fair weather. Visiting cruisers might want to check with The Landings on Skidaway Island for the latest navigational data on this seaward cut before making the jump.

Waterway Anchorage

The correctly charted deep water abutting the western banks of the Skidaway River portion of the ICW south of flashing daybeacon #40 can serve as an overnight anchorage for skippers who are not able to continue north or south to a more protected haven. Depths of 10 feet run to within 50 yards or so of the western shoreline. This anchorage sports fair protection from western winds, but it's open to fresh breezes from any other quarter. You may also be disturbed by the wake of vessels passing on the Waterway, particularly during the early-morning hours.

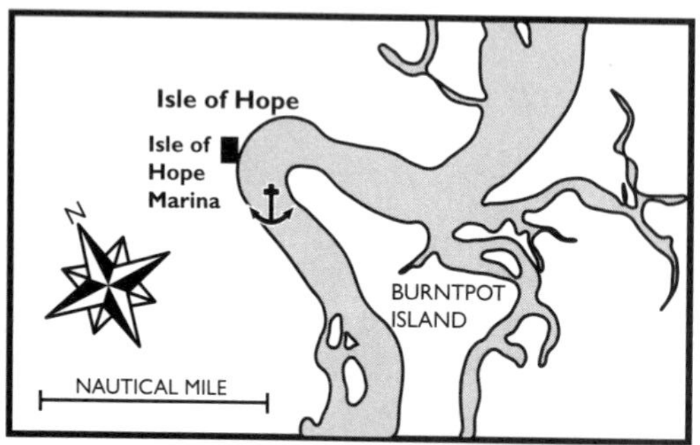

Isle of Hope Marina and Anchorage

After twisting and turning your way down Skidaway River for several more miles, you will come upon the charming village of Isle of Hope, located on the northwestern shore in the body of a hairpin turn northwest of unlighted daybeacon #46. Isle of Hope Marina sits in the heart of the village waterfront, looking much the same as it has for decades and decades. Frequent Waterway travelers will certainly have stopped here many times before. In fact, this writer's mother and father stopped at Isle of Hope Marina when they were bringing their first boat back from Florida in the 1940s.

The present-day version of Isle of Hope Marina features transient dockage at a long, wooden floating-face pier with impressive depths of 15 feet or considerably more. Some of the inner slips, mostly taken up by small power craft, have 11 to 13 feet of water at low tide. Water connections and power connections up to 50 amps are provided at all berths, and gasoline and diesel fuel are at hand. Full mechanical repairs are offered, and vessels up to 50 feet can be hauled out by way of a marine railway. There is a ship's store on the premises that is almost nostalgic in its old-time flavor. A laundromat and showers are available, though this writer found the bathrooms a bit buggy. The marina will provide motorized transportation to the nearby Elegant Pelican Restaurant, and the restaurant will return you to the docks.

Isle of Hope Marina (912) 354-8187

Approach depth: 12+ feet
Dockside depth: 10–15+ feet
Accepts transients: yes
Floating wooden piers: yes
Dockside power connections: 30 and 50 amps
Dockside water connections: yes
Showers: yes
Laundromat: yes
Gasoline: yes
Diesel fuel: yes
Mechanical repairs: yes
Below-waterline repairs: yes
Ship's store: yes
Restaurant: transportation provided

Just behind Isle of Hope Marina, a long row of historic homes fronts onto the river along North Bluff Road. Take a moment to stroll this quiet lane and admire the old homeplaces. They are really quite lovely.

Many Waterway cruisers, particularly sailors, anchor on the ICW's western flank near unlighted daybeacon #46A. Depths seem to run between 8 and 11 feet, with good protection from all but particularly strong northern and southern blows. The Isle of Hope waterfront is a No Wake zone, so you should not be too inconvenienced by passing vessels. Just be sure to drop your hook so as to swing well away from your neighbors.

Moon River Anchorage

South of Skidaway Narrows and flashing daybeacon #74, the ICW quickly enters the headwaters of Burnside River. Between #74 and flashing daybeacon #75, boaters can cut to the northwest on the initial portion of Moon River for overnight anchorage.

Minimum depths of 6 feet extend for only a few hundred yards upstream. Moon River is rather wide, and the all-too-usual marshy shores do not give much protection in fresh breezes. Strong winds from the northwest are a particular problem. Those who anchor might also take some wake from large power craft passing by on the Waterway.

You might be interested to know that this is the same Moon River made famous by the song of the same name. Native son Johnny Mercer wrote the tune about the beautiful body of water then known as Back River. In recognition of the song's seemingly ageless popularity, the Georgia state government officially changed the stream's name to Moon River.

Vernon River

Southwest of flashing daybeacon #79, the Waterway flows into Vernon River and follows this stream generally south to Little Ogeechee River. The Vernon's mostly deep upper reaches, abandoned by the Waterway north-northwest of flashing daybeacon #79, offer at least two good choices for protected overnight anchorage. Vernon River is an attractive body of water, particularly with the warm, golden light of a late-spring afternoon lying along its shores. Cruisers who anchor along this stream in appropriate winds will come away with a cruising memory not soon forgotten.

The first anchor-down spot you might consider is found abeam of the charted village of Beaulieu, where high, well-wooded ground flanks the easterly banks and several attractive modern homes sit along the shore. Depths run from 12 to 20 feet, and there is good protection from easterly winds and fair shelter from northerly breezes. Strong winds blowing from the south straight up the river clearly call for another strategy.

Cruisers can continue a bit farther upstream past the shoal-prone turn at the village of Montgomery and anchor in the body of the next northerly turn. The southwesterly banks sport high, modestly developed shores and provide, as you would expect, good shelter when winds are blowing over this shoreline. Strong breezes from the north blow directly down the river, giving the wind plenty of fetch to foster more than a few waves.

ICW FROM SAVANNAH RIVER TO VERNON RIVER NAVIGATION

Besides several No Wake zones and a restricted bridge, there are few navigational worries other than the typical strong tidal currents between Savannah and Vernon Rivers. The Waterway proceeds along its well-outlined way, and most sidewaters are deep. There are a few shallows to avoid, however, so read the information below and don't be too cavalier with your navigational precautions.

ICW across Savannah River to Wilmington River Boaters exiting Fields Cut at flashing daybeacon #48 should be on maximum alert for strong tidal currents and the possible presence of large oceangoing vessels on Savannah River.

Continue out into Savannah River by setting course directly for flashing buoy #35. Some 30 to 50 yards before reaching this aid to navigation, cut west-northwest and point to come abeam of flashing buoy #36 to its southern side.

As you come abeam of #36, the northeastern entrance to Elba Island Cut will come abeam to the west-southwest. This passage is the ICW's principal southern exodus from Savannah River. Enter Elba Island Cut by coming abeam of and passing flashing daybeacon #2 to its southeastern side. You should then point to come abeam of flashing daybeacon #4 to the same side.

Southwest of #4, the Waterway channel cuts across a portion of the shallow "South Channel." Very shoal water flanks the ICW to the northwest and southeast. Set a careful course from #4 to come abeam of flashing daybeacon #6 to its southeasterly quarter. Watch your stern as you move between #4 and #6 to quickly note any leeway slippage.

Southwest of #6, the Waterway flows through a man-made landcut until it intersects the upper waters of Wilmington River and the mouth of St. Augustine Creek. This latter body of water will be reviewed below.

Boaters cruising south down Savannah River aboard vessels that can clear a 35-foot fixed bridge may make use of the marked "South Channel" cut. This passage is plagued by exceptionally strong tidal currents that can make the various maneuvers required to stay in the sometimes-narrow channel a bit tricky. The northwesterly entrance to this channel lies southeast of Savannah River's flashing buoy #50. Cruise into the canal-like body of water on its mid-width, pointing to pass south-southwest of unlighted daybeacon #A1. Don't cut either corner at the creek's entrance!

Continue downstream by passing red markers to your starboard side and green beacons to port. Southeast of unlighted daybeacon #A8, you will soon approach the 35-foot fixed bridge. If you need more clearance, your only option is to retrace your steps to Savannah River and cruise downstream to Elba Island Cut.

After passing under the 35-foot fixed bridge, slow down! The waters southeast of the span are the most difficult portion of the alternate channel. Set course carefully to come abeam of unlighted daybeacon #A12 to its fairly immediate northeasterly side. You must then follow a sharp cut to the southwest around #A12. Study chart 11507 to illuminate this complicated maneuver.

Once around #A12, point to pass unlighted daybeacon #A15 to its west-northwesterly side. This aid marks the entrance into a dredged canal that in turn leads to the principal ICW passage.

The alternate route's entrance into the Waterway southwest of unlighted daybeacon #A17 is complicated by the presence of a marshy shoal bisecting the stream's mouth. This hazard is covered at high tide or even mid-tide, and it has brought more than one boater to grief. To avoid the shoal, point to pass just south of unlighted daybeacon #A18 and hold course out into the mid-width of the Waterway.

St. Augustine Creek, Bull River, and Associated Waters The entrance to St. Augustine Creek will come abeam on the ICW's southeastern shore near unlighted daybeacon #8. Enter on the mid-width. You need hold to the centerline for good depths only as far as the intersection with Bull River.

Do not attempt to enter Richardson and Turner

Creeks. While the initial portion of the combined creeks is deep, shoal water is encountered as Battery Point is approached.

Continue holding to the centerline as you pass the entrance to the two creeks and cruise into the widening waters of Bull River. For best depths, favor the northeastern shoreline slightly as you pass charted Screvens Point. Soon, you will approach the 20-foot fixed bridge. (Sailcraft and large power vessels that cannot clear the span must retrace their steps up St. Augustine Creek to the Waterway.) Bull River Yacht Club Marina will come abeam to the southwest immediately after the span.

South and east of the fixed span, Bull River snakes its way along an ever-broader course. Good depths stretch to within 100 yards or less of both banks. You need only hold to within shouting distance of the centerline to avoid any fear of grounding.

Bull River eventually turns almost due south and hurries on to a juncture with Lazaretto Creek and its several auxiliary streams. Cruisers who choose to explore these fascinating waters should favor the southern banks slightly when entering Lazaretto Creek from Bull River. Chart 11512 correctly predicts a small shoal abutting the northeastern point.

Continue keeping to the mid-width until reaching Morgan Cut. You must now choose whether to cut northwest and cruise Oyster Creek or turn east into Tybee Creek.

Boaters deciding on Oyster Creek must avoid the charted shoal guarding the upper portion of Lazaretto Creek. This obstruction impinges on the eastern mouth of Oyster Creek. It can be bypassed by slightly favoring the southern shoreline of Oyster Creek's entrance. Excellent depths continue on a broad path straddling the centerline until the creek splits into two branches well upstream. Cruising-size craft are advised to discontinue their gunkholing at this point.

To enter Tybee Creek, follow the mid-width of Morgan Cut to the east-southeast. Soon, you will come upon an area where one stream appears to cut to the south while another strikes east. Don't attempt to enter the southerly passage. While this stream looks good on chart 11512, on-site research proved these waters hard to identify and more than slightly treacherous. Instead, follow the center of the eastward-flowing stream as it cuts first one way and then another.

West of shallow Carter Creek, a shoal abuts Tybee Creek's southwesterly shoreline. Favor the northeasterly banks slightly after passing through the charted turn to the southeast (as you pass the mouth of Carter Creek to the northeast). You can cut back to the centerline after cruising 200 yards or so southeast of Carter Creek's entrance.

East of the intersection with shoaly Chimney Creek, Tybee Creek turns sharply south, and significant shoals begin to shelve out from both shorelines. Hold strictly to the mid-width as you round the turn. Favor the eastern banks as you cruise south past the resort development on Tybee Island. Study chart 11512 and you will quickly note the large, charted patch of shallows on the western banks. You will soon spot the docks of MarLin Marina along the eastern shoreline.

Don't attempt to cruise past the southerly tip of Tybee Island, since mammoth breakers and huge unmarked shoals are soon encountered.

On Bull River Back on the main track of Bull River, passing cruisers will come upon the eastern mouth of Halfmoon River abeam of unlighted daybeacon #4. In spite of the wide entrance channel noted on chart 11512, on-site research revealed that shoaling has now all but closed this cut. Additionally, two large bodies of shallow water flank Halfmoon River's entrance to the north and south. These shallows are a concern to those heading seaward on Bull River. Pass unlighted daybeacon #4 by some 50 yards to its western side. Study chart 11512 for a moment and you will see why this maneuver is so important.

South of #4, the channel remains broad, but there is shallow water to the east and west. Point to eventually come abeam of unlighted daybeacon #3 by some 100 yards to its easterly quarter. Very shoal water lies west of #3.

From #3, point to come abeam of unlighted daybeacon #1 by about the same distance to its northeastern side. Now, the really shallow water shifts to the northeastern side of the channel. Do not stray too far from #1.

You must not continue directly seaward from #1. Rather, you should cut to the southwest and intersect Wilmington River's seaward channel. To achieve this objective, continue cruising southeast past #1 for 100 yards or so, then cut sharply south and point to come abeam of flashing buoy #14 by some 25 yards to its easterly quarter. You can then cruise south from #14 to the heart of the Wilmington River channel. A turn to the southeast leads to the open sea, while a jog to the west carries the cruiser into Wilmington River.

Back on the ICW Boaters entering Wilmington River via the primary Elba Island Cut should favor the southwestern banks, marked by flashing daybeacon #15, as they pass the southwestern entrance of the alternate route abeam of #15. This procedure will help boaters avoid the charted marsh island that bisects the entrance to the alternate passage. High- or even mid-tide waters completely cover this potential obstruction.

At flashing daybeacon #19, the ICW cuts sharply southwest and begins its approach to Causton Bluff and the GA 26 drawbridge. This span has at least 25 feet of vertical clearance, but for boats that need more height, a restrictive opening schedule is still in place. The bridge will not open from 6:30 A.M. to 9:00 A.M. or from 4:30 P.M. to 6:30 P.M., except for scheduled openings at 7:00 A.M., 8:00 A.M., and 5:30 P.M.—and that's if and only if vessels are waiting to pass. At all other times, the span deigns to open on demand for us peon boaters.

Watch the western shores both above and below the bridge for a glimpse of Bonaventure Cemetery perched atop Causton Bluff. Powerboaters operating their craft from the high vantage point of a fly bridge will have the best view.

Thunderbolt South-southwest of unlighted daybeacon #33, the Waterway begins its approach to the Thunderbolt high-rise bridge and the many facilities grouped about the village. Power vessels should slow to No Wake speed and continue this procedure until reaching flashing daybeacon #36.

The high-rise bridge at Thunderbolt has a full 65 feet of vertical clearance and is a welcome addition to the Georgia ICW. Marina facilities line both banks of the Waterway north of the fixed span. South-southwest of the bridge, a number of facilities flank the westerly shoreline.

Herb River Shoal water is building out from Herb River's northwesterly entrance point. Enter the river by favoring the easterly banks.

After working your way upstream for 300 yards or so, cut back to the centerline. Continue holding to the middle until Herb River cuts sharply southwest. Hold scrupulously to the mid-width until the river turns back to the west-northwest. Favor the northeasterly banks slightly as you cruise through this stretch and approach the next southerly turn.

After passing through this final turn, boaters must guard against the correctly charted shoal building out from the easterly banks. Obviously, you should favor the westerly shoreline to avoid this problem.

Don't attempt to cruise past the stream's next hairpin turn. Depths finally begin to deteriorate past this point.

On the ICW Shoal water abuts the Waterway's southwestern flank between flashing daybeacon #37 and unlighted daybeacon #38. Come abeam of flashing daybeacon #37A to its immediate southwestern side.

Continue favoring the northeasterly shoreline as you cruise. Point to pass unlighted daybeacon #38 by some 25 yards (or a bit more) to its northeasterly side. Soon, you will spot the docks and clubhouse of Savannah Yacht Club on the northeasterly banks. You can cruise back to the centerline at this point. Good depths again open out almost from shore to shore.

At flashing daybeacon #40, the Waterway leaves Wilmington River and cuts sharply south-southwest on Skidaway River. Our account will leave the ICW for a few moments to consider the lower Wilmington River and nearby Turner Creek.

Turner Creek Successful entrance into Turner Creek is a bit trickier than a quick study of chart 11507 would indicate. Enter the creek by favoring the high ground of Turners Rock on the northern banks.

You will pass several attractive private homes while you cruise. As you come abeam of the second private dock, immediately begin working your way across the creek, pointing for the mid-width of Sail Harbor Marina's dockage basin. Failing to follow this procedure could well land the hapless boater in the charted 2-foot shoal to the east.

Once abeam of Sail Harbor Marina, you need only cruise upstream on the mid-width to maintain good depths as far as the 35-foot fixed bridge.

Both Palmer's Seafood House Restaurant and Hogan's Marina will come abeam on the eastern banks near facility designation #10A (noted on chart 11507).

Further passage northeast of the 35-foot fixed bridge is strictly not recommended. Low-tide depths of as little as 3 to 4 feet are a distinct possibility.

Lower Wilmington River The southerly portion of Wilmington River, bypassed by the ICW, is a wide, deep stream that is mostly free of navigational hazards short of its inlet passage. This channel is clearly outlined by numerous charted aids to navigation. The fact that these beacons are charted is a good indication that the cut is reasonably stable.

As you leave the Waterway and pass into the lower Wilmington River, watch the easterly banks just south of the Turner Creek entrance for a good view of the Sheraton Savannah Resort and Inn. Flashing daybeacon #29 should be passed well southwest of your course.

South of the charted position of Wilmington Park (on the river's eastern shoreline), a line of shallows flanks the Wilmington's western banks. Simply pass several hundred yards east of flashing daybeacons #25 and #23 to bypass this shoal. Stay well away from #23 in particular. Shallow water seems to be building around this aid.

Soon, Wilmington River begins to curve to the southeast. The Landings on Skidaway Island marina will come abeam at the charted location of Priest Landing just before you enter the river's southeasterly bend.

After cruising through the southeasterly turn, watch for flashing daybeacon #22 along the northeasterly banks. This aid marks a bank of shallow water along this shoreline. Again, simply pass well to the southwest of #22 and you should encounter no difficulty.

As you approach Sister Island, use your binoculars

to pick out flashing daybeacon #19 and unlighted daybeacon #20. Be sure to pass between these two aids. Shallow water lies west of #19 and east of #20.

East and south of #19 and #20, the Wilmington River channel begins its passage to the ocean. The wide channel runs between extensive shoals, but a fair number of markers help boaters keep to the good water. Flashing daybeacon #17 warns against the Salt Pond Shoals, which run out from the southwestern banks. Another large body of shallows associated with Cabbage Island Spit flanks the channel to the northeast.

Past #17, the channel turns almost due east. Point to pass well south of flashing daybeacon #16 and continue to a position between flashing buoy #14 and unlighted can buoy #13.

The inlet channel sweeps to the southeast after passing #14 and #13. Consult the latest edition of chart 11512 for the most recent arrangement of aids to navigation from #14 and #13 to the open sea.

Back on the ICW Flashing daybeacon #40 marks a sharp southern turn of the ICW into the headwaters of Skidaway River. Give #40 a wide berth. Shoal water seems to be building around this marker.

Waterway Anchorage If you decide to make use of the rather open anchorage along the ICW's western shore south of flashing daybeacon #40, simply depart the Waterway as the deep waters come abeam to the west. You can cruise to within 50 yards or so of the western shoreline with good depths.

On the ICW Southwest of flashing daybeacon #43, a large patch of shoals and marsh shoulders its way into the ICW's western and northwestern flanks. Unlighted daybeacons #44 and #44A warn cruisers away from this potential trap. Be sure to pass well southeast of both #44 and #44A.

The Waterway turns sharply northwest at unlighted daybeacon #46 and begins its approach to Isle of Hope. The community sits on the northern and northwestern shores of the hairpin turn in the Waterway north of unlighted daybeacon #46A. Isle of Hope Marina is located on this same shoreline about midway along the village waterfront. The anchorage to the south can usually be picked out by virtue of all the anchored vessels grouped around #46A.

South of Isle of Hope, the ICW runs through a narrow passage known as Skidaway Narrows. Stick strictly to the marked channel between unlighted daybeacons #50 and #60. Very shallow water abuts both sides of the ICW along this stretch.

Southwest of unlighted daybeacon #60, the ICW flows under a bascule bridge with 22 feet of closed vertical clearance. This span currently opens on demand.

Flashing daybeacon #71 marks the ICW's passage from Skidaway Narrows into the upper reaches of Burnside River. Don't attempt to cruise the river northwest of the ICW intersection. This portion of the stream is quite shoal and treacherous.

The well-outlined Waterway channel passes northeast of Marsh Island and then curls around to the southwest at flashing daybeacon #74. Soon, the southeasterly mouth of Moon River will come abeam to the northwest.

Moon River Anchorage Remember that the deep water on Moon River extends only a few hundred yards upstream from its southeasterly entrance. Cruise into the stream on its centerline and drop the hook before proceeding too far!

On the ICW South of flashing daybeacon #74, the Waterway curls back around to the west via a long hairpin turn. Watch for unlighted daybeacon #76 as you come out of this bend. Be sure to pass well southwest of #76. Shallow water lies northeast, north, and northwest of this aid.

A long No Wake zone begins at unlighted daybeacon #76 and stretches west almost to flashing daybeacon #79. This speed-restricted belt was obviously designed to protect the private homes and docks lining Burnside River's northern banks. The homes are associated with the residential community of Vernon View. Since vessels are seldom seen docked at the piers, it leads one to wonder who knew their congressman or county commissioner well enough to get the necessary regulation in place.

Stay well northwest of flashing daybeacon #79. Shoaling from the adjacent point was encroaching on this aid at the time of this writing. Some 6-foot depths were sounded close beside #79 during on-site research.

Flashing daybeacon #79 heralds the end of Burnside River and the Waterway's entrance into Vernon River. The northwesterly portion of this latter stream, bypassed by the ICW, offers at least two anchorage considerations.

Upper Vernon River Boaters entering the northwestern stretch of Vernon River must scrupulously avoid Possum Point, which separates Vernon and Burnside Rivers. A long, mean shoal is building south from this promontory. Otherwise, you can simply hold to the centerline until the high ground at the charted village of Beaulieu comes abeam to the east.

Boaters who decide to continue upriver to the anchorage near Houston Creek should begin heavily favoring the southern banks as Vernon River turns sharply westward north of Beaulieu. Glance at chart 11512 for a moment and notice the large patch of shallows abutting the "Montgomery" (northern) shoreline.

Soon, Vernon River begins to follow a bend back to the north. In the body of this turn, high ground will come abeam to the southwest immediately northwest of charted, shallow Houston Creek. Drop the hook abeam of this high ground.

The real die-hard explorers among us can continue upstream to a position abeam of Vernonberg, but there are no facilities here for pleasure craft, and several unmarked shoals must be avoided along the way. Study chart 11512 should you decide to push your limits.

ICW to Little Ogeechee River The Waterway's route down the lower Vernon River stretches through an unusually wide swath of deep water. There is only one marker along the way, but it would require some inventive navigation to run aground here. Eventually, the ICW skates southeast past flashing daybeacon #81 northeast of your course.

At the foot of Vernon River, come abeam of unlighted daybeacon #82 well to its easterly side. Stay away from #82. This aid marks a long shoal building out from the point separating Vernon and Little Ogeechee Rivers.

Unlighted daybeacon #82 introduces visiting cruisers to the wide confines of Little Ogeechee River and Ossabaw Sound.

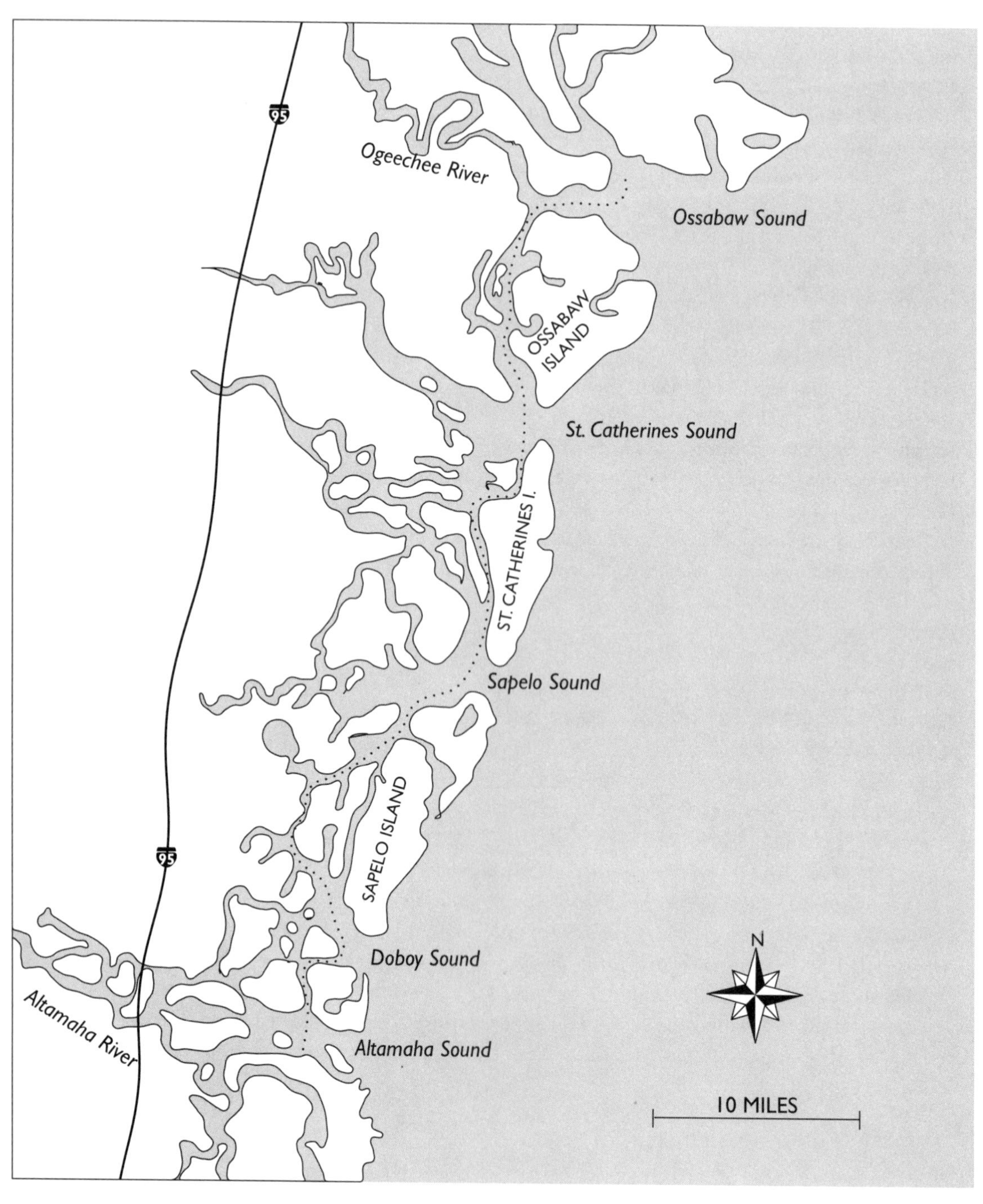

95
Ogeechee River
Ossabaw Sound
OSSABAW ISLAND
St. Catherines Sound
ST. CATHERINES I.
Sapelo Sound
SAPELO ISLAND
95
Doboy Sound
Altamaha River
Altamaha Sound
N
10 MILES

Little Ogeechee River to Altamaha Sound

Little Ogeechee River, Green Island Sound, and Ossabaw Sound introduce southbound boaters on the Georgia ICW to the state's wide sounds and rivers. From the Little Ogeechee to the Florida state line, the Waterway tracks its way across broad, open waters connected by protected landcuts or rivers leading to other large sounds. All of these sounds allow for plenty of wind fetch, which can produce a daunting, occasionally dangerous chop when the weather turns nasty. A cruise of the Georgia coastline south of Vernon River should be planned with a ready ear for the latest NOAA weather forecast.

Marina facilities become sparse, to say the least. In fact, there are only three marinas that welcome the cruising boater between the Little Ogeechee and St. Catherines Sound. A single facility is available between North Newport River and Altamaha Sound. These facilities call for a healthy cruise off the Waterway.

Be sure your tanks are topped off and your craft is in top operating condition before tackling this section of the Georgia coastline. During research, this writer and his mate actually ran out of fuel on Medway River, this in spite of the fact that we filled up at every available stop. Fortunately, a quick call on the VHF brought assistance, but that was some of the most expensive gasoline this writer has ever purchased.

Charts

Boaters will need three charts to cruise the waters of central Georgia:

11507 continues to be the primary ICW chart for all the waters covered in this chapter

11511 is a large-format chart detailing both Ossabaw and St. Catherines Sounds and some sidewaters in between, including Ogeechee, Medway, and North Newport Rivers

11510 is another large chart providing navigational detail for Sapelo and Doboy Sounds

Anchorages, on the other hand, abound all along the Waterway. It would take a truly jaded cruiser not to be intrigued by the potpourri of possible overnight stops far from any sign of civilization.

While undoubtedly a bit more lonely than their northerly counterparts, the waters of central Georgia between the Little Ogeechee and Altamaha Sound display some of the most wonderful natural splendors in the state.

LITTLE OGEECHEE RIVER TO MEDWAY RIVER

There is really little to distinguish the waters between Little Ogeechee and Medway Rivers from their fellows along the central Georgia coastline. Again, anchorages are prolific and marina facilities are about as scarce as the proverbial hen's teeth. The scenery is mostly composed of the usual marsh, though higher ground can lift your eyes up from the low-level banks from time to time. Take your time and enjoy this first real bit of Georgia isolation.

Little Ogeechee River

Little Ogeechee River cuts back to the west from the ICW's unlighted daybeacon #82. In spite of the broad and impressive face this stream presents to passing cruisers, its waters harbor numerous shoals, and the river lacks any aids to navigation. While local boaters, particularly fishermen, use the Little Ogeechee regularly, visiting cruisers should probably relegate this river to that small group of Georgia bodies of water better bypassed.

Green Island Sound and Ossabaw Sound

The ICW leaves Vernon River at unlighted daybeacon #82 and thrusts its way southeast into the combined waters of Vernon and Little Ogeechee Rivers. These waters are designated on chart 11512 as Green Island Sound, but this writer thinks of them simply as the westerly reaches of Ossabaw Sound. This latter body of water sweeps east in a wide, often shallow path to the Atlantic Ocean.

While some aids to navigation outline Ossabaw Sound's seaward passage, they are not nearly prolific enough to warn boaters who lack specific local knowledge to keep away from the surrounding shallows. There are far better inlets to the north and south, so unless you can find a local craft and follow in its wake, it would be better to make another seaward choice.

Delegal Creek Marina

Southwest of flashing daybeacon #86, the Georgia ICW leaves the waters of Green Island and Ossabaw Sounds and cuts through current-plagued Hell Gate, which connects with Ogeechee River. Before leaving Ossabaw Sound behind, boaters have the opportunity to visit amicable Delegal Creek Marina, located on the creek of the same name east-northeast of #86.

The westerly entrance into Delegal Creek

can be rather tricky for first-timers. Be sure to read the navigational instructions presented in the next section of this chapter before attempting first-time entry.

Once you find your way through the entrance cut, minimum depths of 7 to 8 feet can be maintained to the docks. The marina's piers are found on the creek's eastern banks northeast of flashing daybeacon #11. This is a very sheltered setting, with extensive high ground fronting the eastern shoreline.

Big changes have taken place at Delegal Creek Marina since the last edition of this guide went to press. Ownership has now been transferred to The Landings Yacht Club from the private development company that used to manage the complex. The new owners are eager to attract visiting transients. Cruisers can now look for a warm welcome at this advantageously placed facility.

Delegal Creek Marina is clearly a good spot to ride out a heavy blow before tackling the open waters to the south. Overnight berths are found at concrete-decked floating docks with full power and water connections. Minimum dockside depths are 8 feet, with most slips having 10 to 12 feet of water. Gasoline and diesel fuel can be purchased at a pier set aside for this purpose, and mechanical repairs are now available through on-site technicians. The marina maintains a full-line ship's and variety store, showers, and a laundromat. The nearby Upper Crust Restaurant will dispatch a van to pick up boaters and return them to the docks. The new marina management hopes to establish food service on the marina grounds in the near future, but the inception date for this service could not be determined at the time of this writing.

Delegal Creek Marina (912) 598-0023

Approach depth: 6–8 feet (minimum channel depth)
Dockside depth: 8–12 feet (low water)
Accepts transients: yes
Floating concrete piers: yes
Dockside power connections: 30 and 50 amps
Dockside water connections: yes
Showers: yes
Laundromat: yes
Gasoline: yes
Diesel fuel: yes
Mechanical repairs: yes
Ship's and variety store: yes
Restaurant: nearby (transportation provided)

It is also possible to anchor in Delegal Creek above the marina. The creek maintains minimum 6-foot depths, with typical soundings of 8 to 20 feet until the stream splits into several branches west of Ritter Hammock. One of the two best anchorages is found where the charted high ground fronts the western banks just north of the marina, and the other is found abeam of the wooded Ritter Hammock shores along the creek's northern banks west of shallow Franklin Creek. Both refuges have enough swinging room for vessels up to 45 feet. Obviously, if the wind happens to be blowing across the high ground, protection is much enhanced.

Ogeechee River

The ICW flows south through the shoal-prone Hell Gate landcut into Ogeechee River. To the east-southeast, the Ogeechee cuts through a broad but poorly marked channel into Ossabaw Sound, eventually leading to the open sea. Again, this inlet channel is not recommended for strangers.

The Waterway cuts generally west on Ogeechee River for several miles before turning southwest on the so-called Florida Passage at flashing daybeacon #98. A privately marked channel leads upstream on the upper portion of Ogeechee River to Fort McAllister Marina. Most of the markers are small, privately maintained floating buoys. During daylight, you should be able to pick out these aids to navigation with the help of binoculars, but this channel is all but impossible for strangers at night.

If you avoid the surrounding shoals with the help of the private markers, minimum 9-foot depths can be held to Fort McAllister Marina. It is a run of some 5.1 nautical miles from the Waterway to the marina docks.

This facility has one wooden-decked floating dock. The marina management has informed this writer that the pier is often filled during the summer, spring, and early fall by resident boaters and fishermen. It would be a good idea to call ahead of time to check on dockage availability before committing to a stay at Fort McAllister Marina. You should also be on guard against the swift tidal currents when docking.

When space is available, transients are accepted for overnight or temporary dockage. Depths alongside run 9 to 12 feet. Water connections and power connections up to 50 amps are provided. Gasoline and diesel fuel are available dockside, and the marina boasts some low-key showers and a small laundromat. A large ship's, variety, and tackle store is perched just behind the docks. Some low-key mechanical repairs can sometimes be arranged for gasoline engines. There is no restaurant within walking distance.

Fort McAllister Marina (912) 727-2632

Approach depth: 9 feet (minimum)
Dockside depth: 9–12 feet
Accepts transients: limited
Floating wooden dock: yes
Dockside power connections: 30 and 50 amps
Dockside water connections: yes
Showers: yes
Laundromat: yes
Gasoline: yes
Diesel fuel: yes
Mechanical repairs: limited (gasoline only)
Ship's and variety store: yes

Fort McAllister History This guide has already discussed Fort Pulaski's capitulation to Union forces early in the Civil War, ending the era of masonry fortifications. The Confederates soon adapted their defenses, and Fort McAllister, perched on the southern banks of Ogeechee River, is a prime example of the new strategy. Formed of earthen rather than brick walls, this fort was constructed in 1861 to guard the "back door" to Savannah.

From 1862 to 1863, Fort McAllister's defenders successfully repulsed no fewer than seven determined attacks by armored Union warships outfitted with rifled cannon. The post did not capitulate until taken in hand-to-hand combat with the massive Northern force under William Sherman.

With the fall of Fort McAllister, Savannah was encircled and all but lost. The reluctant Confederates soon evacuated the city amidst the fires of scuttled vessels.

Today, Fort McAllister is part of Richmond Hill State Park and is open to the public Tuesday through Saturday from 9:00 A.M. to 5:00 P.M. and Sunday from 2:00 P.M. to 5:30 P.M.

Through the diligent efforts of the Georgia Historic Commission, the fort has been restored to the way it looked in 1865. An on-site museum offers a short movie that is an excellent introduction to the fort's history.

Fort McAllister is within walking distance of Fort McAllister Marina, with 0.75 mile separating the two. Wear comfortable shoes and bring the camera along.

Redbird Creek

The stream known as Redbird Creek cuts the northwestern banks of the ICW's Florida Passage north of flashing daybeacon #99. The creek carries minimum depths of 11 feet for a considerable distance. Boats up to 45 feet can anchor just upstream from the creek's southeastern mouth. For better protection, you can cruise through the creek's first jog to the northwest. After leaving this "knuckle" behind, you will see high ground beginning to flank the western banks some distance back from the shoreline. The wooded banks render good protection when winds are blowing from the west or southwest.

Upper Bear River and Associated Streams

Unlighted nun buoy #102 marks the ICW's exit from the Florida Passage and its entrance into Bear River. The easterly portion of Bear River, bypassed by the Waterway, offers a multitude of good anchorages. East of #102, the initial portion of the river is quite deep, but it is too broad for anything except light-air anchorage. In all but fair weather, boaters will do better to cruise farther east to the point where Bear River splits into Buckhead and Cane Patch Creeks.

Pleasure craft of almost any size can drop the hook short of the river's split in 15 to 25 feet of water. The high ground off to the north gives some protection when winds are blowing from this quarter.

Buckhead Creek boasts minimum depths of 11 feet until it splinters into several streams south of Pine Island. Cruisers will find good anchorage southwest of Pine Island where chart 11507 notes a 13-foot sounding. Shelter is better than average for northeasterly blows.

For this writer's money, Cane Patch Creek is the real anchorage find in this locale. Unadventurous types or those simply not wanting to make too long a cruise from the ICW can drop the hook just inside the stream's western mouth amidst ample swinging room. To minimize the use of a long anchor rode, consider anchoring in the charted 19-foot waters rather than the depths of 30-plus feet at the stream's mouth. The beautifully undeveloped, well-wooded southern shores look as if they have never known the

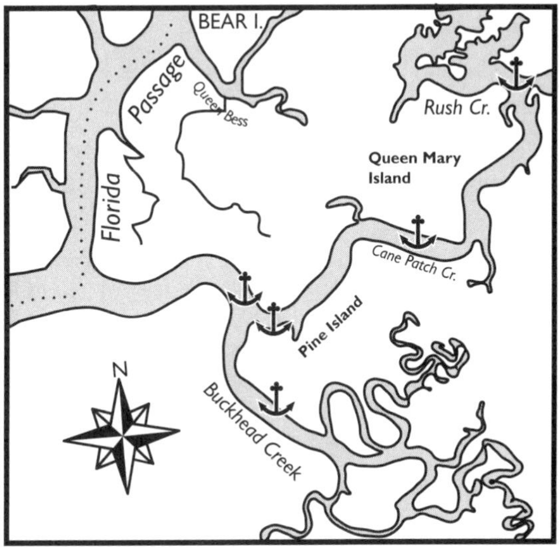

hand of man. This high ground offers good shelter when winds are blowing from the south, southeast, or southwest.

Another good anchorage is found south of charted Queen Mary Island. Again, the scenery is all any nature lover could ask for, and swinging room is plentiful. Depths run 16 to 22 feet.

Finally, for those who, like this author, have a bit of wanderlust in their hearts and are willing to make a substantial trek from the ICW (and who pilot a boat 40 feet or smaller), it is possible to follow Cane Patch Creek to its intersection with Rush Creek. You must pass though one small patch of uncharted 5- to 6-foot low-tide depths to reach this haven, but you may find the extra effort more than justified. Drop the hook as high ground comes abeam to the northeast at the intersection of Cane Patch and Rush Creeks. You can then sit back in the cockpit or fly bridge and contemplate the vastness of nature without the slightest human intrusion.

Ossabaw Island

Cane Patch and Buckhead Creeks pierce a portion of Ossabaw Island and allow boaters a fleeting look at this privately owned, historic Sea Island. Ossabaw Island was the site of the first great plantation empire on the Georgia coast. After early ownership by the Bosomworths (who will be discussed at greater length in the section on St. Catherines Island history), the entire island was acquired by John Morel in 1760. Morel was an experienced planter who had settled along South Carolina's Ashley River in 1730.

Soon, Morel's slaves cleared many fields on Ossabaw Island and planted vast quantities of indigo. It wasn't long before indigo began to yield vast sums to the Morel coffers. As Burnette Vanstory comments in his unforgettable book, *Georgia's Land of the Golden Isles*, "Ossabaw became one of the first great island empires of the Georgia Coast."

During the Revolution, the Morel family took an ardent stand in favor of American independence. During the long British occupation of Savannah, endangered patriots would slip away to Ossabaw Island, where they were invariably provided with secret sanctuary.

Following the war, timbering became a great Ossabaw Island industry, and more fields were cleared for the growth of other agricultural products. Morel Plantation became a kind of self-supporting state, producing everything needed for its sustenance. Late in his life, John Morel divided his island into three plantations, which were eventually inherited by his three sons.

By the early 1800s, Sea Island cotton had been introduced to Ossabaw Island, and as Vanstory comments, "Ossabaw fields were white with cotton, her wharves busy with barges, schooners and boats of happy groups for house parties and hunting parties as the Morels pursued their business and social affairs. . . . In those days when the coastal planters had 'company for breakfast, dinner, tea and supper, and drawing rooms were lighted by whole dozens of spermaceti candles high blazing from glass chandeliers,' a beautiful custom in the Morel family was the molding of the candles of Ossabaw."

By the early 1850s, much of Ossabaw Island had passed out of the Morel family's ownership, bringing to a close the island's most colorful era. During the Civil War, it was evacuated. For a short while, a Union battery was located on the isle's northern tip.

During the early 1900s, Ossabaw Island was used as a hunting preserve by the Wanamaker family of Philadelphia. The old plantation homes were quickly being reclaimed by the forest, and fields that had once waved proudly in Sea Island cotton were overgrown and rank with weeds.

In 1924, Ossabaw Island was acquired by Dr. H. N. Torrey of Michigan. He rounded up the wild cattle and hogs running free on the island and soon began construction of a grand homeplace. Three generations of his family entertained honored guests at this island home, which still stands.

Ossabaw Island finally passed into the hands of Eleanor Torrey West. In 1961, West formed the Ossabaw Foundation, which soon undertook the ambitious Ossabaw Island Project. This effort sponsored several artistic and environmental-research communities on the island. Eventually, the state of Georgia took over the island's management. At one time, students from more than 20 colleges and universities were participating in the foundation's various projects.

Sad to say, most of the Ossabaw Island Project's important ecological work was abandoned during the 1980s due to lack of funds. However, as stated in the Georgia Conservancy's *Guide to the Georgia Coast*, "Ossabaw offers a lesson in how preservation of significant natural areas can be accomplished through a cooperative effort between private landowners, state agencies and private conservation organizations. . . . As a Heritage Preserve, Ossabaw is only to be used for natural, scientific and cultural purposes based on environmentally sound practices. . . . Future use will be managed by the Department of Natural Resources. . . . Ossabaw Foundation projects are based on the premise that people must understand their relationship to the environment, and they should 'look at everything before disturbing anything.' " This writer wishes the foundation the very best in its future efforts.

At the present time, special permission is required for a visit to Ossabaw Island's interior sections. But there is nothing to keep boaters from viewing the isle's shoreline (from the water, that is). Should you find yourself ensconced in a cozy anchorage on Cane Patch Creek, take a moment to gaze upon the lands to the east and ponder all that has gone before you.

Unnamed Anchorage

An unnamed creek cuts north from the ICW's trek down Bear River north of flashing daybeacon #B (itself east of unlighted daybeacon #104C). The creek carries minimum 8-foot depths and offers enough swinging room for boats up to 40 feet in length. While you can certainly anchor just upstream from the creek's southerly mouth, you can also follow the stream around its first turn to the west if you want more shelter. You can then anchor in 15 to 22 feet of water with comparable swinging room.

Big Tom Creek

The stream known as Big Tom Creek makes in to the ICW's eastern banks south of flashing daybeacon #105. This creek offers yet another anchorage possibility for boaters cruising north of St. Catherines Sound. The western reaches boast 9- to 12-foot minimum depths and enough room for a 42-footer.

If the weather demands more protection, consider following Big Tom Creek through its first ultrasharp turn to the north-northeast. The

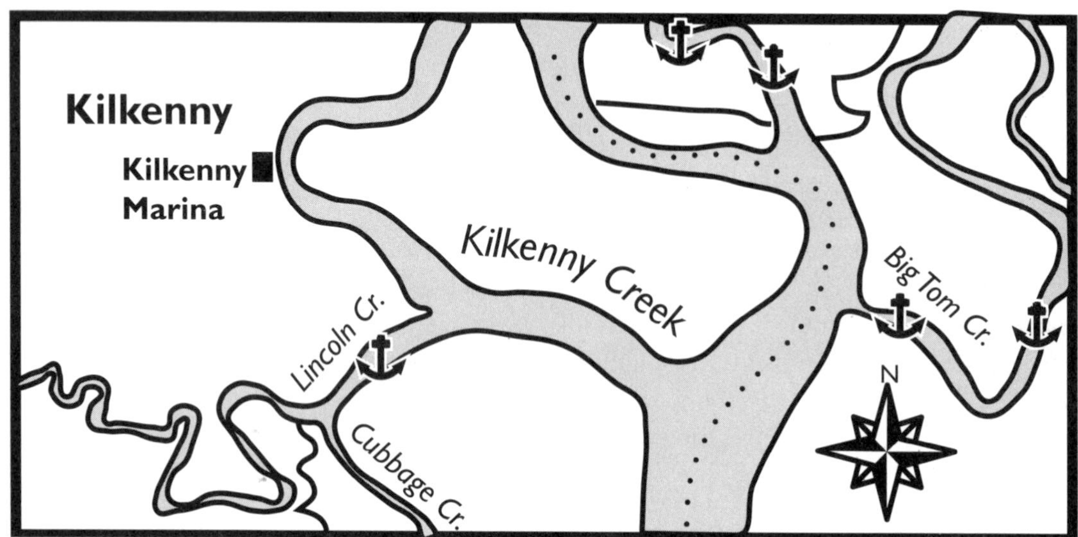

straight stretch beyond this bend is backed by the high ground of Ossabaw Island to the east. If breezes are blowing from this quarter, the banks give a moderate windbreak.

Kilkenny Marina

South of flashing daybeacon #106, Kilkenny Creek runs off to the west. This stream plays host to the last marina facility north of St. Catherines Sound. Minimum 8-foot depths lead up the broad path of Kilkenny Creek to a hairpin turn to the north, and then back to the east and northeast. Kilkenny Marina sits hard by the western banks on the charted high ground designated "Kilkenny" on chart 11511 in the heart of this turn.

Kilkenny Marina, Kilkenny Creek

Those who prefer to anchor-off rather than visit the marina might consider Lincoln Creek, which splits off from Kilkenny Creek well below the hairpin turn. You must avoid an unmarked shoal on Lincoln Creek, but otherwise minimum depths of 7 feet are held, with most soundings ranging from 7 to 12 feet, until the stream splinters into several branches to the southwest. Boats up to 36 feet should find enough elbow room.

Kilkenny Marina is a small but very hospitable facility that caters to boaters passing on the Waterway. Considering its proximity to the ICW in a region of few marina facilities, Kilkenny Marina is clearly an important stop along this portion of the Waterway.

Transients are eagerly accepted at the marina's single wooden-decked floating pier. Dockside depths are 9-plus feet. All power and water connections are available, as are both gasoline and diesel fuel. Showers and laundromat facilities are found just behind the well-stocked variety and tackle store overlooking the docks. Some low-key mechanical service is available for outboards only. There is no restaurant within walking distance, so bring all your own supplies.

Kilkenny Marina (912) 727-2215

Approach depth: 8–25 feet
Dockside depth: 9+ feet
Accepts transients: yes
Floating wooden pier: yes
Dockside power connections: 30 and 50 amps
Dockside water connections: yes
Showers: yes
Laundromat: yes
Gasoline: yes
Diesel fuel: yes
Mechanical repairs: limited
Variety store: yes

St. Catherines Sound

The ICW continues down ever-broadening Bear River until it intersects the truly wide-open waters of St. Catherines Sound just south of flashing daybeacon #112. The Waterway darts southwest across the great sound and into the mouth of North Newport River. Medway River stretches to the west and offers cruising possibilities of its own, which will be considered separately below.

St. Catherines Sound's inlet passage to the east could use a few more aids to navigation, but the channel is deep and very wide. Careful use of your compass and chart 11511 should see you out to sea or safely into inland waters during daylight hours. Nighttime entry by strangers is a definite no-no.

Medway River

Boaters up for a different sort of cruising treat can cut west-northwest short of the ICW's flashing daybeacon #116 and visit beautiful Medway River. While, to be sure, there is plenty of shoal water along the course of Medway River, most of the trouble spots are marked, and cautious mariners should be able to hold minimum 8- to 10-foot depths upstream to some very interesting anchorages.

You might try dropping the hook on Dickinson Creek, which makes off from the Medway's southwestern banks south of the charted position of Sunbury. Minimum depths of 6 feet can be carried well upstream, but there are several shoals to bypass at the creek's entrance. Boats up to 34 feet should find enough swinging room to avoid the shoaly banks.

Most boaters who cruise the Medway with the intention of dropping anchor for the evening will probably want to consider setting the hook abeam of charted Sunbury on the Sunbury Channel portion of the river. While there are no historic sites visible from the water, this is a lovely spot with a few private residences overlooking the high westerly banks. Protection is quite good when winds are blowing from the west, southwest, or northwest. The marsh island to the east gives some shelter from this direction, but strong blows from the north or south will call for a delay in your visit.

Boaters anchoring abeam of Sunbury are encouraged to break out the dinghy and go ashore at a small, public launching area visible on the westerly shoreline. From there, visitors can then walk back up the highway for about 0.25 mile to the Historic Sunbury Site. Watch to the left of the highway for the park's entrance. The hours of operation are from 9:00 A.M. to 5:00 P.M. Tuesday through Saturday and from 2:00 P.M. to 5:30 P.M. Sunday.

Historic Sunbury

According to legend, James Oglethorpe founded the first Masonic lodge in Georgia under a great oak tree in the village of Sunbury. This was but one event from the rich history Sunbury once enjoyed. Sadly, those times all but vanished in the 1800s.

In the 1750s, a community of Puritans from Massachusetts settled a few miles inland from Medway River (then known as Midway River). They had originally migrated to South Carolina, but as the Georgia economy expanded, some of them moved farther south.

It wasn't long before a community of 300 had sprung up and the surrounding plantations were growing rice by the ton. The small town took on the name of Midway, sometimes spelled Medway.

By 1758, there was a real need for a local shipping port. Overland transportation to Savannah was precarious and quite expensive. Thus, the industrious citizens and planters of Midway undertook to build their own port on the banks of Midway River. They dubbed the new town Sunbury.

From the start, Sunbury was a thriving place. Prior to the Revolution, it rivaled Savannah in its waterborne exports. By 1760, Sunbury boasted 80 homes, a custom house, a naval office, and many merchants. William Bartram visited Sunbury on his famous travels through the southeastern United States and described the town as having "pleasant piazzas around [its houses] where the genteel, wealthy planters resorted to partake of the sea breeze, bathing and sporting on the Sea Islands."

When trouble began to brew between the 13 American colonies and England, Georgia as a whole was slow to take up the patriot cause. There was no such hesitation in Sunbury and the entire St. Johns Parish (what we would today call a county). With their staunch New England independence, the citizens of Midway and Sunbury were outspoken in their support for American rights. They agitated for aggressive measures against the mother country.

During the war, British forces invaded Georgia from Florida. After a bloody fight, Sunbury and Midway were taken. When the survivors returned after the war, they found their community devastated and partially burned.

Though Midway was slowly rebuilt and the region's plantations began another rise to prosperity, for some unknown reason Sunbury slowly lost its importance. In the mid-1800s, one visitor described the old port as a "deserted village."

Today, visitors may tour a museum at the site of Fort Morris, a Revolutionary War fortification that defended Sunbury and Midway River. A few headstones standing in the cemetery are the only reminders left of the once-thriving port of Sunbury. This town is now officially listed as one of Georgia's "dead" communities.

LITTLE OGEECHEE RIVER TO ST. CATHERINES SOUND NAVIGATION

As stated earlier, navigation of central Georgia's large sounds and rivers is not a task to be undertaken lightly. Check the latest weather forecast and make sure there is plenty of fuel on board before leaving Isle of Hope too far behind. On some of the sounds, aids to navigation are a bit far apart for eyeball navigation. Prudent skippers will preplot compass courses for these lengthy runs long before they actually enter the wide waters.

There is plenty of shoal water in Georgia's sounds and rivers, often just where you least expect it. Study the various charts and the information presented below carefully.

If you expect the unexpected, before you know it the glinting waters of St. Catherines Sound will appear over the southern horizon of Bear River.

Down Vernon River After leaving Burnside River south of flashing daybeacon #79, boaters should set their course down the broad, deep path of the lower Vernon River. There are no aids to navigation for 1.4 nautical miles, but you should not encounter any difficulty if you stay anywhere near the river's mid-width.

Eventually, flashing daybeacon #81 will come abeam well northeast of your course. Don't approach this marker too closely. It lies hard by the northeastern banks.

From a position abeam of #81, point to pass between unlighted daybeacons #82 and #83. As you make this run, the broad waters of Ossabaw and Green Island Sounds will open out before you. Equally wide Little Ogeechee River sweeps back to the west and is best avoided due to numerous shoals and a lack of markings.

Flashing daybeacon #86 heralds a southwesterly turn into the Waterway preparatory to entering the Hell Gate passage. Before making this run, boaters have the opportunity to visit Delegal Creek Marina to the east.

Delegal Creek Marina On the water, the marked entrance into Delegal Creek does not bear much resemblance to what you might expect from a study of chart 11512. Prudent mariners will contact Delegal Creek Marina on VHF channel 16 to check on the latest channel conditions before attempting entry into the creek. The charted marsh island southwest of the creek's mouth has completely eroded. Even at low tide, it is covered with a thin shelf of water. It's all too easy to wander into these shallow depths.

To avoid the shoal, come abeam of unlighted daybeacon #2 on "Steamboat Cut" to its fairly immediate northerly side. From #2, set a careful course to come abeam of flashing daybeacon #7 to its fairly immediate southerly side. Along the way between #2 and #7, you will pass unlighted daybeacon #5 by some 25 yards to its southerly side.

Once abeam of #7, turn fairly quickly to the north-northwest and enter Delegal Creek. More than one boater has made the mistake of not rounding both #5 and #7 before turning north-northwest into the creek. Such an error can land the unlucky cruiser in less than 3 feet of water.

After making your northward turn, point to pass between flashing daybeacon #10 and unlighted daybeacon #9. Soon, the creek takes a sharp jog to the northeast. Favor the southeasterly shores heavily to avoid the correctly charted shoal northeast of flashing daybeacon #11. You will soon sight the marina docks on the easterly banks.

Delegal Creek continues deep for quite some distance upstream until it splinters into several branches west of Ritter Hammock. Hold to the centerline and avoid cutting short any point of land.

On the ICW Continue tracking your way to the southeast for another 50 yards or so after flashing daybeacon #86 comes abeam to the southwest. You should then cut sharply to the southwest and set course to come abeam of flashing buoy #87 to its northwesterly side. At this point, the entrance to Hell Gate will lie almost dead ahead.

Hell Gate is one of those portions of the ICW that is subject to perennial shoaling and strong, confusing tidal currents. Expect the worst, and approach Hell Gate with a healthy amount of respect.

From #87, point to come abeam of unlighted daybeacon #89 to its westerly quarter. At #89, the ICW turns almost due south and runs on toward Ogeechee River. Study chart 11507 for a moment and you will notice that it is very important not to cut the corner at #89.

Flashing daybeacons #91 and #92 mark the southerly mouth of Hell Gate. Pass #92 by some 20 yards to its easterly quarter and point to come abeam of #91 fairly close to its westerly side. Note the correctly charted shallows west of #92 and a second set of shoals bordering the eastern flank of Hell Gate's southerly mouth. Give both these hazards your most respectful attention. Once abeam of flashing daybeacon #91, the ICW channel turns sharply west.

From #91, the next westerly marker on the ICW is flashing daybeacon #93. The current edition of chart 11507 shows a large shoal north and east of this beacon. Extensive on-site soundings revealed that most or all of this obstruction had been removed, presumably by dredging. It's always better to be safe than sorry, so favor the Waterway's northeasterly flank a bit when passing #93.

Ogeechee River remains wide but reasonably well outlined by daybeacons as the Waterway tracks its way west to the so-called Florida Passage. At flashing daybeacon #96, the ICW begins a long, slow bend to the southwest as it heads for the passage.

Flashing daybeacon #98 denotes the northeasterly entrance of the Florida Passage. Between #96 and #98, cruisers can break off to the west and track their way up Ogeechee River to Fort McAllister Marina.

Ogeechee River to Fort McAllister Marina The channel up Ogeechee River to Fort McAllister Marina is outlined by privately maintained floating buoys. Most are green, but there are a few red markers as well. All are rather small, and you may well need your binoculars to pick out each succeeding one. This writer will not even begin to try to describe all the twists and turns in this passage. Suffice it to say that you should pass all green buoys to your port side and all red markers to starboard. Eventually, you will sight the marina dock along the port-side banks.

On the ICW and the Florida Passage The Florida Passage is a delightfully deep section of the Georgia ICW that leads cruisers generally south to Bear River. Simply stay away from the shoreline and you should have few worries.

Redbird Creek Enter Redbird Creek, north of flashing daybeacon #99, on its mid-width. Simply continue holding to the center for good depths up to the stream's charted limits.

On the ICW Shoals guard the western flank of the Florida Passage's intersection with Bear River. Be *sure* to pass unlighted nun buoy #102 to its eastern side. Very shallow water lies west of #102.

The charted range will help you avoid the shallows. Continue toward the forward range marker until you are within some 100 yards of this aid to navigation. You can then either cut to the west and follow the Waterway down Bear River or turn east and visit the river's delightful upper reaches.

Upper Bear River and Associated Creeks Favor the southerly shores slightly as you enter the wide upper portion of Bear River. As correctly forecast on chart 11507, some shoal water guards the stream's northwesterly entrance point.

Cruise back to the mid-width after proceeding 200 yards upstream. Soon, you will approach the intersection with Cane Patch and Buckhead Creeks.

Should you decide to visit Buckhead Creek, favor the western banks slightly as you cruise through the northern entrance. A small bank of shallows guards the juncture of the two creeks to the east. Soon, Buckhead Creek takes a turn to the southeast. For best depths, begin slightly favoring the southwestern shoreline after coming out of this bend. Discontinue your explorations as the unnamed but charted offshoot comes abeam to the north.

Cane Patch Creek should be entered on its centerline. Hold scrupulously to the middle as you work your way upstream. If you decide to proceed to the anchorage near Rush Creek, watch out for the uncharted patch of 5- to 6-foot waters just south of the intersection with Rush Creek. Don't try to cruise the waters of Rush Creek to the east or west. Depths are much too unreliable for cruising craft.

On the ICW After turning west from a position 100 yards or so north of the forward range marker (south of unlighted nun buoy #102), you will track your way through a short stretch without markers. Avoid the northerly shoreline. It is abutted by a narrow strip of shallows.

Flashing daybeacon #104 marks a sharp southerly turn in Bear River and the ICW. Several charted ranges as well as the various daybeacons help you keep to the channel.

Unnamed Anchorage Boaters choosing to enter the unnamed creek northeast of unlighted daybeacon #104C should cruise into its mid-width. Cruise to within 25 yards of forward range marker #B, then turn due north into the stream. Good depths continue within shouting distance of the centerline for several miles upstream, until the creek intersects the charted "7 FT" offshoot on its southern banks. Past this point, soundings become unreliable.

Big Tom Creek The westerly entrance to Big Tom Creek is found along Bear River's easterly banks south of flashing daybeacon #105. Enter on the mid-width and, as usual, hold to the center until the creek splinters into several branches well upstream. Prudent cruisers will discontinue their gunkholing at this point.

Kilkenny Creek Look at chart 11507 and notice that shoal water 3 to 4 feet deep flanks Kilkenny Creek's southern entrance point, as well as a good portion of the southern banks. Be sure to favor the northern shores when cruising into Kilkenny Creek to avoid this potential trap.

You can cruise back to the mid-width after passing the first small offshoot on the southerly banks. Soon, westbound cruisers on Kilkenny Creek will encounter the entrance to Lincoln Creek. Avoid the point of land separating these two streams. A large shoal is building east from this promontory.

Cruise up Lincoln Creek on its centerline. Most large cruising craft will do well to halt their progress where the stream splits into three branches to the southwest.

Boaters continuing up Kilkenny Creek to Kilkenny Marina should favor the northeasterly (starboard-side) banks for several hundred yards past the intersection with Lincoln Creek. Chart 11511 correctly predicts a large shoal flanking the southwesterly (upstream) banks on this section of the creek. Take this writer's bent prop's word for it—these shallows are for real.

Soon, Kilkenny Creek cuts sharply north, and the marina docks will come abeam on the western shoreline. Watch out for the usual swift tidal currents when pulling up to the pier.

On the ICW South of Kilkenny Creek, Bear River widens perceptibly. This portion of the ICW can indeed be a real "bear" if winds are blowing strongly out of the north or particularly the south.

Use chart 11507 and the various markers to track your way to a position well east of flashing daybeacon #110. Notice the large, charted shoal south of this aid. Boaters must take great care to avoid these unexpected shallows. Set your course to come abeam of flashing daybeacon #112 by at least 200 yards to its easterly side. Don't allow leeway to ease you to the west during this run.

By the time you reach #112, the southerly horizon will have all but disappeared, and the sometimes daunting waters of vast St. Catherines Sound will lie before you. From a position well east of #112, bend your course to the southwest and point to come abeam of flashing daybeacon #114 by several hundred yards to its southeasterly side. You are now in the heart of the sound, with the seaward channel lying to the east, the Waterway cutting southwest across St. Catherines Sound's inner reaches, and Medway River beckoning to the west.

St. Catherines Sound Inlet The spacious St. Catherines Sound inlet channel lies almost due east of the ICW's flashing daybeacon #114. Be sure to have the very latest edition of chart 11511 aboard to help you pick out the various aids to navigation. Preplot your compass courses. Have you ever tried to plot a course in a choppy seaway? This writer doesn't recommend the experience. Be prepared to find new and different markers even if you have the latest chart. This is an inlet, after all, and subject to continual change.

ICW across St. Catherines Sound From flashing daybeacon #114, set course to come abeam of flashing daybeacon #114A by some 100 yards to its southeasterly side. The shoal waters of Medway Spit lie northwest of the gap between #114 and #114A. Be sure to identify the markers correctly and avoid any lateral slippage to the northwest.

Once abeam of #114A, bend your course slightly farther to the south-southwest and point to come abeam of flashing daybeacon #116 well to its southeasterly side. This aid marks a long shoal building southeast from Cedar Point. Stay away from #116.

Flashing daybeacon #116 denotes the ICW's exodus from St. Catherines Sound and entry into the ample waters of North Newport River. Before reaching #116, visiting cruisers can do themselves a big favor by turning northwest into Medway River.

Medway River Successful entry into Medway River is a matter of avoiding the huge patch of shoals comprising Medway Spit, located northeast of the channel, as well as the smaller but equally deadly shoal building out from Cedar Point. Use chart 11511 for navigation on this body of water.

Abandon the ICW about two-thirds of the way between #114A and #116. Strike a careful compass course to the northwest, pointing to come abeam of unlighted daybeacon #2 by several hundred yards to its southwesterly quarter.

Once abeam of #2, continue on the same course for another 0.3 nautical mile. Only then should you cut farther to the north and set course to eventually come abeam of unlighted daybeacon #3 to its northeasterly side. This procedure will help you avoid the shallows of Medway Spit to the northeast. However, you *must also be on guard* against the correctly charted tongue of 2-foot water extending southeast from #3. Once clear of Medway Spit, work your way quickly toward the northerly shores and then turn northwest to avoid this very real and worrisome obstruction.

Favor the northern and northeastern banks of the Medway as you cruise upstream from #3. A quick glance at chart 11511 will reveal the huge field of shoals stretching out from the southwestern shoreline well into the river's center section. After cruising upstream for 1.8 nautical miles from #3, you will begin to approach the mouth of shallow Jones Creek, which makes in to the southwestern banks. Begin heavily favoring the southern shores well east of this intersection. A broad band of shoals bisects the river at this point, and the best water is found along the southern and southwestern banks.

Medway River now begins a very long, slow turn to the north. Eventually, the northeastern entrance of Dickinson Creek will come abeam to the southwest. If you decide to enter, stick strictly to the mid-width. Shoal water guards both points at the stream's mouth. Good depths continue on the center until the creek follows a hairpin turn to the northwest. Cease your explorations before coming out of this turn. Very shoal water is encountered immediately upstream of this point.

Back on Medway River, the great stream is soon split into two channels by an oblong marsh island. The easterly passage is known, appropriately enough, as East Channel, while the westerly cut is called Sunbury Channel.

Boaters seeking overnight anchorage on the Medway should choose Sunbury Channel. Pass well south of the marshy point separating the two cuts. A long shoal is building to the south from the marshy isle.

Work your way up Sunbury Channel on its mid-width and drop the hook as the high ground reaches down to the western banks. Break out the dinghy and go ashore to the small public launch, which sits just beside a private home and a long-closed restaurant.

NORTH NEWPORT RIVER TO ALTAMAHA SOUND

If you thought the run from Vernon River to St. Catherines Sound was a bit lonely, just wait until you meet up with the Waterway between North Newport and Altamaha Rivers. There were three marinas in the last section, but only one graces this passage, and even this facility calls for a long cruise through a shoal-prone river to reach its limited piers.

As usual in coastal Georgia, just the opposite is true of anchorages. The ICW continues to be peppered with interesting overnight stops that many boaters will want to visit time and again as they make their way up or down the so-called ditch.

The trend toward open water continues on this run. Before reaching the Altamaha, itself an ample-sized sound and river, boaters must first pass through the broad confines of Sapelo and

Doboy Sounds. In between these expansive waters, the Waterway follows far more sheltered paths.

There is very little, if any, difference in the shoreside scenery on this portion of the voyage from South Carolina to Florida. Undeveloped marsh-grass banks continue to be the rule. As always, the best and most attractive anchorages are those that cozy up to wooded high ground.

It's worth noting again that all boats, but particularly power craft, should have plenty of fuel aboard before tackling the central Georgia ICW.

If you enjoy cruising waters that look as if they have never known the hand of man, then you will appreciate this run immensely. If not, take heart—St. Simons Island and its many facilities lie but a short hop farther to the south.

Walburg Creek

If it were not for one minor detail, Walburg Creek would deserve a red circle on every cruiser's chart. The stream borders the magnificently wooded shores of historic St. Catherines Island to the east and is bounded by undeveloped marsh to the west. Some of the island's historic buildings and research facilities (see the next section) are visible near the stream's turn to the west, though public landing is not allowed.

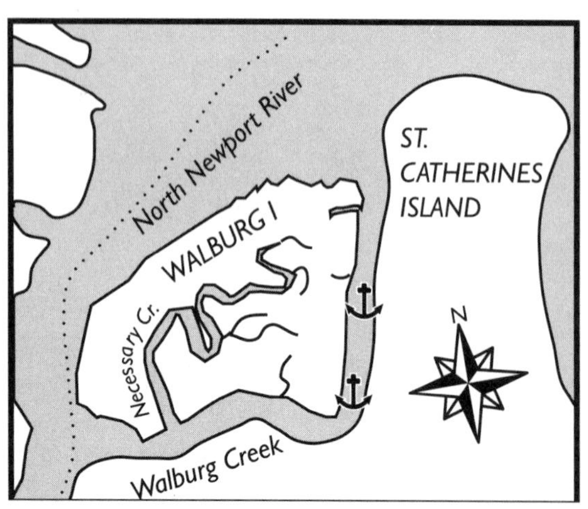

Walburg Creek offers safe and secure anchorage, particularly when winds are blowing from the east, northeast, or southeast over St. Catherines Island. The setting is all that one could desire. Some of this writer's fellow cruisers have argued that Walburg Creek is one of the most appealing anchorages in all of coastal Georgia. Minimum depths run around 12 feet, though there are one or two unmarked shoals to avoid. All of these are found on the east-to-west portion of the creek. They do not impinge on the best anchorages, which are adjacent to St. Catherines Island's high ground.

Now the bad news. The stream's westerly entrance, which makes in to the ICW east of unlighted daybeacon #124 and south of flashing daybeacon #123, is shoal and carries only 4 feet of water at low tide. Boats drawing less than 4 feet might still consider entering here, particularly on a rising tide, but there is no denying that the conditions are less than perfect for easy navigation.

Walburg Creek's northern mouth gazes out upon the southern shores of St. Catherines Sound. While this entrance is quite deep, there is an unmarked shoal to the west, and cruisers must be careful to work their way around several shallows in the sound itself before finding their way to the creek. Still, with sunny skies and winds under 15 knots, many boaters will find this involved route more than justified as the price for experiencing the considerable charms of Walburg Creek.

In easterly winds or light to moderate westerly

breezes, you can anchor on any portion of the north-to-south section of Walburg Creek. Northerly winds over 15 knots or particularly strong southerly blows might be a bit of a problem. There is plenty of swinging room for a 50-footer.

My favorite anchorage is found in the body of the creek's bend to the west. Here, the high ground of St. Catherines Island sweeps briefly to the west, giving some protection from southerly breezes as well. Some of the research facilities on St. Catherines Island are visible along the immediate shoreline. The presence of two private docks amidst the trees will help you recognize these structures.

The east-to-west portion of Walburg Creek leaves the high ground behind, with both banks composed of the usual undeveloped marsh grass. While it is certainly possible to anchor on this portion of the creek, you probably wouldn't want to with the aforementioned havens just a quick hop away.

Necessary Creek makes off to the north near Walburg Creek's westerly exodus into the ICW. Soundings run to as little as 7 feet on this little-sheltered stream, and there is only enough swinging room for boats up to 28 feet.

So there you have it—Walburg Creek is as nice an overnight stop as anyone voyaging the ICW could ever dream. Just make sure to read the navigational information concerning the entrances presented in the next section of this chapter, and make your plans accordingly.

St. Catherines Island

St. Catherines Island, along with St. Simons Island, may hold the distinction of being the most historic of coastal Georgia's Golden Isles. Today, St. Catherines hosts some of the most unusual residents of any Sea Island in all of America.

St. Catherines Island's history predates the earliest European exploration of North and South America. The capital of the Creek Indian confederacy was located on the island, and there were several other Native American settlements on the 25,000-acre body of land as well.

In recognition of the island's importance to the local Indians, Spanish authorities based in Florida established the Santa Catalina Mission on St. Catherines in 1566. Peopled first by Jesuits and then later and more successfully by Franciscan friars, the mission was abandoned by the mid-1600s after several bloody Indian rebellions.

St. Catherines Island lapsed into relative obscurity until James Oglethorpe arrived to establish the English colony of Georgia. A half-Indian–half-white woman named Mary Musgrove who operated a trading post in the area was instrumental in the give and take between the dynamic colonial leader and the Indians. Musgrove later married Thomas Bosomworth, a preacher sent from England to minister to the new colony.

In the negotiations between Oglethorpe and the Indians, it was agreed that the Native Americans would retain the ownership of Ossabaw, St. Catherines, and Sapelo Islands. For her services in making the arrangements, Mary Bosomworth, afterwards known as a "princess" of the tribe, was awarded ownership of these three islands.

With the opening of Georgia to slavery in 1749, these bodies of land took on greater importance as potential plantations. The colony's trustees disputed the Bosomworths' claim to the land, which led to a decade-long legal struggle.

At one point during the proceedings, the Bosomworths and their Indian allies made a show of force. As aptly described in Burnette Vanstory's *Georgia's Land of the Golden Isles*, it must have been an impressive scene indeed: "Led by the princess in her royal trappings and Thomas Bosomworth in his canonical robes, two hundred Indian braves marched into the seaport city [Savannah], where they remained for a fortnight threatening the authorities and intimidating residents."

With the case still in the courts, Thomas and Mary cleared and planted fields on St. Catherines and began construction of a fine home. Finally, in 1760, the Bosomworths were officially granted ownership of St. Catherines Island, while the other isles were purchased by the English Crown.

Princess Mary was able to enjoy the couple's hard-won property for only a few years before she passed away. St. Catherines Island was purchased by one of colonial Georgia's most colorful figures, Button Gwinnett. By 1765, Gwinnett and his family had settled on their new isle and had begun to develop an extensive and profitable plantation.

As the years passed and the conflict between Great Britain and its American colonies became ever more serious, Button Gwinnett was one of Georgia's leading proponents of the patriot cause. Selected to attend the Second Continental Congress, he distinguished himself as intelligent and spirited. He was one of Georgia's signers of the Declaration of Independence.

By 1800, St. Catherines Island was the property of Jacob Walburg. This industrious planter developed two mammoth plantations on the island.

St. Catherines was abandoned during the Civil War. Immediately following the close of the dark conflict, the island was very briefly the site of an independent state set up for freed slaves.

After going through a succession of owners, St. Catherines was bought in 1927 by Howard Coffin, owner of nearby Sapelo Island. Coffin carefully restored and enlarged the so-called Old House, which tradition claims was once the home of Button Gwinnett.

There followed another series of owners until 1943, when St. Catherines was purchased by Edward J. Noble. Following Noble's death, the island came under the ownership of the Edward J. Noble Foundation.

Since 1974, the New York Zoological Society has used St. Catherines Island as a sanctuary for rare and endangered species. Today, such exotic animals as gray zebras, sable antelopes, and hartebeests wander fields that were once snow-white with Sea Island cotton.

Unfortunately, public access to St. Catherines Island is severely restricted. Visitors must obtain special permission, which is not often granted. But should you anchor in Walburg Creek, don't be surprised to awaken the next morning and see a zebra staring at you from the shoreline. This writer has yet to be so lucky, but perhaps you will be more fortunate.

Cedar Creek

Southwest of flashing daybeacon #116, the ICW enters the headwaters of North Newport River. To the west, the unmarked mouth of Cedar Creek may be sighted by careful observers. The channel leading to this sidewater is bordered by extensive shoals. Considering all the other anchorage possibilities along this run, it would probably be better for large craft to bypass this stream entirely.

Timmons River

The broad mouth of Timmons River flanks the ICW west of the gap between flashing daybeacon #119 and unlighted daybeacon #121. Cruising boaters are strictly warned away from this body of water. Numerous unmarked shoals crowd the river's track like grains of sand on a beach. These hazards relegate exploration of the Timmons to our outboard brethren.

Upper North Newport River and Half Moon Marina

After skirting its way around a mammoth shoal, the Georgia Waterway leaves North Newport River and enters Johnson Creek at flashing daybeacon #125. Passing boaters will note several signs on the ICW just short of #125 advertising Half Moon Marina and directing them up the westerly portion of the river, abandoned by the ICW.

Half Moon Marina is the last facility available to cruising boaters north of St. Simons Island. If you need fuel or any other sort of marine supplies, this is the last stop for southbound boaters for the next 40 statute miles.

The path up spacious North Newport River is not exactly a simple trek. The river sports quite a few shoals. There are no on-the-water aids to navigation. Half Moon Marina has erected several funky shoreside markers which indicate the shoreline you are supposed to favor to bypass the shallows. This is a scheme that this writer and his mate had never seen before, and frankly we were not too impressed. Your best means of running the river successfully is by using the latest edition of chart 11511 and careful navigation. If you avoid the shallows, minimum depths run around 10 feet, with typical soundings ranging from 12 to as much as 25 feet. Running the river after dark would be a foolish proposition for strangers.

As you trek to the west and northwest on North Newport River, the stream eventually joins the westward-running waters of Timmons River south of charted Drum Point Landing. You must follow the combined streams for another 1.4 nautical miles before spotting Half Moon Marina perched on the northeastern banks in a hairpin turn in the river near the charted position of Half Moon Landing.

Half Moon is a fairly small marina that sports two face-type wooden-decked floating piers in fair condition. Tidal currents are incredibly swift on this portion of North Newport River, so approach the piers with extreme caution.

Transients are accepted for overnight or temporary dockage, and berths feature full power and water connections, as well as an incredible 25-plus feet of water. Gasoline and diesel fuel can be purchased, and the marina maintains a ship's and variety store on the hill overlooking the docks. Some low-key showers are available. There is no restaurant within walking distance.

Half Moon Marina (912) 884-5819

Approach depth: 10 feet (minimum)
Dockside depth: 25+ feet
Accepts transients: yes
Floating wooden piers: yes
Dockside power connections: 20, 30, and 50 amps
Dockside water connections: yes

Showers: yes
Gasoline: yes
Diesel fuel: yes
Ship's and variety store: yes

Cattle Pen Creek

The stream known as Cattle Pen Creek cuts into the eastern banks of the Waterway's Johnson Creek stretch between unlighted daybeacons #127 and #128. In spite of the soundings shown on chart 11507, some 6½-foot low-water depths can be expected at the stream's entrance. Inside, soundings improve to between 10 and 16 feet. Both of the stream's shores are quite shoal, considerably reducing the apparent swinging room. Vessels larger than 32 feet will definitely be cramped.

Should your craft fit the size requirements, the best spot to drop the hook is upstream of Cattle Pen Creek's first jog to the northeast. High ground sits in back of the southeasterly banks along this stretch of the stream and gives good shelter if winds are blowing from the east or southeast.

South Newport River

Southwest of flashing daybeacon #132, the ICW leaves Johnson Creek behind and enters the southerly section of South Newport River. The northerly portion of this mighty stream is littered with shoals and is best avoided entirely. Even the Waterway is bounded by shoals. You must be careful to follow the markers, or you might spend the afternoon contemplating the value of good coastal navigation while hard aground on a sandbar.

Wahoo River

Wahoo River is an impressive stream that flows into the waters of the ICW section of South Newport River well west of unlighted daybeacon #133. To enter the stream, you must carefully skirt the large shoal west of #133, but cautious navigators should be able to maintain minimum 10-foot depths both while entering and while on the river's interior reaches.

While you can anchor almost anywhere on Wahoo River, there is one spot that rates prime consideration. Break out chart 11510 and study the river's track for a moment. Notice the portion of the stream where the high banks of Wahoo Island border the stream's northerly banks. Some of the island's shoreline is shoal, but dropping the hook just as the island comes abeam to the north (moving east to west) should provide sufficient room for boats up to 45 feet.

This writer cannot stress the beauty of this anchorage too strongly. It is idyllic. It would not be out of place to find a Native American hunting party camping on the deep, wooded banks of Wahoo Island. The isolation is tangible. Believe me, there are few better spots to spend the night far from the madding crowd in all of coastal Georgia.

Sapelo Sound

South of unlighted daybeacon #136, the ever-widening waters of South Newport River discharge the Waterway cruiser into the massive, open waters of Sapelo Sound. The ICW tracks its way west and then southwest on the sound's often choppy waters for some 5.2 nautical miles before cutting into sheltered Front River.

South and east of flashing daybeacon #138, Sapelo Sound's inlet presents a good channel to the open sea. The passage is quite broad and reasonably well marked. Most of the aids to navigation are charted, a sure sign of a stable seaward cut. Boaters with the latest chart in hand and preplotted compass courses should be able to come through with nothing worse than a little salt spray during times of favorable weather.

The ICW's passage west through Sapelo Sound is bounded by shoals along much of its track. To be sure, the Waterway channel is broad and reasonably well marked, but wise boaters will want to plot compass courses between the various aids to navigation. This "better safe than sorry" practice is particularly helpful during inclement weather.

Southwest of unlighted daybeacon #150, the ICW begins its approach to Front River and soon leaves the waters of Sapelo Sound behind. Sapelo River, abandoned by the Waterway, lies to the west and northwest of #150.

Sapelo River

Boaters preparing to make their exit from Sapelo Sound may spot a series of signs beckoning them up Sapelo River to Pelican Point Restaurant. The signs promise dockage and fuel. After tracking several miles up the Sapelo through a marked channel with minimum 7-foot depths, this writer found the restaurant's dockage completely filled by commercial shrimp trawlers, with nary a gas pump in sight. There was not even a place to tie up and go ashore to find out if the restaurant was still in operation. From the water, it was unclear whether it was still serving landside customers.

Considering the lack of sheltered anchorage and the current lack of dockage facilities, this writer suggests leaving Sapelo River behind and continuing south to the many fine anchorages north of Doboy Sound.

Crescent River

The ICW's southbound path works its way down Front River and enters the Creighton Narrows landcut. This is a surprisingly attractive section of the Waterway, with heavily timbered banks. The trees make for a welcome change from the usual brown water and marsh grass.

The Waterway then ducks briefly down the lower reaches of Crescent River before cutting southwest on Old Teakettle Creek.

West of flashing daybeacon #157, the upper Crescent River beckons with superb anchorage. While you must avoid one unmarked shoal at the river's entrance and another farther upstream, good navigators can maintain minimum 11-foot depths as far as the creek's first sharp turn to the west. Just before this bend, the high ground of Creighton Island marches down almost to the northeastern banks. Boats up to 40 feet will find ample elbow room in 11- to 15-foot depths, with excellent shelter from eastern, southeastern, and northeastern winds. This is yet another of those off-the-beaten-path overnight refuges so typical of the Georgia coastline, with the added bonus of timbered banks.

Shellbluff Creek

It will never be mistaken for one of the sterling anchorages of the Georgia coastline, but Shellbluff Creek, south of flashing daybeacon #162, can provide anchorage for boats up to 32 feet. Minimum 8-foot depths hold for the first 100 yards of the stream's westward-tracking path.

New Teakettle Creek

East of unlighted daybeacon #172, New Teakettle Creek strikes generally north and provides reasonably good anchorage amidst the usual marsh. The initial southerly reaches of the stream have depths of 20-plus feet and enough swinging room for vessels as large as 40 feet. Strong southerly breezes blow directly up the creek and can be a problem for boaters anchored in this refuge.

Better sheltered is the stretch beyond the creek's first turn to the northeast. Here, depths range from 8 to 17 feet, and protection is sufficient for all but fresh winds. Boats up to 45 feet will find enough elbow room.

Doboy Sound

The ICW leaves New Teakettle Creek at flashing daybeacon #175 and tracks its way southeast for some 1.1 nautical miles on the wider waters of Doboy Sound before ducking west into sheltered North River.

Doboy Sound is not as large as its sisters to the north and south, but its waters still allow plenty of wind fetch to foster some healthy waves in a fresh breeze. Doboy Sound's seaward passage is reasonably well outlined by aids to navigation, but it has the unfortunate qualities of some 6- to 7-foot depths and persistent shoaling. This writer would choose Altamaha Sound inlet, just a short hop to the south, over the Doboy passage every time. But if you are of a mind to try the cut, be sure to have the latest edition of chart 11510 aboard.

The northwesterly waters of Doboy Sound are seldom visited, as they are circumvented by the Waterway. At least two sidewaters in this region offer anchorage possibilities.

Folly River

Folly River cuts off from Doboy Sound's southwestern banks well west-northwest of the ICW's flashing daybeacon #175. Minimum 13-foot depths lead upstream to an intersection with charted Fox Creek. Vessels up to 48 feet will find enough swinging room for a comfortable stay. The surrounding marshes reminded this writer of the never-ending grass savannas of South Carolina's Cape Romain. Needless to say, these shores do not give the best protection from heavy weather.

Dark Creek

Doboy Sound eventually splits into four different streams northwest of Folly River. Perhaps the most accessible of these bodies of water is Dark Creek, the easternmost branch. Dark Creek boasts minimum 9-foot depths and enough room for a 38-footer. Again, marsh grass comprises the shoreline.

Duplin River

One of the most memorable anchorages between Doboy Sound and the Altamaha is on the waters of Duplin River, located northeast of the ICW's flashing daybeacon #178. This stream is but a short hop from the Waterway's entrance into North River, thus making it very convenient for ICW cruisers.

With caution, boaters can maintain minimum 12-foot depths while traversing the river's southerly entrance. There is a large, unmarked shoal to avoid, and one or two markers would certainly be a welcome addition. However, those who proceed with caution and a wary eye on the sounder should come through without any problems.

Once inside Duplin River, boaters will sight what seems to be a marina on the eastern banks at the charted location of Marsh Landing. This dock is actually associated with the tour facilities on Sapelo Island (see below), and signs warn that no dockage, fuel, or other marine services are available.

But don't worry—continue cruising upstream until the charted high banks of Little Sapelo Island come abeam to the west. The heavily timbered banks make an idyllic backdrop and provide superior protection from western, northwestern, and southwestern breezes. Boats up to 48 feet should find plenty of room in the 12- to 19-foot depths.

This writer and his mate spent an unforgettable evening anchored in this spot one warm May evening. The sunset over Little Sapelo Island was magnificent, and the scene will always remain with us as a fond memory of our Georgia cruises.

Sapelo Island

While cruising Duplin River, boaters will have a fine view of Sapelo Island to the east. This historic sea island has hosted some of the most extraordinary individuals to ever reside amidst the Golden Isles.

Sapelo Island was purchased during the early 1800s by Thomas Spalding, son of a well-to-do Scottish trader. For almost 50 years, Spalding owned virtually all of Sapelo, and he ruled the island like a wise and benevolent king.

Spalding built his homeplace near the island's southern tip and named it South End House. South End House was not a typical Southern plantation home, with tall columns and broad porches. Always a practical man, Spalding built his house low to the ground in order to withstand the fury of the frequent coastal storms.

During his long residence on Sapelo Island, Thomas Spalding undertook the occupations of writer and statesman. A leading proponent of experimental agriculture, he was one of the first planters in coastal Georgia to practice crop rotation. Though his wealth lay in Sea Island cotton, Spalding foresaw that sole reliance on this crop could be devastating. With the coming of the boll weevil following the War Between the States, Spalding's thesis was proved in all too dramatic a fashion.

The master of Sapelo Island was known for his unusually humane treatment of his slaves. He never broke up families or sold slaves from the plantation. While, to be sure, the concept of slavery is indefensible, by all accounts there was a genuine affection between master and slaves on Sapelo Island.

Spalding's overseer was a famous slave known as Ben-Ali, the Mohammedan. Legend tells us that he was born to royalty in the French Sudan. While his fellow blacks little understood his native dialect, Ben-Ali spoke both French and English fluently. Obviously a person of great intellect, he was known for his copper-toned skin and aquiline features. Many of his descendants still bear Ben-Ali's unusual countenance and live in coastal Georgia to this day. They are rightfully proud to tell tales of the "Old Man."

One legend speaks of how Ben-Ali beat off a party of invading British soldiers during the War of 1812. Spalding armed a group of his slaves, an unheard-of practice at the time. Under Ben-Ali's leadership, the group of black soldiers stole through the heavy undergrowth and surprised a

British landing party. The invaders were routed and never returned again.

It is also said of Ben-Ali that his Koran and prayer rug were his most prized possessions. He knew the ways of forest and field and taught his children how to predict tides and prepare medicinal roots.

With the death of Thomas Spalding in 1851, an era came to an end on Sapelo Island. Soon, the Civil War left the great plantation in ruins. Returning after the great conflict, Thomas Spalding II found the old South End House destitute.

In 1911, the founder of Detroit's Hudson Motors, Howard Coffin, chanced to be visiting Savannah and became enraptured with the Georgia coastline. By 1912, he had purchased Sapelo Island and undertaken a complete renovation of South End House. He expanded the home further in 1925 and soon took up permanent residence there. Such famous visitors as Herbert Hoover, Calvin Coolidge, and Charles Lindbergh enjoyed the hospitality of the new South End House.

Howard Coffin died in 1932, and the island was sold to North Carolina tobacco magnate R. J. Reynolds, Jr. Always interested in agriculture, Reynolds continued Coffin's experiments in cattle breeding and large-scale farming.

In 1950, Reynolds opened Sapelo Island as a summer camp for boys. This action led to the endowment of the Sapelo Island Research Foundation in 1954. R. J. Reynolds, Jr. died in 1964, and the state of Georgia purchased the northern half of Sapelo Island in 1969. The remainder of the island was acquired by the state in 1976.

All sorts of environmental research has been conducted on Sapelo since then. The island is now home to the University of Georgia Marine Institute. Historic South End House serves as the institute's headquarters and a vacation home for Georgia's governors. In recent times, Jimmy and Rosalynn Carter made extensive use of the old mansion.

Sapelo Island was opened to public visitation in 1977. No landing is allowed by private pleasure craft, but landlubber visitors are ferried over from the mainland for a modest fee. It's a shame that cruising boaters can't visit the island. The magnificence of South End House is worth the trip alone. Should you ever find yourself near the ferry site, do yourself a big favor and take the trip.

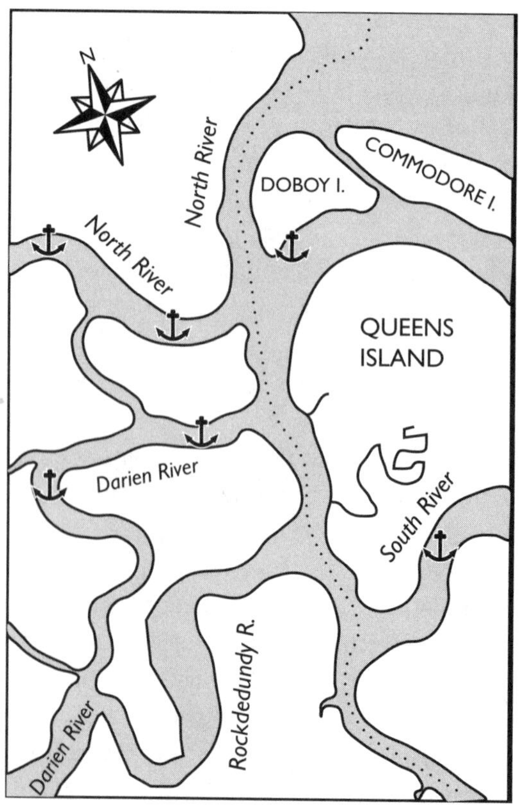

Back River Anchorage

The Waterway follows North River for only a short distance before this stream cuts off to the west and the ICW continues to track its way almost due south down the combined waters of Back, Darien, Rockdedundy, and South Rivers to Little Mud River. Little Mud River leads in turn to vast Altamaha Sound.

Several streams offer good anchorage north of Altamaha Sound. First up is the westerly portion of Back River, located east of unlighted daybeacon #181. By hugging the southerly shores of charted Doboy Island, visiting cruisers can maintain minimum 6-foot depths while paralleling the west-to-east length of the island. Near the channel's westerly limits, high ground will come abeam to the north, thereby significantly improving shelter if winds are blowing from this direction. There should be enough room for boats as large as 40 feet to swing comfortably without impinging upon the charted shallows to the south. Be aware that this anchorage is quite open to strong winds blowing from the southwest and (to a lesser extent) the south and west.

North River Anchorage

West of flashing daybeacon #182, the upper reaches of North River continue on their merry way without the ICW. Minimum depths of 8 feet are held far upstream. Pleasure boats of almost any size can anchor just inside the stream's mouth, but the waters are a bit too broad for comfort unless the fickle wind is blowing lightly.

For better protection, track your way upriver through the first turn to the northwest and then through a second turn to the west. The creek broadens at this point, but you will still find better shelter here than at the downstream haven.

Darien River

Darien River cuts off to the west immediately north of flashing daybeacon #184. This historic stream leads far inland to the old village of Darien, one of the most storied communities in coastal Georgia. Unfortunately, significant shoaling a short distance southwest of charted Catfish Creek has limited cruising opportunities on the upper Darien River to only very small, shallow-draft outboard boats.

On the plus side, the waters short of Catfish Creek can serve as a readily accessible overnight anchorage for Waterway cruisers. By avoiding two shoals, you can maintain minimum depths of 13 feet to a point abeam of Catfish Creek.

This writer's pick for a Darien River anchorage is encountered on the charted 17-foot soundings south of the stream's first southward turn. There is enough room for almost any skipper to anchor his vessel comfortably.

Of course, in fair weather, you can always drop anchor in the initial easterly portion of the stream west of #184. Just be advised that strong easterly breezes blow straight up the creek and can make for a bumpy night.

Rockdedundy River

Boaters are advised to leave off explorations of Rockdedundy River, in spite of its intriguing name. The river's eastern mouth, located west of the gap between flashing daybeacon #185 and unlighted daybeacon #188, is shoal and treacherous.

South River

The waters of South River, located southeast of flashing daybeacon #190, offer the last possibility for sheltered overnight anchorage north of Altamaha Sound. However, unless you arrive during a time of light airs, it might be better to make use of one of the other havens reviewed above.

Boaters on South River must bypass a large bubble of unmarked shallow water at the stream's entrance. Even with this obstruction out of the way, there are more shoals to deal with, and the river is far broader than a cursory study of chart 11507 might lead you to believe. Protection is minimal in winds above 15 knots.

Should you decide to drop the hook here anyway, consider the waters northeast of the entrance shoal and short of the river's first easterly turn.

Altamaha Sound

After a quick trip down Little Mud River, the Waterway disgorges into the spacious waters of Altamaha Sound southeast of unlighted daybeacon #195. The ICW first cuts southeast into the heart of the sound, then darts back to the southwest and parallels the sound's southerly banks as it works its way through acres and acres of shallow water to Buttermilk Sound.

Fortunately, the Waterway is very well outlined by numerous aids to navigation along its course through Altamaha Sound. Daylight navigation should not be too taxing for the alert mariner.

Altamaha Sound's inlet channel lies east of flashing daybeacon #198. This is one of the most straightforward ocean passages south of Savannah River. In fact, the cut runs an almost straight west-to-east line. The channel's aids to navigation are well charted, a sure sign of a stable inlet.

The charted deep water south and west of Dolbow Island may look good on paper, but on-site research revealed that low-water depths at the island's western tip now run to 4 feet. By the way, don't confuse this small island with Doboy Island, located just south of the like-named sound.

Altamaha Sound stretches west and turns into Altamaha River. Don't even think about trying to track your way west on the main body of this river. Altamaha River is one of the most shoal-prone bodies of water in coastal Georgia. It would be a foolhardy gesture indeed to attempt exploration of this stream.

NORTH NEWPORT RIVER TO ALTAMAHA SOUND NAVIGATION

Navigational conditions are pretty much the same on and along the Waterway from North Newport River to Altamaha Sound as they were from Vernon River to St. Catherines Sound. The various sounds are still composed of wide-open waters interconnected by more-sheltered passages. There is really very little to add except to again note the total lack of marina facilities (with one exception) on this portion of the Waterway, a situation that makes proper cruise planning even more important than usual.

ICW through North Newport River From a position abeam of flashing daybeacon #116, set course to follow the mid-width of North Newport River's slow curve to the south. Unlighted daybeacon #117 and flashing daybeacon #119 should be passed well southeast of your course line. These two aids sit hard by the shallows on the river's southeasterly shoreline and should not be closely approached.

After leaving #119 behind, turn a bit farther to the south and point to pass unlighted daybeacon #121 by some 50 yards to its westerly side. Continue cruising almost due south by passing between unlighted daybeacon #122 and flashing daybeacon #123.

Between #119 and #121, the mouth of Timmons River will come abeam to the west. This shoaly stream is better left off your cruising itinerary.

South of #123, the Waterway takes a jog to the south-southeast and bypasses a large patch of shoals shelving out from the western banks. *Be sure* to pass unlighted daybeacon #124 by at least 50 yards to its eastern side. Do not approach #124 closely. It is surrounded by shallow water. East of #124, the southern mouth of Walburg Creek exchanges greetings with the ICW.

Walburg Creek As discussed previously, Walburg Creek's entrances pose a problem. The stream's southwesterly mouth, opposite unlighted daybeacon #124, is bounded by shoals with low-water depths of 4 feet or so. If you draw less than 4 feet, or if you arrive during a rising tide, it might be possible to use this entrance. Consult the tide tables, consider your draft, and make your decision accordingly.

Should you successfully bypass the 4-foot entrance bar, favor the northern and northeastern shores heavily to avoid the large patch of charted shallows abutting the creek's southern shoreline.

Immediately after coming abeam of the first point on the northern shore, cruise toward the southern banks and favor this shoreline as you continue toward the intersection with Necessary Creek.

After Necessary Creek, good depths spread out in a wide swath along Walburg Creek's centerline. Hold scrupulously to the mid-width and you should have good depths all the way upstream to the north-side entrance. Notice the charted 5-foot shoal west of the creek's sharp northerly turn. Favor the northerly banks slightly to be sure of bypassing this hazard.

Many boaters wisely choose to enter Walburg Creek via its northerly mouth, which leads to St. Catherines Sound. The trick to this route is to be sure to pass well east of flashing daybeacon #C. A long shoal identified on chart 11507 as "Middle Ground" is building to the west of #C. For best depths, curl around #C by at least 0.3 nautical mile to its easterly side. You can then cut back to the southwest and find Walburg Creek's northerly mouth.

As you enter northerly Walburg Creek, favor the easterly shoreline. As can be seen from a quick glance at 11507, a 1-foot shoal juts out from the northwesterly entrance point.

Soon after you pass the western shore's northern tip, good depths will spread out almost from shore to shore. You need only hold to the mid-width as far as the creek's sharp turn to the west for excellent soundings.

On the ICW Once you pass unlighted daybeacon #124, continue favoring the easterly banks slightly as you cruise to the south-southwest.

Watch for flashing daybeacon #125, which marks a southeasterly turn in the ICW and its entrance into Johnson Creek. Just north of #125, Newport River sweeps to the west and offers the last marina facility north of Altamaha Sound.

North Newport River to Half Moon Marina The channel up North Newport River to Half Moon Marina is littered with shoals. The only markings are some flag-type signs set along the shoreline to indicate which shore should be favored to avoid the shallows. Frankly, you would do better to follow chart 11511 and the data presented below. Of course, you can certainly watch for the flags to verify your path, but this writer would not recommend using them as a primary source of navigational data.

Depart the Waterway 200 yards north of flashing daybeacon #125 and cruise into the center of the river. Begin working your way toward the northern banks right away. A large shoal has built out from the southern shore just west of the entrance.

West of this shoal, good depths stretch from shore to shore for some 1.2 nautical miles. Shallows begin building out from the northerly banks as Newport River approaches a turn to the north. Favor the southerly shoreline until you make the northerly turn, then begin holding to the easterly banks to avoid the large body of shoals shelving out to the east and northeast from the mouth of South Newport Cut.

Soon, North Newport River intersects Timmons River, and the two streams flow to the west and north together. Cruise 100 yards or so into the mid-width of the combined rivers, then turn 90 degrees to the west. Chart 11511 shows a 5-foot section along this run, but on-site research revealed that 7-foot soundings should be carried.

Be on guard against the large patch of shallows stretching south from charted Drum Point Landing at the juncture of North Newport and Timmons Rivers. To bypass this obstruction, favor the southern and western banks as you follow the river west and then north.

Favor the eastern banks as you begin to enter the large hairpin turn leading to Halfmoon Landing. Glance at chart 11511 and notice that this maneuver will circumvent a 3- to 5-foot shoal along the western shoreline.

The docks of Half Moon Marina will come abeam on the northeastern banks in the body of the hairpin turn. This guide's coverage of the North Newport ends at this point. Should you decide to continue upstream from the marina, make a careful study of the shoals portrayed on 11511.

On the ICW Johnson Creek cuts generally south through the marshy shores of western St. Catherines Island. Navigation of this cut is fairly straightforward, but that fact did not prevent one of the most spectacular groundings this writer and his mate witnessed while exploring Georgia's waters. A large powerboat apparently passed to the eastern side of unlighted daybeacon #131A at full speed just before we came along. The craft's entire hull was exposed, with only the keel buried in the mud. Talk about a bird out of water! We really felt for that skipper and his mate. Fortunately, they were able to get off hours later at high tide.

Cattle Pen Creek The southwesterly mouth of Cattle Pen Creek will come abeam between unlighted daybeacons #127 and #128. Enter the stream on its centerline and continue on the middle as the creek turns to the northeast. Discontinue your explorations well before the stream takes a sharp bend back to the west.

On the ICW Southwest of flashing daybeacon #132, the Waterway quickly makes contact with the wider waters of the southern South Newport River.

From #132, set a careful course to come abeam of unlighted daybeacon #133 by some 30 yards to its northwesterly side. Don't allow leeway to ease you to the west between #132 and #133. The charted shoal running south from the intersection of Johnson Creek and South Newport River seems to be building ever farther. From #133, slightly favor the southeasterly shoreline of South Newport River, but don't approach the banks too closely. Eventually, you should point to come abeam of flashing daybeacon #135 to its westerly side. West and north of #135, one of the finest anchorages on this entire run beckons.

Wahoo River From a position abeam of flashing daybeacon #135, cruise due west until you are within some 300 yards of the westerly banks, then cut sharply north and point to enter Wahoo River's southeasterly entrance on its mid-width. Continue cruising upstream within shouting distance of the stream's center until the river begins to bend sharply to the west. Drop anchor as soon as the high ground to the north comes abeam. Farther to the west, both shorelines exhibit shallower depths, and swinging room is a bit restricted.

ICW to Sapelo Sound It is a good idea to run compass courses down the southerly reaches of South Newport River to Sapelo Sound. The aids to navigation are rather widely spaced. Be sure to stay well east of unlighted daybeacon #136 and flashing daybeacon #138. A huge shelf of shallows lies west of these aids to navigation.

Flashing daybeacon #138 heralds the ICW's entrance into Sapelo Sound. Come abeam of #138 by some 100 yards to its easterly quarter. Farther to the east, shallow water runs south from the north-side entrance point of Sapelo Sound's inlet.

Continue south for several hundred yards past #138 before either cutting west to follow the Waterway or heading east into the sound's inlet channel.

Sapelo Sound's Inlet The real trick to running Sapelo Sound's inlet is to stay well south of charted Experiment Shoal. On the water, this huge patch of shallows is just where you would least expect to find anything but deep water. Boaters should pass well south of unlighted nun buoys #10, #8, and #6 to avoid the shoal. Consult the latest edition of chart 11510 for the configuration of other aids to navigation.

ICW Westward on Sapelo Sound From a position 300 yards or so south of flashing daybeacon #138, cut almost due west and follow the ICW past flashing daybeacons #140 and #142. Stay at least 200 yards south of these aids. The large, charted shoal marked by #140 and #142 seems to be building south and has already encroached upon these two daybeacons. It might be a good idea to run preplotted compass courses through Sapelo Sound to Front River.

Continue on the same course by coming abeam of and passing unlighted daybeacon #143 and flashing daybeacon #145 by at least 100 yards to their northerly sides. These beacons denote yet another large shallow patch, charted as Dog Hammock Spit. Depths of as little as ½ foot wait to trap the navigationally impaired who wander south of these aids.

At flashing daybeacon #145, the ICW bends to the southwest before entering Front River. Be sure to pass unlighted daybeacon #147 to its northwesterly side, as it, too, marks Dog Hammock Spit.

From #147, set course to come abeam of

flashing daybeacon #149 by some 100 yards to its northwesterly side. This beacon sits hard by the northerly shores of Dog Hammock Spit and can sometimes be hard to spot. Southwest of #149, set a careful compass course to pass unlighted daybeacon #150 to its southeasterly side. Shoal water lies to the west of #150.

Don't attempt to run an arrow-straight course from #150 to the next southerly aid to navigation, flashing daybeacon #151. As you will see after a study of the channel on chart 11507, it is better to follow a more gradual turn to the southwest.

Flashing daybeacon #151 marks the ICW's entrance into Front River. Many a boater has breathed a sigh of relief upon leaving the often choppy waters of Sapelo Sound behind.

Sapelo River Remember that there are currently no marina facilities on Sapelo River, whatever the signs might say. If you decide to cruise the stream anyway, depart the Waterway about halfway between flashing daybeacon #149 and unlighted daybeacon #150.

Come abeam of and pass unlighted daybeacon #2 by at least 100 yards to its southerly side. West of #2, your best bet is to simply follow the markers, keeping red beacons to your starboard side and green markers to port, as you would expect. Have chart 11510 handy, and make sure you study the few shoals along the way ahead of time.

The restaurant docks will come abeam on the southerly banks near unlighted daybeacon #8.

On the ICW It's a quick and protected run down Front River and Creighton Narrows to Old Teakettle Creek. Be sure to stay east of unlighted daybeacon #154. Some shallow water lies west of #154.

South of flashing daybeacon #155A, the Waterway begins its approach to Crescent River and Old Teakettle Creek. Stay east of unlighted daybeacon #156 and come abeam of flashing daybeacon #157 fairly close to its westerly quarter. A shoal has built out from the southwesterly point of Creighton Narrows west of #156.

From #157, a set of range markers lying to the south-southeast helps you make your entrance into Old Teakettle Creek.

Just before reaching the forward range marker, veer off a bit to the southwest and pass between unlighted daybeacon #158 and flashing daybeacon #159. Between #157 and the range marker, boaters in search of overnight anchorage can do themselves a big favor by cutting up Crescent River.

Crescent River Favor the southwestern shores of Crescent River as you enter in order to bypass the charted shoal west of unlighted daybeacon #156. Hold to the centerline until the river bends to the north, then begin favoring the eastern banks to avoid the charted 1-foot shoal striking out from the western shoreline.

As the creek curves back to the west, the high ground of Creighton Island marches down to the northeastern banks. This is the best sport to drop the hook. Farther to the west, the Crescent splits into two branches, and depths become suspect.

On the ICW Pass unlighted daybeacons #158A and #160 by at least 55 yards to their southeasterly sides. Shoal water building in from the northwest has encroached on both markers.

Flashing daybeacon #162 marks a southerly turn in Old Teakettle Creek and the ICW. Just south of #162, skippers piloting small cruising craft might check out Shellbluff Creek.

Shellbluff Creek Enter Shellbluff Creek on the mid-width. Discontinue your upstream progress before passing through the stream's first small jog to starboard.

On the ICW Pass close to the western side of unlighted daybeacon #167. Shallows impinge upon the Waterway channel to the east and west near #167.

Northeast of unlighted daybeacon #172, boaters may choose to enter the mostly deep waters of New Teakettle Creek.

New Teakettle Creek From unlighted daybeacon #172, cruise down the Waterway for another 50 yards or so, then turn directly toward the easterly banks. Some 50 yards before meeting up with the shoreline, swing due north and enter the mouth of New Teakettle Creek, favoring the east-side banks slightly. Study chart 11507 and you will quickly see how this plan of action will help you avoid the shoal that has built out from the point separating New and Old Teakettle Creeks.

Once you are on the creek's interior section, hold to the mid-width until you are just south of the juncture with small Mary Creek, which makes in to the eastern shoreline. Favor the western side of New Teakettle Creek as you pass the mouth of Mary Creek. A shoal lies northwest of Mary Creek's western mouth.

Good depths continue on the centerline of

Classic motor yacht on Georgia ICW

New Teakettle Creek all the way to the intersection with shallow Mud River. Most cruisers will choose to stop long before reaching this faraway spot.

On the ICW At flashing daybeacon #175, Old Teakettle Creek and the ICW flow into Doboy Sound. Pass #175 fairly close to its westerly side and immediately set a new course to come abeam of flashing daybeacon #178 by at least 100 yards to its easterly side. Be sure to avoid the point of land northwest of #175 that separates Old Teakettle Creek and Doboy Sound. A long shoal is building south from this quarter.

Between #175 and #178, adventurous cruisers can cut northwest into upper Doboy Sound and visit its various sidewaters. There are no markers on the upper sound, so use your compass and chart 11507 to avoid the shallows.

Folly River Favor the northwesterly side of Folly River as you make your way from Doboy Sound into its interior reaches. Cruise back to the mid-width after leaving the entrance behind. Excellent soundings continue upstream at least as far as the intersection with Dead River. Cruising-size craft should begin to retrace their steps at this juncture.

Dark Creek A long shoal has built southwest from the point of marsh separating Dark and Atwood Creeks. Favor the southeasterly side of Dark Creek's entrance to avoid these shallows. Don't attempt to cruise past the two-way fork in Dark Creek well upstream.

Duplin River Duplin River can be accessed east of flashing daybeacon #178. Cruise into the stream by favoring its southeastern and eastern banks. Notice the large shoal stretching well south and southwest from the point separating Duplin River and Doboy Sound, accurately portrayed on chart 11507.

Continue slightly favoring the eastern shores until you come abeam of the private dock at Marsh Landing. Cruise back to the middle at this point. North of the dock, you need only stay within a stone's throw of the mid-width until Duplin River turns sharply east abeam of Pumpkin Hammock. This upper portion of the river is not recommended for cruising-size craft.

ICW into North River After coming abeam of flashing daybeacon #178 to its easterly side, continue cruising due south on Doboy Sound for another 50 to 75 yards. You should then turn 90 degrees to the west and pick up the charted range at the entrance to North River. Don't allow leeway to ease you north on this run. Shoal water of 3 feet or less guards North River's northerly entrance point west of #178.

Break off from the range some 25 yards before reaching the forward marker and follow North River's slow curve to the south. Continue slightly favoring the northern and northwestern marsh shores to bypass the thin strip of shallows abutting Doboy Island to the south and southeast.

After cruising through the southerly turn, favor the easterly banks just a bit to avoid the correctly charted shoal north and northwest of flashing daybeacon #182.

Just short of unlighted daybeacon #181, the first anchorage on the trek from Doboy Sound to Altamaha Sound will come abeam to the east.

Doboy Island Anchorage Depart the Waterway north of unlighted daybeacon #181 and favor Doboy Island's southern shoreline heavily as you track your way to the east. For maximum protection, drop anchor on the western portion of this run where the high ground of western Doboy Island comes abeam to the north. For more swinging room, continue east until you are past the southern shoal lying east of #181. Don't attempt to cruise past the small stream separating Doboy and Commodore Islands. The waters here are suspect.

North River The westerly reaches of North River, abandoned by the ICW, can be accessed from unlighted daybeacon #181. To cruise the river, cut sharply west upon coming abeam of #181. Enter the stream's mid-width, passing flashing daybeacon #182 to its northerly side in the process. Hold to the middle until the river begins to bend to the north. Begin favoring the southwesterly banks until just before coming abeam of the small, unnamed offshoot on the westerly banks.

Start favoring the easterly banks immediately after passing this small stream. Soon, the river turns back to the west. Stick to the mid-width here. The river then takes a turn to the north and leaves chart 11507. Most boaters will wisely choose to stop before reaching this last northerly jog.

On the ICW Slightly favor the easterly shoreline as you cruise south from flashing daybeacon #182 to flashing daybeacon #183. There is a patch of shallows abutting the westerly banks along this run. To the west of #183, you may choose to explore Darien River for a short distance.

Darien River Enter the eastern mouth of Darien River on its mid-width. Good depths stretch to within several yards of each bank until the river encounters the small, charted, northward-running stream that connects with North River.

If you are simply seeking anchorage, it makes sense to drop the hook east of this intersection. However, those wanting to look over as much of Darien River as possible should begin favoring the northern banks west of the juncture with the small stream. Soon, the river flows through a sharp turn to the south. Begin favoring the northern banks as you approach this turn. Favor the northwestern and western shoreline as you pass through the bend. Continue favoring the western banks for the next 100 yards to the south past the turn. You can then cruise back to the mid-width. Good depths continue upstream on the centerline to a point just short of Catfish Creek. Nothing but small, shallow-draft outboard craft should even consider voyaging upstream past this intersection.

On the ICW South of flashing daybeacon #183, be sure to favor the easterly banks slightly as you track your way to flashing daybeacon #185. A band of shallow water flanks the westerly shoreline along this stretch.

Pass #185 fairly close to its westerly side. A small pool of shallow water lies farther west of #185. Similarly, be sure to pass east of unlighted daybeacon #188, since a small patch of shallow water and marsh is found northwest of #188.

Favor the easterly shores slightly as you cruise from #188 to the next southerly aid to navigation, flashing daybeacon #190.

A well-placed range marker leads northbound boaters on the ICW through the channel between #190 and #185.

South River If you decide to cruise the questionable South River channel, continue southwest on the ICW for 25 yards or so past flashing daybeacon #190. You can then cut southeast and enter the middle of South River's northwesterly mouth.

After proceeding upstream for 100 yards or so,

begin heavily favoring the southerly banks. This maneuver will help you avoid the 3-foot shoal that appears so prominently on 11507.

Soon, the stream follows a small turn to the northeast, then cuts back to the southeast. If you continue through this turn, favor the northern and northeastern banks to bypass the charted shoal abutting the south side of the turn.

Favor the southern banks as you continue downstream toward the intersection with Wolf Creek. Local boats sometimes run the unmarked waters of the eastern South River into Doboy Sound, but this passage is strictly not recommended without very specific local knowledge.

ICW into Altamaha Sound On its way to Altamaha Sound, the Georgia ICW cuts through narrow Little Mud River. This stream is subject to continual shoaling, particularly on its southerly extreme. This writer has found some 4-foot depths immediately adjacent to unlighted daybeacon #194. The best advice is to stick to the mid-width of the channel and not approach any of the various markers too closely. Keep a sharp watch on the sounder and slow to idle speed if depths become dicey.

Eventually, you should point to come between the fairly immediate westerly quarter of unlighted daybeacon #195 and flashing daybeacon #B, which serves as a forward range marker. Don't let leeway push you to the west between #194 and #195. Also note that shoal water lies west and north of #B.

Unlighted daybeacon #195 introduces southbound ICW boaters to the impressive confines of Altamaha Sound. This body of water may not be as wide as some of Georgia's sounds, but it certainly holds the distinction of being the shallowest.

From #195, the ICW channel cuts sharply southeast to bypass a long shoal south of Little Mud River. Set course to pass flashing daybeacon #198 to its northeasterly side. Again, northbound cruisers have the advantage of a good range to help with the run from #198 to #195.

To ensure best possible depths, continue on the same course line past #198 for at least 200 yards. Only then should you curl back around to the west-southwest and point to come abeam of and pass flashing daybeacon #201 to its northerly side.

East of #198, pleasure craft of almost any size and draft may put to sea.

Altamaha Sound Inlet The channel running east from Altamaha Sound to the sea has the distinct advantage of being almost a straight shot. Markers are widely placed, so run a compass course and use your binoculars to pick out the various markers. Have charts 11507 and 11508 at hand to quickly resolve any questions that arise. As with all inlets, be ready to find a different configuration of aids to navigation from what appears on the charts.

ICW from Altamaha Sound to Buttermilk Sound As the Waterway channel cuts along the south side of Altamaha Sound, it runs through what one captain described as "a mess of shoals." It would be pointless to delineate all of these shallows in this account, since they are depicted on chart 11507. What every skipper *must* do, though, is take more than the usual caution to identify all markers and to be *sure* that he or she is about to pass them on the proper side.

By the time you reach flashing daybeacon #209, the Waterway will have led you close by the shores of Little St. Simons Island. The channel now cuts a bit to the northwest on its way to shoal-prone Buttermilk Sound. Watch for the charted range near One-Mile Cut. These markers will lead you safely past unlighted daybeacon #211 (to its northeasterly side) and into the headwaters of Buttermilk Sound. Some 25 yards before reaching the forward range marker, cut off to the west and point to pass flashing daybeacon #213 to its northerly side. A continuing account of the ICW to the Florida border will be presented in the next chapter.

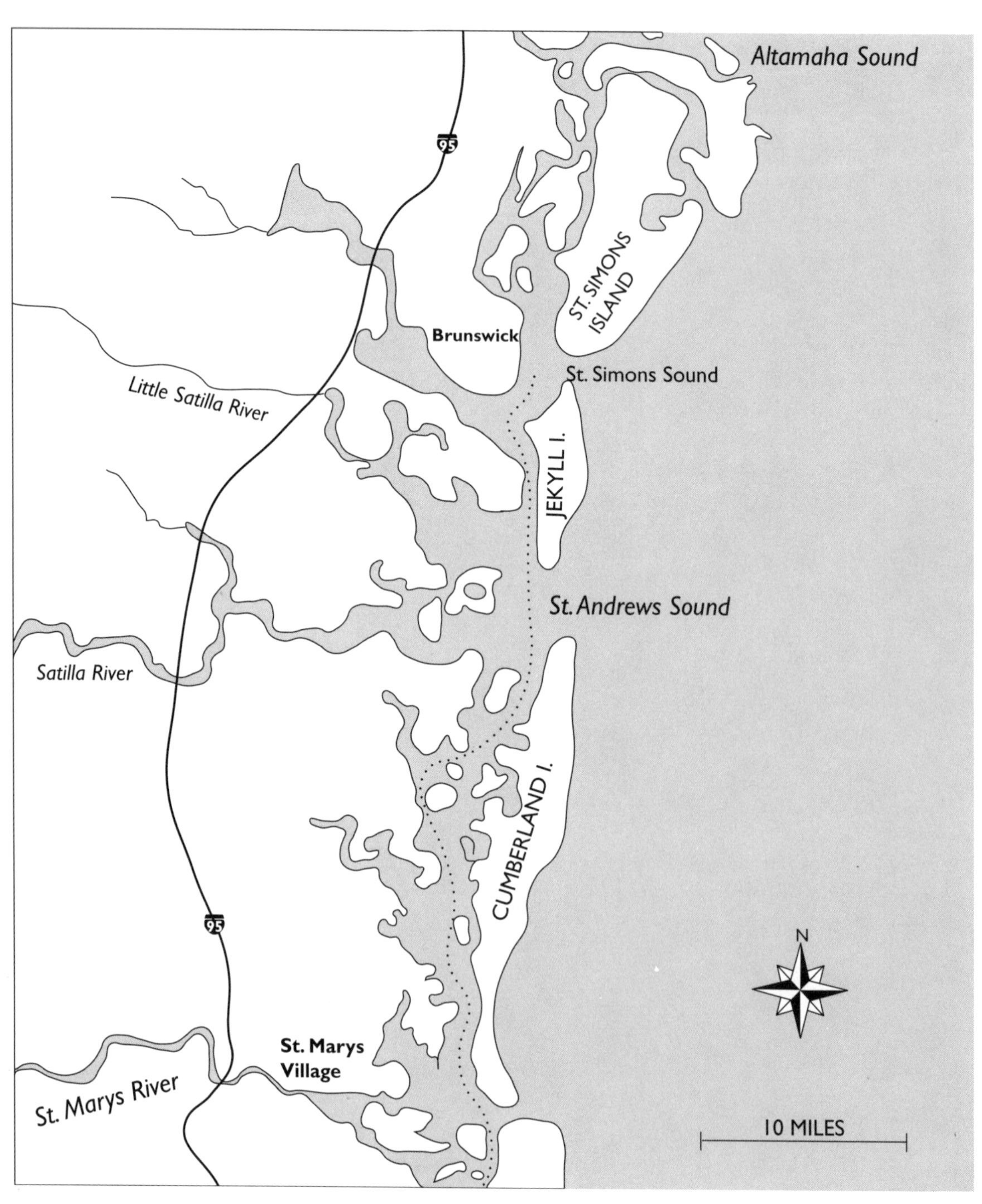

Altamaha Sound
ST. SIMONS ISLAND
Brunswick
St. Simons Sound
Little Satilla River
JEKYLL I.
St. Andrews Sound
Satilla River
CUMBERLAND I.
95
N
St. Marys Village
St. Marys River
10 MILES

Buttermilk Sound to St. Marys River

The waters of southeastern Georgia present a striking two-part contrast for boaters. To the north, numerous marina facilities have proliferated around the resorts of St. Simons, Jekyll, and Sea Islands. The commercial city of Brunswick, with its many paper and pulp mills, its quaint downtown district, and a new marina, overlooks these same waters to the west.

South of huge St. Andrew Sound, the lands surrounding the ICW are very different. The eastern shoreline north of St. Marys River is dominated by gorgeous Cumberland Island. Set amidst a sea of incredibly lush foliage are some of the most enchanting historic sites in coastal Georgia. Cumberland Island is now managed by the National Park Service and is being preserved for all to enjoy. There is even the opportunity to lodge in one of the most prestigious inns to be found anywhere.

The waters of coastal Georgia finally come to an end at St. Marys River. This stream serves as the dividing line between Georgia and Florida. A short cruise to the west on St. Marys River will lead fortunate boaters to the delightful village of the same name, the last stop on the Georgia coast. Formerly overlooked by cruising boaters, the village of St. Marys now features a marina with good dining nearby, along with lodging set in a beautifully preserved historic atmosphere.

While it may lack the length and breadth of the northern coastline, southeastern Georgia clearly has something to offer every style of cruiser. This writer heartily recommends that you take the opportunity to enjoy the comforts and the unique historical perspectives of this timeless land and its waters.

Charts

Several charts are necessary for cruising the waters of southeastern Georgia:

11507 continues to follow the ICW south to a point just short of St. Simons Island's southern tip

11489 details the ICW and surrounding waters throughout the remainder of southeastern Georgia into Florida

11508 covers Altamaha Sound's inlet to the open sea

11506 outlines St. Simons Sound and its inlet, as well as the upper reaches of Turtle River

11504 is a good chart for those putting to sea from St. Andrew Sound

11503 shows the route up St. Marys River to the village of St. Marys, as well as a portion of the river's inlet

BUTTERMILK SOUND TO ST. ANDREW SOUND

The ICW between Buttermilk and St. Andrew Sounds might be termed the resort stretch of the Georgia Waterway. St. Simons, Jekyll, and Sea Islands have all been developed as vacation meccas with the very best taste and preservation techniques.

Jekyll Island is actually owned and managed by the state of Georgia. While St. Simons certainly has its share of development, it is light years from the concrete jungle that is quickly enveloping such resorts as Hilton Head. Tall trees with reindeer moss and virgin forests are still everywhere in evidence on the isle. Some of the most important historical sites in all of Georgia are available to visitors as well. Sea Island is home to The Cloisters, one of the most exclusive inns in the world.

Both St. Simons and Jekyll Islands offer excellent marina facilities that welcome Waterway transients. Rental cars are readily available, allowing visitors to ferry their way easily to the isles' many points of interest.

Flanking the three resort islands to the west is the industrial city of Brunswick, with its potpourri of paper mills. A new marina that welcomes visiting cruisers now offers easy access to the downtown Brunswick historic district.

Once again, boaters generally have the opportunity to drop the hook in more locales than they can count. Some of these overnight stops are truly memorable.

Buttermilk Sound

Buttermilk Sound's chief characteristic for cruising boaters is its penchant for shoaling. During our latest cruise of these waters, this writer and his mate sounded some 9-foot depths, but that of course still offers plenty of room for 98 percent of all pleasure craft. Conditions may change in the future, for better or worse. Proceed with caution.

Hampton River Club Marina

South and east of unlighted daybeacon #222, the westerly mouth of Hampton River strikes off to the north, then cuts back to the east, dividing St. Simons and Little St. Simons Islands. A privately marked channel leads downriver for some 2.8 nautical miles to Hampton River Club Marina. Minimum depths in the river channel are 7 feet. Entry can be a little tricky for first-timers due to a change in the color configuration of the beacons. Be sure to read the navigational information in the next section of this chapter before making your first visit to the river or its marina.

Hampton River Club Marina graces the southwesterly shores of Hampton River northwest of charted Butler Point. This facility can be recognized by its large, metal dry-stack storage building set well back from the docks. As is often the case in coastal Georgia, the marina is part of an

Hampton River Club Marina

exclusive private development, but the marine services are open to all. Transients are accommodated at first-rate concrete floating docks featuring water connections and power connections up to 50 amps. Depths alongside at low tide are an impressive 10 to 15 feet. Gasoline and diesel fuel are readily available dockside, and full mechanical service is offered as well. The marina has showers on the premises, as well as a small ship's and variety store. Future plans call for the installation of waste pump-out. Boats up to 5 tons can be hauled out via the marina's dry-stack forklift. You can walk to the restaurant at the nearby Hampton Club, or motorized transportation can probably be arranged by the accommodating marina staff. All in all, Hampton River Club Marina is a fine facility.

Hampton River Club Marina
(912) 638-1210

Approach depth: 7 feet (minimum)
Dockside depth: 12–15 feet (low water)
Accepts transients: yes
Floating concrete piers: yes
Dockside power connections: 30 and 50 amps
Dockside water connections: yes
Showers: yes
Gasoline: yes
Diesel fuel: yes
Mechanical repairs: yes
Below-waterline repairs: limited (forklift only)
Ship's and variety store: small
Restaurant: nearby

Past the marina, Hampton River continues to snake its way east and south for many miles until it finally makes a shallow entry into the Atlantic. Frankly, this downstream portion of the river is not recommended for visiting cruisers. Unmarked shoals are strewn along the river's path, and the inlet is shallow and dangerous.

It should also be noted that Village Creek breaks off to the south from Hampton River near the latter stream's inlet. Village Creek eventually leads to some low-key docks associated with the exclusive Cloisters development on Sea Island. Depths run to 3 feet, and the creek is quite narrow in places. Also, it is crossed by a low-level fixed bridge. Obviously, this is an "outboards only" sojourn.

Little St. Simons Island

The northern banks of Hampton River are part of Little St. Simons Island, a body of marsh and high ground that boasts unforgettable stories. During the late 1700s and early 1800s, this isle was home to one of the most colorful figures in all of coastal Georgia.

In 1774, Major Pierce Butler of South Carolina purchased Little St. Simons Island and began to plan what would be one of the most efficient plantations in the South. Hampton Plantation employed hundreds of workers who transported materials, supplies, and livestock by boat from South Carolina to the island. Skilled artisans were imported from the Low Country, and work soon began on what became known as the "Big House." Formal gardens were laid out, and outbuildings of all descriptions soon dotted the landscape. It was almost two decades in the making, but by the late 1700s Hampton Plantation had become one of the most prestigious holdings on the Georgia coastline.

Burnette Vanstory comments on Pierce Butler in *Georgia's Land of the Golden Isles*: "The major, austere and dignified autocrat that he was, differed in every way from his easy-going neighbors; and the strict military regulations and discipline at Hampton were in marked contrast to the leisurely atmosphere of the other plantations. . . . The casual visitor arriving by boat must state his name and business to a warden . . . before being escorted to the Big House. Managed with the regimental efficiency that was part of Pierce Butler's nature, Hampton was a model community that produced everything needed in the daily life of its inhabitants."

In 1804, Vice President Aaron Burr visited Hampton Plantation for several weeks following his tragic duel with Alexander Hamilton. He wrote his daughter that the great farm "affords plenty of milk, cream and butter; turkeys, fowls, kids, pigs, geese and mutton; fish of course in abundance; figs, peaches, melons, oranges and pomegranates."

During that same year, a powerful hurricane swept ashore on Little St. Simons Island. One of the plantation's overseers, a man known only as Morris, accurately read the deteriorating weather conditions and rushed everyone inside a strongly fortified structure called the "Hurricane House" before the storm arrived in its full intensity. In recognition of his quick thinking, Morris received a coin-silver tankard from Butler. It was inscribed with a passage commemorating his courage and wisdom. This piece was handed down through many generations of Morris's family. Today, it resides in a museum.

By 1839, the elder Butler had passed on, and ownership of the plantation fell to his son, Pierce Butler II. The younger Butler had married the famous English actress Frances Ann "Fanny" Kemble. Outspoken in her opposition to slavery, she penned her immortal *Journal of a Residence on a Georgian Plantation, 1838–1839* while living on Hampton Plantation. Far more accurate than the famous *Uncle Tom's Cabin*, Kemble's work remains one of the most important documents describing life on an antebellum plantation. She and her husband were divorced in Philadelphia soon after this book's publication.

Hampton Plantation declined during the 1850s. It was occupied and all but destroyed by Union troops during the Civil War. What was left of the Big House's ruins burned in 1871.

In 1900, Little St. Simons was sold to a pencil company, which harvested the abundant red cedar trees growing on the island. For many years thereafter, the isle was left in its natural state. Since World War II, the rustic "Inn on Little St. Simons" has offered its guests some of the most naturalistic lodgings imaginable. It's a very special treat to spend a night or two on this little-discovered island and muse upon the great plantation that has now all but vanished amidst the marsh grass, weeds, and undergrowth.

Sad to say, no dockage by private pleasure craft is permitted at the lodge's pier. Guests must be transported by ferry from Hampton River Club Marina. Contact the inn (912-638-7472) for more information.

Waterway Anchorage

Study chart 11507 for a moment and notice the bubble of deep water west and northwest of unlighted daybeacon #227. While the water is not quite as deep as shown on the chart (on-site research revealed 6-foot depths), boats drawing 5 feet or less can track their way off the ICW for 50 to 75 yards and drop the hook with fair protection from eastern or western blows. There is even some protection to the north, but a bit less to the south. Cruisers selecting this anchorage will be exposed to the wake of all passing vessels. Considering the many other available anchorages, this refuge cannot be looked upon as a prime consideration.

Frederica River's Northern Leg

Until a few years ago, the ICW cut southeast down the northern section of Frederica River at unlighted daybeacon #229. The Waterway now winds its way south down MacKay River, but the older route is still very navigable for vessels drawing less than 6 feet. While minimum depths of 6½ feet hold over most of the river's course, some shoaling has recently occurred near the river's intersection with the ICW at #229. Depths of 5½ to 6 feet at dead low tide can now be expected. Just what the future holds for water depths in this questionable area is unclear, but you can always enter and depart on a rising tide for more depth.

Frederica River is a delightful stream that is far more scenic than the new ICW route down MacKay River. It borders marsh to the west, but the easterly shoreline is composed of St. Simons Island's westerly flank. There are at least three prime considerations for overnight anchorage, but if winds are blowing less than 20 knots, particularly from the east or west, you can suit your fancy.

Moving north to south, you might first want to consider the waters abeam of charted West Point. High ground marches down to St. Simons Island's banks to the east and provides plenty of protection when winds are blowing across the island. Vessels up to 36 feet can be accommodated.

Next up is what is undoubtedly the premier Frederica River anchorage. Boaters piloting craft up to 48 feet in length have the opportunity to anchor just south of charted Fort Frederica National Monument (see the St. Simons Island section below) in 10- to 18-foot depths. Landing at the national monument is strictly prohibited, even for dinghies. You must obtain the use of a rental car from one of the nearby marinas to visit this point of interest. Even so, it is a very special treat indeed to anchor next door to one of the most important historic sites in the southeastern United States. As one park ranger remarked to this writer, "If things had turned out differently at Frederica, we might all be speaking Spanish today." This anchorage is well sheltered from eastern winds courtesy of the high, well-wooded St. Simons banks. The shelter from the east, north, and south should be sufficient for winds under 30 knots.

Finally, boaters seeking shelter from strong southerly blows can drop the hook beside the charted patch of high banks south of Dunbar Creek. Hawkins Island, farther to the south, acts as an additional windbreak. Depths of 30 feet or better call for a prodigious amount of anchor rode to maintain a proper 6-to-1 scope. For this reason, boats larger than 36 feet might find themselves a bit cramped for swinging room. A Bahamian-style mooring would be a wise precaution.

The southern portion of North Frederica River joins back up with MacKay River and the ICW near flashing daybeacon #241. Most cruising boaters who have followed Frederica River south will want to reenter the ICW at this point. The southern branch of the Frederica, while deep, is crossed by a fixed bridge with only 9 feet of vertical clearance. A world-class marina is found on Frederica River southwest of the fixed span, but large boats must access it via the ICW and St. Simons Sound. This marina will be reviewed later in the chapter.

Wallys Leg

Back on the ICW where the preceding discussion of Frederica River began, southbound cruisers will soon come upon the unusually named creek known as Wallys Leg west of flashing daybeacon #231. The initial easterly portion of this creek offers anchorage convenient to the ICW, with minimum 15-foot depths and enough swinging room for vessels up to 45 feet. The bit of charted high ground to the north helps protect boats when breezes are wafting from this direction.

Troup Creek

Boaters can, but probably shouldn't, enter the mouth of Troup Creek northwest of unlighted daybeacon #238. For one thing, it is necessary to bypass an unmarked shoal to enter the stream. For another, a small United States Coast Guard base is perched upstream on Troup Creek, and you could find yourself obstructing a rescue mission if you attempt to anchor on this small creek.

Troup Creek leads past the Coast Guard docks to the less-than-ideal pier of tiny Troup Creek Marina (912-264-3862). This small firm is clearly in the business of serving fishermen, rather than cruising boaters. To give you some idea of the marina's flavor, its main "attraction" is a pool hall. The management claims to accept transients, but no power or water connections are available. Gasoline, but not diesel fuel, can be purchased. There are no other marine or shoreside services except dry-stack storage for small powerboats. My ace research assistant, Kerry, suggested that the marina's motto is probably "Any excuse for a beer."

Man Head Marina

The ICW flows smoothly down the course of MacKay River and passes under a relatively new fixed high-rise bridge south of unlighted daybeacon #242. Immediately after this span, the single concrete floating dock of now-closed Man Head Marina will come abeam to the west-northwest.

Golden Isles Marina

The ICW bids a fond farewell to MacKay River south of flashing daybeacon #245 and flows out into the widening waters of St. Simons Sound. After carefully rounding the protracted shoal stretching south from the intersection of MacKay and Frederica Rivers, you can cruise north through 8-foot minimum depths on the Frederica to Golden Isles Marina, one of the premier boating facilities in all of Georgia.

Golden Isles Marina is not your everyday stop along the ICW. Consider the large retail and dining complex that overlooks the docks. During 1995, Golden Isles changed owners. While in the short run some of the restaurants in the retail center behind the docks have closed, this writer believes that in the long term things will take a turn for the better at this well-respected and well-appointed facility.

The shopping complex still contains several firms that visiting cruisers will want to check out. First on this list is Dunbar Sails (912-638-8573 or 800-282-1411). This ultrafriendly nautical operation maintains a first-class ship's store in the Golden Isles center. Additionally, it offers an ASA-certified sailing school and sailcraft brokerage. This writer simply cannot say enough about the helpful nature of Dunbar Sails and all its knowledgeable personnel. Make their acquaintance for yourself.

The only restaurant currently operating in the Golden Isles center is the Dockside Grill, open for the midday and evening meals. This writer found the food here quite tasty, particularly the sandwiches, even if the cuisine is not what one would term sophisticated. Future plans call for several more on-site restaurants to open, but it could be several months, or even years, before these projects are realized.

The Golden Isles shopping center also contains a dive shop and any number of other private offices, including a radio station. There is no grocery or convenience store available at this time. A quick cab ride or car rental will be necessary to restock your larder. For taxi service, call St. Simons Cab (912-638-3790). Enterprise Rent-A-Car (912-262-1436) can usually be relied upon to deliver cars to the marina for its customers.

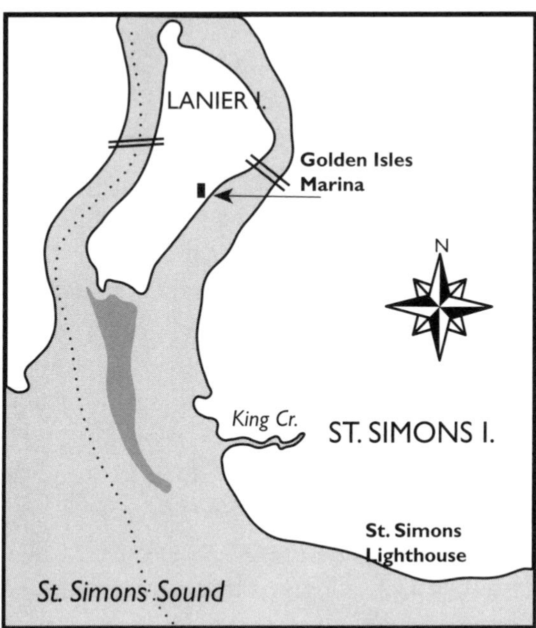

As you are cruising up Frederica River from St. Simons Sound to Golden Isles Marina, you will first sight a single row of docks adjacent to a building designated by an "Inn" sign. Don't mistake this establishment for the marina. The docks here are "boataminiums" that are sold to those who buy permanent space in the inn. By the way, boaters wanting to take a break from the live-aboard routine can usually find temporary lodging in this facility. Ask the accommodating dockmasters at Golden Isles for assistance.

Golden Isles Marina will soon come abeam to the west. The marina features extensive transient dockage at ultramodern wooden-decked floating docks. The harbor is enclosed by an outer dock that acts as a breakwater for the interior piers. In foul weather, try to secure one of the inside berths. Dockside depths at the outer piers run 18 to 20 feet, with 10 to 13 feet of water at the innermost slips. All berths have cable-television and water hookups, as well as power connections up to 50 amps. Shoreside, boaters will find some of the nicest showers and laundromat facilities that this writer has ever reviewed. Gasoline, diesel fuel, and a new waste pump-out service are readily at hand, and mechanical repairs can be arranged by the dockmasters through local mechanics. Advance dockage reservations by either VHF or landline are almost a necessity during the spring and fall transient seasons.

Just to let you know a bit more about the marina staff's super attitude, this writer and his mate were informed that no one goes home until "the last boat is in." We believe it! How many facilities do you know that can honestly make that claim?

Golden Isles Marina (912) 634-1786

Approach depth: 8 feet (minimum)
Dockside depth: 10–20 feet
Accepts transients: yes
Floating wooden piers: yes
Dockside power connections: 30 and 50 amps
Dockside water connections: yes
Showers: yes
Laundromat: yes
Waste pump-out: yes
Gasoline: yes
Diesel fuel: yes
Mechanical repairs: independent contractors
Ship's store: yes
Restaurant: on-site

St. Simons Island

Coastal Sea Islands undergoing development for tourism and resort uses should all turn out just like St. Simons. In fact, it might not be putting too fine a point on it to require all coastal developers to study just what this island has done right.

While, to be sure, more and more private homes and other buildings have gone up on St. Simons over the past several decades due to the island's increasing popularity, the charm remains very much intact. Houses are still mostly single-family dwellings on large lots with a host of venerable oaks and other hardwoods set about the grounds, sporting their beards of gray moss. Even the "pier village" has a distinct lack of fast-food restaurants and garish modern construction. Historic sites are respectfully cared for and outfitted with markers or taped messages to allow every visitor the opportunity to experience as much of this isle's fascinating history as possible. Golf courses dot both St. Simons Island and adjacent Sea Island. One course still boasts the old avenue of oaks planted on Retreat Plantation in the 1800s.

Of all the developed Sea Islands we have visited, this writer and his mate have never discovered another with more grace, charm, and historical character than St. Simons. Do yourself a very big favor and take the opportunity to come to know this enchanted isle. Who knows, you may find yourself drawn back year after year to the snow-white St. Simons Lighthouse, the tall, stately trees, and the peaceful beaches.

It must be noted in passing that none of the many attractions described below are within walking distance of Golden Isles or Hampton River Club Marinas. You will almost certainly need a rental car or taxi to enjoy these points of interest. Consult the previous section for car-rental and taxi information.

St. Simons Island Attractions

Every visit to St. Simons Island should probably begin at the "pier village." This small community is located at the southern tip of St. Simons. It is actually a rather recent settlement, having sprung up in the early part of this century.

Village visitors will find an eclectic selection of shops and restaurants set about a delightful waterside park and fishing pier. Again, there is no dockage for pleasure craft, though you will undoubtedly sight the pier should you cruise into or out of St. Simons Sound's inlet.

If you happen to arrive at mealtime, give every consideration to visiting Coconut Willie's Raw Bar and Grill (121 Mallory Street, 912-

634-6134). This informal dining and drinking establishment serves wonderful food. The fried-shrimp sandwich is outstanding. Come breakfast time, Dressner's Village Cafe (223 Mallory Street, 912-634-1217) offers some of the *best* blueberry pancakes that this writer has ever enjoyed.

It may be written in the Constitution—and if not, there should be an amendment—that every newcomer to the village must tour the nearby St. Simons Lighthouse and keeper's quarters. The original tower on this spot was destroyed during the War Between the States. The present light was built in 1872. The lighthouse was first powered with kerosene, but electricity finally took over in 1934. Beginning in 1971, the old keeper's cottage was converted to a museum memorializing coastal Georgia's history. This interesting exhibit is managed by the Coastal Georgia Historical Society. Patrons have the opportunity to tour the keeper's quarters, which are outfitted according to various themes reflecting island life in the late 1800s and the early part of this century. Then it's time to climb the narrow, winding stairs to the lighthouse's crown. Your legs may be a bit sore from the climb, but the effort is more than justified by the magnificent view of the surrounding land and waters. If you have a bit of acrophobia like this writer, watch out for weak knees.

Any self-respecting lighthouse of venerable years must have its ghost, and St. Simons Lighthouse is no exception. Whispers speak of a murdered light keeper's spirit who paces the spiral steps night after night. A later keeper and his family who spent almost 25 years living at the lighthouse became so used to the ghost that the footsteps seemed commonplace.

It is said that the ascending steps always stop before reaching the uppermost landing, while the descending steps cease before the ground-floor landing. The keeper was often fooled into thinking his wife was coming up to visit him. She in turn frequently thought her husband was coming down to dinner, and she would set out the food, only to learn that he was still high in the tower. Go quietly as you make your climb, and the sound of footsteps may still accompany you up the old tower.

The marker commemorating the historically critical Battle of Bloody Marsh (see the historical account below) is found just off Demere Road well north of the old lighthouse. Stop your

St. Simons Lighthouse, St. Simons Island

car and spend a few moments staring out over the broad expanse of marsh, then listen to the taped message at the nearby "squawk box" and try to imagine the conflict that took place here so many years ago. Those who listen carefully may still hear the crack of muskets and the soldiers' curses uttered both in English and Spanish.

Every caller on St. Simons Island should make an effort to tour old Christ Church, Frederica, near the site of historic Frederica village. The grounds feature luscious green grass overlooked by huge, hoary oak trees with long beards of moss. Take a few moments to tour the cemetery beside and behind the church. Some of the most prominent citizens of old St. Simons were laid to rest here. Listen as the wind sighs through the trees, singing a lament for all those who sleep beneath their limbs. The peace and tranquility of the church grounds are a palatable entity and one that must be experienced to be understood.

Over the years, many have claimed to have seen a light flickering among the old tombstones in Christ Church's graveyard. An old story speaks of a young woman who was so afraid of the dark that she molded hundreds of beeswax candles and always kept her home ablaze with light after sunset. Following her tragic death, her husband was strangely uneasy about his wife's tomb sitting lightless during the dark Georgia nights. He supposedly took a lighted candle to her grave and returned home comforted. Soon, this practice developed into a nightly ritual, which the husband continued until he was at last laid to rest beside his beloved wife. There are those who will tell you that those faithful lights still shine about the old graveyard, but sightings have been scarcer following the enclosure of the cemetery by a brick wall.

Christ Church, St. Simons Island

The church building visible today was extensively rebuilt in 1889 after an earlier structure was vandalized by Union troops. The reconstruction was managed almost exclusively by Anson Phelps Dodge, Jr., in loving memory of his first wife. Dodge eventually became rector of the church. He was buried in the adjacent cemetery after many decades of service.

Respectful visitors are welcome inside the church. The interior is surprisingly small but nevertheless blessed with a warmth and grace so lacking in many modern religious structures.

The partially excavated site of Frederica village, hard by the shores of Frederica River, is one of the most fascinating attractions on this island of almost infinite curiosity. The site is now managed by the National Park Service. Visitors are treated to a short movie that does an excellent job of describing the life and times of Frederica village. This writer recommends that you wander out onto the grounds and look over the many excavated foundations. Conveniently placed placards describe the original structures and their probable use. Work you way down to the old fort by the water, then turn north and visit the remnants of the old troop barracks. Few will count a sojourn to this important historical site as anything but totally fascinating. Be sure to bring along a bit of insect repellent, though. At times, the "no-see-ums" can be absolutely fierce.

Again, it has only been possible to describe a smattering of St. Simons Island's many attractions. Those who would like to learn more before their visit to the island should contact the St. Simons Island Chamber of Commerce (530B Beachview Drive, St. Simons Island, GA 31522, 912-638-9014).

St. Simons Island History Like the other Golden Isles, St. Simons was occupied by Native Americans for many centuries before the first European ship ever crested the Atlantic's horizon. During the 1500s, Spanish authorities based in St. Augustine, Florida, established three missions on what they called the isle of Asao. One of these, San Simon, eventually lent its name to the entire island.

Soon after the founding of Savannah, James Oglethorpe selected the island as the most likely position from which to make a frontal defense against the Spanish. Beginning in 1734, his forces began construction of a fort on the island's western flank near a bend in Frederica River. The fort and the settlement that sprang up around its walls were named Frederica in honor of the Prince of Wales. Another fort was built to guard the island's southern tip. This fortification was known as St. Simons.

The village surrounding the fort eventually grew into a community of 1,000 or more. The first temporary huts were soon replaced by brick and tabby dwellings that were peopled by

Old foundation at Frederica village, St. Simons Island

bricklayers, masons, carpenters, cabinetmakers, locksmiths, silversmiths, watchmakers, millers, bakers, tailors, and others. A substantial community grew up within a few years where there was once nothing but marsh and forest. Today's visitors can view the foundations of these formerly prosperous dwellings.

By all accounts, Frederica was a bustling place, with red-coated British regulars patrolling the streets alongside their quilted Highlander counterparts. Indians were often in town, sporting their moccasins and beaded clothing. Oglethorpe himself maintained a large farm and home near Frederica, which he dubbed Orange Hall.

In the 1730s, England and Spain came into conflict during the "War of Jenkins Ear." The strange name of this dispute comes from its origin. An English citizen by the name of Jenkins was taken prisoner by Spanish soldiers on a stretch of land between Georgia and Florida that was claimed by both governments. His ear was cut off by the Spanish, and England, itching for a chance to wrest Spain's New World possessions away, declared war.

Never one for inaction, Oglethorpe organized a

strong expeditionary force that sailed boldly into St. Augustine's harbor. The English sacked the town, but the coquina-walled Castilla de San Marcos proved all but invulnerable to cannon fire, and Oglethorpe withdrew.

Following this attack, the Spanish authorities were eager for revenge. In 1742, a strong fleet from St. Augustine landed troops on the southern tip of St. Simons. Vastly outnumbered, Oglethorpe's forces marched to meet the invaders as the Spanish pushed north to Frederica. The two armies clashed briefly, and then the English seemed to withdraw. Though accounts are confusing from this point on, it seems that the colonial forces lay in hiding and ambushed the advancing Spanish grenadiers, decimating their ranks with withering musket fire. The brief encounter became known as the Battle of Bloody Marsh. Having lost some of its key officers, the invading fleet withdrew, never to threaten Georgia again.

It is truly amazing how such a short, brief event can have such a dramatic impact on history. Had the Spanish been successful in their campaign, the history of the southeastern United States could have been very different, and written in a disparate language.

Site of Battle of Bloody Marsh, St. Simons Island

With the cessation of Spanish threats, the garrison at Frederica was slowly withdrawn, and the town was eventually abandoned. A fire in 1758 destroyed some of the old settlement's buildings, and the land was sold in 1760. (In 1903, Belle Stevens Taylor deeded the property to the Georgia Society of Colonial Dames of America. A portion of the old fort was repaired, and efforts went forward to have the one-time village declared a national monument. This dream finally became a reality in 1947, when the tract was officially dedicated and the National Park Service took over its management.)

In 1772, James Spalding, the father of Sapelo Island's Thomas Spalding, began a large plantation on St. Simons that was first known as "The General's Farm." Spalding and all the other inhabitants left St. Simons during the Revolution. He returned after the war, only to find his home and farms in ruins.

It was not long before Spalding began to recoup his losses in dramatic fashion. He is credited as being one of the first to cultivate long-staple cotton imported from the West Indies. This was the beginning of the fabled Sea Island cotton empire that came to be an almost unimaginable source of wealth for island planters.

By the early 1800s, a number of successful plantations were situated on St. Simons Island. Luxurious homes were built, and exquisite carriages transported guests to and from the various homeplaces. Many of the planters' children traveled abroad, and the finest books and furnishings were imported from Europe. Some of the planters even had their portraits painted by Thomas Sully of Philadelphia, the foremost

American artist of his day. It was a time of gracious living on St. Simons, and its like would continue until the Civil War.

The foundation for the first St. Simons Lighthouse was laid in 1811. Within a year, British troops invaded the island during the War of 1812. Plantations were sacked, but the returning planters soon set things right by virtue of their continuing wealth from Sea Island cotton.

With the coming of the tragic North-South conflict, Confederate troops were stationed on the southerly tip of St. Simons to guard the inlet. These forces abandoned the island in 1862, blowing up the lighthouse as they left. Union troops soon occupied St. Simons, and during the remainder of the war freed slaves were housed on the island.

The end had come to St. Simons Island's most colorful era. No longer would the fields wave with snow-white cotton. The war and the coming of the boll weevil quickly pushed the old way of life into the past.

The island's economy finally began to revive with the establishment of several sawmills during the 1870s. As the twentieth century approached, St. Simons became one of the most popular summer vacation resorts in the Southeast. Guests initially arrived aboard two steamships, the *Emmeline* and the *Hessie*. They were met at the pier by surreys, but this primitive mode of transportation was soon replaced by a donkey-drawn railroad. Finally, a steam engine replaced the tired animals, and St. Simons entered the twentieth century with a bright future based on tourism.

With the opening of the Torras Causeway in 1924, the average person could now afford to spend a few days or even a week on the island. New building went forward apace, but somehow the wise island leaders always found a way to keep construction in line with St. Simons Island's very special air of enchantment and relaxation. Today, islanders are still optimistic about the future, though they must remain vigilant to guard against massive development. So far, they have been successful, and this writer wishes them well.

Back River

A third stream breaks off to the west from St. Simons Sound and then cuts north into Brunswick. Back River is, quite honestly, one of the least interesting streams in southeastern Georgia, at least to this writer's eye. Fairly heavy development lines much of the southwestern banks northwest of the 40-foot fixed bridge. Charted Terry Creek is actually a little-used barge canal that leads to one of Brunswick's paper mills.

Clubbs Creek is a three-fingered body of water that breaks off to the south near Back River's easterly entrance. In spite of soundings shown on chart 11489, on-site research showed that low-tide depths of 4 feet or even less can be expected.

Should you for some reason decide to ignore all this advice and anchor in Back River anyway, your best bet is to cruise northwest of the fixed span (assuming you can clear it) until the charted high ground comes abeam to the southwest. Drop the hook well southeast of unlighted daybeacon #1 for best swinging room. Here, you will be reasonably well sheltered, especially from western and southwestern breezes. (Of course, winds from this direction will also blow straight over the paper mills toward your craft.)

Swinging room should be sufficient for a 50-footer.

Little River

Little River is aptly named. It is a rather insignificant stream that breaks off to the northeast from Back River. Minimum 8-foot depths can be held as you track your way upstream to a 6-foot fixed bridge. Boats of almost any size can anchor southwest of the span in 9 to 16 feet of water. The protection offered by the marshy shores is not the best, and the paper mills may still be a problem.

St. Simons Sound and Its Inlet

St. Simons Sound is certainly not the largest of coastal Georgia's sounds, but it can still be plenty rough in fresh southern and southwestern winds. The ICW cuts out into the sound's inlet and strikes an arrow-straight path to the southwest on its way to protected Jekyll Creek.

St. Simons Sound's inlet is one of best seaward cuts south of Savannah River. It is well marked and used regularly by large oceangoing vessels that stop at Brunswick's commercial port. If you are planning to enter or return from the ocean north of St. Marys, then this channel is the ticket.

Brunswick

Brunswick River is an immense stream that strikes west and then northwest from St. Simons Sound. For many decades, boaters have admired the huge Sidney Lanier Bridge, which crosses the river just east of Brunswick. This old lift-type span with a closed vertical clearance of 24 feet is an intriguing sight from the water. At the current time, construction has just begun on a new, fixed high-rise span to take the old bridge's place.

Brunswick River leads to the downtown historic district of the like-named community. When this writer and his mate first visited Brunswick several years ago, it lacked any marina facilities, and we came away with the quick impression of a highly industrialized community. In fact, as one fellow cruiser put it to this writer, "You can't swing a dead cat in Brunswick and not hit a pulp and paper mill."

Well, the mills are still there, but we have now discovered there is a bit more to this community than first meets the eye. For one thing, a new marina has opened off East River on the eastern shores of charted Academy Creek (well north of East River's flashing daybeacon #5).

While researching this new facility, we were privileged to make the acquaintance of downtown Brunswick's historic and business district. Here, we found a wealth of lovely old homes. Some stretch back to the antebellum era. The downtown itself has undergone a tasteful renaissance, with many remodeled offices and retail businesses in evidence.

Brunswick Landing Marina's dockage basin is actually located on the easterly shores of Academy Creek opposite the forward charted range marker (near the creek's mouth). A repair yard associated with this firm lies a bit farther upstream, also along the easterly banks, just short of the creek's charted turn to the west. Soon thereafter, Academy Creek is blocked by a dam.

This newly minted facility is eager to attract visiting cruisers. Transients are gratefully accepted for overnight or temporary dockage at ultramodern concrete-decked floating piers. Approach depths run 12 feet or better, with at least 7½ feet of water dockside. All berths feature full power, water, telephone, and cable-television hookups. The shoreside showers and laundromat, located on the southern border of the complex, are extranice. Paid customers have free use of the washer and dryer. There is even an air-conditioned boaters' lounge with color television.

Brunswick Landing's fuel dock (gasoline and diesel fuel) is found on its southernmost rank of piers. Here, you will most likely observe a large "gambling ship" which makes its home at the marina. So far, the crowds patronizing this vessel don't seem to be too much of a problem for cruisers, but only the future will tell.

The repair-yard portion of Brunswick Landing features full-service mechanical repairs for both gasoline and diesel power plants. Haul-outs are accomplished by way of a 50-ton travelift. Judging from the number of vessels on the ways during our visit, this yard's popularity is growing.

While there is no restaurant or grocery store within easy walking distance, you can always call Yellow Cab (912-265-0000). On the other hand, ultrafresh seafood can often be purchased at a commercial seafood dock immediately south of the dockage basin. Future plans call for the construction of an adjacent hotel and restaurant, but these additions are probably some time away.

Taken as a whole, Brunswick Landing Marina has much to offer visiting cruisers. It should be noted that it takes a fairly lengthy cruise from the ICW to reach its piers, but many boaters will find the extra effort more than justified.

Brunswick Landing Marina
(912) 262-9264

Approach depth: 12+ feet
Dockside depth: 7½ feet (minimum)
Accepts transients: yes
Floating concrete piers: yes
Dockside power connections: 30, 50, and 100 amps
Dockside water connections: yes
Showers: yes
Laundromat: yes
Gasoline: yes
Diesel fuel: yes
Mechanical repairs: yes
Below-waterline repairs: yes
Restaurants: taxi ride necessary

Jekyll Island and Its History The ICW departs St. Simons Sound south of flashing daybeacon #2 and enters Jekyll Creek. This stream is named for the storied island that comprises its easterly banks. Jekyll Island is one of the smallest of the Golden Isles, but it is also perhaps the best known, thanks to its status as a dazzling private resort.

James Oglethorpe named Jekyll Island in honor of one of the colony of Georgia's financial sponsors. During those early years, several fields on Jekyll Island were cleared and planted with grain and hops to be used in the production of beer for the troops stationed at Frederica. History doesn't record a mention of the beer's taste, but it must have been a rich brew indeed.

After the Spanish defeat at the Battle of Bloody Marsh, Jekyll Island was used as a military reservation for several years. In the late 1700s, the land passed through several owners until it was acquired by one of the colony's renowned French settlers, Christopher Poulain duBignon. DuBignon built an island empire encompassing 11,000 acres planted in Sea Island cotton. His sumptuous parties and entertainment were legendary, and everybody who was anybody in colonial high society fervently sought an invitation to his estate.

DuBignon's family maintained its home on Jekyll Island for almost 100 years. One of his sons, Colonel Henry duBignon, was an early yacht-racing enthusiast. His *Goddess of Liberty* was a famous racer all along the coastline and won many a prize from those early regattas.

The Civil War drove the duBignon family from its ancestral home, but the gracious living of the antebellum era was but a harbinger of things to come. In 1886, Jekyll Island was bought by the world-renowned Jekyll Island Club. The list of members reads like a who's who of late-nineteenth-century America. The club boasted families with such names as Morgan, Vanderbilt, Astor, Gould, Rockefeller, Armour, Goodyear, Pulitzer, and Macy. Membership was passed on by inheritance, and the privacy of the island's residents was jealously guarded.

Before you could blink an eye, construction began on a magnificent Victorian clubhouse, an apartment complex, and two dozen plush cottages. Soon, a private steamer was ferrying members and guests from Brunswick. Island activities included hunting stocked animals such as deer, turkeys, English pheasants, and wild boar. There was also fishing, swimming, croquet, tennis, and golf on what has been described as one of the finest dune courses in the world.

In 1899, Jekyll Island played host to President William McKinley and his entire administration when he met with Speaker of the House Thomas Reed in a showdown to decide the future presidency. These meetings were moderated by Senator Mark Hanna, one of the most influential political leaders of the day.

The president and his entourage arrived by way of five of the most luxurious cars the railroad could furnish. Met in Brunswick by the secretary of the interior, the president's party continued by steamer to Jekyll Island. Patrol boats prowled the waters to keep off any curious press that might have gotten wind of the meeting. A young reporter at the *Brunswick News*, L. J. Leavy, somehow learned of the political get-together and made a name for himself by wiring the news all over the country.

The next year, Leavy filed a story after he was received in a private railway car by an unnamed but socially prominent female—a female smoking a cigarette! Telegrams questioning the accuracy of this report were flashed to Brunswick from newspapers from New York to San Francisco. Finally satisfied as to its authenticity, the national press reported the scandalous story.

As was true with many old Victorian inns, the Jekyll Island Club lost much of its popularity between the world wars. The entire island was purchased by the state of Georgia in 1947 to be used as a state park. The old Rockefeller cottage was converted into the Jekyll Island Museum, which is still is operation (and strongly recommended by this writer). With the opening of a bridge and causeway connecting Jekyll Island with the mainland in 1954, the island was at last accessible to the general public.

In these latter days, visitors from all levels of American society stay in the rooms and cottages once peopled by the likes of

Rockefellers, Astors, and Vanderbilts. The clubhouse (often called the "Millionaire's Club") was renovated by a private investment group and is operated under a Radisson franchise.

The old days of splendor may now be only a distant memory, but the strains of those days can still be experienced on Jekyll Island. The sensitive visitor can use his mind's eye while strolling Jekyll Island's historic district and gain an imaginative view of what life was like in those days when wealth was concentrated in the hands of a relative few.

Jekyll Island Marina Facilities

East of flashing daybeacon #20, cruisers on the ICW and Jekyll Creek will have to be blind to miss the awe-inspiring towers of the old Millionaire's Club. The marina associated with this complex is now closed, and this writer has been informed that even should it reopen in the future, visitors will most likely not be accepted.

Notable Jekyll Harbor Marina guards the Waterway's eastern shores a short distance south of the 9-foot lift bridge soon to be replaced by a fixed high-rise structure. This facility simply could not do enough to help this writer and his mate with the very best possible information. We will always be grateful for the assistance.

Jekyll Harbor Marina now features extensive

The "Millionaire's Club," Jekyll Island

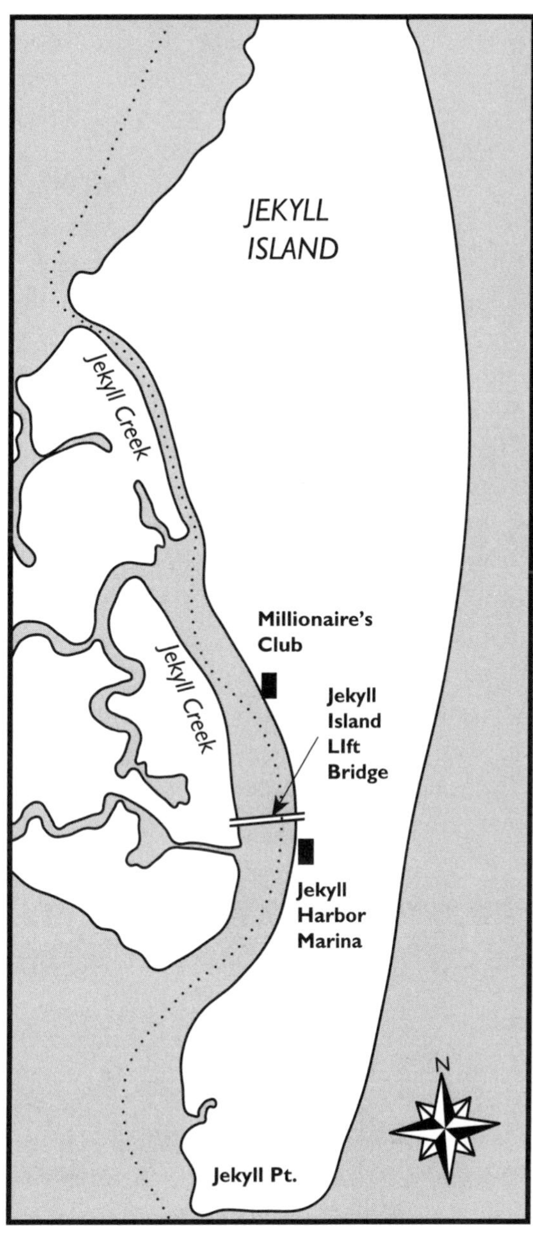

transient dockage at modern, concrete-decked floating piers. Depths alongside run around 10 feet. Full water connections and power hookups (30 and 50 amps) are available at every berth. Gasoline and diesel fuel can be purchased at the floating docks, and waste pump-out is available. Mechanical repairs can be arranged through independent contractors, and dry-stack storage is offered for small power craft.

Shoreside amenities for visiting cruisers include top-notch showers, a full laundromat, a swimming pool, and a Jacuzzi. The marina maintains a small ship's and variety store in the adjacent deli-restaurant. This latter facility is quite attractive and was expanding into a full-service operation at the time of this writing.

To facilitate your visit to other Jekyll Island restaurants or attractions, this marina offers the use of a courtesy car. This service has become all too rare with present-day marine operations. Both a grocery store and a pharmacy are located 0.6 mile from the marina.

The accommodating marina staff will also help with golf and tennis arrangements. In short, you'll find this writer's craft resting comfortably at Jekyll Harbor Marina on every visit to these waters.

Jekyll Harbor Marina (912) 635-3137

Approach depth: 12+ feet
Dockside depth: 10 feet (minimum)
Accepts transients: yes
Floating concrete piers: yes
Dockside power connections: 30 and 50 amps
Dockside water connections: yes
Showers: yes
Laundromat: yes
Waste pump-out: yes
Gasoline: yes
Diesel fuel: yes
Mechanical repairs: yes
Below-waterline repairs: yes
Ship's and variety store: small
Snack bar: yes
Restaurants: transportation arranged

Jekyll Sound

The ICW's southbound path down Jekyll Creek leads to Jekyll Sound. This body of water is really little more than an adjunct of St. Andrew Sound, which lies almost due south.

Boaters can take the direct route and follow the two sounds or make use of a shoaly but protected alternate cut. This portion of the Waterway will be reviewed in the last two sections of this chapter.

BUTTERMILK SOUND TO ST. ANDREW SOUND NAVIGATION

The only remarkable navigational characteristic of the waters between Buttermilk and St. Andrew Sounds is the swift tidal currents often encountered along this run. Otherwise, there is very little to distinguish this section of coastal Georgia from those to the north or south.

The Waterway is a bit more protected in this region, with St. Simons Sound the only really open body of water that boaters must traverse. Don't be too cavalier, though, as these waters can still stir up quite a froth when conditions are right.

Like many pleasure boaters on the ICW, this

writer sometimes just follows the daybeacons and ignores range markers. But you may want to make an exception to this practice for the run from Buttermilk Sound to St. Simons Sound. This is one region where the many ranges, set up for both northbound and southbound craft, are very useful indeed. Some are outlined below, but boaters studying chart 11507 will find many other ranges to help them along the way.

As always, have the latest charts aboard, watch the sounder, and keep a cautious eye out for those tidal currents.

Buttermilk Sound From a position north of flashing daybeacon #213, boaters should follow a concave course to the southwest, favoring the southeasterly shores of charted Broughton Island. Shoal water lies to the southeast.

Buttermilk Sound is noted for periodic shoaling. This writer encountered no problems while following the ICW channel in mid-1995, but conditions could be different by the time of your visit. Proceed with more than the usual caution and keep strictly to the marked channel.

Southwest of #213, unlighted daybeacon #214 marks the ICW's northwestern flank. Obviously, this aid should be passed to its southeastern quarter. Boaters cruising north should be aware that #214 can be hard to spot. Use your binoculars to pick out #214 from the surrounding marsh shores.

After coming abeam of flashing daybeacon #A (the forward marker for a range serving northbound craft), set course to come abeam of unlighted daybeacon #216A to its fairly immediate southeasterly side. Shallow water lies northwest of #216A. Continue on course, pointing to come between flashing daybeacon #218 and unlighted daybeacon #219. Flashing daybeacon #218 is also labeled #B. This aid serves the double role of a standard aid to navigation and a forward marker for a range that primarily benefits skippers cruising north on the Waterway.

Between #218 and #219, the Waterway cuts sharply to the south-southeast. Point to come abeam of unlighted daybeacon #220 to its easterly quarter.

At flashing daybeacon #221, the ICW swerves again, this time to the southeast, and runs to a point between unlighted daybeacon #222 and flashing daybeacon #A (the forward range marker). At last, southbound boaters have the opportunity to use one of the many ranges along this stretch. The pair marked by #A is really quite useful. Shoals shelve out from the southwestern banks between #221 and #222. Stick to the channel and don't allow leeway to ease you to the southwest. South of #222, the entrance to the upper Hampton River will soon come abeam to the east.

Hampton River *Take note*: Hampton River runs all the way east and south to an intersection with the ocean. Boaters entering the river from the ICW are actually traveling *toward* the sea. Anyone familiar with the red-right-returning rule will quickly surmise that this means red markers should be taken to the boater's port side, while green beacons should be waved at to starboard.

The channel is well marked downriver to Hampton River Club Marina. Don't cut any corners, and pass all beacons to their proper side. You should not have any undue difficulty if you follow this simple procedure. Southeast of the marina, the markers cease and depths become more questionable. This portion of Hampton River is not further covered in this guide.

Waterway Anchorage To drop anchor in the bubble of deep water west of unlighted daybeacon #227, simply cut a little west-northwest from

#227 and feel your way along for some 50 to 75 yards. Don't slip to the south or cut due northwest. Those who track their way too far to the west will also find themselves in shoal water.

On the ICW Southwest of unlighted daybeacon #227, a charted range helps southbound boaters keep to the narrow channel. Both sides of the ICW are shoal along this stretch. Watch your sounder and stay on the range. After coming abeam of the forward range marker (flashing daybeacon #C), you can pick up yet another range to the southwest that will lead you to a point just north of unlighted daybeacon #229. This aid marks the strategic intersection of Frederica and MacKay Rivers.

The Georgia ICW now continues down MacKay River, but cruisers with a flair for getting off the beaten path may want to give the Frederica a try. The stream eventually loops to the south and rejoins the Waterway, so you won't actually lose any time, unless it's from gazing too long at the sights on the adjacent shores of St. Simons Island.

Frederica River Frederica River's only real shallow spot is found just southeast of unlighted daybeacon #229, where cruisers may encounter a few 5- to 6-foot soundings at low water. If you need more depth, enter or leave on a rising tide. Otherwise, simply hold to the mid-width as you track your way south to any of the many anchorages described previously.

Eventually, you will sight Fort Frederica National Monument overlooking the river's easterly flank. Take a good look or drop the anchor at your discretion, but please remember that landings are strictly disallowed, even for dinghies.

Frederica River joins back up with MacKay River and the ICW near flashing daybeacon #241. Boaters reentering the Waterway at this point must be on guard against the tongue of shoals extending south from the north-side point of marsh separating the two rivers. Favor the southern point marked by flashing daybeacon #241.

Northbound boaters leaving the ICW and entering Frederica River just northeast of #241 should be aware that the southern mouth of the northern Frederica River is so wide at this intersection that it often causes confusion. Use your compass and chart 11507 to quickly resolve any questions that arise.

It is also possible to continue cruising southeast

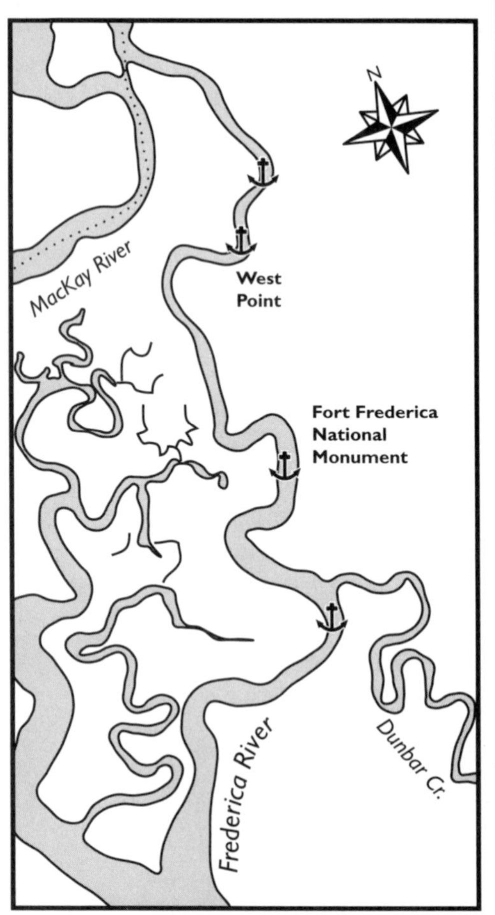

on the southern half of Frederica River. However, this leg of the stream is blocked by a 9-foot fixed bridge short of the facilities at Golden Isles Marina. While you can always anchor near the bridge, this can be a busy refuge, and most boaters will probably be happier anchoring on the northern portion of the river.

Back on the ICW South of unlighted daybeacon #229, the ICW flows through a short landcut into the waters of MacKay River. Pass flashing daybeacon #231 to its westerly quarter as you enter the MacKay. West of #231, boaters can anchor on the broad and deep waters of Wallys Leg.

Wallys Leg The initial portion of Wallys Leg is deep almost from bank to bank. Drop anchor anywhere within spitting distance of the mid-width and you should have plenty of swinging room.

Don't attempt to cruise past the stream's first turn to the north, **as** you will encounter massive unmarked shoals immediately after passing through this turn.

On the Waterway The ICW channel down MacKay River remains well marked and fairly straightforward. Don't accidentally ease to the north between unlighted daybeacon #234 and flashing daybeacon #A. This latter aid is part of a range that will help you avoid the 2-foot shoal to the north.

Similarly, avoid the northwestern banks between unlighted daybeacons #236 and #235A. The charted shoal abutting this shoreline is for real.

Avoid the easterly banks between #235A and flashing daybeacon #237. A 3-foot patch of shallows lies between and to the east of these markers.

South of flashing daybeacon #237, the entrance to Troup Creek will come abeam to the west.

Troup Creek If you decide to enter questionable Troup Creek, favor the northern and northeastern shores heavily. Shoal water extends out for quite some distance from the southwestern shoreline.

Eventually, Troup Creek turns to the west, and good depths spread out in a broad band along the mid-width. As the creek turns to the north, begin favoring the easterly shoreline to avoid the charted shallows. You can cruise back to the middle as the creek takes a small jog to the north-northwest. Soon, the Coast Guard dock will come abeam to the west, followed by Troup Creek Marina.

On the ICW South of flashing daybeacon #239A, the smokestacks of Brunswick will begin popping into view to the southwest. Boaters must approach this portion of the Waterway with genuine caution. The eastern shores drop away where MacKay and Frederica Rivers converge. A long shoal stretches well south from the northern point of marsh separating the two streams. Favor the MacKay's western banks slightly to stay well away from this hazard.

Soon, you will pass unlighted daybeacon #242, followed by the fixed 65-foot high-rise St. Simons Island bridge. Exceptionally strong tidal currents plague the ICW in and around this span. Sailcraft and single-screw trawlers should proceed at maximum alert.

Immediately south of the 65-foot bridge, the eastern and western portions of the old swing bridge have been left in place for the use of local fishermen. The center span has of course been removed to allow easy passage of all vessels.

South Frederica River Boaters entering the southern leg of Frederica River from the ICW and MacKay River at flashing daybeacon #241 should favor the southwestern banks slightly. After coming abeam of Hawkins Creek to the northeast, cruise back to the centerline. Soon, the river is blocked by a fixed bridge with only 9 feet of vertical clearance. A small, private fishing marina will come abeam to the southeast just before the span.

On to St. Simons Sound South of flashing daybeacon #244, the waters widen and the ICW soon flows into the northern portion of St. Simons Sound. An incredibly long tongue of shallows extends south for almost 1 nautical mile from the southern point of Lanier Island, which separates the southernmost portion of Frederica and MacKay Rivers.

Golden Isles Marina Continue following the Waterway until you come abeam of flashing daybeacon #249 to its southwesterly side. *Don't cut this corner.* On the water, it will look as if you are being led well out of your way, but the shoal running south from Lanier Island is nothing to trifle with.

Curl around #249 and set your course east to eventually come abeam of flashing daybeacon #2 by some 100 yards to its westerly quarter. Break out your binoculars and locate the charted range to the north-northwest. This range is hard to spot, but be sure to identify it properly before cutting to the north-northwest. Ignore the two huge rear range markers, which you will spot well east of your course line. These aids are in shoal water.

For best depths, keep your course line slightly to the west of the line marked by the twin ranges. Abandon this course at least 50 yards before reaching the forward range marker. Cut to the north-northeast and point to come abeam of unlighted daybeacon #5 to its immediate southeastern quarter. Continue cruising upstream on the mid-width. You will spy one long pier jutting out into the harbor, backed by a large building with a sign reading "Inn." Ignore this pier, as the slips are private "boataminiums." The extensive harbor of Golden Isles Marina will soon be obvious along the western shore. Just upstream of the marina, the river is blocked by the same 9-foot fixed bridge encountered in the discussion of the southern Frederica River above.

Back River Boaters can also make their entry into Back River from flashing daybeacon #249. Leave the Waterway by curling around to the northwest and enter the river on its mid-width. Don't attempt to enter Clubbs Creek, which soon breaks off to the south. In spite of soundings shown on chart 11489, this three-fingered stream is shoal and dangerous.

Farther upstream, Little River strikes off to the northeast. Avoid this stream's northwesterly entrance point. A shoal is building south from this promontory.

Back River leads under a fixed bridge with 40 feet of vertical clearance. Again, a portion of the old swing bridge, with the center section removed, has been left in place south of the fixed span.

Northwest of the fixed span, the Terry Creek canal will come abeam to the west-southwest. Don't attempt to enter. Northwest of unlighted daybeacons #2 and #3, shoals begin to appear more frequently. Boaters will do well to discontinue their explorations between #2 and #3.

St. Simons Sound Boaters traveling south on the Georgia ICW should set course from flashing daybeacon #249 to pass flashing daybeacon #250 well to its northeasterly side, then come abeam of flashing buoy #20 to its fairly immediate easterly quarter. Buoy #20 sits in the heart of St. Simons Sound. If you are going to encounter rough water, this will be the spot.

East of #20, cruisers can put to sea on the wide and well-marked St. Simons Sound inlet. Be sure to have the latest edition of chart 11506 aboard to check on the current configuration of aids to navigation.

Look north just before coming abeam of flashing buoy #17 for a good view of the snow-white St. Simons Lighthouse. This old sentinel of the sea is a striking sight from the inlet's waters.

Southwest of flashing buoy #20, the ICW follows a portion of the Brunswick large-ships' channel on its way to Jekyll Creek. It is a long run of 1.3 nautical miles from #20 to flashing buoy #22, which should be brought abeam to its southeastern side. It might be a good idea to run a compass course between #20 and #22.

At #22, the ICW departs the large-ships' channel and cuts to the southwest. The large-ships' passage turns west-southwest toward Brunswick and Brunswick River and passes flashing buoy #24 to its southerly side.

Brunswick West-northwest of #24, the commercial channel flows into Brunswick River and eventually leads to downtown Brunswick and its new marina. Cruisers continuing upstream to Brunswick Landing Marina should set course to come abeam of flashing buoy #24 to its southerly side. At this point, the channel follows a jog to the west-northwest and passes between flashing buoys #26 and #27. West of these markers, the cut meets up with the Sidney Lanier lift bridge.

This span, with a closed vertical clearance of 24 feet, is an impressive sight. Fortunately, the bridge currently opens on demand. At the time of this writing, construction had just begun on a new, fixed high-rise which will eventually take the place of the old lift bridge. It's a safe bet that the new bridge will not be open, nor the old span removed, for some time to come.

Once past the lift bridge, point to come abeam of flashing buoy #1 to its northerly side. At this point, East River breaks off to the north-northwest. Enter this stream by passing well east of the flashing (but unnumbered) junction buoy marking the intersection of the two channels. Shallow water and rocks lie north of the junction buoy.

After cruising into East River, hold to the centerline as you work your way upstream. Flashing daybeacons #3 and #5 will be passed to your port side.

Watch ahead and you will sight a pair of range markers in the distance. As you approach to within 50 yards of the forward range marker, break off to the north and enter the mid-width of Academy Creek's southerly mouth. Brunswick Landing Marina's dockage basin will quickly come abeam to the east. The boatyard facilities are found farther upstream, also along the easterly banks, just as the stream begins to swing to the west. Continue holding to the center. A bit farther upstream, a dam blocks Academy Creek.

ICW to Jekyll Creek From a position abeam of flashing buoy #22, set a careful compass course to come abeam of flashing daybeacon #2 to its immediate easterly side. As you have undoubtedly guessed, the numbering sequence of the ICW's aids to navigation begins anew at the northerly mouth of Jekyll Creek.

Slow down! The northerly entrance to Jekyll Creek is one of the most difficult sections of the Georgia ICW. The stream's mouth is bounded by a stone jetty on its westerly flank. Numerous aids and a most fortuitous range help you keep to the good water. Be ready for strong tidal currents that may try to push you out of the channel. Keep an unusually firm hand on the helm and detail one crew member to do nothing but watch the sounder.

Eventually, the channel turns to the southeast and leaves the troublesome waters behind. Hold to the narrow channel's centerline as you track your way downstream to flashing daybeacon #19.

South of #19, the Waterway follows a dredged channel through otherwise shallow waters. Stick strictly to the marked passage, and don't even think about sticking your nose outside the Waterway.

The Jekyll Creek lift bridge, south of #20, has only 9 feet of closed vertical clearance and now sports a restrictive opening schedule. The span opens only on the hour and half-hour, 24 hours a day, 365 days a year. Fortunately, construction is now well under way on a fixed high-rise span to take the old bridge's place. The new structure is scheduled to open in November 1997.

This bridge's restricted opening hours are particularly unfortunate, as the channel is none too wide here, with little maneuvering room in the often swift current.

South of the lift bridge, the ICW channel runs close by the eastern and then southeastern shoreline of Jekyll Island. Don't approach this shoreline too closely either. You will soon spy the docks of Jekyll Harbor Marina just east of the Waterway.

Observe all markers carefully until you come abeam of flashing daybeacon #25 to its northwesterly quarter. Boaters must now decide whether to follow the principal ICW passage, which cuts through St. Andrew Sound out into the open sea, or to continue south by way of the alternate, shoal-prone Umbrella Cut–Floyd Creek route.

ST. ANDREW SOUND TO ST. MARYS RIVER

After successfully traversing the sometimes scary channel through St. Andrew Sound, you will find that the remaining waters of the southern Georgia Waterway are dominated by the idyllic shores of Cumberland Island. Several deep side streams and anchorages allow boaters to have firsthand experience of the many historic sites and the unbelievably lush foliage of this most beautiful Golden Isle.

Finally, the waters of coastal Georgia come to an end at St. Marys River. This storied stream serves as the state line between Georgia and Florida. To the west, the delightful village of St. Marys offers a marina, super restaurants, and several of the most delightful inns to be found anywhere.

There is but a single marina available to boaters between Jekyll Island and Florida. This facility is found in the village of St. Marys on the southernmost portion of this run. Be sure to fuel up and have plenty of supplies on board before bidding farewell to Jekyll Island.

Anchorages are still in plentiful supply. Even the alternate ICW route via Umbrella Creek boasts several overnight stops. The anchorages along the Cumberland Island shoreline are absolutely unforgettable. Even if you usually frequent marinas, be sure to anchor for at least one night on the waters adjacent to this magical isle.

St. Andrew Sound

The ICW passage through St. Andrew Sound is one of the most dreaded sections of the entire Atlantic Intracoastal Waterway from Norfolk to

Miami. What is the reason for all this worry? Simply this: The channel does not just cross the sound. Rather, in order to avoid extensive shallows that guard the sound's mid-width, the ICW cuts east for a short distance on the sound's inlet channel. Waterway cruisers are all but out to sea before turning into more sheltered waters to the southwest. When winds and tide oppose one another in the inlet, this passage can be truly daunting. Whenever possible, pick a fair-weather day to cross St. Andrew Sound.

St. Andrew Sound's inlet is not particularly recommended. Many of the markers are not charted, as they are frequently shifted to follow the ever-moving sands. While it is possible for strangers to run the channel, it can sometimes be a white-knuckle experience. This writer suggests either using the far more reliable St. Simons Sound inlet to the north or following in the wake of a local craft while tracking your way out to sea.

ICW Alternate Route and Satilla River

In recognition of the often rough conditions on St. Andrew Sound, the Army Corps of Engineers has provided a marked alternate passage by way of Little Satilla River, Umbrella Cut, Dover Creek, Satilla River, and Floyd Creek. Unfortunately, the corps has not been too concerned about maintenance of this passage for some time. Currently, boaters can expect low-water soundings of as little as 5 feet, with numerous unmarked shoals cutting out from the various points of land along the way. The passage is also quite narrow in places.

Considering these unfortunate characteristics, this writer cannot really recommend the alternate passage for vessels larger than 42 feet or those drawing more than 5 feet. If you can time your arrival to coincide with a rising tide, so much the better.

On the plus side, there are a number of opportunities to anchor along the alternate passage far from coastal development. South of unlighted daybeacon #A2, the alternate Waterway cuts southwest, but another branch of Umbrella Creek strikes east and then south. This stream sports minimum 18-foot depths and enough swinging room for boats as large as 36 feet. The most sheltered spot is found along the southern-running portion of the creek before it cuts back again to the northeast and broadens considerably.

At unlighted daybeacon #A4, the alternate ICW cuts southeast down a narrow and shoal-prone stream to Dover Creek. Northwest of #A4, boats of almost any size can anchor short of upper Umbrella Creek's first hairpin turn. Depths run 12 to 14 feet.

In light airs, boaters might consider setting anchor south of unlighted daybeacon #A10 on the lower portion of Dover Creek. This is a far larger stream than you might expect from a study of chart 11489. Thanks to Dover Creek's size and the typical marsh-grass shores, protection is not adequate for winds exceeding 15 knots.

This writer's favorite overnight stop along the alternate ICW is found northwest of unlighted daybeacon #A12. For a brief space, high ground flanks the southwesterly shores of upper Dover Creek, bypassed by the ICW. There is an unmarked and uncharted shoal to avoid, but skippers with boats up to 36 feet should find enough swinging room. Protection is good from southwesterly winds.

After traversing a short landcut, the alternate

ICW cuts across a portion of Satilla River. This body of water is yet another of those large coastal Georgia rivers on which shoals are far more numerous than markers. The Satilla has no marina facilities and an unusual lack of sidewater anchorages. Thus, this stream is not further addressed in this guide.

The alternate Waterway leaves Satilla River via Floyd Cut and eventually twists its way into the main body of Floyd Creek. This stream eventually joins the primary ICW cutting southwest down Cumberland River near unlighted daybeacon #40. On-site observations confirmed that passing cruisers often use the southeastern mouth of Floyd Creek as an anchorage. Apparently, the traffic traversing the alternate route is so light as to seldom be a problem. Two sailing yachts were swinging tranquilly on the hook during this writer's visit to the creek. Take note, though, that both were wisely showing bright anchor lights. Depths on this portion of Floyd Creek run 14 to 25 feet, and there is enough elbow room for a 40-footer.

ICW South down Cumberland River

Back on the primary Waterway channel south of St. Andrew Sound, southbound cruisers will find a bare total of four aids to navigation on Cumberland River between the northern tip of Cumberland Island and an intersection with Brickhill River at unlighted daybeacon #40. Fortunately, the channel is broad and allows for plenty of leisure time at the helm to appreciate Cumberland Island's shoreline.

Cumberland Island

I well remember my first sight of Cumberland Island as a gregarious youngster some 30 years ago. Thoughts of exploring under all those tall trees and lush bushes danced in my head like those sugarplum fairies on Christmas Eve. I never got the chance in those days, so it was with a real sense of anticipation that I returned while researching this guide.

My trusty research assistant, Kerry, and I found the Cumberland shoreline unchanged. Here and there, high earthen cliffs march down almost to the water's edge. We spotted several wild horses playing on the beach close to the cliffs. We could only look wonderingly at one another, hoping that the other was enjoying the same sense of wonder. To describe that shoreline's beauty in the golden light of a late-May afternoon falls far beyond this writer's supply of adjectives. Put simply, it was all that a true outdoorsman could ever hope for.

After docking at the National Park Service pier (described below), we went ashore. We exposed countless rolls of film trying to capture the grandeur of the foliage, then hiked down to the site of Dungeness. Later, we dinghied ashore to Plum Orchard mansion. To say that we were captivated by this old homeplace does not do justice to our feelings. This writer strongly suggests that you read the historical write-up below,

Cumberland Island shoreline, with abandoned lighthouse in background

as well as the accounts of the various island anchorages and stops along the way. Be sure to set aside some time to experience for yourself this quintessential Golden Isle.

Cumberland Island History The isle we know today as Cumberland was originally called Missoe, or "Sassafras," by the native Timucuan Indians. The Spanish established a mission here, and for many years the land was known as San Pedro Island.

After the colony of Georgia was founded, James Oglethorpe persuaded Mico (Chief) Tomo-chi-chi of the Creek Indians to return to England with him for a visit. The chief's son, Toonhowie, became fast friends with the young William Augustus, duke of Cumberland. William presented Toonhowie with a gold watch shortly before the party reembarked for America. By all accounts, the chief's son prized the watch over all his other worldly possessions. Upon his return to Georgia, Toonhowie requested that San Pedro be renamed Cumberland in honor of his new friend. Oglethorpe and the colony's leaders were only to happy to comply.

Oglethorpe built a small fort on Cumberland Island's southern tip. He was so impressed with the island's beauty and abundant wildlife that he established a hunting lodge nearby, which was called Dungeness. The name was derived from Oglethorpe's "seat" in the county of Kent, England.

As the threat of Spanish invasion strengthened, Oglethorpe established a second military stronghold, Fort St. Andrew, on the isle's northern section. Much as at Frederica on St. Simons Island, a small village known as Berrimacke grew up around the fort. When the site was abandoned by the military after the Battle of Bloody Marsh, the town of Berrimacke disappeared. It is now only a footnote in Georgia history texts.

Cumberland Island passed through a long series of owners over the next several decades. At least one large plantation was established on the isle during this period. The owner of this large farm, known as Stafford Plantation, employed the unique practice of dividing his land and work force into two independent camps that were encouraged to compete against each other. The winners were awarded prizes and privileges.

Following the victorious close of the American Revolution, a grateful state of Georgia presented General Nathanael Greene, the "George Washington of the South," with a large plantation outside Savannah. Whether through purchase or gift (historians still disagree), Greene also acquired large holdings on Cumberland Island. The war hero personally selected the site for his new island home and laid out plans for extensive gardens and landscaping. He selected the same name as that used by Oglethorpe years before, and the great general looked forward to many happy years on his Dungeness. But before these plans could come to fruition, Greene was tragically struck down by sunstroke in 1786.

In 1796, the general's widow, Catherine "Caty" Littlefield Greene, married Phineas Miller. The new family undertook completion of the grand house that Nathanael Greene had planned on Cumberland Island, and it became a showplace indeed. The house is rumored to have been a 4-story mansion with a foundation of 6-foot tabby walls. It has been described as the most elegant residence on the coast.

Before many years passed, the Greene-Miller household became the center of social activity in southeastern Georgia. Caty was known as the most likable and capable hostess in all of Georgia. Her eldest daughter, Martha, and her youngest, Louisa, both married into prominent Georgia families, and the two young couples made their homes at Dungeness as well. It was a happy and lively time on Cumberland Island.

During the War of 1812, a body of invading British troops surprised the Dungeness household by arriving right in the middle of a large house party. Legend has it that one of the visitors, Ann Couper of Cannons Point Plantation on St. Simons Island, became enraptured with a young English officer, Captain Fraser. This romance has been charmingly chronicled by St. Simons Island's world-class romantic novelist, Eugenia Price.

In 1818, Nathanael Greene's old friend "Light-Horse Harry" Lee arrived at Cumberland to recuperate from a nagging illness. In spite of constant care, the war hero died on the island a scant month later and was laid to rest in the Greene family's burial ground at Dungeness. Years later, his son, the immortal Robert E. Lee, sent a headstone to mark his father's grave. It is said that Robert E. Lee visited the island many times to pay reverence to his father's grave site.

The Greenes' and Millers' many descendants lived happily at Cumberland Island and Dungeness until that dark conflict sometimes called "the War of Northern Aggression." The invading Union troops laid Dungeness in ruins. When the family returned after the war, there was literally nothing to be found of the elegant homeplace.

Cumberland lay more or less deserted until 1882, when millionaire Thomas Carnegie purchased the island. The new owner lost no time in raising a third Dungeness on the site of the Greene homeplace. Carnegie's island home was a huge, turreted Victorian mansion at which guests were in constant attendance. Once again, the shores of bountiful Cumberland Island rang with the laughter and merriment of many a gay party.

Burnette Vanstory's wonderful *Georgia's Land of the Golden Isles* describes Carnegie's Dungeness as having "deep shady verandas with comfortable rocking chairs and hammocks; there were mastiffs and Russian bear hounds and stables of carriage and saddle horses and fat little ponies for the children. Old newspaper clippings tell of hunting and fishing parties and golf on the course with its famous short hole of sixty yards."

The Carnegies maintained their off-and-on residence for almost 50 years. Some of Thomas Carnegie's children built their own island "cottages," chief among them Plum Orchard and Grey Field. The former still stands and is open to the public, while Grey Field is now one of the most elegant and exclusive inns in the United States. After lying idle for several years, the main Dungeness house burned in 1959, bringing to a close one of the island's many colorful eras.

Under private ownership for almost its entire history, Cumberland Island has been spared the blight of modern development. In recognition of its natural wonders and impressive history, the island was declared a National Seashore Park in 1972. Ferry service was established from St. Marys, and a Dungeness museum was developed in the estate's old icehouse.

Today, visitors arriving either by ferry or their own cruising craft have the good fortune of being able to tour magnificent Cumberland Island without hindrance (unless they are attacked by the "no-see-ums"). There is even the possibility of overnight camping, but unfortunately for boaters, no nighttime dockage is available. A hike through the magnificent maritime forests is an experience to be savored for a lifetime.

Don't overlook a visit to the ruins of Dungeness, the Ice House Museum, and Plum Orchard mansion. Of course, a night or two spent at Grey Field Inn can only be relegated to the dreamlike. Truly, those who have not seen the beauty of Cumberland Island have missed the very best that the Golden Isles have to offer.

Waterway Anchorage

In light to moderate easterly winds or light breezes from any other direction, it is possible to anchor in the charted patch of deep water north and east of flashing daybeacon #37. This writer spotted the high cliffs and wild ponies described earlier just south of #37, so it doesn't take much imagination to envision this anchorage's aesthetic attractions.

Plum Orchard mansion, Cumberland Island

You must be careful to bypass the finger of shoal water running northeast of #37, but otherwise minimum 7-foot depths hold to within 150 yards of the eastern shoreline. This anchorage is completely exposed to the wake of all vessels passing on the Waterway, and it is most definitely not the spot to ride out nasty weather.

Brickhill River

Now, things really begin to get good. The northern mouth of Brickhill River cuts south opposite unlighted daybeacon #40. The stream then turns east into the heart of Cumberland Island before snaking its way south and rejoining the ICW near flashing daybeacon #60.

There are only a few shoals to avoid over this stream's entire length. For the most part, visiting cruisers can expect minimum depths of 8 feet, with most soundings considerably deeper.

Protected overnight anchorage is a practical consideration anywhere on Brickhill River, but there are three havens that deserve special recognition. One is absolutely unforgettable.

The deep waters north of Malkintooh Creek border beautiful wooded banks to the east. Swinging room is limited by some shoaling to the west that is not apparent from the water. Boats larger than 36 feet might have a bit of a problem. Also, strong winds from the northwest blow straight in from the ICW and can make for a bumpy night. Of course, there is super shelter from easterly breezes.

Second, you might consider anchoring north of the charted "Table Point" high ground. These timbered banks are set back a bit from the water, but there should still be some protection from fresh southerly winds. There is plenty of swinging room along this portion of the river, and depths run 14 to 23 feet.

Finally, boaters can track their way south (or enter the southerly Brickhill River directly from the ICW at flashing daybeacon #60) and find their way to the charted high ground abeam of the river's first northward-striking loop. This anchorage is directly adjacent to none other than Plum Orchard Plantation, discussed in the section on Cumberland Island's history above. You can anchor directly abeam of the plantation in 10 to 20 feet of water, with enough room for boats up to 42 feet. In fact, a 42-foot Grand Banks trawler was swinging easily on the hook when this writer last visited the stream.

Even more promising is a small dinghy dock on the creek's easterly banks just south of the mansion. This old structure is certainly inadequate for any craft larger than 20 feet, but it is quite acceptable for dinghy dockage. The National Park Service has informed this writer that the Plum Orchard pier is not really public dockage, but that small craft are usually permitted to tie here temporarily unless the ferry happens to call. This usually takes place on Sundays, but sometimes charter groups bring the ferry to the dock at other times. It might be a good idea to tour Plum Orchard in shifts, leaving one crew member with the dinghy in case the ferry comes along.

There is some shoal water to avoid while cruising along Brickhill River's southern exodus into the ICW, but careful mariners should come through with little problem. In short, the stream is simply chock-full of cruising opportunities.

Before dropping everything and making a beeline for the Brickhill, be sure to read the review of the Grey Field–Dungeness channel below. The channel is equally intriguing and offers the added inducement of public dockage.

Shellbine Creek

The stream known as Shellbine Creek cuts into the Waterway's mainland (northwesterly) shoreline north of flashing daybeacon #43. In light to low-moderate winds, boaters can pick from among several spots to anchor.

Minimum depths of 7 to 8 feet can be expected on the initial southeasterly stretch of Shellbine Creek short of its upstream split (after bypassing an unmarked shoal). In light airs, boats up to 50 feet can drop the hook just short of the split in 15 to 22 feet of water. Strong winds from the southeast blow straight across the ICW and into the creek's mouth. These conditions call for another strategy.

For more protection, consider tracking your way a short distance upstream on the southwesterly arm of the creek. Minimum 9-foot depths are held for at least 100 yards from the split. Swinging room is a little more restricted here, but boats up to 42 feet should still find enough room.

Delaroche Creek

Another possible mainland-side anchorage is on the ICW's southwestern shores just northwest of flashing daybeacon #58. Short of Delaroche Creek's two-part split to the west, minimum depths of 11 feet are coupled with enough room for a 38-footer.

Crooked River

Crooked River divides into two streams before it finds its way to an intersection with the ICW. The northerly fork is found west of flashing daybeacon #63. This stream provides a little-protected, questionable anchorage. It is possible to avoid the considerable unmarked shoals flanking the easterly entrance and hold 7-foot depths until approaching the charted marsh island that bisects the stream. However, the river is so wide that even a moderate breeze can bring on unwanted chop. While there is plenty of swinging room here, this writer suggests that you consider other overnight havens.

The southerly branch of Crooked River joins the Waterway considerably farther to the south, near unlighted daybeacon #70. The story is pretty much the same here, except that successful entry of this fork is a far easier proposition than with its northerly counterpart. Minimum 15-foot depths hold at least to the point where the river meets its northerly fork. There is enough swinging room for the *QE II*, but again there is little shelter from inclement weather.

This body of water is close by the Kings Bay Submarine Base. As my friend and research assistant Kerry put it (tongue in cheek, of course), "If you drop anchor and hear a metallic clank, you know you're in big trouble."

Kings Bay Submarine Base

The United States Navy maintains an extensive nuclear submarine base on the wide waters of Kings Bay northwest of unlighted daybeacon #78. Feel free to look as you pass, but don't attempt to take any photographs. There is usually a patrol boat to warn off the curious. The base's waters are strictly off-limits to pleasure craft.

Dungeness–Grey Field Channel

South of Kings Bay, marker colors reverse as the ICW follows a well-outlined large-ships' channel south. At flashing buoy #40, boaters have a last chance (and one of the best chances) to visit Cumberland Island by departing the Waterway and following the wide ribbon of deep water along the island's westerly shoreline. There are practically no markings, but if you simply keep the Cumberland Island shoreline some 75 to 100 yards off your starboard side, minimum 8- to 9-foot depths can be carried north to Grey Field.

The first point of interest that will capture your attention is the dock at the charted position of Dungeness. As was discussed in the section on Cumberland Island's history, the last Dungeness mansion was built by Thomas Carnegie in 1882. The main house burned in 1959. Today, the ruins still make interesting viewing, and the National Park Service maintains a Dungeness museum in the old icehouse. Dockage by private vessels is not permitted at this pier.

North of Dungeness, a second concrete-decked floating pier maintained by the National Park Service welcomes not only the ferry running from St. Marys, but visitors with their own vessels as well. All the locals refer to this facility as the "Sea Camp Dock." Minimum depths alongside run 10 to 11 feet. There are no power or water hookups available. Overnight dockage is *not* permitted, but you can easily tie up during the daylight hours and go ashore to explore

Cumberland Island. You can hike south to Dungeness and north to Plum Orchard or simply admire the island's incredible plant and animal life. From time to time, interpretive programs are offered by the park rangers in a small building just behind this pier.

The last stop north on this channel is Grey Field Inn. Grey Field is one of the most exclusive inns in the United States. A ferry carries inn guests from Florida's Fernandina Beach to a small dock along the channel. Inn guests may also moor their vessels free of charge to this fixed wooden floating pier. Dockage is now permitted for those not staying at the inn, but there is a fee. No power or water connections or any other marine services are available. Depths alongside are 8 feet or better. Call (904) 261-6408 for more information. You might also consider anchoring abeam of the inn for an unforgettable evening.

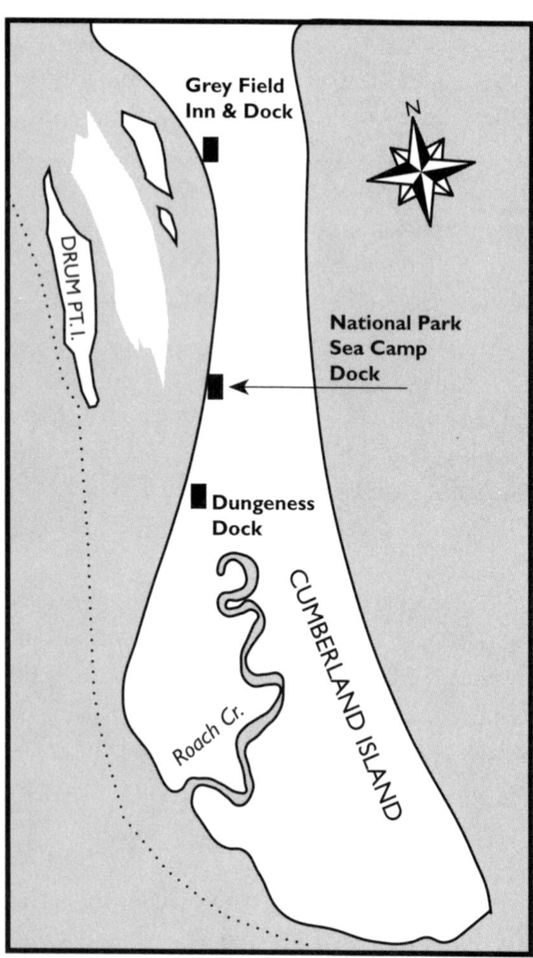

Farther to the north, the Dungeness–Grey Field channel plays out, and shoal water is soon encountered.

St. Marys River

The mouth of St. Marys River lies just west of flashing buoy #35. This impressive stream serves as Florida's northern boundary. It originates in the great Okefenokee Swamp in Georgia, long a source of mystery and romance. The river is deep and easily navigable as far west as the village of St. Marys. It is reasonably well marked and has few shoals to trouble the visitor. Cruising craft of almost any size and draft can explore the eastern portion of St. Marys River with confidence.

The St. Marys shoreline remains delightfully undeveloped saltwater marsh, except for the St. Marys village waterfront. Another exception, and an unfortunate one, is the large pulp-processing mill just north of flashing daybeacon #3. This plant is one of several in the area. When the wind is from the wrong quarter, the smell of progress is not so sweet.

The only marina on the river is located along the St. Marys village waterfront. This facility is anxious to attract passing cruisers.

Along with its two principal auxiliary waters, North and Jolly Rivers, St. Marys River offers several protected overnight anchorages. The broad section of the river east of flashing daybeacon #3 is too open for adequate protection except in the lightest winds. Cruisers will do better to consider the more sheltered spot just west of flashing daybeacon #10 in the river's first sharp northern loop. Even here, the surrounding marsh-grass shores do not provide adequate protection in heavy weather. Another possibility is to anchor abeam of St. Marys village. Protection is particularly good from northern blows, and it is a quick dinghy trip to the village.

Jolly River

The northern entrance to Jolly River lies southwest of flashing daybeacon #2, which is east of Point Peter. Minimum depths of 10 feet can be carried upstream to the charted marsh island in the river's second jog to the south, located northwest of Tiger Basin. While there are a few unmarked shoals along the way, basic navigation skills should see most boaters safely along their way. However, because of the river's lack of markings, it is not recommended for craft over 40 feet long.

Jolly River is much larger than a casual inspection of chart 11489 might lead you to believe. Thanks to the marsh-grass shoreline, high winds can make for an uncomfortable evening swinging on the hook. However, in light or moderate winds, Jolly River can be a delightful place to rest from your travels. The northernmost section of the river is a bit open and should probably be bypassed in favor of the more sheltered areas upstream. A good spot to drop the hook is found in the mid-width of the stream's first cut to the west. Here, you can anchor in some 10 to 16 feet of water with fair protection.

North River

North River makes in to the northern shore of St. Marys River near flashing daybeacon #3. This stream offers a very sheltered place to anchor. Unfortunately, the pulp mill mentioned earlier overlooks the river's western bank at its second bend to the north. In eastern or southern winds, the plant is not too much of a problem, but in a northern blow, you might want to seek shelter elsewhere. Except for the pulp mill, North River's banks are mostly undeveloped. Marsh grass alternates with higher ground, providing an eye-pleasing mix.

Minimum depths of 9 feet can be expected on North River until you reach the charted patch of shallower water north of the pulp mill. Farther upstream, shoaling not noted on the latest edition of chart 11489 has occurred, and there are depths of 4 feet or less. Be sure to discontinue your exploration before reaching the shallows.

One of the best anchorages for large boats is found in the stretch between the North's juncture with the St. Marys and the stream's first bend to the north. Boats up to 50 feet can drop the hook here in some 9 to 16 feet of water with fair protection. Better yet is the mid-width of the first northerly bend. High ground to the east gives good protection in easterly breezes. Craft of 40 feet or less should find adequate swinging room here in some 20 feet of water. Yet another possibility is the area just east of the large wastewood hill shown as a rough circle on chart 11489. This high ground affords good protection in westerly winds, and depths run to about 25 feet. Owing to the large amount of anchor scope necessitated by the deep water, only boats up to 36 feet will find adequate swinging room in this spot.

St. Marys Village

St. Marys village is one of the quaintest and most easygoing ports of call along the Georgia coastline. This writer highly recommends a stroll along its shaded streets, lined by restored historic homes.

St. Marys has facilities for the transient boater. Lang Marina, just west of the village's principal waterfront, welcomes visiting cruisers. This facility features all-concrete floating docks with power and water connections. Depths alongside run 6 feet or better. In gale-force winds, the harbor's protection may not be sufficient for comfort. No fueling services are available at the marina.

After coiling the lines, walk east for several blocks and watch to the south for the offices of Lang's Seafood Company. You can usually find the marina's dockmaster here. If you arrive after 5:00 P.M., check at Seagle's Restaurant, on the northern side of the road, and the staff will be glad to call the dockmaster for you. Better yet, call ahead of time and make advance mooring arrangements.

Lang Marina (912) 882-4432

Approach depth: 12+ feet
Dockside depth: 6 feet (minimum)
Accepts transients: yes
Floating concrete docks: yes
Dockside power connections: 30 and 50 amps
Dockside water connections: yes
Restaurant: nearby

During the last several years, local business people and volunteers have contributed greatly to the renovation, restoration, and revitalization of the downtown business district of St. Marys. There are places to shop, dreamlike historic homes to view, and excellent restaurants to enjoy while you take a break from your life on the water.

For those interested in a unique dining experience, this writer highly recommends Seagle's Restaurant, which occupies the first floor of the Riverview Hotel. This fine dining spot may be a bit noisy, but the seafood is as good as any in Georgia. The massive breakfasts are nothing to sneeze at either.

The Riverview Hotel (912-882-3242) is located atop Seagle's Restaurant at the corner of Osborne and St. Marys Streets, only a short walk east of the Lang Marina docks. Built in 1916 and extensively renovated in 1976, the hotel offers 18 second-story guest rooms and a large veranda.

Just up Osborne Street, two historic bed-and-breakfast inns are well worth your consideration.

Historic Spencer House (912-882-1872) guards the corner of Osborne and Bryant Streets. This massive three-story structure features some of the most delightful rooms that this writer has had the good fortune to occupy. The breakfast is all that a hearty appetite could ask for, and there is even a resident ghost! Ensconced in an 1872 edifice, Spencer House served as a hotel in its previous life. After a stint as an office building, it was magnificently restored into the handsome inn that greets modern-day visitors.

The Goodbread House (912-882-7490) is found just across Osborne Street from Spencer House. This Victorian-era bed-and-breakfast inn prides itself on being the county's first modern inn of this genre. Built in 1870, the old homeplace features seven fireplaces (two in bathrooms) and wide pine floors. The warmth of the welcome is all one could ask for.

The downtown grocery store in St. Marys has long been closed, but there is still much for visiting cruisers to see and do in the historic business district. There are a number of fine gift and antique shops. Anyone interested in coastal Georgia literature will want to visit Once Upon a Bookstore, just south of Spencer House on Osborne Street.

Sightseers and history buffs may be interested in the St. Marys Historical Society. Simply walk north on Osborne Street and watch to your left for impressive Orange Hall. The visitors center has a separate doorway on the ground floor along the right-hand side of the house. Here, local volunteers will be glad to provide you with a pamphlet that outlines a self-guided walking tour.

Spencer House, St. Marys

St. Marys has much to offer considering its small size. Every single boater is urged to take advantage of the village's considerable charms before heading south into the waters of the Sunshine State.

St. Marys History The town of St. Marys stands perched upon a bluff that was once the site of an Indian village. An old legend relates that the tribe was ruled by a queen who was reputed to be the most beautiful Native American in the 13 original colonies.

The lands lying about St. Marys were part of the so-called debatable land, which was contended for by both England and Spain until the Georgia line was extended south to St. Marys River following the Revolution.

In 1787, a group of citizens purchased land on St. Marys River for the express purpose of founding a port. The town's original industry consisted of cutting and exporting lumber. Its population was swelled by the arrival of French-speaking Acadians and refugees from Santo Domingo.

One of the most prominent early citizens of St. Marys was Major Archibald Clark. He moved to the new port in 1802 and opened a law office. Aaron Burr was entertained in Clark's home when he visited St. Marys in 1804. Clark established a host of sawmills in and around the young community. His industry and enterprise went a long way toward ensuring the port's early prosperity.

During the War of 1812, a fort was established at St. Marys. This military depot was overwhelmed by invading English forces in 1815.

Strangely enough, the war had already ended at that point, but the word had not reached either the invaders or the defenders. During the occupation, Major Clark was taken prisoner because of his refusal to disclose the town treasury's hiding place. When it became known that the war was at a negotiated end, Clark was released and became even more of a local hero.

St. Marys grew ever more prosperous in the antebellum period. Early accounts note that cotton, rice, sugarcane, corn, peaches, oranges, lemons, and figs were some of the town's exports. By the 1820s, St. Marys had become the business and cultural center of southeastern Georgia.

In 1828, the old Union Church was reorganized as Independent Presbyterian Church. This stately white structure survives to this day. By 1829, the church members had built a parsonage, which became known as Orange Hall. This classic Greek Revival structure now serves as headquarters for the St. Marys Historical Society. Carved over the fireplace in Orange Hall are words that embody the very special tranquility of this peaceful community:

Happy is the home that shelters a friend.
O turn thy rudder thitherward awhile,
Here may the storm-beat vessel safely ryde!
This is the port of rest from troublous toyle,
The World's sweet Inn from pain and wearisome turmoyle.

By the late 1840s, Georgia's new railroads were stealing much of the commercial traffic from St. Marys' waterfront. The town was abandoned with the arrival of Union forces during the Civil War. The invaders stabled horses in Independent Presbyterian Church, but fortunately most of the historic buildings in the village survived the war.

With her commercial prosperity gone, St. Marys became a sleepy little fishing village. The arrival of the Gilman Paper Company in 1945 breathed some new life into the local economy, even if it did little good for the citizens' breathing.

Modern visitors to downtown St. Marys will find a beautiful village still blessed with many historic buildings. Notice the old oak tree in the middle of Osborne Street. It is called the "Washington Oak," and according to tradition it was planted in 1799 to commemorate our first president's death.

Whether you stop only for a night or tarry for a week, there are few places where you could spend your time more profitably than tranquil St. Marys.

ST. ANDREW SOUND TO ST. MARYS RIVER NAVIGATION

Georgia's southernmost waters continue to show the kind of contrast that is evident throughout the state. In the northern part of this section, boaters have the less-than-auspicious choice of either following the primary ICW passage almost out into the ocean or making use of the shoal-prone, alternate Umbrella Cut–Floyd Creek route. Either way, navigational skills will be challenged. But south of St. Andrew Sound, the Waterway is reasonably well sheltered as it tracks its way down

Cumberland River to St. Marys River and Florida waters. Most of the sidewaters adjoining Cumberland Island are deep and easily navigated, while the mainland streams clearly call for more caution.

Alternate ICW Route Continue cruising southwest from flashing daybeacon #25 for several hundred yards before turning to the west on Little Satilla River. Set course so as to pass well north of unlighted daybeacon #A1A. This marker sits hard by the southern marsh banks.

Use your binoculars to help pick out flashing daybeacon #A1. This aid marks the northern entrance to Umbrella Cut and can be hard to spot from the water. Come abeam of #A1 by at least 100 yards to its northern side, then cut due south and point to pass #A1 to its fairly immediate western side and unlighted daybeacon #A2 to its eastern quarter. From this point south on the alternate Waterway channel, you should take red markers to your starboard side and green beacons to port, just as you would expect.

South of #A2, you can swing to the east on the lower reaches of Umbrella Creek. Hold to the mid-width as the stream sweeps to the south. You will do well to anchor before the creek cuts back to the northeast.

From #A2, the alternate route follows Umbrella Creek for a short distance to the southwest. At unlighted daybeacon #A4, the passage traverses a narrow cut to the southeast. Northwest of #A4, upper Umbrella Creek can also serve as an overnight stop. Again, you should stick to the mid-width. Be sure to cease your explorations before passing the creek's first hairpin turn.

The narrow connecting stream that leads from #A4 to unlighted daybeacon #A10 is one of the shallowest portions of the alternate ICW. Expect some low-water soundings of as little as 5 feet. This writer's best advice is to stick strictly to the passage's mid-width and avoid all points of marsh like the plague.

Unlighted daybeacon #A10 introduces southbound boaters to Dover Creek. Turn northwest and follow the long curve in the creek back to the south, then to the west. Watch for unlighted daybeacon #A12 along the southerly banks. Just before reaching #A12, turn south-southwest into the small connecting stream leading to Satilla River.

You may also consider anchoring northwest of #A12. Cruise upstream on the mid-width for only a short distance until the high ground comes abeam on the southwestern banks. Don't proceed any farther upstream, as unmarked shoals are quickly encountered.

The alternate ICW passage down Satilla River is wide open, and aids to navigation are widely separated. Cut southeast only after cruising out into the main body of the river for at least 100 yards from the southwesterly mouth of the connecting stream.

Follow a compass course designed to let you come abeam of and pass unlighted daybeacon #A14 by *at least* 300 yards to its easterly side. Daybeacon #A14 is completely surrounded by charted shoals. Do not approach this aid closely.

Set a new course once abeam of #A14 to come abeam of #A15, on the river's southerly banks, to its immediate westerly side. This aid marks yet another narrow cut-through, which connects with Floyd Creek.

While cruising between #A14 and #A15, be careful to avoid the tongue of shallow water that extends southeast of #A14 for a short distance. Also, look to the east as you are making this run. The charted marsh shoals are often home to several hundred seabirds.

As you enter Floyd Cut from #A15, favor the

easterly side of the channel slightly. On-site research revealed that a shoal seems to be encroaching on the westerly side of the entrance cut near unlighted daybeacon #A16.

Unlighted daybeacon #A21 marks the entrance of Floyd Cut into Floyd Creek. Slow down! This is a very tricky section indeed.

In spite of what chart 11489 might lead you to believe, the westerly banks must not be closely approached as you round the turn southeast of #A21. This writer ran aground here in a 19-foot I/O power craft.

The remainder of Floyd Creek is mostly deep along its mid-width. You must still take care not to cut any corners or approach any of the points of marsh too closely. At low tide, several shoals building out from the banks are visible.

At one point, a surprising industrial facility overlooks the western banks where the charted high ground runs directly down to the water's edge. It is difficult to guess the purpose of the facility—a secret biological-warfare project, perhaps?

Floyd Creek joins back up with Cumberland River and the primary ICW after passing northeast of unlighted daybeacon #A22. Once abeam of #A22, point to pass *northeast* of unlighted daybeacon #40. Shallow water lies southwest of #40.

ICW through St. Andrew Sound From flashing daybeacon #25, the main ICW passage sweeps south through Jekyll Sound on its way to St. Andrew Sound. The channel favors the easterly shoreline, but there is a thin band of shallows directly adjacent to these banks.

From #25, continue to the southwest. Bend your course slowly to the south and point to pass flashing daybeacon #27 by at least 200 yards to its westerly quarter. This marker sits hard by the easterly banks near the charted "TV TR."

Follow the Jekyll Island shoreline south until you are abeam of Jekyll Point. Prepare for a noticeable increase in wind and waves as you round this promontory. Pass flashing daybeacon #29 well to its southwesterly side. Turn to the southeast and follow the various charted markers out to flashing buoy #32. You are tracking your way toward the open sea along this run, so expect rough conditions. Be sure you don't cut any corners here. The charted shoals to the north, southeast, east, and west are very much for real. Run a careful compass course and have your binoculars close at hand to help spot the various markers.

Come abeam of flashing buoy #32 to its fairly immediate northeasterly side. Don't stray too far to the northeast as you approach #32. As you will see from a quick study of chart 11489, a large shoal lies in this quarter as well.

Curl around #32 and set your course back to the southwest, pointing to come abeam of Cumberland Island's westerly shoreline by at least 200 yards to your easterly quarter. This is a long, markerless stretch of the Waterway, so compass courses should be a prime consideration.

Eventually, you should pass flashing daybeacon #34 well west of your course line. This is yet another aid set in shallow water that you must not approach closely.

Waterway Anchorage To enter the bubble of deep water north and east of flashing daybeacon #37, you must avoid the tongue of 3-foot water stretching north-northeast from #37. Depart the Waterway several hundred yards north of #37 and work your way carefully toward the easterly shoreline. When you are about 200 yards short of the banks, cut south and feel your way along with the sounder. Don't continue south past #37 (to your westerly side).

On the ICW The Waterway sweeps southwest down the broad and mostly deep track of Cumberland River. Markers are a bit few and far between, so be sure to tick off the various daybeacons to keep a running check on your position.

Pass unlighted daybeacon #40 well to its eastern and southeastern side. As discussed in the review of the alternate ICW passage, a lengthy shoal has built out from the shore west of #40. If it keeps shelving out, the shallows will soon encroach on #40 itself.

Brickhill River From unlighted daybeacon #40, cut south and point to enter Brickhill River, favoring the eastern and northeastern shoreline. As clearly shown on chart 11489, a large shoal has built out well to the northeast from the stream's western entrance point (near flashing daybeacon #41). Of course, you should not approach the eastern or northeastern shoreline too closely either.

Mud Creek, which cuts to the southwest, is not particularly recommended, as its entrance is completely surrounded by unmarked shoals. After tracking your way past the Mud Creek entrance on Brickhill River for 100 yards or so, you can cruise back to the mid-width for a short distance.

South of the river's intersection with shallow Hawkins Creek, a broad band of shoal water strikes out from the southwestern banks. Favor the northeastern and then the eastern banks fairly heavily as the river cuts to the south. By the time Brickhill River cuts back to the west, good depths open out almost from bank to bank. The charted patch of 5-foot water on the turn's southern tier did not show up during on-site research, but if your boat draws more than 5 feet and it's near low tide, you might favor one bank or the other to be safe.

Happily, you need only hold to the centerline for a long cruise to the south on Brickhill River. The charted cable area west of Mumford Creek is an underwater crossing. Obviously, you should not anchor anywhere near this spot, but at least sailors will not have to worry with overhead power-line clearance.

South of Mumford Creek, Brickhill River flows through a hairpin turn that eventually leads south. A charted shoal abutting the southeasterly banks on the turn's westerly section can be bypassed by favoring the northwesterly shoreline. Study chart 11489 and this rather complicated maneuver will become clear.

Past the hairpin turn, favor the southwestern shoreline to bypass the charted ½-foot shoal. You need then only hold to the mid-width until you reach Brickhill River's southern mouth. Favor the eastern shores as you cruise back out into the ICW. Leave flashing daybeacon #60 well to your western side.

Shellbine Creek Back on the ICW, boaters can make good their entry into Shellbine Creek, north of flashing daybeacon #43, by favoring the stream's northeastern banks, though this shoreline should not be approached too closely. As shown on chart 11489, a considerable patch of shallows has built out from the creek's southwestern entrance point.

Shellbine Creek soon splits into two branches. Good depths can be maintained on the northerly fork by favoring the westerly banks slightly until the creek divides yet again. Continued cruising past this second split is not recommended.

The southwesterly branch is deep almost from bank to bank for 100 yards or so. Most cruisers will do well to drop the hook here rather than continuing farther upstream and braving the several charted but unmarked shoals.

On the ICW Come abeam of and pass flashing daybeacon #43 well to its northwesterly side. At this point, the Waterway bends farther to the southwest. Pass unlighted daybeacon #45 well to its northwesterly side. These two aids (#43 and #45) mark a considerable shelf of shallow water along the southeasterly banks.

Southwest of flashing daybeacon #46, the marked ICW channel runs hard by the westerly shoreline at charted Cabin Bluff in order to avoid the large patch of shallows and marsh lying to the east. As you leave Cabin Bluff behind, be sure to pick out flashing daybeacon #51A and unlighted daybeacon #52. These two beacons direct boaters toward the northeasterly shore to help them avoid yet another large shoal bisecting the stream's mid-width.

Southeast of flashing daybeacon #55, the channel parallels the southwesterly shores. Be sure to pass to the southwesterly side of unlighted daybeacons #57 and #57A and flashing daybeacon #59. These aids mark a shoal building out from the northeasterly banks.

Delaroche Creek Enter the mouth of Delaroche Creek, north of flashing daybeacon #58, on its centerline. Drop anchor before reaching the charted two-way split to the west.

On the Waterway Some 0.4 nautical mile southeast of flashing daybeacon #59, favor the northeasterly banks and point to eventually pass to the fairly immediate easterly sides of flashing daybeacons #60 and #62A. You should then set course to come abeam of and pass flashing daybeacon #63 to its immediate westerly quarter. Between #62A and #63, the northerly branch of Crooked River is accessible to the west.

Crooked River's Northern Branch Take a few moments to study chart 11489. Notice the long tongue of shallows that thrusts into Crooked River's southern entrance flank. To avoid this potential grounding zone, favor the northern banks when entering the stream. Good depths soon spread out in a broad band, but it's still a good idea to favor the northern side of the river slightly. Discontinue your cruise of Crooked River as you near the charted marsh island that bisects the river.

On the ICW South-southwest of flashing daybeacon #63, the Waterway follows a dredged cut through shoal water and surrounding mud banks. Observe the various markers with the greatest care.

At unlighted daybeacon #66, the ICW turns farther to the south. Set course to pass flashing daybeacon #69 to its fairly immediate westerly quarter. Continue on the same track, pointing to come abeam of and pass unlighted daybeacon #70 by some 35 to 50 yards to its easterly side. A very shallow area has built southeast from the point of marsh separating the ICW and the southerly branch of Crooked River. It has already encroached on #70. Stay well away from this beacon.

Crooked River's Southern Branch The only real trick to successfully navigating the southerly fork of Crooked River is to avoid the long shoal extending southeast from the stream's northeasterly entrance point. This objective is most easily accomplished if you depart the Waterway abeam of unlighted daybeacon #71. You can cruise directly from #71 to the stream's mouth, favoring the southwesterly shores slightly, and keep good water all the way into the river's interior reaches.

Excellent depths continue on a broad band up the middle of the southern branch of Crooked

River until the stream cuts to the west and leaves chart 11489. Cruising boaters are advised to stick to the charted portion of the river.

On the Waterway Come abeam of and pass unlighted daybeacon #72 to its easterly side and continue to flashing daybeacon #74. Shallow water lies west and northwest of #72.

South of #74, the Waterway follows a narrow passage that is subject to shoaling. Fortunately, this route is well marked. Keep chart 11489 in hand as you traverse this tricky section.

The huge Kings Bay Submarine Base will be obvious on the westerly shoreline between #74 and flashing daybeacon #50. Remember not to attempt entry into this government facility.

Immediately **south of** unlighted daybeacons #78 and #79, *marker colors reverse*. You are now following the large-ships' channel to St. Marys Inlet, so green markers should be passed to your starboard side and red beacons to your port quarter.

Cruise southwest for 50 yards or so after passing between #78 and #79, then turn sharply south-southeast and point to pass between flashing buoy #51 and flashing daybeacon #50.

From Kings Bay to St. Marys River, the combined ICW and large-ships' channel is well marked and lit up like a Christmas tree. Keep chart 11489 at hand to help you sort out the prolific aids. Otherwise, if you run aground here, you had better purchase a new edition of *Chapman*'s.

Dungeness–Grey Field Channel For best depths, follow the Waterway south to a point just north of flashing buoy #40. You can then swing back to the northeast and, by staying within 75 yards or so of the Cumberland Island shoreline (to your easterly side), carry good water far north to a position abeam of charted Grey Field Inn.

Moving north along the channel, you will first sight the dock at Dungeness. A bit farther, you will spy the public "Sea Camp" floating pier on the Cumberland Island shoreline. The small dock at Grey Field guards the practical northerly cruising limits on this channel.

On to St. Marys River As you come between flashing buoys #35 and #36, it's just a hop, skip, and jump into Floridian waters. There is one last Georgia body of water that you should seriously consider visiting. Enchanting St. Marys River lies to the west of #35.

St. Marys River If you choose to visit St. Marys River and the charming village of the same name, break off from the ICW's track at flashing buoy #35 and set course due west into the mid-width of the river. Successful navigation of St. Marys River is an elementary matter of following a few navigational beacons until coming abeam of St. Marys village on the northern shore. These beacons mark the few shoal areas of the river's eastern reaches. Simply pass each on the appropriate side, and don't approach them closely. Afterwards, you can take a break from your depth-sounder vigil while on St. Marys River.

Jolly River Jolly River breaks off to the south near St. Marys River's eastern entrance. The mouth of the Jolly is flanked by a large shoal on its western shore. To avoid this considerable hazard, favor the eastern banks when entering. As the river begins to swing to the west, cruise back to the mid-width. Between this point and the stream's next bend to the south is a good place to drop the hook. If you choose to proceed farther, begin favoring the northern shore heavily as you approach the turn to the south. There is some shallow water abutting the turn's southern point. Once through the bend, cruise back to the mid-width. Remember to discontinue your cruise before coming abeam of the charted marsh island that bisects the river. Past this point, the winding channel is much too uncertain for large craft.

North River Enter North River by favoring the western shore slightly. Once on the stream's interior, cruise back to the mid-width until the river swings almost due west as it begins to approach the large pulp mill. Chart 11489 correctly shows a shallow patch along the northern shore in this section. Favor the southern banks until the stream begins to swing back to the north, then reenter the centerline and continue along the middle until reaching the charted shallows north of the mill. Continued passage upstream is not recommended without specific local knowledge.

Farewell to Georgia South of flashing buoys #35 and #36, boaters will quickly pass into the waters of northeastern Florida. A continuing account of the ICW and all its sidewaters is presented in this writer's *Cruising Guide to Eastern Florida*.

It seems a long way since we first met up with the waters of South Carolina at Little River. This writer only hopes that you enjoy the coastline of South Carolina and Georgia as much as I have delighted in bringing it to your attention.

Good luck and good boating!

Index